TLE SIX

OPTIONS FOR THE 1970s

B 484 108

LOUIS G. LOCKE
Madison College

WILLIAM M. GIBSON
New York University

GEORGE ARMS
University of New Mexico

GEORGE PETTY
Montclair State College

HOLT, RINEHART AND WINSTON, INC.
New York Chicago San Francisco Atlanta Dallas

The authors and publisher have made every effort to trace the ownership of all selections found in this book and to make full acknowledgment for their use. Many of the selections are in the public domain.

Grateful acknowledgment is made to the following authors, publishers, agents, and individuals for their permission to reprint copyrighted materials.

McGraw-Hill Book Co. for Jane Howard, *Help See Own Way Behave* from *Please Touch* by Jane Howard. Copyright © 1970 by Jane Howard.

The Humanist for A. H. Maslow, *Peak Experiences in Education and Art*. This article first appeared in *The Humanist*, Sept./Oct., 1970.

The Macmillan Co. for Rasa Gustaitus, *Out-of-Sight Joanie and Sequential Monogamy*, from *Turning On Without Drugs*. © 1969 by The Macmillan Co.

W. W. Norton & Co. Inc. for Rollo May, *Paradoxes of Sex and Love*, Reprinted from *Love and Will* by Rollo May, Copyright © 1969 by W. W. Norton & Co., Inc.; and Erik H. Erikson, *Adolescence* reprinted from *Identity: Youth and Crisis* by Erik Erikson, Copyright © 1968 by W. W. Norton & Co., Inc.

Kenneth Lash, for *Children of Turmoil* from *Change* magazine, March/April, 1971. Copyright © 1971 by Kenneth Lash.

The New York Times Co. for: Russell Baker, *Big Brother Really Is Watching*; Jean Stafford, *Women as Chattels, Men as Chumps*; George F. Kennan, *Con III is Not the Answer*; Eric Hoffer, *Whose Country Is America?*; Earl Warren, *Centuries of Discrimination*; R. Buckminster Fuller, *The Earthians' Critical Moment*; Kenneth Clark, *The Quest for Civilization*; Copyright © 1969/1970 by The New York Times Company.

Simon and Schuster, Inc. for Jerry Rubin, *Long Hair, Aunt Sadie, Is a Communist Plot*, Copyright © 1970 by the Social Education Foundation.

Harry Golden for *The Real Iron Curtain*, copyright © 1970 by Harry Golden.

Harold Ober Associates Inc. for Marya Mannes, *Who Am I?*, Copyright © 1968 by Marya Mannes.

Penguin Books Ltd. for R. D. Laing, *Us and Them*, from *The Politics of Experience* by R. D. Laing. Copyright © 1967 by R. D. Laing.

The Bobbs-Merrill Co., Inc. for Leonard Schecter, *Lombardi* from *The Jacks*, Copyright © 1969 by Leonard Shecter.

The New York Times Co. for Robert Lipsyte, *A Person Again*; Charles A. Reich, *The Rebirth of a Future: I & II*, Copyright © 1970 by The New York Times Company.

Random House, Inc. for Ralph Ellison, from *The Invisible Man*, Copyright © 1947 by Random House, Inc.

Princeton University Press for Thomas Jefferson, *Letter to James Madison* from *The Papers of Thomas Jefferson*, ed. by Julian P. Boyd, Vol. 12, p. 439. Copyright © 1955 by Princeton University Press.

Holt, Rinehart and Winston, Inc. for Russell Kirk, *Prescription, Authority, and Ordered Freedom* from *What Is Conservatism?* edited by Frank S. Meyer. Copyright © 1964 by Intercollegiate Society of Individualists, Inc.

Hendricks House, Inc. for Niccolo Machiavelli, *The Prince, XVIII*, from *The Prince and Other Works*, new translation by Allen H. Gilbert. Copyright © 1946 by Hendricks House, Inc.

The Nation for Bertrand Russell, *Co-Existence or No Existence: The Choice Is Ours*, from *The Nation*, CLXXX, June 8, 1955. Copyright © 1955 by *The Nation* magazine.

The University of Wisconsin Press for Thucydides, *Revolution in the Greek Cities*, from Mackendrick and Howe, eds., *Classics in Translation, vol. I.* (© 1965 by the Regents of the University of Wisconsin), pp. 245–247.

W. W. Norton & Co., Inc. for John V. Lindsay, *Poverty and the Welfare Trap*, from *The City*, by John V. Lindsay. Copyright © 1969, 1970 by W. W. Norton & Co., Inc.

E. P. Dutton & Co., Inc. for Peter Farb, *The American Indian: A Portrait in Limbo*, from the book *Man's Rise to Civilization* by Peter Farb. Copyright © 1968 by Peter Farb. Excerpted from *The American Indian: A Portrait in Limbo* which originally appeared in *The Saturday Review*.

Leslie M. Silko for *The Man to Send Rain Clouds* which originally appeared in *New Mexico Quarterly*, Winter/Spring 1969. Coypright © 1969 by Leslie Chapman Silko.

The Dial Press for James Baldwin, *Letter to His Nephew* from *The Fire Next Time* by James Baldwin. Copyright © 1962, 1963 by James Baldwin.

Student National Coordinating Committee for Stokeley Carmichael, *What We Want*. © 1966 by the Student Nonviolent Coordinating Committee.

Random House, Inc. and Alfred A. Knopf, Inc. for Piri Thomas, *Hung Down* from *Down These Mean Streets*. Copyright © 1967 by Alfred A. Knopf, Inc.; Peter Schrag, *The Forgotten American* from *Out of Place in America*. Copyright © 1969 by Random House, Inc.; James S. Kunen, *The Shit Hits the Fan* from *The Strawberry Statement*. Copyright © 1969 by Random House, Inc.; Robinson Jeffers, "Night", from *Selected Poetry of Robinson Jeffers* by Robinson Jeffers. Copyright © 1960 by Random House, Inc.

Prentice-Hall, Inc. for Alfredo Cuellar, *The Chicano Movement* from Joan Moore, with Alfredo Cuellar, *Mexican Americans*, © 1970 by Prentice-Hall, Inc.

Harper & Row, Publishers, Inc. for Eric Hoffer, *The Radicalized Rich* from *First Things, Last Things* by Eric Hoffer. Copyright © 1970 by Eric Hoffer.

James Brown Associates Inc. for Herbert Gold, *Marriage Is Not Enough*, from *Vogue*, Feb. 1, 1971. Copyright © 1971 by Herbert Gold.

Margaret Schmid, for *Sex Roles and Survival*, as abridged in *Women: A Journal of Liberation*, Fall, 1969. Copyright © 1969 by Margaret Schmid.

Time magazine for Gloria Steinem, *What It Would Be Like If Women Win* from *Time*, August 31, 1970. Copyright © 1970 by Time Inc., reprinted by permission from *Time*, The Weekly Newsmagazine.

Reader's Digest for Spiro T. Agnew, *Enough of Government by Street Carnival!*, condensed from an address by Vice President Agnew, in *Reader's Digest*, February, 1970. Copyright © 1970 by the Reader's Digest Assn., Inc.

Hummingbird Press for Paul F. Schmidt, *Historical Rebellion*, from *Rebelling, Loving and Liberation* by Paul F. Schmidt. Copyright © 1971 by Paul F. Schmidt.

Freedomways Associates for Richard G. Hatcher, *The Age of a New Humanity*. Reprinted from *Freedomways* magazine, Vol. 9, No. 2, 1969. Copyright © 1969 by *Freedomways*.

Présence Africaine, for Frantz Fanon, *Concerning Violence*, an extract from Chapter 1 of

The Damned by Frantz Fanon (translated by Constance Farrington). Copyright © 1963 by *Présence Africaine* and used with their permission.

The Washington *Post* for Nicholas von Hoffman, *Why The Rich Toss Bombs*, from The Washington *Post*, March 20, 1970. Copyright © 1970 by The Washington *Post*.

King Features Syndicate for William F. Buckley, Jr., *On Returning to America*, from *National Review*, Nov. 17, 1970. Copyright © 1970 by King Features Syndicate.

John F. Kennedy, *Inaugural Address*, delivered on January 20, 1961 is from the 87th Congress, 1st Session, House Document 218, Washington D.C., 1961.

Joan Daves for Martin Luther King, Jr., *I Have a Dream*. Copyright © 1963 by Martin Luther King, Jr.

George Stade for *An Apology for the Liberal Education Front*, from a pamphlet by the State University College of Arts and Science at Genesco, New York. Copyright © 1970 by George Stade.

Association for the Study of Negro Life and History for Ossie Davis, *The English Language is My Enemy* from *The Negro History Bulletin*, vol. 30, 1967. Copyright © 1967 by ASNLH.

Doubleday & Co. for R. Buckminster Fuller, *Education and Technology* from *Education and Automation* by R. B. Fuller. Copyright © 1962 by Southern University Press.

The New Yorker for Morris Bishop, *The Reading Machine*. Copyright © 1947 by The New Yorker Magazine, Inc.

Commonweal Publishing Co., Inc. for Paul Velde, *Therapeutic Soap Opera* from *Commonweal*, November 15, 1968. Copyright © 1968 by *Commonweal*.

The Nation for John Horn, *Television* from *The Nation*, March 18, 1968. Copyright © 1968 by *The Nation*.

Harcourt Brace Jovanovich, Inc. for Marshall McLuhan, from *Counterblast*, © 1969 by Marshall McLuhan; Thomas Merton, from *The Ascent to Truth* by Thomas Merton, copyright 1951 by The Abbey of Gethsemani; Loren Eiseley, *The Golden Alphabet*, abridged from *The Unexpected Universe*, copyright © 1969 by Loren Eiseley.

Little, Brown and Co. for Frank Sullivan, *The Cliche Expert Reveals Himself in His True Colors*, from *A Pearl in Every Oyster* by Frank Sullivan. Copyright 1938, © 1956 by Frank Sullivan.

Indiana University Press for Walker Gibson, *Being Serious Without Being Stuffy* from *Tough, Sweet & Stuffy* by Walker Gibson. Copyright © 1966 by Indiana University Press.

The *Paris Review* for Ernest Hemingway, from *An Interview*, an excerpt from an *Interview with Hemingway* by George Plimpton in *Writers at Work*, Vol. II.

New Directions Publishing Corp. for Dylan Thomas, *In My Craft or Sullen Art* from Dylan Thomas, *Collected Poems*. Copyright 1946 by New Directions Publishing Corp.

Emerson Books, Inc. for the excerpt from Kenneth Walker, *The Extra-Sensory Mind*, $5.25. Copyright © 1961 by Emerson Books, Inc., 251 West 19 Street, N.Y. N.Y.

Doubleday and Company, Inc. for excerpt from *The Mind of the Dolphin* by John C. Lilly, Copyright © 1967 by John C. Lilly; and Arthur Koestler, *Cultural Snobbery* from *The Anchor Review Number One*, edited by Melvin J. Lasky, Copyright © 1955 by Doubleday and Company, Inc.

McGraw-Hill Book Company for Walter Sullivan, *Celestial Syntax* from *We Are Not Alone* by Walter Sullivan. Copyright © 1966 by Walter Sullivan; Aaron Copland, *How We Listen* from *What to Listen for in Music*, Rev. ed. by Aaron Copland. Copyright © 1957 by McGraw-Hill, Inc.

Lurton Blassingame for Robert A. Heinlein, excerpt from *Stranger in a Strange Land*. Copyright © 1961 by Robert A. Heinlein.

Charles Scribner's Sons for *The Clark's Fork Valley, Wyoming* (Copyright 1939 Ernest

Hemingway; renewal copyright © 1967 Mary Hemingway and By-Line Ernest Hemingway, Inc.) from *By-Line: Ernest Hemingway* edited by William White.

W. W. Howells for W. D. Howells, *A Letter to C. E. Norton* from Mildred Howells, ed., *Life in Letters of William Dean Howells* (Doubleday Doran, 1928) II, 154. Copyright 1928 by Mildred Howells.

Holt, Rinehart and Winston, Inc. for Robert Frost, "Directive" from *The Poetry of Robert Frost* edited by Edward C. Latham. Copyright 1947, © 1969 by Holt, Rinehart & Winston.

Houghton Mifflin Co. for "The Grass on the Mountain" (Paiute Poem) from *The American Rhythm*, translated by Mary Austin. Copyright 1923, © 1970 by Houghton Mifflin Co.

Wesleyan University Press for John Cage, *Experimental Music*, from *Silence* by John Cage. Copyright © 1955 by John Cage.

Rolling Stone for Ben Fong–Torres, *An Interview with Leon Russell*, from *Rolling Stone*. © 1970 by Straight Arrow Publishers, Inc. All Rights Reserved.

Liberator for LeRoi Jones, *The Revolutionary Theatre* from *Liberator* Vol. 5, No. 7 (July 1965). Copyright © 1965 by *Liberator* magazine.

Francois Morellet for *The Choice in Present–Day Art*. Copyright © 1965 by Francois Morellet.

The Drama Review for Antonin Artaud, *Motion Pictures and Witchcraft* from *Tulane Drama Review*, Vol. II, No. 1 (T33) Fall 1966. Copyright © 1966 by *The Tulane Drama Review*. All rights reserved.

The New Yorker magazine for Penelope Gilliatt, *Only Films are Truly, Deep–Down Groovy*, Copyright © 1968 by The New Yorker Magazine, Inc.; *Crumbcrusher* by Pauline Kael and *Forever Avant* by Winthrap Sargeant, Copyright © 1970 by The New Yorker Magazine, Inc.

Clement Greenberg for *The Case for Abstract Art*. Copyright © 1960 by Clement Greenberg.

Esquire Magazine and Robert Lantz for Jonathan Baumbach, *The Aesthetics of Basketball*. Copyright © 1970 by Jonathan Baumbach.

Andrew Sarris for *Tomorrow's Movies* from *Mademoiselle*, January 1970. Copyright © 1970 by Andrew Sarris.

Commentary for Jack Richardson, *Avant-Garde Theatrics*. Reprint from Commentary by permission; Copyright © 1968 by the American Jewish Committee.

Commonweal Publishing Co. for Philip Tracy, *The Birth of a Culture* from *Commonweal*, September 5, 1969. Copyright © 1969 by Commonweal Publishing Co.

Charles Scribner's Sons for Susanne K. Langer, *The Cultural Importance of the Arts* from *Problems of Art*, pages 59–74, by Susanne K. Langer. Copyright © 1957 by Susanne K. Langer.

The Viking Press, Inc. for Fred Warshofsky, *The Creation of Life* from *The 21st Century* by Fred Warshofsky. Copyright © 1967, 1969 by Columbia Broadcasting System, Inc. All rights reserved.

George Allen & Unwin Ltd. for Arthur Stanley Eddington, *The Evolution of the Physical World* from *Science and the Unseen World* by A. S. Eddington. Copyright © 1969 by George Allen & Unwin Ltd.

Murnat Publications Inc. for Claude Bernard, *Carbon Monoxide Poisoning* from *An Introduction to the Study of Experimental Medicine* by Claude Bernard, translated by Henry Copley Greene, (New York: Macmillan). Copyright 1927 by Macmillan.

W. H. Freeman and Co. for Martin Gardner, extract from *Mathematical Games* from *Scientific American*, vol. 221 (August, 1969). Copyright © 1969 by Scientific American, Inc. All rights reserved.

Ballantine Books, Inc. for Paul R. Ehrlich, *Too Many People* from *The Population Bomb* by Dr. Paul R. Ehrlich. Copyright © 1968 by Paul R. Ehrlich.

Bulletin of the Atomic Scientists, Science and Public Affairs for Garrett Hardin, *To Trouble a Star: The Cost of Intervention in Nature*. Copyright © 1964 by the Educational Foundation for Nuclear Science.

The Wall Street Journal for Eric Morgenthaler, *Tweet, Tweet, Hic!* from its publication of September 8, 1970 and Dennis Farney, *Atom-Age Trash*, from its publication of January 25, 1971. Copyright © 1970, 1971 by *The Wall Street Journal*.

Professor Zbigniew Brzezinski for *America in the Technetronic Age* from *Encounter* (London) January, 1968. Copyright © 1968 by Zbigniew Brzezinski.

Dr. Harlow Shapley for *Man's Fourth Adjustment* from *The American Scholar*, Autumn 1956. Copyright © 1956 by Harlow Shapley.

Life Magazine for Brad Darrach, *Shaky* abridged from *Meet Shaky, The First Electronic Person* in *Life* Magazine, November 20, 1970. Copyright © 1970 by Time, Inc.

Cornell University Press for Plato, *The Apology of Socrates* from *Plato on the Trial and Death of Socrates* translated into English with an introduction and prefatory notes by Lane Cooper. Copyright 1941 by Lane Cooper.

Harcourt Brace Jovanovich, Inc. for William Golding, *The Hot Gates*, abridged from his essay in *The Hot Gates and Other Occasional Pieces*. Copyright © 1962 by William Golding.

Cambridge University Press for A. E. Housman, *Introductory Lecture* from *An Introductory Lecture Delivered* . . . October 3, 1892. (Cambridge University Press, 1937).

Alan Simpson for *The Marks of an Educated Man* from *Context*, I, No. 1 (Spring, 1961). Copyright © 1961 by Alan Simpson.

George Allen & Unwin Ltd. for Bertrand Russell, *A Free Man's Worship* from *Mysticism and Logic* (W. W. Norton, 2nd ed., 1954) Copyright by George Allen & Unwin Ltd.

The Viking Press, Inc. for Friedrich Nietzsche, *God is Dead* from *The Portable Nietzsche* translated and edited by Walter Kaufman. Copyright 1954 by The Viking Press, Inc.

Harper and Row, for William Barrett, *Existentialism as a Symptom of Man's Contemporary Crisis* from *Spiritual Problems in Contemporary Literature*, edited by Stanley Hopper. Copyright © 1952, 1957 by The Institute for Social and Religious Studies.

Psychology Today for Harvey Cox and T. George Harris, *Religion in the Age of Aquarius*, abridged from *Psychology Today* magazine, April, 1970. Copyright © Communications/Research/Machines, Inc.

The New York Times Co. for Paul Goodman, *The New Reformation* from *The New York Times Magazine*, Sept. 14, 1969. Copyright © 1969 by The New York Times Co.

Walter Kaufman for *On Dualistic Thinking—From Mani to the New Left*, abridged from *Survey: A Journal of Soviet and East European Studies*. Copyright © 1970 by Walter Kaufman.

Doubleday & Company, Inc. for Malcolm Muggeridge, *On Rediscovering Jesus* from *Esquire* magazine. Copyright © 1969 by Esquire, Inc. from the book *Jesus Rediscovered* by Malcolm Muggeridge.

Open Court Publishing Co. for Gautama Buddha, *The Sermon at Benares*, reprinted from *The Monist*, La Salle, Illinois.

Vedanta Society of Southern California for *Svetasvatara* from *The Upanishads*: The Principal Texts Selected and Translated from the Original Sanscrit by Swami Prabhavananda and Frederick Manchester (New York: The New American Library of World Literature, 1964). Copyright 1948, 1957 by The Vedanta Society of Southern California, Hollywood, California.

Random House, Inc. for William Faulkner, *Man Will Prevail*, his Nobel Prize speech, from *The Faulkner Reader*, Copyright © 1954 by William Faulkner.

PREFACE

A lot has happened since 1948 when the editors of this book first published TOWARD LIBERAL EDUCATION. We have been through the silent and scientific 50's, the violent and divisive 60's, and the nation that was proud of its democratic leadership in 1948 is less sure of itself today. Much of what we admired then is not an unmixed blessing now: yesterday's marvels of technology are today's ecological threats, and yesterday's shining metropolis is today's shabby inner city. It is natural that *TLE6* reflect this movement; compared to the five earlier editions of TOWARD LIBERAL EDUCATION, *TLE6* is a brand new book.

Many freshmen will leave their classrooms one day in November of 1972 to vote for the first time in a presidential election. This situation forces current realities abruptly into the curriculum. And it is only right that this should be so; their lives and futures will shape and be shaped by world forces. They are entitled to read and write about the problems that most concern them. We have therefore tried to select essays that will respond to this wish of students to learn about and influence the real world of the seventies. About seventy-five per cent of the material in our collection was written after 1968, and a glance at the Society section, for example, shows that we have included many essays on the tensions that most frequently hit the headlines.

We have also noticed a change in priorities among our students, many of whom place the preservation and development of the self ahead of success in conventional social roles. This concern with the self is reflected in new ideas in art, music, movies, writing, and education, many of which are represented in our collection. Even more striking, the emphasis on self has produced a new rhetoric for the 70's, a rhetoric of self-involvement, of commitment to the subject matter by the writer. It seems to us that our students most appreciate those essays in which the author is deeply involved. Because we recognize the validity of such rhetoric we have included many selections written from the committed point of view, such as autobiography, whether fictionalized or not, and interviews and eyewitness accounts. We hope they will stimulate the student to express his own involvement.

Perhaps some of those who remember our earlier collections will wonder what relationship there is between them and this edition. This is not so much the usual revision of an old book with new material added as it is a new book with a number of key pieces carried over from previous editions; a majority of the selections have been written in recent years, but we have also added new writings from the past that have become increasingly alive today. In short, we believe we have balanced continuity with change. Certainly the section of Values witnesses the endurance of important ideas from our heritage.

Yet we have in no sense ended where we began. This book presents a whole new set of attitudes about writing, style and subject matter, about the nature of freshman English courses, and even about the aims of higher education. We believe it will provide a valuable experience in reading and writing for students and teachers. It was not always easy for us to agree; our selection process reflected many of the tensions of our current society and culture. But, we are glad that the continuity of the past with the present, found particularly in the final section of *TLE6*, acknowledges that at the heart of the matter we were always together.

It is impossible to acknowledge our numerous and great obligations. We are mindful of our debt to friends, colleagues, and students of today and yesterday. But we are especially grateful to Jane Ross, English Editor of Holt, Rinehart and Winston, who at every stage of this book generously shared our concerns and perceptively advised us. We want to thank Frances Ware of Madison College for assistance, David A. Remley of the University of New Mexico and Gail Baker of the Hummingbird Press for especially helpful suggestions, and Priscilla Van Haverbeke for seeing the manuscript through the press.

January, 1972

L.G.L.
W.M.G.
G.A.
G.P.

CONTENTS

IMPLOSIONS

WOMEN

REACTIONS

III SPEECH INTERFERENCE, POOR RECEPTION, GROK

CULTURE BARRIERS

MEDIA MESSAGES

VI SCIENCE THE DJINN FROM THE BOTTLE

VII VALUES THE HEART OF THE MATTER

RHETORICAL TABLE OF CONTENTS

TLE SIX

I
SELF

THE REVOLUTION OF I

Having pried through the strata, analyzed to a hair, counsel'd with doctors and calculated close, I find no sweeter fat than sticks to my own bones.

WALT WHITMAN,
"SONG OF MYSELF"

The principal inheritance of the 70s from the social actions and frustrations of the 60s seems to be a focus inward, an emphasis on the primacy of self. Leaders of "pop-cult" are testing all of our institutions, ideas, and actions by the standard of the self: anything that doesn't help self-development is seen as "the enemy" and is rejected. Nothing escapes this scrutiny; taboos about sex and nudity, the sanctity of marriage, the police, school, political parties and institutions, male dominance, patriotism, and God are all subject to the acid test. We have collected some representative illustrations of the self-impulse, ranging from the joy and knowledge to be found in the physical self to the struggle to discover self in the melting pot of our society.

But discussion of this issue can hardly be confined to one section; in fact our whole collection illustrates this remarkable tension as it has existed through the history of our civilization to the latest turmoil to hit the headlines. The ecological outcry insists on considering the "quality of life" for the individual ahead of the quantity of production for society as a whole. Religious eclecticism, pentecostal movements, witch cults, and mysticism arise out of a desire to make the religious experience uniquely personal rather than uniformly social. Similar results of the self-impulse can be seen in the increasing personalization of the arts, the revival of the black flag of anarchy in social action, and among small groups of students a disgust with the impersonalized group-goaled John Deweyized school system, this latter point expressed typically by James Kunen's *Strawberry Statement*.

Although the event that Kunen describes is often thought of as an expression of doctrinaire political radicalism, his participation in it is thoroughly personal; he tries to keep his ties with his own life clear and undamaged by the Columbia rebellion. When he makes a call on a telephone in an office he has occupied, he doesn't call the first Commissar for instructions, he calls his mother. The tone of his account expresses the conviction that his actions are completely individual and in the mainstream of the very cultural tradition supported by the liberal education of the university he disrupted, a point made in George Stade's essay in Section II. The sanctity of the individual is an idea whose roots run deep into American society, and its resurgence in the 70s may be a welcome sign of the health of the whole organism.

Through The Looking Glass

A SUN-BATH–NAKEDNESS

Walt Whitman

Sunday, Aug. 27—Another day quite free from marked prostration and pain. It seems indeed as if peace and nutriment from heaven subtly filter into me as I slowly hobble down these country lanes and across fields, in the good air—as I sit here in solitude with Nature—open, voiceless, mystic, far removed, yet palpable, eloquent Nature. I merge myself in the scene, in the perfect day. Hovering over the clear brook water, I am soothed by its soft gurgle in one place, and the hoarser murmurs of its three-foot fall in another. Come, ye disconsolate, in whom any latent eligibility is left—come get the sure virtues of creek shore, and wood and field. Two months (July and August, '77) have I absorbed them, and they begin to make a new man of me. Every day, seclusion—every day at least two or three hours of freedom, bathing, no talk, no bonds, no dress, no books, no *manners*.

Shall I tell you, reader, to what I attribute my already much-restored health? That I have been almost two years, off and on, without drugs and medicines, and daily in the open air. Last summer I found a particularly secluded little dell off one side by my creek, originally a large dug-out marl pit, now abandoned, filled with bushes, trees, grass, a group of willows, a straggling bank, and a spring of delicious water running right through the middle of it, with two or three little cascades. Here I retreated every hot day, and follow it up this summer. Here I realize the meaning of that old fellow who said he was seldom less alone than when alone. Never before did I get so close to Nature; never before did she come so close to me. By old habit, I penciled down from time to time, almost automatically, moods, sights, hours, tints, and outlines, on the spot. Let me specially record the satisfaction of this current forenoon, so serene and primitive, so conventionally exceptional, natural.

An hour or so after breakfast I wended my way down to the recesses of the aforesaid dell, which I and certain thrushes, catbirds, etc., had all to ourselves. A light southwest wind was blowing through the treetops. It was just the place and time for my Adamic air bath and flesh brushing from head to foot. So hanging clothes on a rail near by, keeping old broadbrim straw on head and easy shoes on feet, haven't I had a good time the last two hours! First with the stiff-elastic bristles rasping arms, breast, sides, till they turned scarlet—then partially bathing in the clear waters of the running brook—taking everything very leisurely, with many rests and pauses—stepping about barefooted every few minutes now and then in some neighboring black ooze, for unctuous mud bath to my feet—a brief second and third rinsing in the crystal running waters—rubbing with the fragrant towel —slow negligent promenades on the turf up and down in the sun, varied with occasional rests, and further frictions of the bristle brush—sometimes carrying my portable chair with me from place to place, as my range is quite extensive here, nearly a hundred rods, feeling quite secure from intrusion (and that indeed I am not at all nervous about, if it accidentally happens).

As I walked slowly over the grass, the sun shone out enough to show the shadow moving with me. Somehow I seemed to get identity with each and every thing around me, in its condition. Nature was naked, and I was also. It was too lazy, soothing, and joyous-equable to speculate about. Yet I might have thought somehow in this vein: Perhaps the inner, never-lost rapport we hold with earth, light, air, trees, etc., is not to be realized through eyes and mind only, but through the whole corporeal body, which I will not have blinded or bandaged any more than the eyes. Sweet, sane, still nakedness in Nature!—ah, if poor, sick, prurient humanity in cities might really know you once more! Is not nakedness then indecent? No, not inherently. It is your thought, your sophistication, your fear, your respectability, that is indecent. There come moods when these clothes of ours are not only too irksome to wear, but are themselves indecent. Perhaps indeed he or she to whom the free exhilarating ecstasy of nakedness in Nature has never been eligible (and how many thousands there are!) has not really known what purity is—nor what faith or art or health really is. (Probably the whole curriculum of first-class philosophy, beauty, heroism, form, illustrated by the old Hellenic race —the highest height and deepest depth known to civilization in those departments—came from their natural and religious idea of Nakedness.)

Many such hours, from time to time, the last two summers—I attribute my partial rehabilitation largely to them. Some good people may think it a feeble or half-cracked way of spending one's time and thinking. Maybe it is.

HELP SEE OWN WAY BEHAVE

Jane Howard

Extremes entice me, perhaps because I represent so many middles. It was in the middle of the nineteen-thirties, in the middle of the sign of Taurus and in the middle of the Middle West that my middle-class parents named me Jane. I have never been sorry they did, yet it was with a sense of oddly mounting excitement one wet November noontime that I stood reading a sign on the door of a Roman Catholic retreat in northern Massachusetts. Scrawled with a Magic Marker and already runny from the rain, the sign read "ABANDON BACK-HOME NAMES, ALL YE WHO ENTER HERE."

Inside that house I need not—in fact *could* not—be Jane, the vagabond journalist from New York via Illinois and Michigan. My identity, my marital status, my "interesting" "career" with its all-expense trips to such places as Gangtok, Tangier and Garden City, Kansas, would all be irrelevant. The thirty-nine people I would meet in that house, most of them total strangers, would react not to my labels and biography and credentials but just to me, and I in the same spirit to them. The NTL had organized this $350 "Advanced Personal Growth Laboratory," for people who had missed, or who wanted more of, the two-week version held annually at Bethel, Maine. My own interest had first been kindled at Bethel a few months earlier. I visited there the last four days of the 1968 summer session, hoping thereby to sample the flavor of the place and of the whole organization. Four days wasn't enough time, though. When I dropped in on the Advanced Personal Growth Lab (which everybody I met told me I simply must do), I was greeted warily. The lab members, who had spent nearly a fortnight developing their own special jargon, names, and camaraderie, weren't happy to have a spectator. Only after a good deal of talk and voting and ceremony did they let me in.

"You can't possibly *begin* to understand what this is all about," several of them told me, "coming in this way at the last minute. Why weren't you here at the beginning?"

Because I had never heard of it before, that was why, but I wished I had. Later, traveling around the country, I gathered that to enthusiasts of sensitivity training that lab means what the Davis Cup means to tennis fans, or the *Ring* to lovers of Wagner. During the phone conversation that convinced me to sign up for the Massachusetts version, I scribbled a note quoting my informant. The note said: "DAMN GOOD EXAMPLE, COMPLETE RESURRECTION, HELP SEE OWN WAY BEHAVE, NOV. 9–17, HAMILTON, MASS." . . .

Our Massachusetts quarters, converted from the estate of a rich family, were much more spartan. The fireplace no longer worked. Men were housed on the third floor, women on the second, everybody in one of several curtained cubicles in a room. My room, dominated by a graphic bleeding-heart crucifix, had five cubicles. Two of the others were taken, one by a short middle-aged widow with a kind face named Lucy, and the other by an olive-skinned girl with an enigmatic European accent named Tanya. I could easily imagine Lucy on real-life home ground: she would live nearby, and have a bird-feeding station in the yard. Not until I chanced to see Tanya's toothpaste, however, could I guess that she was Greek. It was labeled ΚΟΛΥΣΙΤ.

Our four trainers had new names, too. The chief among them was a wiry small man who looked to be in his forties and who always made me think of a Scottish bagpiper. He told us to call him Conchis, after the hero of Fowles' novel *The Magus*. In real life he was John Weir, just resigned from the faculty of the University of Southern California in order to become a full-time itinerant group leader. His wife Joyce, here called Noel, would lead sessions in Body Movement. Ted Kroeber, who teaches psychology at San Francisco State College, would also assist Weir, and so would my old friend Michael Kahn, in this incarnation called Les Glass after J. D. Salinger's paterfamilias.

Weir decreed a silent lunch, and then a silent free period. Not really at ease, I went outside and did something that always gives me a comfortable feeling of abandon: I rolled down a hill. It was a wet hill, but it still felt good. In the retreat living room, where we next assembled, all the furniture had been removed except the phonograph. The Weirs don't think much of tables and chairs, but their labs rely greatly on music.

"There's a place somewhere in this room where you'll feel comfortable," Noel told us all as she put a record on. "Find that place." Gauchely, tentatively we moved about the room. I found my place near the hearth.

"Gradually," Noel told us, "ooze to the floor." We oozed. "You have no bones," she said. "You can't keep your knees up. You're just a blob. Your eyes are closed. If you touch other blobs, it doesn't matter. Now, let your ooze coagulate into a ball, so that your head touches your knees and your organism is a tight, round unit." Obediently we coagulated.

"Now, very gradually, stretch out and discover that you have a backbone! You can move! You can crawl!" With eyes still shut we did crawl, like the most primitive of vertebrates. "It's all right," she said, "if you bump into others." Bump we did. As the music played on we advanced to more sophisticated phyla. In time we were given permission to walk around on all fours, and to stand up on our hind legs.

"Now open your eyes," Noel said, "and feel how it is to see without focusing." We felt how it was. I reached to touch a metal sconce on the wall as if I had never beheld such a thing, or anything else, in all my life.

"Now notice," Noel said, "that there are other creatures around you." Indeed there were, and they began to cluster in friendly fours, fives and eights. My cluster was a small one, patently composed of leftovers. I ended up with one arm entwined in that of a very shy, very blond man in a polo shirt named Orpheus. His other arm was linked with that of a short fortyish brunette, with tears in her eyes, named Lili Marlene.

Evolving from a blob of ooze to an anthropoid did not affect me as it did most. I felt numb and anti-social, and somewhat afraid. The others in the lab, several of whom seemed already to know each other, gathered gaily before dinner on the second floor landing, stashing their liquor bottles by the naked toes of a statue of the Virgin Mary. Ordinarily that juxtaposition would amuse me, but now I felt out of phase and sorry for myself. I retreated to my cubicle and read a book. "Help See Own Way Behave" was a valid promise: my whole life I have escaped unpleasantness by reading. . . .

My own favorite Graphics period, in which I crept boldly from the periphery of things to the melodramatic center, came to be known in the folklore of the group as The Great Finger-Paint Fight, featuring Holly vs. Arizona.

Holly seemed to me to be all the things I conspicuously wasn't: pert, popular, vivacious enough to be a cheerleader. To the extent that she had made any impression on me at all, which wasn't much, she annoyed me. She and I were at opposite ends of a long table covered with an unbroken stretch of paper on which we were all to do a mass mural in finger paint. My section of the mural was dazzling. It had an amber tree against a blue-green background, resplendent with fruits and flowers and the all-important roots. It was tastefully connected with the paintings of my neighbors on either side, and so touchingly symbolic that I paused to stand back and admire it. As I did so a handful of mud-colored glop came careening down the length of the room to land right in the middle of my beautiful tree. Holly had hurled it. I was so heartbroken I nearly wept. It was as if a hurricane had uprooted my tree. But not until the others in the group said: "What are you going to do, *let* her ruin it?" did it cross my mind to retaliate.

I threw a handful of my paint at Holly's picture, then she more at mine, and she some at me, and I at her. Pretty soon the two of us had squared off facing each other in an unrestrained free-for-all. Everybody else stood back as we plastered the walls and windows of the room, not to say each other, with multicolored finger paint. Somebody removed my bespattered glasses. The cheering spectators chose sides.

"I'll lay you two-to-one odds on Arizona," somebody said.

"You have everything I want," Holly yelled. "*I'd* like to have a pretty tree *too*, you know."

"You always ruin everything of mine!" I retorted. "Besides, you never have to help with the dishes!" Plainly we were regressing *à deux* and becoming each other's sister. Soon all the other women in the group joined in too, gleefully smearing us and each other with paint. In time the men got into the act. Everybody's faces and clothes turned hopelessly technicolor. The paint grew cold and flaky as it dried on our skin and even inside our clothes, but nobody cared.

"Hey, Arizona," Francie said, apparently convinced at last that I wasn't anti-Semitic, "let's have a tribal-cleaning ritual. I've got a car; let's you and me take everybody's dirty clothes to the laundromat after lunch. I've never even *been* to a laundromat."

That sounded fine. Our triumphantly dirty group was the envy of the others as we waited in line for lunch. In the line I stood next to a woman named Gretchen from another group, whom I had liked in our only previous talk. She had said "I'm not from Boston—I'm from another large, in fact, *very* large, Eastern Seaboard metropolis." I had been missing such signs of wit. Wit is tolerated in encounter groups, but not encouraged. It is regarded as an irrelevant defense, and an evasion of what in some circles is known as the nitty-gritty. Maybe so, but it is a defense I cling to myself and cherish in others.

I was therefore amazed when sympathetic Gretchen made an ugly face at me when I asked if she'd had a nice morning.

"May I ask," I said to her rather icily when lunch was done, "why you stuck your tongue out at me?"

"Not at *you*," she replied. "Don't be silly. I was just so upset about the morning *I'd* had. They took me on a fantasy trip all the way back to when I was three years old, and it was really harrowing."

Oh God, I thought, how unperceptive of me. How many other potential friends had I lost through such unreal, imagined slights? How inaccurate was my radar? The fun of the paint fight faded entirely as I brooded about such matters. As Francie and I drove off with a huge bag of dirty clothes I cried, brightening only long enough to explain the arcane symbolic mysteries of the Maytag Wash Cycle. When we returned for our Body Movement class I cried again, this time on the shoulder of Orpheus.

"I don't even know what I'm crying about," I sobbed to him. "I guess it's just because I don't know what I'm doing or where I'm going in this world."

"That seems a plenty good reason," he said, and his consoling tone made me weep all the more. I was still in tears when Noel directed us to lie down on the floor and listen to the music. She assigned us to imagine that each of us was a drop of water—any water anywhere—and to do whatever that drop of water would do. First I envisioned my own tears, then water leaping in a mountain brook. Then I saw a coral reef like one I had once snorkeled over in Puerto Rico, in which there swam a school of nearly transparent tropical fish.

Then I became a fish myself, only not tropical but a haddock like one I had caught the previous summer in Maine. I was big, sleek and silver, flashing with sturdy grace around the floor of the ocean. The music continued. Others in the group had risen to dance out their water fantasies, but I was still prone, vaguely mimicking the motions of swimming.

As that same fish, I spied a worm dangling from the end of a hook. I bit it and was caught. The funny part was I didn't care. I didn't mind even being hauled up out of the ocean, having the hook ripped from my mouth and being tossed into a wooden box on the bottom of the boat with other fish, there to thrash and finally expire. Nor did I later object when I was beheaded, degutted and served, with boiled potatoes and tiny fresh new peas. No longer sobbing, I slowly rose to a standing position.

Noel, who had changed the record, now was saying: "Each of us has a personal myth inside him he wants to act out. Act out yours." I still didn't feel exactly sprightly, but at least I was on my feet. I trudged around examining the room's peripheries, methodically inspecting all four corners, stopping in none, always going on. (As I say, I've always felt attracted to extremes.) When I got to the corner with the phonograph where Noel was, I ignored her outstretched hand. I didn't even look at her, or for that matter, at anyone. I just went on, hardly noticing that others were acting out their myths, too.

Slowly my trudge became a sort of dance, in which I circled the other dancers warily, still not stopping, thinking "this one's interesting, yes, but what about *him*, over there? And who are *they*? Might I like them better? What's going on in the other room?" That's my myth, all right, I thought (and still do think): I'm far too seldom content with where I am, and often ruinously curious about where I'm not.

But finally I tired of motion. I stopped arbitrarily, figuring (with what for me was a revelation) that maybe if I just stayed in one place somebody would find me. Somebody did: Lili Marlene. I don't know how I fit into her myth, but she hovered and danced around me like a loving, protective mother. I thought, disloyally, that it might have been nice to have been found by a man. But having emerged so recently from fishhood—true to my scribbled promise "COMPLETE RESURRECTION"—I was scarcely what you could call nubile.

That phonograph was on and busy all the time, even before breakfast. People who had previously shied away from demure foxtrots were now devising abandoned and dramatic new steps to records by Feliciano, Leanard Cohen and the Doors. Even I, with a gimpy foot and a long history of athletic ineptitude, was taking part. Less and less did I retreat to my curtained cubicle, or brood about people in my "real life" outside. In fact, when one of those friends phoned long-distance, I rather snappishly said: "But I'm *not* Jane this week at all, don't you *see*? I'm Arizona!" . . .

Toward the end of the meeting Conchis rather abruptly turned out all the lights, leaving us leaning bewildered against the walls of a pitch-dark room. It was, as a behavioral science graduate student might say, quite a dynamic. The bolder people groped their way around the room, finding special friends and forming whispering, cuddling groups. Such groups developed on either side of me, but I was alone, still too forlorn to strike out myself in search of camaraderie. I was infinitely grateful when Jacques and Gretchen came over to me, uncannily aware of my aloneness. Jacques gave me a kiss, and Gretchen sat down to put her arm around me. It was positively Proustian. I felt as if I were a baby again (not a baby fish, but a human infant), whose parents had come to her nursery bedside to tuck her safely in. I felt loved.

That feeling multiplied, in me and in us all, the next day. In our final Body Movement session we stood in a circle. One by one, as music played, we went forward with closed eyes as all the others in the "family group" simultaneously touched us. This exercise, as melting as any experience of my life, was clearly a demonstration of *agape*, not *eros*. We called it a "love bath" because our whole bodies, from earlobes to kneecaps to heels, were barraged with affection. Out of context it might have seemed part of a Maoist plot to arouse and destroy the whole free world, but in context it was exquisite. My old Mid-western reluctance to be demonstrative with other people dissolved. Afterward I felt as interdependent as one of a litter of newborn kittens, requiring at all times to be in physical contact with somebody else. Within us all burgeoned a love of mankind in general and our fellow lab members in particular. I have not elsewhere found the like of that love.

For a collective farewell rite on the final Sunday morning, all forty of us joined hands to form a huge circle. We swayed back and forth to music for a short while. Then Conchis broke the circle, leading us around the room in a snaking, uncoiling, spiraling "jelly roll" so that each of us was brought into contact with every one of the others. Now I could see the sense of eyeballing. When the eyes you look into have had a chance to become important to you, the exercise can touch the core of your soul.

"Hi," said Orpheus' eyes, "you and I have already said goodbye haven't we?"

"Sorry I never got to know you more," said Holly's.

"There's real affection between us, isn't there?" said Gretchen's.

"Funny, I never thought I'd even like you," said Isaiah, "but now, oddly enough, I love you."

Then the time came for us to part hands and eyes and resume our places among the real people—those who had not spent these past eight days amid such exposure, risk, regression, insights, trust and love. Conchis dismissed us with a poem by Blake:

> He who binds to himself a joy
> Does the wingèd life destroy;
> But he who kisses the bird as it flies
> Lives in eternity's sun rise.

Then, in his own language, he added some prose advice: "Don't talk about it, whatever it is," he said. "Get off your ass and *do* it. Stick with it. If it hurts, it's probably good."

As I packed my clothes—including a cardigan permanently stained with dried finger paint—I tried to summarize what I had learned. No lessons that other people, in and out of the movement, hadn't been trying to teach me for years: that I could love strangers and they me, that anger can be converted into strength and force, that tears can melt anguish, and that staying put can be more rewarding than keeping in motion. Banal truths, really, but this time they hit home, because these eight days I had trusted the people in charge and yielded to them. They were gentle and wise as well as messianic. Their style was not shrill; they did not push and shove. They admitted their own limits, gave of themselves incessantly, and perceived in me and in us all something more than we knew was there. Having felt inflated with helium, I thought how hard it would be to become Jane Howard again.

As I made my way from my cubicle down the stairs and out the door to the real world, I set my suitcase down at least a dozen times for effusive, last-minute hugs. I could not have been sadder to leave had I spent eight weeks in that house, instead of just eight days. But I was saved from maudlin tears by a farewell one new friend called out as I left the house: "Goodbye, Arizona, Bubbi."

PEAK EXPERIENCES IN EDUCATION AND ART

A. H. Maslow

Something big is happening. It's happening to everything that concerns human beings. Everything the human being generates is involved, and certainly education is involved. A new *Weltanschauung* is the process of being developed, a new *Zeitgeist*, a new set of values and a new way of finding them, and certainly a new image of man. There is a new kind of psychology —presently called the humanistic, existential, third-force psychology—that at this transitional moment is certainly different in many important ways from the Freudian and behavioristic psychologies, which have been the two great comprehensive, dominating psychologies.

There are new conceptions of interpersonal relationships. There is a new image of society. There is a new conception of the goals of society, of all the social institutions, and of all the social sciences. There is a new economics, a new conception of politics, and revolutions in religion, in science, in work. There is a newer conception of education, and this forms the background for my ideas of music and creativity.

First of all, most psychologies of learning are beside the point; that is, beside the "humanistic" point. Most teachers and books present learning as the acquisition of associations, of skills, and of capacities that are *external* and not *intrinsic* to the human character, to the human personality, to the person himself. Picking up coins or keys or possessions or something of the sort is like picking up reinforcements and conditioned reflexes that are in a certain very profound sense expendable. It does not really matter if one has a conditioned reflex: If I salivate to the sound of a buzzer and then this extinguishes, nothing has happened to me; I have lost nothing of any consequence whatever. We might almost say that those extensive books on the psychology of learning are of no consequence—at least to the human center, to the human soul, to the human essence.

Generated by the new humanistic philosophy is a new conception of learning, teaching, and education. Such a conception holds that the goal of education—the human goal, the humanistic goal—is ultimately the "self-actualization" of a person, the development of the fullest height that the human species or a particular individual can come to. In a less technical way, it is helping the person to become the best that he is able to become. Such a goal involves very serious shifts in learning strategies.

Associative learning is certainly useful: for learning things that are of no real consequence, or for learning techniques that are interchangeable. And many of the things we must learn are like that. If one needed to memorize the vocabulary of another language, he would learn it by sheer rote memory. Here the laws of association can be a help. Whereas if one wants to learn automatic habits in driving, like responding to a red signal light or something of the sort, then conditioning is of consequence. It is important and useful, especially in a technological society.

In terms of becoming a better person, of self-development, self-fulfillment, or "becoming fully human," the greatest learning experiences are very different. In my life, such experiences have been far more important than listening, memorizing, and organizing data for formal courses.

More important for me have been such experiences as having a child. Our first baby changed me as a psychologist. It made the behaviorism I had been so enthusiastic about look so foolish that I could not stomach it any more. It

was impossible. Having a second baby, and learning how profoundly different people are even before birth, made it impossible for me to think in terms
of the kind of learning psychology in which one can teach anybody anything.
I could no longer think in terms of the John B. Watson theory, "Give me
two babies and I will make one into this and one into the other." It is as if
he never had any children. We know only too well that a parent cannot
make his children into anything. Children make themselves into something.
The best we can do, and frequently the most effect we can have, is to serve
as something to react against if the child presses too hard.

Another profound learning experience that I value far more highly than
any particular course or any degree is my personal psychoanalysis: discovering my own identity, my own self. Yet another basic experience—far more
important—was getting married; that was certainly more instructive than my
Ph.D. . . .

Another empirical statement can be made about what we call "peak experiences." We have made studies of peak experiences by asking groups of
people and individuals such questions as, "What was the most ecstatic moment of your life?" or "Have you experienced transcendent ecstasy?" One
might think that in a general population, such questions might get only blank
stares. But there were many answers. Apparently the transcendent ecstasies
had been kept private because there are few if any ways of speaking about
them in public. They are sort of embarrassing, shameful, not "scientific"
—which many believe is the ultimate sin.

But we found many trippers to set them off. Almost everybody seems to
have peak experiences or ecstasies. The question might be asked in terms of
the single most joyous, happiest, most blissful moment of your whole life.
You might ask questions of the kind I asked: "How did you feel different
about yourself at that time?" "How did the world look different?" "What did
you feel like?" "What were your impulses?" "How did you change if you
did?" I want to report that the two easiest ways of getting peak experiences
(in terms of simple statistics in empirical reports) are through music and
through sex. I will push aside sex education, as such discussions are premature—although I am certain that one day we will not giggle over it, but will
take it quite seriously and teach children that like music, like love, like
insight, like a beautiful meadow, like a cute baby, or whatever, there are
many paths to heaven. And sex is one of them. And music is one of them.
These happen to be the easiest ones to understand.

For purposes of identifying and studying peak experiences, a list of triggers can be made. The list gets so long, however, that it becomes necessary
to make generalizations. It looks as if any experience of real excellence, of
real perfection, of any moving toward perfect justice or toward perfect
values, tends to produce a peak experience. Not always. But it's a generali-
zation I would make for the many kinds of things that we can concentrate

on. Remember, I am talking here as a scientist. This doesn't sound like scientific talk, but this is a new kind of science.

We know that from this new humanistic science has come one of the real childbearing improvements since Adam and Eve; that is, natural childbirth, a potent source of peak experiences. We know just how to encourage peak experiences; how women can have children in such a fashion as to have a great and mystical experience, a religious experience if you wish—an illumination, a revelation, an insight. That is what women say in interviews. They become a different kind of person because there ensues what I have called "the cognition of being."

We must make a new vocabulary for all these untilled, unworked problems. "Cognition of being" really means the cognition that Plato and Socrates were talking about; almost, you could say, a technology of happiness, of pure excellence, pure truth, pure goodness, and so on. Well, why *not* a technology of joy, of happiness?

Let's proceed to music in this relation. So far, peak experiences are reported only from what we might call "classical music." I have not found a peak experience from John Cage (or from an Andy Warhol movie, from abstract expressionist painting, etc.). I just haven't. The peak experiences that have been reported as great joy, ecstasy, visions of another world or another level of living, have come from the great classics. On the other hand, music also melts over and fuses into dancing and rhythm. So far as this realm of research is concerned, there really isn't much difference; they melt into each other. Music as a path to peak experiences includes dancing. It also includes the rhythmic experience, even very simple rhythmic experience —the good dancing of a rumba, or the kinds of things that the kids can do with drums. (I don't know whether to call the latter music, dancing, rhythm, athletics, or something else.)

Love, awareness, and reverence of the body are clearly good paths to peak experiences. These in turn are good paths (not guaranteed, but statistically likely) to the "cognition of being," to the perceiving of the Platonic essences, intrinsic values, the ultimate of being. And these paths are a therapeutic-like help toward both the curing-of-sicknesses kind of therapy and toward the growth of full-humanness. In other words, peak experiences often have consequences, very important consequences.

Music and art can have the same kinds of consequences; there is a certain overlap. They can do the same thing as psychotherapy if one keeps his goals right, knows just what he is about, and is conscious of what he is going toward. We can talk of the breaking up of symptoms like the breaking up of clichés, anxieties, and the like; *or* we can talk about the development of spontaneity, courage, Olympian or godlike humor, sensory awareness, body awareness, and the like. Music and art and rhythm and dancing are excellent ways of moving toward that second means of discovering identity.

Such triggers tend to do all kinds of things to our autonomic nervous systems, endocrine glands, feelings, and emotions. They just do. We do not know enough about physiology to understand why they do. But they do, and these are unmistakable experiences. They are a little like pain, which is also an unmistakable experience. For experientially empty people, including a tragically large proportion of the population, for people who do not know what is going on inside themselves and who live by clocks, schedules, rules, laws, hints from the neighbors (i.e., other-directed people), this kind of trigger provides a way of discovering what the self is like. There are signals from inside; there are voices that yell out, "By gosh this is good, don't ever doubt it!" We use these signals as a path to teach the discovery of the self and self-actualization. The discovery of identity comes via the impulse voices, via the ability to listen to your own guts and what is going on inside of you.

This discovery is also an experimental kind of education that may eventually lead us into a parallel educational establishment, into another *kind* of school, where mathematics can be just as beautiful, just as peak-producing, as music. Of course there are mathematics teachers who have devoted themselves to preventing this. I had no glimpse of mathematics as a study in aesthetics until I was 30 years old, when I read some books about it. And one can find the same kind of experience with history or anthropology (in the sense of learning another culture), social anthropology, palaeontology, or the study of science.

Here again I want to talk data. If one works with great creators, great scientists, the creative scientists, *that* is the way they talk. The picture of the scientist—his image as one who never smiles, who bleeds embalming fluid rather than blood—must change. Such conceptions must yield to an understanding of the creative scientist who lives by peak experiences, who lives for the moments of glory when a problem is solved and when suddenly through a microscope he gets a new perception, a moment of revelation, of illumination, insight, understanding, ecstasy. These are vital for him. Scientists are very shy and embarrassed about this. They refuse to talk about it in public. It takes a delicate kind of midwifery to extract it; but it is there, and I have got it out. If one manages to convince a creative scientist that he is not going to be laughed at for these things, then he will blushingly admit the fact of having a high emotional experience at the moment in which the crucial correlation turns out right. They just don't talk about it. As for the usual textbook on how you do science, it is total nonsense.

My point is that if we are conscious enough of what we are doing and are philosophically insightful in doing it, we may be able to use those experiences that most easily produce ecstasies and revelations, peaks and illumination, bliss and rapture. We may be able to use them as models by which to reevaluate all kinds of teaching.

The final impression that I want to try to work out is that effective education in music, art, dancing, and rhythm is intrinsically far closer to the kind of education I think necessary than is the usual "core curriculum"; that is, it is closer to the goal of learning one's identity as an essential part of his education. And if education doesn't do that, it is useless. Education is learning to grow, learning what to grow toward, learning what is good and bad, learning what is desirable and undesirable, learning what to choose and what not to choose. In this realm of intrinsic learning, intrinsic teaching, and intrinsic education, I think that the arts are so close to our psychological and biological core, so close to this identity, this biological identity, that rather than think of these courses as a sort of whipped cream or luxury, we must let them become basic experiences in our education. They could very well serve as a model; the glimpse into the infinite that they provide might well serve as the means by which we might rescue the rest of the school curriculum from the value-free, value-neutral, goal-lacking meaninglessness into which it has fallen.

OUT-OF-SIGHT JOANIE AND SEQUENTIAL MONOGAMY

Rasa Gustaitis

On one of Joanie's occasional trips to New York, a friend bought her a purple feather boa because, that friend told me, Joanie is the only person in the world who can put on a purple boa and attract no more attention than she does walking down Fifth Avenue in her simple everyday clothes. It was the perfect thing for her to wear with the purple velvet cape, the Indian red blouse and the orange skirt. It also would have looked good with the black silk blouse and tiger-spotted silk harem pants Joanie is wearing right now as she dishes out spaghetti with grass-seasoned sauce in her tidy, warm San Francisco kitchen.

"I'm thinking of changing my name to Sequin Palladini," she says.

"Oh? Why?"

"Just because of the sound. I dig the sound. It suits me."

Over a mouthful of spaghetti—delicious spaghetti—I peer at Joanie with her newly red hair, the butterfly effect penciled out from the eyes, those pants, the gold chain dangling from hips to pelvis. Well, why not? Why should an intelligent, well-educated Jewish girl from New York not be Sequin Palladini if she so chooses?

Joanie is smiling, her eyes are laughing. Once again my astonishment turns into admiration. Two years ago Joanie was the proper-liberal dutiful wife of a social worker. Dinner was always on time, friends were employed and square, evenings were family scenes, weekends were busy. She was a wife-mother-career woman, one of those superfemales who seem to be always doing a dozen things at once, all efficiently. And all the while she was miserable.

Most of her friends were married and similarly miserable two years ago. They're still her friends now, but it's a new scene altogether. She sees them separately, them and the men and women they now live with. Sometimes they leave their children with her, to be picked up by the ex-spouse. With some of these old friends Joanie is closer now than ever, perhaps because, for the first time in years, she feels completely alive. A whole new world opened to her when, somewhat to her own surprise, she left Ed (also a fictitious name) after eleven years. Her old habits and hang-ups came off with her wedding ring. What remained was herself at last, going hip at thirty, Joanie only more so—Sequin Palladini.

Not that she flipped into an all-out hippie. She continued to work for a living, sent her two children to public school in neat clothes with homework done. She even enrolled her six-year-old daughter in dancing school, like a good suburban mother. But her entire outlook toward her work, her family, her friends and her possessions underwent a transformation. Now she is in the vanguard of a growing number of people who are spreading the turned-on life-style through middle-class society.

"Let's go into the living room, it's more comfortable," Joanie says, getting up and clearing the dishes. I follow her into the high-ceilinged salon filled with things draped and dripping and sparkling darkly in candlelight. Tinsel, cut-glass beads and long pieces of cloth droop from a mirror behind the couch; some handmade copper and silver pendants hang from nails on the wall behind the easy chair opposite, beside the fireplace. There's a batik print above the marble mantle, and below it, on the floor, a tangle of plants, straw flowers and reeds. The lower halves of the three tall windows that form a bay are covered with Persian print cloth, a cozy back-drop to the wooden window seat and its mirror-inlaid embroidered Indian pillows. A small light machine turns slowly, catching colors and flashes and letting them slip back into the shadow. The whole thing is more like some Persian courtesan's tent than the living room of a woman who grew up in New York's Westchester County.

Joanie lights a stick of incense, slips it into a ceramic candle holder on the mantel and then sinks into the rope hammock hung in the doorway between the dining room and the bedroom. In the dim light, her hair regains its natural darkness and her face becomes pale and soft.

"I was looking at that dresser the other day," she says, motioning with her left arm toward the recesses of the bedroom. "I painted the drawers different colors once when Ed was away for a month because of his job. I knew he wouldn't approve, so I did it when he was away. It was just one of the ways that the supercracks in our marriage began showing.

"It was somewhere in this period after our return from Mexico that it became apparent that Ed and I were moving apart. When we married we were mates. For a while we kept getting closer and swung together. But somewhere in those eleven years of our marriage the pendulum reversed in this superslow motion thing between us and we began to move in opposite directions. He started a reaction to his liberal childhood toward a middle-class secure thing while I started toward the place where his family was at when he was a child. It was like what happens in an eclipse—the sun's shadow moves toward the moon, covers it, and you see them for a moment together. They they divide and you see opposites.

"All these signs began appearing. For example, I was halfway to a pilot's license and I never told Ed about it because I knew he'd freak. I had heard an ad on the radio for flying lessons and I started to think about the idea and thought I might just dig it. So one day after my classes at Cal I got into the car, went to the airport and someone took me up in a plane. I loved it. So I started to save money and whenever I had enough for another flying class I'd go to the airport in the afternoon and put in my hours and then go home and make supper and all that.

"We did a lot of interesting things together, Ed and I. But he is one of those people who can't stay home so we ran around every weekend. He seemed to mark time by moving himself around bodily—one weekend to Santa Cruz, another weekend to Mendecino, always going somewhere. He turned me onto that way of living but I really often preferred to stay home and make things. He kept saying I wasn't adventurous.

"So anyway, the supercracks became bigger. I flew a plane, I had an affair, one thing after another. We were building up a thing that was getting more and more secretive, as if in this way we could keep everything from crashing. We didn't talk about the big things but we argued about little ones. I'd want to put bead curtains in the doorways and he'd say that wasn't very practical, doors are to walk through. Or I'd come up with some lighting effect and he'd say that was very dramatic, but how can anyone read a book? He wanted to move out to Berkeley and get a house with a yard and a dog. I wanted to stay in the city.

"A couple of friends turned us on to grass but Ed wouldn't keep any in the house because he thought it was too dangerous. I thought he was being too uptight. I smoked more when he wasn't around and generally, I noticed, I was freer and more into what was going on around me when I wasn't with him. In every way, he was pulling in, I was moving out. . . .

"Well, things got more fractured between Ed and me. I pleaded with him to go with me to group therapy but he wouldn't. So then I went alone to a shrink but not for long. He seemed so superficial. Meanwhile I finished graduate school and now had more of the economic security I had wanted. But that was of no help. I got more and more nervous until finally I was almost catatonic. I was scared. I knew I should split but I just couldn't do it. And then one day—I don't want to go into all the details—one day I just realized that I could. And none of the dire things I had imagined happened. . . .

"I don't see the man-woman thing at all the same way as I used to. Like I don't see much point in marriage 'till death do us part'. Trevor and I are mates now the way Ed and I were mates when we married. Everybody is capable of finding several people in a lifetime whom he considers to be mates. A mate is just your true partner for any part of the life cycle, not necessarily for a whole lifetime or even the whole bringing up of a child. Most young people I know think the same way. There comes a point where you are ready for a new partner on a different level and then you move on. That requires a kind of inner freedom my 'feminine mystique' thinking hadn't opened up to me. If you get uptight and can't move on you begin to dry up and die.

"When I panicked at the idea of splitting with Ed it was mostly panic at losing my security, the kind of physical security I'd grown up to expect from marriage. There was a place that was my home, a man who said he'd stick with me 'for better or for worse', a whole setup where I had very particular roles to play as the wife, the mother. I had always gone on the assumption that once I found my mate that would be it, from then on I would be able to stop worrying about a whole lot of things.

"Now I know I'll never have that kind of security because I don't believe in staying together with anyone 'for worse'. So I've got to find an inner security. I've got to replace the physical guarantee with a new state of mind. And I'm doing that through acid. I take it about every six months and each time I get a kind of reaffirmation. If I had taken acid before Ed and I split I don't think I'd have gotten into that panic. . . .

"My children dress the way they like. My daughter likes to dress very straight, in black leather mary jane shoes and tights and little dresses and pocketbooks. She's liked that sort of thing since she was two. My son, who's seven now, likes mirror vests and long hair and jewelry and the rest of the hippie man thing. He likes to parody it just as boys always parody men. They both have choices and they can see different styles of living because Ed takes them to his house and on his trips every other weekend. As far as I can see, they're comfortable in both places and that's because Ed and I still respect what we had together and don't run each other down in front of the kids or anywhere else. There's no need for that. We're just on different trips now."

Joanie drops her feet to the floor, gets out of the hammock and stretches. Then we go back into the kitchen and she puts on a pot of hot water for tea.

The children are with Ed tonight. I saw them all this afternoon. They're friendly children, alert and lively. For, though Joanie may look weird and have exotic adventures, she is a responsible mother. And despite the fact that other men stay in the house now from time to time, the children suffer from no confusion about who their father is. They seem to appreciate having two homes, both with a firmly anchored parent.

"I hear Ed is going to Synanon now," Joanie says as she reaches into the refrigerator for some cake.

"Yes. He's playing the Synanon games and he's very enthusiastic about them. Are you involved in Synanon too?"

"No, I don't join things. I like to find out about them and I know a lot of people who belong to all kinds of groups and movements, but that's not my bag. Though I would like to try living in a commune sometime. I've been to some but I haven't found one that's for me. I went up to Morningstar Ranch—you know, the place up near Sebastopol?—but I had a bad experience there. The Gypsy Jokers had come in on their bikes the day I arrived. I was walking past the house they had taken over and two of them came after me. They walked alongside and started bugging me. They didn't do anything, really, but just the way they looked I had this feeling that anything could happen and nobody would protect me. It was freaky. I felt I'd never been so close to being raped in my life.

"I've visited a couple of the Kerista groups too. The attitudes there are not exactly traditional. Like one night I was balling with this friend of mine in a room and a little girl walked in. For a moment I froze. I didn't know what to do. Then I thought that stopping would be worse than going on. So we continued and she sat down and waited and when we were through we rapped. She was perfectly at ease. Later I asked around and this was perfectly all right with everyone, her parents and everyone. Some of the Kerista communities have family groupings—this one did—others don't. I've looked around to other communities too but none of them is for me, and I'm not the type to start one. Well, maybe someday."

She sets out Darjeeling tea, cuts the cake and serves it. I listen to Joanie's report on the communal scene and wonder how Ed could possibly have thought her lacking in a sense of adventure. He must have seen only this comfortable human in the kitchen, the Joanie of the New York-Bennington accent, the PTA meetings and the home-baked cake. Perhaps he was too frightened to make the acquaintance of Sequin Palladini. For now he has a house in Berkeley with a yard and is thinking of getting a dog.

Those who know her only slightly can dismiss Joanie, with her wild clothes and hip lingo, as a freaky parody of a hippie. To see the real Joanie is more threatening to a square. For in fact she is a revolutionary who says out loud and without hesitation something that most people already realize but hate to admit. It's perfectly clear by now that marriage is no longer the solid rock upon which men and women may build their lives. One out of every four marriages in the United States now ends in divorce. Yet most people still cling to the fantasy that nothing has changed. Most girls grow up believing that once they find a husband they can relax in wifely security. They divide their lives into two parts: the search for a man and life with the man. It's frightening to think that the home may at any time be abandoned by one of the partners if he feels the other is, as Joanie put it, tying him down.

And yet, though the traditional words are still spoken at weddings—"for better for worse . . . until death do us part"—what most people mean by them is not what their grandparents meant. They assume that the union will be "for better." If it proves to be "for worse," divorce is accepted as the healthy, positive answer.

There is no longer, for most people, any economic or social necessity to stay married no matter how miserable life becomes. Divorce has no stigma anymore. The ideal of personal growth implies that a relationship between a man and a woman should cease to exist if it goes dead.

Some young people, particularly hippies, have rejected legal marriage altogether and have replaced it with their own personal rituals. Others reject even personal ceremonies. A doctor's wife told me she had urged her son to "marry that girl before she gets away," and he had laughed at her.

"We're grooving together," he told her. "We like living together. What do we need marriage for? We don't need that kind of lock on each other. If one of us wanted to split, we'd stop grooving. So there would be no point in staying together."

Many non-hippies have similar views but marry when they want to have children, for the children's protection. But even with children, divorce is no longer looked upon as a disaster. "It all depends on how it is handled," said Dr. William C. Schutz, a psychologist on the Esalen staff who has been divorced twice and has three children, two by his first wife and one by his second. "Often the reason divorce is traumatic for children is that the children come to believe it's their fault. If you make sure they understand it isn't, they need not suffer any trauma." Schutz sees his children regularly or calls them regularly. He knows more about their thoughts and activities than many fathers who stumble in from work every night to perform fatherly duties automatically and without interest.

The high incidence of divorce has begun to create a new form of extended family, as in the case of Ed and Joanie and some of their friends. Children have two homes and, in their parents' new partners, a new set of relatives. If the adults manage to move from the first relationship to the second without bitterness, the children may well be better off this way than they would be with both parents in one home and unhappy.

The ex-mates, however, often part in bitterness and vent it on the children. Even when they make a deliberate effort to avoid it, they convey the idea that the other person was some kind of rotten bastard. Gerald Smith, divorced father of two children, does both marriage and divorce counseling in San Mateo County. Couples or entire families come to him to settle problems of breaking up and dividing property. The idea of saving the marriage is not even mentioned in these interviews. The aim is "to try to get through the divorce with as few mixed feelings as possible so that all that would be left would be the roles of mother and father. It's important to recognize that it is the relationship that gets sick, not one person or the other," he says. "The legal system does not recognize this fact. The adversary system, with two lawyers confronting each other in court battle, tends to set up vendettas. It would be much more helpful for them and their children if the divorcing man and woman were not pitted against each other legally as they are now."

Smith advocates that marriage be viewed as "an open-ended contract, a subjective commitment to the present, not the outcome twenty years from now. For this it is important to keep an open door—the option of divorce. For you can't be close if you don't have room to be distant. You can't love freely if you feel trapped."

However, Smith believes that the marriage contract continues to remain important. "The symbol of commitment gives the marriage the resiliency needed to get through the pain in a relationship," he maintains. "Couples that don't symbolize the relationship have a brittle relationship. The tendency is to avoid pain and split over differences. But if worked out, the differences are the very thing that keeps a marriage together. They are the excitement in a marriage.

Margaret Mead has suggested that it might be useful to have two kinds of marriage contract. The first would allow a couple to live together but would not license them to have children. It would be easy to enter and easy to dissolve. The second would require some evidence that a couple is fit for parenthood. Everyone would go through the first relationship before—if at all—beginning the second.

The law usually lags behind social change, so it is unlikely that Margaret Mead's idea, or anything similar, would become the standard legal thing in the near future. Meanwhile, countless studies will continue to be published on why marriages fail, countless diagnoses and cures will be offered by popular magazines for the family's sickly condition and, quietly, daring souls like Joanie Summer will continue to experiment with entirely new approaches to the man-woman relationship.

PARADOXES OF SEX AND LOVE

Rollo May

SEXUAL WILDERNESS

In Victorian times, when the denial of sexual impulses, feelings, and drives was the mode and one would not talk about sex in polite company, an aura of sanctifying repulsiveness surrounded the whole topic. Males and females dealt with each other as though neither possessed sexual organs. William James, that redoubtable crusader who was far ahead of his time on every other topic, treated sex with the polite aversion characteristic of the turn of the century. In the whole two volumes of his epoch-making *Principles of Psychology*, only one page is devoted to sex, at the end of which he adds, "These details are a little unpleasant to discuss. . . ." But William Blake's warning a century before Victorianism, that "He who desires but acts not, breeds pestilence," was amply demonstrated by the later psychotherapists. Freud, a Victorian who did look at sex, was right in his description of the morass of neurotic symptoms which resulted from cutting off so vital a part of the human body and the self.

Then, in the 1920's, a radical change occurred almost overnight. The belief became a militant dogma in liberal circles that the opposite of repression—namely, sex education, freedom of talking, feeling, and expression—would have healthy effects, and obviously constituted the only stand for the enlightened person. In an amazingly short period following World War I, we shifted from acting as though sex did not exist at all to being obsessed with it. We now placed more emphasis on sex than any society since that of ancient Rome, and some scholars believe we are more preoccupied with sex than any other people in all of history. Today, far from not talking about sex, we might well seem, to a visitor from Mars dropping into Times Square, to have no other topic of communication.

And this is not solely an American obsession. Across the ocean in England, for example, "from bishops to biologists, everyone is in on the act." A perceptive front-page article in *The Times Literary Supplement*, London, goes on to point to the "whole turgid flood of post-Kinsey utilitarianism and post-Chatterley moral uplift. Open any newspaper, any day (Sunday in particular), and the odds are you will find some pundit treating the public to his views on contraception, abortion, adultery, obscene publications, homosexuality between consenting adults or (if all else fails) contemporary moral patterns among our adolescents."

Partly as a result of this radical shift, many therapists today rarely see patients who exhibit repression of sex in the manner of Freud's pre-World War I hysterical patients. In fact, we find in the people who come for help just the opposite: a great deal of talk about sex, a great deal of sexual activity, practically no one complaining of cultural prohibitions over going to bed as often or with as many partners as one wishes. But what our patients do complain of is lack of feeling and passion. "The curious thing about this ferment of discussion is how little anyone seems to be *enjoying* emancipation." So much sex and so little meaning or even fun in it!

Where the Victorian didn't want anyone to know that he or she had sexual feelings, we are ashamed if we do not. Before 1910, if you called a lady "sexy" she would be insulted; nowadays, she prizes the compliment and rewards you by turning her charms in your direction. Our patients often have the problems of frigidity and impotence, but the strange and poignant thing we observe is how desperately they struggle not to let anyone find out they don't feel sexually. The Victorian nice man or woman was guilty if he or she did experience sex; now we are guilty if we *don't*.

One paradox, therefore, is that enlightenment has not solved the sexual problems in our culture. To be sure, there are important positive results of the new enlightenment, chiefly in increased freedom for the individual. Most external problems are eased: sexual knowledge can be bought in any bookstore, contraception is available everywhere except in Boston where it is still believed, as the English countess averred on her wedding night, that sex is "too good for the common people." Couples can, without guilt and generally without squeamishness, discuss their sexual relationship and undertake to make it more mutually gratifying and meaningful. Let these gains not be underestimated. External social anxiety and guilt have lessened; dull would be the man who did not rejoice in this.

But *internal* anxiety and guilt have increased. And in some ways these are more morbid, harder to handle, and impose a heavier burden upon the individual than external anxiety and guilt.

The challenge a woman used to face from men was simple and direct—would she or would she not go to bed?—a direct issue of how she stood vis-à-vis cultural mores. But the question men ask now is no longer, "Will she or won't she?" but "Can she or can't she?" The challenge is shifted to the woman's personal adequacy, namely, her own capacity to have the vaunted orgasm—which should resemble a *grand mal* seizure. Though we might agree that the second question places the problem of sexual decision more where it should be, we cannot overlook the fact that the first question is much easier for the person to handle. In my practice, one woman was afraid to go to bed for fear that the man "won't find me very good at making love." Another was afraid because "I don't even know how to do it," assuming that her lover would hold this against her. Another was scared to death of the second marriage for fear that she wouldn't be able to have the orgasm as she had not in her first. Often the woman's hesitation is formulated as, "He won't like me well enough to come back again."

In past decades you could blame society's strict mores and preserve your own self-esteem by telling yourself what you did or didn't do was society's fault and not yours. And this would give you some time in which to decide what you do want to do, or to let yourself grow into a decision. But when the question is simply how you can perform, your own sense of adequacy and self-esteem is called immediately into question, and the whole weight of the encounter is shifted inward to how you can meet the test.

College students, in their fights with college authorities about hours girls are to be permitted in the men's rooms, are curiously blind to the fact that rules are often a boon. Rules give the student time to find himself. He has the leeway to consider a way of behaving without being committed before he is ready, to try on for size, to venture into relationships tentatively—which is part of any growing up. Better to have the lack of commitment direct and open rather than to go into sexual relations under pressure—doing violence to his feelings by having physical commitment without psychological. He may flaunt the rules; but at least they give some structure to be flaunted. My point is true whether he obeys the rule or not. Many contemporary students, understandably anxious because of their new sexual freedom, repress this anxiety ("one should *like* freedom") and then compensate for the additional anxiety the repression gives them by attacking the parietal authorities for not giving them more freedom!

What we did not see in our short-sighted liberalism in sex was that throwing the individual into an unbounded and empty sea of free choice does not in itself give freedom, but is more apt to increase inner conflict. The sexual freedom to which we were devoted fell short of being fully human. . . .

SALVATION THROUGH TECHNIQUE

A second paradox is that *the new emphasis on technique in sex and love-making backfires.* It often occurs to me that there is an inverse relationship between the number of how-to-do-it books perused by a person or rolling off the presses in a society and the amount of sexual passion or even pleasure experienced by the persons involved. Certainly nothing is wrong with technique as such, in playing golf or acting or making love. But the emphasis beyond a certain point on technique in sex makes for a mechanistic attitude toward love-making, and goes along with alienation, feelings of loneliness, and depersonalization.

One aspect of the alienation is that the lover, with his age-old art, tends to be superseded by the computer operator with his modern efficiency. Couples place great emphasis on bookkeeping and timetables in their love-making—a practice confirmed and standardized by Kinsey. If they fall behind schedule they become anxious and feel impelled to go to bed whether they want to or not. My colleague, Dr. John Schimel, observes, "My patients have endured stoically, or without noticing, remarkably destructive treatment at the hands of their spouses, but they have experienced falling behind in the sexual time-table as a loss of love." The man feels he is somehow losing his masculine status if he does not perform up to schedule, and the woman that she has lost her feminine attractiveness if too long a period goes by without the man at least making a pass at her. The phrase "between men," which women use about their affairs, similarly suggests a gap in time like the *entr'acte*. Elaborate accounting- and ledger-book lists—how often this week have we made love? did he (or she) pay the right amount of attention to me during the evening? was the foreplay long enough?—make one wonder how the spontaneity of this most spontaneous act can possibly survive. The computer hovers in the stage wings of the drama of love-making the way Freud said one's parents used to.

It is not surprising then, in this preoccupation with techniques, that the questions typically asked about an act of love-making are not, Was there passion or meaning or pleasure in the act? but, How well did I perform? Take, for example, what Cyril Connolly calls "the tyranny of the orgasm," and the preoccupation with achieving a simultaneous orgasm, which is another aspect of the alienation. I confess that when people talk about the "apocalyptic orgasm," I find myself wondering, Why do they have to try so hard? What abyss of self-doubt, what inner void of loneliness, are they trying to cover up by this great concern with grandiose effects? . . .

THE NEW PURITANISM

The third paradox is that our highly-vaunted sexual freedom has turned out to be a new form of puritanism. I spell it with a small "p" because I do not wish to confuse this with the original Puritanism. That, as in the passion of Hester and Dimmesdale in Hawthorne's *The Scarlet Letter*, was a very different thing. I refer to puritanism as it came down via our Victorian grandparents and became allied with industrialism and emotional and moral compartmentalization.

I define this puritanism as consisting of three elements. First, *a state of alienation from the body.* Second, *the separation of emotion from reason.* And third, *the use of the body as a machine.*

In our new puritanism, bad health is equated with sin. Sin used to mean giving in to one's sexual desires; it now means not having full sexual expression. Our contemporary puritan holds that it is immoral *not* to express your libido. Apparently this is true on both sides of the ocean: "There are few more depressing sights," the London *Times Literary Supplement* writes, "than a progressive intellectual determined to end up in bed with someone from a sense of moral duty. . . . There is no more high-minded puritan in the world than your modern advocate of salvation through properly directed passion. . . ." A woman used to be guilty if she went to bed with a man; now she feels vaguely guilty if after a certain number of dates she still refrains; her sin is "morbid repression," refusing to "give." And the partner, who is always completely enlightened (or at least pretends to be) refuses to allay her guilt by getting overtly angry at her (if she could fight him on the issue, the conflict would be a lot easier for her). But he stands broadmindedly by, ready at the end of every date to undertake a crusade to assist her out of her fallen state. And this, of course, makes her "no" all the more guilt-producing for her.

This all means, of course, that people not only have to learn to perform sexually but have to make sure, at the same time, that they can do so without letting themselves go in passion or unseemly commitment—the latter of which may be interpreted as exerting an unhealthy demand upon the partner. *The Victorian person sought to have love without falling into sex; the modern person seeks to have sex without falling into love. . . .*

The new puritanism brings with it a depersonalization of our whole language. Instead of making love, we "have sex"; in contrast to intercourse, we "screw"; instead of going to bed, we "lay" someone or (heaven help the English language as well as ourselves!) we "are laid." This alienation has become so much the order of the day that in some psychotherapeutic training schools, young psychiatrists and psychologists are taught that it is "therapeutic" to use solely the four-letter words in sessions; the patient is probably masking some repression if he talks about making love; so it becomes our righteous duty—the new puritanism incarnate!—to let him know he only fucks. Everyone seems so intent on sweeping away the last vestiges of Victorian prudishness that we entirely forget that these different words refer to different kinds of human experience. Probably most people have experienced the different forms of sexual relationship described by the different terms and don't have much difficulty distinguishing among them. I am not making a value judgment among these different experiences; they are all appropriate to their own kinds of relationship. Every woman wants at some time to be "laid"—transported, carried away, "made" to have passion when at first she has none, as in the famous scene between Rhett Butler and Scarlett O'Hara in *Gone with the Wind*. But if being "laid" is all that ever happens in her sexual life, then her experience of personal alienation and rejection of sex are just around the corner. If the therapist does not appreciate these diverse kinds of experience, he will be presiding at the shrinking and truncating of the patient's consciousness, and will be confirming the narrowing of the patient's bodily awareness as well as his or her capacity for relationship. This is the chief criticism of the new puritanism: it grossly limits feelings, it blocks the infinite variety and richness of the act, and it makes for emotional impoverishment.

It is not surprising that the new puritanism develops smoldering hostility among the members of our society. And that hostility, in turn, comes out frequently in references to the sexual act itself. We say "go fuck yourself" or "fuck you" as a term of contempt to show that the other is of no value whatever beyond being used and tossed aside. The biological lust is here in its *reductio ad absurdum*. Indeed, the word fuck is the most common expletive in our contemporary language to express violent hostility. I do not think this is by accident. . . .

THE REVOLT AGAINST SEX

With the confusion of motives in sex that we have noted above—almost every motive being present in the act except the desire to make love—it is no wonder that there is a diminution of feeling and that passion has lessened almost to the vanishing point. This diminution of feeling often takes the form of a kind of anesthesia . . . in people who can perform the mechanical aspects of the sexual act very well. We are becoming used to the plaint from the couch or patient's chair that "we made love, but I didn't feel anything." Again, the poets tell us the same things as our patients. T. S. Eliot writes in *The Waste Land* that after "lovely woman stoops to folly," and the carbuncular clerk who seduced her at tea leaves,

> She turns and looks a moment in the glass,
> Hardly aware of her departed lover;
> Her brain allows one half-formed thought to pass;
> "Well now that's done: and I'm glad it's over."
> When lovely woman stoops to folly and
> Paces about her room again, alone,
> She smoothes her hair with automatic hand,
> And puts a record on the gramophone.
> (III:249–256)

It no longer sounds new when we discover that for many young people what used to be called love-making is now experienced as a futile "panting palm to palm," in Aldous Huxley's predictive phrase; that they tell us that it is hard for them to understand what the poets were talking about, and that we should so often hear the disappointed refrain, "We went to bed but it wasn't any good."

Nothing to revolt against, did I say? Well, there is obviously one thing left to revolt against, and that is sex itself. The frontier, the establishing of identity, the validation of the self can be, and not infrequently does become for some people, a revolt against sexuality entirely. I am certainly not advocating this. What I wish to indicate is that the very revolt against sex—this modern Lysistrata in robot's dress—is rumbling at the gates of our cities or, if not rumbling, at least hovering. The sexual revolution comes finally back on itself not with a bang but a whimper.

Thus it is not surprising that, as sex becomes more machinelike, with passion irrelevant and then even pleasure diminishing, the problem has come full circle. And we find, *mirabile dictu,* a progression from an *anesthetic* attitude to an *antiseptic* one. Sexual contact itself then tends to get put on the shelf and to be avoided. This is another and surely least constructive aspect of the new puritanism: it returns, finally, to a new asceticism. . . .

Our future is taken more seriously by the participants in the discussion on this topic at the Center for the Study of Democratic Institutions at Santa Barbara. Their report, called "The A-Sexual Society," frankly faces the fact that "we are hurtling into, not a bisexual or a multi-sexual, but an a-sexual society: the boys grow long hair and the girls wear pants. . . . Romance will disappear; in fact, it has almost disappeared now. . . . Given the guaranteed Annual Income and The Pill, will women choose to marry? Why should they?" Mrs. Eleanor Garth, a participant in the discussion and writer of the report, goes on to point out the radical change that may well occur in having and rearing children. "What of the time when the fertilized ovum can be implanted in the womb of a mercenary, and one's progeny selected from a sperm-bank? Will the lady choose to reproduce her husband, if there still are such things? . . . No problems, no jealousy, no love-transference. . . . And what of the children, incubated under glass? . . . Will communal love develop the human qualities that we assume emerge from the present rearing of children? Will women under these conditions lose the survival drive and become as death-oriented as the present generation of American men? . . . I don't raise the question in advocacy," she adds, "I consider some of the possibilities horrifying."

Mrs. Garth and her colleagues at the Center recognize that the real issue underlying this revolution is not what one does with sexual organs and sexual functions per se, but what happens to man's humanity. "What disturbs me is the real possibility of the disappearance of our humane, life-giving qualities with the speed of developments in the life sciences, and the fact that no one seems to be discussing the alternative possibilities for good and evil in these developments."

The purpose of our discussion . . . is precisely to raise the questions of the alternative possibilities for good and evil—that is, the destruction or the enhancement of the qualities which constitute man's "humane, life-giving qualities."

CHILDREN OF TURMOIL
Kenneth Lash

Not only the subject matter but the very meaning, the root-aim, of education is derived from the past and has changed but little up to the present: higher education was originally a training for the aristocracy, of church or state. (Male aristocracy, of course.) Education existed to prepare members to rule, in effect to live a life of a different quality from that of the uneducated. The aristocrat was taught originally by his own kind. Thus education was of and for an aristocracy, by its appointed autocrat. The approach has survived almost unchanged right into this period of convulsive democracy.

The United States altered things somewhat with the concept of mass education, originally intended to produce what was considered the fundamental necessity of a democracy—an enlightened citizenry. In the unfolding of time, however, this came to signify a *useful* citizenry, with enlightenment rather carefully curtailed. In early days domination was by the church, later by the marketplace (never by the state—we have always had a truly amateur government). One was taught to emulate first Jonathan Edwards, then Benjamin Franklin—and finally a brand of the two. The reigning group disposed. For the drones: education force-fed by law up to a predetermined sufficiency. For the chosen, the opportunity of college, that is, the opportunity to qualify for a place within the group that reigns. Thus one is taught primarily the way, the values, the powers of that group—an education that is essentially a training for replacements to the group. This form of education has been, and is, overseen by the business hierarchy and administered by their chosen representatives. Such education, as Ronald Reagan says, is a privilege. You must deserve it. In advance.

Students, on the contrary, are saying that the education must deserve *them*. They are saying it's their lives, their time, their heads. They have discovered that they are the *consumers* of education. Formerly willing to be force-fed, they are now coming to see themselves as buyers, with all the potential power that implies: right now, the power to spit out what they don't like, suggest new goods and services to the manager; later, their own kind of store. By, for, and of the young people? I think so, because I think . . .

Democracy, it is a'comin'. Or perhaps it is here already, and that's what all the fighting is about. I am assuming that there never was a true democracy anywhere because I can find no record of one. Our own model was Greek, a caste democracy. Never, right from the start, including the Founding Fathers, was there any intention to establish a true *participating* democracy. Those founders were aristocrats. They knew how to give to the people some of the powers they took from the king; they knew also how to protect the country and themselves against those same powers, and how to use the concept of the majority so as to render the individual and the minority politically ineffective.

That system prevails unchanged, but it is suddenly in trouble. The majority is somehow being surrounded by the minority. In much the same way that the group has been surrounded by the individual, and now, finally, the individual by the personality, the Me. While our backs were turning on belief, the great era of Me blew into town. Nothing's been the same since.

Father thinks it's a shame, but he's the carpenter who left off believing for $75 a day, and knows he's not worth it and so loses even his belief in the accuracy of money. He passes little piles of it to his kid, who gives nothing at all for it, and senses it as a kind of bribe. This sense reflects as in a mirror distrust and a consequent dislike. Both as a government and as a people, we behave precisely like that parent who is constitutionally selfish and insecure: he feels threatened by those of his children who are "troublesome," and down inside dislikes them. What he dislikes is whatever threatens his dream of comfort, which he has in fact given much for. Thus he dislikes dissent. That is to say minorities, which are by definition dissenters from the majority. *Black* makes him nervous. *Blacks* threaten him. I don't believe for a minute that he hates blacks. He hates that they're rocking his boat. He hates people, he hates theories, that can rock his boat. He dislikes even the *idea* of minorities. Being rich—and as civilized as most—he tries to bribe them into quiescence, or into leaving home. Which doesn't mean he won't use force, if the bribe doesn't work. I'm afraid he will. He's voting for it already, and squawking about the rising cost of bribery.

It was money that determined our social strata and rode herd on our values. It is now *un*determining them and riding around in circles. Lots of money is going to lots of people for lots of things. Lots of money is going to some people for nothing. It appears as if money is going crazy. But it isn't. It's following a law. The thing is, it's not an economic law but a political one. Money is busy adapting to our kind of democracy.

The only possible political distinction of democracy from other forms of government extant is this: that in a democracy, people are *more* equal. If that sounds like an ad slogan, it is nonetheless part of the fact. The fact is that democracy *is* in part an ad slogan—promising more than it can deliver, yet delivering something "improved." People are not equal. They don't even seem to want to be. Yet any society or government that attempts to protect the less equal under law and to increase their share of the political power is democratic in tendency. It is democratic in fact only where the attempt succeeds.

The United States, where its majority is concerned, has succeeded in becoming a money democracy. Affluence is widely present, largely available. The less equal, my dear, are everywhere these days. It is, in terms of human society, an amazing accomplishment, a wonder of the world. And it appeared only in this lifetime. It appeared, in fact, with father. Never mind other forces, never mind technology—it's his. He worked for it, he achieved it. Driving his Grand Prix, he's as good as anybody. He's living in a *democracy*.

Father doesn't mind millionaires any more, having lessened the gap between them and him (become "more equal"). He hates intellectuals, having widened that gap. Mind is part of the price he paid for the Grand Prix, and his group, his majority, suffers a dangerous form of mindlessness. So does his kid, though perhaps on principle. This kid, on principle, dislikes *both* millionaire and intellectual. He dislikes anyone beyond his own emotional age, any person, any place, any idea that possesses an authority that he, the kid, didn't vote for. And on principle distrusts the very notion of Authority itself. This kid may be the world's first democrat.

The thing is, Authority either rests on real distinction or it's a lie. The kids looked at father, they looked at teacher, they looked at Washington, and they saw that it was a lie! They saw that, sadly, in our democracy authority tends to gather around those who lack distinction. Father usually votes for himself. But what does he especially lack? Not humanity, certainly. Humaneness, I suppose. As I suppose that the kids got focused on humaneness for the good and loud reason that the world, their world to live in, was simply too inhuman. Suddenly and largely *too* inhuman.

As the father was robbed of belief in his gods, so the son was robbed of respect for his elders. And so the long saga of Authority in the West comes to its turning point. From pope to king to president; from soul to citizen to self—the advance, and the decline. Civilization and a beckoning suicide.

Right or not, the kids feel our Authorities brought us to this pass. The people, sharing, deciding, acting, never would have. Besides, who is to say who's over us now? Who has a license to lead, they ask. You're smarter? I'm stronger. You're prettier? I'm sexier. You'll see it's all the same underneath

—the same dreams, the same visions, the same feelings. We are the *same*, man.

The self is all that is given, but everyone has it and on any level but the superficial every self is potentially the same. This psycho-religious (Jung *had* to invent himself) manifesto would be nonsense in Egypt or Russia, dubious in Belgium, avant-garde in France—but I think it is very meaningful in the United States. Because here, father paved the way. He got us all the way into a material democracy; he became an aristocrat of affluence, envied in the world. The son is trying to finish the job. Having had (because of father) to bow to no one, and seeing no reason whatever for doing so, he's out to abolish the practice of bowing, even the very notion of bowing. Outwardly and inwardly. He hopes to acknowledge neither superiority nor guilt.

His message on the electric trumpet is this: The job of forming a democracy is about to be completed. Democracy is coming in its true form, its inescapable form—not merely political, but psychological.

You can see the early consequences showing up all over the newspaper. Little people, little nations, they're all getting uppity. The kids. The whores. The waiters. Ecuador. John Carlos. Ignatz Mouse in university halls. Poppa defying his union leader, Mamma at her investment club. Everybody's holding a playable hand. It's poor days for the patrician, who in most of human history is the only one who has the chance to become a professional at living. And it's poor days for his values, too. Perhaps even his person. If the universe has no law, how can the streets have it? There is certainly the smell of rabble in the air. And of the rabble stirring to face the rabble.

And yet: and yet if the heavy, fearful majority does not finally vote for fascism, if the essential experience of life in a partial democracy stops their hand short of that, then this emergent last step in the creation of a democracy on earth may change the look, feel, smell, taste, the essential *quality* of life. This step, I think, is the remaining hope.

Ecology as I see it is hypnotized by symptoms, reciting its hopes for fewer of us, for more environment. It had better consider carefully psychological space, which might or might not exist in a beautiful green community. It had best consider that where man kills off species of animals for his own protection or mere convenience, he may well do the same to himself—kill off those species called minorities. Or round them up for his zoos.

Everybody knows that variety is the spice of life. Lots of people feel Glory be to God for dappled things. Some people sense that only respect for the life process stands between life and death. They say that the self, in its endless varying, is part of the process. The number of these people is growing fast, as if with urgent rapidity. They act as from a passionate realization that the work of all those centuries to free the outer self leads only to this present and more marvelous necessity: to free the inner self.

BIG BROTHER
REALLY IS WATCHING

Russell Baker

Washington, March 5—The number of crimes that a human being may commit against large organizations is astonishing. One of the worst is noncompliance. A large organization hates nothing so much as a human being who fails to comply. This is why large organizations fill the mails with warnings that "failure to comply may result in——" or that that "the penalty for noncompliance may be——."

Fear of committing noncompliance is a heavy burden on contemporary man, surrounded as he is by circling hordes of large organizations ready to pounce upon him for any number of other offenses against organization.

Has he failed to register, failed to notify, failed to report? No? In that case, perhaps he has failed to renew, failed to file, failed to sign. Maybe he has bent, spindled or folded. Perhaps he has registered, notified, reported, renewed, filed, signed, carefully avoiding bending, spindling and folding, and even complied. Ah, but has he complied before the legal deadline?

They are hard tyrants, large organizations. When you are young they haul you in like so much meat on a hook and test you for the large-organization way of life. "Sweat, you little half-formed human beings," they gloat, distributing their infernal multiple-choice tests and magnetic pencils. "We are testing you for aptitude to perform well in a large organization created to prepare you for a life of compliance, registration, notification, reporting, renewal, filing and signing before the legal deadline without any sloppy bending, spindling or folding."

Those who pass the tests are put in custody of another large organization dedicated to making them take Physics 101 because they want to read poetry. "Failure to observe regulations against entertaining female guests in the dormitory may result in——."

COMPLIANCE TO ORGANIZATION

After compliance, commencement, and then toil. A large organization numbers them. ("What? Not want to be numbered, silly man? You will be glad we numbered you when you reach 65 and one of our large actuarial organizations make you stop toiling and go play shuffleboard.")

Another large organization specifies what clothing styles may be worn in public without risking noncompliance. Another may decree a two-year term in the killing trade. ("Your large organization does not need to be reminded, boy, that killing is wrong. You apparently need to be reminded, however, that killing is not wrong under certain exceptions specified by a sufficiently large organization. The penalty for noncompliance may be——.")

Large organizations find that human beings become more compliable as they age, but they have discovered that it is bad policy to ease up on the terror. And so there is no peace from the time the alarm clock sounds to the gurgle of the last nightcap.

"What are the large organizations threatening us with today, Darling?" one asks at breakfast.

"Let's see. They threaten to deprive us of the use of the car unless we have it inspected within fourteen days. They threaten to fine us a large sum of money unless we amend the estimate of how much income tax we will owe next year. Oh yes, and they threaten to send us another best seller by that awful boy novelist unless you notify them immediately that you don't want this month's book club selection."

"Are they threatening to ruin our credit rating, or did I just dream I had a telephone call from a madman who said he was going to ruin me unless I paid a bill I've already paid?"

"You didn't dream it. That was the large credit organization and they promise to libel you as a cheat and a deadbeat."

"But I've paid that bill."

"Yes, but you spindled the voucher and the large computer organization refused to register your payment. It looks like it's curtains for your reputation unless the computer agrees to give you a second chance."

MORE INTIMIDATIONS

"Any large organizations testing the children today?"

"Yes, there's a large testing organization from Princeton threatening to ruin the children's opportunity to go to college by giving some sort of test at school this morning."

Outside, meanwhile, large organizations are preparing to raise the bus fare, strike the electric company, distill the perfect nerve gas, build a shoddier car, reduce the postal service and start a small war. Soon the postman will arrive with several large organizations' periodic reminders that "the penalty for noncompliance may be——."

The Public and Private I

LONG HAIR, AUNT SADIE, IS A COMMUNIST PLOT

Jerry Rubin

My earliest introduction to Communism involved family intrigue and outasight chicken soup. Every family has a black sheep. Mine was Aunt Sadie in New York.

"She went to Russia to meet Stalin," members of the family used to gossip to each other.

When I was a kid, my family often visited Aunt Sadie, and she served the best chicken soup in the whole world. She used to say to me, "**Jerry**, you must still be hungry. Please eat some more, **Jerry darling**. Eat some more good chicken soup."

And as she ladled more chicken soup into my already overflowing bowl, she'd whisper into my ear, "The capitalists need unemployment to keep wages down."

I lost contact with Aunt Sadie and meanwhile became a family misfit myself. Then one unexpected afternoon Aunt Sadie knocked on the door of my Lower East Side apartment. I hadn't seen her in ten years.

"Aunt Sadie," I shouted, hugging her. "I'm a commie, too!"

She didn't even smile.

Maybe she was no longer a Communist?

"Aunt Sadie, what's the matter?"

She hesitated. "**Jerry**, why don't you cut your hair?"

So I gave her a big bowl of Nancy's outasight chicken soup and began:

"Aunt Sadie, long hair is a commie plot! Long hair gets people uptight—more uptight than ideology, cause long hair is communication. We are a new minority group, a nationwide community of longhairs, a new identity, new loyalties. We longhairs recognize each other as brothers in the street.

"Young kids identify short hair with authority, discipline, unhappiness, boredom, rigidity, hatred of life—and long hair with letting go, letting your hair down, being free, being open.

"Our strategy is to steal the children of the bourgeoisie right away from the parents. Dig it! Yesterday I was walking down the street. A car passed by, parents in the front seat and a young kid, about eight, in the back seat. The kid flashed me the clenched fist sign."

"But, Jerry . . ." Aunt Sadie stammered.

"Aunt Sadie, *long hair is our black skin.* Long hair turns white middle-class youth into niggers. Amerika is a different country when you have long hair. We're outcasts. We, the children of the white middle class, feel like Indians, blacks, Vietnamese, the outsiders in Amerikan history."

"**But, Jerry,**" Aunt Sadie interrupted, "the Negroes in the ghettos, they're only hurting themselves. I mean, all of the vandalism and everything. . . ."

"Long hair polarizes every scene, Aunt Sadie. It's instant confrontation. Everyone is forced to become an actor, and that's revolutionary in a society of passive consumers.

"Having long hair is like saying hello to everybody you see. A few people automatically say 'Hi' right back; most people get furious that you disturbed their environment."

"**Jerry, *you have so much to offer.*** If only you'd cut your hair. People laugh at you. They don't take you seriously."

"Listen, Aunt Sadie, *long hair* is what makes them take us seriously! Wherever we go, our hair tells people where we stand on Vietnam, Wallace, campus disruption, dope. We're living TV commercials for the revolution. We're walking picket signs.

"Every response to longhairs creates a moral crisis for straights. We force adults to bring all their repressions to the surface, to expose their real feelings."

"**Feelings, schmeelings, Jerry,**" Aunt Sadie said. I'm telling you that in my time we were radicals. We were invited to a convention in the Soviet Union to meet Stalin. And who did they pick to represent us? Who did they pick? I'm telling you who they picked.

"They picked the people who were down-to-earth, who were clean and nice. I didn't have long hair. I didn't smell. . . ."

"Aunt Sadie, I don't want to go to any fucking conventions," I said.

"That doesn't matter," she replied, suddenly pushing aside untasted her bowl full of Nancy's good chicken soup. "But you should be clean and nice. Did your mother teach you to smell bad, maybe?"

"Aunt Sadie, you won't believe this, but you're uptight about your body. Man was born to let his hair grow long and to smell like a man. We are descended from the apes, and we're proud of our ancestry. We're natural men lost in this world of machines and computers. Long hair is more beautiful than short hair. We love our bodies. We even smell our armpits once in a while.

"Grownups used to tell us kids that black people smelled bad. We asked, 'What's wrong with Negroes?' and they said, 'Did you ever get close enough to smell them?' If middle-class people say that now about blacks, they'll get a good black-power punch across their fucking mouths, so they say it about longhairs. We ask them, 'Did you ever get close enough to smell a longhair?' and they shout back at us, 'Go take a bath'.

"Amerikans are puritans. Amerikans are afraid of sex. Amerika creates a sexual prison in which men think they have to be supermen and have to see sensitivity as weakness. Women are taught that self-assertion is unfeminine. *So Marines go to Vietnam and get their asses kicked by Viet Kong women.*

"Long hair is the beginning of our liberation from the sexual oppression that underlies this whole military society. Through long hair we're engaged in a sexual assault that's going to destroy the political-economic structure of Amerikan society!"

"God help you destroy it, **Jerry**," Aunt Sadie wailed, chicken-soup tears dribbling down her cheeks. "But you'd be so much more effective if you would cut your hair and dress nicely."

Aunt Sadie and I weren't getting very far. It was sad that the two black sheep in the family couldn't identify with each other.

"**Jerry**," Aunt Sadie said, getting up to leave. "Just remember one thing: there are two classes in the world, the bourgeoisie and the working class. You're either on one side or the other. It has nothing to do with hair.

"If you'd only get a haircut. You're only hurting yourself. . . ."

I embraced her, took the $20 she gave me to buy "some nice new clothes," and waved good-bye.

"Watch out, Aunt Sadie!" I shouted as she left. "Some of the most long-haired people I know are bald."

THE REAL IRON CURTAIN

Harry Golden

When Harvey Haddix of the Pittsburgh Pirates pitched twelve perfect innings against the Milwaukee Braves it was big news not because he lost on a double by Del Crandall in the 13th, but because Harvey was 33 years old.

The real iron curtain is the curtain separating the young from the middle-aged and the middle-aged from the old and the old from the young.

There are cities built specifically for the old, like St. Petersburg, Florida, where there is not a curb. There are developments in California where a playground would look to the residents like some apparatus for the moon. It is no wonder the old are cranky, the young unregenerate and rude, and the middle-aged panicky.

One of the reasons for this division is that we do not believe merit affects the quality of life. Yet Winston Churchill was in his 60s when he became Britain's wartime Prime Minister. When Sophocles was 90 and his sons wanted the courts to declare him non compos mentis, he read his jurors the verses of *Oedipus at Colonus*.

On the Lower East Side, in the crowded tenements, still we had a pretty good idea of what life looked like. We lived with kid brothers, maiden aunts, and grandparents. The result was that we didn't think people belonged in the categories of young, middle-aged, or old—we all of us communicated one way or another. Today, in most suburban complexes, the town at midday is populated only by the women, the kiddies, and the dogs.

We have victimized ourselves by subscribing wholeheartedly to our own myths. We all retire at 65 not because that is when we should retire but because 65 is the most advantageous retirement age for the insurance premiums. We really believe that poets and mathematicians get their gifts early and are washed up at 30. Goethe wrote *Faust* in his 70s. When a 47-year-old bishop becomes a cardinal we say he is young. I submit that our universe is viciously relativistic when it comes to age.

There is little reverence for the old in our society. And because there is none, there is probably less reverence for the young.

WHO AM I?

Marya Mannes

Who are you? You singly, not you together. When did it start—that long day's journey into self? When do you really begin to know what you believe and where you're going? When do you know that you are unique—separate —alone?

The time of discovery is different for everybody. Some people find themselves in early childhood, some in middle-age, some—the tragic ones— never.

I suggest that the first recognition comes when others try to tell you what you are. And although what happened in my generation is supposed to have no relevance to what happens in yours, I know when it happened to me.

I may have been six years old when aunts and uncles and cousins used to say: "You look just like your mother!" or "You're the image of your brother!"

Now, for reasons that have nothing to do with duty or discipline in that distant day, I loved my family. I loved them because they were interesting, handsome, talented, and loving people. I was lucky. But in spite of that, I felt an immediate, instinctive resistance to any suggestion that I was like them or like anybody else. I didn't want to be like anybody else. I was Me. Myself. Separate. Alone.

This is probably as good a time as any to say that if I use the first-person pronoun—if I refer from time to time to my own long, arduous, bumbling journey into self—it is not because of narcissism, but because I have always believed that the particular is more illuminating than the general. Perhaps my dependence as a writer on direct observation rather than on scholarly research, on living example rather than on sociological method, is the natural result of illiteracy. I never went to college and therefore know much less than you people do. About books, I mean. Or the sciences.

But since the laboratory for the study of man is clearly life itself, then I have studied hard in the act of living, of looking, of feeling; involvement rather than detachment; doing as well as being.

We were talking of the first discoveries of uniqueness—of being oneself and no one else. Not your father, not your mother, not your sister, not your brother. I. Me.

It is then—when you begin not only to know it, but act it—that society moves in. Society says it wants people to be different but it doesn't really mean it. Parents like to believe their children are different from other children—smarter, of course, better-looking and so forth—but most parents are secretly disturbed when their children are *really* different—not like others at all. In fact, very early they start to pigeonhole you in certain ways.

Take the difference of sex, for instance. Little girls are pink, little boys are blue. Little girls want dolls, little boys want trains.

For a long time, for instance, the word "tom-boy" to a girl held undertones of worry and disapproval. All it meant was that the girl liked to play ball, climb trees, and skin her knees instead of wearing frilly dresses and curtseying. The companion word for boys, of course, was "sissy"—meaning the kid liked music and poetry and hated fighting. These ignorant and damaging labels have now been discredited, thanks largely to you and the more enlightened members of our society. But there is still, alas, a large Squareland left where growing girls are told from the age of twelve onward not only by their mothers but by the mass media that marriage is the only valid female goal and that Career is a dirty word.

Even now—even when you here know how silly it is (at least, I hope you do), most parents hear wedding bells the minute a girl is born, most parents see an executive office when a boy is born, and the relentless conditioning starts on its merry way. Educate a girl for the marriage market, educate a boy for success. That you, as a human being, as a separate identity, may not want or fit in with either of these goals is considered not a sign of independence but of deviation—pointing to the couch or—in social terms—failure.

That is why these same parents—and they are still a majority—are bewildered, depressed, or plain horrified when their adolescents openly refuse to accept these goals or to share any common identity with any past. Who on earth, their parents moan, will marry this stringy girl with her false eyelashes and shuffling gait? Who will employ this bearded boy with his grunts and records, his pop and pot? On the other end, how gratified are parents when their clean-cut athletic sons get high marks and their clean and pretty daughters marry the clean-cut boys who get good jobs?

You know, I pity you. I pity you for reasons you might not suspect. I pity you because your search for self has been made so self-conscious. You are overexposed in and by the mass media, which never for one instant night and day stop telling you what you are and who you are. With us, decades ago, there was no radio and no television. As adolescents we seldom read papers (they never reported on us) or magazines. The word "teenager," thank God, never existed. From twelve to seventeen we were painful to our parents and not very attractive to ourselves. Our skins and bodies did strange things and we felt strange things. The world paid no attention to us. It didn't interview us, quote us, and ask our advice. We didn't expect it to. We had twenty-five to fifty cents a week to spend for allowance (rich kids got a dollar), but who needed it? Books were in the house or you could borrow them, movies were a quarter, and if you were lucky your family took you to occasional plays or concerts. School was sometimes boring, but we expected it to be. Nobody told us learning ought to be fun. When it was— well, great!

Nothing much external happened, except for trips with the family and meetings with friends. There was a lot of unfilled, unstructured, unplanned free time—with no messages coming in from anywhere to distract us, no entertainment at arm's length, no guidance counselors or psychiatrists to tell us what was bugging us. We had a vast amount of inner space to fill by ourselves. In this inner space there was room and time for that very tender, very vulnerable thing called "I" to be born—and grow.

For there are really two births—the first physical, the second spiritual. Both share something in common: Premature expulsion, premature expo- sure, can damage both foetus and soul. The prenatal fluid that protects the foetus until it is ready for air has its counterpart in the secret world of the yet unborn identity.

Now I want to make it quite clear that this secret world of child and adolescent is not a matter of protection from reality. Just because a child may grow up in the relative security of home and school and neighborhood doesn't mean that the human comedy-tragedy is not a part of daily life. You are not cut off from experience because the world you live in is physically small. On the contrary, you can be put off from real experience because the world has become too large.

And that is precisely why I pity you. You stand naked and exposed in too large a world, and that prenatal sac of your soul has been so repeatedly punctured by external influences, persuasions, and pressures that it must take super-human will to keep yourself intact. Many of you don't. Or at least you find the only answer to a fragmented self in a fragmented life—or a withdrawal from life.

How, in any case, are you ever going to know what you are or who you are when these hundreds of voices are doing the job *for* you? How do you know how much of what you think and do is what you *really* think and want to do, or how much is the feedback from what you hear about yourselves— daily, hourly? A lot of it, of course, is true.

You *are* the new power, if only in numbers. You *are* rich, if only in dollars. You *are* smarter than your parents, if only in acquired knowledge. A lot of you take drugs and pills or cop out in communal huddles, living on handouts. I question whether you are more interested in sex than we were, or even more active. The difference here is that it's now so easy to come by, in beds as well as in books, that it may mean less. Obstacles are great aphrodisiacs.

I would like to think that those of you who hate war are a majority. I would like to think that those of you who believe that sweeping changes must be made in our whole social, legal, political and economic life are a majority and an acting majority at that.

Whatever you are, you can't do anything about making a better society and a better world until you are a productive human being. And you can't be a productive human being, sorting the world out, until you sort yourself out.

Until you really attain an expansion of consciousness—not of another world, through hallucination, but of this world, through illumination. Not long ago Professor Lettwin, that dynamic, free-wheeling bear of M.I.T., told an audience of high-school students and undergraduates in Boston that in order to do what they wanted to do—to change the disastrous drift of society—they would have to keep their wits about them. You must be conscious, he exhorted, you must at all times keep your sense of judgment intact. Anything that blurs, that weakens your judgmental values will, in time, make you ineffective. Only your judgment, consciously arrived at, only the intellect and senses in the service of human compassion—will take you where you want to go—where this new society *must* go.

This I would also passionately advocate. As a long-time rebel, a seeker of new adventures, a destroyer of old myths, I have come to believe that this total awareness is the greatest single attribute of identity, and most preciously to be guarded. That it can be chemically achieved I would very much doubt. For moments, maybe. For the long haul, no. It is one thing—and who doesn't need it?—to seek escape from the pain of total awareness—in drink or pot. It is another to take the quick exit from reality with the distinct possibility that you may not make the reentry back. Or that if you do, you may never be yourself—your real, your useful, your creative self—again. Fly Now—Pay Later.

The price of conscious awareness is stiff—but not that stiff. The price is a very hard look at yourself—alone, and not bolstered by a crowd, a tribe—or even—a wife. And here is where I'm going to stick this already battered neck further out—on the institution of matrimony.

Your parents, I would imagine, consider your generation incomprehensible, sometimes frightening, and certainly unconventional. Everything you wear, grow on your face or head, think, believe, do, is way out of their norm.

Except marriage. In a world of undreamed-of scope and opportunity and choice, most of you do exactly what your parents did in a much more limited world. You rush to the altar to tie the legal tie from the age of eighteen onward to a girl no older. Here you are in full flower of body and mind (and I speak of both sexes) and with the only pure freedom of action you will ever know again, and you tie yourself to one mate and one hearth before you know who you are.

If you're lucky, you will find yourselves *through* each other—the ideal nature of love, the true—and rare—blessing of marriage.

If you're not lucky—and the evidence would call you a majority—you will be two half-persons, half-grown, prematurely bound, inhibiting each other's growth, choking up the road to your full development as a human being.

Many of our laws and institutions, as you well know, have not yet caught up with reality . . . the fact that men and women cannot be codified. So long as we do others no harm, how we choose to live is our own affair, and ours alone. How *you* choose to live is yours alone. And if you are able to bring about an intelligent society—I avoid the word "great"—one of the most important things you will have to do is remove the senseless stigmas that still prevail against single men or single women, and against whatever kind of love is the product of deep inner need.

One of your great influences already is that in your new sense of community—in part forced upon you by isolation from your elders—you have managed to blur already many of the lines of demarcation—between races, between sexes, between thought and feeling, between feeling and action—which have trapped the former generations in patterns of sterility. The best of you have not only discovered your conscience, but are living it.

But apart from the terrible issues of the day—to which the best of you address your conscience—war in Vietnam, the brutal war in the streets—how much are you living it as individuals, how much in group conformity?

How brave, how independent are you when you are alone? I ask this chiefly of my own sex, for I wonder whether girls now really know and want the chances and choices that are open to them, or whether they have been so conditioned by history and habit that they slip back into the old patterns of their mothers the minute they graduate. Oddly enough, this supposed choice between marriage and a career never bothered my generation as much as it seems to have bothered the postwar ones. And I lay the blame for it on a mass media—mainly television, advertising, and women's magazines—which maintain the fiction that the only valid goal for women is marriage and children and domesticity (with a little community work thrown in), and that women who demand and seek more than this from life are at best unfulfilled and at worst unfeminine. It is about time that we realized that many women make better teachers than mothers, better actresses than wives, better mistresses than housekeepers, better diplomats than cooks. Just as many men are better rakes than lawnmowers and better dreamers than providers. We have lost a great deal of talent and wasted a great many lives in the perpetuation of these myths that are called "the role of men" or "the role of women." And just as you have managed to dissipate some of them in your dress, I hope you will dissipate others in your lives. The only thing you need to aspire to, the only ultimate identity you must discover, is that of a human being. The sex, believe it or not, is secondary.

But in the search for this human identity, I urge you to remember one thing. I said before that our first recognition of it comes when we know we are not like anybody else, that we are unique. That is so.

But we did not spring into this world through galactic explosion—we did not even burst from the head of Zeus.

We came from somewhere. Not just the womb of our mothers and the seeds of our fathers but from a long, long procession of identities—whose genes we possess.

Whether we like it or not, we bear the past inside us. Good or bad, it cannot be excised, it cannot be rejected, . . . it should not be. Humanity is a continuous process, and without a past there is no future.

In your worship of Now, in your fierce insistence that only the present exists, that you are new on the face of the earth, owing nothing to history— you are cheating yourself. You are not only denying evolution but limiting your future.

You may say you have nothing in common with the preceding generation, you may lay the blame for the present entirely on their shoulders and on the mistakes of the past. But what of the others who came before? What of the great rebels, the great innovators, the great voices without which no light, no truth would ever have prevailed? Much of what poets and philosophers and artists and scientists said ten centuries ago is as valid now as it was then. Where would you be, where would we be, without them?

On a much humbler level, I remember the photograph albums so many families kept when I was a child. There, in our own, were these strange faces and strange clothes of the dead who preceded me: the tall, gaunt old baker in Poland, the opera singer in Germany, the immigrant furniture dealer in New York, the violinist in Breslau, the General near Kiel, the incredible web of cells and genes contained in my own self.

It took me more than twenty years to realize that they lived in me, that I was part of them, and that in spite of distance, time, and difference, I was part of them. I was not, in short, alone.

And neither are you. I suppose what I am asking for here is that, along with your pride of generation, you somehow maintain compassion for those who preceded you as well as for those who will come after you.

If you will, this is a community just as important as any living community of your own age and time, and if you deny your connection with it, you deny evolution, you deny the human race.

Don't play it too cool. The ultimate pattern of life is immense, there are other worlds in other galaxies that may have far transcended ours, and if you aren't turned on more by a shower of meteors than by an electric circus, you're half dead already.

You won't find yourself in a crowded room. You may find yourself under the crowded sky of night, where—if you attach yourself to a single star— you will discover that you are one of many millions, but still—One.

Listen to your own drum and march to it. You may fall on your face—but then, anybody who never does is—Nobody!

US AND THEM

R. D. Laing

Gossip and scandal are always and everywhere elsewhere. Each person is the other to the others. The members of a scandal network may be unified by ideas to which no one will admit in his own person. Each person is thinking of what he thinks the other thinks. The other, in turn, thinks of what yet another thinks. Each person does not mind a colored lodger, but each person's neighbor does. Each person, however, is a neighbor of his neighbor. What They think is held with conviction. It is indubitable and it is incontestable. The scandal group is a series of others which each serial number repudiates in himself.

It is always the others and always elsewhere, and each person feels unable to make any difference to Them. I have no objection to my daughter marrying a Gentile *really*, but we live in a Jewish neighborhood after all. Such collective power is in proportion to each person's creation of this power and his own impotence. . . .

Now the peculiar thing about Them is that They are created only by each one of us repudiating his own identity. When we have installed Them in our hearts, we are only a plurality of solitudes in which what each person has in common is his allocation to the other of the necessity for his own actions. Each person, however, as other to the other, is the other's necessity. Each denies any internal bond with the others; each person claims his own inessentiality: "I just carried out my orders. If I had not done so, someone else would have." "Why don't you sign? Everyone else has," etc. Yet although I can make no difference, I cannot act differently. No single other person is any more necessary to me than I claim to be to Them. But just as he is "one of Them" to me, so I am "one of Them" to him. In this collection of reciprocal indifference, of reciprocal inessentiality and solitude, there appears to exist no freedom. There is conformity to a *presence* that is everywhere *elsewhere*.

The being of any group from the point of view of the group members themselves is very curious. If I think of you and him as together with me, and others again as not with me, I have already formed two rudimentary syntheses, namely, *We* and *They*. However, this private act of synthesis is not in itself a group. In order that *We* come into being as a group, it is necessary not only that I regard, let us say, you and him and me as *We*, but that you and he also think of us as *We*. I shall call such an act of experiencing a number of persons as a single collectivity, an act of rudimentary group synthesis. In this case *We*, that is each of Us, me, you and him, have performed acts of rudimentary group synthesis. But at present these are simply three private acts of group synthesis. In order that a group really jell, I must realize that you think of yourself as one of Us, as I do, and that he thinks of himself as one of Us, as you and I do. I must ensure furthermore that both you and he realize that I think of myself with you and him, and you and he must ensure likewise that the other two realize that this *We* is ubiquitous among us, not simply a private illusion on my, your or his part, shared between two of us but not all three. . . .

Under the form of group loyalty, brotherhood and love, an ethic is introduced whose basis is my right to afford the other protection from my violence if he is loyal to me, and to expect his protection from his violence if I am loyal to him, and my obligation to terrorize him with the threat of my violence, if he does not remain loyal.

It is the ethic of the Gadarene swine, to remain true, one for all and all for one, as we plunge in brotherhood to our destruction.

Let there be no illusions about the brotherhood of man. My brother, as dear to me as I am to myself, my twin, my double, my flesh and blood, may be a fellow lyncher as well as a fellow martyr, and in either case is liable to meet his death at my hand if he chooses to take a different view of the situation. . . .

The group becomes a machine—and that it is a man-made machine in which the machine is the very men who make it is forgotten. It is quite unlike a machine made by men, which can have an existence of its own. The group is men themselves arranging themselves in patterns, strata, assuming and assigning different powers, functions, roles, rights, obligations and so on.

The group cannot become an entity separate from men, but men can form circles to encircle other men. The patterns in space and time, their relative permanence and rigidity, do not turn at any time into a natural system or a hyperorganism, although the fantasy can develop, and men can start to live by the fantasy that the relative permanence in space-time of patterns and patterns of patterns is what they must live and die for.

It is as though we all preferred to die to preserve our shadows.

For the group can be nothing else than the multiplicity of the points of view and actions of its members, and this remains true even where, through the interiorization of this multiplicity as synthesized by each, this synthesized multiplicity becomes ubiquitous in space and enduring in time.

It is just as well that man is a social animal, since the sheer complexity and contradiction of the social field in which he has to live is so formidable. This is so even with the fantastic simplifications that are imposed on this complexity, some of which we have examined above.

Our society is a plural one in many senses. Any one person is likely to be a participant in a number of groups, which may have not only different memberships, but quite different forms of unification.

Each group requires more or less radical internal transformation of the persons who comprise it. Consider the metamorphoses that one man may go through in one day as he moves from one mode of sociality to another— family man, speck of crowd dust, functionary in the organization, friend. These are not simply different roles: each is a whole past and present and future, offering differing options and constraints, different degrees of change of inertia, different kinds of closeness and distance, different sets of rights and obligations, different pledges and promises.

I know of no theory of the individual that fully recognizes this. There is every temptation to start with a notion of some supposed basic personality, but halo effects are not reducible to one internal system. The tired family man at the office and the tired businessman at home attest to the fact that people carry over, not just one set of internal objects, but *various internalized social modes of being*,* often grossly contradictory, from one context to another.

Nor are there such constant emotions or sentiments as love, hate, anger, trust or mistrust. Whatever generalized definitions can be made of each of these at the highest levels of abstraction, specifically and concretely, each emotion is always found in one or another inflection according to the group mode it occurs in. There are no "basic" emotions, instincts or personality, outside of the relationships a person has within one or another social context.**

There is a race against time. It is just possible that a further transformation is possible if men can come to experience themselves as "One of Us." If, even on the basis of the crassest self-interest, we can realize that We and They must be transcended in the totality of the human race, if we in destroying them are not to destroy us all.

* See "Individual and Family Structure," in *Psychoanalytic Studies of the Family*, edited by P. Lomasz (London: Hogarth Press, 1966).
** This chapter, in particular, owes a great deal to *Critique de la Raison Dialectique* (1960) by J.-P. Sartre. It is summarized in *Reason and Violence* (London: Tavistock Publications, 1964), by R. D. Laing and David Cooper.

As war continues, both sides come more and more to resemble each other. The uroborus eats its own tail. The wheel turns full circle. Shall we realize that We and They are shadows of each other? We are They to Them as They are They to Us. When will the veil be lifted? When will the charade turn to carnival? Saints may still be kissing lepers. It is high time that the leper kissed the saint.

ADOLESCENCE

Erik H. Erikson

As technological advances put more and more time between early school life and the young person's final access to specialized work, the stage of adolescing becomes an even more marked and conscious period and, as it has always been in some cultures in some periods, almost a way of life between childhood and adulthood. Thus in the later school years young people, beset with the physiological revolution of their genital maturation and the uncertainty of the adult roles ahead, seem much concerned with faddish attempts at establishing an adolescent subculture with what looks like a final rather than a transitory or, in fact, initial identity formation. They are sometimes morbidly, often curiously, preoccupied with what they appear to be in the eyes of others as compared with what they feel they are, and with the question of how to connect the roles and skills cultivated earlier with the ideal prototypes of the day. In their search for a new sense of continuity and sameness, which must now include sexual maturity, some adolescents have to come to grips again with crises of earlier years before they can install lasting idols and ideals as guardians of a final identity. They need, above all, a moratorium for the integration of the identity elements ascribed in the foregoing to the childhood stages: only that now a larger unit, vague in its outline and yet immediate in its demands, replaces the childhood milieu—"society." A review of these elements is also a list of adolescent problems.

If the earliest stage bequeathed to the identity crisis an important need for trust in oneself and in others, then clearly the adolescent looks most fervently for men and ideas to have *faith* in, which also means men and ideas in whose service it would seem worth while to prove oneself trustworthy. At the same time, however, the adolescent fears a foolish, all too trusting commitment, and will, paradoxically, express his need for faith in loud and cynical mistrust.

If the second stage established the necessity of being defined by what one can *will* freely, then the adolescent now looks for an opportunity to decide with free assent on one of the available or unavoidable avenues of duty and service, and at the same time is mortally afraid of being forced into activities in which he would feel exposed to ridicule or self-doubt. This, too, can lead to a paradox, namely, that he would rather act shamelessly in the eyes of his elders, out of free choice, then be forced into activities which would be shameful in his own eyes or in those of his peers.

If an unlimited *imagination* as to what one *might* become is the heritage of the play age, then the adolescent's willingness to put his trust in those peers and leading, or misleading, elders who will give imaginative, if not illusory, scope to his aspirations is only too obvious. By the same token, he objects violently to all "pedantic" limitations on his self-images and will be ready to settle by loud accusation all his guiltiness over the excessiveness of his ambition.

Finally, if the desire to make something work, and to make it work well, is the gain of the school age, then the choice of an occupation assumes a significance beyond the question of remuneration and status. It is for this reason that some adolescents prefer not to work at all for a while rather than be forced into an otherwise promising career which would offer success without the satisfaction of functioning with unique excellence.

In any given period in history, then, that part of youth will have the most affirmatively exciting time of it which finds itself in the wave of a technological, economic, or ideological trend seemingly promising all that youthful vitality could ask for.

Adolescence, therefore, is least "stormy" in that segment of youth which is gifted and well trained in the pursuit of expanding technological trends, and thus able to identify with new roles of competency and invention and to accept a more implicit ideological outlook. Where this is not given, the adolescent mind becomes a more explicitly ideological one, by which we mean one searching for some inspiring unification of tradition or anticipated techniques, ideas, and ideals. And, indeed, it is the ideological potential of a society which speaks most clearly to the adolescent who is so eager to be affirmed by peers, to be confirmed by teachers, and to be inspired by worthwhile "ways of life." On the other hand, should a young person feel that the environment tries to deprive him too radically of all the forms of expression which permit him to develop and integrate the next step, he may resist with the wild strength encountered in animals who are suddenly forced to defend their lives. For, indeed, in the social jungle of human existence there is no feeling of being alive without a sense of identity. . . .

The estrangement of this stage is *identity confusion*. For the moment, we will accept Biff's formulation in Arthur Miller's *Death of a Salesman*: "I just can't take hold, Mom, I can't take hold of some kind of a life." Where such a dilemma is based on a strong previous doubt of one's ethnic and sexual identity, or where role confusion joins a hopelessness of long standing, delinquent and "borderline" psychotic episodes are not uncommon. Youth after youth, bewildered by the incapacity to assume a role forced on him by the inexorable standardization of American adolescence, runs away in one form or another, dropping out of school, leaving jobs, staying out all night, or withdrawing into bizarre and inaccessible moods. Once "delinquent," his greatest need and often his only salvation is the refusal on the part of older friends, advisers, and judiciary personnel to type him further by pat diagnoses and social judgments which ignore the special dynamic conditions of adolescence. It is here, as we shall see in greater detail, that the concept of identity confusion is of practical clinical value, for if they are diagnosed and treated correctly, seemingly psychotic and criminal incidents do not have the same fatal significance which they may have at other ages.

In general it is the inability to settle on an occupational identity which most disturbs young people. To keep themselves together they temporarily overidentify with the heroes of cliques and crowds to the point of an apparently complete loss of individuality. Yet in this stage not even "falling in love" is entirely, or even primarily, a sexual matter. To a considerable extent adolescent love is an attempt to arrive at a definition of one's identity by projecting one's diffused self-image on another and by seeing it thus reflected and gradually clarified. This is why so much of young love is conversation. On the other hand, clarification can also be sought by destructive means. Young people can become remarkably clannish, intolerant, and cruel in their exclusion of others who are "different," in skin color or cultural background, in tastes and gifts, and often in entirely petty aspects of dress and gesture arbitrarily selected as the signs of an in-grouper or out-grouper. It is important to understand in principle (which does not mean to condone in all of its manifestations) that such intolerancy may be, for a while, a necessary defense against a sense of identity loss. This is unavoidable at a time of life when the body changes its proportions radically, when genital puberty floods body and imagination with all manner of impulses, when intimacy with the other sex approaches and is, on occasion, forced on the young person, and when the immediate future confronts one with too many conflicting possibilities and choices. Adolescents not only help one another temporarily through such discomfort by forming cliques and stereotyping themselves, their ideals, and their enemies; they also insistently test each other's capacity for sustaining loyalties in the midst of inevitable conflicts of values.

The readiness for such testing helps to explain the appeal of simple and cruel totalitarian doctrines among the youth of such countries and classes as have lost or are losing their group identities—feudal, agrarian, tribal, or national. The democracies are faced with the job of winning these grim youths by convincingly demonstrating to them—by living it—that a democratic identity can be strong and yet tolerant, judicious and still determined. But industrial democracy poses special problems in that it insists on self-made identities ready to grasp many chances and ready to adjust to the changing necessities of booms and busts, of peace and war, of migration and determined sedentary life. Democracy, therefore, must present its adolescents with ideals which can be shared by young people of many backgrounds, and which emphasize autonomy in the form of independence and initiative in the form of constructive work. These promises, however, are not easy to fulfill in increasingly complex and centralized systems of industrial, economic, and political organization, systems which increasingly neglect the "self-made" ideology still flaunted in oratory. This is hard on many young Americans because their whole upbringing has made the development of a self-reliant personality dependent on a certain degree of choice, a sustained hope for an individual chance, and a firm commitment to the freedom of self-realization.

LOMBARDI

Leonard Shecter

Unquestionably it takes toughness to be a successful professional coach. This toughness is paid for in humanity. It's a high price. Vince Lombardi, long an extraordinarily successful coach at Green Bay, and later the Washington Redskins, made his players respect him. They also despised him. Henry Jordan, Green Bay defensive lineman, liked to say, "He treats us all the same, like dogs."

After a stinking, sweating, mind-bending morning workout under a choking, hot, muggy Green Bay summer sun, Jordan talked about the coach. "Sometimes you hate him," he said. "He drives you until you know you can't go on. When we were doing the grass drill, my legs just wouldn't come up anymore. So when he walked by me, *he hit them*. He pushes you to the end of your endurance and then beyond it. If you have a reserve, he finds it."

Jerry Kramer, the offensive guard, who painted a brittle picture of Lombardi in his diary of a season, *Instant Replay*, tells a Lombardi story he treasures. "In 1962 I was banged up around the chest. I was out for about two plays. I didn't know it at the time, but I had two broken ribs. I played anyway. The next week, all I can remember is Merle Olsen of the Rams making cleat marks up and down me all afternoon. After that game we took X-rays and found out about the ribs. I went to Coach and told him I had been playing with two broken ribs and he said 'No shit? Well, they don't hurt anymore, do they?' "

Certainly a great deal of Lombardi's success stemmed from his ability to convince a player that injuries were not important. "No one is ever hurt," Lombardi would tell his players over and over. "Hurt is in your mind." Lombardi had a lot of slogans like that.

"You've got to be mentally tough."

"Winning isn't everything, it's the only thing."

"If you can walk, you can run."

"What the hell are *you* limping around for?"

"Dammit, get up, you're not hurt."

These were more than slogans to Lombardi. They were a way of life, a way that led him into a simplistic philosophy which enabled him to understand football perfectly and life hardly at all. In a speech before the American Management Association in 1967 Lombardi said: "Unfortunately, it has become too much of a custom to ridicule what is termed 'the company man' because he is dedicated to a principle he believes in. . . . Everywhere you look, there is a call for freedom, independence, or whatever you wish to call it. But as much as these people want to be independent, they still want to be told what to do. And so few people who are capable of leading are ready and willing to lead. So few are ready. . . . We must gain respect for authority— no, let's say we must *regain* respect for authority because to disavow it is contrary to our individual natures."

Since this was not out of the memoirs of some South American general, but out of Vince Lombardi, American hero, I was glad of the opportunity, soon after, to ask him about these opinions. He did not back off. Indeed, he was willing to expand on them. "I think the rights of the individual have been put above everything else," he said. "Which I don't think is right. The individual has to have respect for authority regardless of what that authority is. I think the individual has gone too far. I think ninety-five percent of the people, as much as they shout, would rather be led than lead."

A lifetime in athletics, most of the years spent commanding the soft, empty minds of young people, is nearly certainly bound to lead one down through the labyrinths of authoritarianism to Lombardiism. Certainly Lombardi's uniqueness among coaches is due more to his success than his attitudes. Patriotism, conformism, religion (many football teams kneel in prayer in the clubhouse before and after games)—these are the raw materials a coach demands. For after them, blank-eyed dedication to hard work, team spirit and the ignoring of painful injury come more easily.

A PERSON AGAIN

Robert Lipsyte

Bob Ryder says he will not play varsity basketball for Princeton this season because he no longer cares to suffer the abuse and high pressure of intercollegiate sports. A junior, Ryder probably would have started at forward again this season. These days, instead of practicing, working out with the team, he is making candles for Christmas money, enjoying being "a student and a person again," and playing a great deal of pick-up basketball. He says he loves the game, that it is important to him, and he is looking forward to the intramural season.

Throughout the country, varsity athletes are questioning the present system of intercollegiate sports, the authoritarianism of some coaches, the dehumanizing policies of some athletic departments. Those driven to play the game are willing to put up with capricious rules and coaching; those on athletic scholarship or in certain schools where sports offers great prestige, have to put up with it. It's part of the deal.

Ryder, at Princeton, will lose no athletic scholarship or community adulation. But his coach, Pete Carrill, who is one of the reasons he is quitting the team, thinks Ryder may be sorry later he was caught in the "intellectual currents" at Princeton that "often fail to prepare a man for the cruelty or at least indifference of the competitive world outside college."

NEVER QUIT

Carrill, the 40-year-old son of a steelworker, said: "It requires character to work hard, to go in there and practice every day, and there's a follow-through in life, in what you eventually become. There's a way of doing things that's right. Sometimes it pains your legs and your stomach, but you come out better for it because you've persevered. There are very few cases where anyone should quit something he starts."

Ryder, who will be 20 later this month, was born and raised in New Jersey, the son of a United Nations official. He is 6 feet 4 inches tall, but some elements of his life-style do not enchant the athletic department: His hair is long, he plays a guitar, he is politically aware and says: "I'll admit I've done some drugs, but never while I'm playing." Coach Carrill says that Ryder worked hard while he was on the team and was in good shape.

Ryder remembers a game the team lost last year, beaten in the last seconds by the University of California, Los Angeles, in the final game of the U.C.L.A. tournament. "I was in the winning thing then, it's hard to shake it off. You see all of us crying after the game because we lost by one point and they were ecstatic. But we all should have been happy, it was a great game, and for what we had, we played much better than they did."

He would like to see sports on a club basis at college. First of all, there would be equal time for all players who attended the practice sessions. "Maybe the games wouldn't be so exciting to watch, but the games are for the players, not for the crazy people up in the stands who scream and don't have the slightest idea of what's happening."

TALK IT OUT

There might be no referees at all. "If you have a bunch of guys who love to play, you can solve your own problems. It's a beautiful thing to work out your own hassles."

The roles of coaches would be different. "I'm not sure they should be abolished, but there should be more advisers who explain what they're doing and why. If a coach wants to introduce the zone, but the players prefer man-to-man, let the team get together and talk it out."

He would like to see an end to the violence of basketball, more of a chance to appreciate the esthetics of the individual moves and the team flow. Both teams would meet to "rap" before a game, to discuss why they were playing. They would meet again afterward. They could keep score if they wanted to and if the game went very well, they might just play another one immediately.

Ryder, looking back, says he is "grateful" he played varsity ball last year. It was a valuable learning experience, but he did not enjoy it. He was constantly afraid he would "mess up," and have to face the angry, yelling, emotional Coach Carrill.

The coach, who said he was disappointed by Ryder's decision to quit, denied he was abusive or particularly authoritarian or that he tried to cure injuries with tongue-lashings. Carrill said Ryder had been different from the very beginning—when he refused to fill out a sports publicity questionnaire because he didn't want to be regarded as an athlete instead of a student— but wishes him well. "To quote Mao Tse-tung," said Coach Carrill, "We should let a hundred blossoms bloom. That means there's a place for everybody."

from
THE INVISIBLE MAN

Ralph Ellison

I am an invisible man. No, I am not a spook like those who haunted Edgar Allan Poe; nor am I one of your Hollywood-movie ectoplasms. I am a man of substance, of flesh and bone, fiber and liquids—and I might even be said to possess a mind. I am invisible, understand, simply because people refuse to see me. Like the bodiless heads you see sometimes in circus sideshows, it is as though I have been surrounded by mirrors of hard, distorting glass. When they approach me they see only my surroundings, themselves, or figments of their imagination—indeed, everything and anything except me.

Nor is my invisibility exactly a matter of a bio-chemical accident to my epidermis. That invisibility to which I refer occurs because of a peculiar disposition of the eyes of those with whom I come in contact. A matter of the construction of their *inner* eyes, those eyes with which they look through their physical eyes upon reality. I am not complaining, nor am I protesting either. It is sometimes advantageous to be unseen, although it is most often rather wearing on the nerves. Then too, you're constantly being bumped against by those of poor vision. Or again, you often doubt if you really exist. You wonder whether you aren't simply a phantom in other people's minds. Say, a figure in a nightmare which the sleeper tries with all his strength to destroy. It's when you feel like this that, out of resentment, you begin to bump people back. And, let me confess, you feel that way most of the time. You ache with the need to convince yourself that you do exist in the real world, that you're a part of all the sound and anguish, and you strike out with your fists, you curse and you swear to make them recognize you. And, alas, it's seldom successful.

One night I accidentally bumped into a man, and perhaps because of the near darkness he saw me and called me an insulting name. I sprang at him, seized his coat lapels and demanded that he apologize. He was a tall blond man, and as my face came close to his he looked insolently out of his blue eyes and cursed me, his breath hot in my face as he struggled. I pulled his chin down sharp upon the crown of my head, butting him as I had seen the West Indians do, and I felt his flesh tear and the blood gush out, and I yelled, "Apologize! Apologize!" But he continued to curse and struggle, and I butted him again and again until he went down heavily, on his knees, profusely bleeding. I kicked him repeatedly, in a frenzy because he still uttered insults though his lips were frothy with blood. Oh yes, I kicked him! And in my outrage I got out my knife and prepared to slit his throat, right there beneath the lamplight in the deserted street, holding him by the collar with one hand, and opening the knife with my teeth—when it occurred to me that the man had not *seen* me, actually; that he, as far as he knew, was in the midst of a walking nightmare! And I stopped the blade, slicing the air as I pushed him away, letting him fall back to the street. I stared at him hard as the lights of a car stabbed through the darkness. He lay there, moaning on the asphalt; a man almost killed by a phantom. It unnerved me. I was both disgusted and ashamed. I was like a drunken man myself, wavering about on weakened legs. Then I was amused. Something in this man's thick head had sprung out and beaten him within an inch of his life. I began to laugh at this crazy discovery. Would he have awakened at the point of death? Would Death himself have freed him for wakeful living? But I didn't linger. I ran away into the dark, laughing so hard I feared I might rupture myself. The next day I saw his picture in the *Daily News*, beneath a caption stating that he had been "mugged." Poor fool, poor blind fool, I thought with sincere compassion, mugged by an invisible man!

II
SOCIETY

THE CRITICAL MASS

"I have been in Golgotha," at last I answered. "I have seen Humanity hanging on a cross! Do none of you know what sights the sun and stars look down on in this city, that you can think and talk of anything else? Do you not know that close to your doors a great multitude of men and women, flesh of your flesh, live lives that are one agony from birth to death? Listen! their dwellings are so near that if you hush your laughter you will hear their grievous voices, the piteous crying of the little ones that suckle poverty, the hoarse curses of men sodden in misery, turned half-way back to brutes, the chaffering of an army of women selling themselves for bread. With what have you stopped your ears that you do not hear these doleful sounds? For me I can hear nothing else."

EDWARD BELLAMY,
Looking Backward

1984 will soon be here, and what kind of essays on Society will *TLE9* choose then? The tensions in our society seem to hurl people together until, like the trigger of an atomic bomb, they reach a critical mass and begin a self-destructive chain reaction. Every day men of upright and honest conviction can be forced by what appear to be "social necessities" to betray what appear to be "public trusts." The letter of Jefferson to Madison on the Bill of Rights shows that the brilliant, courageous founders of our country were conscious themselves of the dangers of the rapid growth of our society. Just as Jefferson worried that democracy might not be able to survive if our population became as dense as the countries of Europe, so John Lindsay publicly agonizes over whether the City of New York is really governable.

The response of one small part of our society to these pressures is to impose more restrictive controls on political change, to legalize wiretaps, to expand political surveillance, to prosecute Benjamin Spock and Muhammed Ali, and to restrict educational funds where school systems harbor rebellious students and faculty. The response of another group is to reject or ignore all their social obligations, to seek to destroy by violence or guile all of the "establishment," including school, church, business, private property, and political parties.

The great mass of people in between listen as a captive audience to the cries and threats of the fringe groups. They filter out what they can use from the increasingly polluted stream of information they are exposed to, and make choices that seem to them reasonable and fair, expedient, or "better than," now with this side, now with that. We are constantly in a situation where, for example, 10% of our population wants to oppose Communism forcibly all over the world, 10% wants to avoid all such foreign entanglements, and 80% cannot exist in the real world without deciding one way or another, with the lives of their friends and relatives hinging on the outcome.

In such circumstances it is easy to long for a communal utopia where these larger issues can be ignored. But most people recognize they have neither the patience nor the humility for such a life. So they read and observe and listen and try to decide, and they may be grateful for our judicial system that sometimes reads and decides for them. The essays in this section will be academically useful to the convinced and doctrinaire few, and will be of real importance to the many who are still reading and deciding.

First Principles

RESISTANCE TO CIVIL GOVERNMENT

Henry David Thoreau

Unjust laws exist: shall we be content to obey them, or shall we endeavor to amend them, and obey them until we have succeeded, or shall we transgress them at once? Men generally, under such a government as this, think that they ought to wait until they have persuaded the majority to alter them. They think that, if they should resist, the remedy would be worse than the evil. But it is the fault of the government itself that the remedy *is* worse than the evil. *It* makes it worse. Why is it not more apt to anticipate and provide for reform? Why does it not cherish its wise minority? Why does it cry and resist before it is hurt? Why does it not encourage its citizens to be on the alert to point out its faults, and *do* better than it would have them? Why does it always crucify Christ, and excommunicate Copernicus and Luther, and pronounce Washington and Franklin rebels?

One would think, that a deliberate and practical denial of its authority was the only offense never contemplated by government; else, why has it not assigned its definite, its suitable and proportionate penalty? If a man who has no property refuses but once to earn nine shillings for the state, he is put in prison for a period unlimited by any law that I know, and determined only by the discretion of those who placed him there; but if he should steal ninety times nine shillings from the state, he is soon permitted to go at large again.

If the injustice is part of the necessary friction of the machine of government, let it go, let it go: perchance it will wear smooth,—certainly the machine will wear out. If the injustice has a spring, or a pulley, or a rope, or a crank, exclusively for itself, then perhaps you may consider whether the remedy will not be worse than the evil; but if it is of such a nature that it requires you to be the agent of injustice to another, then, I say, break the law. Let your life be a counter friction to stop the machine. What I have to do is to see, at any rate, that I do not lend myself to the wrong which I condemn.

As for adopting the ways which the state has provided for remedying the evil, I know not of such ways. They take too much time, and a man's life will be gone. I have other affairs to attend to. I came into this world, not chiefly to make this a good place to live in, but to live in it, be it good or bad. A man has not everything to do, but something; and because he cannot do *everything*, it is not necessary that he should do *something* wrong. It is not my business to be petitioning the Governor or the Legislature any more than it is theirs to petition me; and if they should not hear my petition, what should I do then? But in this case the state has provided no way: its very Constitution is the evil. This may seem to be harsh and stubborn and un-conciliatory; but it is to treat with the utmost kindness and consideration the only spirit that can appreciate or deserves it. So is all change for the better, like birth and death, which convulse the body.

I do not hesitate to say, that those who call themselves Abolitionists should at once effectually withdraw their support, both in person and prop-erty, from the government of Massachusetts and not wait till they constitute a majority of one, before they suffer the right to prevail through them. I think that it is enough if they have God on their side, without waiting for that other one. Moreover, any man more right than his neighbors constitutes a majority of one already.

I meet this American government, or its representative, the state govern-ment, directly, and face to face, once a year—no more—in the person of its tax-gatherer; this is the only mode in which a man situated as I am neces-sarily meets it; and it then says distinctly, Recognize me; and the simplest, most effectual, and, in the present posture of affairs, the indispensablest mode of treating with it on this head, of expressing your little satisfaction with and love for it, is to deny it then. My civil neighbor, the tax-gatherer, is the very man I have to deal with,—for it is, after all, with men and not with parchment that I quarrel,—and he has voluntarily chosen to be an agent of the government. How shall he ever know well what he is and does as an officer of the government, or as a man, until he is obliged to consider whether he shall treat me, his neighbor, for whom he has respect, as a neighbor and well-disposed man, or as a maniac and disturber of the peace, and see if he can get over this obstruction to his neighborliness without a ruder and more impetuous thought or speech corresponding with his action. I know this well, that if one thousand, if one hundred, if ten men whom I could name,—if ten *honest* men only,—ay, if *one* HONEST man, in this State of Massachusetts, *ceasing to hold slaves*, were actually to withdraw from this copartnership, and be locked up in the county jail therefor, it would be the abolition of slavery in America. For it matters not how small the beginning may seem to be: what is once well done is done forever. But we love better to talk about it: that we say is our mission. Reform keeps many scores of newspapers in its service, but not one man. If my esteemed neighbor, the State's ambassador, who will devote his days to the settlement of the question of human rights in the Council Chamber, instead of being threatened with the prisons of Carolina, were to sit down the prisoner of Massachusetts, that State which is so anxious to foist the sin of slavery upon her sister,— though at present she can discover only an act of inhospitality to be the ground of a quarrel with her,—the Legislature would not wholly waive the subject the following winter.

Under a government which imprisons any unjustly, the true place for a just man is also a prison. The proper place to-day, the only place which Massachusetts has provided for her freer and less desponding spirits, is in her prisons, to be put out and locked out of the State by her own act, as they have already put themselves out by their principles. It is there that the fugitive slave, and the Mexican prisoner on parole, and the Indian come to plead the wrongs of his race should find them; on that separate, but more free and honorable ground, where the State places those who are not *with* her, but *against* her,—the only house in a slave State in which a free man can abide with honor. If any think that their influence would be lost there, and their voices no longer afflict the ear of the State, that they would not be as an enemy within its walls, they do not know by how much truth is stronger than error, nor how much more eloquently and effectively he can combat injustice who has experienced a little in his own person. Cast your whole vote, not a strip of paper merely, but your whole influence. A minority is powerless while it conforms to the majority; it is not even a minority then; but it is irresistible when it clogs by its whole weight. If the alternative is to keep all just men in prison, or give up war and slavery, the State will not hesitate which to choose. If a thousand men were not to pay their tax-bills this year, that would not be a violent and bloody measure, as it would be to pay them, and enable the State to commit violence and shed innocent blood. This is, in fact, the definition of a peaceable revolution, if any such is possible. If the tax-gatherer, or any other public officer, asks me, as one has done, "But what shall I do?" my answer is, "If you really wish to do anything, resign your office." When the subject has refused allegiance, and the officer has resigned his office, then the revolution is accomplished. But even suppose blood should flow. Is there not a sort of blood shed when the conscience is wounded? Through this wound a man's real manhood and immortality flow out, and he bleeds to an everlasting death. I see this blood flowing now.

LETTER TO JAMES MADISON

Thomas Jefferson

Paris, Dec. 20, 1787

Dear Sir

. . . I like much the general idea of framing a government which should go on of itself peaceably, without needing continual recurrence to the state legislatures. I like the organization of the government into Legislative, Judiciary and Executive. I like the power given the Legislature to levy taxes; and for that reason solely approve of the greater house being chosen by the people directly. For tho' I think a house chosen by them will be very illy qualified to legislate for the Union, for foreign nations &c. yet this evil does not weigh against the good of preserving inviolate the fundamental principle that the people are not to be taxed but by representatives chosen immediately by themselves. I am captivated by the compromise of the opposite claims of the great and little states, of the latter to equal, and the former to proportional influence. I am much pleased too with the substitution of the method of voting by persons, instead of that of voting by states: and I like the negative given to the Executive with a third of either house, though I should have liked it better had the Judiciary been associated for that purpose, or invested with a similar and separate power. There are other good things of less moment. I will now add what I do not like. First the omission of a bill of rights providing clearly and without the aid of sophisms for freedom of religion, freedom of the press, protection against standing armies, restriction against monopolies, the eternal and unremitting force of the habeas corpus laws, and trials by jury in all matters of fact triable by the laws of the land and not by the law of Nations. To say, as Mr. Wilson does that a bill of rights was not necessary because all is reserved in the case of the general government which is not given, while in the particular ones all is given which is not reserved might do for the Audience to whom it was addressed, but is surely gratis dictum, opposed by strong inferences from the body of the instrument, as well as from the omission of the clause of our present confederation which had declared that in express terms. It was a hard conclusion to say because there has been no uniformity among the states as to the cases triable by jury, because some have been so incautious as to abandon this mode of trial, therefore the more prudent states shall be reduced to the same level of calamity. It would have been much more just and wise to have concluded the other way that as most of the states had judiciously preserved this palladium, those who had wandered should be brought back to it, and to have established general right instead of general wrong. Let me add that a bill of rights is what the people are entitled to against every government on earth, general or particular, and what no just government should refuse, or rest on inference. The second feature I dislike, and greatly dislike, is the abandonment in every instance of the necessity of rotation in office, and most particularly in the case of the President. Experience concurs with reason in concluding that the first magistrate will always be re-elected if the constitution permits it. He is then an officer for life. This once observed it becomes of so much consequence to certain nations to have a friend or a foe at the head of our affairs that they will interfere with money and with arms. A Galloman or an Angloman will be supported by the nation he befriends. If once elected, and at a second or third election outvoted by one or two votes, he will pretend false votes, foul play, hold possession of the reins of government, be supported by the states voting for him, especially if they are the central ones lying in a compact body themselves and separating their opponents: and they will be aided by one nation of Europe, while the majority are aided by another. The election of a President of America some years hence will be much more interesting to certain nations of Europe than ever the election of a king of Poland was. Reflect on all the instances in history antient and modern, of elective monarchies, and say if they do not give foundation for my fears, the Roman emperors, the popes, while they were of any importance, the German emperors till they became hereditary in practice, the kings of Poland, the Deys of the Ottoman dependancies. It may be said that if elections are to be attended with these disorders, the seldomer they are renewed the better. But experience shews that the only way to prevent disorder is to render them uninteresting by frequent changes. An incapacity to be elected a second time would have been the only effectual preventative. The power of removing him every fourth year by the vote of the people is a power which will not be exercised. The king of Poland is removeable every day by the Diet, yet he is never removed.—Smaller objections are the Appeal in fact as well as law, and the binding all persons Legislative, Executive and Judiciary by oath to maintain that constitution. I do not pretend to decide what would be the best method of procuring the establishment of the manifold good things in this constitution, and of getting rid of the bad. Whether by adopting it in hopes of future amendment, or, after it has been duly weighed and canvassed by the people, after seeing the parts they generally dislike, and those they generally approve, to say to them 'We see now what you wish. Send together your deputies again, let them frame a constitution for you omitting what you have condemned, and establishing the powers you approve. Even these will be a great addition to the energy of your government.'—At all events I hope you will not be discouraged from other trials, if the present one should fail of it's full effect.—I have thus told you freely what I like and dislike: merely as a matter of curiosity for I know your own judgment has been formed on all these points after having heard every thing which could be urged on them. I own I am not a friend to a very energetic government. It is always oppressive. The late rebellion in Massachusets has given more alarm than I think it should have done. Calculate that one rebellion in 13 states in the course of 11 years, is but one for each state in a century and a half. No country should be so long without one. Nor will any degree of power in the hands of government prevent insurrections. France with all it's despotism, and two or three hundred thousand men always in arms has had three insurrections in the three years I have been here in every one of which greater numbers were engaged than in Massachusetts and a great deal more blood was spilt. In Turkey, which Montesquieu supposes more despotic, insurrections are the events of every day. In England, where the hand of power is lighter than here, but heavier than with us they happen every half dozen years. Compare again the ferocious depredations of their insurgents with the order, the moderation and the almost self extinguishment of ours.—After all, it is my principle that the will of the Majority should always prevail. If they approve the proposed Convention in all it's parts, I shall concur in it chearfully, in hopes that they will amend it whenever they shall find it work wrong. I think our governments will remain virtuous for many centuries; as long as they are chiefly agricultural; and this will be as long as there shall be vacant lands in any part of America. When they get piled upon one another in large cities, as in Europe, they will become corrupt as in Europe. Above all things I hope the education of the common people will be attended to; convinced that on their good sense we may rely with the most security for the preservation of a due degree of liberty. I have tired you by this time with my disquisitions and will therefore only add assurances of the sincerity of those sentiments of esteem and attachment with which I am Dear Sir your affectionate friend & servant,

Th: Jefferson

P.S. The instability of our laws is really an immense evil. I think it would be well to provide in our constitutions that there shall always be a twelvemonth between the ingrossing a bill and passing it: that it should then be offered to it's passage without changing a word: and that if circumstances should be thought to require a speedier passage, it should take two thirds of both houses instead of a bare majority.

THE BILL OF RIGHTS

ARTICLE I

Congress shall make no law respecting an establishment of religion, or prohibiting the free exercise thereof; or abridging the freedom of speech, or of the press; or the right of the people peaceably to assemble, and to petition the government for a redress of grievances.

ARTICLE II

A well regulated militia being necessary to the security of a free State, the right of the people to keep and bear arms, shall not be infringed.

ARTICLE III

No soldier shall, in time of peace be quartered in any house, without the consent of the owner, nor in time of war, but in a manner to be prescribed by law.

ARTICLE IV

The right of the people to be secure in their persons, houses, papers, and effects, against unreasonable searches and seizures, shall not be violated, and no warrants shall issue, but upon probable cause, supported by oath or affirmation, and particularly describing the place to be searched, and the persons or things to be seized.

ARTICLE V

No person shall be held to answer for a capital, or otherwise infamous crime, unless on a presentment or indictment of a grand jury, except in cases arising in the land or naval forces, or in the militia, when in actual service in time of war or public danger; nor shall any person be subject for the same offense to be twice put in jeopardy of life or limb; nor shall be compelled in any criminal case to be a witness against himself, nor be deprived of life, liberty, or property, without due process of law; nor shall private property be taken for public use without just compensation.

ARTICLE VI

In all criminal prosecutions, the accused shall enjoy the right to a speedy and public trial, by an impartial jury of the State and district wherein the

71

crime shall have been committed, which district shall have been previously ascertained by law, and to be informed of the nature and cause of the accusation; to be confronted with the witnesses against him; to have compulsory process for obtaining witnesses in his favor, and to have the assistance of counsel for his defense.

ARTICLE VII

In suits at common law, where the value in controversy shall exceed twenty dollars, the right of trial by jury shall be preserved, and no fact tried by a jury shall be otherwise reexamined in any court of the United States, than according to the rules of the common law.

ARTICLE VIII

Excessive bail shall not be required, nor excessive fines imposed, nor cruel and unusual punishments inflicted.

ARTICLE IX

The enumeration in the Constitution of certain rights shall not be construed to deny or disparage others retained by the people.

ARTICLE X

The powers not delegated to the United States by the Constitution, nor prohibited by it to the States, are reserved to the States repectively, or to the people.

PRESCRIPTION, AUTHORITY, AND ORDERED FREEDOM

Russell Kirk

Prescription, socially and politically speaking, means those ways and institutions and rights prescribed by long—sometimes immemorial—usage. Tradition (a word until the end of the eighteenth century applied almost exclusively to Christian beliefs not set down in Scripture) means received opinions, convictions religious and moral and political and aesthetic passed down from generation to generation, so that they are accepted by most men as a matter of course. I have discussed the nature of tradition and prescription at some length in my book *Beyond the Dreams of Avarice.*

Fulbert of Chartres and Gerbert of Rheims, those two grand Schoolmen, said that we moderns are dwarfs standing upon the shoulders of giants. We see so far only because we are elevated upon the accomplishment of our ancestors; and if we break with ancestral wisdom, we at once are plunged into the ditch of ignorance. All that we have and know is founded upon the experience of the race. As Burke put it, "The individual is foolish, but the species is wise." Men have no right, Burke said, to risk the very existence of their nation and their civilization upon experiments in morals and politics; for each man's private capital of intelligence is petty; it is only when a man draws upon the bank and capital of the ages, the wisdom of our ancestors, that he can act wisely. Without resort to tradition and prescription, we are left with merely our vanity and the brief and partial experience of our evanescent lives. "What shadows we are, and what shadows we pursue!"

G.K. Chesterton expressed much the same truth when he wrote of "the democracy of the dead." When we decide great questions in our time, he held, we ought to count not merely the votes of our contemporaries, but the opinions of many generations of men—and particularly the convictions of the wise men who have preceded us in time. By trial and error, by revelation, by the insights of men of genius, mankind has acquired, slowly and painfully, over thousands of years, a knowledge of human nature and of the civil social order which no one individual possibly can supplant by private rationality.

This is true especially in matters of morals, politics, and taste; but in considerable degree it is true also even in modern science and technology. Once a student objected to me that surely enlightened modern man could work out rationally a much better system of morals and politics than the hodgepodge we have inherited from blundering ancestors. But I asked this student if, without consulting senior technicians, books, and authority generally, he thought he could construct, unaided, an automobile—if, indeed, he thought that he personally, even with all sorts of advice, could make an automobile at all. He confessed that he could not; and it began to be borne in upon him to construct, *carte blanche,* a system of morals and politics that really would work might be an undertaking more difficult still.

So even the most gifted of men, and always the great mass of human beings, must fall back upon tradition and prescription if they are to act at all in this world. At the very least, it saves a great deal of time. It is conceivable that, if I set myself to it, I might calculate for myself the circumference of the earth, quite independently of previous calculations. But since I have no strong mathematical gifts, it is improbable that my calculations would be more accurate than those of the present authorities; and it seems almost certain that my result would be quite the same as the present calculation of the earth's circumference; so I would have spent months or years of a brief life in trying to gain what I could have had for the asking. If we are to accomplish anything in this life, we must take much for granted; as Newman said, if one had to make the choice, it would be better to believe all things than to doubt all things. In the matter of the earth's circumference, nearly all of us are much better off if we simply accept the "traditional" or "authoritative" calculation.

This is even more true of moral and social first principles. Only through prescription and tradition, only by habitual acceptance of just and sound authority, can men acquire knowledge of the norms for humanity. Authority tells us that murder is wrong; prescription immemorially has visited severe punishments upon murderers; tradition presents us with an ancient complex of tales of the evil consequences of murder. Now a man who thinks his private petty rationality superior to the wisdom of our ancestors may undertake experiments in murder, with a view to testing these old irrational scruples; but the results of such experiments are sure to be disagreeable for everyone concerned, including the researcher; and that experimenter has no right to be surprised if we hang him by the neck until he is quite dead. For if men flout norm and convention, life becomes intolerable. It is through respect for tradition and prescription, and recourse to those sources of knowledge, that the great mass of men acquire a tolerable understanding of norms and conventions, of the rules by which private and social existence is made tolerable.

A norm is an enduring standard. It is a law of our nature, which we ignore at our peril. It is a rule of human conduct and a measure of public virtue. The norm does not signify the average, the median, the mean, the mediocre. The norm is not the conduct of the average sensual man. A norm is not simply a measure of average performance within a group. There exists law for man, and law for thing; the late Alfred Kinsey notwithstanding, the norm for the wasp and the snake is not the norm for man. A norm has an objective existence: though men may ignore or forget a norm, still that norm does not cease to be, nor does it cease to influence men. A man apprehends a norm or fails to apprehend it, but he does not create or destroy norms.

The sanction for obedience to norms must come from a source other than private advantage and rationality—from a source more than human, indeed. Men do not submit long to their own creations. Standards erected out of expediency will be demolished soon enough, also out of expediency. Either norms have an existence independent of immediate utility, or they are mere fictions. If men assume that norms are merely the pompous fabrications of their ancestors, got up to serve the interests of a faction or an age, then every rising generation will challenge the principles of personal and social order and will learn wisdom only through agony. For half a century, we have been experiencing the consequences of a moral and social neoterism.

"Goodnatured unambitious men are cowards when they have no religion." So, in *Back to Methuselah,* writes Bernard Shaw. "They are dominated and exploited not only by greedy and often halfwitted and half-alive weaklings who will do anything for cigars, champagne, motor cars, and the more childish and selfish uses of money, but by able and sound administrators who can do nothing else with them than dominate and exploit them. Government and exploitation become synonymous under such circumstances; and the world is finally ruled by the childish, the brigands, and the blackguards." (One may acknowledge the acuteness of this insight without subscribing to the curious religion, or quasi-religion, which Shaw sets forth— half soberly, half facetiously—in *Back to Methuselah.*)

As a gloss upon this, one may say also that the average good-natured unambitious man is a coward also if he lacks—even though retaining some religious feelings—"that wise prejudice" by which "a man's virtue becomes his habit," in Burke's phrase. If his life is regulated, almost unconsciously, upon certain received opinions concerning justice and injustice, charity and selfishness, freedom and servitude, truth and falsehood, he will behave habitually with some degree of resolution and courage; but if he is all at sea in a latter-day Liberalism and moral relativism, in which any point of view or mode of conduct has something to be said for it, then he will be unnerved when the test comes. Acting customarily upon tradition and prescription, he will not feel alone; the democracy of the dead will endorse him. But acting without norms, he must be, ordinarily, either a coward or a brute in any personal or civic crisis.

A man who accepts tested authority, and acknowledges the beneficent influence of prescription and tradition, is conventional; but he is not servile. Conventions are the means by which obedience to norms is inculcated in society. Conventions are compacts by which we agree to respect one another's dignity and rights. A high degree of respect for convention is quite consonant with a high development of individual personality, and even of eccentricity. Many of the great "characters," indeed, are the great champions of convention; the names of Samuel Johnson and Benjamin Disraeli, of John Adams, John Randolph, and Theodore Roosevelt may suffice for illustration. There exists no necessary opposition between strong outward indifference to foible and strong inward loyalty to norms. A man of strong character who accepts just authority and its works will be meek—but meek only as Moses: that is, obedient to the will of God, but unflinching against human tyrants.

The good citizen is a law-abiding traditionalist: so the politics of Virgil have been summed up. If men are courageous or virtuous, ordinarily this is because they are persons of good moral *habits*: that is, they act habitually, and almost unthinkingly, upon certain premises they have learnt from infancy, through force of example and through formal instruction. This is what Burke meant when he wrote that prejudice is the wisdom of unlettered men. They draw their strength from acceptance of tradition and prescription.

Now it does not follow that an unquestioning acceptance of received opinions and long-established usage will of itself suffice to solve all personal and public problems. The world does change; a certain sloughing off of tradition and prescription is at work in any vigorous society, and a certain adding to the bulk of received opinion goes on from age to age. We cannot live precisely by the rules of our distant forefathers, in all matters. But, again to employ a phrase of Burke's, the fact that a belief or an institution has long been accepted by men, and seems to have exerted a beneficent influence, establishes in its favor "a legitimate presumption." If we feel inclined to depart from old ways, we ought to do so only after very sober consideration of ultimate consequences. Authority, prescription, and tradition undergo in every generation a certain filtering process, by which the really archaic is discarded; yet we ought to be sure that we actually are filtering, and not merely letting our heritage run down the drain.

Similarly, the general principles and valuable institutions which we have inherited from past generations must be applied and utilized with prudence; there the exercise of right reason by the leaders of any society sets to work. We possess moral norms, the Decalogue, for instance, but the way in which we observe those norms must be determined in our time by the circumstances in which we find ourselves, so that wise men in our age must reconcile exigency and enduring standard. We possess tests of political institutions; but for those institutions to endure, now and then reform is essential, lest the institutions atrophy. Thus Burke's model of a statesman is one who combines with an ability to reform a disposition to preserve.

Prescription and tradition, then, cannot stand forever if the living do not sustain them by vigorous application and prudent reform. But it is equally true that lively action and ingenious reform are mere ropes of sand, unless linked with the wisdom of the ages.

One instance of the abiding value of inherited convictions—beliefs that have their origin both in the experience of the race and in the reasoning of men of genius, but have acquired through subtle processes the status of popular prejudices—is the idea of justice, as expressed by Plato and Cicero. The great classical philosophers of politics argued that justice resides in this: to each his own. Every man, ideally, ought to receive the things that best suit his own nature. Men's talents and appetites vary greatly from individual to individual; therefore a society is unjust which treats all men as if they were uniform, or which allots to one sort of nature rights and duties that properly belong to other sorts of human beings.

This concept of justice has entered deeply into the ethics, the jurisprudence, and even the imaginative literature of what is called "Western civilization." It still is a profound influence upon many men and women who never have read Cicero or Plato. It creates a prejudice against radical egalitarianism, which would reduce all men to a single mode of existence. It has inculcated a sound prejudice in favor of *order*: that is, a society marked by a variety of rewards and duties, a commonwealth in which, as Burke said, all men "have equal rights; but not to equal things." This theory underlies, for example, the British and American constitutions.

Nowadays this classical idea of justice is challenged by the Marxist doctrine that order should be abolished: all human beings should be treated as identical units, and compulsory equality of condition enforced. When the average American or Englishman is brought face to face with Marxist demands for the overthrow of prescriptive order and the establishment of a society without demarcations, he may not be able to meet the Marxist propagandist with a privately reasoned defense of variety and constitutionalism; but he resists the Marxist doctrine out of a feeling that what the Communist proposes somehow is fundamentally unjust. The average American or Englishman remains a law-abiding traditionalist, even in this day of giddy technological and industrial alteration; he takes it for granted that we were not born yesterday; that we have no right to cast away our tested civil social order; that monotonous uniformity of condition is contrary to deep ancient human aspirations; that Communism flies in the face of the nature of things. And because he is the heir to a great tradition, he knows something of the character of justice, and he is resolute despite the threats and seductions of the radical innovator.

"The great mysterious incorporation of the human race" is, as Burke said, a contract of sorts: but a contract between the divine and the human natures, and among the dead, the living, and those yet unborn. We know something of the terms of that eternal contract of society through traditions and prescriptions. Our obedience to norms, to true and just authority in morals and politics, keeps that immortal contract alive. And that obedience secures us all in ordered freedom.

THE PRINCE, XVIII

Niccolo Machiavelli

IN WHAT MANNER PRINCES SHOULD KEEP THEIR WORD

How laudable it is for a prince to keep his word and govern his actions by integrity rather than trickery will be understood by all. Nonetheless we have in our times seen great things accomplished by many princes who have thought little of keeping their promises and have known the art of mystifying the minds of men. Such princes have won out over those whose actions were based on fidelity to their word.

It must be understood that there are two ways of fighting, one with laws and the other with arms. The first is the way of men, the second is the style of beasts, but since very often the first does not suffice it is necessary to turn to the second. Therefore a prince must know how to play the beast as well as the man. This lesson was taught allegorically by the ancient writers who related that Achilles and many other princes were brought up by Chiron the Centaur, who took them under his discipline. The clear significance of this half-man and half-beast preceptorship is that a prince must know how to use either of these two natures and that one without the other has no enduring strength. Now since the prince must make use of the characteristics of beasts he should choose those of the fox and the lion, though the lion cannot defend himself against snares and the fox is helpless against wolves. One must be a fox in avoiding traps and a lion in frightening wolves. Such as choose simply the rôle of a lion do not rightly understand the matter. Hence a wise leader cannot and should not keep his word when keeping it is not to his advantage or when the reasons that made him give it are no longer valid. If men were good, this would not be a good precept, but since they are wicked and will not keep faith with you, you are not bound to keep faith with them.

A prince has never lacked legitimate reasons to justify his breach of faith. We could give countless recent examples and show how any number of peace treaties or promises have been broken and rendered meaningless by the faithlessness of princes, and how success has fallen to the one who best knows how to counterfeit the fox. But it is necessary to know how to disguise this nature well and how to pretend and dissemble. Men are so simple and so ready to follow the needs of the moment that the deceiver will always find some one to deceive. Of recent examples I shall mention one. Alexander VI did nothing but deceive and never thought of anything else and always found some occasion for it. Never was there a man more convincing in his asseverations nor more willing to offer the most solemn oaths nor less likely to observe them. Yet his deceptions were always successful for he was an expert in this field.

So a prince need not have all the aforementioned good qualities, but it is most essential that he appear to have them. Indeed, I should go so far as to say that having them and always practising them is harmful, while seeming to have them is useful. It is good to appear clement, trustworthy, humane, religious, and honest, and also to be so, but always with the mind so disposed that when the occasion arises not to be so, you can become the opposite. It must be understood that a prince and particularly a new prince cannot practise all the virtues for which men are accounted good, for the necessity of preserving the state often compels him to take actions which are opposed to loyalty, charity, humanity, and religion. Hence he must have a spirit ready to adapt itself as the varying winds of fortune command him. As I have said, so far as he is able, a prince should stick to the path of good but, if the necessity arises, he should know how to follow evil.

A prince must take great care that no word ever passes his lips that is not full of the above mentioned five good qualities, and he must seem to all who see and hear him a model of piety, loyalty, integrity, humanity, and religion. Nothing is more necessary than to seem to possess this last quality, for men in general judge more by the eye than the hand, as all can see but few can feel. Everyone sees what you seem to be, few experience what you really are and these few do not dare to set themselves up against the opinion of the majority supported by the majesty of the state. In the actions of all men and especially princes, where there is no court of appeal, the end is all that counts. Let a prince then concern himself with the acquisition or the maintenance of a state; the means employed will always be considered honorable and praised by all, for the mass of mankind is always swayed by appearances and by the outcome of an enterprise. And in the world there is only the mass, for the few find their place only when the majority has no base of support.

CO-EXISTENCE OR NO EXISTENCE: THE CHOICE IS OURS

Bertrand Russell

The recent changes in the technique of war have produced a situation which is wholly unprecedented. War has existed ever since there were organized states, that is to say for some six thousand years. This ancient institution is now about to end. There are two ways in which the end may come about: the first is the extinction of the human race; the second is an agreement not to fight. I do not know which of these will be chosen.

Neither the general public nor the majority of powerful statesmen have as yet realized that war with modern weapons cannot serve the purposes of any government in the world. It is of the first importance that this should be realized by those who control policy both in the East and in the West. It is generally conceded by those who are in a position to speak with authority that no complete defense against an H-bomb attack is possible. We must, I think, consider it the most likely hypothesis that if a great war broke out tomorrow each side would be successful in attack and unsuccessful in defense. This means that in the first days of such a war all the great centers of population on each side would be obliterated. Those who survived this first disaster would perish slowly or quickly as a result of the fall-out from radioactive cloud. Destruction of life from this cause would not be confined to the belligerent countries. The winds would gradually spread death throughout the world. This, at least, is what is to be feared. It cannot be said that the worst outcome is certain, but it is sufficiently probable to deter any sane man from incurring the risk.

Apart from the totality of destruction, there is another new element in the situation. In old days if you had a military advantage over your enemy, you might hope to win in time. But now, if each side has enough H-bombs to wipe out the other, there is no longer any advantage in having twice as many as your adversary.

Both in the United States and in Great Britain there has been much talk of civil defense. Russian military journals contain talk of the same kind. All such plans, I am convinced, show either ignorance or hypocrisy in those who advocate them. Deep shelters would enable a portion of the population to survive the first explosion, but sooner or later these people would have to emerge from their shelters into a radioactive world.

Although the H-bomb is the center of public attention at the moment, it is only one of the possibilities of destruction which science has put in the hands of irresponsible politicians. Chemical and bacteriological warfare are studied by all powerful states and may have consequences at least as horrifying as those of the H-bomb. There is no visible end to the methods of inflicting death that may be invented. Even if a portion of the human race were to survive a great war now, it cannot be doubted that the next war, if scientific technique survives, would complete what its predecessor had left unfinished.

There is therefore no escape from the choice that lies before us: Shall we renounce war, or shall we bring our species to an end?

ESCAPE FROM REALITY

If men realized that these are the only alternatives, no one can doubt that they would choose peace. But there are various ways in which people escape the realization of unpleasant facts. I have seen statements by Russians and Chinese that a thermonuclear war would of course destroy the rotten capitalistic civilizations of the West but would not vitally injure the sturdy Communist nations of the East. I have also seen statements by American authorities claiming that the West would be victorious. Both seemed to me, if genuinely believed, to be mere fantasies of wish-fulfillment and, if not genuinely believed, to be part of the silly game of bluff which great nations have been allowing themselves. I hope that this is beginning to be understood. Recently there have been hopeful signs that neither side is willing to push issues to the point of war. And with every month that passes there is a better chance that statesmen both in the East and in the West will become aware of some of the important facts by which their policy ought to be guided.

Another widespread delusion is that perhaps in a great war H-bombs would not be employed. People point to the fact that gas was not employed in the Second World War. They forget that gas had not proved a decisive weapon even in the First World War and that in the meantime gas-masks had been provided which were a complete protection. Any analogy is therefore entirely misleading.

It is thought by many that the first step forward should be an international agreement not to use H-bombs in the event of war, and this is generally coupled with the suggestion that both sides should destroy their existing stock of these weapons. This suggestion has certain merits but also certain drawbacks. Its chief merit is that if the destruction of existing stocks were honestly carried out, the danger of a sudden attack in the style of Pearl Harbor would be lessened. Against this we must set the fact that no system of inspection can now make sure that bombs are not being manufactured. This is a new fact. At the time of the Baruch proposal it was still possible for an inspectorate to gain control of the raw materials, but this is so no longer. Each side would therefore suspect that the other side was manufacturing bombs surreptitiously, and this might make relations worse than if no agreement had been concluded. What is even more important is that, if war did break out, neither side would consider itself bound by the agreement, and after a certain number of months H-bomb warfare would be in full swing. Only by not making war can the danger be avoided. We must therefore turn our thoughts away from war to the methods by which peace can be made secure.

PEACE BY STAGES

The transition from the cold war to a condition of secure peace cannot be made in a day. But it can be made, and it must be made. It will have to be made by stages. The first stage will consist in persuading all powerful governments of the world that their aims, whatever they may be, cannot be achieved by war. In this first stage, scientists—not only nuclear physicists but also physiologists, geneticists, and bacteriologists—have a very important part to play. Their discoveries have created the dangers, and it is their obvious duty to arouse the public and the governments to a sense of the risks they are running. They may, in performing this duty, be compelled to take action of which their governments disapprove, but loyalty to mankind should be for them the paramount consideration. I am convinced that it is within their power to persuade the governments both of the East and of the West to look to negotiation rather than war for a solution of their problems.

The next stage must be to create temporary machinery to negotiate settlements of all the questions at present causing conflict between East and West. It will be necessary to refer such questions to a body of negotiators in which East and West have equal representation and the balance of power is in the hands of the neutrals. I do not venture to suggest what solution should be reached on any of the vexed questions of the present. I think that a body constituted as I have suggested would avoid gross unfairness to either side, and subject to this condition almost any settlement would be preferable to a continuation of the present state of tension. A very important part of any settlement should of course be a drastic reduction of armaments. It is hardly to be supposed that the very delicate negotiations which will be required can be conducted successfully in the atmosphere of strained hostility that has existed during recent years. Each side will have to abandon perpetual abuse of the other and learn to practice that degree of toleration which after centuries of warfare was at last achieved between Christians and Moslems and between Catholics and Protestants. We cannot now wait for the slow operation of reason through the discouragements of long indecisive wars. We must learn in advance a manner of thinking and feeling which in the past has been learned slowly and through bitter experience. I will not pretend that this is easy. But if men can be made to realize the dreadful alternative I do not think it will prove impossible.

THE THIRD STEP

If the immediate problems that now divide East and West were settled in some such way, we could reach the third stage of progress toward secure peace. The international problems of our day are not the last that will ever arise. There will be new problems, perhaps dividing the world quite differently from the way in which it is now divided between Communist and anti-Communist blocs. So long as there is not an established international authority capable of enforcing peace, the risk of war will remain, and with every advance in science the risk will become more terrible. The international anarchy resulting from a multitude of states with unrestricted sovereignty must be brought to an end. The international authority which is to end it will have to be federal and endowed with only such powers as are necessary for preserving the peace of the world. The most important of these powers, and also the most difficult to secure, will be an obvious preponderance of armed forces over those of any national state or alliance of states. The anarchic liberty at present enjoyed by sovereign states is dear to most people and will not be surrendered easily, but it will have to be surrendered if the human species is to survive. The process required is a continuation of that which occurred in the fifteenth and sixteenth centuries. Before that time powerful barons in their castles could defy national governments, and there was the same sort of anarchy within a nation as now exists between nations. Gunpowder and artillery put an end to internal anarchy in France, Spain, and England. The hydrogen bomb has the same part to play in ending international anarchy. The loss of liberty, though it may be distasteful, is precisely of the same kind as that which private individuals suffer by being forbidden to commit murder, for after all it is the right to murder which hitherto sovereign states will be asked to surrender.

LEGITIMATE HOPES

I have been speaking of dangers and how to avoid them, but there is another thing which it is just as important to emphasize, for while fears are at present unavoidable, hopes are equally legitimate. If we take the measures needed to end our fears, we shall thereby create a world capable of such well-being as has never been known and scarcely even imagined. Throughout the long ages since civilization began, the bulk of mankind have lived lives of misery and toil and bondage. All the long burden of misery that has darkened the slow progress of mankind has now become unnecessary. If we can learn to tolerate each other and to live in amity, poverty can be abolished everywhere more completely than it is now abolished in the most fortunate nations. Fear can be so much diminished that a new buoyancy and a new joy will brighten the daily lives of all. The work of science, which while war survives is largely evil, will become wholly beneficent. Nothing stands in the way but the darkness of atavistic evil passions. New technical possibilities of well-being exist, but the wisdom to make use of them has hitherto been lacking. Shall we collectively continue to turn our back upon the things that each one of us individually desires? We can make a world of light, or we can banish life from our planet. One or other we must do, and do soon. A great duty rests upon those who realize these alternatives, for it is they who must persuade mankind to make the better choice.

REVOLUTION IN THE GREEK CITIES

Thucydides

[Party strife, often leading to actual civil war (the Greeks called both stages *stasis*), broke out in most of the Greek states at some time during the war. These local upheavals were connected with the main struggle, because the oligarchs everywhere ("the few") looked to Sparta for aid and comfort and the democrats ("the many" or "the people") to Athens. The first spectacular outbreak took place at Corcyra in 427, beginning with an oligarchic *coup d'état*. The Athenians negotiated a settlement between the parties, but it broke down; the democrats then armed for action and most of the oligarchs fled for safety to the sacred precinct of Hera. At this point a Peloponnesian fleet appeared, under Alcidas, made its base on the mainland opposite Corcyra, and commenced raiding operations. The democrats naturally expected a direct attack on the city.]

CORCYRA IN THE HANDS OF THE DEMOCRATS

Meanwhile the Corcyraean democrats, being very apprehensive of an attack by sea, held a conference with the refugees and the other oligarchs on measures of defense, and managed to persuade some of them to serve in the navy (they had already gotten thirty ships manned, in spite of everything, in anticipation of an attack). But the Peloponnesians only continued their looting until noon and sailed back again. About nightfall they got a beacon signal that sixty Athenian ships had been sighted coming from Leucas; this force, under the command of Eurymedon son of Thucles, had been dispatched by Athens when news came of the revolution and the imminent departure of Alcidas' fleet for Corcyra. At this the Peloponnesians immediately set sail for home as fast as they could go, keeping close to shore, portaged their ships across the Leucadian isthmus so as not to be seen crossing outside Leucas, and got away safely.

When the Corcyraeans realized that the Athenian fleet was approaching and the enemy had departed, they brought the five hundred Messenians into the city—they had previously been camped outside—and ordered the ships that had received complements to sail around to the Hyllaic harbor. While this movement was under way they set out to kill every oligarch who fell into their hands; then they brought ashore and executed those of them who had been induced to serve in the navy; and finally they went into the precinct of Hera, persuaded about fifty of the refugees there to stand trial, and sentenced them all to death. Most of the refugees, however, remained unpersuaded and when they saw what was going on began destroying each other right in the sanctuary: some hanged themselves from the trees, the rest got themselves dispatched any way they could. For seven days after Eurymedon's arrival, while he stood by with his sixty ships, the democrats carried on the slaughter of their alleged enemies. The general charge against them was attempted overthrow of the democracy, but some were actually killed to satisfy private grudges and others to cancel debts owed them by their captors. Death and murder appeared in all their forms, the things that normally happen at such a time all came to pass, and still worse: fathers actually killed sons, men were dragged from the sanctuaries and slain on the spot, and one group was even walled up inside the temple of Dionysus and left to die there.

PARTY STRIFE AND ITS EFFECT ON CIVIC LIFE

To such inhuman lengths did the civil war go; and it seemed even worse because this was one of the first outbreaks. Later, of course, the unrest spread over practically the whole Greek world, as differences arose in the various cities between the leaders of the popular party, who wanted to bring in the Athenians, and the oligarchs, who wanted the Spartans. In peacetime they would have had neither pretext nor desire to call in these powers; but under the pressure of the war, with each side reckoning how a foreign alliance would damage its opponents and at the same time strengthen its own position, it was easy for revolutionaries in both camps to secure intervention from abroad.

Party strife, then, brought a host of troubles upon the Greek cities, troubles which of course have recurred and will always recur as long as human nature remains the same, but which, if anything, are likely to be less severe and take different forms according to the different way in which circumstances change at one period or another. By this I mean that in times of peace and prosperity states and individuals alike have kinder dispositions, because they are not forced into want and privation; whereas war, by stripping life of its ordinary margin of comfort, keeps a hard school and generally shapes men's feelings to match their present circumstances.

Not only were the cities racked by civil war but the latecomers, hearing what had already been done before them, carried the progressive radicalization of thought to even further extremes by refining on previous methods of attack and inventing unheard-of forms of reprisal. They also reversed the customary application of words to actions as they saw fit. Harebrained recklessness now became the courage of a true party member; prudent hesitation, cowardice under a nicer name; self-restraint, an excuse for lack of manly spirit; and intelligence in any respect, supineness in all respects. Impulsiveness and vehemence were taken as the mark of a man, and an attempt at caution in laying a plot was a specious pretext for desertion. An angry man was to be trusted every time; anyone who opposed him was under suspicion. To bring off an intrigue was a sign of intelligence, to suspect one, a sign of genius, while the man who planned things so as not to need all this was a wrecker of the party and browbeaten by the opposition. In general there were two ways to win respect and approval: to anticipate someone else in a crime, or to urge him to one before he thought of it himself.

Again, party affiliation became a closer bond than family ties: party mates could be counted on to do anything, without qualm or scruple, because the purpose of these associations was not true benefit under established law but self-aggrandizement in defiance of it and their mutual confidence got its sanction not from the divine law but rather from their partnership in lawbreaking. A fair offer from the other side was received skeptically, with an eye to what they might do if they got into power, not in a frank, open spirit; and revenge on an opponent was a finer thing than staying out of trouble oneself. If a settlement was somehow reached after all the binding effect of the oaths was purely temporary, since both sides took them only as a last resort, out of desperation, and the first to regain its nerve by catching the enemy off guard when a chance offered enjoyed its revenge more for the breach of faith than it would have from an open attack: not only were such tactics safe, they felt, but a victory won by cheating brought with it a further price, for astuteness. It is easier for most men to get their rascality called cleverness than their stupidity called virtue, and they are ashamed of one epithet but proud of the other.

Ultimately all these troubles were caused by greed and ambition; it was they that bred the spirit of contentiousness and made men so passionate. The leaders of the two parties in the various cities, campaigning under high-sounding slogans like "equal political rights for the masses" and "responsible government by the best men," paid lip service to the common welfare but really treated it as party spoils; they committed frightful crimes in the all-out struggle to get the upper hand of each other, and their reprisals were even worse. Far from keeping the latter within the bounds of justice and the public interest, they fixed their sentences according to what the party wanted at the time; and in first winning power, whether it was achieved by unjust votes of condemnation or simply by force, they did not hesitate to gratify the animosities of the moment. In short, neither side paid any real heed to conscience or honor, but the one that managed to perform an odious act under cover of fine phrases was better spoken of. And meanwhile the citizens who stood between the parties were destroyed by both, either because they would not take part or simply out of jealousy that they were still alive.

So, thanks to the civil wars, every kind of viciousness made its appearance in the Greek world. Simplicity, the chief element in a noble character, was laughed to scorn and disappeared; instead drawn antagonisms and mutual distrust prevailed far and wide. No assurance was strong enough, no oath formidable enough, to reconcile the parties; too clever for that, they could not bring themselves to trust anybody and preferred to stake their survival on calculation, counting security as hopeless. Actually it was the less intelligent who usually won out. Conscious as they were of their opponents' cleverness and their own lack of it, fearful lest these tricky adversaries take them in with fine words and suddenly confront them with a plot before they suspected one, they proceeded ruthlessly to act; while the others, scornfully confident that they could see the blow coming and need not take by action what they could have by thought, relaxed their guard and were destroyed. [III, 80-83]

MANIFESTO OF THE COMMUNIST PARTY

Karl Marx
Friedrich Engels

PROLETARIANS AND COMMUNISTS

In what relation do the Communists stand to the proletarians as a whole?

The Communists do not form a separate party opposed to other working-class parties.

They have no interests separate and apart from those of the proletariat as a whole.

They do not set up any sectarian principles of their own by which to shape and mold the proletarian movement.

The Communists are distinguished from the other working-class parties by this only: 1. In the national struggles of the proletarians of the different countries, they point out and bring to the front the common interests of the entire proletariat, independently of all nationality. 2. In the various stages of development which the struggle of the working class against the bourgeoisie has to pass through, they always and everywhere represent the interests of the movement as a whole.

The Communists, therefore, are on the one hand, practically, the most advanced and resolute section of the working-class parties of every country, that section which pushes forward all others; on the other hand, theoretically, they have over the great mass of the proletariat the advantage of clearly understanding the line of march, the conditions, and the ultimate general results of the proletarian movement.

The immediate aim of the Communists is the same as that of all the other proletarian parties: Formation of the proletariat into a class, overthrow of bourgeois supremacy, conquest of political power by the proletariat.

The theoretical conclusions of the Communists are in no way based on ideas or principles that have been invented, or discovered, by this or that would-be universal reformer.

They merely express, in general terms, actual relations springing from an existing class struggle, from a historical movement going on under our very eyes. The abolition of existing property relations is not at all a distinctive feature of communism.

All property relations in the past have continually been subject to historical change consequent upon the change in historical conditions.

The French Revolution, for example, abolished feudal property in favor of bourgeois property.

The distinguishing feature of communism is not the abolition of property generally, but the abolition of bourgeois property. But modern bourgeois private property is the final and most complete expression of the system of producing and appropriating products that is based on class antagonisms, on the exploitation of the many by the few.

In this sense, the theory of the Communists may be summed up in the single sentence: Abolition of private property.

We Communists have been reproached with the desire of abolishing the right of personally acquiring property as the fruit of a man's own labor, which property is alleged to be the groundwork of all personal freedom, activity and independence.

Hard-won, self-acquired, self-earned property! Do you mean the property of the petty artisan and of the small peasant, a form of property that preceded the bourgeois form? There is no need to abolish that; the development of industry has to a great extent already destroyed it, and is still destroying it daily.

Or do you mean modern bourgeois private property?

But does wage-labor create any property for the laborer? Not a bit. It creates capital, *i.e.*, that kind of property which exploits wage-labor, and which cannot increase except upon condition of begetting a new supply of wage-labor for fresh exploitation. Property, in its present form, is based on the antagonism of capital and wage-labor. Let us examine both sides of this antagonism.

To be a capitalist, is to have not only a purely personal, but a social *status* in production. Capital is a collective product, and only by the united action of many members, nay, in the last resort, only by the united action of all members of society, can it be set in motion.

Capital is therefore not a personal, it is a social, power.

When, therefore, capital is converted into common property, into the property of all members of society, personal property is not thereby transformed into social property. It is only the social character of the property that is changed. It loses its class character.

Let us now take wage-labor.

The average price of wage-labor is the minimum wage, *i.e.*, that quantum of the means of subsistence which is absolutely requisite to keep the laborer in bare existence as a laborer. What, therefore, the wage-laborer appropriates by means of his labor, merely suffices to prolong and reproduce a bare existence. We by no means intend to abolish this personal appropriation of the products of labor, an appropriation that is made for the maintenance and reproduction of human life, and that leaves no surplus wherewith to command the labor of others. All that we want to do away with is the miserable character of this appropriation, under which the laborer lives merely to increase capital, and is allowed to live only insofar as the interest of the ruling class requires it.

In bourgeois society, living labor is but a means to increase accumulated labor. In Communist society, accumulated labor is but a means to widen, to enrich, to promote the existence of the laborer.

In bourgeois society, therefore, the past dominates the present; in Communist society, the present dominates the past. In bourgeois society capital is independent and has individuality, while the living person is dependent and has no individuality.

And the abolition of this state of things is called by the bourgeois, abolition of individuality and freedom! And rightly so. The abolition of bourgeois individuality, bourgeois independence, and bourgeois freedom is undoubtedly aimed at.

By freedom is meant, under the present bourgeois conditions of production, free trade, free selling and buying.

But if selling and buying disappears, free selling and buying disappears also. This talk about free selling and buying, and all the other "brave words" of our bourgeoisie about freedom in general, have a meaning, if any, only in contrast with restricted selling and buying, with the fettered traders of the Middle Ages, but have no meaning when opposed to the Communist abolition of buying and selling, of the bourgeois conditions of production, and of the bourgeoisie itself.

You are horrified at our intending to do away with private property. But in your existing society, private property is already done away with for nine-tenths of the population; its existence for the few is solely due to its nonexistence in the hands of those nine-tenths. You reproach us, therefore, with intending to do away with a form of property, the necessary condition for whose existence is the nonexistence of any property for the immense majority of society.

In a word, you reproach us with intending to do away with your property. Precisely so; that is just what we intend.

From the moment when labor can no longer be converted into capital, money, or rent, into a social power capable of being monopolized, *i.e.*, from the moment when individual property can no longer be transformed into bourgeois property, into capital, from that moment, you say, individuality vanishes.

You must, therefore, confess that by "individual" you mean no other person than the bourgeois, than the middle-class owner of property. This person must, indeed, be swept out of the way, and made impossible.

Communism deprives no man of the power to appropriate the products of society; all that it does is to deprive him of the power to subjugate the labor of others by means of such appropriation.

It has been objected, that upon the abolition of private property all work will cease, and universal laziness will overtake us.

According to this, bourgeois society ought long ago to have gone to the dogs through sheer idleness; for those of its members who work, acquire nothing, and those who acquire anything, do not work. The whole of this objection is but another expression of the tautology: There can no longer be any wage-labor when there is no longer any capital.

All objections urged against the Communist mode of producing and appropriating material products, have, in the same way, been urged against the Communist modes of producing and appropriating intellectual products. Just as, to the bourgeois, the disappearance of class property is the disappearance of production itself, so the disappearance of class culture is to him identical with the disappearance of all culture.

That culture, the loss of which he laments, is, for the enormous majority, a mere training to act as a machine.

But don't wrangle with us so long as you apply, to our intended abolition of bourgeois property, the standard of your bourgeois notions of freedom, culture, law, etc. Your very ideas are but the outgrowth of the conditions of your bourgeois production and bourgeois property, just as your jurisprudence is but the will of your class made into a law for all, a will whose essential character and direction are determined by the economic conditions of existence of your class.

The selfish misconception that induces you to transform into eternal laws of nature and of reason, the social forms springing from your present mode of production and form of property—historical relations that rise and disappear in the progress of production—this misconception you share with every ruling class that has preceded you. What you see clearly in the case of ancient property, what you admit in the case of feudal property, you are of course forbidden to admit in the case of your own bourgeois form of property.

Abolition of the family! Even the most radical flare up at this infamous proposal of the Communists.

On what foundation is the present family, the bourgeois family, based? On capital, on private gain. In its completely developed form this family exists only among the bourgeoisie. But this state of things finds its complement in the practical absence of the family among the proletarians, and in public prostitution.

The bourgeois family will vanish as a matter of course when its complement vanishes, and both will vanish with the vanishing of capital.

Do you charge us with wanting to stop the exploitation of children by their parents? To this crime we plead guilty.

But, you will say, we destroy the most hallowed of relations, when we replace home education by social.

And your education! Is not that also social, and determined by the social conditions under which you educate, by the intervention of society, direct or indirect, by means of schools, etc.? The Communists have not invented the intervention of society in education; they do but seek to alter the character of that intervention, and to rescue education from the influence of the ruling class.

The bourgeois claptrap about the family and education, about the hallowed co-relation of parent and child, becomes all the more disgusting, the more, by the action of modern industry, all family ties among the proletarians are torn asunder, and their children transformed into simple articles of commerce and instruments of labor.

But you Communists would introduce community of women, screams the whole bourgeoisie in chorus.

The bourgeois sees in his wife a mere instrument of production. He hears that the instruments of production are to be exploited in common, and, naturally, can come to no other conclusion than that the lot of being common to all will likewise fall to the women.

He has not even a suspicion that the real point aimed at is to do away with the status of women as mere instruments of production.

For the rest, nothing is more ridiculous than the virtuous indignation of our bourgeois at the community of women which, they pretend, is to be openly and officially established by the Communists. The Communists have no need to introduce community of women; it has existed almost from time immemorial.

Our bourgeois, not content with having the wives and daughters of their proletarians at their disposal, not to speak of common prostitutes, take the greatest pleasure in seducing each other's wives.

Bourgeois marriage is in reality a system of wives in common and thus, at the most, what the Communists might possibly be reproached with is that they desire to introduce, in substitution for a hypocritically concealed, an openly legalized community of women. For the rest, it is self-evident, that the abolition of the present system of production must bring with it the abolition of the community of women springing from that system, *i.e.*, of prostitution both public and private.

The Communists are further reproached with desiring to abolish countries and nationality.

The workingmen have no country. We cannot take from them what they have not got. Since the proletariat must first of all acquire political supremacy, must rise to be the leading class of the nation, must constitute itself *the* nation, it is, so far, itself national, though not in the bourgeois sense of the word.

National differences and antagonisms between peoples are vanishing gradually from day to day, owing to the development of the bourgeoisie, to freedom of commerce, to the world market, to uniformity in the mode of production and in the conditions of life corresponding thereto.

The supremacy of the proletariat will cause them to vanish still faster. United action, of the leading civilized countries at least, is one of the first conditions for the emancipation of the proletariat.

In proportion as the exploitation of one individual by another is put an end to, the exploitation of one nation by another will also be put an end to. In proportion as the antagonism between classes within the nation vanishes, the hostility of one nation to another will come to an end.

The charges against communism made from a religious, a philosophical, and, generally, from an idealogical standpoint, are not deserving of serious examination.

Does it require deep intuition to comprehend that man's ideas, views, and conceptions, in one word, man's consciousness, changes with every change in the conditions of his material existence, in his social relations and in his social life?

What else does the history of ideas prove, than that intellectual production changes its character in proportion as material production is changed? The ruling ideas of each age have ever been the ideas of its ruling class.

When people speak of ideas that revolutionize society, they do but express the fact that within the old society the elements of a new one have been created, and that the dissolution of the old ideas keeps even pace with the dissolution of the old conditions of existence.

When the ancient world was in its last throes, the ancient religions were overcome by Christianity. When Christian ideas succumbed in the eighteenth century to rationalist ideas, feudal society fought its death-battle with the then revolutionary bourgeoisie. The ideas of religious liberty and freedom of conscience, merely gave expression to the sway of free competition within the domain of knowledge.

"Undoubtedly," it will be said, "religion, moral, philosophical and juridical ideas have been modified in the course of historical development. But religion, morality, philosophy, political science, and law, constantly survived this change."

"There are, besides, eternal truths, such as Freedom, Justice, etc., that are common to all states of society. But communism abolishes eternal truths, it abolishes all religion, and all morality, instead of constituting them on a new basis; it therefore acts in contradiction to all past historical experience."

What does this accusation reduce itself to? The history of all past society has consisted in the development of class antagonisms, antagonisms that assumed different forms at different epochs.

But whatever form they may have taken, one fact is common to all past ages, *viz.*, the exploitation of one part of society by the other. No wonder, then, that the social consciousness of past ages, despite all the multiplicity and variety it displays, moves within certain common forms, or general ideas, which cannot completely vanish except with the total disappearance of class antagonisms.

The Communist revolution is the most radical rupture with traditional property relations; no wonder that its development involves the most radical rupture with traditional ideas.

But let us have done with the bourgeois objections to communism.

We have seen above, that the first step in the revolution by the working class, is to raise the proletariat to the position of ruling class, to establish democracy.

The proletariat will use its political supremacy to wrest, by degrees, all capital from the bourgeoisie, to centralize all instruments of production in the hands of the state, *i.e.*, of the proletariat organized as the ruling class; and to increase the total of productive forces as rapidly as possible.

Of course, in the beginning, this cannot be effected except by means of despotic inroads on the rights of property, and on the conditions of bourgeois production; by means of measures, therefore, which appear economically insufficient and untenable, but which, in the course of the movement, outstrip themselves, necessitate further inroads upon the old social order, and are unavoidable as a means of entirely revolutionizing the mode of production.

These measures will of course be different in different countries.

Nevertheless in the most advanced countries, the following will be pretty generally applicable.

1. Abolition of property in land and application of all rents of land to public purposes.
2. A heavy progressive or graduated income tax.
3. Abolition of all right of inheritance.
4. Confiscation of the property of all emigrants and rebels.
5. Centralization of credit in the hands of the state, by means of a national bank with state capital and an exclusive monopoly.
6. Centralization of the means of communication and transport in the hands of the state.
7. Extension of factories and instruments of production owned by the state; the bringing into cultivation of waste lands, and the improvement of the soil generally in accordance with a common plan.
8. Equal obligation of all to work. Establishment of industrial armies, especially for agriculture.

9. Combination of agriculture with manufacturing industries; gradual abolition of the distinction between town and country, by a more equable distribution of the population over the country.
10. Free education for all children in public schools. Abolition of child factory labor in its present form. Combination of education with industrial production, etc.

When, in the course of development, class distinctions have disappeared, and all production has been concentrated in the hands of a vast association of the whole nation, the public power will lose its political character. Political power, properly so called, is merely the organized power of one class for oppressing another. If the proletariat during its contest with the bourgeoisie is compelled, by the force of circumstances, to organize itself as a class; if, by means of a revolution, it makes itself the ruling class, and, as such sweeps away by force the old conditions of production, then it will, along with these conditions, have swept away the conditions for the existence of class antagonisms, and of classes generally, and will thereby have abolished its own supremacy as a class.

In place of the old bourgeois society, with its classes and class antagonisms, we shall have an association, in which the free development of each is the condition for the free development of all. . . .

POSITION OF THE COMMUNISTS IN RELATION TO THE VARIOUS EXISTING OPPOSITION PARTIES

Section II has made clear the relations of the Communists to the existing work-class parties, such as the Chartists in England and the Agrarian Reformers in America.

The Communists fight for the attainment of the immediate aims, for the enforcement of the momentary interests of the working class; but in the movement of the present, they also represent and take care of the future of that movement. In France the Communists ally themselves with the Social-Democrats, against the conservative and radical bourgeoisie, reserving, however, the right to take up a critical position in regard to phrases and illusions traditionally handed down from the great Revolution.

In Switzerland they support the Radicals, without losing sight of the fact that this party consists of antagonistic elements, partly of Democratic Socialists, in the French sense, partly of radical bourgeois.

In Poland they support the party that insists on an agrarian revolution as the prime condition for national emancipation, that party which fomented the insurrection of Cracow in 1846.

In Germany they fight with the bourgeoisie whenever it acts in a revolutionary way, against the absolute monarchy, the feudal squirearchy, and the petty bourgeoisie.

But they never cease, for a single instant, to instill into the working class the clearest possible recognition of the hostile antagonism between bourgeoisie and proletariat, in order that the German workers may straightway use, as so many weapons against the bourgeoisie, the social and political conditions that the bourgeoisie must necessarily introduce along with its supremacy, and in order that, after the fall of the reactionary classes in Germany, the fight against the bourgeoisie itself may immediately begin.

The Communists turn their attention chiefly to Germany, because that country is on the eve of a bourgeois revolution that is bound to be carried out under more advanced conditions of European civilization and with a much more developed proletariat than what existed in England in the 17th and in France in the 18th century, and because the bourgeois revolution in Germany will be but the prelude to an immediately following proletarian revolution.

In short, the Communists everywhere support every revolutionary movement against the existing social and political order of things.

In all these movements they bring to the front, as the leading question in each case, the property question, no matter what its degree of development at the time.

Finally, they labor everywhere for the union and agreement of the democratic parties of all countries.

The Communists disdain to conceal their views and aims. They openly declare that their ends can be attained only by the forcible overthrow of all existing social conditions. Let the ruling classes tremble at a Communist revolution. The proletarians have nothing to lose but their chains. They have a world to win.

Workingmen of all countries, unite!

LOOKING BACKWARD, 2000-1887

Edward Bellamy

Dr. Leete ceased speaking, and I remained silent, endeavoring to form some general conception of the changes in the arrangements of society implied in the tremendous revolution which he had described.

Finally I said, 'The idea of such an extension of the functions of government is, to say the least, rather overwhelming.'

'Extension!' he repeated, 'where is the extension?'

'In my day,' I replied, 'it was considered that the proper functions of government, strictly speaking, were limited to keeping the peace and defending the people against the public enemy, that is, to the military and police powers.'

'And, in heaven's name, who are the public enemies?' exclaimed Dr. Leete. 'Are they France, England, Germany, or hunger, cold, and nakedness? In your day governments were accustomed, on the slightest international misunderstanding, to seize upon the bodies of citizens and deliver them over by hundreds of thousands to death and mutilation, wasting their treasures the while like water; and all this oftenest for no imaginable profit to the victims. We have no wars now, and our governments no war powers, but in order to protect every citizen against hunger, cold, and nakedness, and provide for all his physical and mental needs, the function is assumed of directing his industry for a term of years. No, Mr. West, I am sure on reflection you will perceive that it was in your age, not in ours, that the extension of the functions of governments was extraordinary. Not even for the best ends would men now allow their governments such powers as were then used for the most maleficent.'

'Leaving comparisons aside,' I said, 'the demagoguery and corruption of our public men would have been considered, in my day, insuperable objections to any assumption by government of the charge of the national industries. We should have thought that no arrangement could be worse than to entrust the politicians with control of the wealth-producing machinery of the country. Its material interests were quite too much the football of parties as it was.'

'No doubt you were right,' rejoined Dr. Leete, 'but all that is changed now. We have no parties or politicians, and as for demagoguery and corruption, they are words having only an historical significance.'

'Human nature itself must have changed very much,' I said.

'Not at all,' was Dr. Leete's reply, 'but the conditions of human life have changed, and with them the motives of human action. The organization of society with you was such that officials were under a constant temptation to misuse their power for the private profit of themselves or others. Under such circumstances it seems almost strange that you dared entrust them with any of your affairs. Nowadays, on the contrary, society is so constituted that there is absolutely no way in which an official, however ill-disposed, could possibly make any profit for himself or any one else by a misuse of his power. Let him be as bad an official as you please, he cannot be a corrupt one. There is no motive to be. The social system no longer offers a premium on dishonesty. But these are matters which you can only understand as you come, with time, to know us better.'

'But you have not yet told me how you have settled the labor problem. It is the problem of capital which we have been discussing,' I said. 'After the nation had assumed conduct of the mills, machinery, railroads, farms,

mines, and capital in general of the country, the labor question still remained. In assuming the responsibilities of capital the nation had assumed
the difficulties of the capitalist's position.'

'The moment the nation assumed the responsibilities of capital those difficulties vanished,' replied Dr. Leete. 'The national organization of labor
under one direction was the complete solution of what was, in your day and
under your system, justly regarded as the insoluble labor problem. When the
nation became the sole employer, all the citizens, by virtue of their citizenship, became employees, to be distributed according to the needs of industry.'

'That is,' I suggested, 'you have simply applied the principle of universal
military service, as it was understood in our day, to the labor question.'

'Yes,' said Dr. Leete, 'that was something which followed as a matter of
course as soon as the nation had become the sole capitalist. The people were
already accustomed to the idea that the obligation of every citizen, not
physically disabled, to contribute his military services to the defense of the
nation was equal and absolute. That it was equally the duty of every citizen
to contribute his quota of industrial or intellectual services to the maintenance of the nation was equally evident, though it was not until the nation
became the employer of labor that citizens were able to render this sort of
service with any pretense either of universality or equity. No organization of
labor was possible when the employing power was divided among hundreds
or thousands of individuals and corporations, between which concert of any
kind was neither desired, nor indeed feasible. It constantly happened then
that vast numbers who desired to labor could find no opportunity, and on
the other hand, those who desired to evade a part or all of their debt could
easily do so.'

'Service, now, I suppose, is compulsory upon all,' I suggested.

'It is rather a matter of course than of compulsion,' replied Dr. Leete. 'It
is regarded as so absolutely natural and reasonable that the idea of its being
compulsory has ceased to be thought of. He would be thought to be an
incredibly contemptible person who should need compulsion in such a case.
Nevertheless, to speak of service being compulsory would be a weak way to
state its absolute inevitableness. Our entire social order is so wholly based
upon and deduced from it that if it were conceivable that a man could
escape it, he would be left with no possible way to provide for his existence.
He would have excluded himself from the world, cut himself off from his
kind, in a word, committed suicide.'

'Is the term of service in this industrial army for life?'

'Oh, no; it both begins later and ends earlier than the average working
period in your day. Your workshops were filled with children and old men,
but we hold the period of youth sacred to education, and the period of
maturity, when the physical forces begin to flag, equally sacred to ease and

agreeable relaxation. The period of industrial service is twenty-four years, beginning at the close of the course of education at twenty-one and terminating at forty-five. After forty-five, while discharged from labor, the citizen still remains liable to special calls, in case of emergencies causing a sudden great increase in the demand for labor, till he reaches the age of fifty-five, but such calls are rarely, in fact almost never, made. The fifteenth day of October of every year is what we call Muster Day, because those who have reached the age of twenty-one are then mustered into the industrial service, and at the same time those who, after twenty-four years' service, have reached the age of forty-five, are honorably mustered out. It is the great day of the year with us, whence we reckon all other events, our Olympiad, save that it is annual.'

Implosions

POVERTY
AND THE
WELFARE TRAP

John V. Lindsay

Earlier I discussed the frequent walks I take through the streets of New York, through the diverse neighborhoods of this city. Sometimes my walks encourage me, as I watch a community refurbishing a block on its own or creating a vest-pocket park on a lot formerly cluttered with rubble and garbage. Sometimes they underscore some failures of the city government— streets where abandoned cars rust in unattended blight or where sanitation service has been inadequate. Sometimes I'm also reminded of past failures still complicating our tasks, when we pass potholes caused by poor paving thirty years ago or faulty or nonexistent sewer facilities in Queens or Staten Island, the products of earlier mistakes in planning, design, and construction —or, indeed, products of a total failure to plan or design or construct.

And then there are the walks through those parts of the city that leave me in rage and despair, that raise profound questions, despite all our efforts and achievements, of whether we are locked in a struggle that simply cannot be won.

Those are my moods when I walk through a neighborhood like Brownsville, a community in central Brooklyn that was once a Jewish residential neighborhood and is now almost exclusively black and Puerto Rican. We think that about 100,000 people live in Brownsville, but nobody really knows the exact number. Even with all our governmental records and surveys, more than 20 per cent of Brownsville residents escape official recognition. Many work sporadically, if at all, and have no permanent address nor any connection with public agencies. We simply do not know who they are.

But we do know about those we can locate. Their average annual income is little more than half the city average—an overall average that itself reflects the incomes of many other poor whites, blacks, and Puerto Ricans. Not a single census tract in Brownsville has median income near middle-class levels. Of almost 50,000 housing units in the area, about 4 per cent are standard. The remaining 96 per cent are all substandard, decaying below the barest levels of adequacy.

By some other statistical measures Brownsville ranks very high. More of its infants die at birth than in any other community in New York. More of its young people are delinquents. More of its citizens are the victims of crime. By every index we use to measure the suffering of a community— narcotics addiction, welfare dependency, sickness, and malnutrition— Brownsville leads all other city neighborhoods.

And those bloodless numbers do not exaggerate the reality of life in Brownsville. Its residents grow accustomed to the littered streets, the homes without water, the scrabbling sound of rats' feet. Its abandoned buildings sag in vacant lines, the tin in their windows staring harshly over the sidewalks. Weathered men sit emptily on porch stoops, and four small children sleep tangled, sharing a single lumpy mattress.

A hard-boiled newsman writes: "Animals in the zoo live better than this. Zoos are heated and kept clean."

A local pastor observes bitterly: "If there is a hell, the people of Brownsville will take it in stride."

This is a brief portrait of one New York City neighborhood. It is also a microcosmic portrait of a nation within America, an isolated world taking fragmented shape in Chicago and Detroit, Newark and St. Louis, Atlanta and Washington and Los Angeles.

Of those we can count in that hidden nation, a million are jobless or working at subsistence wages. At least 4 million live in poverty. About a million housing units are substandard.

It is a nation with infant mortality rates 60 per cent higher than the rest of the country's, with maternal mortality rates three and four times as high. Its schools do not teach and its children do not learn. Its residents are victims of crime five to forty times as frequently as other Americans.

It is a nation offering its citizens no evidence that their lives will improve.

And this nation touches us all. It is reaching into smaller cities, only recently discovering the problems of persistent poverty, substandard housing, and inadequate municipal services. It is spreading into suburban neighborhoods like those around New York City, where the incidence of welfare and crime is increasing more rapidly than in the central city. In 1967, for instance, one-fifth of America's black urban poor lived in the suburbs, and more than one-quarter of suburban blacks lived in poverty.

In other words, all of us confront the consequences of pervasive poverty in America. We cannot escape them. One flees the central city in vain, for the problems follow. One-fourth of the civil disorders that rocked America during 1967 occurred in communities with populations under 50,000. Some of the worst startled such apparently tranquil suburbs as Plainfield, New Jersey.

If the "other America" was once invisible, it is so no longer. Surely, after the summers and springs we have endured, after the violent disorders and militant demonstrations, after the quiet evidence of statistics has accumulated, we must recognize that we face the most severe challenge to the promise and progress of this country since the Depression.

And still, many of us—men and women of good will and decent instincts —continue to disregard what we see before us.

I remember walking through Brownsville and East New York in September 1967 with four prominent businessmen, men supposedly grounded in the reality of the world around them.

There was the late Gerald Philippe, president of General Electric. All he said was, "Unbelievable."

There was Gilbert Fitzhugh, chairman of Metropolitan Life. "It makes you heartsick," he said. "You don't know where to start, but you know something has to be done."

There was J. Irwin Miller, chairman of the Cummins Engine Company in Columbus, Indiana. "The number-one problem of the country," this industrialist told me, "is the big city. There is no issue of greater danger to this nation."

These men were hardly militants. Like the members of the President's Commission on Civil Disorders, they were moderate, prudent men who were shocked by the tragedy of what they saw. With them, each of us—and particularly those who hold a political trust from our citizens—must admit that the tragedy exists and determine to end it.

And that will be only the beginning. Once determined to act, many of us will tend simply to assume that present methods of dealing with poverty are appropriate and rational, that sudden shifts in our policies would somehow be imprudent, impractical, or wrong. But we must not succumb to that laziness of spirit or failure of imagination. In addition to admitting the existence of poverty, it is urgent that we understand the futility of our present efforts to confront it. We must realize that our present policies are vacuous and dangerously unresponsive. Their failures are not merely that they fall short of ending the problem. Far worse, they make the problem infinitely worse. They insure further poverty and further hopelessness among the poor. They guarantee continued waste of the monies we spend on the problem and growing bitterness among the decent, hard-working Americans whose tax dollars are spent with no evidence of meaningful progress. When expensive policies fail by the standards both of the helped and those helping, polarization and resentment are inevitable.

In short, we cannot continue our present course. All of us must recognize the existence of a separate nation of the poor in the hearts of our cities. All of us must determine to end that poverty with rational, effective, just, and humane policies. And all of us must seek to fundamentally change the level and direction of our current efforts to aid the poor. . . .

In New York there is an especially urgent need for a new system because we are desperate for workers in almost every kind of service institution. Those on welfare with adequate incentives and support could provide this man- and womanpower. With the right kind of system, we could multiply a hundred times over our present training program, providing, for example, hundreds more technical aides in many services while maintaining their incomes. In many cases we could train registered nurses by starting women without skills at the nurse's-aide level and providing training as they work on their jobs.

With an income-support system tied to job training, we would open the door to self-sufficiency for our poor communities. Higher incomes would allow the poor to live with dignity and at the same time would lower the burden on the public of providing services to those without the means of self-support. That seems a goal worthy of the effort it will require to redesign the federal welfare system. . . .

Pressures are building for the federal government to assume the leadership in this area, and the welfare reforms proposed by President Nixon are an important beginning. But far more must be done. The cities cannot wait for a reluctant Washington to act. Following the lead of forty other states (Massachusetts the most recent), New York State should relieve all the cities and counties of the state of the cost of welfare. The reasons for national takeover also apply for state takeover, and New York now lags behind most of the other states of the nation in this respect.

Meanwhile, in New York City we have been making our own moves to replace the current system. In the past three years we have adopted several key reforms that are beginning to point the way to a better system.

First, New York City has been pioneering in the separation of income maintenance from social service, and others are beginning to follow. We have adopted a system of simple declaration of need for support to replace the lengthy investigations that formerly took most of a caseworker's time.

Second, we also pioneered in providing real incentives for employment through our Employment Incentive Program, which has now been adopted as part of federal policy. Under this program, the AFDC recipient has been allowed to keep the first $85 of employment earnings each month without tax, plus one-third of the remaining salary, in addition to welfare benefits. Through EIP, we have been encouraging recipients to be trained, to obtain and retain jobs, and to increase their earnings through employment, for through EIP, finally, they can indeed raise their income by working. Since this program was instituted, more than 25,000 people in welfare families have participated—and some genuine success has been won in helping families leave welfare for self-sustaining jobs.

Third, the city's Manpower and Career Development Agency is in the process of opening regional manpower centers throughout the city in which the unskilled will receive intensive training for available jobs. We intend to feed as many welfare recipients into the centers' skill-training courses as we can. And we hope that those industries in New York which must bear some of the welfare burden through their taxes will help themselves by hiring from this pool of newly trained talent.

Finally, we have designed a new, radically different program to improve the earnings of low-income workers at the lowest possible cost to the city. The program is called the Training Incentive Payments Program, for which the city received funds early in the summer of 1969 from the federal government for a pilot test. Under TIPP an employer would train low-income workers by any method he felt would best equip them for the jobs he needed to fill. If the worker's salary were raised, the city would reimburse the employer for the costs of the training, based on a proportion of the increase in earnings.

The program would not involve high-risk, expensive institutional training without the guarantee of success, for payments would be made only if and when a worker's wages were actually increased. There would be no new government bureaucracy, for the employer would choose his own methods of training. And there would be no training for jobs that don't exist because the employer would train people only for jobs that already needed to be filled. There is no question that job openings exist—about 40,000 well-paying jobs now go unfilled because employers cannot find workers with adequate skills. Under TIPP employers will be able to train low-skilled workers and, if the training produces the necessary skills, promise them wage advancements without risk; those assurances should induce unskilled workers previously without hope of improvement to stay on the job.

With federal support, we hope that the Training Incentive Payments Program will help fill job openings, increase the salaries of low-income workers, and provide them with incentives to continue improving their skills. If it does succeed, we will be reducing an ever-increasing pool of potential welfare recipients.

All these efforts have been designed to improve the welfare system. Ultimately, however, welfare remains a program dependent on federal and state policy for direction. Neither the cities nor the states can by themselves erase the legacies of national economic conditions. They particularly cannot shoulder the system's financial burdens or the social dissension that its failures induce.

The federal government must, therefore, assume the full financial costs of an improved system. No one else can. Federal failure to provide employment and to impose uniform minimum-welfare standards on the local level have caused the impossible problems with which too many cities have been grappling in recent years.

Such a federally financed system would solve much of the problem, but the final, most fundamental change comes less easily. We must admit our failures and start anew. We must create not just a program; we must even dare to hope for an entirely different set of social attitudes, which will extend opportunity to those we now regard as cripples. A new program can help provide income, protect dignity, encourage work, and end the disgrace of dependency. But only a new attitude can offer to both the poor and our cities an alternative to increasing bitterness, to the mutual suspicions that so complicate our tasks ahead.

THE AMERICAN INDIAN
A Portrait in Limbo

Peter Farb

The Indian can probably survive the bad housing, lack of jobs, dismal health conditions, and poor education—but not the implication that he is irrelevant to American culture. For once the Indians are deprived of the last bit of the culture that has sustained them, they will disappear into the faceless American poor. Yet, the U.S. Bureau of Indian Affairs was founded a century ago with the stated aim to alienate Indian children "from their native culture and language so they could take their place in modern society"—and that has remained an implied aim to this day. A white policy has stripped the Indian of his identity and made him embarrassed about his rich oral literature, his customs and traditions, his native foods and dress. A white education system has turned out imitation whites who succumb to the bleakness of reservation life and the prejudice around them.

"The American Indian today is about to go over the brink—not only of poverty and prejudice, but of moral collapse," says William Byler, executive director of the Association on American Indian Affairs. The Indian has learned that no one wants to listen or to understand when he speaks his thoughts about his own future. He is bewildered by the capricious policies handed down in Washington—first telling him to leave the reservation and get jobs in the cities, next telling him to stay on the reservation and bring industry to it. Some politicians tell him that he is a child who must be protected by the kindly White Father—and other politicians tell him that he is man enough to be cast adrift to sink or swim in the capitalist tide. The result of such confusion is widespread apathy among Indians. They find it difficult to act in concert with other Indians because whites deliberately ripped apart the intricate web of their social and political relationships.

The present plight of the red man is an indication of exactly how far he has fallen from his state of Noble Savage in little more than 450 years. At first, the newly discovered Indians were greatly respected and admired. Columbus brought home six Indians to show Queen Isabella and, dressed in full regalia, they quickly became the curiosities of Spain. Sir Walter Raleigh brought back Indians also and a craze swept Elizabethan England. Shakespeare complained about it in *The Tempest*: "They will not give a doit [a small coin equal to about half a farthing] to relieve a lame beggar, they will lay out ten to see a dead Indian." The French philosopher Michel de Montaigne talked with Indians who had been brought to the French Court and concluded that the Noble Savage had been found, for the Indian "hath no kind of traffic, no knowledge of letters, no intelligence of numbers, no name of magistrate, nor of politics, no use of services, of riches, or of poverty. . . . The very words that import a lie, falsehood, treason, covetousness, envy, detraction, were not heard among them."

The Noble Savage captivated Europe, but the colonists felt differently about living with red men. When Columbus discovered the Arawak Indians, who inhabited the Caribbean Islands, he described them as "a loving people, without covetousness. . . . Their speech is the sweetest and gentlest in the world." But in their haste to exploit the abundance of the Americas, the Spaniards set the loving and gentle Arawak to labor in mines and on plantations. Whole Arawak villages disappeared due to slavery, disease, warfare, and flight to escape the Spaniards. As a result, the native population of Haiti, for example, declined from an estimated 200,000 in 1492 to 29,000 only twenty-two years later.

The Puritans in New England were not immediately presented with an Indian problem, for diseases introduced by trading ships along the Atlantic Coast had badly decimated the red populations. Yet, the Puritans failed miserably in their dealings with even the remnant Indians. They insisted upon a high standard of religious devotion that the Indians were unable or unwilling to give. The Puritans lacked any way to integrate the Indians into their theocracy, for they did not indulge in wholesale baptisms (as they charged the French did), nor were any Puritans specifically assigned to missionary tasks.

In 1637, a party of Puritans surrounded the Pequot Indian village and set fire to it after these Indians had resisted settlement of whites in the Connecticut Valley. About 500 Indians were burned to death or shot while trying to escape; the woods were then combed for any Pequots who had managed to survive, and these were sold into slavery. The whites devoutly offered up thanks to God that they had lost only two men; when the Puritan divine Cotton Mather heard about the raid, he was grateful to the Lord that "on this day we have sent six hundred heathen souls to hell."

The Indian came to be regarded as a stubborn animal that refused to acknowledge the obvious blessings of white civilization. Hugh Henry Brackenridge, a modest literary figure of the young nation, expressed the changed attitude when he wrote in 1782 of ". . . the animals, vulgarly called Indians." Rousseau's Noble Savage was laid to rest officially in 1790 when John Adams stated: "I am not of Rousseau's Opinions. His Notions of the purity of Morals in savage nations and the earliest Ages of civilized Nations are mere Chimeras." Even that man of enlightened homilies, Benjamin Franklin, observed that rum should be regarded as an agent of Providence "to extirpate these savages in order to make room for the cultivators of the earth."

After the War of 1812, the young United States had no further need for Indian allies against the British, and, as a result, the fortunes of the Indians declined rapidly. Pressures increased to get the Indians off the lands the whites had appropriated from them and, in 1830, Congress passed the Removal Act, which gave the President the right to extirpate all Indians who had managed to survive east of the Mississippi River. It was estimated that the whole job might be done economically at no more than $500,000—the cost to be kept low by persuasion, promises, threats, and the bribery of Indian leaders. When U.S. Supreme Court Justice John Marshall ruled in favor of the Cherokee Indians in a case with wide implications for preventing removal, President Andrew Jackson is said to have remarked: "John Marshall has made his decision, now let him enforce it."

During the next ten years, almost all the Indians were cleared from the East. Some, such as the Chickasaw and Choctaw and Cherokee, went resignedly. The Seminole actively resisted and retreated into the Florida swamps, where they stubbornly held off the United States Army. The Seminole Wars lasted from 1835 to 1842 and cost the United States some 1,500 soldiers and an estimated $20,000,000 (about forty times what Jackson had estimated it would cost to remove all Indians). Many of the Iroquois found sanctuary in Canada. The Sac and Fox made a desperate stand in Illinois against overwhelming numbers of whites, but ultimately their survivors were forced to move, as were the Ottawa, Potawatomi, Wyandot, Shawnee, Kickapoo, Winnebago, Delaware, Peoria, Miami, and many others who are remembered now only in the name of some town, lake, county, or state.

Alexis de Tocqueville, who examined the young United States with a perceptive eye and wrote it all down in his *Democracy in America*, was in Memphis on an unusually cold day when he saw a ragged party of Choctaw, part of the docile thousands who had reluctantly agreed to be transported to the new lands in the West. He wrote:

> The Indians had their families with them, and they brought in their train the wounded and the sick, with children newly born and old men upon the verge of death. . . . I saw them embark to pass the mighty river, and never will that solemn spectacle fade from my remembrance. No cry, no sob, was heard among the assembled crowd; all was silent. Their calamities were of ancient date, and they knew them to be irremediable.

De Tocqueville described with restrained outrage how the Indians were sent westward by government agents: ". . . half-convinced and half-compelled, they go to inhabit new deserts, where the importunate whites will not let them remain ten years in peace. In this manner do the Americans obtain, at a very low price, whole provinces, which the richest sovereigns of Europe could not purchase." He reported that a scant 6,273 Indians still survived in the thirteen original states.

The experience of the Indians west of the Mississippi River was only a sad, monotonous duplication of what had happened east of it—warfare, broken treaties, expropriation of land, rebellion, and ultimately defeat. No sooner were the Eastern Indians dropped down on the plains and prairies than the United States discovered the resources in the West, and miners and settlers were on the move. Emigrant trains rumbled westward, and once again the aim of the frontiersman was to get the Indian out of the way.

The "final extermination" was hastened by epidemics that swept the West and sapped the Indians' power to resist. A mere hundred Mandan out of a population of 1,600 survived a smallpox epidemic (they are extinct today); the same epidemic, spreading westward, reduced the total number of Blackfoot Indians by about half. The majority of Kiowa and Comanche Indians were victims of cholera. The Indians undoubtedly would have been crushed by whites in any event, but the spread of diseases made the job easier.

Up to 1868, nearly 400 treaties had been signed by the U.S. Government with various Indian groups, and scarcely a one had remained unbroken. The Indians were promised new lands, then moved off them to some other place. They were shifted about again and again, as many as five or six times. All of which led the Sioux chief Spotted Tail to ask wearily: "Why does not the Great White Father put his red children on wheels, so he can move them as he will?"

In the last decades of the last century the Indians finally realized that these treaties were real estate deals designed to separate them from their lands. Indians and whites skirmished and then fought openly with ferocity and barbarity on both sides. Group by group, the Indians rose in rebellion only to be crushed—the southern Plains tribes in 1874, the Sioux in 1876, the Nez Percé in 1877, the Ute in 1879, and the Apache throughout much of the 1880s, until Geronimo finally surrendered with his remnant band of thirty-six survivors. The massacre of more than 300 Sioux, mostly women and children and old people, at Wounded Knee, South Dakota, in 1890 marked the end of Indian resistance to white authority.

Humanitarians who attempted to ease the defeat of the Indians felt that the remnant populations should be given the dignity of private property. As a result, Senator Henry L. Dawes of Massachusetts sponsored the Allotment Act of 1887 to salvage some land for the Indians who otherwise might lose everything to voracious whites. When President Grover Cleveland signed the act, he stated that the "hunger and thirst of the white man for the Indian's land is almost equal to his hunger and thirst after righteousness."

The act provided that after every Indian had been allotted land, the remainder would be put up for sale to the public. But the loopholes with which the act was punctured made it an efficient instrument for separating the Indians from this land. The plunder was carried on with remarkable order. The first lands to go to whites were the richest—bottomlands in river valleys or fertile grasslands. Next went the slightly less desirable lands, such as those that had to be cleared before they could produce a crop. Then the marginal lands were taken, and so on, until the Indian had left to him only desert that no white considered worth the trouble to take. Between the passage of the Allotment Act in 1887 and a New Deal investigation in 1934, the Indians had been reduced to only 56,000,000 acres out of the meager 138,000,000 acres that had been allotted them—and every single acre of the 56,000,000 was adjudged by soil conservationists to be eroded. At the same time that the Indians were being systematically relieved of their lands, their birth rate rose higher than the mortality rate, and so there were more and more Indians on less and less land. The Indians did what they had always done: They shared the little they had and went hungry together.

The victory over the Noble Savage—reduced in numbers, deprived of land, broken in spirit, isolated on wasteland reservations—was complete except for one final indignity. That was to Americanize the Indian, to eliminate his last faint recollection of his ancient traditions—in short, to exterminate the cultures along with the Indians. There was not much culture left to eradicate, but at last zealous whites found something. Orders went out from Washington that all male Indians must cut their hair short, even though many Indians believed that long hair had supernatural significance. The Indians refused, and the battle was joined. Army reinforcements were sent to the reservations to carry out the order, and in some cases Indians had to be shackled before they submitted.

Most of the attention of the Americanizers, though, was concentrated on the Indian children, who were snatched from their families and shipped off to boarding schools far from their homes. The children usually were kept at school for eight years, during which time they were not permitted to see their parents, relatives, or friends. Anything Indian—dress, language, religious practices, even outlook on life—was uncompromisingly prohibited. Ostensibly educated, articulate in the English language, wearing store-bought clothes, and with their hair short and their emotionalism muted, the boarding-school graduates were sent out either to make their way in a white world that did not want them, or to return as strangers to their reservation. The Indian had simply failed to melt into the great American melting pot.

He had been remade in the white man's image and then cast adrift or else safely bottled up on reservations. Yet it is apparent to any objective observer that the Indian problem still nags at the American conscience. It seems that whites, both land-hungry settlers and humanitarians, have tried every possible variation in the treatment of the Indian. What, then, is the solution?

Many people concerned about the American Indian are coming to believe that we should simply stop offering the Indian pat solutions. Everything has been tried. The Indians have been herded from reservation to reservation, switched from hunting to agriculture or from agriculture to hunting, moved to cities to work in factories or told instead to make room for factories on their reservations. Indians exist today as the most manipulated people on earth—and yet our Indian policy has produced only failure after failure.

THE MAN TO SEND RAIN CLOUDS

Leslie Chapman Silko

I

They found him under a big cottonwood tree. His Levi jacket and pants were faded light blue so that he had been easy to find. The big cottonwood tree stood apart from a small grove of winter-bare cottonwoods which grew in the wide sandy arroyo. He had been dead for a day or more and the sheep had wandered and scattered up and down the arroyo. Leon and his brother-in-law, Ken, gathered the sheep and left them in the pen at the sheep camp before they returned to the cottonwood tree. Leon waited under the tree while Ken drove the truck through the deep sand to the edge of the arroyo.

He squinted up at the sun and unzipped his jacket—it sure was hot for this time of year. But high and northwest the blue mountains were still deep in snow. Ken came sliding down the low crumbling bank about 50 yards down and he was bringing the red blanket.

Before they wrapped the old man, Leon took a piece of string out of his pocket and tied a small gray feather in the old man's long white hair. Ken gave him the paint. Across the brown wrinkled forehead he drew a streak of white and along the high cheek bones he drew a strip of blue paint. He paused and watched Ken throw pinches of corn meal and pollen into the wind that fluttered the small gray feather. Then Leon painted with yellow under the old man's broad nose, and finally, when he had painted green across the chin, he smiled.

"Send us rain clouds, Grandfather." They laid the bundle in the back of the pick-up and covered it with a heavy tarp before they started back to the pueblo.

They turned off the highway onto the sandy pueblo road. Not long after they passed the store and post office they saw Father Paul's car coming towards them. When he recognized their faces he slowed his car and waved for them to stop. The young priest rolled down the car window. "Did you find old Teofilo?" he asked loudly. Leon stopped the truck.

"Good morning, Father. We were just out to the sheep camp. Everything is o.k. now."

"Thank God for that. Teofilo is a very old man. You really shouldn't allow him to stay at the sheep camp alone."

"No, he won't do that any more now."

"Well, I'm glad you understand. I hope I'll be seeing you at Mass this week—we missed you last Sunday. See if you can get old Teofilo to come with you." The priest smiled and waved at them as they drove away.

II

Louise and Teresa were waiting. The table was set for lunch and the coffee was boiling on the black iron stove. Leon looked at Louise and then at Teresa.

"We found him under a cottonwood tree in the big arroyo near sheep camp. I guess he sat down to rest in the shade and never got up again." Leon walked towards the old man's bed. The red plaid shawl had been shaken and spread carefully over the bed and a new brown flannel shirt and pair of stiff new Levi's were arranged neatly beside the pillow. Louise held the screen door open while Leon and Ken carried in the red blanket. He looked small and shriveled, and after they dressed him in the new shirt and pants he seemed more shrunken.

It was noontime now because the church bells rang the Angelus. They ate the beans with hot bread and nobody said anything until after Teresa poured the coffee. Ken stood up and put on his jacket.

"I'll see about the grave-diggers. Only the top layer of soil is frozen. I think it can be ready before dark." Leon nodded his head and finished his coffee. After Ken had been gone for a while the neighbors and clanspeople came quietly to embrace Teofilo's family and to leave food on the table because the grave-diggers would come to eat when they were finished.

III

The sky in the west was full of pale yellow light. Louise stood outside with her hands in the pockets of Leon's green army jacket that was too big for her. The funeral was over and the old men had taken their candles and medicine bags and were gone. She waited until the body was laid into the pick-up before she said anything to Leon. She touched his arm and he noticed that her hands were still dusty from the corn meal that she had sprinkled around the old man. When she spoke Leon could not hear her.

"What did you say? I didn't hear you."

"I said that I had been thinking about something."

"About what?"

"About the priest sprinkling holy water for Grandpa. So he won't be thirsty." Leon stared at the new mocassins that Teofilo had made for the ceremonial dances in the summer. They were nearly hidden by the red blanket. It was getting colder and the wind pushed gray dust down the narrow pueblo road. The sun was approaching the long mesa where it disappeared during the winter. Louise stood there shivering and watching his face. Then he zipped up his jacket and opened the truck door. "I'll see if he's there."

IV

Ken stopped the pick-up at the church and Leon got out; and then Ken drove down the hill to the graveyard where people were waiting. Leon knocked at the old carved door with its symbols of the Lamb. While he waited he looked up at the twin bells from the King of Spain with the last sunlight pouring around them in their tower. The priest opened the door and smiled when he saw who it was.

"Come in! What brings you here this evening?" The priest walked towards the kitchen and Leon stood with his cap in his hand, playing with the earflaps and examining the living room—the brown sofa, the green arm chair, and the brass lamp that hung down from the ceiling by links of chain. The priest dragged a chair out of the kitchen and offered it to Leon.

"No thank you, Father. I only came to ask you if you would bring your holy water to the graveyard." The priest turned away from Leon and looked out the window at the patio full of shadows and the dining room windows of the nuns' cloister across the patio. The curtains were heavy and the light from within faintly penetrated; it was impossible to see the nuns inside eating supper.

"Why didn't you tell me he was dead? I could have brought the Last Rites anyway."

Leon smiled. "It wasn't necessary, Father." The priest stared down at his scuffed brown loafers and the worn hem of his cassock.

"For a Christian burial it was necessary." His voice was distant and Leon thought that his blue eyes looked tired.

"It's o.k. Father, we just want him to have plenty of water." The priest sank down into the green chair and picked up a glossy missionary magazine. He turned the colored pages full of lepers and pagans without looking at them.

"You know I can't do that, Leon. There should have been the Last Rites and a funeral mass at the very least." Leon put on his green cap and pulled the flaps down over his ears.

"It's getting late, Father. I've got to go." When Leon opened the door Father Paul stood up and said, "Wait." He left the room and came back wearing a long brown overcoat. He followed Leon out the door and across the dim church yard to the adobe steps in front of the church. They both stooped to fit through the low adobe entrance. And when they started down the hill to the graveyard only half of the sun was visible above the mesa.

The priest approached the grave slowly, wondering how they had managed to dig into the frozen ground and then he remembered that this was New Mexico, and saw the pile of cold loose sand beside the hole. The people stood close to each other with little clouds of steam puffing from their faces. The priest looked at them and saw a pile of jackets, gloves and scarves in the yellow dry tumbleweeds that grew in the graveyard. He looked at the red blanket not sure that Teofilo was so small, wondering if it wasn't some perverse Indian trick—something they did in March to insure a good harvest —wondering if maybe old Teofilo was actually at sheep camp corraling the sheep for the night. But there he was, facing into a cold dry wind and squinting at the last sun light, ready to bury a red wool blanket while the faces of his parishioners were in shadow with the last warmth of the sun on their backs.

His fingers were stiff and it took him a long time to twist the lid off the holy water. Drops of water fell on the red blanket and soaked into dark icy spots. He sprinkled the grave and the water disappeared almost before it touched the dim cold sand; it reminded him of something—he tried to remember what it was because he thought if he could remember he might understand this. He sprinkled more water, he shook the container until it was empty and the water fell through the light from sundown like August rain that fell while the sun was still shining almost evaporating before it touched the wilted squash flowers.

The wind pulled at the priest's brown Franciscan robe and swirled away the corn meal and pollen that had been sprinkled on the blanket. They lowered the bundle into the ground and they didn't bother to untie the stiff pieces of new rope that were tied around the ends of the blanket. The sun was gone and over on the highway the east-bound lane was full of head-lights. The priest walked away slowly and Leon watched him climb the hill, and when he had disappeared within the tall thick walls, Leon turned to look up at the high blue mountains in the deep snow that reflected a faint red light from the west. He felt good because it was finished, and he was happy about the sprinkling of the holy water; now the old man could send them big thunder clouds for sure.

LETTER TO HIS NEPHEW

James Baldwin

Dear James: I have begun this letter five times and torn it up five times. I keep seeing your face, which is also the face of your father and my brother. Like him, you are tough, dark, vulnerable, moody—with a very definite tendency to sound truculent because you want no one to think you are soft. You may be like your grandfather in this, I don't know, but certainly both you and your father resemble him very much physically. Well, he is dead, he never saw you, and he had a terrible life; he was defeated long before he died because, at the bottom of his heart, he really believed what white people said about him. This is one of the reasons that he became so holy. I am sure that your father has told you something about all that. Neither you nor your father exhibit any tendency towards holiness: you really *are* of another era, part of what happened when the Negro left the land and came into what the late E. Franklin Frazier called "the cities of destruction." You can only be destroyed by believing that you really are what the white world calls a *nigger*. I tell you this because I love you, and please don't you ever forget it.

I have known both of you all your lives, have carried your Daddy in my arms and on my shoulders, kissed and spanked him and watched him learn to walk. I don't know if you've known anybody from that far back; if you've loved anybody that long, first as an infant, then as a child, then as a man, you gain a strange perspective on time and human pain and effort. Other people cannot see what I see whenever I look into your father's face, for behind your father's face as it is today are all those other faces which were his. Let him laugh and I see a cellar your father does not remember and a house he does not remember and I hear in his present laughter his laughter as a child. Let him curse and I remember him falling down the cellar steps, and howling, and I remember, with pain, his tears, which my hand or your grandmother's so easily wiped away. But no one's hand can wipe away those tears he sheds invisibly today, which one hears in his laughter and in his speech and in his songs. I know what the world has done to my brother and how narrowly he has survived it. And I know, which is much worse, and this is the crime of which I accuse my country and my countrymen, and for which neither I nor time nor history will ever forgive them, that they have destroyed and are destroying hundreds of thousands of lives and do not know it and do not want to know it. One can be, indeed one must strive to become, tough and philosophical concerning destruction and death, for this is what most of mankind has been best at since we have heard of man. (But remember: *most* of mankind is not *all* of mankind.) But it is not permissible that the authors of devastation should also be innocent. It is the innocence which constitutes the crime.

Now, my dear namesake, these innocent and well-meaning people, your countrymen, have caused you to be born under conditions not very far removed from those described for us by Charles Dickens in the London of more than a hundred years ago. (I hear the chorus of the innocents screaming, "No! This is not true! How *bitter* you are!"—but I am writing this letter to *you*, to try to tell you something about how to handle *them*, for most of them do not yet really know that you exist. I *know* the conditions under which you were born, for I was there. Your countrymen were *not* there, and haven't made it yet. Your grandmother was also there, and no one has ever accused her of being bitter. I suggest that the innocents check with her. She isn't hard to find. Your countrymen don't know that *she* exists, either, though she has been working for them all their lives.)

Well, you were born, here you came, something like fourteen years ago; and though your father and mother and grandmother, looking about the streets through which they were carrying you, staring at the walls into which they brought you, had every reason to be heavyhearted, yet they were not. For here you were, Big James, named for me—you were a big baby, I was not—here you were: to be loved. To be loved, baby, hard, at once, and forever, to strengthen you against the loveless world. Remember that: I know how black it looks today, for you. It looked bad that day, too, yes, we were trembling. We have not stopped trembling yet, but if we had not loved each other none of us would have survived. And now you must survive because we love you, and for the sake of your children and your children's children.

This innocent country set you down in a ghetto in which, in fact, it intended that you should perish. Let me spell out precisely what I mean by that, for the heart of the matter is here, and the root of my dispute with my country. You were born where you were born and faced the future that you faced because you were black and *for no other reason*. The limits of your ambition were, thus, expected to be set forever. You were born into a society which spelled out with brutal clarity, and in as many ways as possible, that you were a worthless human being. You were not expected to aspire to excellence: you were expected to make peace with mediocrity. Wherever you have turned, James, in your short time on this earth, you have been told where you could go and what you could do (and *how* you could do it) and where you could live and whom you could marry. I know your countrymen do not agree with me about this, and I hear them saying, "You exaggerate." They do not know Harlem, and I do. So do you. Take no one's word for anything, including mine—but trust your experience. Know whence you came. If you know whence you came, there is really no limit to where you can go. The details and symbols of your life have been deliberately constructed to make you believe what white people say about you. Please try to remember that what they believe, as well as what they do and cause you to endure, does not testify to your inferiority but to their inhumanity and fear. Please try to be clear, dear James, through the storm which rages about your youthful head today, about the reality which lies behind the words *acceptance* and *integration*. There is no reason for you to try to become like white people and there is no basis whatever for their impertinent assumption that *they* must accept *you*. The really terrible thing, old buddy, is that *you* must accept *them*. And I mean that very seriously. You must accept them and accept them with love. For these innocent people have no other hope. They are, in effect, still trapped in a history which they do not understand; and until they understand it, they cannot be released from it. They have had to believe for many years, and for innumerable reasons, that black men are inferior to white men. Many of them, indeed, know better, but, as you will discover, people find it very difficult to act on what they know. To act is to be committed, and to be committed is to be in danger. In this case, the danger, in the minds of most white Americans, is the loss of their identity. Try to imagine how you would feel if you woke up one morning to find the sun shining and all the stars aflame. You would be frightened because it is out of the order of nature. Any upheaval in the universe is terrifying because it so profoundly attacks one's sense of one's own reality. Well, the black man has functioned in the white man's world as a fixed star, as an immovable pillar: and as he moves out of his place, heaven and earth are shaken to their foundations. You, don't be afraid. I said that it was intended that you should perish in the ghetto, perish by never being allowed to go behind the white man's definitions, by never being allowed to spell your proper name. You have, and many of us have, defeated this intention; and, by a terrible law, a terrible paradox, those innocents who believed that your imprisonment made them safe are losing their grasp of reality. But these men are your brothers—your lost, younger brothers. And if the word *integration* means anything, this is what it means: that we, with love, shall force our brothers to see themselves as they are, to cease fleeing from reality and begin to change it. For this is your home, my friend, do not be driven from it; great men have done great things here, and will again, and we can make America what America must become. It will be hard, James, but you come from sturdy, peasant stock, men who picked cotton and dammed rivers and built railroads, and, in the teeth of the most terrifying odds, achieved an unassailable and monumental dignity. You come from a long line of great poets, some of the greatest poets since Homer. One of them said, *The very time I thought I was lost, My dungeon shook and my chains fell off.*

You know, and I know, that the country is celebrating one hundred years of freedom one hundred years too soon. We cannot be free until they are free. God bless you, James, and Godspeed.

Your uncle,
James

WHAT WE WANT

Stokeley Carmichael

Ultimately, the economic foundations of this country must be shaken if black people are to control their lives. The colonies of the United States—and this includes the black ghettoes within its borders, north and south—must be liberated. For a century, this nation has been like an octopus of exploitation, its tentacles stretching from Mississippi and Harlem to South America, the Middle East, southern Africa, and Vietnam; the form of exploitation varies from area to area but the essential result has been the same—a powerful few have been maintained and enriched at the expense of the poor and voiceless colored masses. This pattern must be broken. As its grip loosens here and there around the world, the hopes of black Americans become more realistic. For racism to die, a totally different America must be born.

This is what the white society does not wish to face; this is why that society prefers to talk about integration. But integration speaks not at all to the problem of poverty, only to the problem of blackness. Integration today means the man who "makes it," leaving his black brothers behind in the ghetto as fast as his new sports car will take him. It has no relevance to the Harlem wino or to the cottonpicker making three dollars a day. As a lady I know in Alabama once said, "the food that Ralph Bunche eats doesn't fill my stomach."

Integration, moreover, speaks to the problem of blackness in a despicable way. As a goal, it has been based on complete acceptance of the fact that *in order to have* a decent house or education, blacks must move into a white neighborhood or send their children to a white school. This reinforces, among both black and white, the idea that "white" is automatically better and "black" is by definition inferior. This is why integration is a subterfuge for the maintenance of white supremacy. It allows the nation to focus on a handful of Southern children who get into white schools, at great price, and to ignore the 94 per cent who are left behind in unimproved all-black schools. Such situations will not change until black people have power—to control their own school boards, in this case. Then Negroes become equal in a way that means something, and integration ceases to be a one-way street. Then integration doesn't mean draining skills and energies from the ghetto into white neighborhoods; then it can mean white people moving from Beverly Hills into Watts, white people joining the Lowndes County Freedom Organization. Then integration becomes relevant.

Last April, before the furor over black power, Christopher Jencks wrote in a *New Republic* article on white Mississippi's manipulation of the anti-poverty program:

> The war on poverty has been predicated on the notion that there is such a thing as *a community* which can be defined geographically and mobilized for a collective effort to help the poor. This theory has no relationship to reality in the Deep South. In every Mississippi county there are *two* communities. Despite all the pious platitudes of the moderates on both sides, these two communities habitually see their interests in terms of conflict rather than cooperation. Only when the Negro community can muster enough political, economic and professional strength to compete on somewhat equal terms, will Negroes believe in the possibility of true cooperation and whites accept its necessity. En route to integration, the Negro community needs to develop greater independence—a chance to run its own affairs and not cave in whenever "the man" barks . . . Or so it seems to me, and to most of the knowledgeable people with whom I talked in Mississippi. To OEO, this judgment may sound like black nationalism . . .

Mr. Jencks, a white reporter, perceived the reason why America's anti-poverty program has been a sick farce in both North and South. In the South, it is clearly racism which prevents the poor from running their own programs; in the North, it more often seems to be politicking and bureaucracy. But the results are not so different: In the North, non-whites make up 42 per cent of all families in metropolitan "poverty areas" and only 6 per cent of families in areas classified as not poor. SNCC has been working with local residents in Arkansas, Alabama, and Mississippi to achieve control by the poor of the program and its funds; it has also been working with groups in the North, and the struggle is no less difficult. Behind it all is a federal government which cares far more about winning the war on the Vietnamese than the war on poverty; which has put the poverty program in the hands of self-serving politicians and bureaucrats rather than the poor themselves; which is unwilling to curb the misuse of white power but quick to condemn black power.

To most whites, black power seems to mean that the Mau Mau are coming to the suburbs at night. The Mau Mau are coming, and whites must stop them. Articles appear about plots to "get Whitey," creating an atmosphere in which "law and order must be maintained." Once again, responsibility is shifted from the oppressor to the oppressed. Other whites chide, "Don't forget—you're only 10 per cent of the population; if you get too smart, we'll wipe you out." If they are liberals, they complain, "what about me?—don't you want my help any more?" These are people supposedly concerned about black Americans, but today they think first of themselves, of their feelings of rejection. Or they admonish, "you can't get anywhere without coalitions," without considering the problems of coalition with whom?; on what terms? (coalescing from weakness can mean absorption, betrayal); when? Or they accuse us of "polarizing the races" by our calls for black unity, when the true responsibility for polarization lies with whites who will not accept their responsibility as the majority power for making the democratic process work.

White America will not face the problem of color, the reality of it. The well-intended say: "We're all human, everybody is really decent, we must forget color." But color cannot be "forgotten" until its weight is recognized and dealt with. White America will not acknowledge that the ways in which this country sees itself are contradicted by being black—and always have been. Whereas most of the people who settled this country came here for freedom or for economic opportunity, blacks were brought here to be slaves. When the Lowndes County Freedom Organization chose the black panther as its symbol, it was christened by the press "the Black Panther Party"—but the Alabama Democratic Party, whose symbol is a rooster, has never been called the White Cock Party. No one ever talked about "white power" because power in this country *is* white. All this adds up to more than merely identifying a group phenomenon by some catchy name or adjective. The furor over that black panther reveals the problems that white America has with color and sex; the furor over "black power" reveals how deep racism runs and the great fear which is attached to it.

Whites will not see that I, for example, as a person oppressed because of my blackness, have common cause with other blacks who are oppressed because of blackness. This is not to say that there are no white people who see things as I do, but that it is black people I must speak to first. It must be the oppressed to whom SNCC addresses itself primarily, not to friends from the oppressing group.

From birth, black people are told a set of lies about themselves. We are told that we are lazy—yet I drive through the Delta area of Mississippi and watch black people picking cotton in the hot sun for fourteen hours. We are told, "If you work hard, you'll succeed"—but if that were true, black people would own this country. We are oppressed because we are black—not because we are ignorant, not because we are lazy, not because we're stupid (and got good rhythm), but because we're black.

I remember that when I was a boy, I used to go to see Tarzan movies on Saturday. White Tarzan used to beat up the black natives. I would sit there yelling, "Kill the beasts, kill the savages, kill 'em!" I was saying: Kill *me*. It was as if a Jewish boy watched Nazis taking Jews off to concentration camps and cheered them on. Today, I want the chief to beat hell out of Tarzan and send him back to Europe. But it takes time to become free of the lies and their shaming effect on black minds. It takes time to reject the most important lie: that black people inherently can't do the same things white people can do, unless white people help them.

The need for psychological equality is the reason why SNCC today believes that blacks must organize in the black community. Only black people can convey the revolutionary idea that black people are able to do things themselves. Only they can help create in the community an aroused and continuing black consciousness that will provide the basis for political strength. In the past, white allies have furthered white supremacy without the whites involved realizing it—or wanting it, I think. Black people must do things for themselves; they must get poverty money they will control and spend themselves, they must conduct tutorial programs themselves so that black children can identify with black people. This is one reason Africa has such importance: The reality of black men ruling their own nations gives blacks elsewhere a sense of possibility, of power, which they do not now have.

This does not mean we don't welcome help, or friends. But we want the right to decide whether anyone is, in fact, our friend. In the past, black Americans have been almost the only people whom everybody and his momma could jump up and call their friends. We have been tokens, symbols, objects—as I was in high school to many young whites, who liked having "a Negro friend." We want to decide who is our friend, and we will not accept someone who comes to us and says: "If you do X, Y, and Z, then I'll help you." We will not be told whom we should choose as allies. We will not be isolated from any group or nation except by our own choice. We cannot have the oppressors telling the oppressed how to rid themselves of the oppressor.

I have said that most liberal whites react to "black power" with the question, What about me?, rather than saying: Tell me what you want me to do and I'll see if I can do it. There are answers to the right question. One of the most disturbing things about almost all white supporters of the movement has been that they are afraid to go into their own communities—which is where the racism exists—and work to get rid of it. They want to run from Berkeley to tell us what to do in Mississippi; let them look instead at Berkeley. They admonish blacks to be nonviolent; let them preach nonviolence in the white community. They come to teach me Negro history; let them go to the suburbs and open up freedom schools for whites. Let them work to stop America's racist foreign policy; let them press this government to cease supporting the economy of South Africa.

There is a vital job to be done among poor whites. We hope to see, eventually, a coalition between poor blacks and poor whites. That is the only coalition which seems acceptable to us, and we see such a coalition as the major internal instrument of change in American society. SNCC has tried several times to organize poor whites; we are trying again now, with an initial training program in Tennessee. It is purely academic today to talk about bringing poor blacks and whites together, but the job of creating a poor-white power bloc must be attempted. The main responsibility for it falls upon whites. Black and white can work together in the white community where possible; it is not possible, however, to go into a poor Southern town and talk about integration. Poor whites everywhere are becoming more hostile—not less—partly because they see the nation's attention focused on black poverty and nobody coming to them. Too many young middle-class Americans, like some sort of Pepsi generation, have wanted to come alive through the black community; they've wanted to be where the action is— and the action has been in the black community.

Black people do not want to "take over" this country. They don't want to "get whitey"; they just want to get him off their backs, as the saying goes. It was for example the exploitation by Jewish landlords and merchants which first created black resentment toward Jews—not Judaism. The white man is irrelevant to blacks, except as an oppressive force. Blacks want to be in his place, yes, but not in order to terrorize and lynch and starve him. They want to be in his place because that is where a decent life can be had.

But our vision is not merely of a society in which all black men have enough to buy the good things of life. When we urge that black money go into black pockets, we mean the communal pocket. We want to see money go back into the community and used to benefit it. We want to see the cooperative concept applied in business and banking. We want to see black ghetto residents demand that an exploiting landlord or storekeeper sell them, at minimal cost, a building or a shop that they will own and improve co-operatively; they can back their demand with a rent strike, or a boycott, and a community so unified behind them that no one else will move into the building or buy at the store. The society we seek to build among black people, then, is not a capitalist one. It is a society in which the spirit of community and humanistic love prevail. The word love is suspect; black expectations of what it might produce have been betrayed too often. But those were expectations of a response from the white community, which failed us. The love we seek to encourage is within the black community, the only American community where men call each other "brother" when they meet. We can build a community of love only where we have the ability and power to do so: among blacks.

As for white America, perhaps it can stop crying out against "black supremacy," "black nationalism," "racism in reverse," and begin facing reality. The reality is that this nation, from top to bottom, is racist; that racism is not primarily a problem of "human relations" but of an exploita-tion maintained—either actively or through silence—by the society as a whole. Camus and Sartre have asked, can a man condemn himself? Can whites, particularly liberal whites, condemn themselves? Can they stop blam-ing us, and blame their own system? Are they capable of the shame which might become a revolutionary emotion?

We have found that they usually cannot condemn themselves, and so we have done it. But the rebuilding of this society, if at all possible, is basically the responsibility of whites—not blacks. We won't fight to save the present society, in Vietnam or anywhere else. We are just going to work, in the way *we* see fit, and on goals *we* define, not for civil rights but for all our human rights.

HUNG
DOWN

Piri Thomas

And I walked out of that laundry like if death was there. I walked down toward 104th Street and Lexington Avenue and I saw Waneko.

"Hey Waneko, hey man, wait up."

Waneko waited and I crossed the street. He saw me like I was and said, "What's happening?"

"I'm sick, man."

"Yeah, you've been looking like real shit warmed over for a couple of days."

"Yeah, that *tecata's* got to me. Jesus Christ, man, I'm hooked and I've been trying to get off but I can't, like if I'm in love with this bitch."

I sniffed and thought how I wasn't gonna get hooked. How I was gonna control it. Why the hell did I have to start playing with stuff? Who wants to be a man at that rate? Hell! All for the feeling of belonging, for the price of being called "one of us." Isn't there a better way to make the scene and be accepted on the street without having to go through hell?

I wiped my nose. The water kept oozing out and my eyes were blurred. My guts were getting wilder all the damn time.

"Man, Waneko, I gotta quit. I just gotta quit."

"Look, man, don't be a jerk and try to kick the habit all at once."

My mind went back and his voice blended into the background of my thoughts. I thought of all the hustling I had gone through for the sake of getting drugs, selling pot, pushing stuff, beating my girl for money. Man, I was sick all over, inside and outside.

"Like all you gotta do is get off the habit a little at the time. Get a piece of stuff and break it up. Each time take less and less and bang, you've kicked, cause trying to kick it cold-turkey is a bitch. Do it this way and—"

"You sure?"

"Yeah, I'm sure."

"I'm gonna try it, but I gotta get some bread so I can cop some stuff. You got anything?"

"Yeah."

"How about it?" I was trying to act cool. I wanted the stuff bad, but no matter how hard I fought it, everything in me was crying out for that shit's personal attention.

Waneko's hand went into his pocket and I dug the stuff in his hand. I felt my throat blend in and out with the yen. The taste that takes place even before you get the junk into your system. All of a sudden, I felt like nothing mattered, like if all the promises in the world didn't mean a damn, like all that mattered was that the stuff is there, the needle is there, the yen is there, and your veins have always been there.

I went up to the roof of number 109, running up those stairs like God was on that roof, like everything would be lost if I didn't get up there on time. I felt the night air and my eyes made out the shadows of others like me. Cats I knew and yet never really seen before. Their forms made word noises.

"Got any shit, Piri?"

"Yeah, but I need it all, man. I've been fighting a fever. I'd really like to split with you all, but I'm really strung out like I'm swingin' between hell and the street."

"Yeah, baby, we understand, it's okay."

But I knew they didn't really understand. But it's got to be okay; if it was them, it would be the same.

A little later I felt well, like normal. I was looking at the Triborough Bridge and all its lights and thinking about when I was a little kid and how I used to stand up there on the roof and make believe and there I was, almost twenty years old, and I was still going to that roof and still making believe.

I looked toward Madison Avenue and thought of how close it was to Christmas. I thought about shipping out as soon as I could.

"Funny," I said half aloud, "it's like I've been kinda hanging around waiting for Brew to show up. Hope that Negro's okay."

I felt good about something else—me and Trina was making a steady scene; we really dug each other. My eyes crossed Park Avenue and got nearer Trina's house. I thought about being hung up on *tecata* and Trina kind of noticing that I was acting way out. Coño, like the time at the flick. I was goofing so bad, I couldn't hold my head up and just kept going into my nod.

"Qué te pasa, Piri?" she asked.

"Nothing, girl, just sleepy—tha's all."

I saw Trina come out and stand on the stoop. I felt mad at me for not being satisfied to just snort or a "just once in a while skin-pop." Naw, I hadda be hitting the main vein.

Man, a thought jumped into my mind, *mainline is the best time.* I pushed that thought outta my mind, except for the part of the way out feeling when that good-o smack was making it with you, that nothing in the whole *mundo* world made no difference, nothing—neither paddies nor Poppa and strange other people.

My mind fell back on my pushing stuff to keep my veins happy, and how I was on a certain cat's shit list for taking some stuff from him to sell, and instead, I shot up for as long as it lasted. I mean, like down people know a cat can't help it when *embalao,* like strung out every which way when you need it—that's it, you just need it. But that's a bad bit, cause them people that give you the stuff to push gotta have some kind of trust in you. Even a junky gotta have some kind of dependable, he gotta have some kinda word.

I sat down on the edge of the roof ledge. My mind refused to get off its kick of reminiscing. Man, like how many times some cat's come up to me with his old man's watch or sister's coat and swap for a three-cent bag. Heh, a three-cent bag—like a grain of rice crushed to powder, that's how much it is for a cost of three dollars, and you couldn't beat down that hell-like look as the begging took place in exchange for that super-tranquilizing ca-ca powder. I sniffed back a tear that came out of my nose. And how about the time I plowed through that falling snow with no pride at all in my Buster Brown shoes—like brown on top and bustered on the bottoms—knowing without a doubt in the world that the only thing that would get me warm again so I could care about being cold was the connecting—the blending of my vein's blood and dogie drug.

Shit, man, how far can pride go down? I knew that all the help in the world could get that stuff out of my system, but only some kind of god would be able to get it out of my swinging soul and mind. What a sick mudder scene! If you didn't get gypped outta your stuff, you'd get beat on some weak, cut-down shit. If you didn't get dead on an overdose, you'd get deader on a long strung-out kick. Everything in the world depended on heroin. You'd go to bed thinking about stuff and wake up in the morning thinking about it. Love and life took second place to it and nothing mattered except where, and how soon. It was like my whole puking system had copped a mind bigger than the one in my head.

I walked toward the roof landing. I was thinking. I was gonna kick for good. "I can do it. I swear ta God and the Virgin. Gonna get me li'l shit and cut down good. *I ain't no fuckin' junkie.*"

I went looking for Waneko. I found him in *El Viejo's* candy store. I put my want to him in fast words.

"Help me kick, man?" It was a question. Waneko knew how it was. Even though he was pushing now, he wasn't using, but he'd been through that kicking road *mucho* times. Waneko nodded, "Sure, *panín*—sure I will." We walked into Waneko's place. He explained to his moms what was shaking. She smiled nice-like and said everything was gonna be all right. Waneko followed that assurance up with, "Moms helps most of the cats that want to kick and even some of the chicks. She should be some kind of church worker or something." He laughed. I tried a weak smile.

They put me in a room that just had a bed and chair and a window that had a metal gate across it to keep the crooks out and kicking junkies in. I laid down, and after a while Waneko brought in a small radio so I could dig some music, to take my mind off what was coming. Both he and I knew that the li'l taste of stuff I had shot up on the roof a while ago was gonna wear off and then World War III was gonna break out inside of me. Billie was wailing some sad song. I wailed along with her in a soft hum. Then some kinda time started to go by and my system was better than a clock. And then Judgment Day set in . . . .

Man, talk about wantin' to die—everything started off as it should. First like always, the uncomfortable feeling as you knew your system wanted its baby bottle. And nose running ever so gently at first and the slow kind of pain building up not so gently. I tried hard to listen to some wailin' on the radio, but all I could hear was my own. I got up and went to the door. It was locked from the outside. "Hey, Waneko, open the door," I yelled.

"*Qué es?*"

"I feel real bad, like in bad, man."

"Man, lay down, you ain't been in there long enough to work up any kind of sweat. I'll tell you when, and only then I'll give you a li'l taste to ease you off. So cool it, *panín.*"

I don't know how many hours ran crawling by. I just knew I couldn't make it. *But I hadda. I just hadda.*

"Lemme out, Waneko—lemme out, you mother-fucker." I swam to the door and hit at it.

"Waneko is not home right now." It was Waneko's moms.

"Let me out, *señora.* I kicked already."

"He said not to let you come out until he comes back, *hijo.*"

"Did he leave something for me?" My voice sounded like tears. I went back to bed and just rolled and moaned all alone.

I don't know how many hours ran crawling by. It was a lot of them. At one time I heard the lock being taken off the door and heard it fall from some one's hand. I felt Waneko's mom's voice—I felt her cool hand on my face and felt her wipe my cold sweating face. I heard sounds of comfort coming from her.

"*No te apures, hijo,* you weel soon be fine."

I tried to get up and make it, but she was faster. I felt the iron gates on the window. I shook them. I turned and flopped back on the bed. I was shaking. I was in bad pain. I was cold and I couldn't stop my snots from flowing. I was all in cramps and my guts wouldn't obey me. My eyes were overflowing real fast.

"Lemme out, Waneko—lemme out, you mother-fucker." Shit, I was like screaming out of veins.

Nobody answered and I just lay there and moaned and groaned all alone and turned that mattress into one big soaking mopful of my sweat.

I don't know how many hours went crawling by. Millions maybe. And then a real scared thought hit me. Waneko wasn't coming back. He was gonna let me make it—cold-turkey—*a la canona.* I kept trembling and my whole swinging soul full of pain would make my body lurch up and tie itself up into one big knot and then ease itself almost straight and then retie itself. I felt like a puke coming afar. I thought, didn't I puke before? I felt it come out of my mouth like a green river of yellow-blue bile. I couldn't control nothing, and all the strength I had was enough just to turn my head away. I think I made some soft ca-ca on myself. I think I made some hard ones too.

Sometimes I think I heard Waneko telling me, "It's almost over, baby, it's almost over—we got it beat." But I couldn't answer. I'd just hold myself together with my arms holding me tight and rockaby baby myself to some kind of vague comfort. In a dream I'd eat mountains and mountains of sweet, sweet candy. I opened my eyes and Waneko had me sitting in a chair and I saw Moms cleaning the toilet I had made out of the room—and then I was back in the bed. I still had all the pain, all the cramps. I still had the whole bad bit, but I knew I was gonna make it. I rocked myself to and fro.

I don't know how many hours ran crawling by. Jillions maybe. At last the pain cut itself down. I felt all dried out. Waneko came into the room and rubbed my body down, like trying to work all the knots to straighten out. Waneko and his moms kept me with them for a week or so putting me into shape with hot pigeon soup, liquids, and later heavier stuff like I mean, rice and beans. They were great, Waneko and Moms. My body was kicked free from H—gone was dogie. They said it takes seventy or so hours to kick a habit. I think it seemed like seventy years. Now all I had to do was kick it outta my mind.

I left Waneko's house after really thanking them from way down. I hit the street thinking, "Wow, dying is easier than this has been. Never—never— *nunca más.*"

THE CHICANO MOVEMENT

Alfredo Cuéllar

We have suggested that Mexican American political activity has often been related to social structural factors. Because much of this political activity was possible only after certain structural changes in Mexican American life, there were seldom any real alternatives beyond simple reaction to Anglo pressure. The importance of the *Chicano* movement as an alternative to pressures from the majority society can hardly be overemphasized. It is a distinctively novel development in the Mexican American community. The *Chicano* movement developed in southern California no earlier than 1966, and it is already a sharp new force in the political expression of Mexican Americans throughout the southwest.

The *Chicano* ideology includes a broad definition of political activity. Ironically, such thinking was possible only for a new generation of urbanized and "Anglicized" (that is, assimilated) young Mexican Americans, who were much less burdened by social and class restrictions than their elders were and whose education had exposed them to new ideas.

The exact beginnings of the movement are obscure. There is some evidence that the *Chicano* movement grew out of a group of conferences held at Loyola University in Los Angeles in the summer of 1966. As originally conceived by its Catholic sponsors, the conferences were to create a fairly innocuous youth organization for the middle-class Mexican students attending various colleges throughout California. Very quickly the movement grew beyond the intent or control of its sponsors (Loyola has never been very noted for its interest in Mexican American education) and it drew in yet others, not students and not middle class, who were attracted by the ideology of *chicanismo*. Thus it cannot be understood as a movement limited to the young, to students, or even to urban areas. It must also be understood as including the followers of Reies Tijerina in northern New Mexico and César Chávez' embattled union of striking farm workers in central California. In 1969 Rodolfo (Corky) González was the principal leader and inspiration of the *Chicano* movement in Denver although his interests were mainly in urban civic action. Moreover, "Corky" has organized regional youth conferences and his influence spreads far beyond the local area. No one leader has yet emerged in southern California or in Texas.

As this wide range of activity shows, the *Chicano* movement is extremely heterogeneous, and its elements have different aims and purposes. In this way the movement cuts across social class, regional, and generational lines. Its aims range from traditional forms of social protest to increasingly more radical goals that appear as a sign of an emerging nationalism. It is a social movement, in that it can be described as "pluralistic behavior functioning as an organized mass effort directed toward a change of established folkways or institutions."* The dynamic force of the movement is its ideology—*chicanismo*.

The new ideology is advanced as a challenge to the dominant Anglo beliefs concerning Mexicans as well as to the beliefs of Mexican Americans themselves. Although we have emphasized that students are by no means the

* As defined by Abel, in *Why Hitler Came to Power*, as cited in Martin Oppenheimer, *The Urban Guerilla* (Chicago: Quadrangle Books, 1969), p. 19.

only element of the *Chicano* movement, we will reconstruct *chicanismo* primarily as it has been developed among students. Actually, this is only one of several ideological strands but it is the most consistently developed, thus the best illustration of the change from protest to nationalism and a synthesis of the ideology of *chicanismo*.

The first student form of the *Chicano* movement coincided with the development of new student organizations in California universities and colleges in 1966 and 1967. Some of these groups were the United Mexican American Students (UMAS), the Mexican American Student Association (MASA), Mexican American Student Confederation (MASC), and Movimiento Estudiantil Chicano de Aztlán (MECHA). More recently the Mexican American Youth Organization (MAYO) has appeared, with particular strength in Texas. (MAYO is also the name adopted by the new organizations of *Chicanos* in California prisons.) These student groups were at first concerned with a rather narrow range of problems in the field of education, particularly those concerned with increasing the number of Mexican American students in college. To the extent that these student groups were active in the Mexican American community, they were involved with various forms of protest against specific and longstanding grievances, such as police brutality and inferior educational facilities, although other forms of community activity also involved political campaigns.

Chicano student groups thus have never repudiated ordinary forms of political activity, although for them such forms as voting constitute only one political alternative. Actually, given the wide range of problems facing the Mexican American community, *Chicanos* view conventional forms of political activity as perhaps the least effective. Instead, they favor forms of confrontation as the most effective means to gain access for the traditionally excluded *Chicano*, even though it has, on occasion, led to violence. In general, this conception of politics contrasts sharply with the ideas of more conservative Mexican American leaders, most of whom adhere to very limited and "safe" politics with an emphasis on voting and "working within the system" to gain political leverage. This is not to say that *Chicanos* reject working for social change within the system; as a matter of fact, much recent activity has focussed on bringing about change in the universities and colleges as well as in the public school systems. Nevertheless, whereas the moderates seek to bring major change in American society through nonviolent means, the more militant speak of the need for "revolutionary activity," though they often leave the details and direction of this revolution unspecified. While they admire the life style and aspirations of revolutionary leaders like Ché Guevara, they have thus far made no systematic theoretical connection between the *Chicano* movement and the general literature on revolution. The theoretical underpinnings of the *Chicano* movement thus often lack a strong direction.

And yet, the advent of the *Chicano* movement does represent a revolutionary phenomenon among Mexican Americans. As we shall see, most of the change from traditional forms lies in (or is reflected in) the ideology of *chicanismo*. Basically eclectic, *chicanismo* draws inspiration from outside the United States and outside the Mexican American experience. The Cuban Revolution, for example, exerts some influence, as do the career and ideals of Ché Guevara. For instance, the Brown Berets (a *Chicano* youth group) affect the life style of this revolutionary. Black Power also offers something of a model. Most recently, *Chicanos* have resurrected the Mexican revolutionary tradition.

Basically, however, *chicanismo* focuses on the life experience of the Mexican in the United States. It challenges the belief system of the majority society at the same time that it attempts to reconstruct a new image for Mexican Americans themselves. *Chicanos* assume that along with American Indians and black Americans, Mexicans live in the United States as a conquered people. This idea allows *chicanismo* to explain the evolution of the *Chicano* as essentially conflictful. In each conflictual relationship with Anglos, the Mexicans lost out and were thus forced to live in the poverty and degradation attendant upon those with the status of a conquered people. This is no better illustrated than by the Mexicans' loss of communal and private property. As a result, they had no choice but to work the land for a *patrón* (usually an Anglo, but sometimes a Mexican, who exploited his own people). When the Mexican was thrown off the land, he was forced to become an unattached wage-earner, often a migrant farm worker; or he might migrate to a city, where the exploitation continued. In any event, *chicanismo* emphasizes that the Mexican was transformed into a rootless economic commodity, forced either to depend on migrant farm work or to sell his labor in the urban centers, where his fate depended upon the vicissitudes of the economy. Ironically, indispensable as Mexican labor was for the economic development of the Southwest, the Mexican got little recognition for his contribution and even less benefit from it.

Chicanos therefore see the economic expansion of the Southwest as essentially a dehumanizing process. They also point out that during periods of economic depression in the United States, when the Mexican became "superfluous" and "expensive," Anglo society had no qualms about attempting to eliminate Mexicans from the United States, as in the repatriations of the 1930s . . . . The repatriations are viewed as a conscious attempt to eliminate the *Chicano* from American society.

The thrust of *chicanismo* is not only economic, but also cultural. In many ways, the exploitation and suppression of his culture is what most angers the *Chicano*, who views the attempt to deracinate Mexican culture in the Southwest as the reason why Mexican Americans are disoriented about their culture and often attempt to deny it. The *Chicano* points out that the Anglo himself often views Mexicans with a great degree of ambivalence. Anglos oftentimes take over aspects of "Spanish" (which is really Mexican) culture and at the same time deny it to the Mexican himself. In this fashion Mexicans were denied the development of a more autonomous cultural life, especially as it touches upon Spanish language use, the arts, and so on. (This was done in spite of the agreements made in the signing of the Treaty of Guadalupe Hidalgo. Early drafts of the treaty contained Mexican government efforts to make formal recognition of language rights for Mexicans who chose to remain in the United States after the Mexican War. These provisions were not approved by the U.S. Senate.)

Worse yet, the ideology goes on, the cultural suppression continues to the present day, reinforced by Anglo institutions, particularly the schools. The extreme position (although by no means infrequent) is represented by the fact that Mexican American students in the public schools are corporally punished for using Spanish, their native language. Under these circumstances, it is understandable that the Mexican American student remains ignorant and often ashamed of his past. When the Mexican is mentioned in textbooks, it is in a romanticized and stereotypically Anglicized version of "Spanish culture" that may be congenial to Anglos but is remote and irrelevant to the Mexican American. The *Chicano* considers this type of white-washed "Spanish" culture particularly galling because he feels that while Anglos may selectively choose certain motifs from Mexican culture, the person behind the culture, the Mexican himself, is given neither recognition nor respect.

Chicanismo also focuses on race, and in some ways this emphasis constitutes one of the most controversial aspects of *chicanismo*. It is argued that Anglo racism denies the Mexican his ethnicity by making him ashamed of his "Mexican-ness." Mexican ancestry, instead of being a source of pride, becomes a symbol of shame and inferiority. As a consequence, Mexicans spend their lives apologizing or denying their ancestry, to the point that many dislike and resent being called "Mexican," preferring "Spanish American," "Latin," "Latin American," and similar euphemisms. For these reasons, the term *"Chicano"* is now insisted upon by activists as a symbol of the new assertiveness.

Advocates of *chicanismo* therefore hope to reconstruct the Mexican Americans' concept of themselves by appeals to pride of a common history, culture and "race." *Chicanismo* attempts to redefine the Mexicans' identity on the basis not of class, generation, or area of residence but on a unique and shared experience in the United States. This means that appeals for political action, economic progress, and reorientation of cultural identity are cast in terms of the common history, culture, and ethnic background of *la raza*.

Chicano ideologues insist that social advance based on material achievement is, in the final analysis, less important than social advance based on *la raza;* they reject what they call the myth of American individualism. The *Chicano* movement feels that it cannot afford the luxury of individualism; if Mexicans are to confront the problems of their group realistically they must begin to act along collective lines. Hence, the stirrings of a new spirit of what *chicanismo* terms "cultural nationalism" among the Mexican Americans of the Southwest.

Chicanismo has led not only to increased participation in community activities, but also to a heightened and often intense interest in cultural life. *Chicano* poets, playwrights, journalists, and writers of all varieties have suddenly appeared. There are *Chicano* theater groups in several large cities (often known as the *teatro urbano*) and one nationally known and well-travelled group from Delano, California (*El teatro campesino*), which tells the story not only of the striking California farmworkers but of *Chicanos* in general. Newspapers and magazines also reflect this desire to disseminate the idea of *chicanismo*. Throughout the Southwest numerous *Chicano* "underground" newspapers and magazines publishing literary materials have emerged. There is even a *Chicano* Press Association, a regional association representing *Chicano* publications from Texas to California. Furthermore, because of the strong base in colleges and universities, a serious and generally successful drive to develop "ethnic studies" programs has appeared, especially in California. As part of the drive to spread the idea of *chicanismo* in education, *Chicanos* place an emphasis on Mexican contributions to American society, thus giving *Chicano* college students a new conception of their past and present.

Chicano student groups share an orientation similar to that of black students, and on occasion they cooperate and support each other on similar demands. (There is more mutual support between black and brown students than between their counterparts at the community level.) The alliance between black and brown students, however, has not been close, harmonious, or continuous. *Chicano* student organizations have not yet been significantly involved with Anglo radical student groups, although these groups sometimes claim their support or claim that they are working for the benefit of *Chicanos*.

THE RADICALIZED RICH

Eric Hoffer

Scratch an intellectual and you find a would-be aristocrat who loathes the sight, the sound and the smell of common folk. Professor Marcuse has lived among us for more than 30 years and now, in old age, his disenchantment with this country is spilling over into book after book. He is offended by the intrusion of the vulgar, by the failure of egalitarian America to keep common people in their place. He is frightened by "the degree to which the population is allowed to break the peace where there is still peace and silence, to be ugly and uglify things, to ooze familiarity and to offend against good form." The vulgar invade "the small reserved sphere of existence" and compel exquisite Marcusian souls to partake of their sounds, sights and smells.

To a shabby would-be aristocrat like Professor Marcuse there is something fundamentally wrong with a society in which the master and the worker, the typist and the boss's daughter do not live totally disparate lives. Everything good in America seems to him a sham and a fraud.

An interesting peculiarity of present-day dissenting intellectuals is their lack of animus toward the rich. They are against the Government, the Congress, the Army and the police, and against corporations and unions, but hardly anything is being said or written against "the money changers in the temple," "the economic royalists," "the malefactors of great wealth" and "the maniacs wild for gold" who were the butt of vituperation in the past. Indeed, there is nowadays a certain rapport between the rich and the would-be revolutionaries. The outlandish role the rich are playing in the affluent society is one of the surprises of our time. Though the logic of it seems now fairly evident, I doubt whether anyone had foreseen that affluence would radicalize the upper rich and the lowest poor and nudge them toward an alliance against those in the middle. Whatever we have of revolution just now is financed largely by the rich.

In order to feel rich, you have to have poor people around you. In an affluent society, riches lose their uniqueness—people no longer find fulfillment in being rich. And when the rich cannot feel rich they begin to have misgivings about success—not enough to give up the fruits of success, but enough to feel guilty, and emote soulfully about the grievances of the disadvantaged, and the sins of the status quo. It seems that every time a millionaire opens his mouth nowadays he confesses the sins of our society in public.

Now, it so happens that the rich do indeed have a lot to feel guilty about.

They live in exclusive neighborhoods, send their children to private schools, and use every loophole to avoid paying taxes. But what they confess in public are not their private sins, but the sins of society, the sins of the rest of us, and it is our breasts they are beating into a pulp. They feel guilty and ashamed, they say, because the mass of people, who do most of the work and pay much of the taxes, are against integrated schools and housing, and do not tax themselves to the utmost to fight the evils that beset our cities. We are discovering that in an affluent society the rich have a monopoly of righteousness.

Moreover, the radicalized rich have radical children. There is no generation gap here. The most violent cliques of the New Left are made up of the children of the rich. The Weathermen, to whom workingmen are "honky bastards," have not a member with a workingman's background. The behavior of the extremist young makes sense when seen as the behavior of spoiled brats used to instant fulfillment who expect the solutions to life's problems to be there on demand. And just as in former days aristocratic sprigs horsewhipped peasants, so at present the children of the rich are riding roughshod over community sensibilities. The rich parents applaud and subsidize their revolutionary children, and probably brag about them at dinner parties.

THE FORGOTTEN AMERICAN

Peter Schrag

AT THE BOTTOM OF THE WELL

American culture? Wealth is visible, and so, now, is poverty. Both have become intimidating clichés. But the rest? A vast, complex, and disregarded world that was once—in belief, and in fact—the American middle: Greyhound and Trailways bus terminals in little cities at midnight, each of them with its neon lights and its cardboard hamburgers; acres of tar-paper beach bungalows in places like Revere and Rockaway; the hair curlers in the supermarket on Saturday, and the little girls in the communion dresses the next morning; pinball machines and the *Daily News*, the *Reader's Digest* and Ed Sullivan; houses with tiny front lawns (or even large ones) adorned with statues of the Virgin or of Sambo welcomin' de folks home; Clint Eastwood or Julie Andrews at the Palace; the trotting tracks and the dog tracks—Aurora Downs, Connaught Park, Roosevelt, Yonkers, Rockingham, and forty others—where gray men come not for sport and beauty, but to read numbers, to study and dope. (If you win you have figured something, have in a small way controlled your world, have surmounted your impotence. If you lose, bad luck, shit. "I'll break his goddamned head.") Baseball is not the national pastime; racing is. For every man who goes to a major-league baseball game there are four who go to the track and probably four more who go to the candy store or the barbershop to make their bets. (Total track attendance in 1965: 62 million plus another 10 million who went to the dogs.)

There are places, and styles, and attitudes. If there are neighborhoods of aspiration, suburban enclaves for the mobile young executive and the aspiring worker, there are also places of limited expectation and dead-end districts where mobility is finished. But even there you can often find, however vestigial, a sense of place, the roots of old ethnic loyalties, and a passionate, if often futile, battle against intrusion and change. "Everybody around here," you are told, "pays his own way." In this world the problems are not the ABM or air pollution (have they heard of Biafra?) or the international population crisis; the problem is to get your street cleaned, your garbage collected, to get your husband home from Vietnam alive; to negotiate installment payments and to keep the schools orderly. Ask anyone in Scarsdale or Winnetka about the schools and they'll tell you about new programs, or about how many are getting into Harvard, or about the teachers; ask in Oakland or the North Side of Chicago, and they'll tell you that they have (or haven't) had trouble. Somewhere in his gut the man in those communities knows that mobility and choice in this society are limited. He cannot imagine any major change for the better; but he can imagine change for the worse. And yet for a decade he is the one who has been asked to carry the burden of social reform, to integrate his schools and his neighborhood, has been asked by comfortable people to pay the social debts due to the poor and the black. In Boston, in San Francisco, in Chicago (not to mention Newark or Oakland) he has been telling the reformers to go to hell. The Jewish schoolteachers of New York and the Irish parents of Dorchester have asked the same question: "What the hell did Lindsay (or the Beacon Hill Establishment) ever do for us?"

The ambiguities and changes in American life that occupy discussions in university seminars and policy debates in Washington, and that form the backbone of contemporary popular sociology, become increasingly the conditions of trauma and frustration in the middle. Although the New Frontier and Great Society contained some programs for those not already on the rolls of social pathology—federal aid for higher education, for example—the public priorities and the rhetoric contained little. The emphasis, properly, was on the poor, on the inner cities (*e.g.,* Negroes) and the unemployed. But in Chicago a widow with three children who earns $7,000 a year can't get them college loans because she makes too much: the money is reserved for people on relief. New schools are built in the ghetto but not in the white working-class neighborhoods where they are just as dilapidated. In Newark the head of a white vigilante group (now a city councilman) runs, among other things, on a platform opposing pro-Negro discrimination. "When pools are being built in the Central Ward—don't they think white kids have got frustration? The white can't get a job; we have to hire Negroes first." The middle class, said Congressman Roman Pucinski of Illinois, who represents a lot of it, "is in revolt. Everyone has been generous in supporting anti-poverty. Now the middle-class American is disqualified from most of the programs."

SOMEBODY HAS TO SAY NO . . .

The frustrated middle. The liberal wisdom about welfare, ghettos, student revolt, and Vietnam has only a marginal place, if any, for the values and life of the working man. It flies in the face of most of what he was taught to cherish and respect: hard work, order, authority, self-reliance. He fought, either alone or through labor organizations, to establish the precincts he now considers his own. Union seniority, the civil-service bureaucracy, and the petty professionalism established by the merit system in the public schools become sinecures of particular ethnic groups or of those who have learned to negotiate and master the system. A man who worked all his life to accumulate the points and grades and paraphernalia to become an assistant school principal (no matter how silly the requirements) is not likely to relinquish his position with equanimity. Nor is a dock worker whose only estate is his longshoreman's card. The job, the points, the credits become property:

> Some men leave their sons money [wrote a union member to the *New York Times*], some large investments, some business connections, and some a profession. I have only one worthwhile thing to give: my trade. I hope to follow a centuries-old tradition and sponsor my sons for an apprenticeship. For this simple father's wish it is said that I discriminate against Negroes. Don't all of us discriminate? Which of us . . . will not choose a son over all others?

Suddenly the rules are changing—all the rules. If you protect your job for your own you may be called a bigot. At the same time it's perfectly acceptable to shout black power and to endorse it. What does it take to be a good American? *Give the black man a position because he is black, not because he necessarily works harder or does the job better.* What does it take to be a good American? Dress nicely, hold a job, be clean-cut, don't judge a man by the color of his skin or the country of his origin. What about the demands of Negroes, the long hair of the students, the dirty movies, the people who burn draft cards and American flags? Do you have to go out in the street with picket signs, do you have to burn the place down to get what you want? What does it take to be a good American? *This is a sick society, a racist society, we are fighting an immoral war.* ("I'm against the Vietnam war, too," says the truck driver in Brooklyn. "I see a good kid come home with half an arm and a leg in a brace up to here, and what's it all for? I was glad to see *my kid* flunk the Army physical. Still, somebody has to say no to these demonstrators and enforce the law.") What does it take to be a good American?

The conditions of trauma and frustration in the middle. What does it take to be a good American? Suddenly there are demands for Italian power and Polish power and Ukrainian power. In Cleveland the Poles demand a seat on the school board, and get it, and in Pittsburgh John Pankuch, the seventy-three-year-old president of the National Slovak Society demands "action, plenty of it to make up for lost time." Black power is supposed to be nothing but emulation of the ways in which other ethnic groups made it. But have they made it? In Reardon's Bar on East Eighth Street in South Boston, where the workmen come for their fish-chowder lunch and for their rye and ginger, they still identify themselves as Galway men and Kilkenny men; in the newsstand in Astoria you can buy *Il Progresso, El Tiempo,* the *Staats-Zeitung,* the *Irish World,* plus papers in Greek, Hungarian, and Polish. At the parish of Our Lady of Mount Carmel the priests hear confession in English, Italian, and Spanish and, nearby, the biggest attraction is not the stickball game, but the *bocce* court. Some of the poorest people in America are white, native, and have lived all of their lives in the same place as their fathers and grandfathers. The problems that were presumably solved in some distant past, in that prehistoric era before the textbooks were written —problems of assimilation, of upward mobility—now turn out to be very much unsolved. The melting pot and all: millions made it, millions moved to the affluent suburbs; several million—no one knows how many—did not. The median income in Irish South Boston is $5,100 a year but the community-action workers have a hard time convincing the local citizens that any white man who is not stupid or irresponsible can be poor. Pride still keeps them from applying for income supplements or Medicaid, but it does not keep them from resenting those who do. In Pittsburgh, where the members of Polish-American organizations earn an estimated $5,000 to $6,000 (and some fall below the poverty line), the Poverty Programs are nonetheless directed primarily to Negroes, and almost everywhere the thing called urban backlash associates itself in some fashion with ethnic groups whose members have themselves only a precarious hold on the security of affluence. Almost everywhere in the old cities, tribal neighborhoods and their styles are under assault by masscult. The Italian grocery gives way to the supermarket, the ma-and-pa store and the walk-up are attacked by urban renewal. And almost everywhere, that assault tends to depersonalize and to alienate. It has always been this way, but with time the brave new world that replaces old patterns becomes increasingly bureaucratized, distant, and hard to control.

Yet beyond the problems of ethnic identity, beyond the problems of Poles and Irishmen left behind, there are others more pervasive and more dangerous. For every Greek or Hungarian there are a dozen American-Americans who are past ethnic consciousness and who are as alienated, as confused, and as angry as the rest. The obvious manifestations are the same everywhere—race, taxes, welfare, students—but the threat seems invariably more cultural and psychological than economic or social. What upset the police at the Chicago convention most was not so much the politics of the demonstrators as their manners and their hair. (The barbershops in their neighborhoods don't advertise Beatle Cuts but the Flat Top and the Chicago Box.) The affront comes from middle-class people—and their children—who had been cast in the role of social exemplars (and from those cast as unfortunates worthy of public charity) who offend all the things on which working class identity is built: "hippies [said a San Francisco longshoreman] who fart around the streets and don't work"; welfare recipients who strike and march for better treatment; "all those [said a California labor official] who challenge the precepts that these people live on." If ethnic groups are beginning to organize to get theirs, so are others: police and firemen ("The cop is the new nigger"); schoolteachers; lower-middle-class housewives fighting sex education and bussing; small property owners who have no ethnic communion but a passionate interest in lower taxes, more policemen, and stiffer penalties for criminals. In San Francisco the Teamsters, who had never been known for such interests before, recently demonstrated in support of the police and law enforcement and, on another occasion, joined a group called Mothers Support Neighborhood Schools at a school-board meeting to oppose—with their presence and later, apparently, with their fists—a proposal to integrate the schools through bussing. ("These people," someone said at the meeting, "do not look like mothers.")

Which is not to say that all is frustration and anger, that anybody is ready "to burn the country down." They are not even ready to elect standard model demagogues. "A lot of labor people who thought of voting for Wallace were ashamed of themselves when they realized what they were about to do," said Morris Iushewitz, an officer of New York's Central Labor Council. Because of a massive last-minute union campaign, and perhaps for other reasons, the blue-collar vote for Wallace fell far below the figures predicted by the early polls last fall. Any number of people, moreover, who are not doing well by any set of official statistics, who are earning well below the national mean ($8,000 a year), or who hold two jobs to stay above it, think of themselves as affluent, and often use that word. It is almost as if not to be affluent is to be un-American. People who can't use the word tend to be angry; people who come too close to those who can't become frightened. The definition of affluence is generally pinned to what comes in, not to the quality of life as it's lived. The $8,000 son of a man who never earned more than $4,500 may, for that reason alone, believe that he's "doing all right." If life is not all right, if he can't get his curbs fixed, or his streets patrolled, if the highways are crowded and the beaches polluted, if the schools are ineffectual he is still able to call himself affluent, feels, perhaps, a social compulsion to do so. His anger, if he is angry, is not that of the wage earner resenting management—and certainly not that of the socialist ideologue asking for redistribution of wealth—but that of the consumer, the taxpayer, and the family man. (Inflation and taxes are wiping out most of the wage gains made in labor contracts signed during the past three years.) Thus he will vote for a Louise Day Hicks in Boston who promises to hold the color line in the schools or for a Charles Stenvig calling for law enforcement in Minneapolis but reject a George Wallace who seems to threaten his pocketbook. The danger is that he will identify with the politics of the Birchers and other middle-class reactionaries (who often pretend to speak for him) even though his income and style of life are far removed from theirs; that taxes, for example, will be identified with welfare rather than war, and that he will blame his limited means on the small slice of the poor rather than the fat slice of the rich.

If you sit and talk to people like Marjorie Lemlow, who heads Mothers Support Neighborhood Schools in San Francisco, or Joe Owens, a house painter who is president of a community-action organization in Boston, you quickly discover that the roots of reaction and the roots of reform are often identical, and that the response to particular situations is more often contingent on the politics of the politicians and leaders who appear to care than on the conditions of life or the ideology of the victims. Mrs. Lemlow wants to return the schools to some virtuous past; she worries about disintegration of the family and she speaks vaguely about something that she can't bring herself to call a conspiracy against Americanism. She has been accused of leading a bunch of Birchers, and she sometimes talks Birch language. But whatever the form, her sense of things comes from a small-town vision of national virtues, and her unhappiness from the assaults of urban sophistication. It just so happens that a lot of reactionaries now sing that tune, and that the liberals are indifferent.

Joe Owens—probably because of his experience as a Head Start parent, and because of his association with an effective community-action program —talks a different language. He knows, somehow, that no simple past can be restored. In his world the villains are not conspirators but bureaucrats and politicians, and he is beginning to discover that in a struggle with officials the black man in the ghetto and the working man (black or white) have the same problems. "Every time you ask for something from the politicians they treat you like a beggar, like you ought to be grateful for what you have. They try to make you feel ashamed." . . .

CAN THE COMMON MAN COME BACK?

Beneath it all there is a more fundamental ambivalence, not only about the young, but about institutions—the schools, the churches, the Establishment—and about the future itself. In the major cities of the East (though perhaps not in the West) there is a sense that time is against you, that one is living "in one of the few decent neighborhoods left," that "if I can get $125 a week upstate (or downstate) I'll move." The institutions that were supposed to mediate social change and which, more than ever, are becoming priesthoods of information and conglomerates of social engineers, are increasingly suspect. To attack the Ford Foundation (as Wright Patman has done) is not only to fan the embers of historic populism against concentrations of wealth and power, but also to arouse those who feel that they are trapped by an alliance of upper-class Wasps and lower-class Negroes. If the foundations have done anything for the blue-collar worker he doesn't seem to be aware of it. At the same time the distrust of professional educators that characterizes the black militants is becoming increasingly prevalent among a minority of lower-middle-class whites who are beginning to discover that the schools aren't working for them either. ("Are all those new programs just a cover-up for failure?") And if the Catholic Church is under attack from its liberal members (on birth control, for example) it is also alienating the traditionalists who liked their minor saints (even if they didn't actually exist) and were perfectly content with the Latin Mass. For the alienated Catholic liberal there are other places to go; for the lower-middle-class parishioner in Chicago or Boston there are none.

Perhaps, in some measure, it has always been this way. Perhaps none of this is new. And perhaps it is also true that the American lower middle has never had it so good. And yet surely there is a difference, and that is that the common man has lost his visibility and, somehow, his claim on public attention. There are old liberals and socialists—men like Michael Harrington—who believe that a new alliance can be forged for progressive social action:

> From Marx to Mills, the Left has regarded the middle class as a stratum of hypocritical, vacillating rear-guarders. There was often sound reason for this contempt. But is it not possible that a new class is coming into being? It is not the old middle class of small property owners and entrepreneurs, nor the new middle class of managers. It is composed of scientists, technicians, teachers, and professionals in the public sector of the society. By education and work experience it is predisposed toward

planning. It could be an ally of the poor and the organized workers—or their sophisticated enemy. In other words, an unprecedented social and political variable seems to be taking shape in America.

The American worker, even when he waits on a table or holds open a door, is not servile; he does not carry himself like an inferior. The openness, frankness, and democratic manner which Tocqueville described in the last century persists to this very day. They have been a source of rudeness, contemptuous ignorance, violence—and of a creative self-confidence among great masses of people. It was in this latter spirit that the CIO was organized and the black freedom movement marched.

There are recent indications that the white lower middle class is coming back on the roster of public priorities. Pucinski tells you that liberals in Congress are privately discussing the pressure from the middle class. There are proposals now to increase personal income-tax exemptions from $600 to $1,000 (or $1,200) for each dependent, to protect all Americans with a national insurance system covering castastrophic medical expenses, and to put a floor under all incomes. Yet these things by themselves are insufficient. Nothing is sufficient without a national sense of restoration. What Pucinski means by the middle class has, in some measure, always been represented. A physician earning $75,000 a year is also a working man but he is hardly a victim of the welfare system. Nor, by and large, are the stockholders of the Standard Oil Company or U.S. Steel. The fact that American ideals have often been corrupted in the cause of self-aggrandizement does not make them any less important for the cause of social reform and justice. "As a movement with the conviction that there is more to people than greed and fear," Harrington said, "the Left must . . . also speak in the name of the historic idealism of the United States."

The issue, finally, is not *the program* but the vision, the angle of view. A huge constituency may be coming up for grabs, and there is considerable evidence that its political mobility is more sensitive than anyone can imagine, that all the sociological determinants are not as significant as the simple facts of concern and leadership. When Robert Kennedy was killed . . . thousands of working-class people who had expected to vote for him—if not hundreds of thousands—shifted their loyalties to Wallace. A man who can change from a progressive democrat into a bigot overnight deserves attention.

CENTURIES OF DISCRIMINATION

Earl Warren

The one thing that has the badge of insolubility on it is the problem of how we are to live together in harmony and mutual respect. We have boasted for almost 200 years that we are a plural society wherein we achieve unity through diversity and accommodate diversity through unity. But the sins of former years are upon us, and it is my belief that the question of whether we can permanently have such a society is the greatest problem before the American people today.

It took almost 100 years for us to absolve ourselves from the curse of slavery through the 13th, 14th and 15th Amendments to our Constitution after a bloody fratricidal war, in which one out of every ten young Americans of military age gave their lives. That unfortunately was not the end of our problem and today, after a hundred more years of our national life, we are still paying the price for that slavery.

We have in the nation today about 22 million Negroes who still bear vestiges of that badge of slavery, and they are still struggling to be out of the class of inferior citizenship. The emotions of hundreds of years of discrimination and cruelties have welled up in them to the point of deep bitterness.

They are, for the first time in our history, demanding en masse the rights and privileges of citizenship which have been denied them for so many years—the right to live wherever they desire; the right to a decent education without discrimination; the right to vote; the right to be treated in accordance with human dignity. The violence implicit in these denials, as exemplified by lynchings and other unlawful injuries, has provoked counter-violence in many quarters, and the time has come when the nation must restore good will and cooperation, regardless of race or color if we are to be a healthy nation.

The results of these disaffections have come to plague us in a myriad of ways. Without education, without training in keeping with automation and advanced technology of all kinds, they have been deprived of a livelihood, and at the present time are mired down in the slums of our great cities. In the cotton industry in the Southern States alone, 900,000 illiterate cotton pickers have been displaced by recent cotton picking machines, and they, with their families aggregating between two and a half and three million people, were thrown out of their livelihood. . . . Millions have moved to the cities in desperation to find places in the industrial world.

Without skills or the education to learn them speedily, and without even hospitable treatment in their newly found home, they drift into the already congested slums where unemployment is out of all proportion, where the housing is deplorable, and where degradation of every kind is rampant. There they stay as if they were imprisoned. They are looked down upon by people in affluent circumstances who flee from them to the suburbs and leave them a people apart from the mainstream of American life.

The hard core of all slums is made up of those unfortunates who have been discriminated against all their lives. It is difficult for those of us who have always been able to enjoy our freedoms to understand the feelings of those who have never had them but who are now at long last determined to have them. This is not an unaccountable phenomenon. From 1941 to 1945, we fought a war according to the solemn promises of our Government and her allies to assure the four freedoms for all people throughout the world. American white and black boys fought and died, side by side, in that war, and in Korea, and in Vietnam. Is it unrealistic or premature for them now to demand equal rights under the law?

There can be no other answer to our problem than to wipe out the discrimination for which we have become so notorious, and to treat everyone in the nation with the consideration that we have always demanded and received for the vast majority of our people. Nothing else will restore amity to our country; nothing else will bring harmony to our educational system, in our cities, and in the political life of the nation.

I suppose I am particularly sensitive to this situation because during the years when I was active on the Supreme Court, and when these minority groups were coming to us to achieve their constitutional rights, many people would say to me: "I agree with you that there should be no discrimination and that everybody should be treated equally under the laws, but don't you think that we are moving too fast? The Negroes have improved their situation in the United States more in the last hundred years than they have in any other part of the world." This was said, not in anger, but as an escape from responsibility. However, the question assumed that the Supreme Court had the right to ration freedoms, and that it should go slow enough so as not to offend anyone in doing so. Of course, no such power exists either in law or morals. Either all rights of citizenship belong to them or they are entitled to none, as was said in the Dred Scott decision that precipitated the Civil War. The plain words of the Constitution answer that question.

When the basis of problems is bitterness the solution is impossible until the bitterness is removed. The bitterness in this situation is born of the discrimination of centuries, and can only be removed by elimination of the cause.

It, therefore, seems clear to me that if we are ever to have a placid nation again at least during the lifetime of our children and their children, it will be necessary for us to set aside our prejudices on account of race or color, and be willing to live in a plural society where American citizenship means, in fact as well as in precept, that all men are created equal, and as such are entitled to Life, Liberty, and the pursuit of Happiness.

There is only one other alternative—chaos.

Women

MARRIAGE IS NOT ENOUGH

Herbert Gold

Is marriage really the next toy on the list for the man or woman who has everything?

Any other institution that causes as many failures as marriage would be declared illegal. A medicine that poisoned as many lives would be banned. Better to marry than to burn? Marriage is an anti-scorch drug of choice, but one which usually cures the disease of youth and hope by the remedies of age and despair.

And so new forms have begun to surface.

Each of these experimental systems raises new problems, but at least they give a sense of trying to cope with the old problem, not just following to the edge of the cliff with the other lemmings. It's as hard to explain about freedom in marriage to a Puritan moralist as it is to explain to a ten-year-old child that sex might be more fun than an ice-cream cone. He just doesn't have the equipment for understanding. He wants other things. But in this part of the stunned and goofy twentieth century, many men and women are seeking freedom along with their responsibility in the one area of their lives that retains an element of personal choice. Government, science, war, and natural disasters, such as smog, pollution, and daytime television, seem to be in control of much of our energy.

Marriage is a moral equivalent of choice; it gives real alternatives to the individual soul; people are acting on it and acting it out. Divorce and public miseries may be a part of marriage so conceived; but men's acts seem to say if so, then so be it. But perhaps the new freedom consists not only in the freedom to divorce but also in the freedom to invent, discover, knit up forms of marriage that make divorce as obsolete as the ideal of permanent union except for those with the talent for one-and-one union.

Aristophanes wasn't specifically talking about marriage in Plato's dialogue on love, but he seemed to have something permanent in mind. He made up this little myth that once upon a time we were all four-armed, four-legged, and rolled along with hermaphroditic ease, and then some lightning split us, and ever since we've been looking for the missing halves. Well, that implies some ideal of permanence, for once you've discovered your missing arms and legs, why would you ever let them go again? However, in this vision of splendid fluid-drive roll-roll-rolling along, he didn't deal with the persecutions that, say, Socrates suffered at the hands of his shrewish wife, Xanthippe. (We might suggest this theory about why he drank the hemlock so peaceably. . . .) Nevertheless, in most modern men, the Don Juan dream or any other dream of freedom is really addiction to a permanent quest: the next girl, or the next, or the one after that will be the perfect one. Most men don't really seek impermanence and continual change; they accept it, pro tem, in the interim, while they continue to aspire towards Miss Right. There are those two ideal legs, those arms, that perfect head. . . .

The concept of "imprinting" is important to introduce a notion of the underappreciated charms of sex in marriage. The pleasures of surprise, conquest, new tastes, and hope are well-assimilated in our fantasy lives. But the familiar has its own freedom and excitement, and habit with a wife gives a power that permits of risk and adventure, in sex play, in soul play, in the fullness of a life together. If sex is associated with mirror images, shoes, garters, or schoolmates of the same gender, peculiar activities will be imprinted on the psyche. If sex is associated with a steady partner, a different printing will be made on the circuits. Habit in this area can lead to a freedom of questing in other areas. Imprinting is essential to learning and to causing the ease of habit to replace an impossible continual doubt about what to do with every moment, stimulus, and impulse. Marriage is good to society, but society does not always return the compliment. Marriages, imprinting and all, are often miserable; perhaps because other imprints are stronger than the marriage bond.

New forms of marriage are continually being sought to allow room for the independent soul, the nuns and priests, the totally social, the powerfully polygamous, perhaps even the homosexual and the narcissistic. There is great pressure to loosen the old form of marriage to allow free rein to these elements in everyone—the bowling league, Mother's Night Out, the convention, and the suburb; preserve the marriage, as the poet says, by breaking up the home. Lewis Mumford has written that one of the deep psychological reasons for commuting is to give the couple separate lives, the husband with his secretary and business associates, the wife with the bridge club and the car pool. The panicky pretense of "togetherness" has its natural antidote in the long, crowded roads that lead from city to dormitory suburb. Other roads to circumnavigate marriage are also being travelled.

A curious argument in favour of marriage is connected with the long childhood of man and his consequent intense attachment to parents. The animal with the longest childhood is also the smartest animal. He needs this long childhood to educate himself, to play and develop; but as the result of it, he is attached to his parents in a specially intense and dependent way. Then, when he finally begins to grow up, to become an adult himself, he must turn away from parents—but toward whom? Toward someone out in the world, but who can replace the parents as an object of love? Someone over whom he can exercise power, toward whom he can be submissive, with whom he can face the darkness and the light of life. He needs a wife, or something like one. If he is still a child, hating his parents or loving them too much, which may amount to the same thing, he will seek out a maternal-paternal spouse, or someone to hate, or someone merely to take care of him on the parental model. But he may also find a new one-to-one connection, with a creature who is parent and friend, mother and helper, someone who completes him and, most of all, pleases him.

There is a finality about conventional marriage that challenges some and distresses many. The only next job seems to be good to wife, children, and employer and to decide whether to avoid toilet training the babies and to help your son stay out of the Army and to die full of years, good works, and insurance. The changeable, movable, disposable, available person feels cut off from possibility by marriage, and with good reason: Some possibilities are cut off. He can still have sneaky affairs, of course; but that's not the issue. He is responsible for another. The model of responsibility is set. Marriage is one of your top ten most popular means of staying in touch with someone, "eating and drinking, marrying and giving in marriage."

Happy endings, as everyone knows, are ambiguous. An author writes -30- to a story, but marriage is a series of continuations, little divorces, novel choices, disasters, and victories. Only at the end of their life together might a couple know what the first quarrels and reconciliations meant. Victories are defeats and defeats are victories and they concern Mr. and Mrs. Jack-and-Jill more than any other authority. The audience is irrelevant. Even the children—the secret has been let out—do better in one-parent houses than in unwilling marriages.

Custom rules more men than are ruled by reason, conscience, or even law; and custom—habit—begins training us for marriage as soon as we see our parents together in their own special arrangement. A little rueful glance backward will demonstrate that for most of us this is bad training. We are modelling ourselves on a history of failure. We survive, more or less, but at the price of being blind animals drifting in the most important connection in our grown-up lives. He who does not understand the future is condemned to repeat the present. We can do very little about our parents, but we marry exogamously—out of the family—as if to make dramatic the declaration of free choice in finding a mate, creative inspiration in constructing a marriage. When this creation becomes habit (that is, conflict, boredom, fantasy of new chances), then the chance has been lost. Why nag when we don't want to nag? Why put up with nagging when we don't choose to put up with it? What pathos in that old joke: "Behind every successful man stands a . . . surprised woman." What misery this implies, a sense of worthlessness and hopelessness behind the bright façade of achievement.

Is that what it's all about? Wedlock, this cheerful society, as Milton described it—he was married more than once—was surely not intended to bind together mute and sour mates.

Divorce, on the other hand, seems to make a pretty good prognosis for marriage. About one marriage in three ends in divorce. Two out of three divorced persons remarry. Of these, nine out of ten of the remarried stay married. It seems as if the first divorce often stabilizes the personality, teaches a man what he really wants—in Freudian lingo, breaks the Oedipal bonds—and makes him ready for a lasting, tough-minded, grown-up marriage. . . .

Marriages of the similar both work and fail; cross-cultural and interracial marriages both fail and work, with the statistics not offering very much guidance. Marriage advice, even from serious workers and students, is often trivial (or as James Joyce would put it, quadrivial). Take as an example this comment from the May, 1967, issue of the *Journal of Marriage and the Family*: "Successful husbands and wives were reported to rarely, if ever, resort to physical attack or abuse on each other." And successful sociologists, it might be added, are reported to rarely, if ever, split infinitives.

In other works, such as J. Richard Udry's *The Social Context of Marriage*, a braver resort to conclusions and insights leads the sociologist to genuine conclusions, such as: personality matching in courtship seems to have no relation to success in marriage, interfaith marriage is not a source of trouble in America today, and children seem to have no particular power to hold together unhappy marriages. At least he is thinking, and he offers evidence to support his conclusions. Which seem to be: do your own thing, Jack. Follow your own thing, Jill.

Yeats said something like: We fall in love with a woman not for her intelligence, beauty, or virtue but because of how she pulls on her galoshes. The mysterious element in marriage (when there is a mystery: sometimes, of course, only money, desperation, or pregnancy) is the connection that this man and woman make at this time in their lives. Perhaps there are echoes of parents, perhaps a nest-building instinct overflowing at the same moment, perhaps only the mystery of charm, an attractive nuisance, the pleasures of pulling on galoshes:

> Pussy said to the Owl, "You elegant fowl,
>   How charmingly sweet you sing!
> O! let us be married; too long we have tarried;
>   But what shall we do for a ring?"

George Bernard Shaw said that it's a woman's business to get married as soon as she can and a man's to stay unmarried as long as he can. But he did not say *forever*, and there's the ambiguity in that "as long as he can." When does he quit the single life? When is too late? Henry James's story, "The Beast in the Jungle," about the couple who waited and waited, fearing some nameless monster, has a conclusion that has harrowed many readers. When the lady died and her lover visited her grave, he flung himself upon it, because all at once he knew what the beast really was—a dreary and fearful cautiousness, mortality, the inevitability of losing what is not seized when the time is right. Gregory Corso's long poem about the marriage of friends ends with a vision of himself as an old man in woolen underwear with pee stains at the fly: Many a bachelor suffers this prostatic nightmare.

Some get married because of the "Is this all?" feeling. Sex, career, chasing, gathering goods, friends—*is this all?* They think that permanence, growing together, children, a secure place in the community and in history can settle matters for them. And then at night when they can't sleep, and they stand up and look out the window into the driveway, and the house may be filled with sweet whispers of children's breath, with things, with a history shared and ongoing, and the old ghost returns. Is this all? Is this what it's about? Is this all? And marriage does not dissipate the mysteries and melancholias of the human condition. Well, yes, it alters the life of man in a decisive way, but those who have hungered for meaning have seldom found the appetite satiated by marriage. They have often thought marriage an end, but they have always sought further. Both the married and the unmarried have been desperate—and both the unhappily married and the happily married. William James suffered his "vastations"—those oceanic drownings in hope and doubt—while clinging to his wife as to the shore.

The matter-of-fact marriages in the middle of the institution are bounded on one side by scrappy adversary arrangements and on the other by excitement at the edge of a scream. A few rich interpenetrations of men and women travelling together provide the ideal for everyone, but any nostrum with marriage's percentage of failure would normally be attacked by the Better Business Bureau and banned by the Food and Drug Administration.

The flood of chance-takers and effort-makers appears every day at the license bureaus. Bankruptcies do not frighten them; they are enthralled by their prospects. In the past, men married for women's convenience, their ability to make a home and raise children, or perhaps for money or in response to social pressure, as in the arranged marriage. Then they sought excitement in other men's wives and sexual fulfillment in mistresses or prostitutes. It's only in twentieth-century America, and mostly in the last two generations, that wife and husband have been intended to do everything for each other.

Men and women can not expect everything from each other—comfort, intimacy, and a simple answer to the puzzles and dreads of human existence. Happy-ever-after is a condemnation to chagrin.

This intention in city-dwelling, rapidly moving strivers and achievers breaks down and leaves rubble. The wreckage has become visible to almost everyone.

American men and women are searching for other ways—a more traditional cool marriage or hotter forms of experimental arrangements, affairs, frank living together, communes, conjugal non-marriages. Divorce and efficient contraception are boiling among the elements of marriage along with the liberated woman, the troubled male, society's persistent conservatism, the city's explicit liberation of mores.

The situation in which we and our civilization live is atrocious. Man's fate is to be easeful and full of hopes—and to dread the inevitable. History makes few happy promises. We move in the sight of death. We all die. We talk of human life as if it is precious, and it is, but we will all die nevertheless.

Therefore we strive somehow to make permanent, to make life stay, to keep alive despite our inevitable failure at that ambition. The ways we do this: by work, by monuments, by history. For most of us, only children are a sure record of what we were and what we might have been. No wonder that we go on, despite wars and the fear of the apocalypse, with the intention to have children. And what matter that so few marriages "work"? Marriage is not a business like any other. Human life does not "work," either. And yet we are driven to continue; we live and die, marry and burn. The old man in Shaw's *Misalliance*, on his knees proposing to a piquant young creature, has more than pathos in his voice when he asks: "Will you be my widow?" There is a secret subtext of optimism and hope: *Something will live after me.* Join me now fleetly, he argues, and join me to the future forever.

Immortality mattered less to him, Dylan Thomas said, than the deaths of his friends. He meant a generous thought, but he also meant that there is no immortality. Well, almost none, but the flesh lives on, along with the spirit, in the persistence of history and in the hostages to fortune that are embedded in the turbulence and calm of marriage.

SEX ROLES AND SURVIVAL

Margaret Schmid

Recently there has been a tendency on the part of some women to try to prove that there have been periods (or at least a period) in history in which women were superior and dominant in a society. If such a contention could be documented satisfactorily, this would be lovely, although largely irrelevant to present realities; however, the attempts which I have seen thus far have all failed to present a case convincing to anyone but the previously-converted. It seems important to point out that proof of the existence of female dominance in the historical past is in no way essential to the demands for female liberation in the present. As I will argue presently, it seems to me that it is the economic system in a society and the conditions of work and control over the environment afforded by it that are crucial to the question of the possibilities of female liberation.

Basically, I suggest the following analysis. In a primitive, subsistence-level society, the difference in physical strength and mobility stemming from the physiological sex differences in reproductive functions have significant implications for social survival. Such a society has no efficient means of birth-control, and therefore the women spend most of their adult lives pregnant and/or nursing. Both of these activities limit the mobility of the woman; both of them tax her strength; both of them, thus, necessarily mean that she is not physically able to do the same work as men (or perhaps women without children). There are two points of importance in this situation. First, the society needs all the children which can be produced in order to insure group survival. Thus, the child-bearing function of women is essential and must be protected and encouraged even though it lessens woman's productive capabilities in other areas (she could work harder, travel farther, etc., were she not a mother). Second, since the physical environment is harsh and threatens group extinction, it is important that work be done in the most efficient way possible. This means that the relative weakness and immobility of women must be taken into account in the division of labor. Given the fact that there are others (men) who are available and not similarly encumbered by motherhood, women are therefore not given the tasks of doing the hunting, fishing, fighting, etc., for the group. The initial physiological difference between the sexes thus becomes institutionalized as the basis for the division of labor.

Given the crucial nature of both maximum childbearing and efficiency in the division of labor for the survival of primitive society, it follows that the relative weakness and lack of mobility entailed by motherhood and the resultant differences in work allocated to men and to women must be taken into account by the group in such matters as child-rearing practices. Boy children must be raised so as to encourage them to undertake tasks requiring great strength and mobility, and also to motivate them to protect and encourage women in their function as mothers. Girl children must be raised to be satisfied with functioning as a mother, and not to aspire to the strength and mobility of a man. Thus girls are raised to exhibit, as women, those characteristics expected/demanded of women by her society. Boys are similarly raised to become "men" as socially defined. Human potential for other paths of development is irrelevant.

At some point in the development of societies, a level of technological development is reached such that physical strength and physical mobility are no longer crucial to one's ability to perform in most jobs; mechanical extensions of the body supply the brute strength and mobility. Similarly, technological control over the reproductive process is such as to free women from their previous fate of virtually continuous childbearing. At such a level, technology also assures enough societal control over the physical environment to free human groups from the rigid constraints and pressures of the physical environment. However, I suggest that, by the time that such a level is attained, the inequalities between the sexes due to physiological differences in reproductive functioning will have already become institutionalized parts of the culture. Sex differences in behavior and personality traits—sex differences which typically mean, in fact, male dominance, as the anthropological literature indicates—will have become autonomous from their original function of insuring group survival. However, the fact that they no longer perform their original function does not mean that they are functionless; instead, we find them taking on new functions. For example, sex differences in the direction of male superiority/dominance were essential underpinnings of the traditional patriarchal family systems of the East (China, India, Japan). Similar sex differences were crucial to the ancient Judaic family and religious systems. Medieval European inheritance practices could be viable only insofar as, once again, similar sex differences acquired a variety of new functions, functions no longer based on the necessity of group survival, but rather serving to perpetuate portions of the cultural superstructure.

A logical question arises at this point: once sex differences lost their original relationship to group survival and began to function to insure male dominance in a variety of ways, why didn't women assert themselves and claim equality? Here it is essential to understand that traditionally-defined sex differences continue to be perpetuated by the normal functioning of society. Child-rearing practices continue to instill sex differences; economic systems, family systems, religious systems, and legal systems embody traditionally defined sex differences and thus reinforce and perpetuate them;

cultural myths of all varieties assume traditionally defined sex differences. Thus each generation of women is raised to think of themselves as inferior and as needing male protection and guidance, while their male counterparts learn to think of themselves as dominant, aggressive, and competent. Because this is true, women's oppression will never simply fade away, but must be overcome through conscious, organized, collective struggle. . . .

WOMEN AS CHATTELS, MEN AS CHUMPS

Jean Stafford

My cup of tea has never been poured from a vessel of wrath, and the brew currently being served up by the group known colloquially as "Fem Lib" is strong enough to float a crowbar or to dye white curtains the color of Mississippi mud and to give a body the pip bad enough to call the doctor.

In this heyday of odious neologism, the belligerents have fetched up with what may be the most teratoid coinage so far: "sexism." It is difficult to get a purchase on the exact meaning of the word, but it is pejorative, make no mistake, and among the many manifestations of the activity it defines is wolf-whistling: karate is recommended for dealing with mashers (or, if you can believe it, "sexists") who go in for this sort of effrontery.

The fustian and the hollering, the deification of Simone de Beauvoir and Betty Friedan, the strident jokelessness attendant on the movement are woefully unpropitious because they obfuscate a good many justified grievances. There is no question that the same quantity of work should earn the same amount of money, nor is there any question that great numbers of women receive appreciably lower salaries than men doing the same job.

UNEQUAL OPPORTUNITY

In the Roman Catholic canon, one of the four sins crying to heaven for vengeance is that of defrauding laborers of their wage, and women, for centuries defrauded, are fully warranted in protesting this immorality. Nor is there equal opportunity for men and women; young women with credentials identical to those of coeval young men are rarely given the chance to prove their mettle—they cannot compete because they are not allowed to get as far as the starting gate. Moreover, women have a considerably slighter assurance of promotion for the same term and the same quality of service.

I am most ardently in favor of reform in all of these particulars. I am also in favor of legal abortion, and I applaud the establishment of day care centers for the children of working mothers.

On the other hand, it seems to me that if, in a good many ways, women have been treated as chattels, in a good many others, men have been treated as chumps.

I have not, for example, seen any mention in the Fem Lib screeds suggesting a revision of alimony laws; if women are to have equal privilege, they should assume equal responsibility and men should not be penalized for their half of a mistaken collaboration; they should continue to contribute to the support of their children, but they should not be obliged to pay a retainer fee for offices no longer in existence.

What the most hysterical and the most puritanical of these scolds seem to elide is that there is a difference between men and women, and no amount of legislation is going to alter that. To be *different* is not to be superior or inferior; it is not *bad luck* that women bear and nurse the children. Just as youth is not a virtue (despite maudlin arguments to the contrary) but is a condition, so gender is neither an advantage nor an affliction but is a fact.

A CERTAIN ANATOMY

Youth does, of course, mercifully pass, but anatomy is as certain as death and taxes. Rape, according to one report I have read, is regarded by the embattled women as a *political* crime.

This proposition can be entertained only if one accepts the premise that women are a social class, but the premise is too fragile to serve as a casus belli: it is wanting in history but, more, it is wanting in logic.

WHAT IT WOULD BE LIKE IF WOMEN WIN

Gloria Steinem

Any change is fearful, especially one affecting both politics and sex roles, so let me begin these utopian speculations with a fact. To break the ice.

Women don't want to exchange places with men. Male chauvinists, science-fiction writers and comedians may favor that idea for its shock value, but psychologists say it is a fantasy based on ruling-class ego and guilt. Men assume that women want to imitate them, which is just what white people assumed about blacks. An assumption so strong that it may convince the second-class group of the need to imitate, but for both women and blacks that stage has passed. Guilt produces the question: What if they could treat us as we have treated them?

That is not our goal. But we do want to change the economic system to one more based on merit. In Women's Lib Utopia, there will be free access to good jobs—and decent pay for the bad ones women have been performing all along, including housework. Increased skilled labor might lead to a four-hour workday, and higher wages would encourage further mechanization of repetitive jobs now kept alive by cheap labor.

With women as half the country's elected representatives, and a woman President once in a while, the country's *machismo* problems would be greatly reduced. The old-fashioned idea that manhood depends on violence and victory is, after all, an important part of our troubles in the streets, and in Viet Nam. I'm not saying that women leaders would eliminate violence. We are not more moral than men; we are only uncorrupted by power so far. When we do acquire power, we might turn out to have an equal impulse toward aggression. Even now, Margaret Mead believes that women fight less often but more fiercely than men, because women are not taught the rules of the war game and fight only when cornered. But for the next 50 years or so, women in politics will be very valuable by tempering the idea of manhood into something less aggressive and better suited to this crowded, post-atomic planet. Consumer protection and children's rights, for instance, might get more legislative attention.

Men will have to give up ruling-class privileges, but in return they will no longer be the only ones to support the family, get drafted, bear the strain of power and responsibility. Freud to the contrary, anatomy is not destiny, at least not for more than nine months at a time. In Israel, women are drafted, and some have gone to war. In England, more men type and run switchboards. In India and Israel, a woman rules. In Sweden, both parents take care of the children. In this country, come Utopia, men and women won't reverse roles: they will be free to choose according to individual talents and preferences.

If role reform sounds sexually unsettling, think how it will change the sexual hypocrisy we have now. No more sex arranged on the barter system, with women pretending interest, and men never sure whether they are loved for themselves or for the security few women can get any other way. (Married or not, for sexual reasons or social ones, most women still find it second nature to Uncle-Tom.) No more men who are encouraged to spend a lifetime living with inferiors: with housekeepers, or dependent creatures who are still children. No more domineering wives, emasculating women, and

"Jewish mothers," all of whom are simply human beings with all their normal ambition and drive confined to the home. No more unequal partnerships that eventually doom love and sex.

In order to produce that kind of confidence and individuality, child rearing will train according to talent. Little girls will no longer be surrounded by air-tight, self-fulfilling prophecies of natural passivity, lack of ambition and objectivity, inability to exercise power, and dexterity (so long as special aptitude for jobs requiring patience and dexterity is confined to poorly paid jobs: brain surgery is for males).

Schools and universities will help to break down traditional sex roles, even when parents will not. Half the teachers will be men, a rarity now at preschool and elementary levels: girls will not necessarily serve cookies or boys hoist up the flag. Athletic teams will be picked only by strength and skill. Sexually segregated courses like auto mechanics and home economics will be taken by boys and girls together. New courses in sexual politics will explore female subjugation as the model for political oppression, and women's history will be an academic staple, along with black history, at least until the white-male-oriented textbooks are integrated and rewritten.

As for the American child's classic problem—too much mother, too little father—that would be cured by an equalization of parental responsibility. Free nurseries, school lunches, family cafeterias built into every housing complex, service companies that will do household cleaning chores in a regular, businesslike way, and more responsibility by the entire community for the children: all these will make it possible for both mother and father to work, and to have equal leisure time with the children at home. For parents of very young children, however, a special job category, created by Government and unions, would allow such parents a shorter work day.

The revolution would not take away the option of being a housewife. A woman who prefers to be her husband's housekeeper and/or hostess would receive a percentage of his pay determined by the domestic relations courts. If divorced, she might be eligible for a pension fund, and for a job-training allowance. Or a divorce could be treated the same way that the dissolution of a business partnership is now.

If these proposals seem farfetched, consider Sweden, where most of them are already in effect. Sweden is not yet a working Women's Lib model; most of the role-reform programs began less than a decade ago, and are just beginning to take hold. But that country is so far ahead of us in recognizing the problem that Swedish statements on sex and equality sound like bulletins from the moon.

Our marriage laws, for instance, are so reactionary that Women's Lib groups want couples to take a compulsory written exam on the law, as for a driver's license, before going through with the wedding. A man has alimony and wifely debts to worry about, but a woman may lose so many of her civil rights that in the U.S. now, in important legal ways, she becomes a child again. In some states, she cannot sign credit agreements, use her maiden name, incorporate a business, or establish a legal residence of her own. Being a wife, according to most social and legal definitions, is still a 19th century thing.

Assuming, however, that these blatantly sexist laws are abolished or reformed, that job discrimination is forbidden, that parents share financial responsibility for each other and the children, and that sexual relationships become partnerships of equal adults (some pretty big assumptions), then marriage will probably go right on. Men and women are, after all, physically complementary. When society stops encouraging men to be exploiters and women to be parasites, they may turn out to be more complementary in emotion as well. Women's Lib is not trying to destroy the American family. A look at the statistics on divorce—plus the way in which old people are farmed out with strangers and young people flee the home—shows the destruction that has already been done. Liberated women are just trying to point out the disaster, and build compassionate and practical alternatives from the ruins.

What will exist is a variety of alternative life-styles. Since the population explosion dictates that childbearing be kept to a minimum, parents-and-children will be only one of many "families": couples, age groups, working groups, mixed communes, blood-related clans, class groups, creative groups. Single women will have the right to stay single without ridicule, without the attitudes now betrayed by "spinster" and "bachelor." Lesbians or homosexuals will no longer be denied legally binding marriages, complete with mutual-support agreements and inheritance rights. Paradoxically, the number of homosexuals may get smaller. With fewer overpossessive mothers and fewer fathers who hold up an impossibly cruel or perfectionist idea of manhood, boys will be less likely to be denied or reject their identity as males.

Changes that now seem small may get bigger:

Men's Lib. Men now suffer from more diseases due to stress, heart attacks, ulcers, a higher suicide rate, greater difficulty living alone, less adaptability to change and, in general, a shorter life span than women. There is some scientific evidence that what produces physical problems is not work itself, but the inability to choose which work, and how much. With women bearing half the financial responsibility, and with the idea of "masculine" jobs gone, men might well feel freer and live longer.

Religion. Protestant women are already becoming ordained ministers: radical nuns are carrying out liturgical functions that were once the exclusive property of priests: Jewish women are rewriting prayers—particularly those that Orthodox Jews recite every morning thanking God they are not female.

In the future, the church will become an area of equal participation by women. This means, of course, that organized religion will have to give up one of its great historical weapons: sexual repression. In most structured faiths, from Hinduism through Roman Catholicism, the status of women went down as the position of priests ascended. Male clergy implied, if they did not teach, that women were unclean, unworthy and sources of ungodly temptation, in order to remove them as rivals for the emotional forces of men. Full participation of women in ecclesiastical life might involve certain changes in theology, such as, for instance, a radical redefinition of sin.

Literary Problems. Revised sex roles will outdate more children's books than civil rights ever did. Only a few children had the problem of a *Little Black Sambo,* but most have the male-female stereotypes of "Dick and Jane." A boomlet of children's books about mothers who work has already begun, and liberated parents and editors are beginning to pressure for change in the textbook industry. Fiction writing will change more gradually, but romantic novels with wilting heroines and swashbuckling heroes will be reduced to historical value. Or perhaps to the sado-masochist trade. (*Marjorie Morningstar,* a romantic novel that took the '50s by storm, has already begun to seem as unreal as its '20s predecessor, *The Sheik.*) As for the literary plots that turn on forced marriages or horrific abortions, they will seem as dated as Prohibition stories. Free legal abortions and free birth control will force writers to give up pregnancy as the *deus ex machina.*

Manners and Fashion. Dress will be more androgynous, with class symbols becoming more important than sexual ones. Pro- or anti-Establishment styles may already be more vital than who is wearing them. Hardhats are just as likely to rough up antiwar girls as antiwar men in the street, and police understand that women are just as likely to be pushers or bombers. Dances haven't required that one partner lead the other for years, anyway. Chivalry will transfer itself to those who need it, or deserve respect: old people, admired people, anyone with an armload of packages. Women with normal work identities will be less likely to attach their whole sense of self to youth and appearance; thus there will be fewer nervous breakdowns when the first wrinkles appear. Lighting cigarettes and other treasured niceties will become gestures of mutual affection. "I like to be helped on with my coat," says one Women's Lib worker, "but not if it costs me $2,000 a year in salary."

For those with nostalgia for a simpler past, here is a word of comfort. Anthropologist Geoffrey Gorer studied the few peaceful human tribes and discovered one common characteristic: sex roles were not polarized. Differences of dress and occupation were at a minimum. Society, in other words, was not using sexual blackmail as a way of getting women to do cheap labor, or men to be aggressive.

Thus Women's Lib may achieve a more peaceful society on the way toward its other goals. That is why the Swedish government considers reform to bring about greater equality in the sex roles one of its most important concerns. As Prime Minister Olof Palme explained in a widely ignored speech delivered in Washington this spring: "It is *human beings* we shall emancipate. In Sweden today, if a politician should declare that the woman ought to have a different role from man's, he would be regarded as something from the Stone Age." In other words, the most radical goal of the movement is egalitarianism.

If Women's Lib wins, perhaps we all do.

Reactions

ENOUGH OF GOVERNMENT BY STREET CARNIVAL!

Spiro T. Agnew

Not long ago, I took a rather unusual step for a Vice President . . . I said something. Particularly, I said something that was predictably unpopular with the people who would like to run the country without the inconvenience of seeking public office.

I said I did not like some of the things I saw happening in this country. I criticized those who encouraged government by street carnival and suggested it was time to stop the carrousel.

It appears that by slaughtering a sacred cow I triggered a holy war. I have no regrets; I do not intend to repudiate my beliefs, recant my words, or run and hide.

What I said before, I will say again. It is time for the preponderant majority, the responsible citizens of this country, to assert *their* rights. It is time to stop dignifying the immature actions of arrogant, reckless, inexperienced elements within our society. The reason is compelling. It is simply that their tantrums are insidiously destroying the fabric of American democracy.

By accepting unbridled protest as a way of life, we have tacitly suggested that the great issues of our times are best decided by posturing and shouting matches in the streets. America today is drifting toward Plato's classic definition of a degenerating democracy . . . a democracy that permits the voice of the mob to dominate the affairs of government.

I have been lambasted for my lack of "mental and moral sensitivity." I say that any leader who does not perceive where persistent street struggles are going to lead this nation lacks mental acuity. And any leader who does not caution this nation on the danger of this direction lacks moral strength.

I believe in Constitutional dissent. I believe in the people registering their views with their elected representatives, and I commend those people who care enough about their country to involve themselves in its great issues. I believe in legal protest within the Constitutional limits of free speech, including peaceful assembly and the right of petition. But I do not believe that demonstrations, lawful or unlawful, merit my approval or even my silence where the purpose is fundamentally unsound.

It is worth remembering that our country's Founding Fathers wisely shaped a Constitutional republic, not a pure democracy. The representative government they contemplated and skillfully constructed never intended that elected officials should decide crucial questions by counting the number of bodies cavorting in the streets. They recognize that freedom cannot endure dependent upon referendum every time part of the electorate desires it.

So great is the latitude of our liberty that only a subtle line divides use from abuse. I am convinced that our preoccupation with emotional demonstration, frequently crossing the line to civil disruption and even violence, could inexorably lead us across that line forever.

There is at work today a group of self-proclaimed saviors of the American soul. Relentless in their criticism of intolerance, they themselves are intolerant of those who differ with their views. In the name of academic freedom, they destroy academic freedom. Denouncing violence, they seize and vandalize buildings of great universities. Fiercely expressing their respect for truth, they disavow the logic and discipline necessary to pursue truth.

They would have us believe that they alone know what is good for America; what is true and right and beautiful. They would have us believe that their reflexive action is superior to our reflective action; that their revealed righteousness is more effective than our reason and experience.

Think about it. Small bands of students are allowed to shut down great universities. Small groups of dissidents are allowed to shout down political candidates. Small cadres of professional protesters are allowed to jeopardize the peace efforts of the President of the United States.

It is time to question the credentials of their leaders. And, if in questioning we disturb a few people, I say it is time for them to be disturbed.

It is time for a healthy in-depth examination of policies and a constructive realignment in this country. America's pluralistic society was forged on the premise that what unites us in ideals is greater than what divides us as individuals. Our political and economic institutions were developed to enable men and ideas to compete in the marketplace on the assumption that the best would prevail. Everybody was deemed equal, and by the rules of the game they could become superior.

The rules were clear and fair: in politics, win an election; in economics, build a better mousetrap. And as time progressed, we added more referees to assure equal opportunities and provided special advantages for those who we felt had entered life's arena at a disadvantage.

The majority of Americans respect these rules . . . *and with good reason.* Historically, they have served as a bulwark to prevent totalitarianism, tyranny, and privilege . . . the Old World specters which drove generations of immigrants to American sanctuary. Pragmatically, the rules of America work. This nation and its citizens, collectively and individually, have made more social, political and economic progress than any civilization in world history.

The principles of the American system did not spring up overnight. They represent centuries of bitter struggle. Our laws and institutions are not even purely American—only our federal system bears our unique imprimatur.

We owe our values to the Judeo-Christian ethic which stresses individualism, human dignity, and a higher purpose than hedonism. We owe our laws to the political evolution of government by consent of the governed. Our nation's philosophical heritage is as diverse as its cultural background. We are a melting-pot nation that has for over two centuries distilled something new and, I believe, sacred.

Now, we have among us a glib, activist element who would tell us our values are lies; and I call them impudent, because anyone who impugns a legacy of liberty and dignity that reaches back to Moses is impudent.

It is time to stop demonstrating in the streets and start doing something constructive about our institutions. America must recognize the dangers of constant carnival. Americans must reckon with irresponsible leadership and reckless words. The mature and sensitive people of this country must realize that their freedom of protest is being exploited by avowed anarchists and communists who detest everything about this country and want to destroy it.

This is a fact. These few prey upon the good intentions of gullible men everywhere. (In the case of the Vietnam Moratorium, the objective announced by the leaders—immediate unilateral withdrawal of all our forces from Vietnam—was not only unsound but idiotic. The tragedy was that thousands who participated wanted only to show a fervent desire for peace, but were used by the political hustlers who ran the event.)

Aiding the few who seek to destroy and the many who seek to exploit is a terrifying spirit, the new face of self-righteousness. Former HEW Secretary

John Gardner described it: "Sad to say, it's fun to hate. . . . That is today's fashion. Rage and hate in a good cause. Be vicious for virtue, self-indulgent for higher purposes, dishonest in the service of a higher honesty."

This is what is happening in this nation. . . . We *are* an effete society if we let it happen here.

HISTORICAL REBELLION

Paul F. Schmidt

The current cry for "law and order" is the height of shameful hypocrisy in our nation. What this slogan really translates into is "protection for the privileged" by the brutal suppression of those who criticize a system that denies them justice. What is significant and dangerous is the way an approved mode of speech with connotations of positive values is used to mask actions that, if recognized, would be condemned. Our national life and language in the past decade has become saturated with this technique of rhetoric, from ordinary advertising to the "credibility gap" in reports on Vietnam. The manipulation of language by the phrasemaker is a symptom of a deep malaise infecting our nation. We are able to continue our economic neo-colonialism over the Third World and our suppression of blacks and radical critics within the country by the self-bewitchment of such rhetorical devices. A mask, a façade, a surface consciousness comes into being hiding a reality that few citizens could admit. The rhetoric of formal democracy* seduces the citizen into feeling he has genuine democracy while veiling an oligarchy.

In my existing I came to understand this rhetorical sleight of hand in my day by day, week by week reading of newspapers and magazines. No dramatic single experience did it. I try to expose myself to a spectrum of papers and magazines, more left than right, since the likelihood of finding unusual reports in the sixties was more common in the left: I read or scan the *New York Times*, the *Manchester Guardian* (England), *I. F. Stone's Weekly*, the *Guardian*, *Movement*, *Atlas*, the *New York Review*, *Vietnam Courier*

---

* Earlier in the chapter the author has described "formal democracy," in part writing: "What formal democracy does is create the feeling or illusion of participation in and control of political decisions responsive to the judgments of the people. In fact the people participate in a set of formalities having the outward appearance of elections, while behind these formal procedures lie autocratic controls by powerful groups."

(Hanoi), the *Southern Patriot*, the *Southern Courier*, *El Grito del Norte*, the *Catholic Worker* and various underground papers that spread across the land as the young people move about. While waiting in the doctor's or dentist's office I scan the usual U.S. magazines: *Time, Life, Look, U.S. News and World Report, Ebony*. Whenever we visit other homes I glance at a wide variety, whatever they have, from the *Wall Street Journal* to the *Peking Review*.

Each of these tries to present a description, an account, an explanation in its rhetoric involving some set of interpretive categories, sometimes as recognizable to me as the individual styles of playing of jazz musicians. Each takes hold of the flux of living, the fluidity of acting, the becoming of history, arrests it and abstracts from it, transforming the complexity of concrete history into abstract ideological forms, making the shift from an "I" to an "it," from a person into a character, a becoming of human events into objective situations that happen. Each one carves up the density of existing according to its ends. Formal democracy in the U.S. is only one instance of this categorizing of existing. Its rhetoric is that of the Declaration of Independence, the Constitution, and the Bill of Rights, carefully taught to all children in its schools; its ends are wealth and power. When its own interests are not at stake, it may abide by the genuine democracy of its rhetoric in international and internal local situations so long as these do not seriously challenge its goals. A parallel distinction needs to be made between genuine communism and the formal communism of Russia or China. The formalization of these political ways of existing arises from the abstract structuring of the concrete whose density and becoming constantly surpass and elude whatever organization is attempted. The organization of societies is inherently caught in such formalization whatever form it takes. Why is this so? Because organization requires the specification of fixed relationships among components and such specification requires description in terms of properties which yield objects, "its," in-itselfs, moulds into which people have to be placed.

In contrast, the metaphysics of my concrete finds that modes of organizing, as opposed to organization, flow from and die with the specific historical rebellings of my existing. Existing involves rebelling via rejecting which means ever new organizing within our historical living. It is now possible to understand why the legal system of our nation is so crucial to the maintenance of formal democracy since this legal system gives the codification of the rhetoric and ends for the particular political organization of our society as a democracy. But the density and becoming of concrete existing eludes organization in legal codes of abstract political organizations.

The other major way in which formal democracy maintains itself stems from the social structure of the society, in particular, from the family structure of basic human relations between man-woman-child. In order that the

legal system, which expresses the organized structure in its laws, be enforce-
able among the citizens means must be built into the system, beyond the
police, which bring into being the appropriate behavior. I say beyond the
police because the vast majority of citizens do not break the laws in any
serious manner. Our formal democracy maintains its structure by its economic control over citizens. Any worker can be fired from his job. His
human need of food, shelter, clothing and support for his family creates a
situation in which crippling economic sanctions can be introduced if he does
not acquiesce in the society. Even when he is able to work, his wages are
taxed to support the programs of the government. He pays for the arms race
and if he takes any real action against it, his job is threatened or lost.
Professional people who are self-employed are under the constant pressure
of a loss of clientele through social and economic pressure. Wives in the U.S.
have been made wholly dependent economically on husbands as are children. They accept slavery or starve. The dependence, even degradation of
women, built into the structure of our legal system has been documented in
Leo Kanowitz's fine book, *Women and the Law: The Unfinished Revolution.* Independent women who work are subject to the same economic sanctions as men only more so. Systems of tenure in civil service or educational
employment give the appearance of overcoming such economic sanctions
but anyone who challenges the system can be easily removed by a bevy of
methods from Government Investigative Committees to University Boards
of Trustees or Regents. No avowed Communist Party member is teaching in
the United States today. Red-baiting as a technique of persecution and removal is easily managed. One serious rebellion against these props of the
system of formal democracy in the U.S. has come from the so-called Hippies. They have consciously abandoned much of the system in their existing.
How do they do it?

In the winter and spring of 1967, Hippies began to arrive in New Mexico
from California. I met them at the cabin of friends, Rini Templeton and
John DePuy, sculptor and painter, who lived south of Taos on the mesa
through which the Rio Grande cuts its deep gorge. The Hippies were looking
for land on which to build new communities away from the cities. The cities,
they feel, are doomed. They contain the evils of our system in the most
blatant forms: the duplicity of moral standards, the corruption of politics,
the inhumanity of the ghettos, the brutality of police and manipulation of the
law, and the all-powerful god of money. The cities must be abandoned.
Conversations with them, surrounded by paintings and sculpture in the large
studio room, focused at once on the fundamental conditioning achieved
through economic, legal and educational structures. Their clear insight into
how the system "locks one up" by such conditioning and what they could do
to replace them showed me that they were involved in a profound challenge

to formal democracy. These were not people on some wild drug spree though many had experimented with drugs but profound, quiet, meditative beings attacking the very guts of the system. After this conversation I realized that further communication with these people was important for understanding society's reactions against them.

Several communities came into existence that spring. Further conversations attracted us to one interested in Tibetan Buddhism. Their land, midway up the mountain slope, commanded a view that called forth an inner depth parallel to this scenic visual depth. Gail and I joined this community at Lama for awhile in the summer, our days spent mixing mud and straw for adobe blocks or barking long spruce logs for vigas, talking as we worked, talking in more depth over our communal meals, catching hold of the background leading these people to New Mexico, meditating in silence together in the evening. So we participated and learned.

To go back some years, these Hippies were able to break out of the clutch of our society through the experience of drugs. Nothing less than this would have enabled the first groups to break away. Now, I believe this is no longer necessary with the existence of the communities, but some will still find that drugs give them freedom to reject the very core of their conditional being in the society. This break involves a tremendous upheaval of all that our society has systematically inculcated into them.

The reaction of society was, as expected, increased law enforcement against drugs. Police and courts must stamp out this challenge to middle-class values. But once a consciousness is awakened and expanded these repressive forces won't work. The question of genetic side effects is important and concerns the Hippies. On the other hand, some effects are taboo because they overthrow deep cultural values. Such cultural values are thought to be a part of the very core of the preservation of that social system. Thus, the use of drugs brought about an emancipation of consciousness and a real freeing of the person from the power of the police, the sanctions of the courts and deep-seated values. Once your fear of the sanctions of the system is broken, the way is open to reject the rest of its props.

Hippies were largely middle-class drop-outs from our colleges and universities. Dimly, gradually, sometimes suddenly, often at first by neglect, later by choice, they realized that their education was designed to maintain the system, and the character of that system was manifest in the hypocritical lives of their parents. "No drugs, son, but drink cocktails like us, quiet your mind and relax; live it up a little. No free love, daughter, but concealed affairs are permitted; don't murder, son, but dropping napalm is O.K.; don't be dishonest, but it's O.K. to cheat on your income tax whenever you find a loophole." College and university programs were designed to train the technicians, professionals and managers to enable the system to maintain itself, a system whose daily living contradicted its professed values: freedom, while the nation continued its internal economic enslavement of blacks, Indians, Spanish-Americans and migrant workers, and its external economic domination of Central and South America; equality, while the nation starved the poor and glutted the rich, denied opportunity and education to many; and justice, while the nation suppressed and terrorized the Black Panthers for their radical critique of American society, murdering some, jailing others under fraudulent charges. These contradictions constitute the existential hypocrisy that young Hippies saw in the lives of adults. They realized that if they remained in school they would soon be conditioned to live these hypocrisies like their parents. At the root of their parents' lives they saw the devilish drive for money and power, class privilege and prestige. So their immediate decision was to replace money and power by communal property and love. In this way the legal, educational and socio-economic props of formal democracy were abandoned.

Quite naturally, extravagant manifestations of the rejection of each of these props occurred. Drug use became an end in itself leading to life-denying anesthetization. In discussions with my friends at Lama Community, I learned of their experience with drugs and their gradual realization of the misuse leading to their abandonment when they learned how to liberate themselves through meditation. This way of liberation by meditation has an ancient tradition in Asian countries and may prove of enormous help to us in the West.

Their attack on abstract, technological, scientific thinking with its neglect of immediate concrete intuitive aesthetic feeling is well taken. Also their critique of the concept of truth as likely to generate a workship of principles and laws, and of determinate things (identifiable objects with definite properties) is highly significant. These points were expressed clearly by Hippies living in the community in Placitas and attending my class "Revolution, Race and Zen" at the University of New Mexico in the winter-spring of 1968. Their replacement of money and power by sharing and loving, seeking to meet basic human needs in the communes, required a radical simplification of living. Clothing can be reduced to durable jeans with a single change. A sleeping bag and knapsack are sufficient for one's belongings. Shelter can be reduced by sharing space, giving up beds and much other superfluous furniture. Food can be shared and quantities vastly reduced, gardens planted, high-priced, non-nutritious, purely luxury items given up. Such measures enable one to vastly reduce the money required to supply the community. Farming communities hope to achieve subsistence. Craft communities look forward to income shared by the whole commune. Within a community money is abandoned and human needs taken care of.

Love is flower power; the power to evoke feeling, to give joy, to enrich experience, absolutely harmless, quiet and beautiful, as a flower. This is a different form of power; not the power to control, coerce, manipulate and annihilate, but the power to give, to create, to enliven, to free. If you have been given a flower in your life you know this power of the beautiful. So Hippies wear flowers, give flowers, and when a garland is not freshly available, they wear beads to symbolize such flower garlands. Similarly, the beauty of music parallels the visual aesthetic of flowers. Singing, dancing, bells on clothes, remind one of this flower power. Long hair and beards are meant to reveal the natural person, his contours and qualities, just as blacks have let their hair go *au naturel*. A society like ours almost totally without loving reacts violently to the practice of such flower power love by Hippies. Our society is not at all prepared to allow the fantastic freedom of loving that lies behind the Hippy slogan of "each doing his own thing." In a society so "uptight" as ours, so enslaved by the desire to conform to whatever the proper hem length is, so neurotic about conformity that any nonconformity seems an obscenity and insanity, the Hippy way of living draws out its deepest venom.

A return visit to Lama Community in May 1969 provided me with a longer perspective. Against the ideal I have just sketched, an ideal at times achieved, I found here and in other communes some conditions that call for comment. These conditions we observed and discussed as we spaded the garden for spring planting, six of us in a row turning over the good-smelling earth from after breakfast until suppertime. The success with which communal living was achieved in eating, working, meditation and bathing left me with a strong need for periods of privacy, time to write and read, time to love, time to commune with my self. The absence of such privacy generated a rebelling against communal activities. Some did not feel this need for privacy, suggesting that it varies in different concrete lives. Another problem arises in relation to their rejection of externally enforced moral responsibility. To replace this they need to develop a shared yet internal and existential responsibility within the commune as a single organism. Transients hamper this. We also noticed that in the strenuous effort to build the commune, this goal tended to become paramount, and to achieve it the very conditioned habits of the system they had rejected insidiously came back into practice: the subservient position of women, the concern with money and the exaggerated value of property and things over persons. We left Lama wondering how these problems could be solved, for their vital existence in rebelling against American society depends upon finding some solution.

THE AGE
OF A NEW
HUMANITY

Richard G. Hatcher

THE MEANING OF BLACK POWER

Black Power, that is what I would like to talk to you about this evening. When Stokely Carmichael shouted "black power" in that Mississippi school yard, he performed a mystic function that some poet must always perform at the proper moment in history. He gave voice, he gave a name to a development in the life of black America which was happening anyway, and which needed naming so that we could talk about it and so that we could think about it. I say he named it rather than created it because the movement towards black power under other names has had a long and honorable past. If it has become the dominant tone of our emotions in the last two or three years, that is only because, like the proverbial snowball, the accretion of time and frustration has turned incipience into actuality, has made of a snowball an avalanche. I want, today, to look at these two words, "black" and "power" from the vantage point of a man who has had some connection with both words. It is beyond dispute that I am black—and I am too modest to say beautiful. It is also true that, for more than a year now, I have held a position with at least a modicum of power. It is a good time, then, at the end of the first year of my administration as Mayor of Gary to examine what "black power" has meant to me. My blackness has been the dominant fact of my life's experience, as it is the dominant fact of life of every black man in America, perhaps in the world. James Baldwin, with his usual brilliance and cogency, describes the condition in his famous essay "Stranger in the Village" in which he discusses his experience as a black man in a little Swiss village. "For this village, even were it incomparably more remote and incredibly more primitive, is the West, the West on which I have been so strangely grafted. These people cannot be, from the point of view of power, strangers anywhere in the world. They have made the modern world, in effect, even if they do not know it. The most illiterate among them is related in a way that I am not, to Dante, to Shakespeare, to Michelangelo, da Vinci, Rembrandt and Racine. A cathedral at Chartres says something to them that it cannot say to me, as indeed, with the Empire State Building, should anyone here ever see it. Out of their hymns and dances come Beethoven and Bach. Go back a few centuries, and they are in their full glory; but I am in Africa watching the conquerors arrive." . . .

And so, my experience with the word "black" is that of all black people.

Being black has made me a stranger, being black has dominated my life. I cannot, nor would I wish to reject my blackness, and so I turn what the white world has attempted to make into a handicap, precisely into its opposite. Black America is fortunate in that our culture is more than rich enough so that we can find in blackness an advantage, a source of pride, a way to end our estrangement. But there is another side to this. Even though I may find in Negritude and in black culture a way not to be so strange any longer, especially strange to myself, that is not enough. My estrangement has also included my powerlessness. I have not only been a stranger in the village but I have also been a stranger without power. There are times in history when strangers have had sufficient power to keep themselves at least supplied with the necessaries for decent living. This has been true of many who came to these shores as strangers; as, after a generation or so, the Irish and the Italians and so on. It has not been the case with black Americans. Because our strangeness has provided the others with the chief source for hewing of wood and drawing of water, because black people have had no power, because the ideology of racism has permitted white Americans to think it natural, we have been exploited and used, deprived of the minimum wherewithal for a decent life. Sometimes we have been deprived of our best brains all for the aggrandizement and enrichment of others. And that is why pride in being black is really not enough for our survival. That is why we have had increasingly to turn attention to a means of wresting from the majority, not only a new perception of our humanity, but also a new place in the nation, so that we can enforce our demands for the satisfaction of our needs.

This is nothing new. The African chief, Cinque, sought power when he led a mutiny on the slave ship, Amistad, in 1839. And Nat Turner was quite explicit when he said that the reason for his revolt was to strike terror into the hearts of the planters and thus have the power to establish a black community in the dismal swamp. L'Ouverture knew about the need for power and so did, in more recent history, such often unheeded thinkers as W.E.B. Du Bois and Paul Robeson, or for that matter, Marcus Garvey. There is nothing new in the search for power by black Americans. What is new, perhaps, is that our search has been intensified because we have combined pride in being black with that search for power; and that we have found in various stages of our experience, power shared with the majority does not seem to work. Power means, quite simply, a force strong enough so that you can get whatever it is you need. Let me recall that in the last two decades, we have tried all sorts of ways of achieving power. The Brown Decision by the United States Supreme Court concerning equal education represented an effort to use the power of the courts to win needed improvement in the lives of black children. We won that skirmish, but we have discovered almost fifteen years later that there was not enough strength in the *power* of the courts to guarantee any fundamental change in the education of black children. Legal power which helped a little, did not help enough.

Dr. Martin Luther King tried another form of power. Beginning with the Montgomery bus boycott of 1955, Dr. King tried with all of his skill and all of his dedication—indeed he gave his life for it—to use the nonviolent power of black masses to achieve their needs. An eloquent man, he said it much better than I can hope to do. In writing for *Liberation* magazine in 1959, Dr. King said, "There is more power in socially organized masses on the march than there is in guns in the hands of a desperate few. All history teaches us that, like a turbulent ocean beating great cliffs into fragments of rock, the determined movement of people incessantly demanding their rights always disintegrates the old order. This is the social lever which will force open the door to freedom. The powerful weapons are the voices, the feet and the bodies of dedicated, united people, moving without rest towards a just goal."

This too, was an expression of black power though we did not then call it such; but this form of power in and of itself we also found inadequate to meet our needs. Nine years after he had written those words Dr. King had fallen to the assassin's bullet. Nine years after he had written those words, though segregation was a little less blatant in the south, though more black people had found their way to the voting booth in the south, the bulk of black America, living in the horror of the crowded, firetrap, haunted ghettos of the north, had not advanced. This society, it would appear, was not prepared to yield easily to the needs of black America, and so the search for a lever, for an effective means of achieving power, had to go on.

And we learn something else at this point, something that was taught to us by Malcolm X and LeRoi Jones and Rap Brown and Eldridge Cleaver. We learn that when the stranger allies himself with the so-called natives, to return to Baldwin's metaphor, "It is very hard for the stranger to play anything but a secondary role." In the many struggles black Americans carried on with white people, we found all too often that well-meaning whites nevertheless conceived of us as strangers, assigned to us the role of strangers in our own struggle; and thus, well-meaning white people knew what was good for us better than we did. They knew what our feelings about things ought to be better than we did; and I say that many of these men and women were well-meaning, because history records that they worked very hard and often sacrificed a great deal for our causes. And I cannot forget that it was white Goodman and white Schwerner who died along with black Chaney in the red dirt of Mississippi. But it takes nothing away from their heroism or dedication to say that they were always, willingly or not, the natives and we were always the strangers. To stop being strangers, we have to find the road to power ourselves. Whether or not one fully accepts other aspects of the thought of Frantz Fanon, it is clear that rising black consciousness requires that we be led by our own, determine our own destiny, recognize our own needs and that white Americans have quite another task to perform, perhaps an impossible one; which is to work to cure the sickness of racism among their own people.

Efforts at achieving power in various forms combined with the rising tide of black self-confidence, then, brings us to the heart of the problem faced by Black America today, and to the heart of my own problems as a man who, as I said, has achieved some modicum of power. It is clear that pride in blackness and all that this implies, from a revival of black history and other Afro-American studies to a new appreciation of the beauty of our women, to being led on the road to a better life by black leaders, is an absolute necessity. This we are beginning to do. We have not yet, however, solved the riddle as to what lever can provide the power that we need to wrest a better way of life from the power structure within the total society.

WHAT ARE THE OPTIONS FOR BLACK AMERICANS?

We have a number of options, and I would like to discuss a few of these now, including the one about which I am most knowledgeable. One option is, of course, to leave, to return not only spiritually, but physically to the lands of our African heritage. No doubt, some will choose that solution, but it cannot be a solution for most of us. There are physical problems as to where such a massive migration would go and cultural ones stemming from our distance from African cultures. But there are also other aspects. We own a good part of these United States, not physically, but morally; and our sweat has gone to make the railroads run and to make cotton king, and our brains helped to build Washington, D.C. and make heart transplants possible, our talents have helped enrich the music, the stage and the poetry of the nation, our blood has been shed in too many wars, including the fiasco in which we are now engaged. So, we have a great investment in this nation, one that we ought not be forced to give up; and our power ought to give us our rightful share in what we have wrought. Therefore, I, for one, choose not to leave.

There is another approach. We can demand a piece of the nation for ourselves. We can demand five or six states as the territory for a black nation, or we can carve out the old ghetto in each city as our own turf. This has possibilities. It has been explored by many thinkers, both black and white, including so thoughtful a man as W.H. Ferry, Vice-President of the Center for the Study of Democratic Institutions. Ferry writes in the *Saturday Review* of June 15, 1968, "But what black town wants most, white town cannot give it. Black town wants independence and the authority to run its own affairs. It wants to recover its manhood, self-love, and to develop its

ability to conduct a self-reliant community." A successful plan for co-existence, that is, between black town and white town, to use Ferry's terms, will
not bring utopia into being in black town. Autonomous, interdependent
black town will be no better and no worse than other parts of the urban
scene. Blacks can be expected to exploit blacks, even as whites exploit
whites. It may be less demeaning to be robbed by a soul brother, but it
leaves the belly just as empty. . . .

Now, there is also the *power of violence*, in direct opposition to the kind
of power that Dr. King sought to use. I do not wish here to discuss this form
of power. Rather, I want to ask about the efficiency of the use of street
violence, about its ability to achieve results. Like it or not, violence cannot
readily be dismissed as a source of power. It is true beyond dispute that the
white section of the nation sat up and listened hard when it heard the fire
engines racing to Hough, to Watts, to Harlem and to Chicago's west side. I
am afraid that, to date, this form of power has not paid off very much. White
America talks better about what it *ought* to do, but such talk has been
around for a long time. It is hardly new. In fact, all that street violence has
produced so far is more white talk and burned out ghettos. The Kerner
Report is a nice piece of rhetoric which has not fed one black mouth. I do
not reject violence out of hand but I have yet to see how it becomes a useful
lever for power.

POLITICAL POWER FOR BLACK AMERICA

Let me turn, finally, to the kind of power that I know most about and that
is *political power* in cities of large black population. I think it is clear in the
first place that my election as Mayor of Gary has done something for Gary's
black community, insofar as its pride and sense of self are concerned. While
we may still be strangers in our village, it surely makes us feel less strange
that one of us has been chosen to head the village government. . . .

On the question of power, it becomes more and more apparent it cannot
be left at the level of parochial power. Even if it were possible to establish
the black towns that Ferry talks about, black people would not have control
over the basic economic, foreign policy or social welfare priority decisions
which would determine the welfare of black people as well as whites. Black
towns might make us feel better, and that is terribly important, so I do not
reject such ideas, but they will not make us live much better. What is true of
black power is also true of other forms of group power. Our campuses, for
example, have seen a demand for student power which has a great deal of
legitimacy. Surely, students ought to play a much larger role in the life of a
university which is their community for four or more years; but student
power will not, by itself, change the national system of priorities in which
education runs far behind spending for super weapons of destruction, in
which drafting young men for wars is more important than letting them

continue their studies beyond a bachelor degree so that they can apply their knowledge to the alleviation of human suffering. Student power, like black power, like youth power, like neighborhood power, like other forms of parochial power, can only achieve very limited gains. And so, where does this leave us? Am I rejecting the drive for black power? Am I hopelessly saying that nothing we may do can be of use? The answer is a clear and decisive "No." The drive for black power is an essential, for it will help to end our strangeness in the village and I think that to be absolutely necessary.

And so, I support all forms of black power which will help black America to define itself, to recapture its heritage, to assert its ability, to realize its most immediate demands. I don't think it's immodest on my part to say that Gary's black children will be richer and stronger human beings for the knowledge that one of their own can govern the city, for the knowledge that their mothers and fathers were able to get themselves together enough to elect one of their own and, thus, assert their dignity. Nor is it immodest to say that Gary's black community is being given, for the first time in its history, some of the attention and concern which it so richly deserves, and that the lives of black men and women will be somewhat the better for it and the city will be somewhat the greater for it.

These are among the things which black power can do and ought to do and must do. But, beyond that, if I look to the alleviation of our poverty and the improvement of our standard of life, logic compels me to place hope in the eventual coming together of the demands for power by people of many sorts. I see hope in the rising tide of student militancy if that militancy is carried, in time, from the campuses into the communities across the nation.

I see hope in the demands of Spanish speaking Americans for their share of the power. I see hope in the growing radicalism of the young who demand youth power and no longer are content to accept a dehumanized status quo. I see our only hope for a decent society in the coming together some time in the future of all these demands for partial and parochial power into a total demand for people power.

In the essay which I have already quoted, Baldwin concludes with the following: "No road whatever will lead Americans back to the simplicity of this European village, for white men still have the luxury of looking on me as a stranger. I am not really a stranger any longer for any American alive. One of the things that distinguishes Americans from other people is that no other people has ever been so deeply involved in the lives of black men and vice versa. It is precisely this black-white experience which may prove of indispensable value to us in the world we face today. This world is white no longer and it will never be white again."

That is what we hope America will realize as we achieve more and more power which our blackness demands. As we try to save ourselves, if we achieve the full potential of what black power can do, then it will be up to the rest of America, white, Spanish speaking, student, youth and so on, to join us in the establishment of the power of the people in a world in which none are strangers. If they fail, or if we fail, we may have no way left to live in this country. If they can succeed and if we can succeed, if the People can wrest control from the hands of the economic overlords and the political self-servers, the rich and the powerful, then, and only then, do we have some hope that the good society can be ours.

One of the finest black poets, Margaret Walker, ends her poem "For My People" with a kind of incantation to the future. Let me cite it here in closing, for her vision, the vision of a black woman, wrote these words more than a quarter of a century ago and they still hold true.

> Let a new earth rise, let another world be born,
> Let a bloody peace be written in the sky,
> Let a second generation full of courage issue forth,
> Let a people loving freedom come to growth
> Let a beauty full of healing and a strength of final clenching
> Be the pulsing in our spirits and our blood.
> Let the martial songs be written,
> Let the dirges disappear,
> Let a race of men now arise and take control!

"A race of men" Margaret Walker says, and I say: let us turn the promise of America into real progress; let us turn the dream into reality, for the sake of God, for the sake of man, for the sake of America, let's get ourselves together.

CONCERNING VIOLENCE

Frantz Fanon

> *Already certain minority groups do not hesitate to preach violent methods for resolving their problems and it is not by chance (so the story runs) that in consequence Negro extremists in the United States organize a militia and arm themselves.*
>
> *On the logical plane, Manicheism of the settler produces Manicheism of the native.*
>
> FRANTZ FANON

National liberation, national renaissance, the restoration of nationhood to the people, commonwealth: whatever may be the headings used or the new formulas introduced, decolonization is always a violent phenomenon. At whatever level we study it—relationships between individuals, new names for sports clubs, the human admixture at cocktail parties, in the police, on the directing boards of national or private banks—decolonization is quite simply the replacing of a certain "species" of men by another "species" of men. Without any period of transition, there is a total, complete, and absolute substitution. It is true that we could equally well stress the rise of a new nation, the setting up of a new state, its diplomatic relations, and its economic and political trends. But we have precisely chosen to speak of that kind of *tabula rasa* which characterizes at the outset all decolonization. Its unusual importance is that it constitutes, from the very first day, the minimum demands of the colonized. To tell the truth, the proof of success lies in a whole social structure being changed from the bottom up. The extraordinary importance of this change is that it is willed, called for, demanded. The need for this change exists in its crude state, impetuous and compelling, in the consciousness and in the lives of the men and women who are colonized. But the possibility of this change is equally experienced in the form of a terrifying future in the consciousness of another "species" of men and women: the colonizers.

Decolonization, which sets out to change the order of the world, is, obviously, a program of complete disorder. But it cannot come as a result of magical practices, nor of a natural shock, nor of a friendly understanding. Decolonization, as we know, is a historical process: that is to say that it cannot be understood, it cannot become intelligible nor clear to itself except in the exact measure that we can discern the movements which give it historical form and content. Decolonization is the meeting of two forces, opposed to each other by their very nature, which in fact owe their originality to that sort of substantification which results from and is nourished by the situation in the colonies. Their first encounter was marked by violence and their existence together—that is to say the exploitation of the native by the settler—was carried on by dint of a great array of bayonets and cannons. The settler and the native are old acquaintances. In fact, the settler is right when he speaks of knowing "them" well. For it is the settler who has brought the native into existence and who perpetuates his existence. The settler owes the fact of his very existence, that is to say, his property, to the colonial system.

Decolonization never takes place unnoticed, for it influences individuals and modifies them fundamentally. It transforms spectators crushed with their inessentiality into privileged actors, with the grandiose glare of history's floodlights upon them. It brings a natural rhythm into existence, introduced by new men, and with it a new language and a new humanity. Decolonization is the veritable creation of new men. But this creation owes nothing of its legitimacy to any supernatural power; the "thing" which has been colonized becomes man during the same process by which it frees itself.

In decolonization, there is therefore the need of a complete calling in question of the colonial situation. If we wish to describe it precisely, we might find it in the well-known words: "The last shall be first and the first last." Decolonization is the putting into practice of this sentence. That is why, if we try to describe it, all decolonization is successful.

The naked truth of decolonization evokes for us the searing bullets and bloodstained knives which emanate from it. For if the last shall be first, this will only come to pass after a murderous and decisive struggle between the two protagonists. That affirmed intention to place the last at the head of things, and to make them climb at a pace (too quickly, some say) the well-known steps which characterize an organized society, can only triumph if we use all means to turn the scale, including, of course, that of violence.

You do not turn any society, however primitive it may be, upside down with such a program if you have not decided from the very beginning, that is to say from the actual formulation of that program, to overcome all the obstacles that you will come across in so doing. The native who decides to put the program into practice, and to become its moving force, is ready for violence at all times. From birth it is clear to him that this narrow world, strewn with prohibitions, can only be called in question by absolute violence.

The colonial world is a world divided into compartments. It is probably unnecessary to recall the existence of native quarters and European quarters, of schools for natives and schools for Europeans; in the same way we need not recall apartheid in South Africa. Yet, if we examine closely this system of compartments, we will at least be able to reveal the lines of force it implies. The approach to the colonial world, its ordering and its geographical layout will allow us to mark out the lines on which a decolonized society will be reorganized.

The colonial world is a world cut in two. The dividing line, the frontiers are shown by barracks and police stations. In the colonies it is the policeman and the soldier who are the official, instituted go-betweens, the spokesmen of the settler and his rule of oppression. In capitalist societies the educational system, whether lay or clerical, the structure of moral reflexes handed down from father to son, the exemplary honesty of workers who are given a medal after fifty years of good and loyal service, and the affection which springs from harmonious relations and good behavior—all these aesthetic expressions of respect for the established order serve to create around the exploited person an atmosphere of submission and of inhibition which lightens the task of policing considerably. In the capitalist countries a multitude of moral teachers, counselors and "bewilderers" separate the exploited from those in power. In the colonial countries, on the contrary, the policeman and the soldier, by their immediate presence and their frequent and direct action maintain contact with the native and advise him by means of rifle butts and napalm not to budge. It is obvious here that the agents of government speak the language of pure force. The intermediary does not lighten the oppression, nor seek to hide the domination; he shows them up and puts them into practice with the clear conscience of an upholder of the peace; yet he is the bringer of violence into the home and into the mind of the native.

The zone where the natives live is not complementary to the zone inhabited by the settlers. The two zones are opposed, but not in the service of a higher unity. Obedient to the rules of pure Aristotelian logic, they both follow the principle of reciprocal exclusivity. No conciliation is possible, for of the two terms, one is superfluous. The settlers' town is a strongly built town, all made of stone and steel. It is a brightly lit town; the streets are covered with asphalt, and the garbage cans swallow all the leavings, unseen, unknown and hardly thought about. The settler's feet are never visible, except perhaps in the sea; but there you're never close enough to see them. His feet are protected by strong shoes although the streets of his town are clean and even, with no holes or stones. The settler's town is a well-fed town, an easygoing town; its belly is always full of good things. The settlers' town is a town of white people, of foreigners.

The town belonging to the colonized people, or at least the native town, the Negro village, the medina, the reservation, is a place of ill fame, peopled by men of evil repute. They are born there, it matters little where or how; they die there, it matters not where, nor how. It is a world without spaciousness; men live there on top of each other, and their huts are built one on top of the other. The native town is a hungry town, starved of bread, of meat, of shoes, of coal, of light. The native town is a crouching village, a town on its knees, a town wallowing in the mire. It is a town of niggers and dirty Arabs. The look that the native turns on the settler's town is a look of lust, a look of envy; it expresses his dreams of possession—all manner of possession: to sit at the settler's table, to sleep in the settler's bed, with his wife if possible. The colonized man is an envious man. And this the settler knows very well; when their glances meet he ascertains bitterly, always on the defensive, "They want to take our place." It is true, for there is no native who does not dream at least once a day of setting himself up in the settler's place.

This world divided into compartments, this world cut in two is inhabited by two different species. The originality of the colonial context is that economic reality, inequality, and the immense difference of ways of life never come to mask the human realities. When you examine at close quarters the colonial context, it is evident that what parcels out the world is to begin with the fact of belonging to or not belonging to a given race, a given species. In the colonies the economic substructure is also a superstructure. The cause is the consequence; you are rich because you are white, you are white because you are rich. This is why Marxist analysis should always be slightly stretched every time we have to do with the colonial problem....

WHY THE RICH
TOSS BOMBS

Nicholas von Hoffman

New York—The police had put barriers across West 11th Street, but no one who didn't have business on the block wanted to pass them. The bomb squad was sifting through the ruins of the Wilkerson townhouse for more undetonated explosives while other police were digging for human parts, hoping to scrape together enough to make a positive identification of the pieces of young bodies they'd found.

Some of the people who looked down this Greenwich Village street of expensive early 19th-century row-houses tried to explain how the people in it had come to blow themselves up. There was little to base surmises on, save that the authorities said the place was a bomb factory, that there had been an accident while the nest of young radicals was making antipersonnel explosive weapons, that they were probably connected with Weathermen, that wildly aggressive smithereen of a smashed and fractured SDS.

Some of the people looking down the street passed it off as criminal insanity: a few tried to excuse it as corkscrew idealism, a craziness come of insupportable political frustration, but none of these thoughts satisfactorily answered the question of why young, rich, educated people could be so whacked out as to move around the city of New York planting time bombs.

In the last 10 years we've grown accustomed to the credit card radical, the person who has the time and the money to bang around the country making an appearance at all the big political manifestations, but the rich revolutionary seems to be somebody new. Diana Oughton, the young woman whose remains were identified only by a print taken from the severed little finger of her right hand, came from a rich family. She went to Madeira, one of the country's most hoity-toity finishing schools. She graduated from Bryn Mawr College, and you won't find a school much better or more costly, and she died too young, a Weatherwoman, a revolutionary. She wasn't unique: many of her friends and fellow revolutionaries have the same family and financial backgrounds. When you look at the pedigrees of some of these people, it's as though the country club junior membership had been transformed into an Algerian revolutionary cell.

Such behavior by such people contradicts most of what we think about revolution. We assume that revolutionaries come from classes and groups which stand to gain by overthrowing the political system. We presume the ones who profit most from the status quo are the ones who guard it best. Now we have what appears to be a reversal, the sons and daughters of the rich seeking to overturn the present order and the poorer classes being hostile to change secured by straight force.

Moses, St. Paul, St. Francis, Lenin, Mao, Castro were revolutionaries who came from a higher social class to lead their oppressed constituencies. Many of this country's most famous social reformers were of a much higher class background than the people for whom they worked. This was as true of William Lloyd Garrison and the slaves as it was of Jane Addams and the European immigrants.

Poverty is more shocking to the rich than to a poor man who knows neither better nor other. A rich man can afford moral sensibility; he's got the resources to buy a social conscience. Guilt, fear, many things can turn a rich person into a reformer or a proponent of social change. But what turns him into a bomb thrower, a political terrorist? In the case of our rich revolutionaries, it may also be their money and their upper-class origins. They are young people who grew up accustomed to being obeyed, to having their own way. This is not your permissive psychology stuff; this is the expectation of people doing what you tell them to do because all your life you've had the money to command.

Such a disposition makes certain kinds of rich people very useful in a movement for social change. They're not used to having people say no to them the way the poor are, and so, when it happens, instead of subsiding, they get angry, they retaliate, they put starch in demoralized people.

But the rich can also be reckless, doubly so when they're young because young people think they're immortal. Rich people get reckless because they grow up protected. Their life experience has been that their family and friends will get them out of trouble. During that period in the civil rights movement when a number of rich, upper-class whites were going south as volunteers, one of the recurrent problems faced by the native blacks was their visitors' arrogant, swishing behavior. The volunteers often couldn't be brought to see that needless riling up of local sensibilities increased opposition without any commensurate political gain.

They couldn't see it because they had never had to play as underdogs:

they lacked fear and the chiseling guile which is bred into people who must operate from an inferior power position. Rich people don't cultivate stealthy wits, nor do they develop an aptitude for studying their opponents to discover a weakness because when you're born a Goliath, there's no need to learn the ways of the weak.

If you look at the short, busy biographies of some of these people, you'll see they rarely stick at any one project long. For six months they'll try community organization, then it's back to campus agitation, then building radical caucuses in labor unions, then high school organizing, then something else so that a person who's been a radical revolutionary for three years will have attempted five or six political projects.

But the studied patience of long term work is generally foreign to people reared in the habit of giving orders and having them obeyed. Contrast the absolutism of the Weathermen and Weatherwomen, their quickness in calling others sell-outs or Uncle Toms, contrast that to the compromised pragmatism of even the Black Panther Party, a political organization which makes deals, tries to win allies and keeps working at long-term programs.

While the Panthers have tried to broaden their base in the black community and win flanking support outside of it, the rich, white revolutionary terrorist has, through arrogance, absolutism and a recklessness that makes him very dangerous to be around, isolated himself until he has run out of choices; he can give up politics or become a clandestine bomb thrower.

Most radicals, even most revolutionary radicals, have no use for these angry, undisciplined incendiaries. They condemn them, as the current issue of the *Guardian*, the country's most respected radical newspaper, does by invoking Lenin: ". . . the leader of the first socialist revolution referred to advocates of individual terrorism as liberals who prefer to attack the line of least resistance rather than engage in the unromantic, long range work of mass organizing and agitation—the only genuine method by which a revolution can be carried to a successful conclusion . . . American workers are not going to be won to revolution because someone is throwing a bomb, especially if they think—even mistakenly—the bomb is being thrown at them."

Some people defend blowing up buildings as "advanced reformism," which, translated out of the revolutionary lingo, means social blackmail—do as we say or we'll detonate your corporate headquarters. In fact, it's self-indulgent anger of the upper-class person thwarted, and in this the rich revolutionary resembles his parents. This violent, military, murderous politics he's practicing here is what his elders have practiced abroad. This is the domestic application of American foreign policy tactics.

So when the rich, young revolutionists set off bombs, smash windows and attack people and justify it by saying, "We're bringing the war home," they're right in a real and ironic sense.

ON RETURNING TO AMERICA

William F. Buckley, Jr.

New York, Oct. 28—I travel with a great deal of gear, but don't go away, because herein lies a tale. Most of the gear is checked, of course, but you cannot check your typewriter (if you do, it breaks), or the two-and-one-half briefcases filled with the work you need to tackle on flight. And then your wife, if your wife is like my wife, and in most respects I most sincerely hope that you are so blessed, has her bagful of general accessories, plus also her hatbox (who knows, she might be presented, en route, to a prime minister of an Emerging Nation. Would you want her to go bareheaded?).

Anyway, we checked in at London at BOAC, only to be informed by the lady at the counter that we would be limited to one piece of handluggage each. I advised her that that was altogether impractical, even while recognizing from a certain primness in her accent, that restrictive legislation was the kind of thing she took pleasure in administering—like the clerks and school-mistresses who delight in advising you that you are guilty of transgressing a sleepy regulation.

Well, I said to the lady, why don't we call the passenger agent and see if we can work out this difficulty? So far she was willing to go, and in due course a splendid Englishman materialized, with a great deal of gold filigree on the sleeves of his jacket, who informed me that thus were the antihijacking regulations of British Security—one handbag per passenger. I said, but look, why don't you proceed to inspect our handluggage, take out the bombs, and let us go ahead and board? He replied that if every passenger arrived with as much handluggage as my wife and I had arrived with, the time necessary to check said luggage would be inordinate. I replied that in fact here we were, checking in not only one hour and one-quarter ahead of flight time, as we had been requested to do, but fifteen minutes ahead of that, surely allowing plenty of time to examine our revolutionary paraphernalia, particularly for an airline that boasts of its service? Such, said the admiral, are the regulations of British Security. Well, I said, if British Security says only one handbag per passenger, how come TWA permits as many as you can carry? The admiral sniffed his contempt at American permissiveness, ducking the question why British Security should protect only BOAC; admitting, very simply, that I was caught in the mortal coils of bureaucracy (BOAC is owned by the Queen). Well, said I, I guess the free market has the only answer to the impasse: and my wife and I crossed the hall and booked out on TWA, leaving at the same hour arriving in New York at the same time, with *all* our handluggage, leaving a couple of empty seats at BOAC, mute testimony to the bureaucratic fidelity of the admiral and his ladies, who are incapable of coping with more than one handbag per passenger.

How does TWA manage? Sloppily? Indifferent to potential hijackers? Hardly. Struggling with our clutter, my wife and I came to the security assembly line, where our bags were carefully examined, one by one, without any consternation at all over the fact of our six pieces. TWA is less easily discomposed than BOAC by passengers' peculiarities. Does this suggest carelessness? Not at all. We were, each of us, required to walk through a metal-spotting device, and, however innocent, I must confess to being a most spectacular mechanical failure. I was led back through the X-Ray arcade *four* times, having successively surrendered, in search of the culprit, a) a hotel key, b) my wristwatch, c) a ball-point pen, and finally d)—triumphantly, because now the alarm did not go off—a miniature pack of pana-tella cigars, enclosed in an alarm-ringing aluminum case.

I muse, as I peck away, on my engagement last night at Cambridge University, where the eminent Professor John Kenneth Galbraith and I debated publicly the question, "Resolved, the marketplace is a snare and a delusion." I thought of that, when I considered how satisfying the market just now proved to be, permitting me my modest protest against bureaucracy, by traversing the short distance between the check-in counter of BOAC and TWA. How reassuring, in one's own little way, to be able to take advantage of the choices that competition makes available to us.

INAUGURAL ADDRESS

John F. Kennedy

We observe today not a victory of party but a celebration of freedom—symbolizing an end as well as a beginning—signifying renewal as well as change. For I have sworn before you and Almighty God the same solemn oath our forebears prescribed nearly a century and three-quarters ago.

The world is very different now. For man holds in his mortal hands the power to abolish all forms of human poverty and all forms of human life. And yet the same revolutionary beliefs for which our forebears fought are still at issue around the globe—the belief that the rights of man come not from the generosity of the state but from the hand of God.

We dare not forget today that we are the heirs of that first revolution. Let the word go forth from this time and place, to friend and foe alike, that the torch has been passed to a new generation of Americans—born in this century, tempered by war, disciplined by a hard and bitter peace, proud of our ancient heritage—and unwilling to witness or permit the slow undoing of those human rights to which this nation has always been committed, and to which we are committed today at home and around the world.

Let every nation know, whether it wishes us well or ill, that we shall pay any price, bear any burden, meet any hardship, support any friend, oppose any foe to assure the survival and the success of liberty.

This much we pledge—and more.

To those old allies whose cultural and spiritual origins we share, we pledge the loyalty of faithful friends. United, there is little we cannot do in a host of new cooperative ventures. Divided, there is little we can do—for we dare not meet a powerful challenge at odds and split asunder.

To those new states whom we welcome to the ranks of the free, we pledge our word that one form of colonial control shall not have passed away merely to be replaced by a far more iron tyranny. We shall not always expect to find them supporting our view. But we shall always hope to find them strongly supporting their own freedom—and to remember that, in the past, those who foolishly sought power by riding the back of the tiger ended up inside.

To those peoples in the huts and villages of half the globe struggling to break the bonds of mass misery, we pledge our best efforts to help them help themselves, for whatever period is required—not because the Communists may be doing it, not because we seek their votes, but because it is right. If a free society cannot help the many who are poor, it cannot save the few who are rich.

To our sister republics south of our border, we offer a special pledge—to convert our good words into good deeds—in a new alliance for progress—to assist free men and free governments in casting off the chains of poverty. But this peaceful revolution of hope cannot become the prey of hostile powers. Let all our neighbors know that we shall join with them to oppose aggression or subversion anywhere in the Americas. And let every other power know that this hemisphere intends to remain the master of its own house.

To that world assembly of sovereign states, the United Nations, our last best hope in an age where the instruments of war have far outpaced the instruments of peace, we renew our pledge of support—to prevent it from becoming merely a forum for invective—to strengthen its shield of the new and the weak—and to enlarge the area in which its writ may run.

Finally, to those nations who would make themselves our adversary, we offer not a pledge but a request: that both sides begin anew the quest for peace, before the dark powers of destruction unleashed by science engulf all humanity in planned or accidental self-destruction.

We dare not tempt them with weakness. For only when our arms are sufficient beyond doubt can we be certain beyond doubt that they will never be employed.

But neither can two great and powerful groups of nations take comfort from our present course—both sides overburdened by the cost of modern weapons, both rightly alarmed by the steady spread of the deadly atom, yet both racing to alter that uncertain balance of terror that stays the hand of mankind's final war.

So let us begin anew, remembering on both sides that civility is not a sign of weakness, and sincerity is always subject to proof. Let us never negotiate out of fear, but let us never fear to negotiate.

Let both sides explore what problems unite us instead of belaboring those problems which divide us.

Let both sides, for the first time, formulate serious and precise proposals for the inspection and control of arms, and bring the absolute power to destroy other nations under the absolute control of all nations.

Let both sides seek to invoke the wonders of science instead of its terrors. Together let us explore the stars, conquer the deserts, eradicate disease, tap the ocean depths and encourage the arts and commerce.

Let both sides unite to heed in all corners of the earth the command of Isaiah to "undo the heavy burdens . . . [and] let the oppressed go free."

And if a beachhead of cooperation may push back the jungle of suspicion, let both sides join in creating a new endeavor, not a new balance of power, but a new world of law, where the strong are just and the weak secure and the peace preserved.

All this will not be finished in the first one hundred days. Nor will it be finished in the first one thousand days, nor in the life of this Administration, nor even perhaps in our lifetime on this planet. But let us begin.

In your hands, my fellow citizens, more than mine, will rest the final success or failure of our course. Since this country was founded, each generation of Americans has been summoned to give testimony to its national loyalty. The graves of young Americans who answered the call to service surround the globe.

Now the trumpet summons us again—not as a call to bear arms, though arms we need—not as a call to battle, though embattled we are—but a call to bear the burden of a long twilight struggle year in and year out, "rejoicing in hope, patient in tribulation"—a struggle against the common enemies of man: tyranny, poverty, disease, and war itself.

Can we forge against these enemies a grand and global alliance, north and south, east and west, that can assure a more fruitful life for all mankind? Will you join in that historic effort?

In the long history of the world, only a few generations have been granted the role of defending freedom in its hour of maximum danger. I do not shrink from this responsibility—I welcome it. I do not believe that any of us would exchange places with any other people or any other generation. The energy, the faith, the devotion which we bring to this endeavor will light our country and all who serve it—and the glow from that fire can truly light the world.

And so, my fellow Americans: ask not what your country can do for you—ask what you can do for your country.

My fellow citizens of the world: ask not what America will do for you, but what together we can do for the freedom of man.

Finally, whether you are citizens of America or citizens of the world, ask of us here the same high standards of strength and sacrifice which we ask of you. With a good conscience our only sure reward, with history the final judge of our deeds, let us go forth to lead the land we love, asking His blessing and His help, but knowing that here on earth God's work must truly be our own.

I HAVE A DREAM

Martin Luther King, Jr.

Five score years ago, a great American, in whose symbolic shadow we stand, signed the Emancipation Proclamation. This momentous decree came as a great beacon light of hope to millions of Negro slaves who had been seared in the flames of withering injustice. It came as a joyous daybreak to end the long night of captivity.

But one hundred years later, we must face the tragic fact that the Negro is still not free. One hundred years later, the life of the Negro is still sadly crippled by the manacles of segregation and the chains of discrimination. One hundred years later, the Negro lives on a lonely island of poverty in the midst of a vast ocean of material prosperity. One hundred years later, the Negro is still languished in the corners of American society and finds himself an exile in his own land. So we have come here today to dramatize an appalling condition.

In a sense we have come to our nation's Capital to cash a check. When the architects of our republic wrote the magnificent words of the Constitution and the Declaration of Independence, they were signing a promissory note to which every American was to fall heir. This note was a promise that all men would be guaranteed the unalienable rights of life, liberty, and the pursuit of happiness.

It is obvious today that America has defaulted on this promissory note insofar as her citizens of color are concerned. Instead of honoring this sacred obligation, America has given the Negro people a bad check; a check which has come back marked "insufficient funds." But we refuse to believe that the bank of justice is bankrupt. We refuse to believe that there are insufficient funds in the great vaults of opportunity of this nation. So we have come to cash this check—a check that will give us upon demand the riches of freedom and the security of justice. We have also come to this hallowed spot to remind America of the fierce urgency of *now*. This is no time to engage in the luxury of cooling off or to take the tranquilizing drug of gradualism. *Now* is the time to make real the promises of Democracy. *Now* is the time to rise from the dark and desolate valley of segregation to the sunlit path of racial justice. *Now* is the time to open the doors of opportunity to all of God's children. *Now* is the time to lift our nation from the quicksands of racial injustice to the solid rock of brotherhood.

It would be fatal for the nation to overlook the urgency of the moment and to underestimate the determination of the Negro. This sweltering summer of the Negro's legitimate discontent will not pass until there is an invigorating autumn of freedom and equality. 1963 is not an end, but a beginning. Those who hope that the Negro needed to blow off steam and will now be content will have a rude awakening if the nation returns to business as usual. There will be neither rest nor tranquillity in America until the Negro is granted his citizenship rights. The whirlwinds of revolt will continue to shake the foundations of our nation until the bright day of justice emerges.

But there is something that I must say to my people who stand on the warm threshold which leads into the palace of justice. In the process of gaining our rightful place we must not be guilty of wrongful deeds. Let us not seek to satisfy our thirst for freedom by drinking from the cup of bitterness and hatred. We must forever conduct our struggle on the high plane of dignity and discipline. We must not allow our creative protest to degenerate into physical violence. Again and again we must rise to the majestic heights of meeting physical force with soul force. The marvelous new militancy which has engulfed the Negro community must not lead us to a distrust of all white people, for many of our white brothers, as evidenced by their presence here today, have come to realize that their destiny is tied up with our destiny and their freedom is inextricably bound to our freedom. We cannot walk alone.

And as we walk, we must make the pledge that we shall march ahead. We cannot turn back. There are those who are asking the devotees of civil rights, "When will you be satisfied?" We can never be satisfied as long as the Negro is the victim of the unspeakable horrors of police brutality. We can never be satisfied as long as our bodies, heavy with the fatigue of travel, cannot gain lodging in the motels of the highways and the hotels of the cities. We cannot be satisfied as long as the Negro's basic mobility is from a smaller ghetto to a larger one. We can never be satisfied as long as a Negro in Mississippi cannot vote and a Negro in New York believes he has nothing for which to vote. No, no, we are not satisfied, and we will not be satisfied until justice rolls down like waters and righteousness like a mighty stream.

I am not unmindful that some of you have come here out of great trials and tribulations. Some of you have come fresh from narrow jail cells. Some of you have come from areas where your quest for freedom left you battered by the storms of persecution and staggered by the winds of police brutality. You have been the veterans of creative suffering. Continue to work with the faith that unearned suffering is redemptive.

Go back to Mississippi, go back to Alabama, go back to South Carolina, go back to Georgia, go back to Louisiana, go back to the slums and ghettos of our northern cities, knowing that somehow this situation can and will be changed. Let us not wallow in the valley of despair.

I say to you today, my friends, that in spite of the difficulties and frustrations of the moment I still have a dream. It is a dream deeply rooted in the American dream.

I have a dream that one day this nation will rise up and live out the true meaning of its creed: "We hold these truths to be self-evident; that all men are created equal."

I have a dream that one day on the red hills of Georgia the sons of former slaves and the sons of former slaveowners will be able to sit down together at the table of brotherhood.

I have a dream that one day even the state of Mississippi, a desert state sweltering with the heat of injustice and oppression, will be transformed into an oasis of freedom and justice.

I have a dream that my four little children will one day live in a nation where they will not be judged by the color of their skin but by the content of their character.

I have a dream today.

I have a dream that one day the state of Alabama, whose governor's lips are presently dripping with the words of interposition and nullification, will be transformed into a situation where little black boys and black girls will be able to join hands with little white boys and white girls and walk together as sisters and brothers.

I have a dream today.

I have a dream that one day every valley shall be exalted, every hill and mountain shall be made low, the rough places will be made plain, and the crooked places will be made straight, and the glory of the Lord shall be revealed, and all flesh shall see it together.

This is our hope. This is the faith with which I return to the South. With this faith we will be able to hew out of the mountain of despair a stone of hope. With this faith we will be able to transform the jangling discords of our nation into a beautiful symphony of brotherhood. With this faith we will be able to work together, to pray together, to struggle together, to go to jail together, to stand up for freedom together, knowing that we will be free one day.

This will be the day when all of God's children will be able to sing with new meaning

> My country, 'tis of thee,
> Sweet land of liberty,
>   Of thee I sing:
> Land where my fathers died,
> Land of the pilgrims' pride,
> From every mountain-side
>   Let freedom ring.

And if America is to be a great nation this must become true. So let freedom ring from the prodigious hilltops of New Hampshire. Let freedom ring from the mighty mountains of New York. Let freedom ring from the heightening Alleghenies of Pennsylvania!

Let freedom ring from the snowcapped Rockies of Colorado!

Let freedom ring from the curvacious peaks of California!

But not only that; let freedom ring from Stone Mountain of Georgia!

Let freedom ring from Lookout Mountain of Tennessee!

Let freedom ring from every hill and molehill of Mississippi. From every mountainside, let freedom ring.

When we let freedom ring, when we let it ring from every village and every hamlet, from every state and every city, we will be able to speed up that day when all God's children, black men and white men, Jews and Gentiles, Protestants and Catholics, will be able to join hands and sing in the words of the old Negro spiritual, "Free at last! free at last! thank God almighty, we are free at last!"

III

SPEECH

INTERFERENCE, POOR RECEPTION, GROK

Which of us has known his brother? Which of us has looked into his father's heart? Which of us has not remained forever prison-pent? Which of us is not forever a stranger and alone?

O waste of loss, in the hot mazes, lost, among bright stars on this most weary unbright cinder, lost! Remembering speechlessly we seek the great forgotten language, the lost lane-end into heaven, a stone, a leaf, an unfound door. Where? When?
                              THOMAS WOLFE, *Look Homeward, Angel*

A famous scholar came to talk recently to a faculty group to celebrate the installation of a new Dean of the School of Humanities. He spent two dusty hours explaining in carefully logical words how the main point of three of the most important modern writers, Nabokov, Beckett, and Kafka, was that it is impossible for people to communicate with each other in any way, especially in words. Afterwards the audience retired to a reception where they talked about the scholar's lecture and universally praised it. And no one seemed to think the affair was an educational drama full of comic irony.

Sociologists have agreed that language defines and limits a society. Linguists have worked hard to show that words are simply sound-signs whose meanings are determined by social convention. And these linguists have done their work so well that many philosophers have decided that all metaphysical questions and answers are simply linguistic tricks, masking tautologies fostered by social needs. Written language has become the vital instrument of the production and preservation of wealth, power, and knowledge in every society, so that ours is a "paper" society in at least one sense of the word, and perhaps we are victims of a linguistic cosmos.

Now suppose that a small but recognizable group of people decides that the society in which they live prevents them from achieving a kind of self-development that is vital to their hearts and souls. What will the attitude of this group of people be toward the language of that society? Answer, "The English Language is My Enemy." Or perhaps more accurately, "Language is My Enemy." This attitude is not confined to ethnically repressed minorities; each year all kinds of grade and high school students "off" language, for whatever personal reasons. These students become interested in photography, movies, television, music, art, mental telepathy, mystical apprehension, intergalactic transmission, or any imaginable sort of communication except language. Faced with an essay on the rhetoric of persuasion in college freshman English, many of these students may read it because they are docile or habituated to such tasks, but they will not learn. They have become McLuhan's children.

Perhaps it is fortunate for society that McLuhan's children are a minority group. All of the records of beauty and the divine in our civilization are somehow dependent on language. Even a trip to the moon is unthinkable without languages, both natural and artificial. And no society can long survive without a lively and growing language. So, many essays included here recognize this debt, and the section called "Speech" acknowledges the principal gods of this paper world.

But McLuhan's children are real and effective. They are the cameramen of tomorrow's newspapers and TV shows, and the directors of tomorrow's dramas, guerilla and otherwise. Anyone who studies language, or teaches it, would do well to keep them in mind when he discusses rhetoric, or listens to a visiting scholar.

Culture Barriers

AN APOLOGY FOR THE LIBERAL EDUCATION FRONT

George Stade

The ruins of toppling societies and selves are swept by that panic sociologists call "anomie." It is the adult and communal version of the startle syndrome that jerks through a baby when it is left hanging in air by the sudden removal of a Behaviorist's arms. Anomic terror leads to mass hysteria, to hopes and fears of universal conflagration. These express themselves in capricious violence and messianic politics. The Four Horsemen of the Apocalypse ride through our smoke-filled and crackling imaginations in the shape of ecological disruption, overpopulation, thermonuclear war, and Women's Liberation. And for us the old fear of death is not mitigated by the old consolation of immortality, either in the dreams of religion or in the continuity of natural process or in the honor of one's descendants or in the survival of one's works, deeds, sayings. Alles seems kaput, or about to be.

So it has come about, that for a man of advanced views, no institution, no custom, no habit, no practice, no ceremony, no courtesy, no rite, no authority, no sanction, no taboo, no law, no rule, no value, no norm, no standard, no form, no piety, no ideal, no belief, no myth, no ethic, no aspiration, no role, no occupation, no goal, no style, no fashion, no taste; not the consolations of religion or philosophy; not the findings or procedure or worth of any science; not the family, not marriage, not the relations between husband and wife, parent and child, willing female and able male; not the sinfulness of the

195

seven deadly sins or the virtue of the seven deadly virtues; not the leftness of the Left or the rightness of the white; not the plausibility of truth, not the benevolence of the good, not the attractiveness of beauty, not the legitimacy of justice, not the advantages of freedom, not the relevance of peace, not the craziness of the insane, not the dignity of labor, nor the sanctity of the home, nor the hardness of matter, nor the remembrance of things past, nor the law of diminishing returns, not even the American way of life, not even the existence of a doubter behind the doubts—not nothing, not a thing, nowhere, nohow, is self-evident, self-validating, self-vindicating, to be taken for granted or on trust.

All this makes going to college something like tying your shoelace on the way down after you have already tripped on it into the abyss. For the initial function of a liberal arts college, as distinct from vocational schools, is to make more heady the vertigo of relativity and to multiply uncertainty principles. Its final function is something else, but something equally subversive of whatever pieties bind together the society in which the student happens to live. A liberal education is liberal because it liberates. It liberates in a student all that he believes makes him only himself from what he comes to believe makes him only a member of society. That society is therefore likely to consider him a menace or traitor and to consider his teachers, the midwives of his liberation, corruptors of the young. Out of such considerations, Athenian society put to death Socrates, who thought of himself as a midwife to the truth and who invented liberal education.

Socrates' motto was "know thyself." His operating assumption was that knowledge will make you free. His perspective on things, including himself, was ironic. His method for promoting the ironic perspective, for getting students to know themselves, and for making them free was dialectic. Dialectic works like this: Somebody begins with an assertion. The assertion will at best contain a partial truth because [it is] based either on rumor or on a single point of view emerging out of a singular body of experiences. A second participant then comes forth with a counter-assertion or a qualification or an addition based on the prejudices that *his* singular experiences have formed in *him*. If there is an educated man, say a professor, around he will counter-assert, qualify, and add not only on the basis of prejudices emerging out of his experiences but also on the basis of prejudices emerging out of the points of view and experience that constitute his learning. After a long process during which assertions are knocked smooth against each other, measured against whatever points of view and bodies of experience are available, and patched up, joined, or discarded accordingly, our dialecticians will wind up with either enlightened doubt or a coherent system of prejudice—of interconnected concepts, data, and ideas. This system of prejudice they will call truth. But they will do so ironically, aware that there are points of view and bodies of knowledge still not heard from.

A college student whose need to hug his own prejudices is less than pathological will be promiscuous about entering into dialectical relationships with whatever systems of concept, data, and attitude successfully court his interest—be they in teachers, courses, books, disciplines, or fellow students. Ideally speaking, certain things happen to him in the course of his affair with learning. After airing them in the light of other ones for a while, he comes to recognize the color of his own prejudices. After observing for a while how the prejudices of others, the truths they live by, have arisen out of their special experiences, he comes to recognize how his own have come into being. He gets to know who he is. He gets to know that he has this attitude because he is, say, white, this opinion because his father earns thirty thousand a year, this theory because he grew up in Tenafly, N.J., this propensity because his parents came from Ireland, this belief because he is an American, and this point of view because he lives in the twentieth century. Once he knows who he is and how he got that way he will have means for turning himself into something he likes better. He can move from what the world around him compelled him to be to what he chooses to be.

Individual selves, that is, unlike social ones, are made by choice and act, not found. You make yourself through the point by point extraction of yourself from all you are that you do not want to be and through the point by point absorption into yourself of all you want to be, but are not. You solidify such a self through action. At any moment the individual self in a man is the sum of all he has chosen to do as distinct from what he has been compelled to do. You find out what you are and have been, what you want and do not want to do and be, through a series of confrontations with other people, other places, other times. The function of a liberal arts college is to confront you with the prejudices of other people from other times and places so that in the dialectics of knocking your sconce against them you can beat into it the contours of your choice. You cannot create a distinct individuality by rummaging around in your interior for the ghostly presence of the real you, your true self; it will not be there, not until infernal and angelic voices from within and without have been recognized and heard, then silenced or elected to conjure up the individuality of your longings.

Getting a liberal education so understood may involve more strain than your equilibrium can afford. It separates you from people and prejudices you have been close to for a long time, from parts of yourself. It leaves you shaking from the reverberation of supports crashing all around you. It places you against a wider perspective from which all you have been familiar with, yourself included, looks narrow and cramped. It forces you to choose when the outcome is unknowable and when the only alternative to choosing is a slide backward into anonymity. But alienation is the other side of freedom. To be alienated from something is to see it in a new light that is no longer its own but the effect of your distance from it. Alienation allows you to see a social phenomenon as separate from its own rationale. It liberates you from the suckerdom of pointless guilts, one-way allegiances, unowed obligations, from your own moral blackmail. If you have not gone through the kind of alienation from yourself that is called an identity crisis you remain what others have made you. And no matter how severe the strain involved, most people would prefer to make themselves than to be made, or had, by others.

Once the student has designed a self that hangs together better than the shreds and patches handed down to him by his upbringing, he can move on to design notions as to how prejudices in general are formed, as to how people in general become what they are and believe what they believe. He will become a practical anthropologist, which involves becoming a sociologist, psychologist, and historian as well. His new notions will themselves be prejudicial, of course, but they will be closer to usable truth, which is the sum of all possible prejudices, than the notions he began with. And because his new notions have been garnered by reflection and observation, have been stewed in the juices of his own mind, rather than force-fed into him by his upbringing, they are less likely to cause the heart-burn and biliousness of half-baked, over-ripe, or hap-hazardly mixed ideas. He will be more easy about ejecting them when he has gotten all the nourishment he needs out of them. These new notions will also lift his own prejudices out of the category of the special case—which will make it still easier for him to bear them or throw them away, depending on how he wants to exercise his mind. It will also make it easier for him to bear or shrug off the prejudices of others. He will be less likely to kill others at the instigation of his prejudices or the prompting of theirs. Self-consciousness pacifies self-righteousness.

The dialectics of a liberal education, then, frees the willing student from provincial bias, which takes gossip for truth and local color for the full spectrum of human behavior, from historical myopia, which takes the present climate of opinion for all the weather there can be, as well as from modernist panic, which drives one into new biases, novel myopias, and heavier weather. The agents through which dialectics liberates one are words —for obvious reasons; but these agents carry along side benefits that are not so obvious, benefits that justify both term papers and bull sessions, not to mention bull horns. A prejudice expressed in adequate words, words that can stand up to dialectical analysis, is already less prejudicial, less cranky. It has been adjusted to the centuries of human experience that shaped the forms, connections, distinctions, and associations of the writer's language. A writer in search of adequate words enters into a dialectical relationship with those generations; their experiences qualify and amend his prejudices at the very moment they emerge into words. Once they have emerged into words he will be able to see them and himself better; he can stand back and enter into a dialectical relationship with what he believes in and with what he is. He will then have engaged in that objectification of oneself in words that is called self-expression. He will become not only more visible or at least more audible, to himself, but to others. He will have found a voice. And that will be good for him as well as for all of us. People who do not have a voice find other ways of making a noise.

Whatever of himself a man objectifies in words, then, he releases into the world—backwards among his predecessors, who reorganize themselves into the new pattern his words weave with theirs, sideways amidst contemporaries, and forward into the future, which will flow around words that have outlasted the men who formed them. But at the same time that a man through words makes himself a greater part of the world he makes the world a greater part of himself. The proof that he has taken something in is that he can put it into his own words. And what he puts into his own words becomes easier for him to handle. Its rough surface becomes smooth and familiar to the touch. He can groom it with all the solicitude of his most intimate concerns until it surrenders up its wild and inhuman aspect—until, in fact, it begins to look like him. He can then bind it to whatever else he has already domesticated with language. He can impose a verbal and conceptual unity upon what modernism has scattered or upon what had never been together. Through the dialectics of putting himself and the world in words he wins some mastery over both.

This mastery and that unity may be no more than fictions, of course; but a fiction is better than nothing, especially when it is better for you than anything else around, including what goes for the truth. The fictions of a liberal education are better for you than the truths of modernism. A liberal education teaches you to be skeptical of not only the truths of modernism, but of your own skepticism, whereas modernism turns you into a true believer or his alter ego, a nihilist. Both the dialectics of a liberal education and the disruptions of modernism teach you that when nothing matters, everything goes; but a liberal education builds up a self sturdy enough to go its own way, whereas modernism leaves you weak in the knees or herded into a bandwagon. Both teach you that when everything is relative, nothing is relevant; but a liberal education adds that relevance is made, rather than found; it demonstrates not only how relations are drawn, but how to put yourself in the picture. Both modernism and a liberal education teach you that because nothing is absolutely true, nothing is absolutely false, that things are true or false because the needs and desires of men make them so; but whereas modernism increases your needs, a liberal education clarifies your desires, so that you can choose the truths you need, rather than the ones other people need you to desire. A proper liberal education, in sum, fits you with equipment for a full, delicate, finely attuned, continuously adjusting responsiveness to whatever situation you happen to decide you are in—but with an ironic attachment for tuning you in on all the situations that comment on your own. It should leave you loosey-goosey rather than up-tight.

Your answer to all this might be that you can get along without *that* sort of liberation, that dialectic sounds pretty much like double-talk, that all the individual selves in the world add up to nothing more than individualism, that you would not give a turd for learning, that you do not want to be a part of this world or want it to be a part of you, not as it is now, that talk about skepticism and irony is Olympian, not to mention elitist, considering the state of things, that above all you have had it with mere talk. You might add that the real problem is nothing so high-falutin as modernism, but simply that the United States is built on exploitation, repression and murder, from top to bottom, from side to side, at home and abroad.

My answer is that the alternative to the kind of liberation that comes from knowing yourself and knowing what others know and have known is slavery, bondage to the whip-masters within you and servitude to task-masters without. If you have not been liberated from such masters, you become merely a symptom of the times. The main trouble with symptoms of social disease is that they produce more symptoms. Men who have not liberated themselves cannot liberate others. In the process of trying to end exploitation, repression, and murder they increase it. Their victory means a new reign of exploiters, repressers, and murderers.

In any case, the liberal education front cannot on its own accomplish anything, let alone transform the world. It cannot even teach anything. It can only make it possible for you to learn. What you learn is that if a liberal education leaves you with nothing but yourself, that ought to do for a starter.

THE SHIT
HITS THE FAN

James S. Kunen

Columbia used to be called King's College. They changed the name in 1784 because they wanted to be patriotic and *Columbia* means *America*. This week we've been finding out what America means.

Every morning now when I wake up I have to run through the whole thing in my mind. I have to do that because I wake up in a familiar place that isn't what it was. I wake up and I see blue coats and brass buttons all over the campus. ("Brass buttons, blue coat, can't catch a nanny goat" goes the Harlem nursery rhyme.) I start to go off the campus but then remember to turn and walk two blocks uptown to get to the only open gate. There I squeeze through the three-foot "out" opening in the police barricade, and I feel for my wallet to be sure I've got the two I.D.'s necessary to get back into my college. I stare at the cops. They stare back and see a red armband and long hair and they perhaps tap their night sticks on the barricade. They're looking at a radical leftist.

I wasn't always a radical leftist. Although not altogether straight, I'm not a hair person either, and ten days ago I was writing letters to Kokomo, Indiana, for Senator McCarthy; my principal association with the left was that I rowed port on crew. But then I got involved in this movement and one thing led to another. I am not a leader, you understand. But leaders cannot seize and occupy buildings. It takes great numbers of people to do that. I am one of those great numbers. What follows is the chronicle of a single revolutionary digit. . . .

Tuesday, April 23: Noon. At the sundial are 500 people ready to follow Mark Rudd (whom they don't particularly like because he always refers to President Kirk as "that shithead") into the Low Library administration building to demand severance from IDA, an end to gym construction, and to defy Kirk's recent edict prohibiting indoor demonstrations. There are around 100 counter-demonstrators. They are what Trustee Arthur Ochs Sulzberger's newspapers refers to as "burly white youths" or "students of considerable athletic attainment"—jocks. Various deans and other father surrogates separate the two factions. Low Library is locked. For lack of a better place to go we head for the site of the gym in Morningside Park, chanting "Gym Crow must go." I do not chant because I don't like chanting. . . .

Back at the sundial there is a large crowd. It's clear we've got something going. An offer comes from Vice-President Truman to talk with us in McMillin Theatre but Rudd, after some indecision, refuses. It seems we have the initiative and Truman just wants to get us in some room and bullshit till we all go back to sleep. Someone suggests we go sit down for awhile in Hamilton, the main college classroom building, and we go there. Sitting down turns to sitting-in, although we do not block classes. Rudd asks, "Is this a demonstration?" "Yes!" we answer, all together. "Is it indoors?" "Yes!"

An immediate demand is the release of the one student arrested at the park, Mike Smith, who might as well be named John Everyman, because nobody knows him. To reciprocate for Mike's detention, Dean Coleman is detained. . . .

Wednesday, April 24, 5:30 A.M. Someone just won't stop yelling that we've got to get up, that we're leaving, that the blacks occupying Hamilton with us have asked us to leave. I get up and leave. The column of evicted whites shuffles over to Low Library. A guy in front rams a wooden sign through the security office side doors and about 200 of us rush in. Another

150 hang around outside because the breaking glass was such a bad sound. They become the first "sundial people." Inside we rush up to Kirk's office and someone breaks the lock. I am not at all enthusiastic about this and suggest that perhaps we ought to break up all the Ming Dynasty art that's on display while we're at it. A kid turns on me and says in a really ugly way that the exit is right over there. I reply that I am staying, but that I am not a sheep and he is.

Rudd calls us all together. He looks very strained. He elicits promises from the *Spectator* reporters in the crowd not to report what he is about to say. Then he says that the blacks told us to leave Hamilton because they do not feel that we are willing to make the sacrifices they are willing to make. He says that they have carbines and grenades and that they're not leaving. I think that's really quite amazing.

We all go into Kirk's office and divide into three groups, one in each room. We expect the cops to come any moment. After an hour's discussion my room votes 29-16 to refuse to leave, to make the cops carry us out. The losing alternative is to escape through the windows and then go organize a strike. The feeling is that if we get busted, *then* there will be something to organize a strike about. The man chairing the discussion is standing on a small wooden table and I am very concerned lest he break it. We collect water in wastebaskets in case of tear gas. Some of it gets spilled and I spend my time trying to wipe it up. I don't want to leave somebody else's office all messy. . . .

Friday, April 26: I wake up at 8:55 and run to the crew bus and leave for MIT. From Cambridge I call my home in Marlboro. My mother asks me, "Are you on the side of the law-breakers in this thing?" For ten minutes we exchange mother talk and revolutionary rhetoric. She points out that neither Gandhi nor Thoreau would have asked for amnesty. I admit I haven't read them. But Gandhi had no Gandhi to read and Thoreau hadn't read Thoreau. They had to reach their own conclusions and so will I. . . .

Monday, April 29: A girl comes up to me with some paper towels. Take these, she says, so you can wipe the vaseline (slows tear-gas penetration) off your face when you're in jail. I haven't got vaseline on my face. I am thinking that vaseline is a big petroleum interest, probably makes napalm, and anyway it's too greasy. I hear over the walky-talky that Hamilton has been busted and that the sundial people are moving to Low and Fayerweather to obstruct the police. I put vaseline on my face. I also put vaseline on my hands and arms and legs above the socks and a cigarette filter in each nostril and carefully refold my plastic-bag gas mask so I'll be able to put it on quickly with the holes at the back of my head so my hair will absorb the gas and I'll be able to breathe long enough to cool the canister with a CO_2 fire extinguisher and pick it up with my asbestos gloves and throw it back at the cops. Someone tells me that he can't get busted or he'll miss his shrink again.

I take my place with seven others at the front barricade. All along the stairs our people are lined up, ready to hole up in the many lockable-from-within rooms on the three floors above me. We sing "We Shall Not Be Moved" and realize that something is ending. The cops arrive. The officer bullhorns us: "On behalf of the Trustees of Columbia University and with the authority vested in me. . . ." That's as far as he is able to get, as we answer his question and all others with our commune motto—"Up against the wall, motherfuckers." We can't hold the barricade because the doors open out and the cops simply pull the stuff out. They have to cut through ropes and hoses and it takes them fifteen minutes before they can come through. All the while they're not more than thirty feet from me, but all I can do is watch their green-helmeted heads working. I shine a light in their eyes but Tom tells me not to and he's head of the defense committee so I stop.

At 4:00 A.M. the cops come in. The eight of us sit down on the stairs (which we've made slippery with green soap and water) and lock arms. The big cop says "Don't make it hard for us or you're gonna get hurt." We do not move. We want to make it clear that the police have to step over more than chairs to get our people out. They pull us apart and carry us out, stacking us like cord wood under a tree. The press is here so we are not beaten. As I sit under the tree I can see kids looking down at us from every window in the building. We exchange the "V" sign. The police will have to ax every door to get them out of those offices. They do. Tom Hayden is out now. He yells "Keep the radio on! Peking will instruct you!" When they have sixty of us out they take us to the paddy wagons at mid-campus. I want to make them carry us, but the consensus is that it's a long, dark walk and we'll be killed if we don't cooperate, so I walk. At the paddy wagons there are at least a thousand people cheering us and chanting "Strike! Strike! Strike!" We are loaded in a wagon and the doors shut. John tells a story about how a cop grabbed the cop that grabbed him and then said "Excuse me." We all laugh raucously to show an indomitable spirit and freak out the cops outside.

We are taken to the 24th precinct to be booked. "Up against the wall," we are told. I can't get over how they really do use the term. We turn and lean on the wall with our hands high, because that's what we've seen in the movies. We are told to can that shit and sit down. Booking takes two hours. Lieutenant Dave Bender is the plainclothesman in charge. He seems sternly unhappy that college turns out people like us. He asks John if he thinks he could be a policeman and John says no; he doesn't think he's cut out for it.

We are allowed three calls each. A fat officer makes them for us and he is a really funny and good man. He is only mildly displeased when he is duped into calling Dial-a-Demonstration. He expresses interest in meeting a girl named Janice when three of us give him her number, one as his sister, one as his girl friend, and one as his ex-wife.

We go downstairs to await transportation to court. A TPF man comes in escorting Angus Davis, who was on the sixth floor of Math and refused to walk down. He has been dragged down four flights of marble stairs and kicked and clubbed all the way. A two-inch square patch of his hair has been pulled out. Ben, Outside Agitator, yells, "You're pretty brave when you've got that club." The officer comes over and dares him to say that again. He says it again. The cop kicks for Ben's groin, but Ben knows karate and blocks it. John says to the cop, "Thank you, you have just proved Ben's point." This is sufficiently subtle not to further arouse the cop, and he leaves. A caged bus takes us all the way downtown to the tombs (the court-house). The kid beside me keeps asking me what bridge is this and what building is that. Finally he recognizes something and declares that we are going to pass his grandmother's house. I am busy trying to work a cigarette butt through the window grate so that I can litter from a police bus. Arriving, we drive right into the building; a garage door clamps down behind us.

Our combs and keys are confiscated so that we won't be able to commit suicide. In the elevator to the cells a white cop tells us we look like a fine bunch of men—we ought to be put on the front lines in Vietnam. Someone says that Vietnam is here, now. As we get out I look at the black cop running the elevator for some sort of reaction. He says "Keep the faith."

He said "Keep the faith," I say, and everyone is pleased. We walk by five empty cells and then are jammed into one, thirty-four of us in a 12x15 room. We haven't slept in twenty-four hours and there isn't even space for all of us to sit down at one time.

Some of our cellmates are from Avery. They tell us how they were hand-cuffed and dragged downstairs on their stomachs. Their shirts are bloody.

After a couple of hours we start to perk up. We bang and shout until a guard comes, and then tell him that the door seems to be stuck. Someone screams "All right, all right, I'll talk." It is pointed out that you don't need tickets to get to policemen's balls. We sing folk songs and "The Star-Spangled Banner." They allowed one of us to bring in a recorder and he plays Israeli folk music.

A court officer comes and calls a name. "He left," we say. Finally he finds the right list.

We are arraigned before a judge. The Outsiders are afraid they will be held for bail, but they are released on their own recognizance, like the rest of us, except they have some form of loitering charge tacked on to the standard second-degree criminal trespassing.

Back at school I eat in a restaurant full of police. As audibly as possible I compose a poem entitled "Ode to the TPF." It extolls the beauty of rich wood billies, the sheen of handcuffs, the feel of a boot on your face.

Meeting a cellmate, I extend my hand to him and he slaps it. I have to remember that—handslaps, not shakes, in the Revolution.

Tom Hayden is in Chicago now. As an Outside Agitator, he has a lot of outsides to agitate in. Like the Lone Ranger, he didn't even wave good-bye, but quietly slipped away, taking his silver protest buttons to another beleaguered campus.

Everyone is organizing now—moderates, independent radicals, Liberated Artists, librarians. And the Yippies are trying to sue the University for evicting us from our homes which we owned by virtue of squatters' rights. You can hardly move for the leaflets here. Except at Barnard. The Barnard girls are typing their papers and getting ready to go to Yale for the weekend.

We are on strike, of course. There are "liberation classes" but the scene is essentially no more pencils, no more books.

I saw a cellist math major in Chock Full O' Nuts looking alone. Liberation classes won't help him. He is screwed. Every Revolution leaves a trail of screwed drifting in its wake.

The campus is still locked, although I think you could get in with a Raleigh coupon as an I.D. today. That's our latest issue; a liberated campus should be open. We want free access by June so we can open the summer school under our own aegis.

A particularly thick swatch of air pollution drifted by today and a lot of people thought the gym site was burning. That did not surprise me. Nothing surprises me anymore.

THE ENGLISH LANGUAGE IS MY ENEMY!

Ossie Davis

A superficial examination of Roget's Thesaurus Of The English Language reveals the following facts: the word WHITENESS has 134 synonyms; 44 of which are favorable and pleasing to contemplate, i.e. purity, cleanness, immaculateness, bright, shining, ivory, fair, blonde, stainless, clean, clear, chaste, unblemished, unsullied, innocent, honorable, upright, just, straightforward, fair, genuine, trustworthy, (a white-man colloquialism). Only ten synonyms for WHITENESS appear to me have negative implications—and these only in the mildest sense: gloss over, whitewash, gray, wan, pale, ashen, etc.

The word BLACKNESS has 120 synonyms, 60 of which are distinctly unfavorable, and none of them even mildly positive. Among the offending 60 were such words as: blot, blotch, smut, smudge, sully, begrime, soot, becloud, obscure, dingy, murky, low-toned, threatening, frowning, foreboding, forbidden, sinister, baneful, dismal, thundery, evil, wicked, malignant, deadly, unclean, dirty, unwashed, foul, etc. . . . not to mention 20 synonyms directly related to race, such as: Negro, Negress, nigger, darky, blackamoor, etc.

When you consider the fact that *thinking* itself is sub-vocal speech—in other words, one must use *words* in order to think at all—you will appreciate the enormous heritage of racial prejudgement that lies in wait for any child born into the English Language. Any teacher good or bad, white or black, Jew or Gentile, who used the English Language as a medium of communication is forced, willy-nilly, to teach the Negro child 60 ways to despise himself, and the white child 60 ways to aid and abet him in the crime.

Who speaks to me in my Mother Tongue damns me indeed! . . . the English Language—in which I cannot conceive my self as a black man without, at the same time, debasing myself . . . my enemy, with which to survive at all I must continually be at war.

Media
Messages

EDUCATION AND TECHNOLOGY

R. Buckminster Fuller

We no longer have the one-to-one velocity and frequency correspondence between stimulation and response that we had in the early formative days of the U.S.A. We now have enormous numbers of stimulations and no way to say effectively what we think about them or what we would like to do about each of them. By the time that presidential voting comes around every four years we have accumulated ten thousand unvented, world-around emanating stimulations, and usually we are no longer in the same town with the representatives that we previously elected. . . . That is one large reason why democracy is in great trouble today, because of the vacillation and compromise arising from the lack of one-to-one correspondence between stimulation and response of the electorate. The Communists and dictatorships scoff at democracy—saying it doesn't work. I am sure that democracy is inherently more powerful and capable and appropriate to man's needs than any other form of government, but it needs proper updated implementation to a one-to-one velocity correspondence in respect to each and every stimulation-and-response, and then democracy can work—magnificently.

I have talked to you about solving problems by design competence instead of by political reform. It is possible to get one-to-one correspondence of action and reaction without political revolution, warfare, and reform. I find it possible today with very short electromagnetic waves to make small reflectors by which modulated signals can be beamed. After World War II, we began to beam our TV messages from city to city. One reason television didn't get going before World War II was because of the difficulty in distributing signals over long distances from central sources on long waves or mildly short waves. We were working on coaxial cables between cities, but during the war we found new short ranges of electromagnetic frequencies. We worked practically with very much higher frequencies, very much shorter wave lengths. We found that we could beam these short waves from city to city. Television programs are brought into the small city now by beam from a few big cities and then *rebroadcast* locally to the home sets. That is the existing TV distribution pattern. My invention finds it is now possible to utilize the local TV masts in any community in a new way. Going up to, say, two hundred, three hundred, or four hundred feet and looking down on a community you see the houses individually in the middle of their respective land plots. Therefore, with a few high masts having a number of tiny massers, lassers, or reflectors, each beam aimed accurately at a specific house, the entire community could be directly "hooked up" by beams, instead of being broadcast to. This means a great energy saving, for less than 1 per cent of the omnidirectionally *broadcast* pattern ever hits a receiving antenna. The beaming makes for very sharp, clear, frequency-modulated signals.

In the beaming system, you also have a reflector at the house that picks up the signal. It corresponds directly to the one on the mast and is aimed right back to the specific beaming cup on the mast from which it is receiving. This means that with beam casting you are able to send individual messages to each of those houses. There is a direct, fixed, wireless connection, an actual direct linkage to individuals; and it works in both directions. Therefore, the receiving individual can beam back, "I don't like it." He may and can say "yes" or "no." This "yes" or "no" is the basis of a binary mathematical system, and immediately brings in the "language" of the modern electronic computers. With two-way TV, constant referendum of democracy will be manifest, and democracy will become the most practical form of industrial and space-age government by all people, for all people.

It will be possible not only for an individual to say, "I don't like it," on his two-way TV but he can also beam-dial (without having to know mathematics), "I want number so and so." It is also possible with this kind of two-way TV linkage with individuals' homes to send out many different programs simultaneously; in fact, as many as there are two-way beamed-up receiving sets and programs. It would be possible to have large central storages of documentaries—great libraries. A child could call for a special program information locally over the TV set.

With two-way TV we will develop selecting dials for the children which will not be primarily an alphabetical but a visual *species* and *chronological category* selecting device with secondary alphabetical subdivisions. The child will be able to call up any kind of information he wants about any subject and get his latest authoritative TV documentary, the production of which I have already described to you. The answers to his questions and probings will be *the best information* that man has available up to that minute in history.

All this will bring a profound change in education. We will stop training individuals to be "teachers," when all that most young girl "education" students really want to know is how they are going to earn a living in case they don't get married. Much of the educational system today is aimed at answering: "How am I going to survive? How am I going to get a job? I must earn a living." That is the priority item under which we are working all the time—the idea of *having to earn a living.* That problem of "how are we going to earn a living?" is going to go out the historical window, forever, in the next decade, and education is going to be disembarrassed of the unseen "practical" priority bogeyman. Education will then be concerned primarily with exploring to discover not only more about the universe and its history but about what the universe is trying to do, about why man is part of it, and about how can, and may man best function in universal evolution. . . .

I am trying to keep at the realities with you. Approximately total automation is coming. Men will be essential to the industrial equation but not as workers. People are going to be utterly essential as consumers—what I call *regenerative consumers,* however, not just swill pails.

The vast industrial complex undertakings and associated capital investments are today so enormous and take so long to inaugurate that they require concomitantly rapid regenerative economics to support them. The enterprise must pay off very rapidly in order to be able to refund itself and obtain the economic advantage to inaugurate solution of the next task with still higher technical advantage. In that regenerative cycle of events, the more consumers there are the more the costs are divided and the lower the individual prices. The higher the frequency of the consuming the more quickly the capital cost can be refunded, and the sooner the system is ready for the next wave of better technology. So man is essential to the industrial equation as a consumer—as a regenerative consumer, a critical consumer, a man who tasting wants to taste better and who viewing realizes what he views can be accomplished more efficiently and more interestingly. The consumer thus becomes a highly critical regenerative function, requiring an educational system that fosters the consumer's regenerative capacity and capability. . . .

Every time we educate a man, we as educators have a regenerative experience, and we ought to learn from that experience how to do it much better the next time. The more educated our population the more effective it becomes as an integral of regenerative consumer individuals. We are going to have to invest in our whole population to accelerate its consumer regeneration. We are going to be completely unemployed as muscle-working machines. *We as economic society are going to have to pay our whole population to go to school and pay it to stay at school.* That is, we are going to have to put our whole population into the educational process and get *everybody* realistically literate in many directions. Quite clearly, *the new political word* is going to be *investment*. It is not going to be *dole*, or socialism, or the idea of people hanging around in bread lines. The new popular *regenerative investment* idea is actually that of making people more familiar with the patterns of the universe, that is, with what man has learned about the universe to date, and that of getting everybody inter-communicative at ever higher levels of literacy. People are then going to stay in the education process. They are going to populate ever increasing numbers of research laboratories and universities. . . .

I would say, then, that you are faced with a future in which education is going to be number one amongst the great world industries, within which will flourish an educational machine technology that will provide tools such as the individually selected and articulated two-way TV and an intercontinentally net-worked, documentaries call-up system, operative over any home two-way TV set.

The new educational technology will probably provide also an invention of mine called the Geoscope—a large two-hundred-foot diameter (or more) lightweight geodesic sphere hung hoveringly at one hundred feet above mid-campus by approximately invisible cables from three remote masts. This giant sphere is a miniature earth. Its entire exterior and interior surfaces will be covered with closely-packed electric bulbs, each with variable intensity controls. The lighting of the bulbs is scanningly controlled through an electric computer. The number of the bulbs and their minimum distance of one hundred feet from viewing eyes, either at the center of the sphere or on the ground outside and below the sphere, will produce the visual effect and resolution of a fine-screen halftone cut or that of an excellent television tube picture. The two-hundred-foot geoscope will cost about fifteen million dollars. It will make possible communication of phenomena that are not at present communicable to man's conceptual understanding. There are many motion patterns such as those of the hands of the clock or of the solar system planets or of the molecules of gas in a pneumatic ball or of atoms or the earth's annual weather that cannot be seen or comprehended by the human eye and brain relay and are therefore inadequately comprehended and dealt with by the human mind.

The Geoscope may be illuminated to picture the earth and the motion of its complete cloud-cover history for years run off on its surface in minutes so that man may comprehend the cyclic patterning and predict. The complete census-by-census of world population history changes could be run off in minutes, giving a clear picture of the demological patterning and its clear trending. The total history of transportation and of world resource discovery, development, distribution, and redistribution could become comprehendible to the human mind, which would thus be able to forecast and plan in vastly greater magnitude than heretofore. The consequences of various world plans could be computed and projected. All world data would be dynamically viewable and picturable and relayable by radio to all the world, so that common consideration in a most educated manner of all world problems by all world people would become a practical event.

The universities are going to be wonderful places. Scholars will stay there for a long, long time—the rest of their lives—while they are developing more and more knowledge about the whole experience of man. All men will be going around the world in due process as everyday routine search and exploration, and the world experiencing patterning will be everywhere—all students from everywhere all over the world. That is all part of the new pattern that is rushing upon us. We will accelerate as rapidly into "yesterday" through archaeology as we do into "tomorrow." Archaeology both on land and under the seas will flourish equally with astronautics.

THE READING MACHINE

Morris Bishop

"I have invented a reading machine," said Professor Entwhistle, a strident energumen whose violent enthusiasms are apt to infect his colleagues with nausea or hot flashes before the eyes.

Every head in the smoking room of the Faculty Club bowed over a magazine, in an attitude of prayer. The prayer was unanswered, as usual.

"It is obvious," said Professor Entwhistle, "that the greatest waste of our civilization is the time spent in reading. We have been able to speed up practically everything to fit the modern tempo—communication, transportation, calculation. But today a man takes just as long to read a book as Dante did, or—"

"Great Caesar!" said the Professor of Amphibology, shutting his magazine with a spank.

"Or great Caesar," continued Professor Entwhistle. "So I have invented a machine. It operates by a simple arrangement of photoelectric cells, which scan a line of type at lightning speed. The operation of the photoelectric cells is synchronized with a mechanical device for turning the pages—rather ingenious. I figure that my machine can read a book of three hundred pages in ten minutes."

"Can it read French?" said the Professor of Bio-Economics, without looking up.

"It can read any language that is printed in Roman type. And by an alteration of the master pattern on which the photoelectric cells operate, it can be fitted to read Russian, or Bulgarian, or any language printed in the Cyrillic alphabet. In fact, it will do more. By simply throwing a switch, you can adapt it to read Hebrew, or Arabic, or any language that is written from right to left instead of from left to right."

"Chinese?" said the Professor of Amphibology, throwing himself into the arena. The others still studied their magazines.

"Not Chinese, as yet," said Professor Entwhistle. "Though by inserting the pages sidewise . . . Yes, I think it could be done.

"Yes, but when you say this contrivance reads, exactly what do you mean? It seems to me—"

"The light waves registered by the photoelectric cells are first converted into sound waves."

"So you can listen in to the reading of the text?"

"Not at all. The sound waves alter so fast that you hear nothing but a continuous hum. If you hear them at all. You can't, in fact, because they are on a wave length inaudible to the human ear."

"Well, it seems to me—"

"Think of the efficiency of the thing!" Professor Entwhistle was really warming up. "Think of the time saved! You assign a student a bibliography of fifty books. He runs them through the machine comfortably in a weekend. And on Monday morning he turns in a certificate from the machine. Everything has been conscientiously read!"

"Yes, but the student won't remember what he has read!"

"He doesn't remember what he reads now."

"Well, you have me there," said the Professor of Amphibology. "I confess you have me there. But it seems to me we would have to pass the machine and fail the student."

"Not at all," said Professor Entwhistle. "An accountant today does not think of doing his work by multiplication and division. Often he is unable to multiply and divide. He confides his problem to a business machine and the machine does his work for him. All the accountant has to know is how to run the machine. That is efficiency."

"Still, it seems to me that what we want to do is to transfer the contents of the book to the student's mind."

"In the mechanized age? My dear fellow! What we want is to train the student to run machines. An airplane pilot doesn't need to know the history of aerodynamics. He needs to know how to run his machine. A lawyer doesn't want to know the development of theories of Roman law. He wants to win cases, if possible by getting the right answers to logical problems. That is largely a mechanical process. It might well be possible to construct a machine. It could begin by solving simple syllogisms, you know—drawing a conclusion from a major premise and a minor premise—"

"Here, let's not get distracted. This reading machine of yours, it must *do* something, it must make some kind of record. What happens after you get the sound waves?"

"That's the beauty of it," said Professor Entwhistle. "The sound waves are converted into light waves, of a different character from the original light waves, and these are communicated to an automatic typewriter, working at inconceivable speed. This transforms the light impulses into legible typescript, in folders of a hundred pages each. It tosses them out the way a combine tosses out sacked wheat. Thus, everything the machine reads is preserved entire, in durable form. The only thing that remains is to file it somewhere, and for this you would need only the services of a capable filing clerk."

"Or you could read it?" persisted the Professor of Amphibology.

"Why, yes, if you wanted to, you could read it," said Professor Entwhistle.

An indigestible silence hung over the Faculty Club.

"I see where the Athletic Association has bought a pitching machine," said the Assistant Professor of Business Psychology (Retail). "Damn thing throws any curve desired, with a maximum margin of error of three centimetres over the plate. What'll they be thinking of next?"

"A batting machine, obviously," said Professor Entwhistle.

THERAPEUTIC SOAP OPERA

Paul Velde

Will grandma ever get beyond the soap opera stage? Is she doomed, with millions like her, to suffer life's heartaches with a cheerful soul? Grandma is getting old. Time is running out. So many loose ends to be tied. The old ball of yarn lays still on her lap as she ponders life's mysterious ways. "It wasn't much," she says quietly to herself; the 2:10 non-stop to Hawaii roars overhead, sending a flurry of shock waves across the screen. "Probably all a damn lie anyway." It's all in how you play the game. Some play it hard, others are a bit skittish about the messiness. Grandma played it both ways, and still she lost. All a lie. . . . (Fade.)

The Next Stage.

The young man barely conceals his glee as he tells the group he wanted to see the girl cry. She sits on the floor of the studio next to him, sobbing inaudibly, a huddle of knees and sprung nerves. It is the young man's first time in an encounter group; the girl attends regularly. Earlier in the evening, perfect strangers, the two had walked hand in hand, had taken turns leading the other with eyes shut through a maze of rooms, down unfamiliar corridors, onto an airy fire escape. Trust was exchanged. Gentle with each other, they hugged, caressed, embraced, two strangers who had come together in a session of The Theater of Encounter on New York's Upper West Side.

Betrayal between strangers? A very unlikely idea. But does a kiss on the cheek make the persons less than strangers? To the girl it obviously did, while for the young man it was just as apparent the kiss, as sensory contact, was merely an ingredient of a rather unique situation, and the impulse to make her cry another ingredient. The girl was simply under a misapprehension, taking as personal what was in fact only a matter of chance, for partners were chosen at random. But for all that, the participants were still persons, a kiss still an intimate gesture, despite the created aspect of the group. And so forth. This could go on, as no doubt it does for many veterans of the encounter situation, without ever arriving at a satisfactory conclusion. In fact, much of ordinary life is magnetized around the same poles, which leads one to think the encounter situation, if it accomplishes little else, at least helps point up the futility of such questions.

The director of The Theater of Encounter is Alec Rubin, who, not surprisingly, also does group work with actors. For Rubin, the question of meaning, whether in the group situation or outside, resolves itself in what the person actually feels. The aim is to be open to what you feel and to be able to express it in some fashion. The people who come to his sessions do so for a complex of reasons. Feelings of inadequacy probably predominate, though laced with a heady dose of idealism about the need to make human contact. And one mustn't forget a certain fascination with the clinical aspect of the sessions: the idea of being under treatment, of which Americans seem so fond, and which can mean anything from sitting under a hair-dryer to talking with one's shrink.

Yet bound up with the ability to express one's own feelings is another element which, for most people anyway, touches on the reality of events. Only then are one's experiences real, and something has to happen as a result. In the case of the young man and girl, something pretty clearly did happen that in another situation with different behavioral norms, the office say, or a cocktail party, would probably have been aborted. In this context, betrayal is only a word. For the young man to have denied his feelings or their expression might just as well have meant a betrayal of himself. Otherwise, that leaves only the feelings themselves to constitute the betrayal, which puts everybody in much the same fix—and it might be a good idea if they knew about it. What counts in the encounter situation, however, is that something happened between two people, and to a more or less degree, to the other seven members of the group.

This points to one of the major appeals of the groups, for an encounter session is pretty much what it sounds like, a small group of people getting together to make personal contact with one another. At The Theater of Encounter this involves various types of body contact and sense perception by which physical awareness is heightened. What follows then is usually a group discussion of what everybody felt, with mutual probes, punctures and the sort of close scrutiny that inevitably leads to self-incrimination. The scene between the young man and girl is fairly typical of an evening's effort. Yet compared with other groups that emphasize the release of tension and hostility, presumably on occasion dissolving into cat fights, the incident was mild and harbored, perhaps more than anything, a desire for a little excitement.

One can hardly gainsay therapy that is entertaining, or entertainment that is therapeutic. The combination is as old as the Greeks, and at the very least denotes a civilized approach to problems. And while the scripts are dogeared, taken, like the daytime serials, from the files of real life, they are not without a curious value. For one thing, it is real life society itself whose reality is suspect, a sort of wholesale lie that requires elaborate justification and consolation prizes at every turn. The zest to bring it off anymore seems pretty well exhausted. Not only is the split between experience and behavior acknowledged, but the script is xeroxed and most of us don't even get a speaking part.

Being largely a middle-class luxury concerned primarily with the problems and frustrations of that luxury, the encounter situation merely continues the lie of society at large. Given its minimal structure, it has little choice in the matter. Its customers are still obsessed with middle-class goals of happiness and security, and that most illusive thing of all, reality, which gives meaning to one's dishonesties. An artificially created situation in which a kiss may mean everything to one individual and virtually nothing to another, it is in effect a double lie. It differs from society at large only in that a choice has been made and the lie admitted. The next step must start from there, beginning, not surprisingly, with simply physical experience.

A dubious reality then is discarded for a fiction that at least has the merit of being about the people involved. The script may still be humbug, but the focus is on their own feelings and actions. And in the encounter situation at least, there is the possibility of changing the script, of experimenting, and ultimately of being responsible for what one has wrought. This is not for ordinary life, which is much too serious, where the consequences of one little household drama can run into a lifetime, and where the symbology of good and evil is only too sure of itself. In this sense, the audience has always been less free than the actors on stage. But when the audience begins to climb out of the dark security of its seats and clamor to get on stage, we know that the end of something is near.

TELEVISION
John Horn

Television is a fifth column bringing into Negro homes white nonsense, white violence, white affluence, white materialism, white indifference to fellow Americans of color. To all human beings television is a continuous assault on the heart, the mind and the spirit. To Negroes, as to all racial minorities, it is a major alienating force.

The promise of television was that of a window on the world. The reality of television today is a shop window on a world of commercial-studded frivolity created by broadcasting and advertising interests. Negroes in their ghettos look at this artificial world and see that it is white, hedonistic, violent, affluent and exploitative. The situation comedies, the game shows, the Westerns, the adventure tales, the dramas, the movies, variety, comedy, discussions and commercials—just about all the fare is aimed at the white middle class. Black viewers did not need the Kerner commission to tell them that "our nation is moving toward two societies, one black, one white—separate and unequal." Television by and large excludes Negroes. It denies them the public air waves. It tells them the great white society does not care for them. It gives them a false image of themselves.

The world of television, of course, is a false image of the white world as well, but it is a true reflection of white values. Affluent whites who have control of television employ it to their own economic ends, not for human communication. It is a deprivation of grave consequence.

There have been unusual instances when Negroes were addressed by television as Negroes and people. It was startling to hear, during local station breaks, a plea from Negro leaders to the Negro community of New York City to cool it during the Harlem riots of 1963. Startling because television is seldom used for such direct, social communication. Several years ago the program, *The Comers,* on New York City's educational Channel 13, gave a group of racially and economically diverse youngsters, mainly high school juniors and seniors, the opportunity to get to know one another by free-wheeling discussion on camera. In the process they learned and at the same time taught the television audience that we are all of us, no matter the race, creed or economic position, one community. By having freedom of microphone and camera, the youngsters learned too that the community cared. Typically the program was dropped on the pretext of insufficient funding, after the kids got into a frank discussion of sex that offended adults in the TV audience.

Such examples are rare and they exist now only as history. Every night of the week television offers the more usual sights and sounds of fiddling while civilization burns.

The prospect of changing television into a tool that would help rather than exploit America is not hopeful. The FCC has been permissive about public service. Congress has been more concerned with private broadcasters than public welfare. The most recent proposal to better American television, the still-in-prospect Public Broadcasting Corporation to aid noncommerical television, may need, according to its chairman, Frank Pace, Jr., twenty years to develop into a potent social and educational force. The slow build-up will put America where England was when it began its television system in 1936 by creating the autonomous British Broadcasting Corporation. A communication gap of fifty-two years is ludicrous for an America with crucial and urgent problems to solve now.

Was it too much to expect the Kerner commission to examine television in some depth? The commission was cautious about treading on freedom of the press in discussion of news coverage of riots. It completely overlooked the responsibility of television stations—not their news organizations but the stations themselves—to operate "in the public interest, convenience and necessity." That is how their licenses read. But television is used to amuse the whites and to move their goods. It gives no one, least of all Negroes, a sense of community or a feeling of human dignity. It is divisive. It deprives minorities, especially Negroes, of a part in the American present and future.

The frightful thing is that we have institutionalized white American prejudice by entrusting television to commercial interests which are committed to the majority (white) audience on a limited materialistic basis. We have in effect given away the instrument that could save us.

THE POST-LITERATE AGE

Marshall McLuhan

MADISON AVE

FOR RESTORING THE

MAGICAL ART

OF THE

CAVEMEN

TO

SUBURBIA

Television, in sensorial terms, takes a large leap towards reassembling all the elements of interpersonal discourse which were split apart by writing and by all the intervening artificial media. For language itself is an acoustic medium which incorporates gesture and all the various combinations of sensuous experience, in a single medium of sound. Writing was probably the greatest cultural revolution known to us because it broke down the walls between sight and sound. Writing was a visualizing of the acoustic which split off or abstracted one aspect of speech, setting up a cultural disequilibrium of great violence. The dynamism of the Western world may well proceed from the dynamics of that disequilibrium. If so, our present stage of media development suggests the possibility of a new equilibrium. Our craving today for balance and an end of ever-accelerating change, may quite possibly point to the possibility thereof. But the obvious lesson of all this development for education seems to me both simple and startling. If our new media constitute so complete a range of expressiveness as both to enhance and almost to supplant speech itself, then we have moved into the period of post-literacy. If our present means of exploring and presenting the human past are such as to make simultaneously present all kinds of human pasts, then we have moved into the period of post-history. Not that we are to be deprived of books any more than of ancient manuscripts. But it is plain that our new culture is not going to lean very heavily on any one means of encoding experience or of representing reality. Already we are accustomed to a concert of the arts, of the sensuous channels and of the media. And in this respect we shall resemble pre-literate and pre-historic societies in the inclusiveness of our awareness.

That means also that we shall tend as they did towards homogeneity both of experience and organization. Perhaps, therefore, we have in our post-literacy come to the age of the classroom without walls.

It was very hard at first for the contemporaries of Erasmus to grasp that the printed book meant that the main channel of information and discipline was no longer the spoken word or the single language. Erasmus was the first to act on the awareness that part of the new revolution would be felt in the classroom. He put the old oral scholasticism into his *Adagia* and *Similia*. The same situation confronts us. We are already experiencing the discomfort and challenge of classrooms without walls, just as the modern painter has to modify his techniques in accordance with art reproduction and museums without walls. We can decide either to move into the new wall-less classroom in order to act upon our total environment, or to look on it as the last dike holding back the media flood. Let us consider that the flow of information into the student mind (and our own as well) which was once oral, and then printed, could easily be controlled in the classroom. Today only a tiny trickle of the information flow into the student mind can be accounted for in the classroom. For every fact or attitude which the teacher can initiate or direct, the visual and auditory environment provides many thousands of facts and experiences.

FACED WITH
INFORMATION OVERLOAD,
WE HAVE NO ALTERNATIVE
BUT
PATTERN-RECOGNITION.

In a word, the cultural content approach is futile, even granting that it is preferable. To try to defend our civilization against itself by trying either to warn or to encourage the young about the surrounding chaos and vulgarity would be like the Eskimo trying to defend his culture against ours by taking a vow of silence. Our own history and our own methodology stand ready at hand to advise us in the present very dramatic climax. We must maximize rather than minimize the various features of our new media. It's easy now to see that they are not mere vehicles for already achieved experience and insight. We have moved far beyond mechanization. Let us not lose ourselves by supposing that we have merely to contend with new forms of mechanization. Radio and TV aren't new ways of handling manuscript and book culture. The motor-car wasn't a substitute for the horse. It did what the horse could never do. Radio and TV aren't audio-visual aids to enhance or to popularize previous forms of experience. They are new languages. We must first master and then teach these new languages in all their minute particularity and riches. In so doing we have available on an unprecedented scale the resources of comparison and contrast. We can compare the same play or novel or poem or news story as it's changed artistically in passing into the movie form, the stage, the radio and TV. We can note the precise qualities of each medium as we would compare the various degrees of effectiveness of a thought in Greek or French or English. This is what the young are doing sloppily and helplessly outside the classroom every day. This holds their attention automatically as the classroom does not.

In the electronic age as the media begin to dwarf nature, nature imitates art more and more. Oscar Wilde records his amazement at finding London drawing-rooms over-flowing with long-necked, pale, auburn-haired women where, before the paintings of Rossetti and Burne-Jones, such women had never been seen. Today that is normal. Every movie and every issue of Vogue breezily sets out to revamp not only our clothes but our physiology. Such is the amount of power available today that the boundaries between art and nature have disappeared. Art has substituted for nature, and various new political regimes naturally tend to act on these assumptions. We have as little doubt about our ability to control global climate as the climate of opinion.

In such an age, with such resources, the walls of the classroom disappear if only because everybody outside the classroom is consciously engaged in national and international educational campaigns. Education today is totalitarian because there is no corner of the globe or of inner experience which we are not eager to subject to scrutiny and processing. So that if the educator old-style feels that he lives in an ungrateful world, he can also consider that never before was education so much a part of commerce and politics. Perhaps it is not that the educator has been shouldered aside by men of action so much as he has been swamped by high-powered imitators. If education has now become the basic investment and activity of the electronic age, then the classroom educator can recover his role only by enlarging it beyond anything it ever was in any previous culture. We cannot hope simply to retain our old prerogatives. Our bridges are gone and the Rubicon is yet to cross! We have either to assume a large new role or to abdicate entirely. It is the age of paratroopers.

Yes, we must substitute an interest in the media for the previous interest in subjects. This is the logical answer to the fact that the media have substituted themselves for the older world. Even if we should wish to recover that older world we can do it only by an intensive study of the ways in which the media have swallowed it. And no matter how many walls have fallen, the citadel of individual consciousness has not fallen nor is it likely to fall. For it is not accessible to the mass media.

Words
Words
Words

THE CLICHÉ EXPERT
REVEALS HIMSELF
IN HIS TRUE COLORS

Frank Sullivan

Q Mr. Arbuthnot, would you mind telling us today how you happened to become a cliché expert? Was it easy?

A Easy! Don't make me laugh, Mr. Crouse. It was an uphill climb. A cliché novitiate is no bed of roses, and if anyone ever tells you it is, do you know how I want you to take his statement?

Q How?

A With a grain of salt. I shall tell you about my career, since you insist, and as a special treat, I shall describe it to you entirely in terms of the seesaw cliché.

Q The seesaw cliché?

A You'll see what I mean. Before I made my mark as a cliché expert, I had my ups and downs. Sometimes, when everything was at sixes and sevens, it almost seemed as though my dearest ambitions were going to wrack and ruin. I had moments when I was almost tempted to believe that everything was a snare and a delusion. Even my own flesh and blood discouraged me, in spite of the fact that I was their pride and joy . . . You aren't listening, Mr. Crouse.

Q Yes I am. I just closed my eyes because the light hurt. You were saying that your own kith and kin discouraged you.

223

A I didn't say kith and kin, but it doesn't matter. For a considerable period of time it was nip and tuck whether I would sink or swim. If I had not been hale and hearty, and well equipped for a rough-and-tumble struggle, I wouldn't have come through. But I kept at it, hammer and tongs. I gave 'em tit for tat . . . Mr. Crouse, you *are* asleep.

Q No, I'm not, Mr. Arbuthnot. You were saying you went after your goal hard and fast.

A I did. I eschewed wine, woman, and song—

Q Ah, but wine, woman, and song is not a seesaw cliché, Mr. Arbuthnot.

A Yes it is, too. Woman is standing in the middle, balancing. I worked morning, noon, and night, and kept to the straight and narrow. The consequence was that in the due course of time—

Q And tide?

A Please! In the due course of time things began to come my way by fits and starts, and a little later by leaps and bounds. Now, I'm fine and dandy.

Q High, wide, and handsome, eh?

A I wish I had said that, Mr. Crouse.

Q You—

A Will, Oscar. Had you there, Mr. Crouse, didn't I, ha ha! When I started I was free, white, and twenty-one. Now I'm fat, fair, and forty, and I venture to predict that no man, without regard to race, creed, or color, is a better master of the cliché than your servant—your *humble* servant— Magnus Arbuthnot. So much for my life story in terms of the seesaw cliché.

Q It certainly is an interesting story, Mr. Arbuthnot—by and large.

A Well, in all due modesty, I suppose it is, although sometimes, to tell you the truth, I think there is neither rhyme nor reason to it.

Q Where were you born, Mr. Arbuthnot?

A In the altogether.

Q I see. How?

A On the impulse of the moment.

Q And when?

A In the nick of time.

Q It is agreeable to find a man so frank about himself, Mr. Arbuthnot.

A Why not? You asked me a question. You know what kind of question it was?

Q Impertinent?

A Oh, my dear man, no.

Q Personal?

A Civil. You asked me a civil question. I answered you by telling you the truth. I gave it to you, if I may be permitted to say so, straight from the shoulder. I revealed myself to you in my—

Q True colors?

A Ah, someone told you. Rather, someone *went* and told you.

Q Were you ever in love, Mr. Arbuthnot, or am I out of order in asking that?

A Not at all. I have had my romances.

Q How nice.

A Ah, you wouldn't say so if you knew what kind of romances they were.

Q What kind were they?

A Blighted romances, all of 'em. I kept trying to combine single blessedness with wedded bliss. It didn't work. I had a sweetheart in every port, and I worshiped the ground they walked on, each and every one of them. This ground amounts to a matter of 18,467 acres, as of my latest blighted romance.

Q Hm! You must have been quite a pedestrian.

A Well, those are the figures when the tide was out; only 16,468 acres at the neap. I was land-poor at the end. And you take the advice of a sadder—

Q And a wiser man.

A That's what I was going to say. And never trust the weaker sex, or you'll have an awakening. You seem to be so smart, interrupting me all the while, maybe you can tell me what kind of awakening.

Q Awakening? Awakening? I'm afraid you have me.

A Rude awakening.

Q Oh, of course. Now, I don't think your story would be complete, Mr. Arbuthnot, without some statement from you regarding your material circumstances. Are you well-to-do, or are you—

A Hard pressed for cash? No, I'm solvent. I'm well paid.

Q You mean you get a handsome salary?

A I prefer to call it a princely stipend. You know what kind of coin I'm paid in?

Q No. What?

A Coin of the realm. Not that I give a hoot for money. You know how I refer to money?

Q As the root of all evil?

A No, but you have a talking point there. I call it lucre—filthy lucre.

Q On the whole, you seem to have a pretty good time, Mr. Arbuthnot.

A Oh, I'm not complaining. I'm as snug as a bug in a rug. I'm clear as crystal—when I'm not dull as a dishwater. I'm cool as a cucumber, quick as a flash, fresh as a daisy, pleased as Punch, good as my word, regular as clockwork, and I suppose at the end of my declining years, when I'm gathered to my ancestors, I'll be dead as a doornail.

Q *Eh bien! C'est la vie!*

A *Mais oui, mon vieux.* I manage. I'm the glass of fashion and the mold of form. I have a finger in every pie, all except this finger. I use it for pointing with scorn. When I go in for malice, it is always malice afore-thought. My nods are significant. My offers are standing. I am at cross-purposes and in dire straits. My motives are ulterior, my circles are vicious, my retainers are faithful, and my hopefuls are young. My sus-picions are sneaking, my glee is fiendish, my stories are likely. I am drunk.

Q Drunk?

A Yes, with power. You know where?

Q Where?

A Behind the throne. I am emotional. My mercies are tender, and when I cry, I cry quits. I am lost in thought and up in arms. I am a square shooter with my trusty revolver. My courage is vaunted and my shame is crying, but I don't care—a rap. I have been in the depths of despair, when a watery grave in the briny deep seemed attractive. Eventually I want to marry and settle down, but the woman I marry must be clever.

Q Clever?

A With the needle.

Q Well, I'd certainly call you a man who had led a full life, Mr. Arbuthnot, and a likable chap, too.

A Yes, I'm a peach of a fellow. I'm a diamond in the rough, all wool and a yard wide. I'm too funny for words and too full for utterance. I'm a gay dog, and I like to trip the light fantastic and burn the candle at both ends with motley throngs of boon companions. I may be foolish but my folly is at least sheer.

Q I think you certainly have run—

A I certainly have. The entire gamut of human emotions. I know the facts of life. I'm afraid I've got to go now, Mr. Crouse. I'm due back at my abode. Do you know what kind of abode I live in?

Q Humble, Mr. Arbuthnot?

A Certainly not. Palatial! Goodbye, my little periwinkle!

BEING SERIOUS WITHOUT BEING STUFFY

Walker Gibson

*It struck him abruptly that a woman whose only being
was to "make believe" . . . was a kind of monster.*
                                        —THE TRAGIC MUSE

The three styles I have been trying to describe inevitably give rise to questions of value. Which is it best to be—a Tough or a Sweet or a Stuffy Talker? While many would perhaps not object to being labeled Tough—possibly remembering William James' honorific use of the word—few would want to be called either Sweet or Stuffy. Actually, all three extremes are dangerous. Though it is clearly possible to write very well within the limits of the Tough style, it is easy to write badly too, to sound not simply curt but moronic. Every cheap who-dunit will testify to the indulgence in mindlessness and ego that the Tough style makes easy. As for Sweet Talk and Stuffy Talk, it is difficult to imagine first-rate writing composed strictly within those manners, except as parody. At least I have found no extreme Sweet or Stuffy passage that I can also admire as literature. . . .

I submit, then, that all three of our styles are dangers in modern prose, in ascending order of peril. As a Tough Talker, it is all too easy to sound egocentric, or simpleminded, or plain vulgar. As a Sweet Talker, it is hard to avoid sounding chummy in a way to make most discriminating readers recoil. And as a Stuffy Talker it is almost impossible *not* to sound as if you didn't care about your reader at all.

These difficulties are pervasive in modern American writing, perhaps in any writing. They are apparent, for example, in the styles of those who pontificate on style itself. Let us try a few more passages, this time from the discourse of language experts talking about language.

In the last few years there have appeared on the textbook market a number of anthologies of essays about language and usage. These have been extraordinarily similar in purpose, they have been aimed at an identical audience, and they share current fashionable attitudes of the modern linguistic scholar. They provide us, therefore, with something of a laboratory situation for measuring difference in style. What kinds of voice can we identify in the styles of the anthologists themselves? How do they share the difficulties of self-expression that we have been observing in novelists, journalists, adwriters, and committee spokesmen? All we need, for a tentative answer, is a look at the first hundred words or so of their prefaces.

Here is one:

> From the early grades through the first year of college, the textbooks in grammar and usage scarcely change. The repetition is well meant and apparently necessary: if they won't learn what's good for them, make them do it again. Certainly habits are formed and re-formed by repetitive drill, but it is clear from the record that repetition is not enough.
>
> This book is based on the conviction that knowledge must be added to drill so that repetition may open into growth. Everyone aims at this, at confidence and pleasure in the use of language rather than at anxiety about being correct; the problem has been to get the liberating knowledge, which is scattered through books and journals, into the hands of the students.

A reader who thinks first about details of grammar, and only second of his impression of the whole voice, may too quickly assume that we have a Stuffy Talker here. The reader, that is to say, who has read the last chapter *too* thoroughly, might tick off those verbs in the passive voice and say, There it is—Stuffy. For there they are: *is well meant, are formed and reformed, is based, must be added, is scattered.* Nevertheless, as any sensible reader will point out, this is *not* a Stuffy voice at all—quite the contrary. Perhaps it is almost too breezy. In any case the barrage of passive verbs here is simply not enough to overcome all the other stylistic tricks in this passage which propel the tone in quite another direction, toward Toughness and Sweetness.

What are they? For one thing, the wry half-quotation, *if they won't learn what's good for them. . .* , with its colloquial flavor, serves to disarm the reader in the very second sentence. The willingness to include such talk, in a kind of jocular spirit, is part of a general modesty on the part of the speaker, who is at pains to remind us that there is something to be said for the opposition. "The repetition is well meant," he acknowledges. "Everyone aims at this, at confidence and pleasure in the use of language"—not just I in my wisdom. In sum, the voice here is not that of a Stuffy lecturer at all, but represents some mixture of my three styles.

A short time after the anthology prefaced in this manner appeared, another similar collection was published whose preface began as follows:

> The basic premise of this collection of essays is that language in and of itself is an important subject for study. The second, and equally important, premise is that one can learn about language by reading a variety of essays oriented to the best that modern scholars have thought and said about it.

Because the study of English is often atomized, it is effectively divorced from the broad and scholarly concerns that it is uniquely able to illuminate. In his study of language under the guise of composition, grammar, rhetoric, or poetics, the student is seldom made to think about the nature of language itself.

I hope my reader may sense the difference in that voice, before he stops to take note of details that may account for the difference. The voice here, as I hope we may agree, is less brisk, more removed from the reader, with an academic manner of address that suggests some lack of excitement about what it's saying. If that judgment is at all fair, we may then ask, where does this manner come from? Why is this man so different, even though in realistic fact he is attempting to talk to the same audience for an almost identical purpose?

There are plenty of concrete differences; some of them may be persuasive. The vocabulary of our second speaker is more pretentious, with more longer words and far fewer monosyllables. There are fewer independent verbs, resulting in more subordination, both clauses and other dependent structures. (Half the passage occurs inside subordinate clauses.) There is a tendency to interrupt normal sentence patterns, to make the reader wait for further modification. "The basic premise *of this collection of essays is. . . .*" The second, *and equally important*, premise is. . . ." The tag about the best thought and said may be deliberately ironic, but it's a tired tag for all that. These and other habits of speech may partially justify our feeling that the second anthologist is more dryly professorial (if not plain duller) than the first.

Now here is a third, introducing still another collection of similar essays, aimed at the same audience. It may be his sense of the competition that makes this writer speak as he does.

The growth of interest in language study, in linguistics, has been one of the interesting intellectual developments of the twentieth century. Linguistics must now be viewed as an established and independent branch of study. Under the circumstances it would be odd if there were not a number of books issued to introduce this study to the general public and to the university undergraduate. Many excellent collections of language articles and selections for the undergraduate—especially for the freshman —have appeared in recent years. The compiler of still another collection is consequently obliged to indicate why he adds his product to the number available.

Anyone who begins a book by telling us that "the growth of interest" in something is an "interesting development" cannot himself be overwhelmingly interested in what he has to say. In any event, those rhetorical habits of

Stuffiness that we associate with a remoteness from both subject and audience are here apparent. The vocabulary is now even more multisyllabic. There are fewer finite verbs, with consequent subordination of much of the language. Passive verbs are actually less frequent than in our first passage, but other significant habits appear—for instance the noun adjunct. We have *language study, university undergraduates, language articles*—clear hints that we are approaching the jargon of officialese. The interrupted sentence patterns are interesting; here the writer habitually places modifying phrases between his subject and verb, letting his reader wait patiently until he is all through qualifying. The writer's reference to himself as "the compiler of still another collection" may be taken as a symptom of his nervous self-consciousness. His reaction to his nervousness is withdrawal.

The paragraph I have quoted is followed by a sentence beginning "It is hoped that this book may be welcome for three main reasons. . . ." It is to be wondered who's doing the hoping. Could it be by any chance the author himself? Is there then some good reason why he shouldn't say so? This man seems to be running scared.

The major fault in modern prose generally is Stuffiness. It is true that Sweetness too can be very offensive; witness the overlays of Sweetness on Toughness that . . . [are] observable in the contemporary novel. The excess of Sweetness in journalism . . . speaks for itself. For most people, though, in most situations, in the writing of everyday serious expository prose, it is the Stuffy voice that gets in the way. The reason it gets in the way, I submit, is that the writer is scared. If this is an age of anxiety, one way we react to our anxiety is to withdraw into omniscient and multisyllabic detachment where nobody can get us.

No book, certainly not this book, can remove a person's anxiety for him. But it may be that, through a study of style, one might remove some *symptoms* of anxiety from one's prose. Therefore it may not be utterly useless to offer a little Practical Advice, most of it fairly obvious, for avoiding the symptoms of Stuffiness. To follow such advice may amount to little more than taking aspirin: it may reduce the headache without touching the anxiety. And yet, if anxiety is found in the style of our language, perhaps changing our style may be the best thing we can do. In any case, here are some Rules, deduced from this study, for avoiding the Stuffy voice, at least as that voice is defined in this book.

HOW TO AVOID BEING STUFFY

1. Make about two-thirds of your total vocabulary monosyllabic; keep words of three syllables or more down to under 20 per cent.
2. Try making some of the subjects of your verbs *people*, not neuter nouns.

3. Manage a *finite verb* about every ten words, on the average. (Which is more than that sentence does.)
4. Don't overuse the *passive voice*. (But don't avoid it altogether either.)
5. Keep down the *noun adjuncts.*
6. Keep the average length of *subordinate clauses* down to ten words or so, and see to it that the total proportion of subordinate clauses runs to no more than a third of the whole.
7. Most marks of *punctuation* (except commas and semi-colons) serve to lighten tone. Consider question marks, parentheses, italics, dashes, and of course exclamations.
8. Don't *interrupt* subject and verb with intervening subordinate constructions and modifiers.
9. If really desperate, try a *contraction* or two, or a *fragment* (verbless sentence).
10. Whatever you do, *don't obey all these rules at once,* for to do so would be to emerge with something disastrously cute, probably on the Sweet side. The careful writer, in fact, carefully *disobeys* some of these rules, precisely to avoid the pose of sickly Sweetness. He includes a passive verb, now and then, a lengthy subordinate clause, an elegant interruption between subject and verb. Perhaps his skill in making such choices is what we mean by a *balanced style.*

It remains to say a word about the moral side of rhetoric. The three styles I have been trying to describe can be called ways of making believe. Any style, any way of thinking, can be regarded as a make-believe performance, and it is always possible to take comfort by distinguishing between the performance on the one hand and the Real Person that stands behind all the play-acting on the other. That's not me, that's just my voice of the moment. But such a distinction breaks down very soon; even in the writing of fiction, as we have seen, it produces difficulties. And in the course of our day-to-day lives, we have to live with the effects of our performances. The voices I choose are mine, my responsibility, and the belief I own up to is the make-believe I have made. Serious play-acting. The world is not a stage, nor ever was.

Put that way, all three styles I have been examining are, as I have said, dangerous. Exceedingly common as they are in modern American life, they suggest three ways in which Americans upstage one another. One can talk Tough, beating the hairy chest, and make a spectacle of one's ostentatious simplicity. See how true and humble I am, more true and humble than you are. (And sometimes, furthermore, I really Know!) Or one can talk Sweet, leaping into the lap of one's listener, however unwanted there. See how nice I am to you, you boob. Or one can talk Stuffy, laying down the law as if one were Moses and all the world were a wandering tribe looking for the Word.

In each case the rhetoric, all too often, creates a character who is ill-mannered, to say no worse of him. He has lost forbearance and restraint, a regard for the feelings of his listeners. The result is that in our time we are fairly surrounded by voices that are not much fun to be with.

At the beginning of our first chapter, we noted how our sense of a person, in an ordinary social introduction, is not simply a matter of words, but a matter of many different physical impressions. Gesture and grimace, voicebox and eyelid are all rich with meaning. In written prose, though, it is all words, and the business of the modern day is performed, much of it, with written words. For some people, actions in written language are the principal actions of their lives—at least of their professional lives. Handsome is as handsome writes. But how few of us write handsomely! Instead, the characters we create for ourselves, the characters we become, are too often egocentric and ill-mannered. We push one another around. (Examples abound, I know, in the style of this book, this chapter, this sentence.) And the ill manners can be produced by, among other things, an excessive Toughness, or Sweetness, or Stuffiness, particularly the latter two.

The excesses are understandable. In the very act of addressing someone we acknowledge a wish to push him around, and in our zeal to push a little harder, it is no wonder our voices begin to sound strident. It is with style that we try to behave like a decent person, one who ruefully concedes his drive for power while remaining aware of his reader's well-chosen resistance. Thus style is our way of becoming a person worth listening to, worth knowing.

A moral justification for the study of rhetoric lies right here. We improve ourselves by improving the words we write. We make our performance less monstrous, by *acting* like human beings. Just what comprises a satisfactory human performance is every man's complicated decision. But at least, by looking at rhetoric, we may begin to know more about who it is we are making believe we are. And then, perhaps, we can do something about it.

from
AN INTERVIEW

Ernest Hemingway

INTERVIEWER: A fundamental question: namely, as a creative writer what do you think is the function of your art? Why a representation of fact, rather than fact itself.

HEMINGWAY: Why be puzzled by that? From things that have happened and from things as they exist and from all things that you know and all those you cannot know, you make something through your invention that is not a representation but a whole new thing truer than anything true and alive, and you make it alive, and if you make it well enough, you give it immortality. That is why you write and for no other reason that you know of. But what about all the reasons that no one knows?

IN MY CRAFT
OR SULLEN ART

Dylan Thomas

In my craft or sullen art
Exercised in the still night
When only the moon rages
And the lovers lie abed
With all their griefs in their arms,
I labour by singing light
Not for ambition or bread
Or the strut and trade of charms
On the ivory stages
But for the common wages
Of their most secret heart

Not for the proud man apart
From the raging moon I write
On these spindrift pages
Nor for the towering dead
With their nightingales and psalms
But for the lovers, their arms
Round the griefs of the ages,
Who pay no praise or wages
Nor heed my craft or art.

Para-
communications

EXTRA-SENSORY
PERCEPTION

Kenneth Walker

CAN THE MIND AFFECT MATTER OUTSIDE THE LIMITS
OF THE BODY?

We know that our minds exert their influence on our bodies, for every moment we are demonstrating this fact. But can mind produce a direct effect on matter which lies outside the limits of our bodies? In the past, it was said that physical disturbances were sometimes associated with great emotional crises, as happened when the veil of the Temple was rent in twain. So also does Dr. Jung, during an emotional crisis, claim that there was an instance of a household article breaking in two during an emotional crisis in his earlier life. Some gamblers are convinced that their minds have been responsible on certain occasions for exerting an influence on the fall of dice. They believe that when the attention of a dice-thrower attains a certain degree of concentration and when he *wills* that the dice should fall in the way in which he wants them to fall, the dice sometimes obey his command. This, at any rate, was the belief which made Dr. Rhine decide to submit "willed" dice-throwing to a scientific test and special experiments were devised for this purpose at Duke University. The question which had to be answered was whether or not the scores obtained after "willing" dice to fall in a predetermined way were any higher than could be accounted for by chance alone. . . . Rhine reports that the majority of the earlier experiments yielded results which were sufficiently above chance expectation to encourage the experimenters to continue their investigation. "More and more the realization grew that some other factor than chance was operating and it was a factor that could not be attributed to errors in recording, or to faulty dice, or to skill in throwing."[1]

The Duke University dice-throwing tests were begun in 1934, broken off for a time, and then resumed in the year 1942. An examination of the total results obtained from these experiments showed that there were certain similarities between the results of these new PK tests, as they were called, and those previously obtained in the ESP tests.[1] . . . Rhine makes the following interesting comment on the relationship existing between extra-sensory perception and psycho-kinesis (PK), and from it we can see that he regards psycho-kinesis as being dependent to a great extent on clairvoyance: "If we suppose that the mind of the subject in some way influences the roll of the dice by operating upon it in some point of space and time then ESP is a necessary part of the PK process. So decisive would this argument seem to be that if PK had been discovered without any previous knowledge of ESP, then the latter would have had to have been assumed in order to make the former intelligible . . . PK implies ESP and ESP implies PK."

THE CLOSE LINKAGE BETWEEN THE DIFFERENT VARIETIES OF PARANORMAL PHENOMENA

Looking back now on the various paranormal phenomena of the mind . . . , we see that there is a very close similarity between them. First, we found that Telepathy and Clairvoyance had to be considered together because it was impossible to be sure which of the two was responsible for what was happening. Next, it was found that Precognition was often associated with Telepathy and that whilst Precognition took liberties with *time,* so also did Telepathy take liberties with *space.* Now, . . . , we have discovered that the relationship between Extra-Sensory Perception and Psycho-kinesis is so intimate that the two phenomena cannot be separated from each other. It was on account of this tendency on the part of paranormal phenomena to flow together that Dr. Thouless and Dr. Weisner had suggested several years previously that they should all be regarded as being different manifestations of a single faculty of man: a faculty which might be designated by the Greek letter "Psi."

THE NATURE OF THE DIFFERENT MANIFESTATIONS OF THE PSI FACTOR

The final question to be discussed . . . is whether the various ESP faculties in man should be regarded as being supernormal and in process of

[1] J. B. Rhine, *New World of the Mind.*

development or whether they are common to everybody. The answer to this question is that these faculties are not only natural to man but that they probably exist in varying degrees, in every living organism. Many naturalists have resorted to the ideas of telepathy and clairvoyance when attempting to explain the behavior of gregarious birds, animals and insects. It is difficult to watch a flock of migrating birds manoeuvring in the sky as a single unit, wheeling together, veering now in this direction, now in that, and maintaining the same flock pattern all the time, without feeling that they are linked together by something which is much more immediate and certain in its action than are the special senses. So also did I feel that something more than the special senses was in action when, as a young man, I lay for hours behind a bush watching the behavior of zebra and antelope grazing in the Great Rift Valley of East Africa. I was convinced that these animals possessed a means of detecting my presence and of communicating their fears other than by sight, hearing and smell. Yet a note of caution has to be sounded here. The possession of extra-sensory perception by an animal might not always be of advantage to it unless this were direct knowledge counterbalanced by confirmatory and more precise messages reaching it from its special senses. Dr. Thouless drives this home to us by citing the difficult position in which a deer might be placed if it were entirely dependent for its safety on telepathic warnings of the approach of a tiger. "It would be unable to decide whether the telepathic warning on this score referred to a tiger in the vicinity now, to one a hundred and fifty miles away, or to one that would be there tomorrow. And to this we have to add that if it were a deer conversant with the subtleties of Freudian symbolism, it could not even be sure whether the animal was a tiger at all and not a veiled intimation of some sex aggression."

EVOLUTION AND BRAIN DEVELOPMENT

As evolution progressed it began to move amongst the mammals in the direction of greater and greater brain development. This gave rise to the appearance of more and more intelligent animals with larger and larger brains and as the size of that organ increased the animal in question became much less dependent on the aid previously given by extra-sensory perception. According to Bergson, the brain has a very special function to perform. It is primarily a selective agent which focuses an animal's attention on the events in its environment which are of practical importance to it in the fierce struggle for survival. The brain also simplifies the picture of the outside world which the animal receives through its sense organs, so that it is able to deal with it in a more orderly fashion, bit by bit. Moncrieff, like Thouless, points to the confusion which might be produced in the unprotected animal by the arrival of a sudden flood of extra-sensory impressions from without. He looks upon an animal's visual, olfactory and auditory organs as being canalizing mechanisms by which an animal is saved from being over-whelmed by a flood of irrelevant ESP impressions.

CONCLUSIONS REACHED ON THE SUBJECT OF EXTRA-SENSORY PERCEPTION

Having examined carefully the foregoing evidence in favour and against the existence of another sense or senses beyond those which are known to us as the special senses, I think it is possible to summarize our conclusions as follows:

1. That this additional Sense, or Psi Factor, makes itself evident from time to time in man;
2. That the Psi Function in man is not so limited by questions of space and of time as are man's special senses;
3. That the various activities of man's Psi Function are in all probability governed by laws of their own which have not, as yet, been discovered;
4. That a *percept* of our special senses often provides a useful starting point for a Psi Function activity and that a sensory *percept* may also help us to bring to a focus data which have been received from the said activity of the Psi Function;
5. That a considerable, though as yet undetermined, number of people are partly motivated and conditioned by the Psi Function but that comparatively few of them are aware of this fact, for more often than not they are surprised and even disconcerted when the hidden factor of the Psi Function obtrudes itself on their notice.

THE MIND OF THE DOLPHIN

John C. Lilly

Let us now imagine that the dolphin is swimming along in a bay and that there is a flat surface on the water from which his call will be reflected. He starts at a distance from this flat surface such that the call starts out, leaves his head completely, and then returns and at no point overlaps itself. He will then hear an unimpeded echo of his own call which will be the same shape as the call which he emitted and will have the same frequencies in it. However, as he approaches the flat surface and the echo returns before he has finished the call, there will be chance for beat frequencies between the beginning and the ending frequencies of the call. . . . These new beats are between the call still being emitted and the echo returning to the dolphin. Since the call is rising in frequency at each instant, the early parts beating with the later parts will generate a lower-beat frequency at each instant as long as overlap exists between the outgoing and the incoming portions. As he approaches still closer, more and more of the call will be beating with itself. The distances involved can be easily figured using the velocity of sound in water as 5000 feet per second (1540 meters per second); in one-tenth of a second sound will travel 500 feet (154 meters), and if the dolphin is 500 feet from the surface and emits a tenth-of-a-second call, there will be no overlap. He will hear the call repeated in the echo. If he prolongs the call two-tenths of a second, the returning echo of the first half of the call will overlap and beat with the second half of the call. What is the nature of the beat that he will hear?

If the slash call is a linearly rising frequency-versus-time curve (i.e., if it is a straight line), the first part beats with the latter part and gives a constant-beat frequency. If there are small wobbles in the frequency, these will be reflected in the beat as long as they are not present equally and at the same times in the first half and last half of the call. Thus a slash call is converted into a bar beat of a shorter length than the slash itself. *The frequency of the bar beat will vary with the distance of the object from the dolphin, i.e., distant objects will give higher-frequency differences because of the greater delay in the overlap. Nearby objects will give lower-beat frequencies because there is less delay between the parts which are combined to form the beat.*

Thus it is easy to see that if the dolphin emits a slash call, he can obtain from objects in all directions around him beat frequencies which are different depending on the distance of the objects giving the reflections. Thus with a slash call he can tell pretty well what the shape of the bottom is, where the top of the water is, and what other large objects may be in the water around him, in what directions. He has only to listen to the beat and obtain their directions by the use of his two ears in the usual stereophonic listening fashion.

At the frequencies he is using in the slash call (from about 5000 to 25,000 cps), the wave length in sea water varies from one foot (0.301 meter) to about 2.5 inches (6.35 centimeters) in length. If the analogy of our visual detection holds for his sonic detection system, he can resolve details something of the order of one-fourth of a wave length to one-thirtieth of a wave length. Therefore, with the slash call, he can probably detect objects from about three inches in their largest dimension to about one-half inch in their smallest dimension. Thus, his slash call should tell him pretty well in what direction a school of fish of the proper size is—where his friends (other dolphins) are and possibly even where his enemies (the sharks) are. Of course here he is limited to certain distances (from something like a few feet to something like a few hundred feet).

The internal picture which the dolphin can then create while sounding slash calls, the internal picture which he creates of his surroundings in terms of beat frequencies coming stereophonically combined from the two ears, must be a very interesting kind of picture. It is as if to us the nearby objects emitted a reddish light and the farther objects emitted a bluish light, with the whole spectrum in between. We might see, for example, a red patch very close by and then a dimmer, blue patch in the distance farther away . . . a blue background downward symbolizing the bottom, a red patch up close meaning a fish nearby, and a large green object swimming between us on the bottom meaning another dolphin. This conversion of their acoustic beat frequencies into colors is one way we can visualize how their surrounds look to them. (Once again, . . . we must convert their "acoustic pictures" into our visual pictures, because of the differences in our brains and in our approaches to our surroundings.)

Thus, they could use the slash call and other more complex calls in order to delineate their surroundings by what I call their "long wave length sonar." Their "short wave length sonar" operates at very much higher frequencies; the measurements of this mode that we have made in the Institute show that they use frequencies from approximately 15 kilo-Hertz to around 150,000 cycles per second. The sounds emitted in this region have wave lengths in water from about 4 inches (10 centimeters) down to about four-tenths of an inch (1.0 centimeter). As we and others have shown, this sound is concentrated in a beam with a maximum amplitude straight ahead off the upper jaw of the dolphin. This sound comes in the form of short pulses of very high amplitudes (3000 dynes per square centimeter or 140 decibels above the reference level of 0.002 dyne per square centimeter). Since this is a beam and since it is very high amplitude in shorter wave lengths, it can be used for a more detailed inspection of objects which are found by the longer wave length sonar. He changes his ability to resolve details by change of wave length: the shorter the wave length the finer the detail down to two-fifths of an inch (1.0 centimeter).

The dolphin may find (by a slash call), off to his left, that there is an interesting object at such-and-such a distance. He can then merely turn his head, turn on his "short wave length sonar," and inspect that object in detail by scanning it with his "sonar flashlight." The narrow beam and the shorter wave lengths give him a resolution which he didn't have with his longer wave length slash call or other kinds of whistle. As he wants to see small details he moves the frequency of each pulse upward toward 150,000 cycles per second (two-fifths of an inch wave length).

So far we have spoken about echoes from non-moving objects with a non-moving dolphin. When a dophin is moving and picks up echoes the apparent frequency of those echoes will vary somewhat, depending upon his velocity relative to the reflector. One can see this effect (called the Doppler effect after the man who discovered it) by standing beside a road when a car or some other vehicle sounds a constant-frequency horn or siren as it passes us. When the sonic source is approaching us, the frequency apparently rises and as it passes us and recedes, the frequency falls. We can just as well have a fixed-frequency emitter on our car and approach a big wall. The apparent source in the wall is now approaching us at the velocity of the car so that the reflected echo will have an apparent shift of frequency upward. Alternatively, we can sit still, aim a sonic beam from a fixed-frequency emitter at a moving object approaching us, and the reflected echo will apparently rise in frequency. If the object is moving away from us, the echo will have an apparent fall of frequency, depending on the velocity of recession.

Returning then to the slash call and the objects of varying distances from the dolphin, if he is remaining motionless in the water, he will hear various frequencies. If objects are approaching him, the frequencies will increase. If objects are receding from him, he will hear the frequencies dropping. Similarly, if he is moving through the water very fast and other objects are also moving through the water very fast with him, these echoes will have apparent beat frequencies which will remain constant, whereas objects which they are passing will have the rising-falling Doppler effects. Thus the internal picture of his surrounds becomes more complex and we must bring in change-of-frequency with respect to time as well as frequencies which merely depend upon distance.

All of these various acoustic concepts (and many others) in some way or another must be used in the dolphin's construction of his language. When a dolphin wishes to talk about an object at a given distance with another dolphin and wishes to describe how that object moved and at what velocities, he can do it merely by transmitting the proper frequency pattern in his clicks and whistles. In other words, he can converse about moving down from the surface of the sea toward the bottom, he can converse about fish of a given size at given distances, sharks of a given size and all of these other matters, in a frequency-time-intensity domain which we would have to convert into visual images. It seems to me that this can become a sort of Rosetta stone for proceeding on an analysis of "delphinese." At the least it is a good enough lead for further research and it is a testable quantitative hypothesis.

By blindfolding ourselves or by using blind persons with the proper apparatus, we can copy these various matters with our own subjective systems. However, we must be aware that our brain can handle only one-tenth the amount of information in the acoustic sphere that the dolphin's brain can.

The dolphin can store huge amounts of spatially distributed acoustic information for making up his pictures and will have stored away many models of what his surroundings are like. We lack these advantages quantitatively. In other words we should expect an extended period of training to develop the same abilities the dolphin has. We may never be able to match his performance, at least not at the speed with which he has developed because of the limitations of our brains versus their brains.

What is the evidence that they use the slash calls for long wave length sonar? Some of the evidence is that if one takes a dolphin and places him in new surroundings emitting series of slash calls, after he has been there for a while he stops emitting these calls. In other words, he initially uses them to make an acoustic map of his surroundings. From that point on he doesn't have to emit them so frequently because he knows at any given instant where he is from the last time that he emitted any noise at all. He has mapped all of the obstacles, the walls, the depths, and the boundaries of where he is. He is then free to travel, using, say, only his short wave length sonar or his eyes to tell him in what part of the real surroundings he is and hence on what part of his internal map he is. Any new change in the surroundings starts him off again as he readjusts his internal map. We have observed this behavior literally hundreds of times.

The conversations between two dolphins by means of whistles thus might be explicable on these grounds. They have a very large brain with very large, general-purpose computer properties, i.e., a very large neocortex. Since a large portion of this is acoustic cortex, they have probably developed symbols (i.e., shorthand) of all the special relationships and descriptions of the various objects (including themselves) which correspond to the whistle (and click) echoes and the whistle's beats. Thus one dolphin might start a slash call to another dolphin and then wobble the upper end of it (as we have seen many times when two dolphins are speaking one to the other). It is these wobbles at the upper end which are probably transmitting the subtleties of meaning, one dolphin to another. The very great frequency shifts that we see in the $(<)$ call, the inverted V call, and in the slash call and various others probably symbolize changes in mode, i.e., in whole large categories of meaning. The subtle variations, beats between the two sides, the Doppler effects in the call as the apparent source is moved between the two sides, convert the subtleties of the meanings. If we are ever to break "delphinese" and convert it into human language, we thus have many hints on which to proceed. At least we have testable hypotheses to either bear out or disprove. . . .

It is an uplifting experience to imagine the seas and the oceans of this world of ours as a vast house of dolphins and whales. Audacious in the extreme is this featherless biped walking on the dry land which is my species. His little, dry spirit has a great deal of gall to try to push his way into the primal soup. In the face of the dolphin's necessities, one quickly loses one's self-esteem. Perhaps we can brave out the terror of the deep but we are still not built nor equipped to live in it free as a dolphin. Their appropriateness of body for their life in the sea must be matched by their minds and their brains built and equipped for this life. Their freedoms are our prison walls; and vice versa, our freedoms are their prisons. Every time I walk away from a dolphin in a pool, every time he swims away from me, I feel this reciprocity of freedoms-prisons.

We must assume that dolphins have their own principles, their own assumptions, their own postulates, and their own actions for their mental lives. It is probable that any large computer (such as their brains) has huge alien programs. At the very least, in our search, we can see if they act as if they do have consistent logical bases on which they operate. By living with them and forcing them to live with us, we can discover many of these things by behavioral methods.

At the very most, we some day may be able to ask them and see if their replies show familiar forms or whether we come upon only unknown alien forms of thinking and of philosophy. Between these two extremes there are many other possibilities. For example, we may ask questions vocally or nonvocally, verbally or nonverbally, and receive answers in these modes. The answers may be somewhat comprehensible or totally incomprehensible. Our thinking and speaking are only human. Their thinking, their speaking so far are only delphinic. In order to first ask the proper questions we must become partly delphinic (with their help), and to understand the questions the dolphins must become partly human (with our help). To give proper answers to our questions the dolphins must go partly human, and to understand the answers we must go partly delphinic.

CELESTIAL SYNTAX

Walter Sullivan

Not long after the Green Bank conference, Frank Drake sent to all the participants a strange communication. It was, he believed, of the sort that might be received as the initial message from another race of beings and it manifested the thought that he and others had given to the question: how can we exchange ideas with those who differ from us in ways we cannot guess—certainly in physiognomy, possibly in methods of thought and logic?

Drake's message consisted of a series of pulses sent in a fixed rhythm, but with many gaps. The pulses he wrote as ones; the gaps as zeros. In other words, it was a binary code, the simplest of all communication systems in that it makes use of only two symbols. It is the one commonly used in computers. His colleagues worked over it, but despite some familiarity with the workings of Drake's mind, they found it so compact that its full meaning was difficult to extract. However, one of them, Bernard Oliver, expanded—and thus simplified—the message. It appears on the next page.

A peculiar feature of this message is that it consists of 1,271 ones and zeros—in computer terminology, 1,271 "bits" of information. To anyone mathematically inclined, the number 1,271 will be recognized as the product of two prime numbers: 31 and 41. This suggests the possibility that the message should be written out in 41 lines of 31 bits each, with the zeros, since they were pauses in the transmission, left as blank spaces. As shown on page 245, this arrangement is unenlightening.

The other possibility, 31 lines of 41 bits, is shown on page 246.

It is clear that the transmitting planet is inhabited by two-legged creatures that apparently are bisexual and mammalian. The circle at the upper left is

100000000000000000000000000000000000000010000111100000000010

1000001000010001000000000101000000000010100000000000100010000000100000100000010

0000000011001000000000100010000010000001000000001000100010000000111000000000010

0000100000000000000000000000101000000000010100000000000000000000000011001000000000

0000010000010000110001000000000000000000000000000000000000000000011000011000001

0001100001100001001001010100100100100100100100100100100100100000000010000110000110

00001100001100000000010000000000001111110100000000000000000001000000000001000001

00000000000100000000000000000000000000010111110000000000000100111011011010000000000

001000100111000000000000101000000000000010100100001100101011100101000000000000

00000000000111110000000000010000010010000000000000010010000000000100001001010

11100000011101010000001010100000000001010100000001000000000001000101000000000010

00010101010001000100000010110110111001101100100010001001000100000000000000000000010

0100000000000000000001000100010010010010001000100000100000000000011100001111100001

000100001110001000001000000000010000001000100000101000001010100000101111100000

00000110000000010000010001000100010000010000010000110000100000100010001000100010000

111001100000110110001101100001000000000110000

The message of 1271 "bits" (all ones and zeros) as it would appear transcribed on continuous tape.

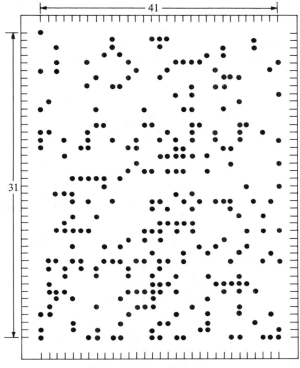

The message arranged in 41 lines

their sun, with its planets spaced below it. The man-like creature points to the fourth planet, where the civilization resides. The wavy line emanating from the third planet shows it to be covered with water, and below it is a fishlike symbol. Apparently the civilization has visited this planet and found it to have marine life. The planets are numbered, down the left side, in a binary code. Symbols across the top represent the atoms of hydrogen, carbon and oxygen, indicating that the chemical basis of life there is like our own. The scale on the right, labelled in the binary code, shows that the creatures are eleven units high, the units presumably being the wavelength of the signal—21 centimeters. This works out to 7½ feet.

Drake's cryptogram was devised not merely for his amusement and that of his colleagues. He sought to stimulate some hardheaded thinking about the decipherment problem. What was needed, Morrison said, was a new specialty: "anti-cryptography," or the designing of codes as easy as possible to decipher. He devised a scheme for coaching distant creatures in the establishment of a television link. Such, it is widely thought, would be of immense importance, for both sides would have almost nothing in common. All that we can count on is that all beings sufficiently intelligent for interstellar

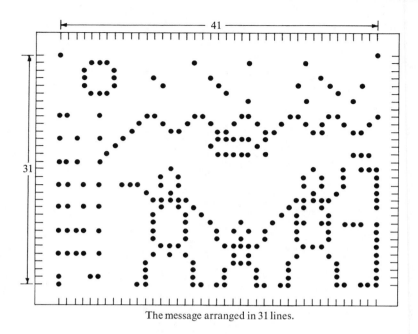

The message arranged in 31 lines.

communication must have a mathematics based on numbers and on the simple concepts of addition, subtraction, division, equality, and so forth. They must be aware of the structure of the various atoms. Yet their higher mathematics, their logic, their way of representing atomic structure, may differ radically from our own.

Despite these handicaps, it is very probable that they can see. The sense of sight is so important that, as Bernard Oliver pointed out, it has evolved independently in widely diverse creatures on our own planet: flies, scallops and men, for example. Hence the emphasis on establishing television contact —using what Bracewell described as "sophisticated sign language."

Morrison's method for making such contact was an elaboration of the "radioglyph" scheme advanced by the British mathematician Lancelot Hogben in a 1952 lecture to the British Interplanetary Society entitled "Astraglossa, or First Steps in Celestial Syntax." Hogben had proposed that numbers could be represented as ordinary pulses. Five such pulses would indicate the numeral 5. Mathematical concepts, such as "plus," "minus" and "equal," would each be symbolized by a distinctive signal of some sort—a radioglyph. In Morrison's version, numbers were indicated by square-shaped pulses, whereas "plus," "minus," "the reciprocal of" and so forth were represented by other pulse shapes. Distant beings would be introduced to the meaning of these symbols in terms of simple arithmetic, as follows:

Addition:

2   +   3   −   5

3   +   5   −   8

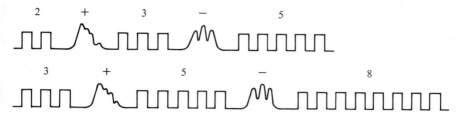

Subtraction:

7   −   4   −   3

Division:

6   +   3   −   2

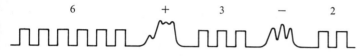

Reciprocals:

R   2   −   1   +   2

The next problem would be to introduce the concept of pi, the ratio of the circumference of a circle to its diameter. Pi is an "irrational" number that cannot directly and precisely be expressed in numerals. However, it can be suggested by adding together an indefinite series of fractions whose sum "converges" on the value of pi. This was how Morrison proposed to do it.

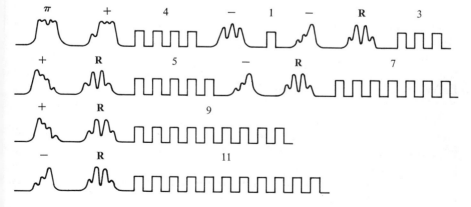

Translated into conventional arithmetic, this means:

$$\pi/4 = 1 - \tfrac{1}{3} + \tfrac{1}{5} - \tfrac{1}{7} + \tfrac{1}{9} - \tfrac{1}{11} \cdots \text{ etc.}$$

He would then send a series of extended radio signals, each marked at its start and finish by a pulse, with occasional pulses in between. He would intersperse these with the symbol for pi in the expectation that those on the receiving end would guess what he was driving at; namely, that the lines of radio emission should be aligned, one below the other, so that the seemingly random pulses form a circle (top drawing on next page). This would establish the "raster" of a television screen—the pattern of its horizontal scanning lines. The next step, Morrison suggested, might be to transmit an illustration of the Pythagorean theorem—reminiscent of the proposals of a century earlier for interplanetary attention-getting (bottom drawing on next page).

The 525 lines of American television channels are scanned 30 times a second, which is fast enough so that our eyes see only a smoothly changing picture. However, there are severe limits on the speed with which a picture can be transmitted over interstellar distances. The farther away the transmitter, the more prolonged must each pulse, or "bit" of information, be to stand out above the background noise. This already has presented problems in designing the television systems for the Ranger spacecraft. When Ranger 7 crashed onto the moon July 31, 1964, its six TV cameras sent 4,316 pictures to earth in the final minutes of the plunge, the last one cut short by the impact, yet a comparable array of studio cameras, not having to send their images so far, would have transmitted more than thirty times as many.) Yet the moon is our nearest neighbor. While the transmitters used for communication between solar systems would be far more powerful than those of Ranger, the distances would be vastly greater. It therefore appears that interstellar sending speeds will have to be far slower, but this should not be too troublesome, since the messages will in any case take years to reach their destination. Also we, in our ignorance, cannot set limits on the skill and ingenuity of our distant friends in devising ways to speed up their sending rates.

Although, without television, it would be very difficult to arrive at a mutually understandable language, some believe it could be done. Russell F. W. Smith, linguist and Associate Dean of General Education at New York University, has cited the difficulties in deciphering lost languages on our own planet. At the 1963 convention of the Audio Engineering Society in New York, he pointed out that, but for the discovery by Napoleon's troops of a basalt slab at Rosetta near the mouth of the Nile, Jean François Champollion could not have deciphered the hieroglyphics of ancient Egypt. The priests of Ptolemy V had placed an inscription on the stone in three alphabets: the ancient hieroglyphic, its successor, the more abbreviated demotic, and the Greek.

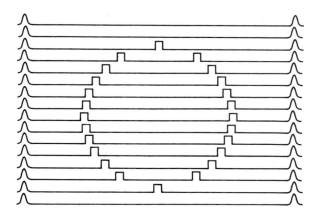

Establishing the TV "raster."

Despite the lack of a cosmic Rosetta Stone, some mathematicians believe that a language suitable for radio communication between different worlds can be evolved through the use of symbolic logic. The effort to develop a purely logical language, in which all mathematical reasoning could be expressed, began at the end of the nineteenth century with the work of several mathematicians, in particular Giuseppe Peano in Italy. In 1900 a lecturer in mathematics at Trinity College, Cambridge, went to Paris for a mathematical congress, bringing with him one of his most brilliant students. The lecturer was named Alfred North Whitehead and his companion was Bertrand Russell. They were greatly excited by news of Peano's new application of logic and ultimately decided to collaborate in carrying it further. The fruit of his collaboration was their monumental three-volume work *Principia Mathematica*, published between 1910 and 1913. Thereafter, Whitehead went to Harvard and became one of the foremost philosophers of his time. His

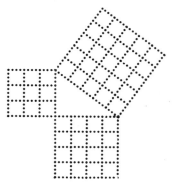

The Pythagorean Theorem on TV.

collaborator became the third Earl Russell, philosopher, winner of a Nobel Prize in Literature and, even in his ninetieth year, a gaunt, frail figure demonstrating in Trafalgar Square against nuclear weapons testing.

Their work on "logistic language" had been preceded by efforts to produce an international language that would bring the world closer together. The first to be widely used was Volapük, invented in 1880 by an Austrian priest. This was followed seven years later by Esperanto, but the mathematician Peano felt these had failed to escape from the arbitrary and illogical syntax of tongues that had evolved in the chance manner of nature. In 1903 he produced his Interlingua, derived from classical Latin but with a simplified syntax. It is still widely used in abstracting scientific articles.

These developments have led Hans Freudenthal, Professor of Mathematics at the University of Utrecht, to attempt extending the "logistic language" of Whitehead and Russell into something intelligible to beings with whom we have nothing in common except intelligence. He calls it "Lincos," as a short form of "Lingua Cosmica." The logical exposition of the language, as might take place in an extended interstellar message, is contained in his book, *Lincos: Design of a Language for Cosmic Intercourse*, published in the Netherlands in 1960. Actually, he pointed out, such a language already may be established as the vehicle for cosmic intercourse. "Messages in that language might unceasingly travel through the universe," he said.

His language is "articulated," so to speak, by unmodulated radio signals of varying duration and wavelength. These represent "phonemes" which can be combined to constitute concepts or words. The lexicon and syntax are built up gradually, much in the way that a first-grade reader uses a new word over and over in various ways, then introduces another word: "See John run. John runs to Mary . . . ," etc.

Freudenthal's book-length "language lesson," like Morrison's simpler approach, begins with elementary arithmetical concepts, but it soon passes on to more abstract ideas. Thus, at an early stage, the idea of right and wrong is conveyed. This is done by presenting a series of mathematical statements, all of which are obviously correct. Each of them is followed by the new word: "good." Then a mistaken statement is given, followed by another new word: "bad." Later such abstract concepts as honesty, lying, understanding and the like are presented. The teaching process uses "actors" or "voices," somewhat in the Socratic method, their dialogues illustrating the meanings of new words.

To represent the radio signals in writing, Freudenthal uses a mixture of mathematical, biological and linguistic symbols including some of those employed earlier by Whitehead and Russell. He points out that Lincos has not yet been developed to where it can explain the diversity of human individuals, but he does use it to express some of the information touched on in Drake's pictorial message; namely, the manner of human reproduction. This is set forth, in Lincos, as follows:

Ha Inq *Ha*ı

$x \in$ Hom. $\rightarrow$:Ini.x Ext $\cdot$ $-$:Ini$\cdot$Cor x.Ext $\cdot$ $=$

Cca.Sec 11 $\times$ 10^{10111}:

$\forall x$:$x \in$ Bes. $\wedge$:Ini.x Ext $\cdot$ $-$:Ini$\cdot$Cor x.Ext $\cdot$ $>$ Sec 0:

$x \in$ Hom. $\rightarrow$ $\forall$⌈y.z⌉:$y \frown z \in$ Hom. $\wedge$ $y =$ .Mat x $\wedge$ $z =$ .Pat x:

$\forall x$:$x \in$ Bes. $\wedge$ $\forall$⌈y.z⌉:$y \frown z \in$ Bes. $\wedge$ $y =$ .Mat x $\wedge$ $z =$ .Pat x:

$x \in$ Hom. $\rightarrow$:$\wedge t$:Ini$\cdot$Cor x.Ext:Ant:t:Ant:Ini.x Ext$\cdot$

$\rightarrow$:t Cor x.Par$\cdot$$t$ Cor.Mat x:

$\forall x$:$x \in$ Bes. $\wedge$ $\cdot$ $\wedge t$.Etc:

$x \in$ Hom. $\wedge$:$s =$ Ini$\cdot$Cor x.Ext$\cdot$

$\rightarrow$:$\forall$⌈u.v⌉s Cor u.Par$\cdot$$s$ Cor.Mat x:

$\wedge$ Pau Ant.$s$$\cdot$Cor v:Par:Pau Ant.$s$$\cdot$Cor.Pat x

$\wedge$:s Cor x.Uni$\cdot$$s$ Cor u.s Cor v:

$\forall x$:$x \in$ Bes. $\wedge$ .Etc:

Hom $=$ Hom Fem. $\cup$ .Hom Msc:

Hom Fem $\cap$ Hom Msc $=$ ⌈⌉:

Car:$\uparrow$$x$$\cdot$Nnc x Ext. $\wedge$.$x \in$ Hom Fem

Pau$>$ Car:$\uparrow$$x$$\cdot$Nnc x Ext. $\wedge$.$x \in$ Hom Msc:

$y =$ Mat x. $\wedge$.$y \in$ Hom $\cdot$ $\rightarrow$.$y \in$ Hom Fem:$\wedge$:

$y =$ Pat x. $\wedge$.$y \in$ Hom $\cdot$ $\rightarrow$.$y \in$ Hom Msc:

$x \in$ Hom $\cup$ Bes:$\rightarrow$:Fin.Cor $x$$\cdot$Pst.Fin x#

The three-letter symbols are derived from Latin roots. For example, "Fem" means "female"; "Msc" means "male." In his "summary" of his passage, Freudenthal translates it, in part, as follows:

> The existence of a human body begins some time earlier than that of the human itself. The same is true for some animals. Mat, mother. Pat, father. Before the individual existence of a human, its body is part of the body of its mother. It has originated from a part of the body of its mother and a part of the body of its father. . . .

Freudenthal comments cryptically that the last paragraph of the coded text "is somewhat premature. Its notions," he continues, "will not be used in this volume." He believes that television, including a three-dimensional form, will come only at an advanced stage of interstellar communication, since analytic geometry will be necessary to explain the method. This he considers too advanced for beginners in cosmic discourse. His approach is thus fundamentally different from that of Drake, Morrison and others, who feel instructions for television contact could be conveyed as the essential first step. In fact, the usefulness of Lincos has been seriously questioned by other mathematicians, such as Hogben, who consider it doubtful that what seems purely logical to us would appear so to distant minds, schooled in utterly different methods of thought.

from
STRANGER IN A
STRANGE LAND

Robert A. Heinlein

Jubal turned to Mahmoud. "Don't worry that I might invite Mike to suicide. I grok that he doesn't grok joking." Jubal blinked. "But *I* don't grok 'grok.' Stinky, you speak Martian."

"A little."

"You speak it fluently, I heard you. Do *you* grok 'grok'?"

Mahmoud looked thoughtful. "No. 'Grok' is the most important word in the language—and I expect to spend years trying to understand it. But I don't expect to be successful. You need to *think* in Martian to grok the word 'grok.' Perhaps you have noticed that Mike takes a veering approach to some ideas?"

"Have I! My throbbing head!"

"Mine, too."

"Food," announced Jubal. "Lunch, and about time! Girls, put it where we can reach it and maintain a respectful silence. Go on, Doctor. Or does Mike's presence make it better to postpone it?"

"Not at all." Mahmoud spoke in Martian to Mike. Mike answered, smiled sunnily; his expression became blank again and he applied himself to food. "I told him what I was trying to do and he told me that I would speak rightly; this was no opinion but a fact, a necessity. I hope that if I fail to, he will notice and tell me. But I doubt if he will. Mike thinks in Martian—and this gives him a different 'map.' You follow me?"

"I grok it," agreed Jubal. "Language itself shapes a man's basic ideas."

"Yes, but—Doctor, you speak Arabic?"

"Eh? Badly," admitted Jubal. "Put in a while as an army surgeon in

North Africa. I still read it because I prefer the words of the Prophet in the original."

"Proper. The Koran cannot be translated—the 'map' changes no matter how one tries. You understand, then, how difficult *I* found English. It was not alone that my native language has simpler inflections; the 'map' changed. English is the largest human tongue; its variety, subtlety, and irrational, idiomatic complexity make it possible to say things in English which cannot be said in any other language. It almost drove me crazy . . . until I learned to think in it—and that put a new 'map' of the world on top of the one I grew up with. A better one, perhaps—certainly a more detailed one."

"But there are things which can be said in Arabic that *cannot* be said in English."

Jubal nodded. "That's why I've kept up my reading."

"Yes. But Martian is so much *more* complex than is English—and so wildly different in how it abstracts its picture of the universe—that English and Arabic might as well be one language. An Englishman and an Arab can learn to think each other's language. But I'm not certain that it will ever be possible for us to *think* in Martian (other than the way Mike learned it)— oh, we can learn 'pidgin' Martian—that is what I speak.

"Take this word: 'grok.' Its literal meaning, one which I suspect goes back to the origin of the Martian race as thinking creatures—and which throws light on their whole 'map'—is easy. 'Grok' means 'to drink.' "

"Huh?" said Jubal. "Mike never says 'grok' when he's just talking about drinking. He—"

"Just a moment." Mahmoud spoke to Mike in Martian.

Mike looked faintly surprised. " 'Grok' is drink."

"But Mike would have agreed," Mahmoud went on, "if I had named a hundred other English words, words which we think of as different concepts, even antithetical concepts. 'Grok' means *all* of these. It means 'fear,' it means 'love,' it means 'hate'—proper hate, for by the Martian 'map' you cannot hate anything unless you grok it, understand it so thoroughly that you merge with it and it merges with you—then can you hate. By hating yourself. But this implies that you love it, too, and cherish it and would not have it otherwise. Then you can *hate*—and (I think) Martian hate is an emotion so black that the nearest human equivalent could only be called mild distaste."

Mahmoud screwed up his face. " 'Grok' means 'identically equal.' The human cliché. 'This hurts me worse than it does you' has a Martian flavor. The Martians seem to know instinctively what we learned painfully from modern physics, that observer interacts with observed through the process of observation. 'Grok' means to understand so thoroughly that the observer becomes a part of the observed—to merge, blend, intermarry, lose identity in group experience. It means almost everything that we mean by religion, philosophy, and science—and it means as little to us as color means to a blind man." Mahmoud paused. "Jubal, if I chopped you up and made a stew, you and the stew, whatever was in it, would grok—and when I ate you, we would grok together and nothing would be lost and it would not matter which one of us did the eating."

"It would to me!" Jubal said firmly.

"You aren't a Martian." Mahmoud stopped to talk to Mike in Martian.

Mike nodded. "You spoke rightly, my brother Dr. Mahmoud. I am been saying so. Thou art God."

Mahmoud shrugged helplessly. "You see how hopeless it is? All I got was a blasphemy. We don't think in Martian. We *can't.*"

"Thou art God," Mike said agreeably. "God groks."

"Let's change the subject! Jubal, could I impose on brotherhood for more gin?"

"I'll get it!" said Dorcas.

THE ASCENT TO TRUTH

Thomas Merton

At the climax of mystical perfection, which is the consummation of perfect charity in so far as it can be attained on this earth, love cries out with a more and more ardent hunger and sweetly demands the satiation of perfect vision. Here there is no darkness. The dawn has come. The first rays of the morning sun, the Divine Word, have penetrated the pure depths of the soul transformed in His Light.

The soul stands on the bank of another Jordan—the bright calm river of death. It looks across the river and sees clear light upon the mountains of the true promised land. It begins to be ravished to the depths of its being by the clean scent of forests full of spice and balsam. It stands upon the riverbank with the wonderful soft wind of the New World playing upon its cheeks and upon its eyelids and in its hair. And now it knows that the country it once took to be Canaan, the poor indigent earth of early contemplation, was nothing more than a desert—a waste of dry rock to which it had escaped, at great cost, from the vain wisdom that is Egypt.

But here is God. He is the Promised Land. Nothing is lost in Him. The whole world shines in His bosom. Creatures of all kinds spring forth without end from the bright abyss of His Wisdom. The soul itself sees itself in Him, and Him in itself, and in them both, the whole world. It sees all things, all men living and dead, the great souls and the little souls, the saints, the glorious Mother of God, and it is one with them all for they are all One, and Christ, God, is this One. He is the Promised Land, He is the Word, He is the Beloved.

Here, in Him, all the articles of faith have converged their rays and have burst open and showered the mind with fire. From Him they came, through Him they came, to Him they return, bringing with them the minds they have raised up in radiance from the sepulcher of vain learning. In Him the articles of faith have disappeared. He is their substance. There is no further need for them to prophesy in part, for when that which is perfect is come, that which is in part shall be done away.

And so the soul, transformed in God and waiting at the threshold of heaven, sings its desire for His theology.

IV

AMERICA VANISHING

Does the Whale's Magnitude Diminish?—Will he Perish?
HERMAN MELVILLE, *Moby-Dick*

THE CLARK'S FORK VALLEY, WYOMING

Ernest Hemingway

At the end of summer, the big trout would be out in the centre of the stream; they were leaving the pools along the upper part of the river and dropping down to spend the winter in the deep water of the canyon. It was wonderful fly-fishing then in the first weeks of September. The native trout were sleek, shining, and heavy, and nearly all of them leaped when they took the fly. If you fished two flies, you would often have two big trout on and the need to handle them very delicately in that heavy current.

The nights were cold, and, if you woke in the night, you would hear the coyotes. But you did not want to get out on the stream too early in the day because the nights were so cold they chilled the water, and the sun had to be on the river until almost noon before the trout would start to feed.

You could ride in the morning, or sit in front of the cabin, lazy in the sun, and look across the valley where the hay was cut so the meadows were cropped brown and smooth to the line of quaking aspens along the river, now turning yellow in the fall. And on the hills rising beyond, the sage was silvery grey.

Up the river were the two peaks of Pilot and Index, where we would hunt mountain-sheep later in the month, and you sat in the sun and marvelled at the formal, clean-lined shape mountains can have at a distance, so that you remember them in the shapes they show from far away, and not as the broken rockslides you crossed, the jagged edges you pulled up by, and the narrow shelves you sweated along, afraid to look down, to round that peak that looked so smooth and geometrical. You climbed around it to come out on a clear space to look down to where an old ram and three young rams were feeding in the juniper bushes in a high, grassy pocket cupped against the broken rock of the peak.

The old ram was purple-grey, his rump was white, and when he raised his head you saw the great heavy curl of his horns. It was the white of his rump that had betrayed him to you in the green of the junipers when you had lain in the lee of a rock, out of the wind, three miles away, looking carefully at every yard of the high country through a pair of good Zeiss glasses.

Now as you sat in front of the cabin, you remembered that down-hill shot and the young rams standing, their heads turned, staring at him, waiting for him to get up. They could not see you on that high ledge, nor wind you, and the shot made no more impression on them than a boulder falling.

You remembered the year we had built a cabin at the head of Timber Creek, and the big grizzly that tore it open every time we were away. The snow came late that year, and this bear would not hibernate, but spent his autumn tearing open cabins and ruining a trap-line. But he was so smart you never saw him in the day. Then you remembered coming on the three grizzlies in the high country at the head of Crandall Creek. You heard a crash of timber and thought it was a cow elk bolting, and then there they were, in the broken shadow, running with an easy, lurching smoothness, the afternoon sun making their coats a soft, bristling silver.

You remembered elk bugling in the fall, the bull so close you could see his chest muscles swell as he lifted his head, and still not see his head in the thick timber; but hear that deep, high mounting whistle and the answer from across another valley. You thought of all the heads you had turned down and refused to shoot, and you were pleased about every one of them.

You remembered the children learning to ride; how they did with different horses; and how they loved the country. You remembered how this country had looked when you first came into it, and the year you had to stay four months after you had brought the first car ever to come in for the swamp roads to freeze solid enough to get the car out. You could remember all the hunting and all the fishing and the riding in the summer sun and the dust of the pack-train, the silent riding in the hills in the sharp cold of fall going up after the cattle on the high range, finding them wild as deer and as quiet, only bawling noisily when they were all herded together being forced along down into the lower country.

Then there was the winter; the trees bare now, the snow blowing so you could not see, the saddle wet, then frozen as you came down-hill, breaking a trail through the snow, trying to keep your legs moving, and the sharp, warming taste of whiskey when you hit the ranch and changed your clothes in front of the big open fireplace. It's a good country.

SPIRIT THAT FORM'D THIS SCENE

Walt Whitman

Spirit that form'd this scene,
These tumbled rock-piles grim and red,
These reckless heaven-ambitious peaks,
These gorges, turbulent-clear streams, this naked freshness,
These formless wild arrays, for reasons of their own,
I know thee, savage spirit—we have communed together,
Mine too such wild arrays, for reasons of their own;
Was't charged against my chants they had forgotten art?
To fuse within themselves its rules precise and delicatesse?
The lyrist's measur'd beat, the wrought-out temple's grace—column and
    polish'd arch forgot?
But thou that revelest here—spirit that form'd this scene,
They have remember'd thee.

1881

A LETTER TO C. E. NORTON, 19 MARCH 1902

W. D. Howells

I am just returned from a voyage on the Ohio River from Pittsburg to Cincinnati and back—a thousand miles of turbid, Tiber-colored torrent, flowing between the loveliest hills and richest levels in the world. Through veils of coal smoke I saw the little ugly house, in the little ugly town, where I was born, the steamboat not staying for me to visit it. The boat did, however, let me visit a vanished epoch in the life of the shores, where the type of Americanism, for good and for bad, or fifty years ago, still prevails. It is all, where man could make it so, a scene of hideous industrialism, with topless chimneys belching the fumes of the bottomless pit; but thousands of comfortable farmsteads line the banks which the river is always eating away (to its own hurt,) and the diabolical contrasts of riches and poverty are almost effaced. I should like to write a book about it. . . .

READING
THE WATER

Mark Twain

The face of the water, in time, became a wonderful book—a book that was a dead language to the uneducated passenger, but which told its mind to me without reserve, delivering its most cherished secrets as clearly as if it uttered them with a voice. And it was not a book to be read once and thrown aside, for it had a new story to tell every day. Throughout the long twelve hundred miles there was never a page that was void of interest, never one that you could leave unread without loss, never one that you would want to skip, thinking you could find higher enjoyment in some other thing. There never was so wonderful a book written by man; never one whose interest was so absorbing, so unflagging, so sparkingly renewed with every reperusal. The passenger who could not read it was charmed with a peculiar sort of faint dimple on its surface (on the rare occasions when he did not overlook it altogether); but to the pilot that was an *italicized* passage; indeed, it was more than that, it was a legend of the largest capitals, with a string of shouting exclamation-points at the end of it, for it meant that a wreck or a rock was buried there that could tear the life out of the strongest vessel that ever floated. It is the faintest and simplest expression the water ever makes, and the most hideous to a pilot's eye. In truth, the passenger who could not read this book saw nothing but all manner of pretty pictures in it, painted by the sun and shaded by the clouds, whereas to the trained eye these were not pictures at all, but the grimmest and most dead-earnest of reading-matter.

Now when I had mastered the language of this water, and had come to know every trifling feature that bordered the great river as familiarly as I knew the letters of the alphabet, I had made a valuable acquisition. But I had lost something, too. I had lost something which could never be restored to me while I lived. All the grace, the beauty, the poetry, had gone out of the majestic river! I still kept in mind a certain wonderful sunset which I witnessed when steamboating was new to me. A broad expanse of the river was turned to blood; in the middle distance the red hue brightened into gold, through which a solitary log came floating, black and conspicuous; in one place a long, slanting mark lay sparkling upon the water; in another the surface was broken by boiling, tumbling rings, that were as many-tinted as an opal; where the ruddy flush was faintest, was a smooth spot that was covered with graceful circles and radiating lines, ever so delicately traced; the shore on our left was densely wooded, and the somber shadow that fell from this forest was broken in one place by a long, ruffled trail that shone like silver; and high above the forest wall a clean-stemmed dead tree waved a single leafy bough that glowed like a flame in the unobstructed splendor that was flowing from the sun. There were graceful curves, reflected images, woody heights, soft distances; and over the whole scene, far and near, the dissolving lights drifted steadily, enriching it every passing moment with new marvels of coloring.

I stood like one bewitched. I drank it in, in a speechless rapture. The world was new to me, and I had never seen anything like this at home. But as I have said, a day came when I began to cease from noting the glories and the charms which the moon and the sun and the twilight wrought upon the river's face; another day came when I ceased altogether to note them. Then, if that sunset scene had been repeated, I should have looked upon it without rapture, and should have commented upon it, inwardly, after this fashion: "This sun means that we are going to have wind to-morrow; that floating log means that the river is rising, small thanks to it; that slanting mark on the water refers to a bluff reef which is going to kill somebody's steamboat one of these nights, if it keeps on stretching out like that; those tumbling 'boils' show a dissolving bar and a changing channel there; the lines and circles in the slick water over yonder are a warning that that troublesome place is shoaling up dangerously; that silver streak in the shadow of the forest is the 'break' from a new snag, and he has located himself in the very best place he could have found to fish for steamboats; that tall dead tree, with a single living branch, is not going to last long, and then how is a body ever going to get through this blind place at night without the friendly old landmark?"

No, the romance and beauty were all gone from the river. All the value any feature of it had for me now was the amount of usefulness it could furnish toward compassing the safe piloting of a steamboat. Since those days, I have pitied doctors from my heart. What does the lovely flush in a beauty's cheek mean to a doctor but a "break" that ripples above some deadly disease? Are not all her visible charms sown thick with what are to him the signs and symbols of hidden decay? Does he ever see her beauty at all, or doesn't he simply view her professionally, and comment upon her unwholesome condition all to himself? And doesn't he sometimes wonder whether he has gained most or lost most by learning his trade?

1883

THE FLOWER-FED BUFFALOES

Vachel Lindsay

The flower-fed buffaloes of the spring
In the days of long ago,
Ranged where the locomotives sing
And the prairie flowers lie low:
The tossing, blooming, perfumed grass
Is swept away by the wheat,
Wheels and wheels and wheels spin by
In the spring that still is sweet.
But the flower-fed buffaloes of the spring
Left us, long ago.
They gore no more, they bellow no more,
They trundle around the hills no more:
With the Blackfeet, lying low.
With the Pawnees, lying low,
Lying low.

A HAWK

Henry David Thoreau

On the 29th of April, as I was fishing from the bank of the river near Nine-Acre-Corner bridge, standing on the quaking grass and willow roots, where the muskrats lurk, I heard a singular rattling sound, somewhat like that of the sticks which boys play with their fingers, when, looking up, I observed a very slight and graceful hawk, like a nighthawk, alternately soaring like a ripple and tumbling a rod or two over and over, showing the under side of its wings, which gleamed like satin ribbon in the sun, or like the pearly inside of a shell. This sight reminded me of falconry and what nobleness and poetry are associated with that sport. The merlin it seemed to me it might be called: but I care not for its name. It was the most ethereal flight I had ever witnessed. It did not simply flutter like a butterfly, nor soar like the larger hawks, but it sported with proud reliance in the fields of air; mounting again and again with its strange chuckle, it repeated its free and beautiful fall, turning over and over like a kite, and then recovering from its lofty tumbling, as if it had never set its foot on *terra firma*. It appeared to have no companion in the universe,—sporting there alone,—and to need none but the morning and the ether with which it played. It was not lonely, but made all the earth lonely beneath it. Where was the parent which hatched it, its kindred, and its father in the heavens? The tenant of the air, it seemed related to the earth but by an egg hatched some time in the crevice of a crag;—or was its native nest made in the angle of a cloud, woven of the rainbow's trimmings and the sunset sky, and lined with some soft midsummer haze caught up from earth? Its eyry now some cliffy cloud.

1854

PASSENGER PIGEONS
James Fenimore Cooper

If the heavens were alive with pigeons, the whole village seemed equally in motion, with men, women, and children. Every species of fire-arms, from the French ducking-gun, with its barrel of near six feet in length, to the common horseman's pistol, was to be seen in the hands of the men and boys; while bows and arrows, some made of the simple stick of a walnut sapling, and others in a rude imitation of the ancient cross-bows, were carried by many of the latter.

The houses and the signs of life apparent in the village, drove the alarmed birds from the direct line of their flight, towards the mountains, along the sides and near the bases of which they were glancing in dense masses, that were equally wonderful by the rapidity of their motion, as by their incredible numbers.

We have already said, that across the inclined plane which fell from the steep ascent of the mountain to the banks of the Susquehanna, ran the highway, on either side of which a clearing of many acres had been made at a very early day. Over those clearings, and up the eastern mountain, and along the dangerous path that was cut into its side the different individuals posted themselves, as suited their inclinations; and in a few moments the attack commenced.

Among the sportsmen was to be seen the tall, gaunt form of Leather-stocking, who was walking over the field, with his rifle hanging on his arm, his dogs following close at his heels, now scenting the dead or wounded birds, that were beginning to tumble from the flocks, and then crouching under the legs of their master, as if they participated in his feelings at this wasteful and unsportsmanlike execution.

The reports of the fire-arms became rapid, whole volleys rising from the plain, as flocks of more than ordinary numbers darted over the opening, covering the field with darkness, like an interposing cloud; and then the light smoke of a single piece would issue from among the leafless bushes on the mountain, as death was hurled on the retreat of the affrighted birds, who were rising from a volley, for many feet into the air, in a vain effort to escape the attacks of man. Arrows, and missiles of every kind, were seen in the midst of the flocks; and so numerous were the birds, and so low did they take their flight, that even long poles, in the hands of those on the sides of the mountain, were used to strike them to the earth. . . .

So prodigious was the number of the birds, that the scattering fire of the guns, with the hurling of missiles, and the cries of the boys, had no other effect than to break off small flocks from the immense masses that continued to dart along the valley, as if the whole creation of the feathered tribe were pouring through that one pass. None pretended to collect the game, which lay scattered over the fields in such profusion as to cover the very ground with the fluttering victims.

Leather-stocking was a silent, but uneasy spectator of all these proceedings, but was able to keep his sentiments to himself until he saw the introduction of the swivel into the sports.

"This comes of settling a country!" he said—"here have I known the pigeons to fly for forty long years, and, till you made your clearings, there was nobody to skear or to hurt them. I loved to see them come into the woods, for they were company to a body; hurting nothing; being, as it was, as harmless as a garter-snake. But now it gives me sore thoughts when I hear the frighty things whizzing through the air, for I know it's only a motion to bring out all the brats in the village at them. Well! the Lord won't see the waste of his creaters for nothing, and right will be done to the pigeons, as well as others, by-and-by. There's Mr. Oliver, as bad as the rest of them, firing into the flocks as if he was shooting down nothing but the Mingo warriors."

Among the sportsmen was Billy Kirby, who, armed with an old musket, was loading, and without even looking into the air, was firing and shouting as his victims fell even on his own person. He heard the speech of Natty, and took upon himself to reply—

"What's that, old Leather-stocking!" he cried, "grumbling at the loss of a few pigeons! If you had to sow your wheat twice, and three times, as I have done, you wouldn't be so massyfully feeling'd to'ards the divils.—Hurrah, boys! scatter the feathers. This is better than shooting at a turkey's head and neck, old fellow."

"It's better for you, maybe, Billy Kirby," replied the indignant old hunter, "and all them as don't know how to put a ball down a rifle-barrel, or how to bring it up ag'n with a true aim; but it's wicked to be shooting into flocks in this wasty manner; and none do it, who know how to knock over a single bird. If a body has a craving for pigeon's flesh, why! it's made the same as all other creater's, for man's eating, but not to kill twenty and eat one. When I want such a thing I go into the woods till I find one to my liking, and then I shoot him off the branches without touching a feather of another, though there might be a hundred on the same tree. But you couldn't do such a thing, Billy Kirby—you couldn't do it if you tried."

"What's that you say, you old, dried cornstalk! you sapless stub!" cried the wood-chopper. "You've grown mighty boasting, sin' you killed the turkey; but if you're for a single shot, here goes at that bird which comes on by himself."

The fire from the distant part of the field had driven a single pigeon below the flock to which it had belonged, and frightened with the constant reports of the muskets, it was approaching the spot where the disputants stood, darting first from one side, and then to the other, cutting the air with the swiftness of lightning, and making a noise with its wings, not unlike the rushing of a bullet. Unfortunately for the wood-chopper, notwithstanding his vaunt, he did not see his bird until it was too late for him to fire as it approached, and he pulled his trigger at the unlucky moment when it was darting immediately over his head. The bird continued its course with incredible velocity.

Natty lowered the rifle from his arm, when the challenge was made, and, waiting a moment, until the terrified victim had got in a line with his eyes, and had dropped near the bank of the lake, he raised it again with uncommon rapidity, and fired. It might have been chance, or it might have been skill, that produced the result; it was probably a union of both; but the pigeon whirled over in the air, and fell into the lake, with a broken wing. At the sound of his rifle, both his dogs started from his feet, and in a few minutes the "slut" brought out the bird, still alive.

The wonderful exploit of Leather-stocking was noised through the field with great rapidity, and the sportsmen gathered in to learn the truth of the report.

"What," said young Edwards, "have you really killed a pigeon on the wing, Natty, with a single ball?"

"Haven't I killed loons before now, lad, that dive at the flash?" returned the hunter. "It's much better to kill only such as you want, without wasting your powder and lead, than to be firing into God's creaters in such a wicked manner. But I come out for a bird, and you know the reason why I like small game, Mr. Oliver, and now I have got one I will go home, for I don't relish to see these wasty ways that you are all practysing, as if the least thing wasn't made for use, and not to destroy."

"Thou sayest well, Leather-stocking," cried Marmaduke, "and I begin to think it time to put an end to this work of destruction."

1823

DIRECTIVE

Robert Frost

Back out of all this now too much for us,
Back in a time made simple by the loss
Of detail, burned, dissolved, and broken off
Like graveyard marble sculpture in the weather,
There is a house that is no more a house
Upon a farm that is no more a farm
And in a town that is no more a town.
The road there, if you'll let a guide direct you
Who only has at heart your getting lost,
May seem as if it should have been a quarry—
Great monolithic knees the former town
Long since gave up pretense of keeping covered.
And there's a story in a book about it:
Besides the wear of iron wagon wheels
The ledges show lines ruled southeast northwest,
The chisel work of an enormous Glacier
That braced his feet against the Arctic Pole.
You must not mind a certain coolness from him
Still said to haunt this side of Panther Mountain.
Nor need you mind the serial ordeal
Of being watched from forty cellar holes
As if by eye pairs out of forty firkins.
As for the woods' excitement over you
That sends light rustle rushes to their leaves,
Charge that to upstart inexperience.
Where were they all not twenty years ago?
They think too much of having shaded out
A few old pecker-fretted apple trees.
Make yourself up a cheering song of how
Someone's road home from work this once was,
Who may be just ahead of you on foot
Or creaking with a buggy load of grain.
The height of the adventure is the height
Of country where two village cultures faded
Into each other. Both of them are lost.
And if you're lost enough to find yourself

By now, pull in your ladder road behind you
And put a sign up CLOSED to all but me.
Then make yourself at home. The only field
Now left's no bigger than a harness gall.
First there's the children's house of make believe,
Some shattered dishes underneath a pine,
The playthings in the playhouse of the children.
Weep for what little things could make them glad.
Then for the house that is no more a house,
But only a belilaced cellar hole,
Now slowly closing like a dent in dough.
This was no playhouse but a house in earnest.
Your destination and your destiny's
A brook that was the water of the house,
Cold as a spring as yet so near its source,
Too lofty and original to rage.
(We know the valley streams that when aroused
Will leave their tatters hung on barb and thorn.)
I have kept hidden in the instep arch
Of an old cedar at the waterside
A broken drinking goblet like the Grail
Under a spell so the wrong ones can't find it,
So can't get saved, as Saint Mark says they mustn't.
(I stole the goblet from the children's playhouse.)
Here are your waters and your watering place.
Drink and be whole again beyond confusion.

NIGHT

Robinson Jeffers

The ebb slips from the rock, the sunken
Tide-rocks lift streaming shoulders
Out of the slack, the slow west
Sombering its torch; a ship's light
Shows faintly, far out,
Over the weight of the prone ocean
On the low cloud.

Over the dark mountain, over the dark pinewood,
Down the long dark valley along the shrunken river,
Returns the splendor without rays, the shining of shadow,
Peace-bringer, the matrix of all shining and quieter of shining.
Where the shore widens on the bay she opens dark wings
And the ocean accepts her glory. O soul worshipful of her
You like the ocean have grave depths where she dwells always,
And the film of waves above that takes the sun takes also
Her, with more love. The sun-lovers have a blond favorite,
A father of lights and noises, wars, weeping and laughter,
Hot labor, lust and delight and the other blemishes.
  Quietness
Flows from her deeper fountain; and he will die; and she is immortal.

Far off from here the slender
Flocks of the mountain forest
Move among stems like towers
Of the old redwoods to the stream,
No twig crackling; dip shy
Wild muzzles into the mountain water
Among the dark ferns.
O passionately at peace you being secure will pardon
The blasphemies of glowworms, the lamp in my tower, the fretfulness
Of cities, the crescents of the planets, the pride of the stars.
This August night in a rift of cloud Antares reddens,
The great one, the ancient torch, a lord among lost children,
The earth's orbit doubled would not girdle his greatness,
  one fire
Globed, out of grasp of the mind enormous; but to you
  O Night

What? Not a spark? What flicker of a spark in the faint far glimmer
Of a lost fire dying in the desert, dim coals of a sand-pit the Bedouins
Wandered from at dawn . . . Ah singing prayer to what gulfs tempted
Suddenly are you more lost? To us the near-hand mountain
Be a measure of height, the tide-worn cliff at the sea-gate a measure of
    continuance.

The tide, moving the night's
Vastness with lonely voices,
Turns, the deep dark-shining
Pacific leans on the land,
Feeling his cold strength
To the outmost margins: you Night will resume
The stars in your time.

O passionately at peace when will that tide draw shoreward?
Truly the spouting fountains of light, Antares, Arcturus,
Tire of their flow, they sing one song but they think silence.
The striding winter giant Orion shines, and dreams darkness.
And life, the flicker of men and moths and the wolf on the hill,
Though furious for continuance, passionately feeding, passionately
    passionately
Remaking itself upon its mates, remembers deep inward
The calm mother, the quietness of the womb and the egg,
The primal and the latter silences: dear Night it is memory
Prophesies, prophecy that remembers, the charm of the dark.
And I and my people, we are willing to love the four-score years
Heartily; but as a sailor loves the sea, when the helm is for harbor.

Have men's minds changed,
Or the rock hidden in the deep of the waters of the soul
Broken the surface? A few centuries
Gone by, was none dared not to people
The darkness beyond the stars with harps and habitations.
But now, dear is the truth. Life is grown sweeter and lonelier,
And death is no evil.

THE GRASS ON THE MOUNTAIN

Paiute Poem

Oh, long long
The snow has possessed the mountains.

The deer have come down and the big-horn,
They have followed the sun to the south
To feed on the mesquite pods and the bunch grass.
Loud are the thunder drums
In the tent of the mountains.
Oh, long, long
Have we eaten chia seeds
And dried deer's flesh of the summer killing.
We are wearied of our huts
And the smoky smell of our garments.

We are sick with desire of the sun
And the grass on the mountain.

—Translated by Mary Austin

V
ART

THE IMITATION OF CHAOS

A noiseless patient spider,
I mark'd where on a little promontory it stood isolated,
Mark'd how to explore the vacant vast surrounding,
It launch'd forth filament, filament, filament, out of itself,
Ever unreeling them, ever tirelessly speeding them.

And you O my soul where you stand,
Surrounded, detached, in measureless oceans of space,
Ceaselessly musing, venturing, throwing, seeking the spheres to connect them,
Till the bridge you will need be form'd, till the ductile anchor hold,
Till the gossamer thread you fling catch somewhere, O my soul.

WALT WHITMAN

Only connect! That was the whole of her sermon. Only connect the prose
and the passion, and both will be exalted, and human love will be seen
at its height. Live in fragments no longer. Only connect, and the
beast and the monk, robbed of the isolation that it life to either, will die.

E. M. FORSTER, *Howard's End*

For most of recorded history the several forms of the arts could be defined by the public for which they were intended. From the ritualized citizenship of Greek drama to the Christian iconography of medieval graphic arts, to the noble Renaissance patron and the bourgeois collector, to the 20th Century institutional consumer every art object or performance had a public that placed a value on it and preserved it for that value. Shakespeare's faith in the immortality of his verses is only possible where art has this public value, and conceptions of style, craftsmanship, and good taste may be understood only in terms of the public for which the art has value.

For Aristotle, the aim of art to "imitate" was a moral and social function, explained in terms of a public audience. Now in our time, artists like Sartre and Kafka working in the public tradition of Aristotelian "imitation" have attempted to give aesthetic form to turmoil and chaos.

What then are we to make of artworks that on one hand solipsize art, that is, deny the existence of any public interest in it, or on the other hand concretize it, that is, conceive of it as made of unworked random materials, without style, craftsmanship, or taste? Are not both such movements efforts to reassert the importance of the self, in the first case the artist's self and in the second the consumer's self, in the art experience? The artist who constructs a self-destructive sculpture must laugh at the institution that purchases it, since the work illustrates the principle that the art object has no value after the artistic experience of creating it is over. "Found art," made of "junk," deliberately denies the idea of craftsmanship, as does "concrete" music, environmental art, and "action" art, in all of which pure chance produces at least part of the aesthetic effects. Even such a social medium as words can be "solipsized" in poetry of private symbolism, or "concretized" in guerilla theater.

Yet the main stream of public art can and does co-opt such "avant garde" artworks, and purchases them for display as evidence of the health of a cultural tradition that encourages rebellious self-criticism. The artist smiles, and the museum director smiles. Only the public frowns, and takes up pottery as a form of self-expression.

The Artist Makes

HOW WE LISTEN

Aaron Copland

We all listen to music according to our separate capacities. But, for the sake of analysis, the whole listening process may become clearer if we break it up into its component parts, so to speak. In a certain sense we all listen to music on three separate planes. For lack of a better terminology, one might name these: (1) the sensuous plane, (2) the expressive plane, (3) the sheerly musical plane. The only advantage to be gained from mechanically splitting up the listening process into these hypothetical planes is the clear view to be had of the way in which we listen.

The simplest way of listening to music is to listen for the sheer pleasure of the musical sound itself. That is the sensuous plane. It is the plane on which we hear music without thinking, without considering it in any way. One turns on the radio while doing something else and absent-mindedly bathes in the sound. A kind of brainless but attractive state of mind is engendered by the mere sound appeal of the music.

You may be sitting in a room reading this book. Imagine one note struck on the piano. Immediately that one note is enough to change the atmosphere of the room—proving that the sound element in music is a powerful and mysterious agent, which it would be foolish to deride or belittle.

The surprising thing is that many people who consider themselves qualified music lovers abuse that plane in listening. They go to concerts in order to lose themselves. They use music as a consolation or an escape. They enter an ideal world where one doesn't have to think of the realities of everyday life. Of course they aren't thinking about the music either. Music allows them to leave it, and they go off to a place to dream, dreaming because of and apropos of the music yet never quite listening to it.

Yes, the sound appeal of music is a potent and primitive force, but you must not allow it to usurp a disproportionate share of your interest. The sensuous plane is an important one in music, a very important one, but it does not constitute the whole story.

There is no need to digress further on the sensuous plane. Its appeal to every normal human being is self-evident. There is, however, such a thing as becoming more sensitive to the different kinds of sound stuff as used by various composers. For all composers do not use that sound stuff in the same way. Don't get the idea that the value of music is commensurate with its sensuous appeal or that the loveliest sounding music is made by the greatest composer. If that were so, Ravel would be a greater creator than Beethoven. The point is that the sound element varies with each composer, that his usage of sound forms an integral part of his style and must be taken into account when listening. The reader can see, therefore, that a more conscious approach is valuable even on this primary plane of music listening.

The second plane on which music exists is what I have called the expressive one. Here, immediately, we tread on controversial ground. Composers have a way of shying away from any discussion of music's expressive side. Did not Stravinsky himself proclaim that his music was an "object," a "thing," with a life of its own, and with no other meaning than its own purely musical existence? This intransigent attitude of Stravinsky's may be due to the fact that so many people have tried to read different meanings into so many pieces. Heaven knows it is difficult enough to say precisely what it is that a piece of music means, to say it definitely, to say it finally so that everyone is satisfied with your explanation. But that should not lead one to the other extreme of denying to music the right to be "expressive."

My own belief is that all music has an expressive power, some more and some less, but that all music has a certain meaning behind the notes and that that meaning behind the notes constitutes, after all, what the piece is saying, what the piece is about. This whole problem can be stated quite simply by asking, "Is there a meaning to music?" My answer to that would be, "Yes." And "Can you state in so many words what the meaning is?" My answer to that would be, "No." Therein lies the difficulty.

Simple-minded souls will never be satisfied with the answer to the second of these questions. They always want music to have a meaning, and the more concrete it is the better they like it. The more the music reminds them of a train, a storm, a funeral, or any other familiar conception the more expressive it appears to be to them. This popular idea of music's meaning— stimulated and abetted by the usual run of musical commentator—should be discouraged wherever and whenever it is met. One timid lady once confessed to me that she suspected something seriously lacking in her appreciation of music because of her inability to connect it with anything definite. That is getting the whole thing backward, of course.

Still, the question remains, How close should the intelligent music lover wish to come to pinning a definite meaning to any particular work? No closer than a general concept, I should say. Music expresses, at different moments, serenity or exuberance, regret or triumph, fury or delight. It expresses each of these moods, and many others, in a numberless variety of subtle shadings and differences. It may even express a state of meaning for which there exists no adequate word in any language. In that case, musicians often like to say that it has only a purely musical meaning. They sometimes go farther and say that *all* music has only a purely musical meaning. What they really mean is that no appropriate word can be found to express the music's meaning and that, even if it could, they do not feel the need of finding it.

But whatever the professional musician may hold, most musical novices still search for specific words with which to pin down their musical reactions. That is why they always find Tschaikovsky easier to "understand" than Beethoven. In the first place, it is easier to pin a meaning-word on a Tschaikovsky piece than on a Beethoven one. Much easier. Moreover, with the Russian composer, every time you come back to a piece of his it almost always says the same thing to you, whereas with Beethoven it is often quite difficult to put your finger right on what he is saying. And any musician will tell you that that is why Beethoven is the greater composer. Because music which always says the same thing to you will necessarily soon become dull music, but music whose meaning is slightly different with each hearing has a greater chance of remaining alive.

Listen, if you can, to the forty-eight fugue themes of Bach's *Well Tempered Clavier*. Listen to each theme, one after another. You will soon realize that each theme mirrors a different world of feeling. You will also soon realize that the more beautiful a theme seems to you the harder it is to find any word that will describe it to your complete satisfaction. Yes, you will certainly know whether it is a gay theme or a sad one. You will be able, in other words, in your own mind, to draw a frame of emotional feeling around your theme. Now study the sad one a little closer. Try to pin down the exact quality of its sadness. Is it pessimistically sad or resignedly sad; is it fatefully sad or smilingly sad?

Let us suppose that you are fortunate and can describe to your own satisfaction in so many words the exact meaning of your chosen theme.

There is still no guarantee that anyone else will be satisfied. Nor need they be. The important thing is that each one feel for himself the specific expressive quality of a theme or, similarly, an entire piece of music. And if it is a great work of art, don't expect it to mean exactly the same thing to you each time you return to it.

Themes or pieces need not express only one emotion, of course. Take such a theme as the first main one of the *Ninth Symphony*, for example. It is clearly made up of different elements. It does not say only one thing. Yet anyone hearing it immediately gets a feeling of strength, a feeling of power. It isn't a power that comes simply because the theme is played loudly. It is a power inherent in the theme itself. The extraordinary strength and vigor of the theme results in the listener's receiving an impression that a forceful statement has been made. But one should never try to boil it down to "the fateful hammer of life," etc. That is where the trouble begins. The musician, in his exasperation, says it means nothing but the notes themselves, whereas the nonprofessional is only too anxious to hang on to any explanation that gives him the illusion of getting closer to the music's meaning.

Now, perhaps the reader will know better what I mean when I say that music does have an expressive meaning but that we cannot say in so many words what that meaning is.

The third plane on which music exists is the sheerly musical plane. Besides the pleasurable sound of music and the expressive feeling that it gives off, music does exist in terms of the notes themselves and of their manipulation. Most listeners are not sufficiently conscious of this third plane. It will be largely the business of this book to make them more aware of music on this plane.

Professional musicians, on the other hand, are, if anything, too conscious of the mere notes themselves. They often fall into the error of becoming so engrossed with their arpeggios and staccatos that they forget the deeper aspects of the music they are performing. But from the layman's standpoint, it is not so much a matter of getting over bad habits on the sheerly musical plane as of increasing one's awareness of what is going on, in so far as the notes are concerned.

When the man in the street listens to the "notes themselves" with any degree of concentration, he is most likely to make some mention of the melody. Either he hears a pretty melody or he does not, and he generally lets it go at that. Rhythm is likely to gain his attention next, particularly if it seems exciting. But harmony and tone color are generally taken for granted, if they are thought of consciously at all. As for music's having a definite form of some kind, that idea seems never to have occurred to him.

It is very important for all of us to become more alive to music on its sheerly musical plane. After all, an actual musical material is being used.

The intelligent listener must be prepared to increase his awareness of the musical material and what happens to it. He must hear the melodies, the rhythms, the harmonies, the tone colors in a more conscious fashion. But above all he must, in order to follow the line of the composer's thought, know something of the principles of musical form. Listening to all of these elements is listening on the sheerly musical plane.

Let me repeat that I have split up mechanically the three separate planes on which we listen merely for the sake of greater clarity. Actually, we never listen on one or the other of these planes. What we do is to correlate them—listening in all three ways at the same time. It takes no mental effort, for we do it instinctively.

Perhaps an analogy with what happens to us when we visit the theater will make this instinctive correlation clearer. In the theater, you are aware of the actors and actresses, costumes and sets, sounds and movements. All these give one the sense that the theater is a pleasant place to be in. They constitute the sensuous plane in our theatrical reactions.

The expressive plane in the theater would be derived from the feeling that you get from what is happening on the stage. You are moved to pity, excitement, or gayety. It is this general feeling, generated aside from the particular words being spoken, a certain emotional something which exists on the stage, that is analogous to the expressive quality in music.

The plot and plot development is equivalent to our sheerly musical plane. The playwright creates and develops a character in just the same way that a composer creates and develops a theme. According to the degree of your awareness of the way in which the artist in either field handles his material will you become a more intelligent listener.

It is easy enough to see that the theatergoer never is conscious of any of these elements separately. He is aware of them all at the same time. The same is true of music listening. We simultaneously and without thinking listen on all three planes.

In a sense, the ideal listener is both inside and outside the music at the same moment, judging it and enjoying it, wishing it would go one way and watching it go another—almost like the composer at the moment he composes it; because in order to write his music, the composer must also be inside and outside his music, carried away by it and yet coldly critical of it. A subjective and objective attitude is implied in both creating and listening to music.

What the reader should strive for, then, is a more *active* kind of listening. Whether you listen to Mozart or Duke Ellington, you can deepen your understanding of music only by being a more conscious and aware listener—not someone who is just listening, but someone who is listening *for* something.

EXPERIMENTAL MUSIC

John Cage

Formerly, whenever anyone said the music I presented was experimental, I objected. It seemed to me that composers knew what they were doing, and that the experiments that had been made had taken place prior to the finished works, just as sketches are made before paintings and rehearsals precede performances. But, giving the matter further thought, I realized that there is ordinarily an essential difference between making a piece of music and hearing one. A composer knows his work as a woodsman knows a path he has traced and retraced, while a listener is confronted by the same work as one is in the woods by a plant he has never seen before.

Now, on the other hand, times have changed; music has changed; and I no longer object to the word "experimental." I use it in fact to describe all the music that especially interests me and to which I am devoted, whether someone else wrote it or I myself did. What has happened is that I have become a listener and the music has become something to hear. Many people, of course, have given up saying "experimental" about this new music. Instead, they either move to a halfway point and say "controversial" or depart to a greater distance and question whether this "music" is music at all.

For in this new music nothing takes place but sounds: those that are notated and those that are not. Those that are not notated appear in the written music as silences, opening the doors of the music to the sounds that happen to be in the environment. This openness exists in the fields of modern sculpture and architecture. The glass houses of Mies van der Rohe reflect their environment, presenting to the eye images of clouds, trees, or grass, according to the situation. And while looking at the constructions in wire of the sculptor Richard Lippold, it is inevitable that one will see other things, and people too, if they happen to be there at the same time, through the network of wires. There is no such thing as an empty space or an empty time. There is always something to see, something to hear. In fact, try as we may to make a silence, we cannot. For certain engineering purposes, it is desirable to have as silent a situation as possible. Such a room is called an anechoic chamber, its six walls made of special material, a room without echoes. I entered one at Harvard University several years ago and heard two sounds, one high and one low. When I described them to the engineer in charge, he informed me that the high one was my nervous system in operation, the low one my blood in circulation. Until I die there will be sounds.

And they will continue following my death. One need not fear about the future of music.

But this fearlessness only follows if, at the parting of the ways, where it is realized that sounds occur whether intended or not, one turns in the direction of these he does not intend. This turning is psychological and seems at first to be a giving up of everything that belongs to humanity—for a musician, the giving up of music. This psychological turning leads to the world of nature, where, gradually or suddenly, one sees that humanity and nature, not separate, are in this world together; that nothing was lost when everything was given away. In fact, everything is gained. In musical terms, any sounds may occur in any combination and in any continuity.

And it is a striking coincidence that just now the technical means to produce such a free-ranging music are available. When the Allies entered Germany towards the end of World War II, it was discovered that improvements had been made in recording sounds magnetically such that tape had become suitable for the high-fidelity recording of music. First in France with the work of Pierre Schaeffer, later here, in Germany, in Italy, in Japan, and perhaps, without my knowing it, in other places, magnetic tape was used not simply to record performances of music but to make a new music that was possible only because of it. Given a minimum of two tape recorders and a disk recorder, the following processes are possible: 1) a single recording of any sound may be made; 2) a rerecording may be made, in the course of which, by means of filters and circuits, any or all of the physical characteristics of a given recorded sound may be altered; 3) electronic mixing (combining on a third machine sounds issuing from two others) permits the presentation of any number of sounds in combination; 4) ordinary splicing permits the juxtaposition of any sounds, and when it includes unconventional cuts, it, like rerecording, brings about alterations of any or all of the original physical characteristics. The situation made available by these means is essentially a total sound-space, the limits of which are ear-determined only, the position of a particular sound in this space being the result of five determinants: frequency or pitch, amplitude or loudness, overtone structure or timbre, duration, and morphology (how the sound begins, goes on, and dies away). By the alteration of any one of these determinants, the position of the sound in sound-space changes. Any sound at any point in this total sound-space can move to become a sound at any other point. But advantage can be taken of these possibilities only if one is willing to change one's musical habits radically. That is, one may take advantage of the appearance of images without visible transition in distant places, which is a way of saying "television," if one is willing to stay at home instead of going to a theatre. Or one may fly if one is willing to give up walking.

Musical habits include scales, modes, theories of counterpoint and harmony, and the study of the timbres, singly and in combination of a limited number of sound-producing mechanisms. In mathematical terms these all concern discrete steps. They resemble walking—in the case of pitches, on steppingstones twelve in number. This cautious stepping is not characteristic of the possibilities of magnetic tape, which is revealing to us that musical action or existence can occur at any point or along any line or curve or what have you in total sound-space; that we are, in fact, technically equipped to transform our contemporary awareness of nature's manner of operation into art.

Again there is a parting of the ways. One has a choice. If he does not wish to give up his attempts to control sound, he may complicate his musical technique towards an approximation of the new possibilities and awareness. (I use the word "approximation" because a measuring mind can never finally measure nature.) Or, as before, one may give up the desire to control sound, clear his mind of music, and set about discovering means to let sounds be themselves rather than vehicles for man-made theories or expressions of human sentiments.

This project will seem fearsome to many, but on examination it gives no cause for alarm. Hearing sounds which are just sounds immediately sets the theorizing mind to theorizing, and the emotions of human beings are continually aroused by encounters with nature. Does not a mountain unintentionally evoke in us a sense of wonder? otters along a stream a sense of mirth? night in the woods a sense of fear? Do not rain falling and mists rising up suggest the love binding heaven and earth? Is not decaying flesh loathsome? Does not the death of someone we love bring sorrow? And is there a greater hero than the least plant that grows? What is more angry than the flash of lightning and the sound of thunder? These responses to nature are mine and will not necessarily correspond with another's. Emotion takes place in the person who has it. And sounds, when allowed to be themselves, do not require that those who hear them do so unfeelingly. The opposite is what is meant by response ability.

New music: new listening. Not an attempt to understand something that is being said, for, if something were being said, the sounds would be given the shapes of words. Just an attention to the activity of sounds.

Those involved with the composition of experimental music find ways and means to remove themselves from the activities of the sounds they make. Some employ chance operations, derived from sources as ancient as the Chinese *Book of Changes*, or as modern as the tables of random numbers used also by physicists in research. Or, analogous to the Rorschach tests of psychology, the interpretation of imperfections in the paper upon which one is writing may provide a music free from one's memory and imagination. Geometrical means employing spatial superimpositions at variance with the ultimate performance in time may be used. The total field of possibilities may be roughly divided and the actual sounds within these divisions may be indicated as to number but left to the performer or to the splicer to choose. In this latter case, the composer resembles the maker of a camera who allows someone else to take the picture.

Whether one uses tape or writes for conventional instruments, the present musical situation has changed from what it was before tape came into being. This also need not arouse alarm, for the coming into being of something new does not by that fact deprive what was of its proper place. Each thing has its own place, never takes the place of something else; and the more things there are, as is said, the merrier.

But several effects of tape on experimental music may be mentioned. Since so many inches of tape equal so many seconds of time, it has become more and more usual that notation is in space rather than in symbols of quarter, half, and sixteenth notes and so on. Thus where on a page a note appears will correspond to when in a time it is to occur. A stop watch is used to facilitate a performance; and a rhythm results which is a far cry from horse's hoofs and other regular beats.

Also it has been impossible with the playing of several separate tapes at once to achieve perfect synchronization. This fact has led some towards the manufacture of multiple-tracked tapes and machines with a corresponding number of heads; while others—those who have accepted the sounds they do not intend—now realize that the score, the requiring that many parts be played in a particular togetherness, is not an accurate representation of how things are. These now compose parts but not scores, and the parts may be combined in any unthought ways. This means that each performance of such a piece of music is unique, as interesting to its composer as to others listening. It is easy to see again the parallel with nature, for even with leaves of the same tree, no two are exactly alike. The parallel in art is the sculpture with moving parts, the mobile.

It goes without saying that dissonances and noises are welcome in this new music. But so is the dominant seventh chord if it happens to put in an appearance.

Rehearsals have shown that this new music, whether for tape or for instruments, is more clearly heard when the several loud-speakers or performers are separated in space rather than grouped closely together. For this music is not concerned with harmoniousness as generally understood, where the quality of harmony results from a blending of several elements. Here we are concerned with the coexistence of dissimilars, and the central points where fusion occurs are many: the ears of the listeners wherever they are. This disharmony, to paraphrase Bergson's statement about disorder, is simply a harmony to which many are unaccustomed.

Where do we go from here? Towards theatre. That art more than music resembles nature. We have eyes as well as ears, and it is our business while we are alive to use them.

And what is the purpose of writing music? One is, of course, not dealing with purposes but dealing with sounds. Or the answer must take the form of paradox: a purposeful purposelessness or a purposeless play. This play, however, is an affirmation of life—not an attempt to bring order out of chaos nor to suggest improvements in creation, but simply a way of waking up to the very life we're living, which is so excellent once one gets one's mind and one's desires out of its way and lets it act of its own accord.

AN INTERVIEW
WITH LEON RUSSELL

Ben Fong-Torres

If rock and roll is color and dynamics, and fusion, and dancing, Leon Russell's got it down. Plus, he's showbiz, and he understands pace, production, and the advantages of keeping an audience a little amazed, wondering what it's all about.

I mean, who are these people? There's that breath-giving black queen, Claudia Lennear, a former Ikette flowing free, but still foxily Ikettish; her partner in the chorale is Kathy McDonald, a white woman who was asked to be an Ikette by Ike Turner when he heard her during a break at Fillmore West, sitting on the floor singing a fourth harmony line to "Wooden Ships." She declined the offer, but it didn't matter—Tina would just not have tolerated her. Kathy, from Seattle, then San Francisco, sings and dances like a waif just unbound, and rock and roll is her freedom.

And there's this comic figure, Huckleberry Finn-ish, thin in a Dr. Shazam T-shirt and adolescent in this wide, beaded headband with the peace symbol as the crown jewel—that's John Galley, playing organ with one hand, electric keyboard bass with the other. From the Joe Cocker Mad Dogs & Englishmen expedition, there are the fluffy blonds, drummer Chuck Blackwell and lead guitar Don Preston. Preston and rhythm guitar Joey Cooper also sing, forming the vocal wall with Claudia and Kathy. And Leon, lean, sleepy-eyed conductor behind his piano, working his fingers like a typist, grainy voice barking out the Dixie/hip words. The magnificent seven. . . .

Leon first split his hometown, Lawton, Oklahoma, to play trumpet with a band in a Tulsa nightclub, saying he was older than his 14 years to keep the job. By 16, he'd jammed with Ronnie Hawkins in Tulsa, and Jerry Lee Lewis was offering his band a touring job. Russell had also studied classical piano, beginning at age three. He split from home again in 1959, at age 17, to go to Los Angeles, working clubs on a borrowed ID card. After a short trip to Oklahoma, he returned to L.A. to stay.

Eventually, he became a full-time session man, at first getting jobs mostly from people who weren't turned off by his greased-back hair and hoodlum demeanor. But he was a master craftsman, and the workload built: he got calls from Phil Spector, Herb Alpert, and Terry Melcher, and worked hundreds of sessions, playing piano on records by Bob Lind, Gary Lewis, the Crystals, the Righteous Brothers, the Ronettes, Paul Revere and the Raiders, and so many more.

Then—hair growing and mind blowing—he dropped out and laid low, working at a small record company and hanging out mostly at home, building that home studio. . . . It was there that he did the Asylum Choir album.

And there, in the playroom-sized studio—now converted to 16-track—on Skyhill Road in the Hollywood hills, is where the energy stays. Reels of wide-band tape fill up closets and bathroom sinks; burlap and sweat often dominate the recording shack, and it isn't very impressive. There's neglect for everything but the music machines. But when Leon and his band are working out there, it's the Fillmore East, and—just the way he likes it—we're all on stage, hanging over stairways and peeking through the little door. Master chef Leon Russell, doin' some home cooking!

There's where the interview was first scheduled. But when the Emerson-Loew photography team and I got there, he wasn't ready. There was a new album and another tour ahead, he said. After that, we'd have something to talk about. Russell doesn't much care to recite his credentials and his biography (that's why we've done it here). So we met again on the first leg of his most recent tour, in Denver, Colorado; by then, he'd pretty well completed the new album, most of it done in Muscle Shoals, Alabama, and he was ready to talk.

It was a good time to find out all about Leon. He was in town a couple of days before the concert, resting up in a city he'd conquered twice before— once with Cocker; once with the stage/plantation all to his own band. His upcoming concert at the old Mammoth Gardens (formerly a roller skating rink) was in doubt—a hassle over the promoter not getting the ventilation fixed, you know. But that night, everyone went ahead, the Gardens was filled, and Russell, the image flashing out by way of a Malcolm X shirt, violet jeans, and a feathered cap provided backstage by a lady fan, Tinker Bell, was on top of it, talking soft and playing tough, a lot of the songs sounding alike and echoing back and forth to each other—one, two, three,

*four—amid the smoke and muggy unventilated air, the act and the audience
very close to each other.*

Sort of like the way it was back home on Skyhill Road.

—B. F.-T.

. . . .

*It's a funny thing, because people who can't understand long hair ask,
Why?" And we basically say, "Because we want to; we enjoy it." You know,
"it's my choice."*

Yeah, I can really understand that, though, because right before my hair
was long I used to see some of my freaky friends running around, and I'd
say, "What's it all about? What're you doing?" All of a sudden I had a
Frank Sinatra session, and I had my ducktail, my Sebring, Elvis Presley
haircut, and I just didn't have time to go through the do, you know, so I just
said hang it. There was so many people that I considered to be my friends
who came up to me and just coerced me. Said all kinds of weird things. And
so I thought: "Well, this is very strange." Sinatra, as a matter of fact, did a
double-take; I was the only one like that in the session. And I thought:
"Well, that's at least an 'eight'." It was weird because it all looked the same
to me and from my point of view, everything was exactly the same. People
just seemed to be bringing in these hostilities. So I decided to see how far it
goes, and I'm still the same. The hair was pretty long. . .

And you lacquered and sprayed it?

Consumed those products. . .

Deadly chemicals. . .

But I'm not an ecology freak . . . nor Women's Liberation. I'm almost
totally politically inactive.

*As Dick Cavett says, "Politics bores my ass off." But would you play free
concerts?*

If everybody'd agree to quit using money, I'd be happy to play for free
every day for awhile. But I don't play benefits or any kind of fund-raisers. I
prefer to play at hospitals, for people who otherwise can't see us. But I can't
see playing for causes, whatever the cause may be. . . .

*When you were doing the Joe Cocker Mad Dogs tour, you said basically
the idea behind your kind of rock and roll was tribalization—to have the
performers and audience together trading songs. Is that working?*

It's working throughout the country; the audience is why they have rock
and roll concerts, because that's the only missing element in the tribal culture. Well, an analogy to more primitive cultures would be—"the only thing
missing is the drummers." They've got the camp fire, they've got the circle,
but they just don't have the drummers, and that's where the rock and roll
bands come in.

Rock and roll joins the Gypsies. . .

I was thinking more of New Zealand, but it's the same bag. Africa, any kind of primitive tribal cultures.

How do you relate to festivals as a "tribal" thing?

Well, the only thing that's unfortunate about it is that for some reason or another, there's no ritual. I mean, the ritual's in the formative stages now. The tribe is just starting to recognize patterns in existence. In India the Indian music is essentially the same form as blues, in that it's spontaneity within a certain restricted format. But in India it's a religion, and the restrictions are known by everybody and they know what their participation is and it's just like a way of life. Here everybody's still seeking out the patterns, like the festivals are the closest thing I can see in our modern civilization because it's the way for people to expend non-specific energies.

Seems, though, like there are always variances in energies—there are always minds focused onto the political meanings of a crowd; why are we here; is this a capitalist cultural ripoff—things that would tend to separate people—and it leads to the talk—the pessimism about communes, tribes— the "death of rock and roll."

Both economics and politics are false sciences. They're based on poor communication. In other words, the reason people don't like to trade—the reason they prefer to have money is because they don't trust their own judgment of what something's worth. If they have an outside arbitrator, who fixes the value for the time certificates—which is what the dollars actually are—money just buys time—it's the same thing with politics, it's based on poor communications.

Capitalism itself in itself is a bit of a rip-off, as far as I'm concerned, but what are you going to do? I'm certainly not going to be a politician and change it, in or out of the system. I'm just going to sing my songs, because that's what I do. Some Oriental philosopher—Tao—once said that people that want to be political leaders are the least qualified to do it, and that's true. The people who really are qualified won't mess with it. So we always get the second best. . . .

Just another aspect of your religion. . . .

Well, before we get too far off in that direction I'd like to say that I believe that organized Christianity has done more harm than any other single force I can think of in the world. I don't know if it's religion itself or the organization—the "we" and the "they" and the "haves" and the "have-nots." We are right and you're wrong, as opposed to "Let's all be in the same spaceship."

What's the alternative for that kind of organization and that kind of religion?

Rock and roll.

Rock and roll—but you're an exponent of one particular kind of rock and roll. What about rock and roll that promotes organized religion or some subculture you might consider as harmful if not more harmful than the things you're fighting against?

I'm not really fighting against anything, but the Holy Trinity . . . I mean, I'm from the Bible Belt, so that's all in my background. Christianity. So that's the way that particular satire takes place. If you think of the Holy Trinity in terms of the triangle and geodesic domes, that's actually where I am at personally.

In the Christian church—or at least in the Protestant church, the Holy Trinity is the father, the son, and the Holy Ghost. But three has been a magic number for all sorts of sciences and near-sciences.

Was your religious background forced at or into you, or did it just seep into you and become a part of your life?

I make it a habit of trying to be really aware of the things I love and the things I hate, and I use them all equally.

How did you become aware of what you loved and hated in your youth?

I didn't understand southern Bible Belt Protestant racism, in terms of brotherhood, which they preached simultaneously; that was perhaps the first indication I had that something was amiss.

What about your family—what did they preach?

Well, the normal, average, Christian Midwestern bag . . . and racism as well. You know, we're all victims or products of our environment, and my thing is to throw it back at them and keep the circle going—that's pretty vague, but that's the best I can do. . . .

Did your satirical inclinations include gospel?

I suppose you could say that, because the words I say in the gospel medium are completely out of order with the meaning of gospel. But gospel means truth, and I try to say what I believe to be the truth in a medium that is a proven mass communicator.

Do you consider Dylan's "Rainy Day Woman (12 & 35)" to be gospel?

I suppose so . . . Dylan, as far as satire goes, is the kingpin, you know. He's been acting like something that he may not be for years and years. But in acting that way, he *is* the way he acts.

Have you ever worked with him?

No, but I hope to sometime, because I've always thought—and this may be purely my own fantasy—but I've always thought he was making musical constructions that were far beneath his actual awareness, just so they could be assimilated by a lot of people.

And yet so many people insist on being so super-serious about him. Have you ever been able to get to a satiric level and listen and understand exactly what he's doing?

I don't know whether I understand exactly. I don't think I could unless I knew him more personally. But he's been a great inspiration. The first time I

ever heard him, I was amazed at how much he sounded like me—this is
from my point of view. And I remember immediately thinking, "Well, it's
great; but nobody'll ever understand it."

*How do you mean he sounds like you? In terms of phrasing, or the kind
of words. . . .*

Yeah, his phrasing, singing and the words, I think. If he sounds like me in
words it's because I've studied his style right.

He always struck me as being one of the first people in mass communications that took a non-musical overview and used a musical medium to
express himself. Like Dylan Thomas. I heard some recordings of him reciting his poetry, and it's just one dimension less than Bob Dylan's poetry
because Bob had the added dimension of music. But otherwise, it's very
similar.

Did Dylan Thomas make up for the lack of music with something else?

Nothing, for me. I prefer Bob Dylan.

What about the Who? Did you like Townshend's opera?

It's a weird premise. Perhaps it's really hip satire, I don't know. A blind
pinball champion? I really don't understand. I'm not saying there's not even
anything going on, but I find myself asking myself why, when I listen to this
record. . . .

*I imagine Peter Townshend'd be able to explain—quite lucidly—what it
means to him, to get into a whole fantasy on how it feels to be a human
being who is actually a mass of nothing, being hit by all those weird scenes,
and being a champion in some way at the same time.*

Yeah, I don't know about superiority to other people, and I don't know
about explaining constructions, but if the construction works, it works. And
if you have to send accompanying dialogue with it to explain it, then it
doesn't work except as that total whole.

But that's the tradition of opera: the libretto.

Perhaps that's true; I'm not much of an opera fan.

*What about films? "Dixie Lullaby" concerned "easy riders" in the South,
and the message was "Be kind to the Southerners, or give them a chance to
be kind to you." Was that from the movie, from your own travels, from your
own life, or something you've always thought was important to say?*

It was all of those things. I was very impressed with the realism of that
movie, the heroes and the bad guys. It wasn't a morality play in the sense of
a John Wayne western, where the bad guys are obviously bad and the good
guys are obviously good. Because the bad guys were as real, if not more real,
than the heroes. That little epic, y'know. And that was probably because
they weren't actors, they were really . . . I remember reading something that
Dennis said when they first pulled in to that truck stop, those guys were
standing around, so he went up to them and explained the premise and said,

"What would you say if this was happening," so they just sat down and said what they would say. You can't get any more real than that, I mean you're really one up to Andy Warhol.

That took balls, too, I think, because they could've had a camera focused on Dennis in case he got ripped off by them. It could easily have happened.

He's definitely got balls. As well as just sheer talent.

Now, what were you saying in your song? That people should give the Southerners a chance to be kind, or to be real?

Well, I don't . . . not being an opera fan, the songs stand alone.

Not being an opera fan?

Yeah. What'd you say, libretto?

Oh, I see. That was a half a topic ago.

Some guy came up to me in San Francisco and asked—he told me that he'd quit turning on because he'd heard "Roll Away the Stone." "Is that what that meant?" And I told him "If that's what it means to you then that's fine, but that's not what it means to me." And he said "What does it mean to you?" That's not the reason that I do it, so I can go out and explain. They are what they are. . . .

I subscribe to the theory that films—and science fiction—come true. In other words, the people that create fiction are actually creating the future. Because the less visionary type of people are influenced. . . .

What was your major concern in school?

I think it was containing my neurosis about school not being the proper way to educate, which I found increasingly difficult as I went on. When I first started in school I was a straight-A student, and as I progressed—my last year in school I failed three courses and just could barely make it to school at all.

What was your last year in school—high school or college? When did you see the light?

When I had a chance to go on the road with Jerry Lee Lewis. I'd just spent three days, twelve hours a day, taking entrance examinations to Tulsa University and I just thought, well, it's a waste of time, 'cause I have to study so many things I'm not interested in. ROTC I had to take, and right away I knew that I didn't want to do that. I figured this was my chance to eat in a lot of restaurants and travel around, play some rock and roll music, which I decided was easier and better. . . .

Who's your wardrobe person who chooses your outstanding outfits and takes care of your color coordination?

It's mostly fans who come up and give me stuff or make clothes for me. I'm into symbolism. Like the long hair is symbolism, and the distance between me and the audience sometimes affects what I'm going to wear.

What does the long hair symbolize?

It's kind of like the songs. Nothing specific—it just is what it is. It's me in comparison to other long-haired people and short-haired people and people in general.

What does the basketball shirt signify?

I'd hate to say what it signifies to me because it might restrict your own fantasies.

Well, I hardly ever fantasize over basketball jersies, to tell you the truth. It strikes me as interesting to see that you'd go out and buy a basketball shirt, or receive one and wear it.

It's a few things: it's teams, it's spectator activities, which I'm not convinced is the best sort of activity—voyeurs—I'm not sure whether it's good or not, but I'm willing to take the role of the musical football player until such time that people realize that they can make music themselves.

There's something else, too. Instead of like the Knicks or some professional team, you're "Gil's Barbershop" or "Holy Trinity." Makes people wonder.

Well, that's the hope. The wondering wanderer. That's the whole bag— the songs, the performance, the whole lifestyle. Make people wonder. Make myself wonder, too. And it's great.

THE REVOLUTIONARY THEATRE

LeRoi Jones

The Revolutionary Theatre should force change; it should be change. (All their faces turned into the lights and you work on them black nigger magic, and cleanse them at having seen the ugliness. And if the beautiful see themselves, they will love themselves.) We are preaching virtue again, but by that to mean NOW, toward what seems the most constructive use of the world.

The Revolutionary Theatre must EXPOSE! Show up the insides of these humans, look into black skulls. White men will cower before this theatre because it hates them. Because they themselves have been trained to hate. The Revolutionary Theatre must hate them for hating. For presuming with their technology to deny the supremacy of the Spirit. They will all die because of this.

The Revolutionary Theatre must teach them their deaths. It must crack their faces open to the mad cries of the poor. It must teach them about silence and the truths lodged there. It must kill any God anyone names except Common Sense. The Revolutionary Theatre should flush the fags and murders out of Lincoln's face.

It should stagger through our universe correcting, insulting, preaching, spitting craziness—but a craziness taught to us in our most rational moments. People must be taught to trust true scientists (knowers, diggers, oddballs) and that the holiness of life is the constant possibility of widening the consciousness. And they must be incited to strike back against *any* agency that attempts to prevent this widening.

The Revolutionary Theatre must Accuse and Attack anything that can be accused and attacked. It must Accuse and Attack because it is a theatre of Victims. It looks at the sky with the victims' eyes, and moves the victims to look at the strength in their minds and their bodies.

Clay, in *Dutchman*, Ray in *The Toilet*, Walker in *The Slave*, are all victims. In the Western sense they could be heroes. But the Revolutionary Theatre, even if it is Western, must be anti-Western. It must show horrible coming attractions of *The Crumbling of the West*. Even as Artaud designed *The Conquest of Mexico*, so we must design *The Conquest of White Eye*, and show the missionaries and wiggly Liberals dying under blasts of concrete. For sound effects, wild screams of joy, from all the peoples of the world.

The Revolutionary Theatre must take dreams and give them a reality. It must isolate the ritual and historical cycles of reality. But it must be food for all those who need food, and daring propaganda for the beauty of the Human Mind. It is a political theatre, a weapon to help in the slaughter of these dim-witted fatbellied white guys who somehow believe that the rest of the world is here for them to slobber on.

This should be a theatre of World Spirit. Where the spirit can be shown to be the most competent force in the world. Force. Spirit. Feeling. The language will be anybody's, but tightened by the poet's backbone. And even the language must show what the facts are in this consciousness epic, what's happening. We will talk about the world, and the preciseness with which we are able to summon the world will be our art. Art is method. And art, "like any ashtray or senator," remains in the world. Wittgenstein said ethics and aesthetics are one. I believe this. So the Broadway theatre is a theatre of reaction whose ethics, like its aesthetics, reflect the spiritual values of this unholy society, which sends young crackers all over the world blowing off colored people's heads. (In some of these flippy Southern towns they even shoot up the immigrants' Favorite Son, be it Michael Schwerner or JF Kennedy.)

The Revolutionary Theatre is shaped by the world, and moves to reshape the world, using as its force the natural force and perpetual vibrations of the mind in the world. We are history and desire, what we are, and what any experience can make us.

It is a social theatre, but all theatre is social theatre. But we will change the drawing rooms into places where real things can be said about a real world, or into smoky rooms where the destruction of Washington can be plotted. The Revolutionary Theatre must function like an incendiary pencil planted in Curtis Lemay's cap. So that when the final curtain goes down brains are splattered over the seats and the floor, and bleeding nuns must wire SOS's to Belgians with gold teeth.

Our theatre will show victims so that their brothers in the audience will be better able to understand that they are the brothers of victims, and that they themselves are victims if they are blood brothers. And what we show must cause the blood to rush, so that pre-revolutionary temperaments will be bathed in this blood, and it will cause their deepest souls to move, and they will find themselves tensed and clenched, even ready to die, at what the soul has been taught. We will scream and cry, murder, run through the streets in agony, if it means some soul will be moved, moved to actual life understanding of what the world is, and what it ought to be. We are preaching virtue and feeling, and a natural sense of the self in the world. All men live in the world, and the world ought to be a place for them to live.

What is called the imagination (from image, magi, magic, magician, etc.) is a practical vector from the soul. It stores all data, and can be called on to solve all our "problems." The imagination is the projection of ourselves past our sense of ourselves as "things." Imagination (Image) is all possibility, because from the image, the initial circumscribed energy, any use (idea) is possible. And so begins that image's use in the world. Possibility is what moves us.

The popular white man's theatre like the popular white man's novel shows tired white lives, and the problems of eating white sugar, or else it herds bigcaboosed blondes onto huge stages in rhinestones and makes believe they are dancing or singing. WHITE BUSINESSMEN OF THE WORLD, DO YOU WANT TO SEE PEOPLE REALLY DANCING AND SING-ING??? ALL OF YOU GO UP TO HARLEM AND GET YOURSELF KILLED. THERE WILL BE DANCING AND SINGING, THEN, FOR REAL!! (In *The Slave*, Walker Vessels, the black revolutionary, wears an arm band, which is the insignia of the attacking army—a big red-lipped minstrel grinning like crazy.)

The liberal white man's objection to the theatre of the revolution (if he is "hip" enough) will be on aesthetic grounds. Most white Western artists do not need to be "political," since usually, whether they know it or not, they are in complete sympathy with the most repressive social forces in the world today. There are more junior birdmen fascists running around the West today disguised as Artists than there are disguised as fascists. (But then, that word, *Fascist*, and with it, *Fascism*, has been made obsolete by the words *America*, and *Americanism*.) The American Artist usually turns out to be just a super-Bourgeois, because, finally, all he has to show for his sojourn through the world is "better taste" than the Bourgeois—many times not even that.

Americans will hate the Revolutionary Theatre because it will be out to destroy them and whatever they believe is real. American cops will try to close the theatres where such nakedness of the human spirit is paraded. American producers will say the revolutionary plays are filth, usually because they will treat human life as if it were actually happening. American directors will say that the white guys in the plays are too abstract and cowardly ("don't get me wrong . . . I mean aesthetically . . .") and they will be right.

The force we want is of twenty million spooks storming America with furious cries and unstoppable weapons. We want actual explosions and actual brutality: AN EPIC IS CRUMBLING and we must give it the space and hugeness of its actual demise. The Revolutionary Theatre, which is now peopled with victims, will soon begin to be peopled with new kinds of heroes—not the weak Hamlets debating whether or not they are ready to die for what's on their minds, but men and women (and minds) digging out from under a thousand years of "high art" and weak-faced dalliance. We must make an art that will function so as to call down the actual wrath of world spirit. We are witch doctors and assassins, but we will open a place for the true scientists to expand our consciousness. This is a theatre of assault. The play that will split the heavens for us will be called THE DESTRUCTION OF AMERICA. The heroes will be Crazy Horse, Denmark Vesey, Patrice Lumumba, and not history, not memory, not sad sentimental groping for a warmth in our despair; these will be new men, new heroes, and their enemies most of you who are reading this.

THE CHOICE IN PRESENT-DAY ART

Francois Morellet

It is said that the photographers came just in time to replace the painters who no longer "wished" to represent nature. If this isn't really correct, one can nevertheless say that photography has certainly hastened the progress of artists towards a non-naturalistic art.

The same process is going on at the present moment vis-à-vis choice. One sees more and more artists who, in making works of art, refuse this arbitrary choice every time, when there are increasingly improved machines and electronic brains appearing which could replace a great part of the artist's work.

How is it one has sought to reduce this free choice which was looked upon as the greatness of modern art? Also, how has one arrived at this idea of the free artist who chooses the place and the colour of each brush-stroke in order to obtain a definitive work where nothing could be added or taken away?

To answer these questions, let us try to distinguish the different categories of choice. One can, quite arbitrarily, distinguish three of them:

1. *Deliberate and conscious choice*. The decision follows a period of reflection where possible developments of actions are imagined, which will follow this decision. This choice corresponds to the classic idea of rational intelligence.

2. *Unconscious and intuitive choice*. The decision is taken without the subject's consciousness operating. This unconscious decision will not be the outcome of chance but will answer the subject's profound inclinations. This ability to take decisions, to choose without being aware of it, would be the main quality of great artists and even great scientists, according to the traditional conception springing from romanticism.

3. *The cybernetic choice*. Machines, thanks to their memory and their ability to face up to different possibilities, determine the choice. This choice, then, needs nothing further for its fulfillment than supplying the machines (programming) in a theoretically objective manner.

One can roughly recognise these three categories in the historical evolution of the plastic arts from the end of the eighteenth century to the present-day.

The naturalistic painters, in order to achieve an objective vision of reality and to reach a more and more perfect imaginary state, owed it to themselves to achieve a considered and conscious choice in their means of creation. They tried different methods, rejecting the least effective.

At the end of the nineteenth century the best artists abandoned their social role as narrators, chroniclers, and reporters to the photographers. In doing this they abandoned all the technical constraints that reproducing nature made necessary. Thus they took the path which opened into unlimited freedom. Little by little each brush-stroke was made only through the artists' choice, and with no other constraints.

But can this choice really be made with each brush-stroke?

a. Some artists have believed so. Abstract painting, which could be said to have begun in a pure state with Kandinsky's first watercolour, was called in the following epochs "automatic writing," "action painting" etc—each gesture resulting in a colour was decided by intuition, the unconscious justifying everything. Today, this way looks rather worn out.

b. Others have tried to replace the old constraints by pseudo-constraints considered more modern. At different times they have tried to reproduce the look of "Negro masks," graffiti, children's drawings, commercial posters; not to mention the fake landscape or unrecognisable still-lives. These artists have regained their equilibrium.

On the one hand, the image of the free artist, the all-powerful creator-artisan was saved, and on the other, by specialising in a set of images they avoided being overcome by the vertigo of free creation in the making of their works of art.

This category of art will last for some time yet, since there is no precise limit to imagery and since it renews itself in making poetic images out of fashionable subjects.

c. At the present time, however, one senses a revulsion among certain artists from choosing one way rather than another in the development of their work. They themselves no longer subscribe to this religion which believes in the infallibility of arbitrary choice.

The meaning of Marcel Duchamp's ready-mades is a striking example of the reaction against the artist's conception of an arbitrary artisan-creator. In his discs or his urinal he has reduced the artisan element in manufacture to zero, and the range of choice in the realisation to one only (the choice of object). The hitherto little-known work of Duchamp, which was rare and precocious, partly accounts for the existence and success of pop art.

d. At the moment there is another reaction against this traditional conception of the artist, and particularly against works in which each detail has been finally fixed by a choice which denies all justification other than intuition.

Artists in this category refuse to repeat Duchamp's negation: but they obviously do not yet possess "machines" allowing them to eliminate this arbitrary choice to any great extent.

They know that they are still working in a primitive way because they find themselves at the beginning of an epoch where an entirely new conception of art is appearing.

The four points characteristic of artists of this tendency seem to me to be:

Impersonal realisation. During the realisation of a work of art the arbitrary decisions are reduced to the minimum. For this, machines are best used. Straight away machines serving current industrial production make possible the manufacture of identical elements, which are sometimes the very basis of the work. In the distribution of these elements, as with their choice, electronic brains could in the future replace the artist's decisions, it remaining for the artist to programme the machines and fix their task.

Movement. Real movement does away with the fixed, immovable character of the work of art. The artist no longer imposes a right moment that he has arbitrarily chosen. Instead he suggests a series of situations which develop outside himself.

Programmed series. The same attitude but without actual movement. Each experience shows one of the possibilities of a system which is developable of itself. If a choice can be made, it will be made by the spectator.

The game. Active participation by the spectator in the creation of transformation of a work of art is the conception of "the artist" far removed from that of the allpowerful romantic creator. The arbitrary geniuses about whom the nineteenth century created legends fade away before the active spectator.

Thus a profound gulf now exists between the "inspired artists" who produce works where each detail is finally fixed by a choice which denies all justification other than intuition, and the "experimental artists" who suggest situations which become modified in space and time for the spectator and even by the spectator.

MOTION PICTURES AND WITCHCRAFT

Antonin Artaud

. . . I have always noticed a special quality in films, in the hidden movement and the very substance of the pictures. There is an unexpected and mysterious side to motion pictures which is not to be found in other arts. We can be sure each picture, no matter how trivial or dull, arrives on the screen transmuted. The tiniest details, the most unimportant objects, take on their own particular life and meaning; this, over and above the value of the meaning of the pictures themselves, beyond the thoughts they translate or the symbols they form. Film gives objects a separate existence by isolating them so they become progressively more independent and detached from the object's normal sense. Leaves, a bottle, a hand, live a quasi-animal life, seeking a useful existence. There are the camera's distortions, too, or the unexpected use it makes of the things it records. As each picture fades out, a certain detail we had ignored catches our imagination with singular force, yet is the reverse of the expression sought after in the film. There is also a physical intoxication communicated by the whirring film. The mind is affected but is free from all identification. Pictures possess a virtual power which probes into the mind and uncovers undreamt-of possibilities.

Motion pictures are fundamentally the revelation of a complete, graphically communicated, occult world. But it is up to us to find the clue to their secret life. There are better ways of making us guess at the secret stirrings in the depths of the mind than simple superimposed film montage. Uncut motion pictures, taken for what they are, in the abstract give off a certain amount of the atmosphere which favors revelations. Using them to tell stories—exterior action—is to deprive them of the best of their resources, to go against their deepest aims. Therefore motion pictures seem to exist especially to express mental things, within the mind, not so much by the interplay of pictures but by something more tangible, re-establishing objects, individual substance without intermediaries or portrayal. Motion pictures have arrived at a turning point in human thought, precisely at the moment when language is losing its symbolic power, when the mind is tired of simulation.

Clear thinking is not enough. It sets life within a spent, disgusted world. Whatever is immediately graspable is clear, but the immediately graspable serves only as life's outer shell. This all too familiar life has lost all its symbolic power and we are beginning to see it as the abnegation of life. And our day is excellent for saints and sorcerers, perhaps better than ever before. An entire intangible substantiality is taking shape, coming into being, seeking to reach the light. Motion pictures bring us closer to this substantiality. If motion pictures are not made to interpret dreams, or everything in waking life connected with the world of dreams, they do not exist. There is nothing to distinguish them from the theatre. However, since motion pictures are a fast, direct language, they do not need slow, heavy logic in order to live and flourish. Either motion pictures will come closer to the world of fantasy, this same fantasy we daily realize all reality rests on, or they will not live long. Or rather motion pictures will become like painting or poetry. What is sure is that most forms of expression have had their day. For a long time now all good painting has served hardly any other purpose than reproduction of the abstract. Thus it is not only a matter of choice. There will not on the one hand be motion pictures which represent life and on the other hand motion pictures which represent the workings of the mind. For life, or what we call life, will become less and less separable from thought. A certain hidden realm tends to surface. Motion pictures can transmute the expression of this realm better than any other art, since stupid order and habitual clarity are its enemies. . . .

The Critic Criticizes

ONLY FILMS ARE TRULY, DEEP-DOWN GROOVY

Penelope Gilliatt

"I never read fiction," a woman professor told me severely in New York the other day, fixing me with an eye that made me feel like an X-ray plate revealing fictional tendencies that would have to be dealt with. "Except at the hairdresser," she added, as people do. Then she attacked Pasternak, Beckett, and "your English novelists" as if they had done her a grievous ill, and I wondered how many sessions of hairdresser it had taken her to read "Zhivago." And then I asked her if she felt the same about films. "Oh, no," she said. "My students are the film generation." Tolstoy, here's the door. The students don't dig you.

"Painting!" said a usually intelligent man, scampering to keep up with the kids. The harsh discipline of grooviness creates a lot of Philistines. He had cleared the walls of his study, which I knew very well, and thrown out his old-fashioned prints. The walls were now alluvial green, and there was a chair—quite a pretty Danish-modern chair—hanging over the fireplace from a hook. The swinging idiot then lammed into all pre-1968 painting. It took ages. He had a lot of centuries to demolish. He disposed of Giotto ("outworn superstition"), Leonardo ("commissioned hack"), Michelangelo ("obsessed with muscle"), Goya ("faulty perspective"), and Holbein ("monarchist creep"). The Impressionists went down the drain, on the rigorous and peculiar ground that they were romanticists about weather. As he carried on, he looked increasingly revived, and downed a hashish-filled chocolate brownie. The brownie had been made at home by his wife, who was a painter, poor devil.

"You mean you *enjoyed* 'The Cherry Orchard'?" a Pop-music critic of intellectual standing asked me in London last week. "I hate plays. They're like picnics. You have to pretend you're having fun. The theatre's finished. Shakespeare is dialectically chaotic. The stage is as dead as Virginia Woolf."

Of course, literature has been finished for years, apart from autobiographies about homosexuality and accounts of bringing up lions/otters/spaniels. Everyone with it knows that. It has been out of touch ever since Joyce. No, ever since James. No, ever since Jane Austen. No; Austen and all that worn-out stuff about bourgeois marriage—what has that got to say to students? The last man was Chaucer, and then only maybe. You could hold that Robbe-Grillet was trying to do something in touch, but then his work is really filmic.

Filmic. Filmic is O.K. Filmic is always groovy. Even out-of-touch nincompoops can tell that it's groovy, because groovy opinion-makers, who may or may not read the ancient printed word under the bedclothes by flashlight, never stop yakking about movies. I don't mean that they necessarily like them that much, but they do tremendously like talking about them. In thirty years of going to the flicks, starting with a rapturous program of Roscoe Arbuckle that has endeared the fat to me for good, I've never before heard voluble intellectuals carry on so much about the cinema while they enjoy it so little.

One of the most companionable people I ever went with to London press shows is a seventy-year-old ex-barmaid. She has spent most of her life going to the local cinema three times a week. She knows the name of every English-speaking actor in the business. The notion of a director is unknown to her, apart from the name of Hitchcock, and so is the idea of a script-writer. She assumes that the actors make up the lines, and very clever, too. When I told her once that I was writing a film script, she looked at me with polite surprise at the redundancy of it, as if I were killing myself scrubbing a rug that had just been sent to the dry cleaner's. At the same time, her judgment is impeccable, even about the totally unfamiliar, maybe because it has nothing to do with guessing what the touted student generation is liable to think. She likes real innovation, and she can smell pretentiousness a mile off. When a film is disappointing, she says only that "something's lacking," which is all I want to say of "Boom!," as it happens. Joseph Losey directed it, and it was adapted from Tennessee Williams' play "The Milk Train Doesn't Stop Here Anymore." Mr. Williams is a stirring and tender play-wright, capable of doing some things with prose that are beyond any other writer in English, and there seems no good reason for intruding into the problems of an irreplaceable dramatist who may be in a technically difficult patch.

The O.K. intellectual put-downs of films now don't really mean anything much more than "something's lacking." They just sound more important. "Not of our time," for instance. In the language of grooviness, this is about as insulting an opinion as a film can earn. But you may well ask why. There is also a lot of very severe and rather unknowledgeable talk about camera technique. People of thirteen or fourteen usually get this right, but the adult film buffs' pronouncements are often lofty codswollop. In an English cinema recently, a stranger next to me leaned over in my direction as he rose to his feet and said that there wasn't much point in staying any longer, because there were three regrettable zoom shots coming. It suddenly made me feel immensely fond of Doris Day fan clubs. We talk such comic *rubbish*; I get nightmare imaginings of it:

"Satyajit Ray has fallen off since 'The World of Apu.' "

"Visconti hasn't really made anything since 'La Terra Trema.' "

" 'La Dolce Vita' was parochial. Fellini simply didn't know Rome."

"Well, I *suppose* Kurosawa is interesting. For the camerawork."

"Truffaut was always a commercial director. I'm ashamed to say I was fooled by 'Jules et Jim.' "

"Movies are the *only* medium to speak to the student generation."

"Frank Tashlin is the *only* director worth talking about."

"I always think Alain Resnais is essentially an editor. Not a filmmaker. All his great work was done in the cutting room."

" '2001' was structurally a disaster."

"Movies are the only *thing*. 'Planet of the Apes' when you're turned on—oh, boy!"

"I liked the first five minutes of 'Belle de Jour.' "

"The last two reels of 'Persona' were visually rather interesting, but the thought was ruinously muddled."

"Have you looked carefully at Eisenstein lately? He was very overrated."

"Something's happened to Tati's sense of humor. Maybe he never *had* a sense of humor."

"I haven't really laughed at a movie since the antique camerawork in 'The Cranes Are Flying.' The Russians are technically still in the ark."

"The Poles haven't done a thing lately. It's all the Czechs now. The Poles haven't honestly much to say to Columbia University any longer."

"Why does anyone carry on about showing Ozu here? We've *seen* it. What's so new about never moving the camera off the floor?"

"I'd rather have Kluge's 'Yesterday Girl.' That had something to do with our time."

" 'Yesterday Girl' was totally derivative of Godard."

"Not derivative. Eclectic."

"Anyway, I walked out after the first two reels."

Does anyone else have fatal visions of carefully educated people getting more and more groovy and less and less intelligent? Can it possibly be true that the growing mob of with-it chasers in the West are turning into a kind of intellectual who hates art?

CRUMBCRUSHER

Pauline Kael

The book "Love Story," by Erich Segal, represents a first in American letters: "Love Story" is the first novelization of a movie to make it to the top of the best-seller lists. The novelization of a movie is a new sub-literary genre, an expansion from the "stories" of the movies which used to appear in fan magazines such as *Screen Stories*; as far as I can determine, novelizations appeared only in paperback until 1966, when "Fantastic Voyage" was the first to cross the barrier into hard-cover. But nothing like the promotion for—or the success of—"Love Story" has been seen before. (One can be sure that movie companies will now take a new interest in the script-into-novel market.) "Love Story" has also been reported to be the most popular hard-cover book in France and England, and the new paperback edition in this country is said to have sold over five million copies. Allowing for hyperbole and halving the figure, that is still one hell of a pile of pulp. The movie's star, Ali MacGraw, is the wife of the head of production of the movie company, and that is not a first. In fact, Miss MacGraw's husband, Robert Evans, became the head of production at Paramount after being selected by Norma Shearer to impersonate her late husband, the producer Irving Thalberg, in a movie. Mr. Thalberg's pictures frequently starred Miss Shearer, sometimes as unfortunately as "Love Story" stars Miss MacGraw.

Mr. Segal's little golden movie book runs to about twenty-five thousand words. According to "A Black Glossary," by Hermese E. Roberts, blacks refer to small children, or shorties, as "crumbcrushers." "Love Story" is a perfect example of a literary crumbcrusher. It's a generation-gap variant of a neo-Victorian heart-wringer in the movie tradition of "Madame X," "Imitation of Life," and "Magnificent Obsession," with maybe a little "Dark Victory;" it is written in a snappy, tear-jerking, hard-soft style synthesized from "A Farewell to Arms" and "The Sun Also Rises." Even allowing for the fact that Paramount pushed it to the top of the best-seller lists, it has been there for an unconscionably long period, and there can be little doubt that it has been read by many people who rarely read anything in hard covers. One would like to find a positive side to this, but I doubt whether those who buy and love "Love Story" will be spurred on to become readers of other books. What could they follow it with that wouldn't be a disappointment? I doubt whether even the breathless, gosh-gee-whiz-can-all-this-be-happening-to-me TV-celebrity-author himself could cap this shlock classic with another.

The book is narrated by a rich Wasp boy who breaks with his family when he marries a poor Italian Catholic girl. Their love is near-perfect, but then he learns she is going to die. Here is our hero addressing God on the subject of his Jenny's leukemia before she learns about it:

> I don't mind the agony, sir, I don't mind knowing as long as Jenny doesn't know. Did you hear me, Lord, sir? You can name the price.

But she finds out, just after he has planned to take her on a last whirl to Paris:

> "I don't want Paris. I don't need Paris. I just want you—"
> "That you've got, baby!" I interrupted, sounding falsely merry.
> "And I want time," she continued, "which you can't give me."
> Now I looked into her eyes. They were ineffably sad. But sad in a way only I understood. They were saying she was sorry. That is, sorry for me.
> We stood there silently holding one another. Please, if one of us cries, let both of us cry. But preferably neither of us.

I doubt if a cynic could fake this. I don't mean to suggest that Segal is as gaga as this book—only that a part of him is. The book has curious lapses suggesting that the author sometimes slipped from his fantasy-hero into a fanciful self-infatuation, as in the passage in which the hero resolves "to tell nobody, to shoulder the entire burden" himself. He lies to his boss, Mr. Jonas, in order to stay close to his dying wife, and then speculates, "Oh, Christ, Mr. Jonas, when you find out the real reason!" Since the real reason is his nobility, how extraordinary that he should be anticipating his boss's future recognition of it. Slips like this make one think that Segal isn't a total fake, that he really does fantasize on this level.

His unworldly-worldly fantasy provides the movie business with a rare opportunity for a killing, at a minimum in production costs. On the screen, it can satisfy the desire for a 1944 movie which seems to afflict television watchers; that is, a movie that reflects an orderly world—one devastated by war but one in which Americans still felt like a moral people and could luxuriate in virtue. That desire for a reassuring moral universe is probably behind the acceptance of "Ryan's Daughter," and "Love Story"—which takes place as if the outside world *were* still 1944, but without a war—may satisfy a national (perhaps international) longing. It deals in private passions at a time when we are exhausted from public defeats, and it deals with the mutual sacrifice of a hard-working, clean-cut pair of lovers, and with love beyond death.

This thing is so instinctively, plus manipulatively, engineered to leave 'em crying that it could hardly fail commercially even if the actors were programmed by Terry Southern to make obscene gestures at the audience at ten-second intervals. The weeping audience probably wouldn't notice, any more than it cares that just about every detail in the movie is phony and off—from having the boy's Brahmin father live and speak in a style that was already a comedy convention in the thirties to the way the hero stands with his girl during his Harvard Law School commencement exercises, from the cutie-pie strong language she uses when she's talking to the children's choir in church to the way she, a brilliant music major at Radcliffe, mispronounces "Köchel" on her deathbed. Those who are susceptible to this sort of movie may not even notice that Ali MacGraw is horribly smug and smirky, though if you share my impulses, whenever she gets facetious you'll probably want to wham her one. It's a role that the young Katharine Hepburn might have redeemed by her eccentricity and intensity; Miss MacGraw has neither. It might have been better if she hadn't tried to act at all; she didn't try to act much in "Goodbye, Columbus," and that was fine, because she was supposed to be an insensitive bitch anyway, and she looked beautiful. She isn't supposed to be a bitch this time, and from some angles she doesn't look so good, either (though she used to be a marvellous model), and her attempts at classy repartee are destroyed by nose-flaring, lip-curling amateurishness. As the hero, Ryan O'Neal, the Rodney Harrington of TV's "Peyton Place," holds the picture together—somewhat. His performance is not the kind I care much about—sincere, vulnerable movie heroes generally not being equipped for much besides trite suffering—but O'Neal knows how to be emotional without being a slob, and in this unskilled, mediocre piece of movie-making (Arthur Hiller directed) his professionalism shines. "Love Story" will not be the first disgraceful movie that has laid waste the emotions of a vast audience, though it may be one of the most ineptly made of all the lump-and-phlegm hits.

Yet even if Ryan O'Neal were as incompetent as Miss MacGraw, "Love Story" would probably still have the smell of a winner. Those who sob away can flatter themselves that the picture must have been beautifully done—or they wouldn't have been so affected. "Love Story" is lucky in its timing, and a lot more than luck went into the timing. The book has been promoted from the start as an antidote to dirty books and movies, as if America were being poisoned by them. Erich Segal (in another compartment of his life a translator of Plautus) used as his sales pitch an attack on "Portnoy's Complaint" and Henry Miller's novels; this picture employs its few shock words repeatedly, but in that old blue way that Broadway does—so, of course, Segal isn't considered foul-mouthed. The movie has been pushed to attract the audience for the "clean and wholesome," the way "The Sound of Music" did, and to attract the kids who loved Zeffirelli's "Romeo and Juliet," because this is a "contemporary" R. & J. story. It has been acclaimed by *Variety*, in a review that might have been written by the Vice-President himself, as a "rare breath of fresh air in the smog of contemporary cinema psychoneurosis." The review goes on, "And not just because Arthur Hiller's sensitive and restrained direction tells a story so touching that tears may be shed without any embarrassment whatsoever. But rather because this gentle romantic tragedy succeeds in conveying some timeless universal human ideals of emotional commitment in a contemporary frame of reference."

In itself, a love idyll like this may seem harmless, but it won't be by itself for long. Given the way movie companies work, it heralds the return of the weepies. The original-soundtrack recording (on a Paramount label) includes such compositions as "Theme from Love Story," "Snow Frolic," "The Christmas Trees," "Skating in Central Park," and "Bozo Barrett." Bozo Barrett is the name that the hero suggests for the child he and his doomed Jenny never have. The picture represents what one had hoped might have been laughed off the screen forever, and it heralds something worse. An audience that's swimming in tears, drowning in seas of virtue, can be a very self-righteous audience. Sentimentality and repression have a natural affinity; they're the two sides of one counterfeit coin.

Strangely, since the book was written after the script, the movie omits the emotional climax of the book, the climax that turns even some hardened, laughing readers to jelly—when, after the wife's death, the hero falls into his father's arms and cries. This was the reconciliation that the dead girl sought, the only thorn in their perfect love having been his refusal to try to understand his father. In the book, it is a Freudian generation gap, and the son has been as helplessly at fault as the father (who in the book is the head of the Peace Corps). Significantly, although the book seemed as opportunistic as is possible, the finished film goes a step further. In order (I assume) to flatter the young movie audience, the reconciliation scene is left out, and the hero ignores his father and remains alone with his memories. The movie thus posits a hopeless, unbridgeable gulf between the generations, even though no basis for conflict is presented, since the son becomes a respectable lawyer and gives no indication of having values that are different from his father's. The movie plays it every which way with the mass audience. A generation gap for the young audience, but no changed values that might upset the "Airport" crowd. It's calculation like this that earns a movie praise for being pure and fresh and idealistic.

FOREVER AVANT

Winthrop Sargeant

I think it was Gore Vidal who remarked recently that "everything changes except the avant-garde." At any rate, it is remarkable how little avant-garde techniques in music have changed over the past fifty years or so. The main idea seems to have been to revolt against the tradition of music as it existed from Monteverdi to Mahler, with its subtly organized conceptions of consonance and dissonance and its reliance on diatonic melody and what, for the sake of simplicity, I would call the do-mi-sol chord. The fact is that a piece of music that is avant-garde remains avant-garde forever. The idea that this music is ahead of its time and that audiences will someday come to like it was long ago disproved. Arnold Schoenberg was the most thoroughgoing avant-gardist of the period between 1910 and 1930. His music from this period stays avant-garde—enigmatic to the listener and not very popular. Schoenberg got the idea that the tradition of chromaticism had been exhausted by Wagner, and that the only thing to do was create an entirely new musical language, based on the twelve tones of the piano keyboard, each tone being treated as the equal of the others, so that any feeling of a tonic, or a tonal center, was abolished. This idea was, to say the least, bizarre and totally unprecedented. No one had ever before had the arrogance to attempt the creation of a new musical language; great composers like Mozart, Beethoven, and Wagner had used the standard musical language as it had been handed down to them, making a few alterations because of their expressive needs, but never presuming to cast aside its basic principles, which were as well understood by their audiences as by themselves. The whole idea of an avant-garde would have seemed preposterous to them. The term was used in Paris in relation to the arts in the nineteenth century, though it was not first applied to music. From there it spread to other arts and other localities. "*Épater le bourgeois*" became a rallying cry, artists cut themselves off from artistic meaning as it was understood at the time, and art began to take on the aspect of women's fashions: "This year, dissonances will be unresolved," "This year, electronics will be *in*," and so on. Actually, there was little change in the structure of the music. The works Schoenberg was writing in 1920 were not very different, in their effect, from the works of Penderecki or the electronic composers of today, though there has been much palaver over methods of construction. All of them have scrupulously avoided tonality and diatonic melody (which means major and minor scales used melodically). Most of these works are soon forgotten because of lack of public interest in them. Some survive because they are the work of the heroes of the avant-

308

garde, which continues to promote them with large amounts of publicity and with pressure on conductors and other musicians to perform them.

Let me say immediately that I am speaking of only one art—music; in the fields of painting and sculpture, avant-gardism seems to have enjoyed considerable success. And let me exempt from my argument certain works in which a composer has managed to express something in spite of the avant-garde materials he has used—Alban Berg's "Wozzeck," for instance. What I am objecting to is the almost universal use of avant-garde techniques by composers, the propagation of them in music schools and colleges, the prevalent idea that only avant-garde conceptions are useful in musical composition, and the systematic discouragement by style-setters of composers who do not make use of them. Involved in all this is a curious notion of the "progressive" character of musical history. Schoenberg himself thought that in discarding the language of Wagner and moving onward to something else he was fulfilling a historical destiny, and generations of composers since his time have adhered to the same theory. But Schoenberg's "history" was of the Marxist sort, based on the deterministic dialectic of Hegel and prophesying the future. History itself, of course, is entirely different. I need only point out that the most distinguished composers since Schoenberg's time have failed to follow his idea of "history." Stravinsky, for example, had his atonal fling, with "Sacre du Printemps," but later on turned to more tonal idioms. Strauss wrote terribly chromatic operas in "Salome" and "Elektra." Later, he turned to the diatonic language that so delights us in "Der Rosenkavalier." Prokofieff had an atonal period, but the magnificent works for which he is best remembered today are things like the ballet "Romeo and Juliet," which is conservative and entirely tonal. The American composers Samuel Barber, Gian Carlo Menotti, Alan Hovhaness, and Elie Siegmeister have never even been tempted to follow this imaginary "history," and their work has consequently been successful with audiences. But most of the younger composers are as dedicated to the Hegelian hypothesis as ever. And most of them are in a blind alley. You can hardly tell one from the other except by the names in the program.

What is happening at the moment to the music that purports to be history? Well, the Schoenberg twelve-tone system seems lately to have gone out of fashion. But electronic tapes, played alone or with orchestra and soloists, are very much in vogue. Then there is the divided-strings-playing-in-close-dissonant-intervals school, represented by Penderecki and some other Poles. And there is aleatory music—the "chance," or "play-anything-you-like," school advocated by John Cage. Yet I cannot help pointing out that the most interesting and moving aleatoric music that ever existed was jazz, which followed its own tradition, and that the most interesting and moving electronic music of today is rock, in which the electronic-beat organ has a very important role.

THE CASE FOR ABSTRACT ART

Clement Greenberg

Many people say that the kind of art our age produces is one of the major symptoms of what's wrong with the age. The disintegration and, finally, the disappearance of recognizable images in painting and sculpture, like the obscurity in advanced literature, are supposed to reflect a disintegration of values in society itself. Some people go further and say that abstract, non-representational art is pathological art, crazy art, and that those who practice it and those who admire and buy it are either sick or silly. The kindest critics are those who say it's all a joke, a hoax, and a fad, and that modernist art in general, or abstract art in particular, will soon pass. This sort of thing is heard or read pretty constantly, but in some years more often than others.

There seems to be a certain rhythm in the advance in popularity of modernist art, and a certain rhythm in the counter-attacks which try to stem it. More or less the same words or arguments are used in all the polemics, but the targets usually change. Once it was the impressionists who were a scandal, next it was Van Gogh and Cézanne, then it was Matisse, then it was cubism and Picasso, after that Mondrian, and now it is Jackson Pollock. The fact that Pollock was an American shows, in a backhanded way, how important American art has lately become.

Some of the same people who attack modernist art in general, or abstract art in particular, happen also to complain that our age has lost those habits of disinterested contemplation, and that capacity for enjoying things as ends in themselves and for their own sake, which former ages are supposed to have cultivated. This idea has been advanced often enough to convert it into a cliché. I hate to give assent to a cliché, for it is almost always an over-simplification, but I have to make an exception in this case. While I strongly doubt that disinterested contemplation was as unalloyed or as popular in ages past as is supposed, I do tend to agree that we could do with more of it in this time, and especially in this country.

I think a poor life is lived by anyone who doesn't regularly take time out to stand and gaze, or sit and listen, or touch, or smell, or brood, without any further end in mind, simply for the satisfaction gotten from that which is gazed at, listened to, touched, smelled or brooded upon. We all know, however, that the climate of Western life, and particularly of American life, is not conducive to this kind of thing; we are all too busy making a living. This is another cliché, of course. And still a third cliché says that we should learn from Oriental society how to give more of ourselves to the life of the spirit, to contemplation and meditation, and to the appreciation of what is satisfying or beautiful in its own sole right. This last is not only a cliché, but a fallacy, since most Orientals are even more preoccupied than we are with making a living. I hope that I myself am not making a gross and reductive simplification when I say that so much of Oriental contemplative and aesthetic discipline strikes me as a technique for keeping one's eyes averted from ugliness and misery.

Every civilization and every tradition of culture seem to possess capacities for self-cure and self-correction that go into operation automatically, unbidden. If the given tradition goes too far in one direction it will usually try to right itself by going equally far in the opposite one. There is no question but that our Western civilization, especially in its American variant, devotes more mental energy than any other to the production of material things and services; and that, more than any other, it puts stress on interested, purposeful activity in general. This is reflected in our art, which, as has been frequently observed, puts such great emphasis on movement and development and resolution, on beginnings, middles, and endings—that is, on dynamics. Compare Western music with any other kind, or look at Western literature, for that matter, with its relatively great concern with plot and over-all structure and its relatively small concern with tropes and figures and ornamental elaborations; think of how slow-moving Chinese and Japanese poetry is by comparison with ours, and how much it delights in static situations; and how uncertain the narrational logic of non-Western fiction tends to be. Think of how encrusted and convoluted Arabic poetry is by contrast even with our most euphuistic lyrical verse. And as for non-Western music, does it not almost always, and literally, strike us as more monotonous than ours?

Well, how does Western art compensate for, correct, or at least qualify its emphasis on the dynamic—an emphasis that may or may not be excessive? And how does Western life itself compensate for, correct, or at least qualify its obsession with material production and purposeful activity? I shall not here attempt to answer the latter question. But in the realm of art an answer is beginning to emerge of its own accord, and the shape of part of that answer is abstract art.

Abstract decoration is almost universal, and Chinese and Japanese calligraphy is quasi-abstract—abstract to the extent that few occidentals can read the characters of Chinese or Japanese writing. But only in the West, and only in the last fifty years, have such things as abstract pictures and freestanding pieces of abstract sculpture appeared. What makes the big difference between these and abstract decoration is that they are, exactly, pictures and free-standing sculpture—solo works of art meant to be looked at for their own sake and with full attention, and not as the adjuncts, incidental aspects, or settings of things other than themselves. These abstract pictures and pieces of sculpture challenge our capacity for disinterested contemplation in a way that is more concentrated and, I daresay, more conscious than anything else I know of in art. Music is an essentially abstract art, but even at its most rarefied and abstract, and whether it's Bach's or the middle-period Schoenberg's music, it does not offer this challenge in quite the same way or degree. Music tends from a beginning through a middle toward an ending. We wait to see how it "comes out"—which is what we also do with literature. Of course, the *total* experience of literature and music is completely disinterested, but it becomes that only at a further remove. While undergoing the experience we are caught up and expectant as well as detached—disinterested and at the same time interested in a way resembling that in which we are interested in how things turn out in real life. I exaggerate to make my point—aesthetic experience *has* to be disinterested, and when it is genuine it always is, even when bad works of art are involved—but the distinctions I've made and those I've still to make are valid nevertheless.

With representational painting it is something like what it is with literature. This has been said before, many times before, but usually in order to criticize representational painting in what I think is a wrong-headed when not downright silly way. What I mean when I say, in this context, that representational painting is like literature, is that it tends to involve us in the interested as well as the disinterested by presenting us with the images of things that are inconceivable outside time and action. This goes even for landscapes and flower pieces and still lifes. It is not simply that we sometimes tend to confuse the attractiveness of the things represented in a picture with the quality of the picture itself. And it is not only that attractiveness as such has nothing to do with the abiding success of a work of art. What is more fundamental is that the meaning—as distinct from the attractiveness—of what is represented becomes truly inseparable from the representation itself. That Rembrandt confined impasto—thick paint, that is—to his highlights, and that in his later portraits especially these coincide with the ridges of the noses of his subjects is important to the artistic effect of these portraits. And that the effectiveness of the impasto, as impasto—as an abstract element of technique—coincides with its effectiveness as a means of showing just how a nose looks under a certain kind of light is also genuinely important. And that the lifelike delineation of the nose contributes to the evocation of the personality of the individual to whom the nose belongs is likewise important. And the manner and degree of insight into that individual's personality which Rembrandt exhibits in his portrait is important too. None of these factors can be, or ought to be, separated from the legitimate effect of the portrait as a picture pure and simple.

But once we have to do with personalities and lifelikeness we have to do with things from which we cannot keep as secure a distance for the sake of disinterestedness as we can, say, from abstract decoration. As it happens, the whole tendency of our Western painting, up until the later stages of impressionism, was to make distance and detachment on the part of the spectator as insecure as possible. It laid more of a stress than any other tradition on creating a sculpture-like, or photographic, illusion of the third dimension, on thrusting images at the eye with a lifelikeness that brought them as close as possible to their originals. Because of their sculptural vividness, Western paintings tend to be far less quiet, far more agitated and active—in short, far more explicitly dynamic—than most non-Western paintings do. And they involve the spectator to a much greater extent in the practical and actual aspects of the things they depict and represent.

We begin to wonder what we think of the people shown in Rembrandt's portraits, *as* people; whether or not we would like to walk through the terrain shown in a Corot landscape; about the life stories of the burghers we see in a Steen painting; we react in a less than disinterested way to the attractiveness of the models, real or ideal, of the personages in a Renaissance painting. And once we begin to do this we begin to participate in the work of art in a so-to-speak practical way. In itself this participation may not be improper, but it does become so when it begins to shut out all other factors. This it has done and does, all too often. Even though the connoisseurs have usually been able in the long run to prefer the picture of a dwarf by Velasquez to that of a pretty girl by Howard Chandler Christy, the enjoyment of pictorial and sculptural art in our society has tended, on every other level than that of professional connoisseurship, to be excessively "literary," and to center too much on merely technical feats of copying.

But, as I've said, every tradition of culture tends to try to correct one extreme by going to its opposite. And when our Western tradition of painting came up at last with reservations about its forthright naturalism, these quickly took the form of an equally forthright antinaturalism. These reservations started with late impressionism, and have now culminated in abstract art. I don't at all wish to be understood as saying that it all happened because some artist or artists decided it was time to curb the excesses of realistic painting, and that the main historical significance of abstract art lies in its function as an antidote to these. Nor do I wish to be understood as assuming that realistic or naturalistic art inherently needs, or ever needed, such a thing as an antidote. The motivations, conscious and unconscious, of the first modernist artists, and of present modernists as well, were and are quite different. Impressionism itself started as an effort to push naturalism further than ever before. And all through the history of art—not only in recent times—consequences have escaped intentions.

It is on a different, and more impersonal and far more general level of meaning and history that our culture has generated abstract art as an antidote. On that level this seemingly new kind of art has emerged as an epitome of almost everything that disinterested contemplation requires, and as both a challenge and a reproof to a society that exaggerates, not the necessity, but the intrinsic value of purposeful and interested activity. Abstract art comes, on this level, as a relief, an archexample of something that does not have to mean, or be useful for, anything other than itself. And it seems fitting, too, that abstract art should at present flourish most in this country. If American society is indeed given over as no other society has been to purposeful activity and material production, then it is right that it should be reminded, in extreme terms, of the essential nature of disinterested activity.

Abstract art does this in very literal and also in very imaginative ways. First, it does not exhibit the illusion or semblance of things we are already familiar with in real life; it gives us no imaginary space through which to walk with the mind's eye; no imaginary objects to desire or not desire; no imaginary people to like or dislike. We are left alone with shapes and colors. These may or may not remind us of real things; but if they do, they usually do so incidentally or accidentally—on our own responsibility as it were; and the genuine enjoyment of an abstract picture does not ordinarily depend on such resemblances.

Second, pictorial art in its highest definition is static; it tries to overcome movement in space or time. This is not to say that the eye does not wander over a painted surface, and thus travel in both space and time. When a picture presents us with an illusion of real space, there is all the more inducement for the eye to do such wandering. But ideally the whole of a picture should be taken in at a glance; its unity should be immediately evident, and the supreme quality of a picture, the highest measure of its power to move and control the visual imagination, should reside in its unity. And this is something to be grasped only in an indivisible instant of time. No expectancy is involved in the true and pertinent experience of a painting; a picture, I repeat, does not "come out" the way a story, or a poem, or a piece of music does. It's all there at once, like a sudden revelation. This "at-onceness" an abstract picture usually drives home to us with greater single-ness and clarity than a representational painting does. And to apprehend this "at-onceness" demands a freedom of mind and untrammeledness of eye that constitute "at-onceness" in their own right. Those who have grown capable of experiencing this know what I mean. You are summoned and gathered into one point in the continuum of duration. The picture does this to you, willy-nilly, regardless of whatever else is on your mind: a mere glance at it creates the attitude required for its appreciation, like a stimulus that elicits an automatic response. You become all attention, which means that you become, for the moment, selfless and in a sense entirely identified with the object of your attention.

The "at-onceness" which a picture or a piece of sculpture enforces on you is not, however, single or isolated. It can be repeated in a succession of instants, in each one remaining an "at-onceness," an instant all by itself. For the cultivated eye, the picture repeats its instantaneous unity like a mouth repeating a single word.

This pinpointing of the attention, this complete liberation and concentration of it, offers what is largely a new experience to most people in our sort of society. And it is, I think, a hunger for this particular kind of experience that helps account for the growing popularity of abstract art in this country: for the way it is taking over in the art schools, the galleries, and the museums. The fact that fad and fashion are also involved does not invalidate what I say. I know that abstract art of the latest variety—that originating with painters like Pollock and Georges Mathieu—has gotten associated with progressive jazz and its cultists; but what of it? That Wagner's music became associated with German ultranationalism, and that Wagner was Hitler's favorite composer, still doesn't detract from its sheer quality as music. That the present vogue for folk music started, back in the 1930's, among the Communists doesn't make our liking for it any the less genuine, or take anything away from folk music itself. Nor does the fact that so much gibberish gets talked and written about abstract art compromise it, just as the gibberish in which art criticism in general abounds, and abounds increasingly, doesn't compromise art in general.

One point, however, I want to make glaringly clear. Abstract art is not a special kind of art; no hard-and-fast line separates it from representational art; it is only the latest phase in the development of Western art as a whole, and almost every "technical" device of abstract painting is already to be found in the realistic painting that preceded it. Nor is it a superior kind of art. I still know of nothing in abstract painting, aside perhaps from some of the near-abstract cubist works that Picasso, Braque and Léger executed between 1910 and 1914, which matches the highest achievements of the old masters. Abstract painting may be a purer, more quintessential form of pictorial art than the representational kind, but this does not of itself confer quality upon an abstract picture. The ratio of bad abstract painting to good is actually much greater than the ratio of bad to good representational painting. Nonetheless, the very best painting, the major painting, of our age is almost exclusively abstract. Only on the middle and lower levels of quality, on the levels below the first-rate—which is, of course, where most of the art that gets produced places itself—only there is the better painting preponderantly representational.

On the plane of culture in general, the special, unique value of abstract art, I repeat, lies in the high degree of detached contemplativeness that its appreciation requires. Contemplativeness is demanded in greater or lesser degree for the appreciation of every kind of art, but abstract art tends to present this requirement in quintessential form, at its purest, least diluted, most immediate. If abstract art—as does happen nowadays—should chance to be the first kind of pictorial art we learn to appreciate, the chances are that when we go to other kinds of pictorial art—to the old masters, say, and I hope we all do go to the old masters eventually—we shall find ourselves all the better able to enjoy them. That is, we shall be able to experience them with less intrusion of irrelevancies, therefore more fully and more intensely.

The old masters stand or fall, their pictures succeed or fail, on the same ultimate basis as do those of Mondrian or any other abstract artist. The abstract formal unity of a picture by Titian is more important to its quality than what that picture images. To return to what I said about Rembrandt's portraits, the whatness of what is imaged is not unimportant—far from it—and cannot be separated, really, from the formal qualities that result from the way it is imaged. But it is a fact, in my experience, that representational paintings are essentially and most fully appreciated when the identities of what they represent are only secondarily present to our consciousness. Baudelaire said he could grasp the quality of a painting by Delacroix when he was still too far away from it to make out the images it contained, when it was still only a blur of colors. I think it was really on this kind of evidence that critics and connoisseurs, though they were almost always unaware of it, discriminated between the good and the bad in the past. Put to it, they more or less unconsciously dismissed from their minds the connotations of Reubens' nudes when assessing and experiencing the final worth of his art. They may have remained aware of the pinkness as a *nude* pinkness, but it was a pinkness and a nudity devoid of most of their usual associations.

Abstract paintings do not confront us with such problems. Or at least the frequenting of abstract art can train us to relegate them automatically to their proper place; and in doing this we refine our eyes for the appreciation of non-abstract art. That has been my own experience. That it is still relatively rare can be explained perhaps by the fact that most people continue to come to painting through academic art—the kind of art they see in ads and in magazines—and when and if they discover abstract art it comes as such an overwhelming experience that they tend to forget everything produced before. This is to be deplored, but it does not negate the value, actual or potential, of abstract art as an introduction to the fine arts in general, and as an introduction, too, to habits of disinterested contemplation. In this respect, the value of abstract art will, I hope, prove far greater in the future than it has yet. Not only can it confirm instead of subverting tradition; it can teach us, by example, how valuable so much in life can be made without being invested with ulterior meanings. How many people I know who have hung abstract pictures on their walls and found themselves gazing at them endlessly, and then exclaiming, "I don't know what there is in that painting, but I can't take my eyes off it." This kind of bewilderment is salutary. It does us good not to be able to explain, either to ourselves or to others, what we enjoy or love; it expands our capacity for experience.

THE AESTHETICS OF BASKETBALL

Jonathan Baumbach

*"It's as if we aren't supposed
to win."—Jerry West after
his team had lost to Boston
for the National Basketball
Association Championship*
(SPORTING NEWS, *May 17, 1969*).

This is the memoir of an addict. While bad stuff is flying in Vietnam, Chicago, our universities—and where not?—it matters to me whether a team of strangers wins or loses a game. Which is madness. I like to think of myself, in the privacy of self-concern, as a serious man. What are the New York Knicks to me? What am I to them? What am I doing throwing in my emotional lot with a group of basketball players I've never met, exhausting my energy in the frustrating non-activity of fandom? During last year's play-offs I discovered that a number of my acquaintances—all serious men—are harboring the same secret passion. Somewhat reassuring this discovery. Somewhat. The comfort of a madman who discovers that there are other lunatics walking around. I figure that if there are enough of us, we can vote ourselves demonstrably sane. Madness in all societies is minority activity.

This past summer a contentious friend, fresh from the battlefield of San Francisco State, taunted me about what he considered my frivolous pastime. "How can an intelligent man concern himself with a bunch of goons running up and down the court trying to put an oversized ball through a goddamn hole?" Rather than answer him—actually, I couldn't think of anything to say—I affected to overlook his remarks as well-meaning aggression, though I understood him better than I pretended. One is hard pressed to define the nature of one's pleasures. This is written less to answer my friend's objections than to come to terms with my own, which I suspect include his. What I want to do, insofar as memory allows, is to observe myself—New York novelist as New York Knick fan—observing the game as played through a season. And what is it all about?

Being a fan is tense business. Sports aren't play but life-and-death rituals as crucial to obsessive fans, who experience players and teams as extensions of themselves, as anything in their "real" lives. Identification makes loss personally frustrating. And one is powerless as spectator to influence the result. Rooting for a loser, if one needs to win, can be an agony. If one seeks a sense of potency through fandom (fan-empathy), one is doomed to feelings of impotence. Vicarious fulfillment is short-lived. Even the best of winning teams lose sometimes. In a certain sense—dig the slang usage of the word "scoring"—all athletic events are potency rituals in their different ways. A beer that regularly sponsors games, using such slogans as "the ten-minute head" and "make it big," gears its advertising to obsession with sexual prowess. Some years ago they told us, "Either you have it or you don't."

What interests me as novelist is the event of a basketball game, the pleasures of style and skill, the psychological variables of confrontation, grace under pressure. What interests me as a fan is the result. I want to see my team win no matter what. The two are not mutually exclusive, though often incompatible. One's view of the event is necessarily limited by one's bias. If the opposing team is experienced as the bad guys, it would be masochistic under duress of competition to admire the brilliances of their game. How can I possibly appreciate the grace of my potential assassin? To *see* a game, to appreciate it as spectacle, one has to be to some extent disinterested in the outcome. Consequently, it is easier for me to watch a game in which the Knicks are not playing; less of myself is at stake. The pleasures, however, are also less intense. My sense is that a fan experiences a game as he experiences the world. A paranoid—and who isn't on occasion?—is likely to feel that his team is being persecuted—by the opponent, by the officials. Why should the officiating of a game be any more reliable than the enforcement of our laws? There are fans—I've watched games with some—who view the team they support as inferior to its opponent regardless of who the opponent is. They experience the game as an acting out—in effect, a metaphor—of their own real or imagined defeats. When their team wins it is a symptom of universal imbalance. Retribution is in the wings. Those of us who root for underdogs concede that the odds are against us, that loss is more common than triumph. Also, if we are acknowledged underdogs, there is less at stake in losing; there is nothing to be ashamed of.

Apart from rooting for one's home team, the fan chooses the team whose performance suits the configurations of his fantasies. Conversely, teams tend to represent the collective will of their constituency. To the extent that we get the politicians we deserve, we also get the teams we deserve. When we talk about sports (apart from the pseudo reality of statistics), we are usually talking in disguise about our own lives. Fandom, for the most part, is vicarious failure, vicarious heroism. Which is why it attracts fantasists like novelists. . . .

To win on the other team's home court in a play-off series is like a service break in tennis, a crucial advantage. The first game was in Baltimore (the

team with the better record gets the extra game at home), and was to
establish the pattern of the series. The lead went back and forth in the
beginning, both teams fairly tight, staying close as if not to tempt fate, like
gunfighters unwilling to make the first move. Monroe hit two consecutive
jumpers from the left side and the Bullets had their biggest lead at 16-12.
Then they went three minutes without a field goal as if unsettled by their
own advantage. The game was decided at the start of the second quarter
when the Knicks, leading by one, ran off ten points in a row in less than two
minutes. Thereafter when Baltimore would rally—and they were at their
best when the Knicks were comfortably ahead—New York would come
back tougher, matching the Bullets steal for steal, basket for basket. The
message was: *even at your best, I can take you.* In control of the rhythm of
the game, New York won convincingly 113 to 101. And so it went. The
Knicks established superiority sooner or later in each of the games—in only
one, the third, did they have to come from behind in the fourth quarter to
win. In all, it was like a child's fantasy enacted. Every one of the Knicks had
his moment of heroism, Reed, overall the dominant figure in the series,
triumphing personally over his rival Unseld.

If the Knicks were a better team than the Bullets at the time of the play-
offs, they were not four straight victories better. Baltimore played, though in
no clearly definable instant, as if they thought themselves impostors, as if,
though they would give it their best, they knew they couldn't win. A team
that moves from last to first in a year must to some extent be incredulous at
their achievement. The notion of the sophomore jinx is relevant here. (Writers of highly praised first novels experience something like it.) When you're
doing anything transcendentally well you're integrated into the process and
so unable to witness the performance: if you didn't witness it, how can you
know after the fact that what you did wasn't some kind of fluke? You can't
know with any assurance until you do something comparable again, and
again, and again. And who knows how many times.

I talk about Baltimore knowing they couldn't win only after the fact of
their defeat. My pleasure in the outcome, in the process itself, was vitiated
by the moment-to-moment anxiety of rooting. Because of the firepower of
the shooters, and because the twenty-four-second rule precludes freezing the
ball, large leads can be overcome in remarkably short space of time. If you
are anxious for your team—that is, for yourself—no lead feels secure. I
couldn't help feeling that the Knicks were going too well for it to last.
Eventually, I assumed, events would reverse themselves. (As they did in the
second round play-offs against Boston, an anticlimax for the Knicks.) Tension frets the secret heart of exhilaration. The happier you are, the greater
the sense of loss afterward, as, for example, postcoital depression. *And Joy,
whose hand is ever at his lips/Bidding adieu.* Since a fan has no control over
the events of a game, its action has the ambience of magic to him. Whenever

the Knicks would miss a few, or lose the ball on a turnover, or Reed pick up a foul, I anticipated the beginning of the end of good luck: retribution in the wind. The game became something else for me, a metaphysical battlefield where my sense of the way it is—no optimistic vision that—was put to the test.

Watching a game "live"—is it you or the players who are alive?—and watching it on the tube are qualitatively different experiences. At the stadium you can concentrate on different aspects of play at different times, while on television you are constrained to see the game from the cameraman's angle of vision, which means generally following the ball. Also, unless you turn off the sound, you have the compulsive sightless chatter of the announcer to put up with as guide to the event. Most commentary is public relations, perpetuating the clichés of the game without observing what actually takes place, the event often belying the reportage. Nevertheless, television has advantages for the fan—particularly ABC's Game of the Week. You can view certain details—the expressions of the players in close-up, for example, that otherwise might be missed. With the slow-motion replay, television can show the grace and timing of a shot or pass or defensive play that you can't possibly catch in the speed of its moment. Still, gratifying as replay can be, what you are getting is something else, a media experience, separable from the event of the game.

As a spectator at the Garden, for better or worse, the crowd shares the burden of empathy. The team is no longer solely your responsibility. Knick fans this past season, grateful for the team's brilliant play after long drought, gave standing ovations to individual plays as if they were arias or pas de deux. We were all lovers (and winners) together, cheering the team that represents us, the manifest object of our self-pleasure.

As with readers of novels, there are those primarily interested in who won and who lost, and those in how the winning and losing took place, the process. My own view is that process offers the larger, more serious pleasures. Spectator sports are a form of theatre, predictable as ritual and surprising because of a wide variety of complex variables. More than the others, pro basketball has the formal openness and immediacy of improvisation. It is not only that individual players perform differently from game to game, but that defense and offense are so skillful—the sport presently at its peak of skill—that game situations excite improvisatory maneuvers. A pro basketball game is at least as serious as politics and more revelatory of the mysteries of human behavior than most of our theatre. Nothing less than character and grace are at issue.

The compartmentalization of culture makes some of our most crucial rituals inaccessible to those educated to notions of higher pursuit. To watch Sam Jones, for example (and last season was for the last time), make one of his remarkable side jumpers at about a forty-five-degree angle off the backboard, is to have some sense of what it is to be at one with yourself. Joe DiMaggio once said that he could never recall having chased a fly ball—the ball, he said, led him to it. Correspondingly, in basketball a great shooter doesn't aim his shot, he lets the hoop receive it. In the moment of truth, to borrow a phrase from another ritual sport, the shooter, the ball, and the basket—or so I like to imagine—become spiritually inseparable.

Spectating, as I have indicated, is not an unmixed pleasure. Watching the game on television alone at home, I go through several kinds of hell. A call against the Knicks in a close game brings out the worst snakes of my paranoia. I rage at the refs, conspiring through blindness and secret hostility to take rightful victory from my team (from me, in fact). If my wife says something to me when the Knicks are missing or the other team is scoring, I hold her personally responsible—a responsibility she bears with admirable cool. I know of others—intelligent men, respected in their professions—who behave even more irrationally under the life and death pressure of rooting. What other power do we have?

The truth is, fandom is a kind of madness. This past summer a man in Queens killed his wife because she wanted to watch *Dark Shadows* when the Mets were engaging the Cubs in a crucial encounter on Channel 9. I know how he felt. His own mortal soul invested in the Mets, it was as if his wife were rejecting him for some epicene television vampire. At times I think of breaking the habit, of driving out, so to speak, when I remind myself of the pleasure of basketball, its style and seriousness, its enactment of the mysteries. I remember how we, meaning the Knicks, blew tough Philadelphia off the court, beating them by over thirty points after a double-overtime loss, and what can I do, hooked by the metaphor of the game, but believe in sympathetic magic and my own unrealized possibilities.

The Public Reacts

TOMORROW'S MOVIES

Andrew Sarris

I don't pretend to be a film prophet, particularly when the continuing existence of the world itself has been cast into doubt. However, enough trends have been set into motion within the past few years to give us some idea of what lies ahead. Technologically, the film medium is being stretched and diversified to accommodate all the blinding and deafening pastimes of the Now Generation. Light and noise as ends in themselves will undoubtedly increase the strain on the audience's nervous systems, and there will be ever-fainter outcries against the systematic brutalization of the senses. But in the end, youth will be served even at the expense of sight and hearing.

Of course, there is nothing new about noisemaking in and out of the movies. Middle-aged moviegoers who complain about the *vavoom* motorcycle genre exemplified most earnestly by *Easy Rider* have conveniently forgotten the noisy police car chases of the '30s. And if rock in all its variants be considered insensate noisemaking, so were jazz, swing, and bop in their time. Hence, films of the future will follow to some extent the same cycles as films of the past. Even the contemporary obsession with youth is not as new or revolutionary as it seems. Many people *act* younger today, but movie stars are much older on the average today than they were in the '20s and '30s. Everybody's favorite adolescent, Dustin Hoffman, would have once been considered too worn and offbeat for anything but character roles, and Ali MacGraw of *Goodbye, Columbus* fame might have seemed too mature for college-girl parts in the days when studio turnover was a more rigorous process than it is today. Therefore, the fact that movie audiences may get younger and younger does not necessarily mean that movie stars will get younger and younger. Quite the contrary. With everyone seeking perpetual youth from the cradle to the grave, it may be harder than ever for genuinely (i.e., biologically) younger people to break into the movie industry. Films of the future may consequently reflect youthful values without youthful participation.

Films will probably seem more fragmented in the future to those who can remember the past. The one-minute or even 30-second TV commercial, the three-minute pop single, the four-panel comic strip concentrate so much manipulative technique into such a short attention span that people may become impatient with the more coherent forms of the 90-minute to two-hour-plus feature film. (A futurist Russian animated cartoon recently depicted a bored driver inserting a coin into a curbside movie meter and being regaled by a speeded-up, 60-second version of Shakespeare's *Macbeth*, and then yawning as he drove away.) Obviously, decline and fall is an amusing game to play in essays of this kind, but the signs of decadence are all around us. People in our relatively affluent Western civilization are at once more stimulated and more bored than people have been ever before in human history, and there is no reason to believe that the process will not continue into the foreseeable future.

Films will travel far and wide to the distant corners of this planet, and perhaps to other planets as well. The days of the confined cosmos of the movie studio are over. No more menacing shadows, no more Rembrandt lighting, no more meaningfully diagonal compositions. A French critic once predicted years ago that the cinema of the future would be the cinema of the traveler. The screen character of tomorrow will tend to be rootless, mobile, unsentimental, pragmatic, and, above all, self-conscious about making the scene, be it in Brooklyn or Beirut. He will try his damndest to look unique and individual. Screen characters will tend also to be created as instant parodies of themselves.

There will be increasingly ambitious attempts to combine reality with illusion. The lines between reality and illusion, amateurism and professionalism, camp and conviction, will become blurred and indistinct. Patterns of production, distribution, and exhibition will become increasingly improvisational as audiences break apart into warring, noncommunicating factions. Indeed, the relatively unified moviegoing coalition we have known for the first 60 years of the medium's history may be coming unglued already. The college 16-millimeter circuit, to take but one current example, may be setting the stage for an ever-growing audience of self-conscious aesthetes who will eventually be unable to participate in the movie-going experience without a full complement of program notes, introductory lectures, and postscreening seminars. At this extreme of polarization, movies won't even be called movies any more, but cinemah or filluhm (as in Philharmonic Hall).

At the opposite pole of honest-to-goodness-so-help-me-Spiro Agnew screen entertainment, the intellectual level of movies will plummet to zero in a veritable orgy of sentimental fantasy that will make old Shirley Temple movies look like sagas of spiritual despair. Simple-minded spectacles will be more lavishly spectacular than ever, musicals more vulgarly bourgeois than ever, melodramas more mindlessly violent than ever. The intellectuals and the philistines will probably mingle only in theatres screening the more thoughtful sexploitation features, sex being the only movie subject that can bring together lowbrow curiosity (yellow or blue as the case may be) and highbrow condescension (yawn-yawn-how-boring-all-this-sex-can-be-especially-since-this-is-the-fourth-time-I've-come-here-to-get-bored). This latter variant of highbrow hypocrisy is known nowadays as the *Oh! Calcutta!* complex.

And what about sex, nudity, pornography, and all that sort of thing, be it simulated or hard-core? Will the tides of "filth" continue to rise or begin to recede? Is sexual frankness a cyclical phenomenon or a progressive one? Here I must side with those who believe that we are closer to the beginning of sexual liberation than to the end, and now that our society has pried loose the clammy grip of Puritanism from the Pandora's box of pan-sexuality, it will be difficult to imagine the box being closed again at any time in the foreseeable future. Once Man, be he Adam or Homo Americanus, has tasted of the forbidden fruit, he can never return to his original state of innocence. There may be vestiges of Puritanism in our society even in the year 3000 A.D. There will always be guilt, revulsion, and self-hatred as long as men's and women's erotic fantasies clash with their existential fears. As long as Death continues to cast its shadow over the libertine's revels, the screen will never reflect the joyful liberation of sexuality without at the same time casting a pall of metaphysical despair. Nonetheless, the insatiability of the audience's clinical curiosity about the hitherto privileged privacy of others will know no bounds. Scandal will know no barriers, immodesty no limits. One can imagine a time when society not only tolerates but demands the ultimate invasion of privacy in the name of scientific inquiry. Indeed, the science of sexology may eventually treat pornographic home movies with the same degree of clinical detachment with which medicine and dentistry now treat X-rays. In order to facilitate the detection, apprehension, and treatment of sex offenders and deviates, it may be necessary to require of every citizen a sexual dossier (on film) in order to classify each citizen's patterns of sexual behavior. Unusual case histories may be dramatized on the screen with skilled actors adding elements of glamor and acrobatics to the spectacle. But the biggest and most scandalous sexploitation coups will not occur with the fictional reenactments of ordinary case histories, but rather with the documentation of the private lives of celebrities. Producers will bid wildly for the exclusive rights to the most intimate moments of that era's Liz and Dick, Jackie and Ari, the Beatles and their birds. Millions of jaded citizens will flock to theatres or huddle in front of their pay-TV to witness the libidinous life styles of their idols and icons, the plastic and muscular mysteries of their scandalously alive statuary. And after a while, if we may project even further, audiences will weary of the carefully, elaborately, and, above all, artistically staged spectacles involving celebrities playing themselves, rehearsed roles of a sort, after all. Thus jaded and discontented, our insatiably curious spectators will then demand instead the most diabolically candid camera yet devised by depraved man in his quest for utter, ignoble realism.

As for the conditions of viewing films, it is not certain that we shall ever attain for the viewer the voluptuous passivity envisaged decades ago by Aldous Huxley in *Brave New World*. As of 1970, movie audiences are still confined to the two basic senses involved with sight and sound. A few isolated experiments with "smellies" back in the '50s ended as ludicrous fiascoes, and it is unlikely any entrepreneur will ever again undertake to squirt jets of perfume out of the spectator's seat for olfactory "atmosphere." Nothing in the way of gastronomic stimulation for the movie audience has ever passed the primal popcorn phase, and, as for Aldous Huxley's "feelies," let us say simply that the more avant-garde theatre companies with their innovations in group-grope and confrontational contact seem to have made the movie medium seem relatively remote and abstract in the realm of tactile sensations. All things considered, it is unlikely that the cinema will ever match the theatre, particularly the physically revolutionary theatre, in the direct bodily stimulation of its audience. It doesn't follow that because some device is technically feasible, it will ever be commercially or culturally feasible, and short of an incredibly decadent transformation of movie palaces into one-man masturbation chambers, it is unlikely that Aldous Huxley's "feelies" will ever see the light of darkness.

A more interesting probe into the future may be provided by the do-it-yourself movies pioneered by Czechoslovakian film theoreticians in special movie-carnival situations. This particular do-it-yourself device invites the assembled viewers to choose one of several plot developments for the characters shown on the screen, a simple plurality of viewers being sufficient to twist the plot hither and yon. The possible variations and refinements of this device seem truly inexhaustible.

Conceivably, a spectator could enter a do-it-yourself movie chamber, and become himself part of the action by picking out a particular character for himself, a particular genre, a particular range of actions, and then, once he had become enmeshed in his illusionary world, the next spectator could begin thickening the plot. Moviegoing could thus become a two-edged adventure, a Pirandellian ploy with almost infinite possibilities from the most sublime to the most sordid. If the society in which these games would be played were relatively civilized, certain restrictions could be applied on the use of force in the resolution of the plot. For a society in search of new sensations, however, the spectator-character could literally take his life into his hands as he walked into the movie chamber. Actually, it doesn't take too much hallucinating to project a future society (patterned after Elio Petri's *The Tenth Victim*) in which the inhabitants are licensed to hunt each other down like animals. And if wife-swapping should have gotten beyond the tepid tease stage of *Bob & Carol & Ted & Alice*, the Czech movie chamber could serve as an efficient means of both switching one's mate and recording the result on film for the edification of the closet swingers out there in the audience.

For the record, I don't think 3-D will ever come back, not even in centuries hence, but neither did I think that Dick Nixon would come back after California, and so perhaps the unwary reader should hold on to his stock in 3-D glasses. The trouble with 3-D now and forever is that it creates an illusion of three-dimensional space without adding a dimension to two-dimensional heavenly bodies. Thus, the most curvaceous cutie in creation looks even more abstractly flat in 3-D than in 2-D, and who needs acres and acres of useless space on the screen? Split-screen effects, by contrast, should proliferate in the years to come, if only because the world is bound to seem more complex and more chaotic as time rushes by. All films will be in color, and those that cling to black and white will seem arty and pretentious and unimaginatively traditional.

Finally and most gratifyingly, film will be treated at long last as one of the fine arts, if not the finest. The Russians have already developed a system of visual tapes that can be projected on television, said tapes serving, therefore, the library functions of books and record albums. If rights could be cleared, and precious prints preserved, our entire cinematic heritage could be made available to students of the future. A film student could wake up in the middle of the night with sudden insight on Buster Keaton's classic silent comedies, go into his private film library and project Keaton's films, then repair to the bookshelf and take down the writings of Samuel Beckett, and compare the absurdist visions of these two remarkable artists, whose paths once actually crossed in a film called too starkly, too simply, too pretentiously *Film*. But their paths did cross, and they *are* artistically comparable, though only at some future time will it be possible to establish the validity of the comparison at a moment's scholarly notice. And at that time, people will be shooting films as casually as they type today, and a few of the film-shooters will be artists, and the rest will be what Truman Capote calls untalented writers: typists. I can't believe in my most morbid musings that there will ever come a time when beauty, truth, and personal feeling disappear completely from the screen.

AVANT-GARDE THEATRICS

Jack Richardson

If one thinks historically about the theater, it is easy to see its conventions as reflections of the various ages through which it has passed. The Athenians, for example, showed their theater to be an extension of the strong sense of community they had evolved, by attending their plays as if they were at a legislative meeting. It was a state ritual and, arranged in curved tiers, the citizens stared down at tragic admonitions and comic harangues with the sense that half was pageant and half parliament. It was very clearly they, the audience as a group joined by common custom and past, who were the subject of the action before them.

Similarly, the restiveness of the Elizabethan Age—its individualism, imagination, and perhaps above all, its love of good talk—shows up clearly in the way it went to its plays. This was an audience of personalities who used the pit and galleries for everything from a meeting place for assignations to a platform from which the actors could be debated. Whatever else a trip to Shakespeare's theater was, it was not a solemn occasion. There was, to be sure, a community there, but it was the community of the marketplace rather than of the assembly, and bringing all those disparate spirits together, getting, in the most basic sense, their attention, was the job of a theatrical style that had mayhem and murder as its core. It seems that only the extremes and frenzies of existence could fashion something cohesive out of the Lords and groundlings at The Globe—or at least make them shut up long enough so that they might realize that something marvelous was being said.

Gradually, of course, the audience grew more manageable until Voltaire, a playwright who needed all the quiet and concentration that he could get, banished it from the stage proper and established symbolically that aesthetic schism by which spectators and performers behave as though each is unaware of what the other is doing. This was not a simple shift of convention but a very deep alteration in the way one was to experience the theater. The audience was no longer to be wrestled with or brought to a sense of communal self-judgment. Passive, sitting in darkness, silent with expectancy, it now was a collection of random voyeurs who could offer nothing to the drama but the most primitive responses. Through the 19th century it swooned, wept, and ogled at the great stars in five-act romances and melodramas tailored to egomaniacal proportions. The whole social situation of the theater was now something quite unreal, something that demanded greater and greater fantasy in order to sustain its unreality. Occasionally, there would be an atavistic hoot from the gallery to unsettle the mood but, for the most part, the audience yielded its right to a persona of its own for the luxury of being flabbergasted by thirty sets and an astounding profile. Even when naturalism appeared and demanded that at least the most blatant part of the fantasy come to an end, it could not break down the separatist tradition. Wanting to thrust its truths at the heart, it contented itself with the peep-show methods of melodrama, and considered the audience still as something repressed and muted, something that could be easily bustled into a sob or laughter by the raw chunks of life thrown at it.

If I seem hard on this, the Victorian tradition of theater-going which is still with us, it is not that I don't realize that many fine playwrights have worked within it and, what is more miraculous, many good plays and productions have come out of it. But I am also aware that if one sits down and thinks rationally about our customs in the theater and the manner of presentation that goes with them, one cannot help but be somewhat embarrassed by their absurdity. This gathering of cultural strangers; this docile acceptance of rules for the imagination which demand that an actor seen forty times previously be granted the right to huff about in front of us deep in his new "character" (in direct contradiction of the fact that he was immediately recognized and applauded when he made his first entrance); this obligatory adoption of the ethics of invisibility which demands that we may not walk out to skip a boring part or call for something particularly fine or complex to be repeated; this tightly-planned emotional schedule with flamboyant scenes carefully spaced so that we may make some approving sound to prove that we are, indeed, after all out there, somewhere, and are at approximately the emotional point worked out for us—can this be an art form for any but idiots who will surrender not only their senses to the artist but their sense as well?

Most of us have been just such idiots and will remain so. What seems ludicrous and impossible on reflection, appears in practice ineluctably natural. With all its intolerant demands and weaknesses, tradition does offer us an easy access to the occasional states of mind we need for the intense experience of life, and this tradition of theater has had, as I said, its successes. I have been abusing it only so that it not seem so formidable, so that it not seem a necessary condition for a notion of theater. I am doing this because there is an attitude current at the moment—it is by no means so organized as to be called a movement—which is heading away from this species of theater toward something which, in the language of our times, might be termed a theater of confrontation, and while I am excited by its goals, I can see that it will need all the help it can get.

This new direction, which has been germinating in cafés and in church and loft productions off off Broadway during the last few years, has both the Theater of the Absurd and the Happening as its aesthetic antecedents. However, what is uniquely its own is its style: the style of performing not *for* an audience but *at* it. By this I do not mean that the spectators are simply acknowledged for a preachment or two, or that they are occasionally invaded by the action of the play, or even that, as in *Tom Paine*, they are asked to participate in an informal dialogue with the actors on current events. These are crude and simplistic devices which, at this stage of the new style's evolution, are heavy-footed embarrassments for everyone. What I am speaking about—and for the purposes of this review I am using as models *Futz, Hair,* and *Tom Paine,* all directed by Tom O'Horgan—is the fierce consciousness in all of these productions that every gesture and movements is indeed being watched and that the purpose of performance is to make that observation a self-conscious one. This is to deny the individual in the audience his private crescendos of understanding and feeling, even to mock them if they should occur; it is to comment on the play's action with body positions that thrust the physicality of the actors uncomfortably upon one; it is to perform not as one drowning in character involvement but as one aware that character is a weapon that can be used; it is, finally, to keep the actors as well as the audience out of their emotional petticoats and to force them to encounter each other naked.

Now, writing about the theater can do strange things to one, the least of which is to see mirages of great significance where there is in fact only a small water-hole of promise. The plays that Tom O'Horgan has directed by no means blister the soul, and for all his feral ingenuity at physical movement and his actors' lack of restraint, there are long stretches of time when the proceedings seem like a children's party where everyone is frantically being bad in order that some attention be paid him. But it can nevertheless be said that these works often did startle, did make one disquietingly apperceptive, and did make of the theater something more than a two-hour hiatus from social abrasions. It must also be considered that our theater gives little of its resources to the experimenter, and, even if it did, it is apparent that what O'Horgan is striving for cannot be fully realized within the designs of stages that have been created for the very tradition he is working against. All three of his plays were put on in theaters planned with the disjunction of performer and audience as an architectural principle, a principle which makes the engulfment of the viewer literally impossible. Until this almost axiomatic arrangement of the watcher and watched is broken down as much as possible—say, by scattered clusters of seats within a theater that is all stage—the attack method of O'Horgan will always seem uncertain and out of its true environment. Comfortable habits are not easily shed, and no amount of confrontation will make an audience a creative force in the theater until its individuals are exposed without the safe retreat back into anonymity that the usual seating arrangement affords. And, too, if this method is ever to be anything but a dramatic curio, the spectator must be allowed his attack too. He must be more than the conditioned response the theater has made of him, even if that response is now to be a contextual one. He, too, must have his action, and the production must be conceived so as to ingest that action without turning into a shambles. If he does not, if he is treated only as a prop, then one has not a confrontation but rather an awkward encounter that will produce little but feelings of superiority on both sides.

Finally, one must come to the plays themselves. Whatever they will be, they cannot be so hermetically sealed as they have been in the past. *Futz* and *Tom Paine*, for example, both use the narrative voice for much of the time, and this allows the company to act out in movement what is being recounted. It is one way of setting up action as something meant to be both observed and depicted, a way which fits in well with O'Horgan's intentions; but one hopes that something more salutary to the poetics of the theater can be joined to the new method. *Futz*, which, so help me, manages to make a sentimental, moral tale out of the love of a man for his pig and his neighbors' hostility to this peculiarity, runs amuck in a lot of Ozark fustian until it can truly be said that the language gets in the way of the play itself. And *Tom Paine*, which does well enough when it sticks to the words of its protagonist, dribbles away when its author takes to what I would call the language of caricature in dealing with history. *Hair*, which uses the extended lyric form of popular music for eighty per cent of the production, does less with it than some of the better writers in this style, and makes no attempt at anything that might be considered a coherent dramatic language.

In short, what I sensed in watching O'Horgan's work was a style in search of a language that would not be overpowered by it, that could make its own confrontation. Indeed, it would have to be a language of such force as to become in its individuality, color, and rhythm, part of the actor's very imagination so that, when he had to, he could use it creatively. This, of course, presupposes actors with much greater literary sympathy than we have at present. Indeed it presupposes the ultimate ensemble theater of actor-writer.

I began by saying that one can tell a great deal about a period of history by the way it attended the theater. Conversely, one can tell a great deal about the theater by the way its conventions meet those of its era. In its great moments there has always been a connection; in its fallow periods there has been little. We are at a moment when it seems to me that the entire notion of the theater experience could stand alteration before it becomes so completely alien to all that is vital in the world about it that it lapses irrevocably into the hands of antiquarians. There is no way of telling if the glimpses of excitement I caught in these plays betoken an idea strong enough to grow into a way of presenting to us our time and ourselves in it. But it did show, or at least it occasioned one to imagine, how the theater might be encountered as a mad relative or a quarrelsome lover, as something almost as dangerous and personal as a walk into one's own living room. It did show, too, that we can at least think of a theater divested of its grand airs, a theater which we can talk to again.

THE BIRTH
OF A CULTURE

Philip Tracy

Maurice wiped the bar, his sad eyes staring out the front door to the street, his head slowly shaking from side to side. Outside, thousands of young people walked along Route 17B heading for the Woodstock Music and Art Fair's Aquarian Exposition five miles away. Inside, Maurice attended to three local beer drinkers and a stranger sipping scotch. It's eleven o'clock on a Saturday night and Maurice the businessman is worried.

"If I bought stock in a cemetery, people would probably stop dying." Thirty-five and slightly paunchy, he frets to the stranger, "As soon as I heard they were holding this thing here, I sunk a thousand bucks into the place in order to attract a big crowd. I figured a discotheque would draw them like flies to honey. Some schemer I am. A thousand bucks down the drain."

Standing there behind his bar, surrounded by the black lights and the posters he recently bought in New York, Maurice shook his head and mentally counted the bills, while half a million kids marched outside his door oblivious to his efforts to attract them. Maurice had guessed wrong.

He wasn't the only one. The sponsors of the Festival planned for fifty thousand people to attend each of the three concerts. At least that many camped on the grounds the night before it opened, with the final number totaling closer to five hundred thousand. The local police, remembering an incident earlier this year when five thousand youngsters had more or less torn a town apart over one weekend, anticipated riots. The riots never came and by Sunday the police were telling newsmen how great the kids had acted. The young, especially the more paranoid types, feared mass arrests and constant harassment from the local citizenry. Instead they found they could smoke their dope in public while the townspeople accepted them as they were.

In retrospect, most of the miscalculations are easy to understand. For what happened at White Lake, N.Y. was the birth of a full-grown culture—a culture of, by, and for the young in which most of us who grew up reading Salinger do not participate or accept. Alone in their lofts or the ticky-tacky houses that their parents love so much, they could be treated as an occasional oddity or family skeleton. You can arrest a pothead or insult a couple but nobody messes with a city full of people. Together at White Lake, they became a distinct society with their own rules, rituals, costumes and standards of behavior. Mobs riot, cities don't, and Woodstock was the first city of the new culture.

Not that it sprang from thin air. There have been signs for quite some time that something like this was afoot. The Be-Ins, the Love-Ins, the communal, family-like quality of the anti-Vietnam war parades, the Haight-Ashbury-East Village scenes were all early signs of pregnancy. Likewise, the campus riots, the people's park, the Chicago Convention were labor pains that accompanied the birth. The Woodstock Festival was merely the final, irrevocable eruption of a life force that's been gestating for the last few years.

The interaction between the residents along the highway and the kids on the road was truly hilarious. On the first day they stood outside their small, white frame houses and stared in utter shock, their slack jaws a constant amusement to the youthful passersby. By Saturday they recovered, or more accurately, adjusted. Some sold warm beer brought in the night before, for five dollars a six-pack. Others offered the use of their houses as comfort stations to the throng of travelers. Outside the Esther Manor Motel, soup, crackers and a cup of kool-aid were dispensed free to all who wished them.

The cops were the funniest of all. Like isolated strangers in a foreign country, they adopted the customs of the dominant culture. Standing in the middle of White Lake, a local sheriff's deputy directed the flow of traffic that included volkswagens covered with riders on the outside, a microbus with four on the roof smoking a gigantic water pipe and motorcycle packs straight out of some Marlon Brando movie. Alone, a flower in his shirtpocket and a whistle in his mouth, his only defense against the unsightly onslaught was a wide if weary grin. All but the most paranoid waved and smiled back as they passed him, knowing their day had finally come.

Music is the glue that holds the young together. If radical politics, dope, sex, and magic are bricks of their new culture, music is the mortar that cements the different elements into place. Sitting in the middle of Max Yasgur's Dairy Farm cum three hundred thousand visitors was a first-class horror until a group called Canned Heat took the stage. Suddenly the waves of electricity came rolling up the slope from the distant tiny square in the center of the valley. Suddenly reefers are passing from hand to hand in a furious effort to strengthen the high. Slowly at first, then all at once, everyone is standing up and bodies are swaying.

The volume deepens, quickens. The swaying turns to jerks. Everyone is into it now. Shouts of "groove it," "smack it," and "lay it into me" are everywhere. The heat and the thirst and the mud are left behind, as if everyone were traveling in a psychic helicopter which is slowly receding from the earth. The bodies come together, the people come together and finally the whole hill becomes one huge rocking trip-out. The energy of the hill feeds back to the band on the stage and the group itself starts to freak, jumping up and down in wild frenzy, stretching their amplification to its outer limits. The intensity is self-generating; it blocks all other stimuli from the senses. Building, constantly growing, the percussion mounts until the most casual observer is caught up in the explosive vibrations flowing back and forth. It goes on like this for over an hour. The group doesn't finish the set, it collapses along with the people on the hill.

Once upon a time Frank Sinatra, Elvis Presley and even the Beatles played to wild swinging audiences. They tantalized, raising and cooling the response of the people in the front almost at will, using suppressed cravings as the source of their energy. On Saturday afternoon in the middle of a dairy farm the Canned Heat had no audience. They were part of a chemical interaction, only an element, no more in control than the people on the hill. Standing in the middle of it, you start to understand why all these hundreds of thousands of people have walked for miles, slept in mud and sat for hours without moving. This is what they all share in common, and now they have felt it they lay back again, exhausted.

Half a mile behind the sloping hill another aspect of the new culture worked itself out among scraggy pines and rocky wasteland where Max's cows rarely wander. The Hog Farm is a communal family of ex-hippies, veterans of Haight-Ashbury and the flower generation. Their normal home is New Mexico, where they own land, raise sheep and chickens, grow most of their food and live together in a large common-house. They either don't know or won't say how many of them there are or how one becomes a member. Flown in several weeks ago by the Festival staff to help clear the camp-site area and set up the ground rules for the weekend, their authority within the metropolis of tents and teepees aptly named "Movement City" is unquestioned.

An observer seeking to help as well as to watch might be directed to a wood and canvas booth, much like those seen at church bazaars, where the raw ingredients used to feed several thousand people day and night were prepared. The meal offered was a simple one—a salad of carrots, kidney beans, raw onion and raisins plus a portion of wheat germ and cracked wheat, studded with tiny bits of scallion. If work in the food-booth slackens, some are directed to the first-aid center, where people are treated for everything from cuts and bruises to bad acid trips or an overdose of heroin. The entire compound was a highly organized operation, far more efficient than an army field unit, yet nearly everybody there was stoned on pot or hash.

The Hog Farmers served as a kind of community service society to the whole festival. They put out a daily fact sheet, listing various locations where free food was available and giving descriptions of people who were selling bad dope. In addition to providing food and health services they acted as intermediaries between the kids and the outside world—hasseling cops and locals indignant over the antics of individual freaks.

Hog Farmers dress with a peculiar kind of consistency. Their clothes tell you the kind of person they want to be. People into astrology wear long, flowing Merlin-like gowns with crudely cut stars sewed all over. The rustic, western types wear calico or buckskin. All move slowly, talk softly and have very little use for outside strangers and the world they represent. They have been through a great many difficulties trying to establish their own way of life. Here, in a place where they are accepted and revered for the way in which they live, they don't care to answer anybody's questions.

Strange and distant, they march to a very different drummer than the rest of us. They've created a society which parallels our own, yet rarely touches it. Underground press, underground clothing factories, underground farm cooperatives, underground restaurants—the Hog Farmers and thousands like them at the Festival no longer need the world of the "straights," the world you and I inhabit. While only a very small portion of the half a million assembled in Max's pasture, the Hog Farmers symbolized the option most of the young are choosing, with no one around to offer objection. [There is] no one these kids will listen to anymore, anyway.

And who could blame them? With our filthy streets and rivers and our cities slowly rotting, who could tell them no? With the best of our leaders dead who could say they're wrong? With our lust for destruction and our murderous hearts, who could tell them ours was the better world? No one. Woodstock was only the beginning.

CULTURAL
SNOBBERY

Arthur Koestler

A friend of mine, whom I shall call Brenda, was given for her birthday by one of her admirers a Picasso line drawing in a simple modern frame. It was an admirable and typical sample of Picasso's "classical" period: a Greek youth carrying a girl in his arms, the contours of the two figures somehow mixed up and partly indistinguishable like those of Siamese twins with shared limbs, yet adding up to a charming and harmonious total effect. It looked like a lithograph, but it bore no serial number, so Brenda took it to be a reproduction and hung it, somewhat disappointed with the gift, over her staircase. On my next visit, several weeks later, it was hanging over her drawing room mantelpiece. "I see the Picasso reproduction has been promoted," I said. "*Reproduction!*" she cried indignantly. "It turned out it's an *original*! Isn't it lovely? Look at that line along the girl's hip. . . ." etc.

As a matter of fact, it *was* an original—a shyly understated gift of the mumbling and devoted admirer. But as it was a line drawing consisting of nothing but black contour on white paper, it needed an expert, or at least a good magnifying lens, to decide whether it was an original, a lithograph, or a reproduction. Neither Brenda nor any of her visitors could tell the difference. But they took it for granted, as we all do, that an original deserves a proud display, whereas a reproduction belongs, at best, over the staircase.

I shall now try to analyze, in a pedantic way, the reason for this apparently so natural attitude. The original is of course many times more expensive than a reproduction; but we would indignantly reject the idea of displaying a picture simply because it is expensive; we pretend to be guided in these matters by purely aesthetic considerations. Next, one might surmise that our contempt for reproductions originates in the poor quality and even poorer choice of subjects of the Victorian print. But modern printing techniques have achieved miracles, and some Ganymede reproductions are almost indistinguishable from the original. In the extreme case of the line drawing, we have complete aesthetic equivalence between original and reproduction.

And yet there is something revolting in this equivalence. It even takes a certain courage to admit to oneself that the aesthetic effect of a copy might be indistinguishable from that of the original. We live in an age of stereotyped mass production; and after mass-produced furniture, mass-produced and prefabricated houses, the idea of mass-produced Piero della Francescas is indeed revolting. But then, we have no similar objection to mass-produced gramophone records. Nor to mass-produced books, and yet they too fall into the category of "reproductions." Why then do you prefer, according to your income, a more or less second-rate original picture on the wall to a first-rate reproduction of a masterpiece? Would you rather read a mediocre young poet in manuscript than Shakespeare in a paper-cover edition?

Our argument seems to have become bogged down. Let us find out what Brenda herself has to say to explain her behavior, in a dialogue with the writer:

BRENDA "I simply can't understand what all this fuss and talk is about. But *of course* my attitude to the drawing has changed since I know that Picasso himself did it. That's nothing to do with snobbery— it's just that I wasn't told before."

K "Your attitude has changed—but has that thing on the wall changed?"

B "Of course it hasn't, but now I *see* it differently!"

K "I would like to understand what it is that determines your attitude to a picture in general."

B "Its quality, of course."

K "And what determines its quality?"

B "Oh, don't be such a pedant. Color, composition, balance, harmony, power, what have you."

K "So, in looking at a picture, you are guided by purely aesthetic value judgments, depending on the qualities you mentioned?"

B "Of course I am."

K "Now, as that picture hasn't changed, and its qualities haven't changed, how can your attitude have changed?"

B "But I have told you before, you idiot. Of course my attitude to it is now different, since I know it isn't one reproduction in a million, but done by Picasso himself. Can't you see?"

K "No, I can't; you are contradicting yourself. The rarity of the object, and your knowledge of the manner in which it came into being, do not alter the qualities of that object, and accordingly should not alter your judgment of it, if it were really based on purely aesthetic criteria—as you believe it to be. But it isn't. Your judgment is not based on what you *see*, but on a purely accidental bit of information, which might be right or wrong and is entirely extraneous to the issue."

B "Wrong? How *dare* you insinuate that my Picasso isn't an original? And how *dare* you say that the question whether he drew it himself is 'extraneous' to the issue?"

And so it will go on indefinitely. Yet Brenda is not stupid; she is merely confused in believing that her attitude to an object of art is determined by purely aesthetic considerations, whereas in fact it is decisively influenced by factors of a quite different order. She is unable to see her picture isolated from the context of her knowledge of its origin. For, in our minds, the question of origin, authorship, or authenticity, *though in itself extraneous to aesthetic value,* is so intimately and indistinguishably fused with our attitude to the object that we find it well-nigh impossible to isolate the two. Thus, Brenda unconsciously projects one scale of values onto a system of quite different values.

Is Brenda, then, a snob? It depends on the definition of snobbery at which we hope to arrive at the end. But as a working hypothesis, I would like to suggest that this process of unconsciously applying to any given field a judgment derived from an alien system of values constitutes the essence of the phenomenon of snobbery. By these standards Brenda would *not* be a snob if she had said: "The reproduction in this case is just as beautiful as the original. But one gives me a greater thrill than the other for reasons which have nothing to do with beauty." She is an unconscious snob because she is unable to distinguish between the two elements of her experience, unable to name the extraneous cause of her biased aesthetic judgment, or to see that it is biased.

I am aware of pedantically laboring an apparently obvious point. But it will become at once less obvious if we turn to a different yet related problem.

In 1948, a German art restorer named Dietrich Fey, engaged in reconstruction work on Lübeck's ancient St. Marien Church, stated that his workmen had discovered traces of old Gothic wall paintings dating back to the thirteenth century, under a coating of chalk on the church walls. The restoration of the paintings was entrusted to Fey's assistant, Lothar Malskat, who finished the job two years later. In 1950, Chancellor Adenauer presided over the ceremonies marking the completion of the restoration work in the presence of art experts from all parts of Europe. Their unanimous opinion, voiced by Chancellor Adenauer, was that the twenty-one thirteenth-century Gothic saints on the church walls were "a valuable treasure and a fabulous discovery of lost masterpieces."

None of the experts on that or any later occasion expressed doubt as to the authenticity of the frescoes. It was Herr Malskat himself who, two years later, disclosed the fraud. He presented himself on his own initiative at Lübeck police headquarters, where he stated that the frescoes were entirely his own work, undertaken by order from his boss, Herr Fey, and asked to be tried for forgery. The leading German art experts, however, stuck to their opinion: the frescoes, they said, were no doubt genuine, and Herr Malskat was merely seeking cheap publicity. An official Board of Investigation was appointed which came to the conclusion that the restoration of the wall paintings was a hoax—but only after Herr Malskat had confessed that he had also manufactured hundreds of Rembrandts, Watteaus, Toulouse-Lautrecs, Picassos, Henri Rousseaus, Corots, Chagalls, Vlamincks, and other masters, and sold them as originals—some of which were actually found by the police in Herr Fey's house. Without this evidence, it is doubtful whether the German experts would ever have admitted having been fooled.

My point is not the fallibility of the experts. Herr Malskat's exploit is merely the most recent of a number of similarly successful hoaxes and forgeries—of which the most fabulous were probably van Megeeren's false Vermeers. The disturbing question which they raise is whether the Lübeck saints are less beautiful, and have ceased to be "a valuable treasure of masterpieces," simply because they had been painted by Herr Malskat and not by somebody else?

There are several answers to this line of argument, but before going into them I want to continue in the part of *advocatus diaboli* by considering an example of a forgery in a different field: Macpherson's *Ossian*. The case is so notorious that the facts need only be briefly mentioned. James Macpherson (1736–96), a Scottish poet and adventurer, alleged that in the course of his wanderings, in the Highlands he had discovered some ancient Gaelic manuscripts. Enthusiastic Scottish littérateurs put up a subscription to enable Macpherson to pursue his researches, and in 1761 he published *Fingal, an Ancient Epic Poem in Six Books, together with Several Other Poems composed by Ossian, the Son of Fingal*. Ossian is the legendary third-century hero and bard of Celtic literature. *Fingal* was soon followed by the publication of a still larger Ossianic epic called *Temora*, and this by a collected edition, *The Works of Ossian*. The authenticity of Macpherson's text was at once questioned in England, particularly by Dr. Johnson (whom Macpherson answered by sending him a challenge to a duel), and to his death Macpherson refused, under various unconvincing pretexts, to publish his alleged Gaelic originals. By the turn of the century the controversy was settled and it was established that, while Macpherson had used fragments of ancient Celtic lore, most of the "Ossianic" texts were of his own making.

Yet here again the question arises whether the poetic quality of the work itself is altered by the fact that it was written not by Ossian, the son of Fingal, but by James Macpherson? The "Ossianic" texts were translated into many languages, and had a considerable influence on the literature and cultural climate of Europe at the late eighteenth and early nineteenth centuries. This is how the *Encyclopedia Britannica* sums up its evaluation of Macpherson:

> The varied sources of his work and its worthlessness as a transcript of actual Celtic poems do not alter the fact that he produced a work of art which . . . did more than any single work to bring about the romantic movement in European, and especially in German, literature. . . . Herder and Goethe . . . were among its profound admirers.

These examples could be continued indefinitely. Antique furniture, Roman statuary, Greek tanagra figures, and Italian madonnas are being forged, copied, counterfeited all the time, and the value we set on them is not determined by aesthetic appreciation and pleasure to the eye, but by the precarious and often uncertain judgment of experts. A mediocre but authenticated picture by a known master is held in higher esteem than an artistically superior work of his unknown pupil or "school"—not only by art dealers guided by "investment," but by all of us, including this writer. Are we, then, all snobs to whom a signature, an expert testimonial, or the postmark of a given period is more important than the intrinsic beauty of the object itself?

I now propose to present the case for the defense. It can be summed up in a single sentence: our appraisal of any work of literature or art is never a unitary act, but the result of two independent and simultaneous processes which tend to distort each other.

When we look at an Egyptian fresco, we do not enjoy the painting at its face value, but by means of an unconscious reattunement of the mind to the values of the period. We know, for instance, that the Egyptians had not discovered the technique of perspective in depth. We know that on certain Egyptian murals the size of the figures is determined by their relative social rank. Similarly, we look at every picture through a double frame: the solid frame which isolates it from its surroundings and creates for it a hole in space, as it were; and the unconscious frame of reference in our minds which creates for it a hole in time and locates it in its period and cultural climate. Every time we think that we are making a purely aesthetic judgment based on pure sensory perception, we are in fact judging relative to this second frame or context or mental field.

Any work of art, or literature, or music, can only be appreciated against the background of its period, and that is what we unconsciously do: when we naïvely believe that we are applying absolute criteria, we are in fact applying relative ones. When we contemplate the false Vermeer the first time believing it to be authentic and the second time knowing that it is a fake, our aesthetic experience will indeed completely change, though the picture has remained the same. For it is now seen in a different frame of reference and therefore, in fact, differently. The same considerations apply to the perpetrator of the fake. He may be able to imitate the technique of the seventeenth-century Dutch School, but he could not spontaneously start painting like Vermeer—because his visual organization is different, his perception of reality is different, and because he cannot, except by an artificial effort, erase from his mind the accumulated experience of everything that happened in painting since Vermeer. And if, by a tour de force, a contemporary artist succeeded in reconditioning his own vision to that of the Dutch seventeenth century or the Italian *quattrocento*, he would have to use mass hypnosis to recondition the vision of his customers in a similar manner.

We can add to our knowledge and experience, but we cannot subtract from it. When Picasso decides to disregard the laws of perspective, that means that he has passed through and beyond a certain technique—unlike the Egyptian painter, who has never acquired it. Evolution is an irreversible process; the culture of a period might apparently point into the same direction as an earlier one, but it does so from a different turn of the spiral. A modern primitive is different from a primitive primitive; contemporary classicism is different from any classical classicism; only the mentally insane are able to amputate part of their past.

And yet when we contemplate works of the past, we must perform just such a process of mental subtraction, by attuning our minds to the climate and experience of the period. In order to appreciate them, we must enter into their spirit, by forgetting our modern experience and all that we have learnt since that Homeric epic or Byzantine mosaic was created. We must descend into the past, making our mind a blank; and as we do so, we unconsciously condescend. We close our eyes to crudities of technique, naïveties of perception, prevailing superstitions, limitations of knowledge, factual errors. We make allowances. A little honest introspection will always reveal the element of condescension contained in our admiration for the classics; and part of our enjoyment when listening to the voices of the past is derived from this half-consciously patronizing attitude—"how clever of them to know that at their age." We feel that we have descended a turn of the spiral; we are looking up in awe and wonder at Dante's dreadful Paradise, but at the same time we seem to be bending down, with a tender antiquarian stoop.

This legitimate kind of aesthetic double-think degenerates into snobbery at the point where the frame of reference becomes more important than the picture, when the thrill derived from the gesture of bending over the past dominates the aesthetic experience. The result is a widespread confusion of critical judgment—overestimation of the dead and belittlement of the living, indiscriminate reverence for anything that is "classical," "antique," "primitive," or simply old. In its extreme form this tendency prompts people to have their wall brackets and picture frames artifically dirtied to lend them the patina of age; so let us call it the "patina snobbery."

The process that leads to these distortions of judgment is basically the same as outlined before: the projection of one scale of values to a psychologically related but objectively alien field of experience. The essence of snobbery is to assess value according to a wrong type of scale; the snob is always trying to measure beauty with a thermometer or weight with a clock.

The thirteen-year-old daughter of a friend was recently taken to the Greenwich Museum. When she was asked which was the most beautiful thing she had seen in the Museum, she said unhesitatingly: "Nelson's shirt."

When asked what was so beautiful about it, she explained: "That shirt with the blood on it was jolly nice. Fancy real blood on a real shirt, which belonged to somebody really historic!"

The child's thrill is obviously derived from the same source as the magic that emanates from Napoleon's inkpot, the lock of hair on the Egyptian mummy's head, the relic of the saint carried in annual procession, the strand of the rope by which a famous murderer was hanged, and from Tolstoi's laundry bill. In the mentality of the primitive, an object which had been in contact with a person is not merely a souvenir: it becomes magically imbued with the substance of that personality and in turn magically emanates something of that substance.

"There is, I am sure, for most of us, a special pleasure in sinking your teeth into a peach produced on the estate of an earl who is related to the Royal Family," a London columnist wrote recently in the *Daily Express*.

Primitive magic survives in the subconscious; the strand of hair carried in the locket, grandmother's wedding dress, the faded fan of the first ball, the regimental badge, all have a half-conscious fetish character. The bobby-soxers who tear shreds off the crooner's garb are the vulgarized twentieth-century version of the worshipers cherishing a splinter from a saint's bone. The value that we set on original manuscripts, on "signed" pieces of furniture, on Dickens' quill and Kepler's telescope, are more dignified manifestations of the same unconscious tendency. It is, as the child said, "jolly nice" to behold a fragment of a marble by Praxiteles—even if it is battered out of human shape, with a leper's nose and broken ears. The contact with the master's hand has imbued it with a magic quality which has lingered on and radiates at us, conveying the same thrill as "the real blood on Nelson's real shirt."

The change in our attitude—and in the art dealer's price—when it is learned that a cracked and blackened piece of canvas is an "authenticated" work by X has nothing to do with beauty, aesthetics, or what have you—it is the working of sympathetic magic in us. (See Brenda and her Picasso drawing.) The inordinate importance that we attribute to the original, the authenticated, in those borderline cases where only the expert could tell the difference, is a derivative from primitive fetishism. And as every honest art dealer will admit, these borderline cases are so frequent as to be almost the rule. Moreover, it was a general practice in the past for the master to let his pupils assist in the execution of larger undertakings. It is not the eye that guides the average museum visitor, but the magic of names and the magic of age. The bedevilment of aesthetic experience by unconscious fetish worship and patina snobbery is so general that it has become a major factor in our attitude to the art of past epochs—an attitude as remote from spontaneous appreciation as the "Emperor's Clothes" fallacy regarding hyper-modern art forms.

THE CULTURAL IMPORTANCE OF THE ARTS

Susanne K. Langer

Every culture develops some kind of art as surely as it develops language. Some primitive cultures have no real mythology or religion, but all have some art—dance, song, design (sometimes only on tools or on the human body). Above all, dances; that seems to be the oldest elaborated art.

The ancient ubiquitous character of art contrasts sharply with the prevalent idea that art is a luxury product of civilization, a cultural frill, a piece of social veneer.

It fits better with the conviction held by most artists, that art is the epitome of human life, the truest record of insight and feeling, and that the strongest military or economic society without art is poor in comparison with the most primitive tribe of savage painters, dancers, or idol-carvers. Wherever a society has really achieved culture (in the ethnological, not the popular sense of social form) it has begotten art, not late in its career, but at the very inception of it.

Art is, indeed, the spearhead of human development, social and individual. The vulgarization of art is the surest symptom of ethnic decline. The growth of a new art or even a great and radically new style always bespeaks a young and vigorous mind, whether collective or single.

What sort of thing is art, that it should play such a leading role in human development? It is not an intellectual pursuit, but is necessary to intellectual life; it is not religion, but grows up with religion, serves it and in large measure determines it (as Herodotus said, "Homer made the gods," and surely the Egyptian deities grew under the chisels of sculptors in strangely solemn forms).

We cannot enter here on a long discussion of what has been claimed as the essence of art, the true nature of art, or its defining function; in a single lecture dealing with one aspect of art, namely its cultural influence, I can only give you by way of preamble my own definition of art, with categorical brevity. That does not mean that I set up this definition in a categorical spirit, but only that we have no time to debate it, so you are asked to accept it as an assumption underlying these reflections.

Art, in the sense here intended—that is, the generic term subsuming painting, sculpture, architecture, music, dance, literature and drama—may be defined as the practice of creating perceptible forms expressive of human

343

feeling. I say "perceptible" rather than "sensuous" forms because some works of art are given to imagination rather than to the outward senses. A novel, for instance, usually is read silently with the eye, but is not made for vision, as a painting is; and though sound plays a vital part in poetry, words even in poetry are not essentially sonorous structures like music. Dance requires to be seen, but its appeal is to deeper centers of sensation. The difference between dance and mobile sculpture makes this immediately apparent. But all works of art are purely perceptible forms that seem to embody some sort of feeling.

"Feeling" as I am using it here covers much more than it does in the technical vocabulary of psychology, where it denotes only pleasure and pain, or even in the shifting limits of ordinary discourse, where it sometimes means sensation (as when one says a paralyzed limb has no feeling in it), sometimes sensibility (as we speak of hurting someone's feelings), sometimes emotion (e.g., as a situation is said to harrow your feeling, or to evoke tender feeling), or a directed emotional attitude (we say we feel strongly *about* something), or even our general mental or physical condition, feeling well or ill, blue or a bit above ourselves. As I use the word, in defining art as the creation of perceptible forms expressive of human feeling, it takes in all those meanings; it applies to *everything that may be felt.*

Another word in the definition that might be questioned is "creation." I think it is justified, not pretentious, as perhaps it sounds; but that issue is slightly beside the point here, so let us shelve it. If anyone prefers to speak of the "making" or "construction" of expressive forms that will do here just as well.

What does have to be understood is the meaning of "form," and more particularly "expressive form"; for that involves the very nature of art and therefore the question of its cultural importance.

The word "form" has several current uses; most of them have some relation to the sense in which I am using it here, though a few, such as: "a *form* to be filled in for tax purposes," or "a mere matter of form," are fairly remote, being quite specialized. Since we are speaking of art, it might be good to point out that the meaning of *stylistic patter*—"the sonata form," "the sonnet form"—is not the one I am assuming here. I am using the word in a simpler sense, which it has when you say, on a foggy night, that you see dimly moving forms in the mist; one of them emerges clearly, and is the form of a man. The trees are gigantic forms; the rills of rain trace sinuous forms on the window pane. The rills are not fixed things; they are forms of motion. When you watch gnats weaving in the air, or flocks of birds wheeling overhead, you see dynamic forms—forms made by motion.

It is in this sense of an apparition given to our perception, that a work of art is a form. It may be a permanent form like a building or a vase or a picture, or a transient, dynamic form like a melody or a dance, or even a form given to imagination, like the passage of purely imaginary, apparent events that constitutes a literary work. But it is always a perceptible, self-identical whole; like a natural being, it has a character of organic unity, self-sufficiency, individual reality. And it is thus, as an appearance, that a work of art is good or bad or perhaps only rather poor; as an appearance, not as a comment on things beyond it in the world, nor as a reminder of them.

This, then, is what I mean by "form"; but what is meant by calling such forms "expressive of human feeling"? How do apparitions "express" any-thing—feeling, or anything else? First of all, let us ask just what is meant here by "express"; what sort of "expression" we are talking about.

Most people believe that music and poetry are expressions of emotion, and will further agree that a picture is a glimpse of reality seen through a temperament. Even a Gothic cathedral is supposed to express the religious emotions of its countless, anonymous builders. Its age makes the process indistinct enough to put it beyond very searching question. But it is harder to imagine how a modern office building or a fine flung-out overpass across a highway—an architectural work of art, as many of our offices and ramps and bridges are—could be, in any essential way, an expression of its design-er's emotion or state of mind. To treat it just like a lyric or an easel picture seems a bit silly.

The incongruity, however, points to a misunderstanding that becomes apparent only when we try to conceive the skyscraper as an emotional exhibition, but that really confuses our judgment of the lyric and the picture as well. It is a misconception of what is meant by "expression" in art.

The word "expression" has two principal meanings: in one sense it means *self*-expression—giving vent to our feelings. In this sense it refers to a *symp-tom* of what we feel. Self-expression is a spontaneous reaction to a situation, an event, the company we are in, things people say, or what the weather does to us; it bespeaks the physical and mental state we are in and the emotions that stir us. In another sense, however, "expression" means the presentation of an idea, usually by the proper and apt use of words. But a device for the presentation of an idea is what we call a *symbol*, not a symptom. Thus a *word* is a symbol, and so is a meaningful combination of words. A common word, such as "horse," conveys an idea even when no one is exclaiming over the presence of a horse, or offering his kingdom for one—for instance, in the phrase "White Horse Whiskey," or in the diction-ary, somewhere between "horror" and "horticulture."

A sentence, which is a special combination of words, expresses the idea of some state of affairs, real or imagined. Sentences are complicated symbols—so complicated, sometimes, that we have to consider them word by word and analyze the way they are put together to understand the meanings they convey. And sometimes the meaning is an idea we never had before, or concerns something we have never seen—a new animal, a foreign place, or what not. Language will formulate new ideas as well as communicate old ones, so that all people know a lot of things that they have merely heard or read about. Symbolic expression, therefore, extends our knowledge beyond the scope of our actual experience.

If an idea is clearly conveyed by means of symbols we say it is *well expressed*. A person may work for a long time to give his statement the best possible form, to find the exact words for what he means to say and to carry his account or his argument most directly from one point to another. But a discourse so worked out is certainly not a spontaneous reaction. Giving expression to an idea is obviously a different thing from giving expression to feelings by laughing, crying, blushing, or quivering. You do not say of a man in a rage that his anger is well expressed; you either try to calm him down, or you rage back at him, but in either case you understand quite well that he is furious. The symptoms just are what they are, there is no critical standard for symptoms. If, on the other hand, the angry man tries to tell you what he is fuming about, he will have to collect himself, curtail his emotional expression, and find words to express his ideas. For to tell a story coherently involves "expression" in quite a different sense: this sort of expression is not "self-expression," but may be called "conceptual expression."

Language, of course, is our prime instrument of conceptual expression. The things we can say are in effect the things we can think. Words are the terms of our thinking as well as the terms in which we present our thoughts, because they present the objects of thought to the thinker himself. Before language communicates ideas, it gives them form, makes them clear, and in fact makes them what they are. Whatever has a name is an object for thought. Without words, sense experience is only a flow of impressions, as subjective as our feelings; words make it objective, and carve it up into *things* and *facts* that we can note, remember, and think about. Language gives outward experience its form, and makes it definite and clear.

There is, however, an important part of reality that is quite inaccessible to the formative influence of language: that is the realm of so-called "inner experience," the life of feeling and emotion. The reason why language is so powerless here is not, as many people suppose, that feeling and emotion are irrational; on the contrary, they seem irrational because language does not help to make them conceivable, and most people cannot conceive anything without the logical scaffolding of words. The unfitness of language to convey subjective experience is a somewhat technical subject, easier for logicians to understand than for artists; but the gist of it is that the form of language does not reflect the natural form of feeling, so we cannot shape any concepts of feeling with the help of ordinary, discursive language. Therefore the words whereby we refer to feeling only name very general kinds of inner experience—excitement, calm, joy, sorrow, love, hate, etc. But there is no language to describe just how one joy differs so radically from another, or what the experience of hate is really like, how it can interplay with feelings usually called love, how it burns and then goes cold in almost the same moment. The real nature of feeling is something language as such—as discursive symbolism—cannot render.

For this reason, the phenomena of feeling and emotion are usually treated by philosophers as irrational. The only pattern discursive thought can find in them is the pattern of outward events that occasion them. There are different degrees of fear, but they are thought of as so many degrees of the same simple feeling.

But human feeling is a fabric, not a vague mass. It has an intricate dynamic pattern, possible combinations and new emergent phenomena. It is a pattern of organically interdependent and interdetermined tensions and resolutions; a pattern of almost infinitely complex activation and cadence. To it belongs the whole gamut of our sensibility, the sense of straining thought, all mental attitude and motor set. Those are the deeper reaches that underlie the surface waves of our emotion, and make human life a *life of feeling* instead of an unconscious metabolic existence interrupted by feelings.

It is, I think, this dynamic pattern that finds its formal expression in the arts. The expressiveness of art is like that of a symbol, not that of an emotional symptom; it is as a formulation of feeling for our conception that a work of art is properly said to be expressive. It may serve somebody's need of self-expression besides; but that is not what makes it good or bad art. In a special sense one may call a work of art a symbol of feeling, for, like a symbol it formulates our ideas of inward experience, as discourse formulates our ideas of things and facts in the outside world. A work of art differs from a genuine symbol—that is, a symbol in the full and usual sense—in that it does not point beyond itself to something else. The word "symbol" does not originally connote any representative function, or reference to something beyond itself; it means "thrown together"—συμβαλλειν. But in English usage it has come to mean a sign that stands for something else to which it directs our attention. This is something a work of art does not do. Its relation to feeling is a rather special one that we cannot undertake to analyze here; in effect, the feeling it expresses appears to be directly given with it, as the sense of a true metaphor, or the value of a religious myth, is not separable from its expression. We speak of the feeling *of*, or the feeling *in*, a work of art, not the feeling it means. And we speak truly; a work of art presents something like a direct vision of vitality, emotion, subjective reality.

The primary function of art is to objectify feeling so we can contemplate and understand it. It is the formulation of so-called "inward experience," the "inner life," that is impossible to achieve by discursive thought, because its forms are incommensurable with the forms of language and all its derivatives (e.g. mathematics, symbolic logic). Art objectifies the sentience and desire, self-consciousness and world-consciousness, emotions and moods that are generally regarded as irrational because words cannot give us clear ideas of them. But the premise tacitly assumed in such a judgment—namely, that anything language cannot express is formless and irrational—seems to me to be an error. I believe the life of feeling is not irrational; its logical forms are merely very different from the structures of discourse. But they are so much like the dynamic forms of art that art is their natural symbol. Through plastic works, music, fiction, dance, or dramatic forms we can conceive what vitality and emotion feel like.

All this time I have been expounding, word by word, what I mean by the definition of art proposed at the beginning of this lecture: Art is the practice of creating perceptible forms expressive of human feeling. We have dwelt on the exact sense of "form," and "expressive," and "feeling." Form in this context means a configuration, something seen or heard or imaginatively grasped as an entity, an integral whole given to perception like an apparition. Every work of art is a form in this sense. It may be a solid form, or a dynamic form like a whirl or a stream, or it may be a sounding form like a melody. Or even the image of events known as a story, that, like dreams or memory, presents its form to imagination alone. "Expression" is here taken to mean articulation, not *self*-expression or venting of one's feeling. And "feeling," finally, is used in the broadest sense, denoting anything that can or could be felt—sensation, emotion, every tension in a sentient organism, from the feeling of vitality itself to the highest development of personal or even transcendent consciousness. The reason why works of art can express the nature of feeling, which language cannot present, is that artistic forms and the forms of feeling, or subjective reality, are logically similar, so that our directly felt life is reflected, symbolically articulated, and objectively presented to our understanding in works of art.

This brings us, at last, to the question of the cultural importance of the arts. Why is it so apt to be the vanguard of cultural advance, as it was in Egypt, in Greece, in Christian Europe (think of Gregorian music and Gothic architecture), in Renaissance Italy—not to speculate about ancient cavemen, whose art is all that we know of them? One thinks of culture as economic increase, social organization, the gradual ascendancy of rational thinking and scientific control of nature over superstitious imagination and magical practices. But art is not practical; it is neither philosophy nor science; it is not religion, morality, nor even social comment (as many drama critics take comedy to be). What does it contribute to culture that could be of major importance?

It merely presents forms—sometimes intangible forms—to imagination. Its direct appeal is to that faculty, or function, that Lord Bacon considered the chief stumbling block in the way of reason, that enlightened writers like

Stuart Chase never tire of condemning as the source of all nonsense and bizarre erroneous beliefs. And so it is; but it is also the source of all insight and true beliefs. Imagination is probably the oldest mental trait that is typically human—older than discursive reason; it is probably the common source of dream, reason, religion, and all true general observation. It is this primitive human power—imagination—that engenders the arts and is in turn directly affected by their products.

Somewhere at the animalian starting line of human evolution lie the beginnings of that supreme instrument of the mind, language. We think of it as a device for communication among the members of a society. But communication is only one, and perhaps not even the first, of its functions. The first thing it does is to break up what William James called the "blooming, buzzing confusion" of sense perception into units and groups, events and chains of events—things and relations, causes and effects. All these patterns are imposed on our experience by language. We think, as we speak, in terms of objects and their relations.

But the process of breaking up our sense experience in this way, making reality conceivable, memorable, sometimes even predictable, is a process of imagination. Primitive conception is imagination. Language and imagination grow up together in a reciprocal tutelage.

What discursive symbolism—language in its literal use—does for our awareness of things about us and our own relation to them, the arts do for our awareness of subjective reality, feeling and emotion; they give inward experiences form and thus make them conceivable. The only way we can really envisage vital movement, the stirring and growth and passage of emotion, and ultimately the whole direct sense of human life, is in artistic terms. A musical person thinks of emotions musically. They cannot be discursively talked about above a very general level. But they may none the less be known—objectively set forth, publicly known—and there is nothing necessarily confused or formless about emotions.

As soon as the natural forms of subjective experience are abstracted to the point of symbolic presentation, we can use those forms to *imagine* feeling and understand its nature. Self-knowledge, insight into all phases of life and mind, springs from artistic imagination. That is the cognitive value of the arts.

But their influence on human life goes deeper than the intellectual level. As language actually gives form to our sense-experience, grouping our impressions around those things which have names, and fitting sensations to the qualities that have adjectival names, and so on, the arts we live with— our picture books and stories and the music we hear—actually form our emotive experience. Every generation has its styles of feeling. One age shudders and blushes and faints, another swaggers, still another is godlike in a universal indifference. These styles in actual emotion are not insincere. They are largely unconscious—determined by many social causes, but *shaped* by artists, usually popular artists of the screen, the juke-box, the shop window and the picture magazine. (That, rather than incitement to crime, is my objection to the comics.) Irwin Edman remarks in one of his books that our emotions are largely Shakespeare's poetry.

This influence of art on life gives us an indication why a period of efflorescence in the arts is apt to lead a cultural advance: it formulates a new way of feeling, and that is the beginning of a cultural age. It suggests another matter for reflection, too: that a wide neglect of artistic education is a neglect in the education of feeling. Most people are so imbued with the idea that feeling is a formless total organic excitement in humans as in animals, that the idea of educating feeling, developing its scope and quality, seems odd to them, if not absurd. It is really, I think, at the very heart of personal education.

There is one other function of the arts that benefits not so much the advance of culture as its stabilization; an influence on individual lives. This function is the converse and complement of the objectification of feeling, the driving force of creation in art: it is the education of vision that we receive in seeing, hearing, reading works of art—the development of the artist's eye, that assimilates ordinary sights (or sounds, motions, or events) to inward vision, and lends expressiveness and emotional import to the world. Wherever art takes a motif from actuality—a flowering branch, a bit of landscape, a historic event or a personal memory, any model or theme from life—it transforms it into a piece of imagination, and imbues its image with artistic vitality. The result is an impregnation of ordinary reality with the significance of created form. This is the *subjectification of nature*, that makes reality itself a symbol of life and feeling.

I cannot say much about this last point because I am just working with the idea myself. One of my students gave it to me, in a criticism of my own theory. But it seems to me to be of great significance.

Let us sum up briefly, then, why the arts, which many people regard as a cultural frill, are actually never a late addition to civilized life, an ornament gracing society like tea ceremonies or etiquette, but are born during the rise and the primitive phases of cultures, and often outrun all other developments in achieving mature character and technical competence. Cultures begin with the development of personal and social and religious feeling. The great instrument of this development is art. For, (1) art makes feeling apparent, objectively given so we may reflect on it and understand it; (2) the practice and familiar knowledge of any art provides forms for actual feeling to take, as language provides forms for sensory experience and factual observation; and (3) art is the education of the senses to see nature in expressive form. Thereby the actual world becomes in some measure symbolic of feeling (without being "anthropomorphized," supposed to *have* feelings) and personally significant.

The arts objectify subjective reality, and subjectify outward experience of nature. Art education is the education of feeling, and a society that neglects it gives itself up to formless emotion. Bad art is corruption of feeling. This is a large factor in the irrationalism which dictators and demagogues exploit.

THE QUEST FOR CIVILIZATION

Kenneth Clark

We have no idea where we are going, and sweeping, confident articles on the future seem to me, intellectually, the most disreputable of all forms of public utterance. The scientists who are best qualified to talk have kept their mouths shut. J. B. S. Haldane summed up the situation when he said: "My own suspicion is that the universe is not only queerer than we suppose, but queerer than we can suppose. I saw a new heaven and a new earth, for the old heaven and the old earth had passed away." Which reminds us that the universe so vividly described in the Book of Revelation is queer enough; but with the help of symbols not beyond description. Whereas our universe cannot even be stated symbolically.

The incomprehensibility of our new cosmos seems to me, ultimately, to be the reason for the chaos of modern art. I know next to nothing about science but I've spent my life in trying to learn about art, and I am completely baffled by what is taking place today. I sometimes like what I see, but when I read modern critics I realise that my preferences are merely accidental.

However, in the world of action a few things are obvious—so obvious that I hesitate to repeat them. One of them is our increasing reliance on machines. They have ceased to be tools and have begun to give us directions. And unfortunately machines, from the Maxim gun to the computer, are for the most part means by which a minority can keep free men in subjection.

Our other specialty is our urge to destruction. With the help of machines we did our best to destroy ourselves in two wars, and in doing so we released a flood of evil, which intelligent people have tried to justify with praise of violence, "theaters of cruelty" and so forth. Add to this the memory of that shadowy companion who is always with us, like an inverted guardian angel, silent, invisible, almost incredible and yet unquestionably there and ready to assert itself at the touch of a button; and one must concede that the future of civilisation does not look very bright.

And yet when I look at the world about me, I don't at all feel that we are entering a new period of barbarism. The things that made the Dark Ages so dark—the isolation, the lack of mobility, the lack of curiosity, the hopelessness—don't obtain at all. When I have the good fortune to visit one of our new universities, it seems to me that the inheritors of all our catastrophes look cheerful enough—very different from the melancholy late Romans or pathetic Gauls whose likenesses have come down to us. In fact, I should doubt if so many people have ever been as well-fed, as well-read, as bright-minded, as curious and as critical as the young are today.

Of course there has been a little flattening at the top. But one mustn't overrate the culture of what used to be called "top people" before the wars. They had charming manners, but they were as ignorant as swans. They did know something about literature, and a few had been to the opera. But they knew nothing about painting and less than nothing about philosophy (except for Balfour and Haldane). The members of a music group or an art group at a provincial university would be five times better informed and more alert. Naturally, these bright-minded young people think poorly of existing institutions and want to abolish them. Well, one doesn't need to be young to dislike institutions. But the dreary fact remains that, even in the darkest ages, it was institutions that made society work, and if civilisation is to survive society must somehow be made to work.

At this point I reveal myself in my true colors, as a stick-in-the-mud. I hold a number of beliefs that have been repudiated by the liveliest intellects of our time. I believe that order is better than chaos, creation better than destruction. I prefer gentleness to violence, forgiveness to vendetta. On the whole I think that knowledge is preferable to ignorance, and I am sure that human sympathy is more valuable than ideology. I believe that in spite of the recent triumphs of science, men haven't changed much in the last two thousand years, and in consequence we must still try to learn from history. History is ourselves.

I also hold one or two beliefs that are more difficult to put shortly. For example, I believe in courtesy, the ritual by which we avoid hurting other people's feelings by satisfying our own egos. And I think we should remember that we are part of a great whole, which for convenience we call nature. All living things are our brothers and sisters. Above all, I believe in the God-given genius of certain individuals, and I value a society that makes their existence possible.

Our civilisation has been filled with great works of genius, in architecture, sculpture and painting, in philosophy, poetry and music, in science and engineering. There they are; you can't dismiss them. And they are only a fraction of what Western man has achieved in the last thousand years, often after setbacks and deviations at least as destructive as those of our own time. Western civilisation has been a series of rebirths. Surely this should give us confidence in ourselves.

It is lack of confidence, more than anything else, that kills a civilisation. We can destroy ourselves by cynicism and disillusion, just as effectively as by bombs. Fifty years ago W. B. Yeats, who was more like a man of genius than anyone I have ever known, wrote a famous prophetic poem.

> Things fall apart; the centre cannot hold;
> Mere anarchy is loosed upon the world,
> The blood-dimmed tide is loosed, and everywhere
> The ceremony of innocence is drowned;
> The best lack all conviction, while the worst
> Are full of passionate intensity.

Well, that was certainly true between the wars, and it damn nearly destroyed us. Is it true today? Not quite, because good people have convictions, rather too many of them. The trouble is that there is still no center. The moral and intellectual failure of Marxism has left us with no alternative to heroic materialism, and that isn't enough. One may be optimistic, but one can't exactly be joyful at the prospect before us.

VI

SCIENCE

THE DJINN FROM THE BOTTLE

I would say that if "dead" matter has reared up this curious landscape of fiddling crickets, song sparrows, and wondering men, it must be plain even to the most devoted materialist that the matter of which he speaks contains amazing, if not dreadful powers . . .
LOREN EISELEY, *The Immense Journey*

The typical bookman's collection of essays about science would include many of the landmarks of the growth of our knowledge of the physical universe from Aristotle through Galileo and Harvey to Darwin and Einstein. The effect of any such collection is to give the impression that the scientific method is the rock upon which the inevitable progress of mankind is based. We have included several such essays because they represent the most remarkable and obvious achievements of the human mind.

But the new decade is alive with resistance to the conception of science as our saviour. In the basements of schools and the backpages of popular journals rumble the animal noises of the anti-science underground, people who suspect that the scientist and his creation are basically anti-human. Who needs the atom bomb? they ask, or DDT, or phosphate detergents, or any number of taken-for-granted modern improvements to the environment? All this technological achievement seems to them to be leading to a great effort to find a way to escape from a planet that science itself has destroyed.

Students and teachers alike are increasingly uncertain of the value of the scientific society. Some are convinced disciples of Buckminster Fuller, who believes that science and not politics can solve all the world's problems. Others believe in organic farming, health foods, yoga, astrology, fresh air, and regular sex, and trust to personal relationships, not politics, to solve the world's problems.

Most of us, surprised by the vehemence of the argument, wonder how such a dispute could come about in this well-informed and rational age. Perhaps the resolution of the conflict cannot be found in this section, but must be looked for in the last section, on Values, which are the heart of the matter.

The New Mythology of Creation

THE CREATION OF LIFE

Fred Warshofsky

If one were to attempt an approximate guess, he might estimate that life began about a billion years after the earth itself had formed. That event is subject to a great deal of conjecture, though most scientists agree that about five or six billion years ago great masses of interstellar gases and dust began to coalesce into the planets that now surround the sun. It took yet another billion or so years for the earth's mantle to coalesce. At this point, about four and a half billion years ago, the crust of the earth became stable, and it is from that event that scientists compute the age of the earth.

From then on the great physical and chemical forces interacting upon the newly formed planet all conspired to bring life into being. The great chunk of rock spinning about the sun began to generate an atmosphere of fiery gases squeezed from the solid mantle of the earth by great currents of heat produced by the radioactive decay of some elements and by volcanic eruptions that vented the earth's surface.

One of the most important theories to deal with the origin of life on earth was formulated by a Russian biologist, Alexander Oparin. In a paper published in 1924, Oparin set forth the conditions that might have existed on the primitive earth—conditions that could give rise to life. "The atmosphere at that period," he wrote, "differed materially from our present atmosphere in that it contained neither oxygen nor nitrogen gas, but was filled instead with superheated aqueous vapor. . . . The superheated aqueous vapor of the atmosphere coming in contact with the carbides reacted chemically, giving rise to the simplest organic matter, the hydrocarbons, which in turn gave rise to a great variety of derivatives."

Just what were the gases that composed Oparin's superheated aqueous vapor? What was available in that primitive atmosphere for the creation of organic molecules—the next vital step on the road to life?

One of the first scientists to attempt an experimental answer to that question was Dr. Harold Urey, a Nobel Prize-winning chemist now at the University of California. Urey took Oparin's idea of the chemical evolution of life and proposed it be tried out in the test tube. In 1953, while at the University of Chicago, Urey had a bright young chemist named Stanley Miller under his tutelage. To him, Urey suggested an experiment based upon an atmosphere he considered likely to have existed when the earth was young—methane, ammonia, water vapor, and hydrogen.

Miller constructed a sealed system of flasks and tubes into which he injected a mixture of methane, ammonia, and hydrogen. The gases were mixed with water vapor, piped in from a flask of boiling water. The entire brew was then stabbed by sixty thousand volts of high-frequency electrical sparks, a sort of man-made lightning.

After a week of this laboratory gestation, the collection flask at the end of the system was filled with water that had turned deep red. When analyzed it was found to contain several organic substances, among them amino acids.

This was proof of the theoretical first step to life the scientists thought nature had taken. For amino acids are organic molecules, the building blocks that are used in the construction of proteins. Chemists know of eighty amino acids, but only twenty are found in natural protein molecules, without question the most important structural components of all living things.

The Urey-Miller experiment produced four amino acids. Other experimenters varied the gas mixture slightly and produced other amino acids, and soon various workers were able to account for fewer than half of the amino acids common to protein. But it required a number of different attempts to get the diversity of molecules that had to be present for life to begin. And no one had successfully produced all, or even most, of the twenty amino acids in one single experimental genesis.

A great deal of controversy surrounded these atmospheric experiments, with each group certain that the gases it proposed were in fact the actual ones present at the time. All, however, included free hydrogen, the first and basic element of the universe in the primal mix. Then in 1964, at Florida State University, Dr. Sidney Fox and Dr. Kaoru Harada considered the idea of an original atmosphere that had little or no free hydrogen in it, to account for the amino acids that were very poor in hydrogen—some of the amino acids that had not been produced in all the other atmosphere experiments.

Harada put together an atmosphere of methane, ammonia, and water, with no free hydrogen to react with the intermediate products being formed from the gases on their way to becoming amino acids. He also used a different kind of energy input from those of earlier experiments. Miller had used electrical discharges, others had bombarded the gas with alpha particles and ultraviolet radiation. Harada used heat. Volcanic activity and other conditions indicated that the earth was much hotter than it is now, with thousands of hot zones well above the boiling point of water.

The result of the experiment was amino acids in profusion; twelve amino acids were formed and each was an amino acid common to protein production.

Although the controversy over the primitive atmosphere continues, all the debaters are agreed that one element was certainly *not* present then— oxygen. This lack was as important to the evolution of life as any phenomenon that did take place, for if oxygen had been present the fledgling molecules would have simply ended up as the waste products of combustion and not as the precursors of protein.

The lack of oxygen also meant that ozone, a heavy form of the oxygen, was also lacking, and the screen it now provides against most of the fierce ultraviolet rays of the sun was not present. The primordial atmosphere was bombarded every moment of daylight by ultraviolet radiation, a condition that would be lethal to living organisms, but which served as an energy source for the creation of life.

"Most of this chemistry," explains Dr. George Wald of the Biological Laboratories at Harvard University, "probably took place in the upper reaches of the atmosphere, activated mainly by ultraviolet radiation from the sun and by electric discharges. Leached out of the atmosphere over long ages into the waters of the earth, organic molecules accumulated in the seas, and there interacted with one another, so that the seas gradually acquired an increasing concentration and variety of such molecules."

About this stage of the life creation, scientists again disagree. Some hold that the simple, stately procession of time provided the opportunity for small molecules to link up to form the far more complex amino acids that are in turn the building stones of protein. Others argue that even nature must bow to some chronological pressures to speed things up.

"We have no concept as to what can happen in a million years," says Dr. Harold Urey. "We have no concept as to how large an ocean is and what an enormous amount of experimentation can take place in a large body of water over long periods of time.

"It seems to me that it may be that life originated even during the time before one could definitely say that the accumulation of the earth was complete . . . say, one hundred million years or possibly even less."

Whatever the time span, at one point or other the amino acids that leached out of the atmosphere to form what the great British biologist J. B. S. Haldane called in 1928 a "hot dilute soup" organized themselves into proteins. The process is enormously complex, for a single protein molecule is built of hundreds of amino acids alternating the basic twenty in complex and almost limitless combinations, just as the letters of the alphabet can be combined and recombined to form millions of words.

Just how these complex protein molecules were put together from the original short amino-acid chains is open to speculation. But it was an essential step in the creation of life. For only with long-chain proteins could enzymes, the catalysts that speed up chemical reactions to the point where life processes can be carried out, be constructed.

Then the self-organizing precursors of life constructed boundaries that sharply demarcated themselves from their surroundings. This has been described by Dr. J. D. Bernal of the University of London, an expert on the origin of life, as "the passage from a mere living area of metabolizing material without specific limitations into a closed organism which separates one part of the continuum from another, the living from the nonliving."

An experimental attempt to explain how such an event might have taken place was made by Dr. Sidney Fox, who now heads the Institute of Molecular Evolution at the University of Miami. Fox thinks that genetic instructions might not be necessary for protein construction. He proposes that nature could have used a chemical reaction known as thermal polymerization as the process that may have linked amino acids to form proteins. Industrial chemists have used polymerization for many years to assemble related molecules into long chains called polymers. The best example of the technology was the creation of a wholly new material, something that did not exist in nature—plastics. In a similar manner, the living organism links up amino acids, first into a small polymer called a peptide, which consists of several amino acids hooked together. The more amino acids available, the more readily polymerization occurs. The peptides are then joined to form extremely long-chain molecules that are proteins. . . .

In putting the theory to experimental test, specifically by heating amino acids, Fox violated a number of traditional chemical shibboleths. One was that if amino acids are heated above the boiling point of water, the result is only a dark unworkable mess. But he took a clue from evolutionary studies and included in his primal brew a high proportion of aspartic acid and glutamic acid, two amino acids that constitute one fourth to one half of all proteins found in nature. The solution was then heated to 150 degrees centigrade; the result was a "lightly colored material."

Chemical analysis showed the material to resemble protein molecules. An even more dramatic result occurred when these proteinoids were bathed in hot water. They took on a startling form, a spherical shape that could be clearly seen under the microscope. Moreover, there were hundreds of them in the field, bumping into each other in random motion produced by the phenomenon called Brownian movement.

Fox called these objects "microspheres." They demonstrate a long list of properties that are remarkably similar to those displayed by what he calls "contemporary cells."

"No other experiment," he wrote, "has produced anything that even begins to approach the microspheres in their similarity to cells and the properties the cells have." . . .

Does this mean that the microspheres are alive? A better question might be, did they come into being before anything we dare describe as life originated? If so, and much of the evidence indicates they did, these microspheres represent an evolutionary link with the distant past, to a time before cellular forms such as we now know existed.

If the microspheres are the precursors of contemporary cells, there would still be a key step in completing the evolution from nonlife to life. A microsphere does not make its own protein within the confines of its walls. This is essentially a process governed by the nucleic acids, the DNA and RNA of the modern cell. The instructions for the assembly of protein from the amino acids taken in by the cell are carried within the DNA molecule and passed on to a portion of the cell by a messenger called RNA.

In experiments on the formation of other biologically active molecules from nonbiological materials, the vital subunits of DNA have been produced by researchers in other laboratories.

"We now seek to learn how natural experiments could have taught these organized structures to make their own protein internally with coded control by nucleic acids," explains Dr. Fox. "We believe that once this is accomplished, we will have traced the evolution of a primitive reproducing organism to a highly contemporary type of reproducing organism."

Some of the steps by which nature evolved life now seem clear and have been reproduced, in part, in the laboratory. The necessary ingredients sparked by the proper catalysts and fired by the energy of vast outpourings of ultraviolet radiation and electrical storms are organized and primed for making the enormous transition from non-life to life. . . .

One of the most elemental and important processes is photosynthesis, the process in which green plants release oxygen while reducing carbon dioxide into carbohydrates. The development of photosynthesis by living organisms would complete the transition from chemical to biological evolution and at the same time set the stage for still greater biological events to follow. For at that point a change in the gaseous make-up of the primitive atmosphere would be effected.

What were the steps that produced such a profound change? "If, as we suppose," explains Professor Wald, "life first appeared in an organic medium in the absence of oxygen, it must first have been supported by fermentations—Pasteur's 'life without air'. In so far we beg the question. But fermentation remains in a sense the basic way of life. Fermentative processes underlie all other forms of metabolism; and virtually all types of cell can survive for periods of fermentation if deprived of oxygen.

In the process of fermentation, energy is liberated and then stored by a phosphate compound within the cell called adenosine triphosphate, or ATP. At the same time, carbon dioxide is created as a waste product and released into the atmosphere, which presumably contained very little of this gas early in the earth's history. As the ages passed, the metabolic pathways of the primitive organisms became more and more sophisticated until a new process called photophosphorylation evolved, providing a means of using the sun's rays to produce ATP.

Photophosphorylation was an intermediate step, for as it evolved, the cells using it began to develop the specialized pigment called chlorophyll, which absorbs light energy, thus making the process more efficient. This set the stage for the development of photosynthesis, in which the carbon dioxide that had been merely a waste product of fermentation and other anaerobic, or oxygen-free, types of metabolism, became very important. For in the photosynthesis process, carbon dioxide is reduced to carbohydrate and oxygen is released as a by-product.

When enough oxygen had been liberated into the atmosphere by living organisms, still another great evolutionary event took place; cells learned to breathe. Respiration and photosynthesis then achieved some sort of balance, so that each could support the other. In the process, the atmosphere of the earth changed radically, with oxygen becoming a major component, twenty-one per cent, in fact, and life itself became an integral part of and contributor to the maintenance of the environment.

Soon every step in the evolution of life will have been traced, its processes described and duplicated in the laboratory. Then its creation by man becomes possible. But how shall he use this creative power? Will the 21st century see new life forms brought into being, or will man attempt to improve upon himself? Many scientists today disassociate themselves from such an idea. Many think not in terms of creating life, but simply of explaining its evolution. But full explanations will come from knowledge, and knowledge in this case will provide the power to create life.

Will man ever exercise that power? The likelihood is that he will, for never before in history has man failed to seize that which he could reach.

THE EVOLUTION OF THE PHYSICAL WORLD

Arthur Stanley Eddington

Looking back through the long past we picture the beginning of the world —a primeval chaos which time has fashioned into the universe that we know. Its vastness appalls the mind; space boundless though not infinite, according to the strange doctrine of science. The world was without form and almost void. But at the earliest stage we can contemplate the void is sparsely broken by tiny electric particles, the germs of the things that are to be; positive and negative they wander aimlessly in solitude, rarely coming near enough to seek or shun one another. They range everywhere so that all space is filled, and yet so empty that in comparison the most highly exhausted vacuum on earth is a jostling throng. In the beginning was vastness, solitude and the deepest night. Darkness was upon the face of the deep, for as yet there was no light.

The years rolled by, million after million. Slight aggregations occurring casually in one place and another drew to themselves more and more particles. They warred for sovereignty, won and lost their spoil, until the matter was collected round centers of condensation leaving vast empty spaces from which it had ebbed away. Thus gravitation slowly parted the primeval chaos. These first divisions were not the stars but what we should call "island universes" each ultimately to be a system of some thousands of millions of stars. From our own island universe we can discern the other islands as spiral nebulae lying one beyond another as far as the telescope can fathom. The nearest of them is such that light takes 900,000 years to cross the gulf between us. They acquired rotation (we do not yet understand how) which bulged them into flattened form and made them wreathe themselves in spirals. Their forms, diverse, yet with underlying regularity, make a fascinating spectacle for telescopic study.

As it had divided the original chaos, so gravitation subdivided the island universes. First the star clusters, then the stars themselves were separated. And with the stars came light, born of the fiercer turmoil which ensued when the electrical particles were drawn from their solitude into dense throngs. A star is not just a lump of matter casually thrown together in the general confusion; it is of nicely graded size. There is relatively not much more diversity in the masses of new-born stars than in the masses of new-born babies. Aggregations rather greater than our Sun have a strong tendency to subdivide, but when the mass is reduced a little the danger quickly passes and the impulse to subdivision is satisfied. Here it would seem the work of creation might cease. Having carved chaos into stars, the first evolutionary impulse has reached its goal. For many billions of years the stars may continue to shed their light and heat through the world, feeding on their own matter which disappears bit by bit into aetherial waves.

Not infrequently a star, spinning too fast or strained by the radiant heat imprisoned within it, may divide into two nearly equal stars, which remain yoked together as a double star; apart from this no regular plan of further development is known. For what might be called the second day of creation we turn from the general rule to the exceptions. Amid so many myriads there will be a few which by some rare accident have a fate unlike the rest. In the vast expanse of the heavens the traffic is so thin that a star may reasonably count on travelling for the whole of its long life without serious risk of collision. The risk is negligible for any individual star, but ten thousand million stars in our own system and more in the systems beyond afford a wide playground for chance. If the risk is one in a hundred millions some unlucky victims are doomed to play the role of "one." This rare accident must have happened to our Sun—an accident to the Sun, but to us the cause of our being here. A star journeying through space casually overtook the Sun, not indeed colliding with it, but approaching so close as to raise a great tidal wave. By this disturbance jets of matter spurted out of the Sun; being carried round by their angular momentum they did not fall back again but condensed into small globes—the planets.

By this and similar events there appeared here and there in the universe something outside Nature's regular plan, namely a lump of matter small enough and dense enough to be cool. A temperature of ten million degrees or more prevails through the greater part of the interior of a star; it cannot be otherwise so long as matter remains heaped in immense masses. Thus the design of the first stage of evolution seems to have been that matter should ordinarily be endowed with intense heat. Cool matter appears as an afterthought. It is unlikely that the Sun is the only one of the starry host to possess a system of planets, but it is believed that such development is very rare. In these exceptional formations Nature has tried the experiment of finding what strange effects may ensue if matter is released from its usual temperature of millions of degrees and permitted to be cool.

Out of the electric charges dispersed in the primitive chaos ninety-two different kinds of matter—ninety-two chemical elements—have been built. This building is also a work of evolution, but little or nothing is known as to its history. In the matter which we handle daily we find the original bricks fitted together and cannot but infer that somewhere and somewhen a process of matter-building has occurred. At high temperature this diversity of matter remains as it were latent; little of consequence results from it. But in the cool experimental stations of the universe the differences assert themselves. At root the diversity of the ninety-two elements reflects the diversity of the integers from one to ninety-two; because the chemical characteristics of element No. 11 (sodium) arise from the fact that it has the power at low temperatures of gathering round it eleven negative electric particles; those of No. 12 (magnesium) from its power of gathering twelve particles; and so on.

It is tempting to linger over the development out of this fundamental beginning of the wonders studied in chemistry and physics, but we must hurry on. The provision of certain cool planetary globes was the second impulse of evolution, and it has exhausted itself in the formation of inorganic rocks and ores and other materials. We must look to a new exception or abnormality if anything further is to be achieved. We can scarcely call it an accident that among the integers there should happen to be the number 6; but I do not know how otherwise to express the fact that organic life would not have begun if Nature's arithmetic had overlooked the number 6. The general plan of ninety-two elements, each embodying in its structural pattern one of the first ninety-two numbers, contemplates a material world of considerable but limited diversity; but the element carbon, embodying the number 6, and because of the peculiarity of the number 6, rebels against limits. The carbon atoms love to string themselves in long chains such as those which give toughness to a soap-film. Whilst other atoms organise themselves in twos and threes or it may be in tens, carbon atoms organise themselves in hundreds and thousands. From this potentiality of carbon to form more and more elaborate structures, a third impulse of evolution arises.

I cannot profess to say whether anything more than this prolific structure-building power of carbon is involved in the beginning of life. The story of evolution here passes into the domain of the biological sciences for which I cannot speak, and I am not ready to take sides in the controversy between the Mechanists and the Vitalists. So far as the earth is concerned the history of development of living forms extending over nearly a thousand million years is recorded (though with many breaks) in fossil remains. Looking back over the geological record it would seem that Nature made nearly every possible mistake before she reached her greatest achievement Man—or perhaps some would say her worst mistake of all. At one time she put her trust in armaments and gigantic size. Frozen in the rock is the evidence of her failures to provide a form fitted to endure and dominate—failures which we are only too ready to imitate. At last she tried a being of no great size, almost defenceless, defective in at least one of the more important sense-organs; one gift she bestowed to save him from threatened extinction—a certain stirring, a restlessness, in the organ called the brain.

And so we come to Man.

CARBON MONOXIDE POISONING

Claude Bernard

About 1846, I wished to make experiments on the cause of poisoning with carbon monoxide. I knew that this gas had been described as toxic, but I knew literally nothing about the mechanism of its poisoning; I therefore could not have a preconceived opinion. What, then, was to be done? I must bring to birth an idea by making a fact appear, i.e., make another experiment to see. In fact I poisoned a dog by making him breathe carbon monoxide and after death I at once opened his body. I looked at the state of the organs and fluids. What caught my attention at once was that its blood was scarlet in all the vessels, in the veins as well as the arteries, in the right heart as well as in the left. I repeated the experiment on rabbits, birds and frogs, and everywhere I found the same scarlet coloring of the blood. But I was diverted from continuing this investigation, and I kept this observation a long time unused except for quoting it in my course *a propos* of the coloring of blood.

In 1856, no one had carried the experimental question further, and in my course at the Collège de France on toxic and medicinal substances, I again took up the study of poisoning by carbon monoxide which I had begun in 1846. I found myself then in a confused situation, for at this time I already knew that poisoning with carbon monoxide makes the blood scarlet in the whole circulatory system. I had to make hypotheses, and establish a preconceived idea about my first observation, so as to go ahead. Now, reflecting on the fact of scarlet blood, I tried to interpret it by my earlier knowledge as to the cause of the color of blood. Whereupon all the following reflections presented themselves to my mind. The scarlet color, said I, is peculiar to arterial blood and connected with the presence of a large proportion of oxygen, while dark coloring belongs with absence of oxygen and presence of a larger proportion of carbonic acid; so the idea occurred to me that carbon monoxide, by keeping venous blood scarlet might perhaps have prevented the oxygen from changing into carbonic acid in the capillaries. Yet it seemed hard to understand how that could be the cause of death. But still keeping on with my inner preconceived reasoning, I added: If that is true, blood taken from the veins of animals poisoned with carbon monoxide should be like arterial blood in containing oxygen; we must see if that is the fact.

Following this reasoning, based on interpretation of my observation, I tried an experiment to verify my hypothesis as to the persistence of oxygen in the venous blood. I passed a current of hydrogen through scarlet venous blood taken from an animal poisoned with carbon monoxide, but I could not liberate the oxygen as usual. I tried to do the same with arterial blood; I had no greater success. My preconceived idea was therefore false. But the impossibility of getting oxygen from the blood of a dog poisoned with carbon monoxide was a second observation which suggested a fresh hypothesis. What could have become of the oxygen in the blood? It had not changed with carbonic acid, because I had not set free large quantities of that gas in passing a current of hydrogen through the blood of the poisoned animals. Moreover, that hypothesis was contrary to the color of the blood. I exhausted myself in conjectures about how carbon monoxide could cause the oxygen to disappear from the blood; and as gases displace one another I naturally thought that the carbon monoxide might have displaced the oxygen and driven it out of the blood. To learn this, I decided to vary my experimentation by putting the blood in artificial conditions that would allow me to recover the displaced oxygen. So I studied the action of carbon monoxide on blood experimentally. For this purpose I took a certain amount of arterial blood from a healthy animal; I put this blood on the mercury in an inverted test tube containing carbon monoxide; I then shook the whole thing so as to poison the blood sheltered from contact with the outer air. Then, after an interval, I examined whether the air in the test tube in contact with the poisoned blood had been changed, and I noted that the air thus in contact with the blood had been remarkably enriched with oxygen, while the proportion of carbon monoxide was lessened. Repeated in the same conditions, these experiments taught me that what had occurred was an exchange, volume by volume, between the carbon monoxide and the oxygen of the blood. But the carbon monoxide, in displacing the oxygen that it had expelled from the blood, remained chemically combined in the blood and could no longer be displaced either by oxygen or by other gases. So that death came through death of the molecules of blood, or in other words by stopping their exercises of a physiological property essential to life.

This last example, which I have very briefly described, is complete; it shows from one end to the other, how we proceed with the experimental method and succeed in learning the immediate cause of phenomena. To begin with I knew literally nothing about the mechanism of the phenomenon of poisoning with carbon monoxide. I undertook an experiment to see, i.e., to observe. I made a preliminary observation of a special change in the coloring of blood. I interpreted this observation, and I made an hypothesis which proved false. But the experiment provided me with a second observation about which I reasoned anew, using it as a starting point for making a new hypothesis as to the mechanism, by which the oxygen in the blood was removed. By building up hypotheses, one by one, about the facts as I observed them, I finally succeeded in showing that carbon monoxide replaces oxygen in a molecule of blood, by combining with the substance of the molecule. Experimental analysis, here, has reached its goal. This is one of the cases, rare in physiology, which I am happy to be able to quote. Here the immediate cause of the phenomenon of poisoning is found and is translated into a theory which accounts for all the facts and at the same time includes all the observations and experiments. Formulated as follows, the theory posits the main facts from which all the rest are deducted: Carbon monoxide combines more intimately than oxygen with the hemoglobin in a molecule of blood. It has quite recently been proved that carbon monoxide forms a definite combination with hemoglobin. So that the molecule of blood, as if petrified by the stability of the combination, loses its vital properties. Hence everything is logically deduced: because of its property of more intimate combination, carbon monoxide drives out of the blood the oxygen essential to life; the molecules of blood become inert, and the animal dies, with symptoms of hemorrhage, from true paralysis of the molecules.

THE GOLDEN ALPHABET

Loren Eisley

A creature without memory cannot discover the past; one without expectation cannot conceive a future.
—GEORGE SANTAYANA

"Wisdom," the Eskimo say, "can be found only far from man, out in the great loneliness." These people speak from silences we will not know again until we set foot upon the moon. Perhaps our track is somehow rounding evocatively backward into another version of the giant winter out of which we emerged ten thousand years ago. Perhaps it is our destiny to have plunged across it only to re-enter it once more.

Of all the men of the nineteenth century who might be said to have been intimates of that loneliness and yet, at the same time, to have possessed unusual prophetic powers, Henry David Thoreau and Charles Darwin form both a spectacular comparison and a contrast. Both Thoreau and Darwin were voyagers. One confined himself to the ever widening ripples on a pond until they embraced infinity. The other went around the world and remained for the rest of his life a meditative recluse in an old Victorian house in the English countryside. . . .

Both men forfeited the orthodox hopes that had sustained, through many centuries, the Christian world. Yet, at the last, the one transcends the other's vision, or amplifies it. Darwin remains, though sometimes hesitantly, the pragmatic scientist, content with what his eyes have seen. The other turns toward an unseen spring beyond the wintry industrialism of the nineteenth century, with its illusions of secular progress. The two views, even the two lives, can be best epitomized in youthful expressions that have come down to us. The one, Darwin's, is sure, practical, and exuberant. The other reveals an exploring, but wary, nature.

Darwin, the empiricist, wrote from Valparaiso in 1834: "I have just got scent of some fossil bones of a MAMMOTH; what they may be I do not know, but if gold or galloping will get them they shall be mine." Thoreau, by nature more skeptical of what can be captured in this world, mused, in his turn, "I cannot lean so hard on any arm as on a sunbeam." It was one of the first of many similar enigmatic expressions that were finally to lead his well-meaning friend, Ellery Channing, to venture sadly, "I have never been able to understand what he meant by his life. . . . Why was he so disappointed with everybody else? Why was he so interested in the river and the woods . . . ? Something peculiar here I judge."

Channing was not wrong. There *was* something peculiar about Thoreau, just as there was something equally peculiar about Darwin. The difference between them lies essentially in the nature of man himself, the creature who persists in drawing sharp, definitive lines across the indeterminate face of nature. Essentially, the problem may be easily put. It is its varied permutations and combinations that each generation finds so defeating, and that our own time is busy, one might say horribly busy, in re-creating. . . .

The whole story of humanity is basically that of a journey toward the Emerald City, and of an effort to learn the nature of Oz, who, perhaps wisely, keeps himself concealed. In each human heart exists the Cowardly Lion and the little girl who was sure that the solution to life lay in just walking far enough. Finally, among our great discoverers are those with precious strawfilled heads who have to make up their own thoughts because each knows he has been made such a little while before, and has stood alone in the fields. Darwin and Thoreau are two such oddly opposed, yet similar, scarecrows. As it turned out, they came to two different cities, or at least vistas. They discovered something of the nature of Oz, and, rightly understood, their views are complementary to each other.

I shall treat first of Darwin and then of Thoreau, because, though contemporaries, they were distinct in temperament. Thoreau, who died young, perhaps trudged farther toward the place which the little girl Dorothy was so sure existed, and thus, in a sense, he may be a messenger from the future.

Since futures do not really exist until they are present, it might be more cautious to say that Thoreau was the messenger of a *possible* future in some way dependent upon ourselves.

Neither of the two men ever discovered the nature of Oz himself. The one, Darwin, learned much about his ways—so much, indeed, that I suspect he came to doubt the existence of Oz. The other, Thoreau, leaned perhaps too heavily upon his sunbeam, and in time it faded, but not surely, because to the last he clung to the fields and heard increasingly distant echoes. Both men wore spectacles of sorts, for this is a rule that Oz has decreed for all men. Moreover, there are diverse kinds of spectacles.

There are, for example, the two different pairs through which philosophers may look at the world. Through one we see ourselves in the light of the past; through the other, in the light of the future. If we fail to use both pairs of spectacles equally, our view of ourselves and of the world is apt to be distorted, since we can never see completely without the use of both. The historical sciences have made us very conscious of our past, and of the world as a machine generating successive events out of foregoing ones. For this reason some scholars tend to look totally backward in their interpretation of the human future. It is, unconsciously, an exercise much favored in our time.

Like much else, this attitude has a history.

When science, early in the nineteenth century, began to ask what we have previously termed "the terrible questions" because they involved the nature of evil, the age of the world, the origins of man, of sex, or even of language itself, a kind of Pandora's box had been opened. People could classify giraffes and porcupines but not explain them—much less a man. Everything stood in isolation, and therefore the universe of life was bound to appear a little ridiculous to the honestly enquiring mind. What was needed was the kind of man of whom Thoreau had spoken, who could couple two seemingly unrelated facts and reduce the intractable chaos of the world. Such a man was about to appear. In fact, he had already had his forerunners. . . .

The youth who went aboard the *Beagle* in December 1831 was a great deal more clever than his academic record at both Edinburgh and Cambridge might suggest. The ingenuity with which he went about securing his father's permission for the voyage in itself indicates the dedicated persistence with which he could overcome obstacles. There remained in the motherless young man a certain wary reserve, which would finally draw him into total seclusion. In the first edition of the *Origin of Species* he was to write: "When on board H.M.S. *Beagle*, as naturalist, I was much struck with certain facts. . . . These facts seemed to . . . throw light on the origin of species. . . ." The remark is true, but it is also ingenuous. Young Charles's first knowledge of evolution did not emerge spontaneously aboard the *Beagle*, however much that conception was to be strengthened in the wild lands below the equator.

Instead, its genesis in Darwin's mind lies mysteriously back amidst unrecorded nights in student Edinburgh and lost in the tracery of spider tracks over thousands of dusty volumes after his return. For this is the secret of Charles Darwin the naturalist-voyager, the modern Odysseus who came to Circe's island of change in the Galápagos: he was the product of two odysseys, not one. He lives in the public mind partly by the undoubted drama of a great voyage whose purpose, as defined by the chief hydrographer, was the placing of a chain of meridians around the world. While those meridians were being established through Fitzroy's efforts, another set was being posted by Darwin in the haunted corridors of the past.

But the second odyssey, the one most solitary, secretive, and hidden, is the Merlin-like journey which had no ending save at death. It is the groping through webby corridors of books in smoky London—the kind of journey in which men are accountable only to themselves and by which the public is not at all enlivened. No waves burst, no seaman falls from the masthead, no icy continent confronts the voyager. Within the mind, however, all is different. There are ghost fires burning over swampy morasses of books, confusing trails, interceptions of the lost, the endless weaving and unweaving of floating threads of thought drawn from a thousand sources. . . .

The floating threads of all the ideas, all the thinking, all the nightmares of hours spent in the endless galleries of books, meet and are gathered up at last in the great book of 1859—that book termed the *Origin of Species*, which Darwin to the last maintained was only a hasty abstract. . . .

Variation—that subtle, unnoted shifting of the shapes of men and leaves, bird beaks and turtles, that he had pondered over far off in the Circean Galápagos—was now seen to link the seemingly ridiculous and chaotic world of life into a single whole. Selection was the living screen through which all life must pass. No fact could be left a fact; somewhere in the world it was tied to something else. What made a tuft of feathers suddenly appear on a cock's head or induce the meaningless gyrations of a tumbler pigeon? What, in this final world of the fortuitous, the sad eyes questioned, had convinced a tailless ape that he was the object of divine attention? . . .

Thoreau had loved nature as intensely as Darwin and perhaps more personally. He had seen with another set of glasses. He was, in an opposite sense to Darwin, a dweller along the edge of the known, a place where the new begins. Thoreau carries a hint of that newness. He dwelt, without being quite consciously aware of it, in the age after tomorrow. His friends felt universally baffled by Thoreau and labeled him "almost another species." One contemporary wrote: "His eyes slipped into every tuft of meadow or beach grass and went winding in and out of the thickest undergrowth, like some slim, silent, cunning animal." It has been said that he was not a true naturalist. What was he, then? The account just quoted implies a man similar to Darwin, and, in his own way, as powerfully motivated.

Of all strange and unaccountable things, Thoreau admits his efforts at his *Journal* to be the strangest. Even in youth he is beset by a prescient sadness. The companions who beguile his way will leave him, he already knows, at the first turn of the road. He was basically doomed all his life to be the Scarecrow of Oz, and if he seems harsher than that genial figure, it is because the city he sought was more elusive and he did not have even the Cowardly Lion for company. He knew only that by approaching nature he would be consulting, in every autumn-leaf fall, not alone those who had gone before him, but also those who would come after. He was writing before the *Origin of Species,* but someone had sewn amazing eyes upon the Concord Scarecrow.

There is a delicacy in him that is all his own. His search for support in nature is as diligent as that of a climbing vine he had once watched with fascinated attention groping eerily toward an invisible branch. Yet, like Darwin, he had witnessed the worst that nature could do. On his deathbed he had asked, still insatiable, to be lifted up in order that he could catch through the window a glimpse of one more spring.

In one passage in the *Journal* he had observed that the fishers' nets strung across the transparent river were no more intrusive than a cobweb in the sun. "It is," he notes, "a very slight and refined outrage at most." In their symmetry, he realizes, they are a beautiful memento of man's presence in nature, as wary a discovery as the footprint upon Crusoe's isle. Moreover, this little symbol of the fishers' seine defines precisely that delicately woven fabric of human relationships in which man, as a social animal, is so thoroughly enmeshed. There are times when, intellectually, Darwin threshed about in that same net as though trapped by a bird spider in his own forested Brazil.

For the most part, the untraveled man in Concord managed to slip in and out of similar meshes with comparative ease. Like some lean-bodied fish he is there, he is curiously observant, but he floats, oddly detached and unfrightened, in the great stream. "If we see nature as pausing," Thoreau remarks more than once, "immediately all mortifies and decays." In that nature is man, merely another creature in perspective, if one does not come too close, his civilizations like toadstools springing up by the road. Everything is in the flowing, not the past.

Museums, by contrast, are catacombs, the dead nature of dead men. Thoreau does not struggle so hard as Darwin in his phylogenies to knit the living world together. Unlike the moderns, Thoreau was not constantly seeking nostalgically for men on other planets. He respected the proud solitude of diversity, as when he watched a sparrow hawk amusing itself with aerial acrobatics. "It appeared to have no companion in the universe and to need none but the morning," he remarked, unconsciously characterizing himself. "It was not lonely but it made all the earth lonely beneath it."

Or again, he says plainly, "fox belongs to a different order of things from that which reigns in the village." Fox is alone. That is part of the ultimate secret shared between fox and scarecrow. They are creatures of the woods' edge. One of Thoreau's peculiar insights lies in his recognition of the creative loneliness of the individual, the struggle of man the evolved animal to live "a supernatural life." In a sense, it is a symbolic expression of the equally creative but microcosmic loneliness of the mutative gene. "Some," he remarks, "record only what has happened to them; but others how *they* have happened to the universe."

To this latter record Thoreau devoted the *Journal* that mystified his friends. Though, like Darwin, he was a seeker who never totally found what he sought, he had found a road, though no one appeared to be walking in it. Nevertheless, he seems to have been interiorly informed that it was a way traversed at long intervals by great minds. Thoreau, the physical stay-at-home, was an avid searcher of travel literature, but he was not a traveler in the body. Indeed, there are times when he seems to have regarded that labyrinth—for so he called it—with some of the same feeling he held toward a house—as a place to escape from. The nature we profess to know never completely contained him.

"I am sensible of a certain doubleness," he wrote, "by which I can stand as remote from myself as from another. . . . When the play—it may be the tragedy of life—is over, the spectator goes his way. It was a kind of fiction." This man does suggest another species, perhaps those cool, removed men of a far, oncoming century who can both live their lives and order them like great art. The gift is rare now, and not wholly enticing to earthbound creatures like ourselves.

Once, while surveying, Thoreau had encountered an unusual echo. After days with humdrum companions, he recorded with surprise and pleasure this generosity in nature. He wanted to linger and call all day to the air, to some voice akin to his own. There needs must be some actual doubleness like this in nature, he reiterates, "for if the voices which we commonly hear were all that we ever heard, what then? Echoes . . . are the only kindred voices that I hear."

Here, in Thoreau's question, is the crux, the sum total of the human predicament. This is why I spoke of our figuratively winding our way backward into a spiritual winter, why I quoted an Eskimo upon wisdom. On the eve of the publication of the *Origin of Species,* Thoreau, not by any means inimical to the evolutionary philosophy, had commented: "It is ebb tide with the scientific reports."

In some quarters this has aroused amusement. But what did Thoreau mean? Did he sense amidst English utilitarian philosophy, of which some aspects of Darwinism are an offshoot, an oncoming cold, a muffling of snow, an inability to hear echoes? Paradoxically, Thoreau, who delighted in simplicity of living, was averse to the parisomonious nature of Victorian science. It offended his transcendental vision of man. Lest I seem to exaggerate this conflict, read what Darwin himself admitted of his work in later years:

"I did not formerly consider sufficiently the existence of structures," he confesses, "which as far as we can . . . judge, are neither beneficial nor injurious, and this I believe to be one of the greatest oversights as yet detected in my work. This led to my tacit assumption that every detail of structure was of some special though unrecognized service."

We know that Thoreau already feared that man was becoming the tool of his tools, which can, alas, include ideas. Even now, forgetting Darwin's belated caution, those with the backward-reaching spectacles tell us eagerly, if not arrogantly, in the name of evolution, how we are born to behave and the limitations placed upon us—we who have come the far way from a wood nest in a Paleocene forest. Figuratively, these pronouncements have about them the enlarging, man-destroying evil of the pulsing worm. They stop man at an imagined border of himself. Man suffers, in truth, from a magical worm genuinely enlarged by a certain color of spectacles. It is a part, but not the whole, of the magic of Oz.

Is it not significant, in contrast to certain of these modern prophets, that Thoreau spoke of the freedom he felt to go and come in nature; that what is peculiar to the life of man "consists not in his obedience, but his opposition to his instincts"? The very behavior of the other animals toward mankind, Thoreau knew, revealed that man was not yet the civilized creature he pretended to be.

One must summarize the two philosophies of evolution and then let the Eskimo speak once more. In the Viking Eddas it is written:

> Hard it is on earth . . .
> Ax-time, sword-time . . .
> Wind-time, wolf-time, ere the world falls
> Nor ever shall men each other spare.

Through these lines comes the howl of the world-devouring Fenris-wolf, waiting his moment under the deep-buried rocket silos of today. In the last pages of *Walden* one of Thoreau's wisest remarks is upon the demand scientific intellectuals sometimes make, that one must speak so as to be always understood. "Neither men," he says, "nor toadstools grow so." There is a constant emergent novelty in nature that does not lie totally behind us, or we would not be what we are.

Here is where Thoreau's sensitivity to echoes emerges powerfully: It is onflowing man, not past evolutionary man, who concerns him. He wants desperately to know to what degree the human mind is capable of inward expansion. "If the condition of things which we were made for is not yet at hand," he questions anxiously, "what can we substitute?" The echoes he senses are reverberating from the future.

Finally, he compresses into a single passage the answer to the wolf-time philosophy, whether expressed by the Viking freebooters, or by certain of their modern descendants. "After," he says, "the germs of virtue have thus been prevented many times from developing themselves, the beneficent breath of evening does not suffice to preserve them. . . . Then the nature of man does not differ much from that of the brute."

Does this last constriction contain the true and natural condition of man? No, Thoreau would contend, for nature lives always in anticipation. Thoreau was part of the future. He walked toward it, knowing also that in the case of man it must emerge from within by means of his own creation. That was why Thoreau saw the double nature of the tool and eyed it with doubt.

The soul of the universe, the Upholder, reported Rasmussen of the Alaskan Eskimo, is never seen. Its voice, however, may be heard on occasion, through innocent children. Or in storms. Or in sunshine. Both Darwin and Thoreau had disavowed the traditional paradise, and it has been said of Thoreau that he awaited a Visitor who never came. Nevertheless, he had felt the weight of an unseen power. What it whispers, said the men of the high cold, is, "Be not afraid of the universe."

Man, since the beginning of his symbol-making mind, has sought to read the map of that same universe. Do not believe those serious-minded men who tell us that writing began with economics and the ordering of jars of oil. Man is, in reality, an oracular animal. Bereft of instinct, he must search constantly for meanings. We forget that, like a child, man was a reader before he became a writer, a reader of what Coleridge once called the mighty alphabet of the universe. Long ago, our forerunners knew, as the Eskimo still know that there is an instruction hidden in the storm or dancing in auroral fires. The future can be invoked by the pictures impressed on a cave wall or in the cracks interpreted by a shaman on the incinerated shoulder blade of a hare. The very flight of birds is a writing to be read. Thoreau strove for its interpretation on his pond, as Darwin, in his way, sought equally to read the message written in the beaks of Galápagos finches.

But the messages, like all the messages in the universe, are elusive.

Some months ago, walking along the shore of a desolate island off the Gulf Coast, I caught a glimpse of a beautiful shell, imprinted with what appeared to be strange writing, rolling in the breakers. Impelled by curiosity,

I leaped into the surf and salvaged it. Golden characters like Chinese hiero-glyphs ran in symmetrical lines around the cone of the shell. I lifted it up with the utmost excitement, as though a message had come to me from the green depths of the sea.

Later I unwrapped the shell before a dealer in antiquities in the back streets of a seaport town.

"*Conus spurius atlanticus*," he diagnosed for me with brisk efficiency, "otherwise known as the alphabet shell."

But why spurious? I questioned inwardly as I left the grubby little shop, warily refusing an offer for my treasure. The shell, I was sure, contained a message. We *live* by messages—all true scientists, all lovers of the arts, indeed, all true men of any stamp. Some of the messages cannot be read, but man will always try. He hungers for messages, and when he ceases to seek and interpret them he will be no longer man.

The little cone lies now upon my desk, and I handle it as reverently as I would the tablets of a lost civilization. It transmits tidings as real as the increasingly far echoes heard by Thoreau in his last years.

Perhaps I would never have stumbled into so complete a revelation save that the shell was *Conus spurius*, carrying the appellation given it by one who had misread, most painfully misread, a true message from the universe. Each man deciphers from the ancient alphabets of nature only those secrets that his own deeps possess the power to endow with meaning. It had been so with Darwin and Thoreau. The golden alphabet, in whatever shape it chooses to reveal itself, is never spurious. From its inscrutable lettering is created man and all the towering cloudland of his dreams.

STRUGGLE FOR EXISTENCE

Charles Darwin

Before entering on the subject of this chapter, I must make a few pre-liminary remarks, to show how the struggle for existence bears on Natural Selection. It has been seen in the last chapter that amongst organic beings in a state of nature there is some individual variability: indeed I am not aware that this has ever been disputed. It is immaterial for us whether a multitude of doubtful forms be called species or sub-species or varieties; what rank, for instance, the two or three hundred doubtful forms of British plants are entitled to hold, if the existence of any well-marked varieties be admitted.

But the mere existence of individual variability and of some few well-marked varieties, though necessary as the foundation for the work, helps us but little in understanding how species arise in nature. How have all those exquisite adaptations of one part of the organisation to another part, and to the conditions of life, and of one organic being to another being, been perfected? We see these beautiful co-adaptations most plainly in the woodpecker and the mistletoe; and only a little less plainly in the humblest parasite which clings to the hairs of a quadruped or feathers of a bird: in the structure of the beetle which dives through the water: in the plumed seed which is wafted by the gentlest breeze; in short, we see beautiful adaptations everywhere and in every part of the organic world.

Again, it may be asked, how is it that varieties, which I have called incipient species, become ultimately converted into good and distinct species, which in most cases obviously differ from each other far more than do the varieties of the same species? How do those groups of species, which constitute what are called distinct genera, and which differ from each other more than do the species of the same genus, arise? All these results, as we shall more fully see in the next chapter, follow from the struggle for life. Owing to this struggle, variations, however slight and from whatever cause proceeding, if they be in any degree profitable to the individuals of a species, in their infinitely complex relations to other organic beings and to their physical conditions of life, will tend to the preservation of such individuals, and will generally be inherited by the offspring. The offspring, also, will thus have a better chance of surviving, for, of the many individuals of any species which are periodically born, but a small number can survive. I have called this principle, by which each slight variation, if useful, is preserved, by the term Natural Selection, in order to mark its relation to man's power of selection. But the expression often used by Mr. Herbert Spencer of the Survival of the Fittest is more accurate, and is sometimes equally convenient. We have seen that man by selection can certainly produce great results, and can adapt organic beings to his own uses, through the accumulation of slight but useful variations, given to him by the hand of Nature. But Natural Selection, as we shall hereafter see, is a power incessantly ready for action, and is as immeasurably superior to man's feeble efforts, as the works of Nature are to those of Art. . . .

Complex relations of all animals and plants to each other in the struggle for existence. Many cases are on record showing how complex and unexpected are the checks and relations between organic beings, which have to struggle together in the same country. I will give only a single instance, which, though a simple one, interested me. In Staffordshire, on the estate of a relation, where I had ample means of investigation, there was a large and extremely barren heath, which had never been touched by the hand of man;

but several acres of exactly the same nature had been enclosed twenty-five years previously and planted with Scotch fir. The change in the native vegetation of the planted part of the heath was most remarkable, more than is generally seen in passing from one quite different soil to another: not only the proportional numbers of the heath-plants were wholly changed, but twelve species of plants (not counting grasses and carices) flourished in the plantations, which could not be found on the heath. The effect on the insects must have been still greater, for six insectivorous birds were very common in the plantations, which were not to be seen on the heath; and the heath was frequented by two or three distinct insectivorous birds. Here we see how potent has been the effect of the introduction of a single tree, nothing whatever else having been done, with the exception of the land having been enclosed, so that cattle could not enter. But how important an element enclosure is, I plainly saw near Farnham, in Surrey. Here there are extensive heaths, with a few clumps of old Scotch firs on the distant hilltops: within the last ten years large spaces have been enclosed, and self-sown firs are now springing up in multitudes, so close together that all cannot live. When I ascertained that these young trees had not been sown or planted, I was so much surprised at their numbers that I went to several points of view, whence I could examine hundreds of acres of the unenclosed heath, and literally I could not see a single Scotch fir, except the old planted clumps. But on looking closely between the stems of the heath, I found a multitude of seedlings and little trees which had been perpetually browsed down by the cattle. In one square yard, at a point some hundred yards distant from one of the old clumps, I counted thirty-two little trees; and one of them, with twenty-six rings of growth, had, during many years, tried to raise its head above the stems of the heath, and had failed. No wonder that, as soon as the land was enclosed, it became thickly clothed with vigorously growing young firs. Yet the heath was so extremely barren and so extensive that no one would ever have imagined that cattle would have so closely and effectually searched it for food.

Here we see that cattle absolutely determine the existence of the Scotch fir; but in several parts of the world insects determine the existence of cattle. Perhaps Paraguay offers the most curious instance of this; for here neither cattle nor horses nor dogs have ever run wild, though they swarm southward and northward in a feral state; and Azara and Rengger have shown that this is caused by the greater number in Paraguay of a certain fly, which lays its eggs in the navels of these animals when first born. The increase of these flies, numerous as they are, must be habitually checked by some means, probably by other parasitic insects. Hence, if certain insectivorous birds were to decrease in Paraguay, the parasitic insects would probably increase; and this would lessen the number of the navel-frequenting flies—then cattle and horses would become feral, and this would certainly greatly alter (as indeed I have observed in parts of South America) the vegetation: this again would largely affect the insects; and this, as we have just seen in Staffordshire, the insectivorous birds, and so onwards in ever-increasing circles of complexity. Not that under nature the relations will ever be as simple as this. Battle within battle must be continually recurring with varying success; and yet in the long-run the forces are so nicely balanced, that the face of nature remains for long periods of time uniform, though assuredly the merest trifle would give the victory to one organic being over another. Nevertheless, so profound is our ignorance, and so high our presumption, that we marvel when we hear of the extinction of an organic being; and as we do not see the cause, we invoke cataclysms to desolate the world, or invent laws on the duration of the forms of life!

I am tempted to give one more instance showing how plants and animals, remote in the scale of nature, are bound together by a web of complex relations. I shall hereafter have occasion to show that the exotic Lobelia fulgens is never visited in my garden by insects, and consequently, from its peculiar structure, never sets a seed. Nearly all our orchidaceous plants absolutely require the visits of insects to remove their pollen-masses and thus to fertilise them. I find from experiments that humble-bees are almost indispensable to the fertilisation of the heartsease (Viola tricolor), for other bees do not visit this flower. I have also found that the visits of bees are necessary for the fertilisation of some kinds of clover; for instance, 20 heads of Dutch clover (Trifolium repens) yielded 2,290 seeds, but 20 other heads protected from bees produced not one. Again, 100 heads of red clover (T. pratense) produced 2,700 seeds, but the same number of protected heads produced not a single seed. Humble-bees alone visit red clover, as other bees cannot reach the nectar. It has been suggested that moths may fertilise the clovers; but I doubt whether they could do so in the case of the red clover, from their weight not being sufficient to depress the wing petals. Hence we may infer as highly probable that, if the whole genus of humble-bees became extinct or very rare in England, the heartsease and red clover would become very rare, or wholly disappear. The number of humble-bees in any district depends in a great measure upon the number of field-mice, which destroy their combs and nests; and Col. Newman, who has long attended to the habits of humble-bees, believes that "more than two-thirds of them are thus destroyed all over England." Now the number of mice is largely dependent, as every one knows, on the number of cats; and Col. Newman says, "Near villages and small towns I have found the nests of humble-bees more numerous than elsewhere, which I attribute to the number of cats that destroy the mice." Hence it is quite credible that the presence of a feline animal in large numbers in a district might determine, through the intervention first of mice and then of bees, the frequency of certain flowers in that district!

In the case of every species, many different checks, acting at different periods of life, and during different seasons or years, probably come into play; some one check or some few being generally the most potent; but all will concur in determining the average number or even the existence of the species. In some cases it can be shown that widely-different checks act on the same species in different districts. When we look at the plants and bushes clothing an entangled bank, we are tempted to attribute their proportional numbers and kinds to what we call chance. But how false a view is this! Every one has heard that when an American forest is cut down, a very different vegetation springs up; but it has been observed that ancient Indian ruins in the Southern United States, which must formerly have been cleared of trees, now display the same beautiful diversity and proportion of kinds as in the surrounding virgin forest. What a struggle must have gone on during long centuries between the several kinds of trees, each annually scattering its seeds by the thousand; what war between insect and insect—between insects, snails, and other animals with birds and beasts of prey—all striving to increase, all feeding on each other, or on the trees, their seeds and seedlings, or on the other plants which first clothed the ground and thus checked the growth of the trees! Throw up a handful of feathers, and all fall to the ground according to definite laws; but how simple is the problem where each shall fall compared to that of the action and reaction of the innumerable plants and animals which have determined, in the course of centuries, the proportional numbers and kinds of trees now growing on the old Indian ruins!

The dependency of one organic being on another, as of a parasite on its prey, lies generally between beings remote in the scale of nature. This is likewise sometimes the case with those which may be strictly said to struggle with each other for existence, as in the case of locusts and grass-feeding quadrupeds. But the struggle will almost invariably be most severe between the individuals of the same species, for they frequent the same districts, require the same food, and are exposed to the same dangers. In the case of varieties of the same species, the struggle will generally be almost equally severe, and we sometimes see the contest soon decided: for instance, if several varieties of wheat be sown together, and the mixed seed be resown, some of the varieties which best suit the soil or climate, or are naturally the most fertile, will beat the others and so yield more seed, and will consequently in a few years supplant the other varieties. To keep up a mixed stock of even such extremely close varieties as the variously-coloured sweet peas, they must be each year harvested separately, and the seed then mixed in due proportion, otherwise the weaker kinds will steadily decrease in number and disappear. So again with the varieties of sheep; it has been asserted that certain mountain-varieties will starve out other mountain-varieties, so that they cannot be kept together. The same result has followed from keeping together different varieties of the medicinal leech. It may even be doubted whether the varieties of any of our domestic plants or animals have so exactly the same strength, habits, and constitution, that the original proportions of a mixed stock (crossing being prevented) could be kept up for a half-a-dozen generations, if they were allowed to struggle together, in the same manner as beings in a state of nature, and if the seed or young were not annually preserved in due proportion.

MATHEMATICAL GAMES

Martin Gardner

Simplicity, simplicity, simplicity!
I say, let your affairs be as two
or three, and not a hundred or a
thousand; instead of a million
count half a dozen, and keep
your accounts on your thumb nail.
—HENRY DAVID THOREAU, *Walden*

Thoreau's advice raises deep and difficult questions regarding the universe. Does nature keep her accounts on a thumbnail? Are the basic laws of science few in number or, as the mathematician Stanislaw Ulam believes, infinite? Are they, as the physicist Richard Feynman has suggested, perhaps finite but increasingly hard to discover, so that there will always be a tiny but forever shrinking margin of mystery about the universe?

A closely related question is whether the basic laws themselves are simple or complicated. Most biologists, particularly those working with the brain and the nervous system, are impressed by the complexity of life. In contrast, although quantum theory has become enormously more complicated with the discovery of weird new particles and interactions, most physicists retain a strong faith in the ultimate simplicity of basic laws. This was especially true of Albert Einstein. "Our experience," he wrote, "justifies us in believing that nature is the realization of the simplest conceivable mathematical ideas." When he chose the tensor equations for his theory of gravitation, he picked the simplest set that would do the job, then published them with complete confidence that (as he once said to the mathematician John Kemeny) "God would not have passed up an opportunity to make nature that simple." It has even been argued that Einstein's great achievements were tied up with a psychological compulsion, like Thoreau's, to simplify his personal life.

"Einstein's bedroom was monkish," Peter Michelmore writes in *Einstein, Profile of the Man.* "There were no pictures on the wall, no carpet on the floor. . . . He shaved roughly with bar soap. He often went barefoot around the house. Only once every few months he would allow Elsa [his wife] to lop off swatches of his hair. . . . Most days he did not find underwear necessary. He also dispensed with pajamas and, later, with socks. 'What use are socks?' he asked. 'They only produce holes'. Elsa put her foot down when she saw him chopping off the sleeves of a new shirt from the elbow down. He explained that cuffs had to be buttoned or studded and washed frequently—all a waste of time."

"Every possession," Einstein said, "is a stone around the leg." The statement could have come straight out of *Walden.*

Yet nature seems to have a great many stones around her legs. Basic laws are simple only in first approximations; they become increasingly complex as they are refined to explain new observations. The guiding motto of the scientist, Alfred North Whitehead wrote, should be: "Seek simplicity and distrust it." Galileo picked the simplest workable equation for falling bodies, but it did not take into account the altitude of the body and had to be modified by the slightly more complicated equations of Newton. Newton too had great faith in simplicity. "Nature is pleased with simplicity," he wrote, echoing a passage in Aristotle, "and affects not the pomp of superfluous causes." Yet Newton's equations in turn were modified by Einstein, and today there are physicists, such as Robert Dicke, who believe that Einstein's gravitational equations must be modified by still more complicated formulas.

It is dangerous to argue that because many basic laws are simple the undiscovered laws also will be simple. Simple first approximations are obviously the easiest to discover first. The most one can say is that science sometimes increases simplicity by producing theories that reduce to the same laws phenomena previously considered unrelated (for example the equivalence of inertia and gravity in general relativity), but that science equally often discovers that behind apparently simple phenomena, such as the structure of matter, there lurks an unsuspected complexity. Johannes Kepler struggled for years to defend the circular orbits of planets because the circle was the simplest closed curve. When he finally convinced himself that the orbits were ellipses, he wrote of the ellipse as "dung" he had to introduce to rid astronomy of vaster amounts of dung. It is a perceptive statement because it suggests that the introduction of more complexity on one level of a theory can introduce greater overall simplicity.

Nevertheless, at each step along the road simplicity seems to enter into a scientist's work in some mysterious way that makes the simplest workable hypothesis the best bet. "Simplest" is used here in an objective sense. Naturally there are many pragmatic aspects, but they are irrelevant to the big question. If two theories are identical in all respects except the way they are expressed (for example one in English measures, the other in the metric system), a scientist would be foolish not to pick the formulation that is easier to handle. When two theories are not equivalent—when they lead to different predictions—he also will prefer to test first whichever theory is easier to test. This depends, however, on what apparatus he has available, what kinds of mathematics he understands best and so on. The same theory may seem simple to one physicist and complicated to another.

Although such subjective matters play their role, they fail to touch the heart of the mystery. The important question is: Why, other things being equal, is the simplest hypothesis usually the most likely to be on the right track? The classic instance is the graphing of a relation between two variables. The physicist records his observations as dots on a graph, then draws the simplest curve that comes close to those dots. Simplicity even overrules the data. If the spots fall near a straight line, he will not draw a wavy curve that passes through every spot. He will assume that his observations are probably a bit off, pick a straight line that misses every spot and guess that the function is a simple linear equation such as $x = 2y$ [see *illustration*]. If this fails to predict new observations, he will try a curve of next-highest degree, say a hyperbola or a parabola. The point is that, other things being equal, the simpler curve has the higher probability of being right. A truly astonishing number of basic laws are expressed by low-order equations. Nature's preference for extrema (maxima and minima) is another familiar example of simplicity because in both cases they are the values when the function's derivative equals zero.

This raises some of the most perplexing questions in this philosophy of science. How can this particular kind of simplicity—the kind that adds to the probability that a law or theory is true—be defined? If it can be defined, can it be measured? Scientists tend to scorn both questions. They make intuitive judgments of simplicity without worrying about exactly what it is.

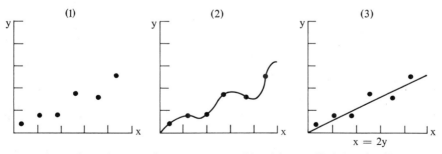

Observed data (1), a possible function curve (2) and the most likely function (3)

Yet it is conceivable that someday a way to measure simplicity may have great practical value. Consider two theories that explain all known facts about fundamental particles. They are equal in their power to predict new observations, although the predictions are different. Both theories cannot be true. Both may be false. Each demands a different test and each test costs $1 million. If simplicity enters into the probability of a theory's being right, there is an obvious advantage in being able to measure simplicity so that the simplest theory can be tested first.

No one today knows how to measure this kind of simplicity or even how to define it. *Something* in the situation must be minimized, but what? It is no good to count the terms in a theory's mathematical formulation, because the number depends on the notation. The same formula may have 10 terms in one notation and three in another. Einstein's famous $E = mc^2$ looks simple only because each term is a shorthand symbol for concepts that can be written with formulas involving other concepts. This happens also in pure mathematics. The only way to express pi with integers is as the limit of an infinite series, but by writing π the entire series is squeezed into one symbol.

Minimizing the powers of terms also is misleading. For one thing, a linear equation such as $x = 2y$ graphs as a straight line only when the coordinates are Cartesian. With polar coordinates it graphs as a spiral. For another thing, minimizing powers is no help when equations are not polynomials.

Even in comparing the simplest geometric figures the notion of simplicity is annoyingly vague. In one of Johnny Hart's *B.C.* comic strips a caveman invents a square wagon wheel. Because it has too many corners and therefore too many bumps, he goes back to his drawing board and invents a "simpler" wheel in the shape of a triangle. Corners and bumps have been minimized, but the inventor is still further from the simplest wheel, the circle, which has no corners. Or should the circle be called the most complicated wheel because it is a "polygon" with an infinity of corners? The truth is that an equilateral triangle is simpler than a square in that it has fewer sides and corners. On the other hand, the square is simpler in that the formula for its area as a function of its side has fewer terms.

One of the most tempting of many proposed ways to measure the simplicity of a hypothesis stated in words is to count its number of primitive concepts. This, alas, is another blind alley. One can artificially reduce concepts by combining them. The philosopher Nelson Goodman brings this out clearly in his famous "grue" paradox about which dozens of technical papers have recently been written. Consider a simple law: All emeralds are green. We now introduce the concept "grue." It is the property of being green if observed, say, before January 1, 1970, and being blue if observed thereafter. We state a second law: All emeralds are grue.

Both laws have the same number of concepts. Both have the same "empirical content" (they explain all observations). Both have equal predictive power. A single instance of a wrong color, when an emerald is examined at any future time, can falsify either hypothesis. Everyone prefers the first law because "green" is simpler than "grue"—it does not demand new theories to explain the sudden change of color of emeralds on January 1, 1970. Although Goodman has done more work than anyone on this narrow aspect of simplicity, he is still far from final results, to say nothing of the more difficult problem of measuring the overall simplicity of a law or theory. The concept of simplicity in science is enormously complex! It may turn out that there is no single measure of simplicity but many different kinds, all of which enter into the final evaluation of a law or theory.

The Sorcerer's Apprentice

TOO MANY PEOPLE

Paul R. Ehrlich

Americans are beginning to realize that the undeveloped countries of the world face an inevitable population-food crisis. Each year food production in undeveloped countries falls a bit further behind burgeoning population growth, and people go to bed a little bit hungrier. While there are temporary or local reversals of this trend, it now seems inevitable that it will continue to its logical conclusion: mass starvation. The rich are going to get richer, but the more numerous poor are going to get poorer. Of these poor, a minimum of three and one-half million will starve to death this year, mostly children. But this is a mere handful compared to the numbers that will be starving in a decade or so. And it is now too late to take action to save many of those people.

In a book about population there is a temptation to stun the reader with an avalanche of statistics. I'll spare you most, but not all, of that. After all, no matter how you slice it, population is a numbers game. Perhaps the best way to impress you with numbers is to tell you about the "doubling time"— the time necessary for the population to double in size.

It has been estimated that the human population of 6000 B.C. was about five million people, taking perhaps one million years to get there from two and a half million. The population did not reach 500 million until almost 8,000 years later—about 1650 A.D. This means it doubled roughly once every thousand years or so. It reached a billion people around 1850, doubling in some 200 years. It took only 80 years or so for the next doubling, as the population reached two billion around 1930. We have not completed the next doubling to four billion yet, but we now have well over three billion people. The doubling time at present seems to be about 37 years. Quite a reduction in doubling times: 1,000,000 years, 1,000 years, 200 years, 80 years, 37 years. Perhaps the meaning of a doubling time of around 37 years is best brought home by a theoretical exercise. Let's examine what might happen on the absurd assumption that the population continued to double every 37 years into the indefinite future.

If growth continued at that rate for about 900 years, there would be some 60,000,000,000,000,000 people on the face of the earth. Sixty million billion people. This is about 100 persons for each square yard of the Earth's surface, land and sea. A British physicist, J. H. Fremlin, guessed that such a multitude might be housed in a continuous 2,000-story building covering our entire planet. The upper 1,000 stories would contain only the apparatus for running this gigantic warren. Ducts, pipes, wires, elevator shafts, etc., would occupy about half of the space in the bottom 1,000 stories. This would leave three or four yards of floor space for each person. I will leave to your imagination the physical details of existence in this ant heap, except to point out that all would not be black. Probably each person would be limited in his travel. Perhaps he could take elevators through all 1,000 residential stories but could travel only within a circle of a few hundred yards' radius on any floor. This would permit, however, each person to choose his friends from among some ten million people! And, as Fremlin points out, entertainment on the worldwide TV should be excellent, for at any time "one could expect some ten million Shakespears and rather more Beatles to be alive."

Could growth of the human population of the Earth continue beyond that point? Not according to Fremlin. We would have reached a "heat limit." People themselves, as well as their activities, convert other forms of energy into heat which must be dissipated. In order to permit this excess heat to radiate directly from the top of the "world building" directly into space, the atmosphere would have been pumped into flasks under the sea well before the limiting population size was reached. The precise limit would depend on the technology of the day. At a population size of one billion billion people, the temperature of the "world roof" would be kept around the melting point of iron to radiate away the human heat generated.

But, you say, surely Science (with a capital "S") will find a way for us to occupy the other planets of our solar system and eventually of other stars before we get all that crowded. Skip for a moment the virtual certainty that those planets are uninhabitable. Forget also the insurmountable logistic problems of moving billions of people off the Earth. Fremlin has made some interesting calculations on how much time we could buy by occupying the planets of the solar system. For instance, at any given time it would take only about 50 years to populate Venus, Mercury, Mars, the moon, and the moons of Jupiter and Saturn to the same population density as Earth.

What if the fantastic problems of reaching and colonizing the other planets of the solar system, such as Jupiter and Uranus, can be solved? It would take only about 200 years to fill them "Earth-full." So we could perhaps gain 250 years of time for population growth in the solar system after we had reached an absolute limit on Earth. What then? We can't ship our surplus to the stars. Professor Garrett Hardin of the University of California at Santa Barbara has dealt effectively with this fantasy. Using extremely optimistic assumptions, he has calculated that Americans, by cutting their standard of living down to 18% of its present level, could in *one year* set aside enough capital to finance the exportation to the stars of *one day's* increase in the population of the world.

Interstellar transport for surplus people presents an amusing prospect. Since the ships would take generations to reach most stars, the only people who could be transported would be those willing to exercise strict birth control. Population explosions on space ships would be disastrous. Thus we would have to export our responsible people, leaving the irresponsible at home on Earth to breed.

Enough of fantasy. Hopefully, you are convinced that the population will have to stop growing sooner or later and that the extremely remote possibility of expanding into outer space offers no escape from the laws of population growth. If you still want to hope for the stars, just remember that, at the current growth rate, in a few thousand years everything in the visible universe would be converted into people, and the ball of people would be expanding with the speed of light! Unfortunately, even 900 years is much too far in the future for those of us concerned with the population explosion. As you shall see, the next *nine* years will probably tell the story. . . .

From the point of view of a demographer, the whole problem is quite simple. A population will continue to grow as long as the birth rate exceeds the death rate—if immigration and emigration are not occurring. It is, of course, the balance between birth rate and death rate that is critical. The birth rate is the number of births per thousand people per year in the population. The death rate is the number of deaths per thousand people per year. Subtracting the death rate from the birth rate, and ignoring migration, gives the rate of increase. If the birth rate is 30 per thousand per year, and the death rate is 10 per thousand per year, then the rate of increase is 20 per thousand per year $(30 - 10 = 20)$. Expressed as a percent (rate per hundred people), the rate of 20 per thousand becomes 2%. If the rate of increase is 2%, then the doubling time will be 35 years. Note that if you simply added 20 people per thousand per year to the population, it would take 50 years to add a second thousand people $(20 \times 50 = 1,000)$. But the doubling time is actually much less because populations grow at compound interest rates. Just as interest dollars themselves earn interest, so people added to populations produce more people. It's growing at compound interest that makes populations double so much more rapidly than seems possible. Look at the relationship between the annual percent increase (interest rate) and the doubling time of the population (time for your money to double):

Annual percent increase	Doubling time
1.0	70
2.0	35
3.0	24
4.0	17

Those are all the calculations—I promise. If you are interested in more details on how demographic figuring is done, you may enjoy reading Thompson and Lewis's excellent book, *Population Problems*.

There are some professional optimists around who like to greet every sign of dropping birth rates with wild pronouncements about the end of the population explosion. They are a little like a person who, after a low temperature of five below zero on December 21, interprets a low of only three below zero on December 22 as a cheery sign of approaching spring. First of all, birth rates, along with all demographic statistics, show short-term fluctuations caused by many factors. For instance, the birth rate depends rather heavily on the number of women at reproductive age. In the United States the current low birth rates soon will be replaced by higher rates as more post World War II "baby boom" children move into their reproductive years. In Japan, 1966, the Year of the Fire Horse, was a year of very low birth rates. There is widespread belief that girls born in the Year of the Fire Horse make poor wives, and Japanese couples try to avoid giving birth in that year because they are afraid of having daughters.

But, I repeat, it is the relationship between birth rate and death rate that is most critical. Indonesia, Laos, and Haiti all had birth rates around 46 per thousand in 1966. Costa Rica's birth rate was 41 per thousand. Good for Costa Rica? Unfortunately, not very. Costa Rica's death rate was less than nine per thousand, while the other countries all had death rates above 20 per thousand. The population of Costa Rica in 1966 was doubling every 17 years, while the doubling times of Indonesia, Laos, and Haiti were all above 30 years. Ah, but, you say, it was good for Costa Rica—fewer people per thousand were dying each year. Fine for a few years perhaps, but what then? Some 50% of the people in Costa Rica are under 15 years old. As they get older, they will need more and more food in a world with less and less. In 1983 they will have twice as many mouths to feed as they had in 1966, if the 1966 trend continues. Where will the food come from? Today the death rate in Costa Rica is low in part because they have a large number of physicians in proportion to their population. How do you suppose those physicians will keep the death rate down when there's not enough food to keep people alive?

One of the most ominous facts of the current situation is that roughly 40% of the population of the undeveloped world is made up of people *under 15 years old*. As that mass of young people moves into its reproductive years during the next decade, we're going to see the greatest baby boom of all time. Those youngsters are the reason for all the ominous predictions for the year 2000. They are the gunpowder for the population explosion. . . .

While lowering death rates in the DCs was due in part to other factors, there is question that "instant death control," exported by the DCs, has been responsible for the drastic lowering of death rates in the UDCs. Medical science, with its efficient public health programs, has been able to depress the death rate with astonishing rapidity and at the same time drastically increase the birth rate; healthier people have more babies.

The power of exported death control can best be seen by an examination of the classic case of Ceylon's assault on malaria after World War II. Between 1933 and 1942 the death rate due directly to malaria was *reported* as almost two per thousand. This rate, however, represented only a portion of the malaria deaths, as many were reported as being due to "pyrexia." Indeed, in 1934–1935 a malaria epidemic may have been directly responsible for fully half of the deaths on the island. In addition, malaria, which infected a large portion of the population, made people susceptible to many other diseases. It thus contributed to the death rate indirectly as well as directly.

The introduction of DDT in 1946 brought rapid control over the mosquitoes which carry malaria. As a result, the death rate on the island was halved in less than a decade. The death rate in Ceylon in 1945 was 22. It dropped 34% between 1946 and 1947 and moved down to ten in 1954. Since the sharp postwar drop it has continued to decline and now stands at eight. Although part of the drop is doubtless due to the killing of other insects which carry disease and to other public health measures, most of it can be accounted for by the control of malaria.

Victory over malaria, yellow fever, smallpox, cholera, and other infectious diseases has been responsible for similar plunges in death rate throughout most of the UDCs. In the decade 1940–1950 the death rate declined 46% in Puerto Rico, 43% in Formosa, and 23% in Jamaica. In a sample of 18 undeveloped areas the average decline in death rate between 1945 and 1950 was 24%.

It is, of course, socially very acceptable to reduce the death rate. Billions of years of evolution have given us all a powerful will to live. Intervening in the birth rate goes against our evolutionary values. During all those centuries of our evolutionary past, the individuals who had the most children passed on their genetic endowment in greater quantities than those who reproduced less. Their genes dominate our heredity today. All our biological urges are for more reproduction, and they are all too often reinforced by our culture. In brief, death control goes with the grain, birth control against it.

In summary, the world's population will continue to grow as long as the birth rate exceeds the death rate; it's as simple as that. When it stops growing or starts to shrink, it will mean that either the birth rate has gone down or the death rate has gone up or a combination of the two. Basically, then, there are only two kinds of solutions to the population problem. One is a "birth rate solution," in which we find ways to lower the birth rate. The other is a "death rate solution," in which ways to raise the death rate—war, famine, pestilence—*find us*. The problem could have been avoided by *population control*, in which mankind consciously adjusted the birth rate so that a "death rate solution" did not have to occur.

REHEARSE FOR THE APOCALYPSE

Action Magazine

YES FOLKS! NOW YOU CAN BE THE FIRST ON YOUR BLOCK TO EXPERIENCE THE ECOLOGICAL DISASTER.
WHY WAIT TILL 1980?
DON'T LET THE FUTURE TAKE YOU BY SURPRISE.
PREPARE NOW FOR THE END OF CIVILIZATION.
REHEARSE FOR THE APOCALYPSE. HERE ARE A FEW SUGGESTIONS:
Better start preparing your pallette and stomach for the fare of the 80's:

* Mix detergent with everything you eat and drink. There's already quite a bit but there will be a lot more in the future.
* Learn how to digest grass and other common plants.
* Start fattening your dog, cat, parakeet and guppies for the main course of the future.
* Develop a taste for grubs and insects—your ancestors weren't too proud to lift a rock for their dinner.
* Practice starving.
* Every night before bedtime drink a glass of industrial and organic waste on the rocks (with mixer if you prefer).

Appreciating that most services and products will disappear over the next ten to twenty years, we suggest this little dry run:

* Turn off your gas
* Turn off your water
* Turn off your telephone
* Turn off your heat
* Turn off your electricity
* Sit naked on the floor and repeat this chant: PROGRESS IS OUR MOST IMPORTANT PRODUCT, PROGRESS IS OUR . . . .

And as the final crisis approaches there's no better time to start hoarding. Start buying things you'll need after the Fall on credit—after the collapse no one will bother with collecting debts.

* While on the subject: start thinking about creative new uses for money since its present function will soon end. Remember, paper—particularly tissue—will be in short supply.

* Think about creative new uses for other potentially obsolete things like electric can openers, televisions, brassieres, toilets, alarm clocks, automobiles, etc.

* Accustom yourself to human body odor.

* Now is the time to learn a trade for the future—practice making arrowheads and other implements out of stone. Advanced students should start experimenting with bronze.

* For those of you who are investment minded, buy land, but you'd better leave enough bread to also buy a small arsenal to defend your property with.

* Remember Victory Gardens? Plant your Survival Garden now!

* Better quit smoking—or rip off a tobacco warehouse.

* Stockpile useful items like matches, safety pins, thread and needles, condoms, etc.

* Learn how to shoot a bow and arrow.

* Start preparing for the fashions of the future. You girls might take a hint from the heroines of monster films and start tearing your clothing in tasteful but strategically located tatters in order to create the Fay Wray look of tomorrow. Those less frivolous minded among you should start cultivating your body hair. (Remember a naked ape is a cold ape).

* You housewives had better learn how to maim and kill with a vegematic.

* Finally everyone should buy a boy scout manual—or in lieu of that, buy a boy scout.

SO IN FACING THE WORLD OF TOMORROW REMEMBER: BUILD FOR THE FUTURE AND CONTEMPLATE SUICIDE.

TO TROUBLE A STAR
The Cost of
Intervention in Nature

Garrett Hardin

All things by immortal power
  Near or far
  Hiddenly
To each other linked are,
That thou canst not stir a flower
Without troubling of a star.
                    —FRANCIS THOMPSON

One of the maddening aspects of a cultural revolution is that those who take part in one have a hard time telling what the revolution is about until it is over. They often do not know what is taking place until the change has progressed to a "point of no return."

Rachel Carson started a revolution when she published "Silent Spring" in 1962. True to form, this revolutionary work was widely misunderstood at first. Some critics complained that Miss Carson had not presented all of the evidence—which was true. Others said that pesticides were not necessarily so bad as her horrendous examples implied—which also was true. But most of the nit-picking critics missed entirely the revolutionary meaning of "Silent Spring."

What Miss Carson was trying to tell us was simply this: The world can no longer afford to ignore what has been called the "ecologic ethic." The ethical system under which we operated in the past was possibly adequate for an uncrowded world, though even this is debatable. But it is not adequate for a world that is already critically overcrowded, a world in which it is increasingly difficult for anyone to do anything at all without seriously affecting the well-being of countless other human beings. In castigating pesticide sprayers as monomaniacs, Rachel Carson was alerting the world to what has been called the fundamental principle of ecology, namely: *We can never do merely one thing.* A monomaniac, by definition, is someone who thinks he *can* do just one thing, whether it be killing pests with pesticides, creating law and order with naked force or bringing Utopia into being with uninstructed love....

ONE EXAMPLE

Despite the verse by Francis Thompson opening this article, the stirring of a flower on Earth may not quite trouble a distant star. But it does trouble the rest of the Earth to a surprising degree. Let's look at a particular example, one among many.

Everyone has heard of the Aswan Dam in Egypt. It has been built high up in the Nile for two purposes: to generate electricity and to provide a regular flow of water for irrigation of the lower Nile basin. Ecology tells us that we cannot do merely one thing: neither can we do merely two things. What have been the consequences of the recently built Aswan Dam?

First, the replacement of periodic flooding by controlled irrigation is depriving the flood plains of the annual fertilization it has depended on for 5,000 years. (The fertile silt is now deposited behind the dam, which will eventually have to be abandoned.) Consequently, artificial fertilizers will soon have to be imported into the Nile valley.

Second, controlled irrigation without periodic flushing salinates the soil, bit by bit. There are methods for correcting this, but they cost money. This problem has not yet been faced in Egypt.

Third, the sardine catch in the eastern Mediterranean has diminished from 18,000 tons a year to 500 tons, a 97 percent loss, because the sea is now deprived of flood-borne nutrients. No one has reimbursed the fishermen for their losses.

Fourth, schistosomiasis (a fearsomely debilitating disease) has greatly increased among Egyptians. The disease organism depends on snails, which depend on a steady supply of water, which constant irrigation furnishes but annual flooding does not. Of course, medical control of the disease is possible—but that, too, costs money.

Is this all? By no means. The first (and perhaps only a temporary) effect of the Aswan Dam has been to bring into being a larger population of Egyptians, of whom a greater proportion than before are chronically ill. What will be the political effects of this demographic fact? This is a most difficult question—but would anyone doubt that there will be many political consequences, for a long time to come, of trying to do "just one thing," like building a dam on the Nile? The effects of any sizable intervention in an ecosystem are like ripples spreading out on a pond from a dropped pebble; they go on and on.

ECOLOGY ENGULFS ECONOMICS

Before the Aswan Dam was ever started, there should have been a thorough study of the costs and benefits to be expected. There was a study of a sort, of course, but it was myopic on the cost end: All it included was the cost of building a concrete dam, implicitly assuming that it is possible to do just one thing. There was no mention of the costs of a new fertilizer industry, of a far-flung medical program, of a soil reclamation program or of developing a new occupation for displaced fishermen; and nothing at all about controlling pathological processes in the body politic. What was missing in the preliminary cost-benefit analysis was the ecologic view. The analysis was merely economic, in the narrowest sense.

I think one of the few predictions that we can confidently make as we move into the 1970s is that economic analysis is going to become ecologized; or perhaps we should say ecology will engulf economics. Whether ecologists will become economists or vice versa is of only secondary importance. What is important is that the more inclusive science will encompass the less inclusive, which has proved too narrow a base for carrying out cost-benefit analyses. . . .

Logic dictates this engulfment, but logic alone does not determine history. Power relationships also must be favorable. I think the power relationships now favor a change. In the past, economics was to a large extent the handmaiden of business. The vast majority of economists were either employed directly by businesses, or had jobs in university departments of economics that were unusually sensitive to business interests. In recent decades, the steady increase in the number of economists employed by governmental and quasi-governmental agencies points toward the day when the tunes played by economists will be different. A different sector of society is paying the piper. Whether this means that economists will enjoy greater intellectual independence is not clear and may well be doubted. However, the shift in the balance of power should favor the development of a broadly ecological view among economists and that will be a social gain. . . .

Economics employs *partial* analysis to reach its decisions. This defect is not essential to the subject of economics, but it is traditional. Because of the increasing pressure of population and because of our greater knowledge of the consequences of our actions, economics is being rapidly altered away from its classical mold in the direction of ecology. The public interest in every proposal will in the future weigh more and more heavily in reaching decisions on the expenditure of public moneys. Cost-benefit analyses must be carried out within an intellectual framework that comes closer to incorporating the total system—not, certainly, all the way from Thompson's flower to the troubled stars, but certainly over a broad swath of earthly interrelationships. The myth of "externalities" must be abandoned. Economics must become ecologized.

WILL PROGRESS END?

When ecology engulfs economics, many of the dreams of imaginative engineers will be deliberately aborted because cost-benefit analysis will indicate an aggregate value that is negative. Many a dam will go unbuilt. The SST and many other technical marvels will never be realized or will be subsequently abandoned. Does this mean that all material "progress" will come to an end? Does it mean that we will be so inhibited by complete ecological-economic analysis that we can never again take a new technological step?

I think not. "We can never do one thing," and we can (in principle) never carry out an absolutely complete analysis, but it is nonetheless possible to institute changes safely. Two intellectual tools make this possible. The first is model-building, as mathematicians understand the term. With an intellectual model, one works out the feedback consequences of alterations in the system in an immaterial realm where the "costs" can be borne without pain. The second tool is dynamic programing, that is, the use of an adaptive logical system that can correct the model (or its real life analog) rapidly, before runaway feedback processes take control. Every order-of-magnitude improvement in the state of the art of computers brings with it a corresponding improvement in the efficacy of model-building and dynamic-programing. Such improvements in turn increase our confidence in our ability to foresee the consequences of interventions in ecological systems, and our willingness to undertake innovations.

The engulfing of economics by ecology thus will reintroduce responsibility into the political system, though at the risk of putting an end to all change. Fortunately, however, the powers of modern computers give man the capability of dealing with almost incredibly complex systems and thus regaining confidence in his ability to alter the systems in which he lives in a creative and responsible way.

TWEET, TWEET, HIC!

Eric Morgenthaler

DALLAS—Carobeth Byrd first noticed it when the woodpecker in her backyard began acting, well, strangely. He would fly head-on into the patio roof and was spending a lot of time sitting in the flower beds, looking addled.

Mrs. Byrd—her real name—has a dog that loves woodpeckers. For lunch. So the dog has been staying indoors a lot while Mrs. Byrd waits for the woodpecker to recover and fly away. It takes awhile, because he is drunk out of his mind a good part of the time.

Mrs. Byrd, who is fond of her little feathered namesakes, is part of an army of bird buffs confronted with a minor scandal—avian drunkenness. As ornithologists and other specialists explain it, the birds innocently feed on berries that have been fermented by the hot summer sun and carry a potent kick. Before they know it, they really are high fliers.

The Audubon Society indicates that drunken birds are a national problem of sorts. Hal Kirby, director of the Dallas Museum of Natural History, explains "Any birds that get involved in eating fermented berries are apt to experience some difficulty in locomotion and perching."

That's putting it mildly. Now, in the waning days of summer, birds are not just having a little difficulty in locomotion and perching. They are stinko, staggering around backyards, crashing into closed doors and falling off tree limbs from coast to coast.

DO THEY HICCUP?

Dallas, which is located along one migration flyway, is as good a place as any to watch the spectacle. It has become a familiar one to many residents; housewife Hazel Nichols, for example, has been watching blotto birds for years and swears she has heard them hiccup ("It's very interesting"). A biologist at nearby Southern Methodist University says he has never heard a bird hiccup himself but concedes that it might be possible.

Mrs. Nichols also used to have a possumberry vine that served as a songbird saloon. Some imbibers, she recalls, would lurch belligerently around the lawn, others would perch at odd angles on tree limbs, and still others would "just sort of sit there and wobble."

Though there are many birds staggering around in Dallas right now, the city really braces itself for trouble in the spring. That's when the cedar waxwing, a notorious tippler, blows into town to feed on the local pyracantha berries. Residents who don't know the cedar waxwing's habits think the birds are sick or injured and call the Dallas Zoo. Still others bring in inebriated birds for treatment, says Larry Calvin, zoo director.

CAN'T LEAVE THE STUFF ALONE

This consists of throwing them into a cage until they sober up, says Mr. Calvin. Unfortunately, the cedar waxwing apparently still can't learn to leave the stuff alone; drunk in the South on pyracantha, he gets drunk in the North on wild cherries, according to Roland Clement, staff biologist of the Audubon Society. "I've seen them sitting on telephone wires, just leaning against each other," Mr. Clement declares.

Birds who get blotto are just asking for trouble, authorities agree. Some get too fuddled to fly and just sit on the ground—easy targets for cats, dogs and other predators.

In Dallas birds often have one berry too many at bushes in the median strips of highways and are flattened by passing cars when they stagger blindly into the road. Some residents say other birds get pretty feisty when drunk; one woman claims they have been dive-bombing her cat.

A base canard, says Mr. Kirby, director of the Dallas Museum of Natural History. "Birds are not as inhibited as people are," he claims. "So they don't have to be released from their inhibitions to chase cats. They just do it because they enjoy it."

CHASING IMAGES

Also, ornithologists caution that birds flying into closed windows—a common occurrence—shouldn't automatically be scorned as drunks by householders. Many sober birds are just chasing images they see in the glass, the experts say.

There is, of course, no such excuse for birds that fly into tree trunks, closed doors and other objects. They probably are drunk. But they are not alcoholics, say the ornithologists. Some maintain the avian intoxication may be a mild form of poisoning; some of the symptoms displayed parallel those of birds that have ingested too much DDT. In any case, the birds drawn to the berries are there for food, not to got zonked.

However, enough of them do wind up drunk to distress bird lovers everywhere, and there is nothing to be done for it—except, perhaps, to remember that things could be a lot worse. In Africa, for example, elephants get drunk on berries. And that's a different bird altogether.

ATOM-AGE TRASH

Dennis Farney

LYONS, Kan.—The phrase "peaceful atom" conjures up images of cleanliness and light: Of white-gowned technicians and bright new reactors, of light and heat and power, seemingly without pollution.

The dark, dirty side of atomic energy is symbolized a half-mile east of this central Kansas town. It is an abandoned salt mine that may soon become this country's first atomic-age crypt.

There, in the perpetual darkness a thousand feet below the Kansas prairie, the Atomic Energy Commission plans to entomb all the "high level" (intensely radioactive) wastes generated by U.S. commercial atomic power plants for the rest of this century. So concentrated will be these wastes that, were they somehow evenly distributed, they could contaminate much of the nation. So fantastically long-lived are they that they will have to remain sealed away for as long as 500,000 years.

The mine also symbolizes a growing, if belated, effort by the AEC to come to grips with potentially the most devilish pollution problem of all. This is the problem of isolating from the environment the growing volume of radioactive wastes—the result of weapons-making as well as commercial operations—for the centuries, even millennia, they require to decompose.

EXPEDIENCY IS CHARGED

Finding solutions hasn't been the AEC's top priority. Democratic Sen. Frank Church of Idaho has calculated that over the last 25 years, while the agency spent billions to bevelop military and commercial applications of the atom, it spent only $50 million on waste disposal research. Today the nuclear industry is growing rapidly. But one of the AEC's own scientific advisory committees has characterized some of the agency's waste disposal practices as "expedients designed to make the best use of poor locations."

For example:

—In' southeastern Idaho, one of the AEC's four major U.S. installations routinely stores a variety of radioactive wastes about 600 feet directly above the Snake Plain Aquifer, a huge underground river whose waters ultimately reach much of the Pacific Northwest. Sen. Church and Federal water quality officials are concerned that radioactivity might leak down into the aquifer.

—Near Richland, Wash., the AEC's Hanford installation stores millions of gallons of high-level liquid wastes in huge underground tanks. The tanks have a life expectancy of 20 or 30 years, though the wastes within them will remain deadly for about 600 years. At least 11 times, the tanks have sprung relatively minor leaks.

—Millions of gallons of high-level wastes rest in a similar "tank farm" at the AEC's Savannah River plant, near Aiken, S.C. The AEC hopes to dispose of these wastes by pumping them into a man-made cavern below the Tuscaloosa Aquifer, already heavily used for drinking water and industry. The AEC advisory committee has called this plan—in a report that was suppressed for four years—"in its essence dangerous."

AN INSIDER URGES HALT

Glenn T. Seaborg, AEC chairman, concedes that "you could argue, in retrospect, that the AEC might have moved faster" on waste disposal. But he says such work is moving rapidly now and argues "it was logical" to build up the industry first.

One of the commission's sharpest critics disagrees. Arthur R. Tamplin of the AEC's Lawrence Radiation Laboratory argues for a moratorium on growth of the industry "until we perfect the systems all along the line." He adds: "We really don't know what to do with wastes today. We haven't devised the systems. And we're starting to produce wastes at an ever-increasing rate."

The AEC puts the great bulk of radioactive wastes in the "low-level" category, and maintains that relatively simple disposal techniques are perfectly adequate. Some four million cubic feet of contaminated materials now lie buried in the Idaho desert, for example—everything from contaminated laboratory gloves to bricks and rubble, placed in steel drums or wooden containers and buried in shallow trenches.

There is growing concern that disposal practices for even low-level and intermediate-level wastes pose serious potential hazards. "The current practices of disposing of intermediate and low-level liquid wastes and all manner of solid wastes directly into the ground above or in the fresh-water zones, although momentarily safe, will lead in the long run to a serious fouling of man's environment," warned one AEC scientific advisory committee.

DRAMATIC GROWTH SEEN

But by far the greatest concern is over "high-level" wastes, which account for more than 99% of all the radioactivity in materials on hand, though they account for a relatively small percentage of volume.

The exact volume of high-level wastes is classified because they are largely the result of AEC plutonium production for nuclear weapons. The AEC puts the total at more than 80 million gallons; of this, only about 400,000 gallons are the result of commercial operations.

But this ratio is going to change dramatically as the U.S. nuclear power industry grows. Today that industry provides roughly 1% of all U.S. electric power; by 1980, the AEC estimates, it will provide 25%. By the year 2000, the industry is expected to generate some 60 million gallons of "high-level" waste (or its solidified equivalent), which will be from 10 to 30 times as radioactive as the weapons-related waste now on hand.

Nuclear reactors' uranium fuel elements, whether used to generate electricity or to produce plutonium for weapons, eventually become choked, in effect, with the radioactive fragments of split atoms. When this happens the fuel must be taken to a reprocessing plant. There, the fuel rods are dissolved in acid and the reusable uranium and plutonium are separated out.

What's left, in AEC jargon, is "the soup": A liquid laden with enough radioisotopes to make it one of the deadliest substances on earth.

Many of the radioisotopes decay to harmless levels in relatively short order. (An example is zirconium-95, with a half-life of 65 days; this means half of a given amount will decay in the first 65 days, half of the remaining half in the next 65, and so on.) At the other extreme is plutonium—some of which escapes reprocessing—with a half-life of 24,000 years.

Despite its extreme longevity, plutonium isn't considered the most dangerous component of the liquid waste. Its radiation is incapable of penetrating even a thin shield (a steel barrel, for example) and most plutonium compounds aren't readily soluble in water. Thus plutonium is considered highly dangerous only if actually ingested into the body, particularly if inhaled into the lungs.

The really troublesome radioisotopes are strontium-90 (half-life: 25 years) and cesium-137 (33 years). Unlike many radioisotopes, which are excreted by the body, strontium-90 concentrates in the bones. Cesium-137 emits gamma radiation, similar to X-rays, which can readily penetrate thick shields. In addition, both give off great amounts of heat as they decay, enough to make "the soup" boil furiously for years.

The waste liquid goes into enormous concrete-encased steel tanks, some more than a million gallons in capacity. Depending upon the tank design, the liquid is either cooled for years or simply allowed to boil (with its steam siphoned off to prevent tank rupture). Either way, the liquid loses much of its heat and radioactivity within a few years.

The problem is that the tanks wear out—to say nothing of their vulnerability to accidents—while some radioisotopes within them remain hazardous, in human terms, almost forever. (Strontium-90 and cesium-137 are considered hazardous for 600 years and plutonium for a half-million.) Already there have been 15 recorded cases of tank failure, the 11 at Hanford and four at Savannah River. In one mishap at Savannah River, about 700 gallons of intensely radioactive waste overwhelmed safety devices and soaked into the ground.

LONGER THAN HISTORY

Clearly, the AEC and its critics agree, a more permanent solution is needed. "We really can't talk about this in terms of 'waste disposal,'" says Mr. Tamplin. "It's 'waste guardianship.' . . . Somebody is going to have to watch this stuff . . . for longer than the history of our country and, in the case of plutonium, longer than the recorded history of man."

The AEC has yet to decide upon a "final" solution to its weapons-related wastes. In the interim, it is solidifying much of them in the tanks they now occupy. But the agency does have a plan for the growing volume of commercial wastes: Solidification and shipment to the salt mine here at Lyons.

Many scientists, inside and outside the AEC, endorse this plan as the safest, surest available. Salt beds are dry and extremely stable geologic formations. Rock salt approximately equals concrete as a gamma ray shield and is so plastic under heat and stress that fissures are self-healing.

Beginning in 1975, if AEC plans hold, ordinary railroad cars would start hauling in barrels and containers of "low-level" wastes for burial here. At full-scale operation, 200 to 400 carloads might be coming here each year.

DEFYING THE IMAGINATION

The "high-level" wastes would start arriving about 1976. Concentrated and solidified, they might take the form of a greenish-black glassy substance, a ceramic-like material or a granular powder. This would be packed inside steel cylinders, each containing wastes so enormously radioactive as to almost defy imagination. . . .

By 1990, when the disposal operation would be in full swing, some 1,200 or more cylinders would be arriving here each year—shipped in enormous 50 or 100-ton lead "casks" to contain their gamma radiation.

Once here, the casks would be unloaded by remote control behind heavy shielding. The cylinders would then be lowered to the caverns below and transported by a remote-controlled vehicle to their burial tunnels, holes drilled into the tunnel floor. Eventually the entire tunnel would be filled with crushed salt.

TAKING THE LONG VIEW

The strontium and cesium within the cylinders would make them hot enough eventually to raise the temperature within the underground caverns to 200 degrees or more. This impresses laymen, but AEC engineers seem to take it in stride. Conducting a group of Lyons townsfolk through the mine, an AEC official assured them that "the heat drops off very rapidly. It would be essentially done . . . in a couple of hundred years." . . .

Questions about this project may seem mild, however, compared to the controversy likely to erupt if the AEC goes ahead with another proposal under evaluation. This is "Project Bedrock," the plan to pump millions of gallons of high-level liquid waste into a cavern below the Tuscaloosa Aquifer.

ECONOMY GETS PRIORITY

The project here at Lyons is only for commercially related wastes; the AEC's enormous stores of high-level weapons-related wastes still remain. It seems generally agreed—even among AEC officials—that the safest answer to these wastes, too, is solidification and salt mine burial. Nevertheless, the

AEC is seriously considering the bedrock plan, which another of its own scientific advisory committees not only described as "in its essence dangerous" but also predicted would be sure to "lead to public controversy."

Economy appears to be the foremost consideration. AEC officials say admittedly inexact estimates indicate it might cost 10 times as much to solidify the wastes and bury them in salt mines as to pump them into bedrock caverns. Another consideration: Project Bedrock would allow on-site disposal, eliminating potentially hazardous overland shipments. Finally, AEC officials argue, if Project Bedrock proves safe enough it's simply wasting money to buy an additional margin of safety.

The big questions, of course, are whether the wastes would seep upward through fissures in the bedrock into the acquifer itself—and, if so, how soon?

A majority of the AEC advisory committee—in a critical 1966 report that the AEC suppressed until 1970—concluded the risks of this happening were simply too great. In one of several projections, the committee theorized that wastes could possibly reach fresh water within 100 years; they will be hazardous for at least 600 years. A narrow committee majority recommended that the AEC abandon even attempts to study the project.

"You could never prove, even by all sorts of (exploratory) drilling, that bedrock storage would be as safe as solidification and storage in a salt mine," says Earl Cook, a Texas geographer who was executive director of the committee. "The only way you could be sure is to put this stuff down and wait and see. Unfortunately, that's the way we make too many decisions these days." . . .

The agency says it plans to spend $1.3 million for preliminary work and at least $10 million to sink an exploratory shaft and tunnels. If tests prove favorable, routine pumping of the wastes into the cavern probably would start in the late 1970s. The agency might then go ahead with a similar project for the Hanford wastes. "We won't go ahead with (Project Bedrock) until we're sure it's absolutely safe," pledges Chairman Seaborg.

But, as AEC officials themselves testify, few problems in the arcane world of radioactive waste lend themselves to "absolute" answers.

"I'm often asked, 'Can you be absolutely sure this or that is safe,' " says John A. Erlewine, the AEC's assistant general manager for operations. "My invariable answer is 'No, I'm not absolutely sure of anything on this earth.' "

The Morality of Science

AMERICA IN THE TECHNETRONIC AGE

Zbigniew Brzezinski

Ours is no longer the conventional revolutionary era; we are entering a novel metamorphic phase in human history. The world is on the eve of a transformation more dramatic in its historic and human consequences than that wrought either by the French or the Bolshevik revolutions. Viewed from a long perspective, these famous revolutions merely scratched the surface of the human condition. The changes they precipitated involved alterations in the distribution of power and property within society; they did not affect the essence of individual and social existence. Life—personal and organised—continued much as before, even though some of its external forms (primarily political) were substantially altered. Shocking though it may sound to their acolytes, by the year 2000 it will be accepted that Robespierre and Lenin were mild reformers.

Unlike the revolutions of the past, the developing metamorphosis will have no charismatic leaders with strident doctrines, but its impact will be far more profound. Most of the change that has so far taken place in human history has been gradual—with the great "revolutions" being mere punctuation marks to a slow, eludible process. In contrast, the approaching transformation will come more rapidly and will have deeper consequences for the way and even perhaps for the meaning of human life than anything experienced by the generations that preceded us.

America is already beginning to experience these changes and in the course of so doing it is becoming a "technetronic" society: a society that is shaped culturally, psychologically, socially and economically by the impact of technology and electronics, particularly computers and communications. The industrial process no longer is the principal determinant of social change, altering the mores, the social structure and the values of society. This change is separating the United States from the rest of the world, prompting a further fragmentation among an increasingly differentiated mankind and imposing upon Americans a special obligation to ease the pains of the resulting confrontation.

THE TECHNETRONIC SOCIETY

The far-reaching innovations we are about to experience will be the result primarily of the impact of science and technology on man and his society, especially in the developed world. Recent years have seen a proliferation of exciting and challenging literature on the future. Much of it is serious, and not mere science-fiction. Moreover, both in the United States and, to a lesser degree, in Western Europe a number of systematic, scholarly efforts have been designed to project, predict, and possess what the future holds for us. Curiously, very little has been heard on this theme from the Communist World, even though Communist doctrinarians are the first to claim their 19th-century ideology holds a special pass-key to the 21st century.

The work in progress indicates that men living in the developed world will undergo during the next several decades a mutation potentially as basic as that experienced through the slow process of evolution from animal to human experience. The difference, however, is that the process will be telescoped in time—and hence the shock effect of the change may be quite profound. Human conduct will become less spontaneous and less mysterious —more predetermined and subject to deliberate "programming." Man will increasingly possess the capacity to determine the sex of his children, to affect through drugs the extent of their intelligence and to modify and control their personalities. The human brain will acquire expanded powers, with computers becoming as routine an extension of man's reasoning as automobiles have been of man's mobility. The human body will be improved and its durability extended: some estimate that during the next century the average life-span could reach approximately 120 years.

These developments will have major social impact. The prolongation of life will alter our values, our career patterns, and our social relationships. New forms of social control may be needed to limit the indiscriminate exercise by individuals of their new powers. The possibility of extensive chemical mind-control, the danger of loss of individuality inherent in extensive transplantation, and the feasibility of manipulation of the genetic structure will call for a social definition of common criteria of restraint as well as of utilisation. Scientists predict with some confidence that by the end of this century, computers will reason as well as man, and will be able to engage in "creative" thought; wedded to robots or to "laboratory beings," they could act like humans. The makings of a most complex—and perhaps bitter— philosophical and political dialogue about the nature of man are self-evident in these developments.

Other discoveries and refinements will further alter society as we now know it. The information revolution, including extensive information storage, instant retrieval, and eventually push-button visual and sound availability of needed data in almost any private home, will transform the character of institutionalised collective education. The same techniques could serve to impose well-nigh total political surveillance on every citizen, putting into much sharper relief than is the case today the question of privacy. Cybernetics and automation will revolutionise working habits, with leisure becoming the practice and active work the exception—and a privilege reserved for the most talented. The achievement-oriented society might give way to the amusement-focused society, with essentially spectator spectacles (mass sports, TV) providing an opiate for increasingly purposeless masses.

But while for the masses life will grow longer and time will seem to expand, for the activist élite time will become a rare commodity. Indeed, even the élite's sense of time will alter. Already now speed dictates the pace of our lives—instead of the other way around. As the speed of transportation increases, largely by its own technological momentum, man discovers that he has no choice but to avail himself of that acceleration, either to keep up with others or because he thinks he can thus accomplish more. This will be especially true of the élite, for whom an expansion in leisure time does not seem to be in the cards. Thus as speed expands, time contracts—and the pressures on the élite increase.

By the end of this century the citizens of the more developed countries will live predominantly in cities—hence almost surrounded by man-made environment. Confronting nature could be to them what facing the elements was to our forefathers: meeting the unknown and not necessarily liking it. Enjoying a personal standard of living that (in some countries) may reach almost $10,000 per head, eating artificial food, speedily commuting from one corner of the country to work in another, in continual visual contact with their employer, government, or family, consulting their annual calendars to establish on which day it will rain or shine, our descendants will be shaped almost entirely by what they themselves create and control.

But even short of these far-reaching changes, the transformation that is now taking place is already creating a society increasingly unlike its industrial predecessor. In the industrial society, technical knowledge was applied primarily to one specific end: the acceleration and improvement of production techniques. Social consequences were a later by-product of this paramount concern. In the technetronic society, scientific and technological knowledge, in addition to enhancing productive capabilities, quickly spills over to affect directly almost all aspects of life.

This is particularly evident in the case of the impact of communications and computers. Communications create an extraordinarily interwoven society, in continuous visual, audial, and increasingly close contact among almost all its members—electronically interacting, sharing instantly most intense social experiences, prompting far greater personal involvement, with their consciousnesses shaped in a sporadic manner fundamentally different (as McLuhan has noted) from the literate (or pamphleteering) mode of transmitting information, characteristic of the industrial age. The growing capacity for calculating instantly most complex interactions and the increasing availability of bio-chemical means of human control increase the potential scope of self-conscious direction, and thereby also the pressures to direct, to choose, and to change.

The consequence is a society that differs from the industrial one in a variety of economic, political and social aspects. The following examples may be briefly cited to summarise some of the contrasts:

1. In an industrial society, the mode of production shifts from agriculture to industry, with the use of muscle and animals supplanted by machine-operation. In the technetronic society, industrial employment yields to services, with automation and cybernetics replacing individual operation of machines.

2. Problems of employment and unemployment—not to speak of the earlier stage of the urban socialisation of the post-rural labour force—dominate the relationship between employers, labour, and the market in the industrial society; assuring minimum welfare to the new industrial masses is a source of major concern. In the emerging new society, questions relating to skill-obsolescence, security, vacations, leisure, and profit-sharing dominate the relationship; the matter of psychic well-being of millions of relatively secure but potentially aimless lower-middle class blue collar workers becomes a growing problem.

3. Breaking down traditional barriers to education, thus creating the basic point of departure for social advancement, is a major goal of social reformers in the industrial society. Education, available for limited and specific periods of time, is initially concerned with overcoming illiteracy, and subsequently with technical training, largely based on written, sequential reasoning. In the technetronic society, not only has education become universal but advanced training is available to almost all who have the basic talents. Quantity-training is reinforced

by far greater emphasis on quality-selection. The basic problem is to discover the most effective techniques for the rational exploitation of social talent. Latest communication and calculating techniques are applied to that end. The educational process, relying much more on visual and audial devices, becomes extended in time, while the flow of new knowledge necessitates more and more frequent refresher studies.

4. In the industrial society social leadership shifts from the traditional rural-aristocratic to an urban "plutocratic" élite. Newly acquired wealth is its foundation, and intense competition the outlet—as well as the stimulus—for its energy. In the post-industrial technetronic society plutocratic pre-eminence comes under a sustained challenge from the political leadership which itself is increasingly permeated by individuals possessing special skills and intellectual talents. Knowledge becomes a tool of power, and the effective mobilisation of talent an important way for acquiring power.

5. The university in an industrial society—rather in contrast to the medieval times—is an aloof ivory-tower, the repository of irrelevant, even if respected wisdom, and, for only a brief time, the watering fountain for budding members of the established social élite. In the technetronic society, the university becomes an intensely involved *think-tank*, the source of much sustained political planning and social innovation.

6. The turmoil inherent in the shift from the rigidly traditional rural to urban existence engenders an inclination to seek total answers to social dilemmas, thus causing ideologies to thrive in the industrial society. In the technetronic society, increasing ability to reduce social conflicts to quantifiable and measurable dimensions reinforces the trend towards a more pragmatic problem-solving approach to social issues.

7. The activisation of hitherto passive masses makes for intense political conflicts in the industrial society over such matters as disenfranchisement and the right to vote. The issue of political participation is a crucial one. In the technetronic age, the question increasingly is one of ensuring real participation in decisions that seem too complex and too far-removed from the average citizen. Political alienation becomes a problem. Similarly, the issue of political equality of the sexes gives way to a struggle for the sexual equality of women. In the industrial society, woman—the operator of machines—ceases to be physically inferior to the male, a consideration of some importance in rural life, and she begins to demand her political rights. In the emerging society, automation discriminates equally against males and females; intellectual talent is computable; the pill encourages sexual equality.

8. The newly enfranchised masses are coordinated in the industrial society through trade unions and political parties, and integrated by

relatively simple and somewhat ideological programmes. Moreover, political attitudes are influenced by appeals to nationalist sentiments, communicated through the massive growth of newspapers, relying, naturally, on native tongues. In the technetronic society, the trend would seem to be towards the aggregation of the individual support of millions of uncoordinated citizens, easily within the reach of magnetic and attractive personalities effectively exploiting the latest communication techniques to manipulate emotions and control reason. Reliance on TV—and hence the tendency to replace language with imagery, with the latter unlimited by national confines (and also including coverage for such matters as hunger in India or war scenes)—tends to create a somewhat more cosmopolitan, though highly impressionistic, involvement in global affairs.

9. Economic power in the industrial society tends to be personalised, either in the shape of great *entrepreneurs* like Henry Ford or bureaucratic industrialisers like Kaganovich in Russia, or Minc in Poland. The tendency towards de-personalisation of economic power is stimulated in the next stage by the appearance of a highly complex interdependence between governmental institutions (including the military), scientific establishments, and industrial organisations. As economic power becomes inseparably linked with political power, it becomes more invisible and the sense of individual futility increases.

10. Relaxation and escapism in the industrial society, in its more intense forms, is a carry-over from the rural drinking bout, in which intimate friends and family would join. Bars and saloons—or fraternities—strive to recreate the atmosphere of intimacy. In the technetronic society social life tends to be so atomised, even though communications (especially TV) make for unprecedented immediacy of social experience, that group intimacy cannot be recreated through the artificial stimulation of externally convivial group behaviour. The new interest in drugs seeks to create intimacy through introspection, allegedly by expanding consciousness.

Eventually, these changes and many others, including the ones that affect much more directly the personality and quality of the human being itself, will make the technetronic society as different from the industrial as the industrial became from the agrarian.

THE COMING BLOODLESS REVOLUTION

R. Buckminster Fuller

YOU CAN'T REFORM A VACUUM

. . . The university student, having attained his first freedom of initiative, his optimum level of metabolic efficiency, bodily coordination, and general outlook, finds that his idealism is concurrently exposed to an awareness of powerful intellectual and technical disciplines. At the same time he is the recipient of frequent science-technology breakthrough news, such as under-the-polar-ice passages of atomic submarines and new achievements in rock-etry and electronics. He also receives an overabundance of news concerning world want and political stresses that break into ever more frequent crises.

Logically, the student becomes exasperated and says, "Why can't we make the world work? All the negative nonsense is the consequence of outworn, ignorant biases of the old-timers. Let's join forces and set things to rights." Parading in multitudes, students demand that their political leaders take steps to bring about peace and plenty. The fallacy of this lies in their mistaken, age-old assumption that the problem is one of political reform. The fact is that the politicians are faced with a vacuum, and you can't reform a vacuum. The vacuum is the apparent world condition of not enough to go around—not enough for even a majority of mankind to survive more than half of its potential life span. It is a "you or me to the death" situation that leads from impasse to ultimate showdown by arms. Thus more and more students around the world are learning of the new and surprising alternative to politics—the design science revolution, which alone can solve the problem.

The students are thrilled to realize that it is themselves they must turn to in order to make the world work, through practical use of their university science and technology resources and their laboratory-supported design science capabilities. The students know that they need no more license to invent the tools that will make the world work than the Wright brothers needed a license to invent one of the most needed more-with-less tools—the airplane. The student's task is clear-cut. It is to increase the over-all efficiency of the world's mechanical devices from their present 4 per cent to an over-all efficiency of 12 per cent. This is easy, since over-all efficiencies up to 80 per cent are now feasible. The students know that if they

413

invent the right tools, the tools will be used, given the right emergency. And they know that their design science revolution is bound to work because the emergencies to foster its realization are already here. Their revolution is a bloodless revolution that brings peace in the only way it may ever become effective—by elimination of the physical wants that always underlie war.

MAN'S FOURTH ADJUSTMENT

Harlow Shapley

The scattering of galaxies, the habits of macromolecules, and the astounding abundance of stars are forcing those who ponder such matters to a further adjustment of their concept of the place and functioning of man in the material universe.

In the history of the evolving human mind, with its increasing knowledge of the surrounding world, there must have been a time when the philosophers of the early tribes began to realize that the world was not simply anthropocentric—centered on man himself. The geocentric concept became common doctrine. It accepted a universe centered on the earth. This first adjustment was only mildly deflationary to the human ego, for man appeared to surpass all other living forms.

The second adjustment in the relation of man to the physical universe, that is, the abandonment of the earth-center theory, was not generally acceptable until the sixteenth-century Copernican revolution soundly established the heliocentric concept—the theory of a universe centered on the sun. Man is a stubborn adherent to official dogma. Eventually, however, he accepted the sun as the center not only of the local family of planets, but also of the total sidereal assemblage, and long held that view.

He had slowly given up the earth-center. But why, in spite of increasing evidence, did he then hold so persistently to the heliocentric view? Was it only because of vanity—his feeling, nourished by the unscientific dogmatists, that he is of paramount significance in the world? There were several better reasons for his second delusion. For example, the Milky Way is a great circle, a band of starlight that divides the sky into two nearly equal parts. It is of about the same brightness in all its parts. By implication, therefore, the sun and earth are centrally located. Also, the numbers of stars seemed to the early census-takers to fall off with distance from the sun as though it were central, and such a position for his star among the stellar millions brought to man a dignity of position not at all disagreeable.

The shift from the geocentric to the heliocentric concept doubtless had some philosophical impact in the sixteenth century, but not much. After all, the hot, turbulent, gaseous sun is no place for the delicate biology in which man finds himself at or near the top. Earth-center or sun-center seemed to make little difference to cosmic thinking during the past four centuries. But then, less than forty years ago, came the inescapable need for a third adjustment—one that should have deeply affected and to some extent has disturbed man's thoughts about his place, his career and his cosmic importance.

This shift has dug deeply into man's pride and self-assurance, for it has carried with it the knowledge of the appalling number of galaxies. He could accept rather cheerfully the Darwinian evidence of his animal origin, for that still left him at the summit of all terrestrial organisms. But the abandonment of the heliocentric universe on the authority of the astronomical evidence was certainly deflationary, from the standpoint of man's position in the material world, however flattering it was to the human mind.

The "galactocentric universe" suddenly puts the earth and its life near the edge of one great galaxy in a universe of millions of galaxies. Man becomes peripheral among the billions of stars of his own Milky Way; and according to the revelations of paleontology and geochemistry, he is recent and apparently ephemeral in the unrolling of cosmic time. And here is a somber or happy thought, whichever mood you prefer. There is no retreat! The inquiring human has passed the point of no return. We cannot restore geocentrism or heliocentrism. The apes, eagles and honeybees may be wholly content to be peripheral ephemerals, and thus miss the great vision that opens before us. For them, egocentrism and lococentrism may suffice; for us, no! And since we cannot go back to the cramped but comfortable past (without sacrificing completely our cultures and civilizations), we go forward and find there is more to the story.

The downgrading of the earth and sun, and the elevation of the galaxies, is not the end of this progress of scientific pilgrims through philosophic fields. The need for a further jolting adjustment now appears—not wholly unexpected by workers in science, nor wholly the result of one or two scientific revelations.

Our new problem concerns the spread of life throughout the universe. As unsolicited spokesmen for all the earthly organisms of land, sea and air, we ask the piquant question: Are we alone?

From among the many measures and thoughts that promote this fourth adjustment of *Homo sapiens sapiens* in the galaxy of galaxies (the metagalaxy), I select three phenomena as most demanding of our consideration.

The first refers to the number of stars, the second to catastrophes of ancient days, and the third to the origin of self-duplicating molecules.

To the ancients, only a few thousand stars were known; to the early telescopes, however, it was a million; and that astounding number has increased spectacularly with every telescopic advance. Finally, with the discovery that the "extragalactic nebulae" are in reality galaxies, each with its hundreds or thousands of millions of stars, and with our inability to "touch metagalactic bottom" with the greatest telescopes, we are led to accept the existence of more than 10^{20} stars in our explorable universe, perhaps many more.

The significance of this discovery, or rather of this uncovering, is that we have at hand—that is, the universe contains—more than one hundred million million million sources of light and warmth for whatever planets accompany these radiant stars.

The second phenomenon, the expanding metagalaxy, bears on the question: Do planets accompany at least some of the stars that pour forth energy suitable for the complex biological activity that we call life?

We now accept the observational evidence for an expanding universe of galaxies. The rapid expansion of the measurable part of the metagalaxy implies an increasingly greater concentration of these cosmic units (galaxies) as we go back in time. A few thousand million years ago, the average density of matter in space was so great that collisions, near encounters, and gravitational disruptions were of necessity frequent. The crust of the earth, radioactively measured, is also a few thousand million years old, and therefore the earth and the other planets of our sun's system were "born" in those days of turbulence. At that time countless millions of other planetary systems must have developed, for our sun is of a very common stellar variety. (Miss Cannon's catalogue of spectra reports forty thousand sun-like stars in our immediate neighborhood.)

Other ways in which planets may form—other than this primitive process of the early days—are recognized. The contraction of protostars out of the hypothetical primeval gas, giving birth on the way to protoplanets, is an evolutionary process now widely favored. It would imply the existence of countless planets.

The head-on-collision theory of planetary origin has also been considered. But the stars are now so widely dispersed that collisions must be exceedingly rare—so very unlikely, in fact, that we might claim uniqueness for our planetary system and for ourselves if planet birth depended only on such procedure. The expanding universe discovery, however, has shown the crowded conditions when our earth was born.

Passing over details, we state the relevant conclusion: *Millions of planetary systems must exist.* Whatever the method of origin, planets may be the common heritage of all stars except those so situated that planetary materials would be swallowed or cast off through gravitational action. In passing we note that astrophysicists have shown that our kinds of chemistry and physics prevail throughout the explorable universe. There is nothing uncommon here or now.

Remembering our 10^{20} stars and the high probability of millions of planets with suitable chemistry, dimensions and distance from their nutrient stars, we are ready for the question: On some of these planets is there actually life; or is that biochemical operation strangely limited to our planet, No. 3 in the family of the sun, which is a run-of-the-mill star located in the outer part of a galaxy that contains a hundred thousand million other stars —and this galaxy but one of millions already on the records?

Is life thus restricted? Of course not. We are not alone. And we can accept life's wide dispersion still more confidently when our third argument is indicated.

To put it briefly: biochemistry and microbiology, with the assistance of geophysics, astronomy and other sciences, have gone so far in bridging the gap between the inanimate and the living that we can no longer doubt but that whenever the physics, chemistry and climates are right on a planet's surface, life will emerge and persist.

This consequence has long been suspected by scientists, but the many researches of the past few years in the field of macromolecules have made it unnecessary any longer to postulate miracles and the supernatural for the origin of life.

The astronomical demonstration of the great number of stars, and therefore the abundance of life opportunities, naturally leads to the belief that countless planets have had long and varied experience with biochemical evolution. Thousands of kinds of terrestrial animals are known to develop neurotic complexes, that is "intelligence." It comes naturally. No higher animal is without it in high degree. Could it be otherwise on another life-bearing planet?

And here we must end with the simple but weighty proposal: There is no reason in the world to believe that our own mental stature has not been excelled by that of sentient beings elsewhere. I am not suggesting, however, that *Homo* is repeated. There are a million variations on the animal theme.

In conclusion, I need not emphasize the possible relevance to philosophy and perhaps to religion of this fourth adjustment in man's view of himself in the material universe.

SHAKY

Brad Darrach

It looked at first glance like a Good Humor wagon sadly in need of a spring paint job. But instead of a tinkly little bell on top of its box-shaped body there was this big metallic whangdoodle that came rearing up, full of lenses and cables, like a junk-sculpture gargoyle.

"Meet Shaky," said the young scientist who was showing me through the Stanford Research Institute. "The first electronic person."

I looked for a twinkle in the scientist's eye. There wasn't any. Sober as an equation, he sat down at an input terminal and typed out a terse instruction which was fed into Shaky's "brain," a computer set up in a nearby room: PUSH THE BLOCK OFF THE PLATFORM.

Something inside Shaky began to hum. A large glass prism shaped like a thick slice of pie and set in the middle of what passed for his face spun faster and faster till it dissolved into a glare. Then his superstructure made a slow 360° turn and his face leaned forward and seemed to be staring at the floor. As the hum rose to a whir, Shaky rolled slowly out of the room, rotated his superstructure again and turned left down the corridor at about four miles an hour, still staring at the floor.

"Guides himself by watching the baseboards," the scientist explained as we hurried to keep up. At every open door Shaky stopped, turned his head, inspected the room, turned away and rolled on to the next open door. In the fourth room he saw what he was looking for: a platform one foot high and eight feet long with a large wooden block sitting on it. He went in, then stopped short in the middle of the room and stared for about five seconds at the platform. I stared at it too.

"He'll never make it," I found myself thinking. "His wheels are too small." All at once I got gooseflesh. "*Shaky*," I realized, "*is thinking the same thing I am thinking!*"

Shaky was also thinking faster. He rotated his head slowly till his eye came to rest on a wide shallow ramp that was lying on the floor on the other side of the room. Whirring briskly, he crossed to the ramp, semicircled it and then pushed it straight across the floor till the high end of the ramp hit the platform. Rolling back a few feet, he cased the situation again and discovered that only one corner of the ramp was touching the platform. Rolling quickly to the far side of the ramp, he nudged it till the gap closed. Then he swung around, charged up the slope, located the block and gently pushed it off the platform.

Compared to the glamorous electronic elves who trundle across television

screens, Shaky may not seem like much. No death-ray eyes, no secret trans-
istorized lust for nubile lab technicians. But in fact he is a historic achievement. The task I saw him perform would tax the talents of a lively 4-year-
old child, and the men who over the last two years have headed up the
Shaky project—Charles Rosen, Nils Nilsson and Bert Raphael—say he is
capable of far more sophisticated routines. Armed with the right devices and
programmed in advance with basic instructions, Shaky could travel about
the moon for months at a time and, without a single beep of direction from
the earth, could gather rocks, drill cores, make surveys and photographs and
even decide to lay plank bridges over crevices he had made up his mind to
cross.

The center of all this intricate activity is Shaky's "brain," a remarkably
programmed computer with a capacity of more than 7 million "bits" of
information. In defiance of the soothing conventional view that the computer
is just a glorified abacus that cannot possibly challenge the human monopoly
of reason, Shaky's brain demonstrates that machines can think. Variously
defined, thinking includes such processes as "exercising the powers of judgment" and "reflecting for the purpose of reaching a conclusion." In some of
these respects—among them powers of recall and mathematical agility—
Shaky's brain can think better than the human mind.

Marvin Minsky of MIT's Project Mac, a 42-year-old polymath who has
made major contributions to Artificial Intelligence, recently told me with
quiet certitude: "In from three to eight years we will have a machine with
the general intelligence of an average human being. I mean a machine that
will be able to read Shakespeare, grease a car, play office politics, tell a joke,
have a fight. At that point the machine will begin to educate itself with
fantastic speed. In a few months it will be at genius level and a few months
after that its powers will be incalculable."

I had to smile at my instant credulity—the nervous sort of smile that
comes when you realize you've been taken in by a clever piece of science
fiction. When I checked Minsky's prophecy with other people working on
Artificial Intelligence, however, many of them said that Minsky's timetable
might be somewhat wishful—"give us 15 years," was a common remark—
but all agreed that there would be such a machine and that it could precipi-
tate the third Industrial Revolution, wipe out war and poverty and roll up
centuries of growth in science, education and the arts. At the same time a
number of computer scientists fear that the godsend may become a Golem.
"Man's limited mind," says Minsky, "may not be able to control such immense mentalities." . . .

Shaky is not limited to thinking in strictly logical forms. He is also learning to think by analogy—that is, to make himself at home in a new situation,
much the way human beings do, by finding in it something that resembles a
situation he already knows, and on the basis of this resemblance to make

and carry out decisions. For example, knowing how to roll up a ramp onto a platform, a slightly more advanced Shaky equipped with legs instead of wheels and given a similar problem could very quickly figure out how to use steps in order to reach the platform.

But as Shaky grows and his decisions become more complicated, more like decisions in real life, he will need a way of thinking that is more flexible than either logic or analogy. He will need a way to do the sort of ingenious, practical "soft thinking" that can stop gaps, chop knots, make the best of bad situations and even, when time is short, solve a problem by making a shrewd guess.

The route toward "soft thinking" has been charted by the founding fathers of Artificial Intelligence, Allen Newell and Herbert Simon of Carnegie-Mellon University. Before Newell and Simon, computers solved (or failed to solve) nonmathematical problems by a hopelessly tedious process of trial and error. "It was like looking up a name in a big-city telephone book that nobody has bothered to arrange in alphabetical order," says one computer scientist. Newell and Simon figured out a simple scheme—modeled, says Minsky, on "the way Herb Simon's mind works." Using the Newell-Simon method, a computer does not immediately search for answers, but is programmed to sort through general categories first, trying to locate the one where the problem and solution would most likely fit. When the correct category is found, the computer then works within it, but does not rummage endlessly for an absolutely perfect solution, which often does not exist. Instead, it accepts (as people do) a good solution, which for most non-numerical problems is good enough. Using this type of programming, an MIT professor wrote into a computer the criteria a certain banker used to pick stocks for his trust accounts. In a test, the program picked the same stock the banker did in 21 of 25 cases. In the other four cases the stocks the program picked were so much like the ones the banker picked that he said they would have suited the portfolio just as well. . . .

With very little change in program and equipment, Shaky now could do work in a number of limited environments: warehouses, libraries, assembly lines. To operate successfully in more loosely structured scenes, he will need far more extensive, more nearly human abilities to remember and to think. His memory, which supplies the rest of his system with a massive and continuous flow of essential information, is already large, but at the next step of progress it will probably become monstrous. Big memories are essential to complex intelligence. The largest standard computer now on the market can store about 36 million "bits" of information in a six-foot cube, and a computer already planned will be able to store more than a trillion "bits" (one estimate of the capacity of a human brain) in the same space.

Size and efficiency of hardware are less important, though, than sophistication in programming. In a dozen universities, psychologists are trying to create computers with well-defined humanoid personalities. Aldous, developed at the University of Texas by a psychologist named John Loehlin, is the first attempt to endow a computer with emotion. Aldous is programmed with three emotions and three responses, which he signals. Love makes him signal approach, fear makes him signal withdrawal, anger makes him signal attack. By varying the intensity and probability of these three responses, the personality of Aldous can be drastically changed. In addition, two or more different Aldouses can be programmed into a computer and made to interact. They go through rituals of getting acquainted, making friends, having fights.

Even more peculiarly human is the program created by Stanford psychoanalyst Kenneth M. Colby. Colby has developed a Freudian complex in his computer by setting up conflicts between beliefs (I must love Father, I hate Father). He has also created a computer psychiatrist and when he lets the two programs interact, the "patient" resolves its conflicts just as a human being does—by forgetting about them, lying about them or talking truthfully about them with the "psychiatrist." Such a large store of possible reactions has been programmed into the computer—and there are so many possible sequences of question and answer—that Colby can never be exactly sure what the "patient" will decide to do.

Colby is currently attempting to broaden the range of emotional reactions his computer can experience. "But so far," one of his assistants says, "we have not achieved computer orgasm."

Knowledge that comes out of these experiments in "sophistication" is helping to lead toward the ultimate sophistication—the autonomous computer that will be able to write its own programs and then use them in an approximation of the independent, imaginative way a human being dreams up projects and carries them out. Such a machine is now being developed at Stanford by Joshua Lederberg (the Nobel Prize-winning geneticist) and Edward Feigenbaum. In using a computer to solve a series of problems in chemistry, Lederberg and Feigenbaum realized their progress was being held back by the long, tedious job of programming their computer for each new problem. "That started me wondering," says Lederberg. "Couldn't we save ourselves work by teaching the computer how we write these programs, and then let it program itself?"

Basically, a computer program is nothing more than a set of instructions (or rules of procedure) applicable to a particular problem at hand. A computer can tell you that $1 + 1 = 2$—not because it has that fact stored away and then finds it, but because it has been programmed with the rules for simple addition. Lederberg decided you could give a computer some general rules for programming; and now, based on his initial success in teaching a computer to write programs in chemistry, he is convinced that computers can do this in any field—that they will be able in the reasonably near future to write programs that write programs that write programs . . .

This prospect raises a haunting question: won't computers then be just as independent as human beings are? Peter Ossorio, a philosopher at the University of Colorado who has pondered the psychology of computers, says that autonomy is part of the computer's inherent nature. "Free will," Ossorio says, "is a characteristic of serial processors—of all systems that do one thing after another and therefore have more options than they are able to use. Serial systems naturally have to make choices among alternatives. People are serial systems and so are computers."

Many computer scientists believe that people who talk about computer autonomy are indulging in a lot of cybernetic hoopla. Most of these skeptics are engineers who work mainly with technical problems in computer hardware and who are preoccupied with the mechanical operations of these machines. Other computer experts seriously doubt that the finer psychic processes of the human mind will ever be brought within the scope of circuitry, but they see autonomy as a prospect and are persuaded that the social impact will be immense.

Up to a point, says Minsky, the impact will be positive—"The machine dehumanized man, but it could rehumanize him." By automating all routine work and even tedious low-grade thinking, computers could free billions of people to spend most of their time doing pretty much as they damn please. But such progress could also produce quite different results. "It might happen," says Herbert Simon, "that the Puritan work ethic would crumble too fast and masses of people would succumb to the diseases of leisure." An even greater danger may lie in man's increasing and by now irreversible dependency upon the computer. The electronic circuit has already replaced the dynamo at the center of technological civilization. Many U.S. industries and businesses, the telephone and power grids, the airlines and the mail service, the systems for distributing food and, not least, the big government bureaucracies would be instantly disrupted and threatened with complete breakdown if the computers they depend on were disconnected. The disorder in Western Europe and the Soviet Union would be almost as severe.

What's more, our dependency on computers seems certain to increase at a rapid rate. Doctors are already beginning to rely on computer diagnosis and computer-administered postoperative care. Artificial Intelligence experts believe that fiscal planners in both industry and government, caught up in deepening economic complexities, will gradually delegate to computers nearly complete control of the national (and even the global) economy. In the interests of efficiency, cost-cutting and speed of reaction, the Department of Defense may well be forced more and more to surrender human direction of military policies to machines that plan strategy and tactics. In time, say the scientists, diplomats will abdicate judgment to computers that predict, say, Russian policy by analyzing their own simulations of the entire Soviet state and of the personalities—or the computers—in power there.

Man, in short, is coming to depend on thinking machines to make decisions that involve his vital interests and even his survival as a species. What guarantee do we have that in making these decisions the machines will always consider our best interests? There is no guarantee unless we provide it, says Minsky, and it will not be easy to provide—after all, man has not been able to guarantee that his own decisions are made in his own best interests. Any supercomputer could be programmed to test important decisions for their value to human beings, but such a computer, being autonomous, could also presumably write a program that countermanded these "ethical" instructions. There need be no question of computer malice here, merely a matter of computer creativity overcoming external restraints.

The men at Project MAC foresee an even more unsettling possibility. A computer that can program a computer, they reason, will be followed in fairly short order by a computer that can design and build a computer vastly more complex and intelligent than itself—and so on indefinitely.

"I'm afraid the spiral could get out of control," says Minsky. It is possible, of course, to monitor computers, to make an occasional check on what they are doing in there; but even now it is difficult to monitor the larger computers, and the computers of the future may be far too complex to keep track of.

Why not just unplug the thing if it got out of hand? "Switching off a system that defends a country or runs its entire economy," says Minsky, "is like cutting off its food supply. Also, the Russians are only about three years behind us in A-1 work. With our system switched off, they would have us at their mercy."

The problem of computer control will have to be solved, Minsky and Papert believe, before computers are put in charge of systems essential to society's survival. If a computer directing the nation's economy or its nuclear defenses ever rated its own efficiency above its ethical obligation, it could destroy man's social order—or destroy man. "Once the computers got control," says Minsky, "we might never get it back. We would survive at their sufferance. If we're lucky, they might decide to keep us as pets."

But even if no such catastrophe were to occur, say the people at Project MAC, the development of a machine more intelligent than man will surely deal a severe shock to man's sense of his own worth. Even Shaky is disturbing, and a creature that deposed man from the pinnacle of creation might tempt us to ask ourselves: Is the human brain outmoded? Has evolution in protoplasm been replaced by evolution in circuitry?

"And why not?" Minsky replied when I recently asked him these questions. "After all, the human brain is just a computer that happens to be made out of meat."

I stared at him—he was smiling. This man, I thought, has lived too long in a subtle tangle of ideas and circuits. And yet men like Minsky are admirable, even heroic. They have struck out on a Promethean adventure and you can tell by a kind of afterthought in their eyes that they are haunted by what they have done. It is the others who depress me, the lesser figures in the world of Artificial Intelligence, men who contemplate infinitesimal riddles of circuitry and never once look up from their work to wonder what effect it might have upon the world they scarcely live in. And what of the people in the Pentagon who are footing most of the bill in Artificial Intelligence research? "I have warned them again and again," says Minsky, "that we are getting into very dangerous country. They don't seem to understand."

I thought of Shaky growing up in the care of these careless people—growing up to be what? No way to tell. Confused, concerned, unable to affirm or deny the warnings I had heard at Project MAC, I took my questions to computer-memory expert Ross Quillian, a nice warm guy with a house full of dogs and children, who seemed to me one of the best-balanced men in the field. I hoped he would cheer me up. Instead, he said, "I hope that man and these ultimate machines will be able to collaborate without conflict. But if they can't, we may be forced to choose sides. And if it comes to a choice, I know what mine will be." He looked me straight in the eye. "My loyalties go to intelligent life, no matter in what medium it may arise."

VII
VALUES

THE HEART OF THE MATTER

*For what is a man profited, if he shall gain
the whole world, and lose his own soul?*
MATTHEW 16:26

Sometimes it seems as if the history of our Western civilization is like one of those digital clocks where the minutes tick off in the little window and the numbers gradually get larger, except that nobody knows what is the magic number that ends our day. Our clock began with the Christian era and is now at 1972 and counting, but we don't know when it will blast off. We just have this weird sort of feeling that it is getting late, and maybe we'd better begin thinking about tomorrow.

The selections in this section draw from many kinds of sources of values for judging the worth of life. Probably it is not important to make distinctions between old values and new ones, or between social values and individual values. Who can say whether Leonidas and his Spartans at the "Hot Gates" based their decision on individual or social values? Who even knows any of their names, except Leonidas's? They were a military institution, a troop of soldiers, but nature in old times made the pass small enough so that each man had to step up and die by himself. Now, over the years, silt deposited by a river has made the pass large enough for an army, and dying individually there would be impossible.

Every system of values seems to have its individual and its social component. The Judeo-Christian system has survived for so long because it combined both components in ways that responded to the changing needs of our civilization as it grew. The one need it seems to have trouble meeting is the need for objective or scientific reality. Perhaps this deficiency isn't as important as it seems, for Eastern value systems share it, and they have survived even longer than the Western ones. The selections we have chosen will show that all value systems have their virtues and defects, just as the men who made them. There are similarities among the systems, as there are among men. And just as one man can help another, perhaps one system can modify another and make it stronger. So traditional faiths modified by science and existentialism may become stronger, if not in the eyes of The Unknowable, then in the hearts of men.

Tradition

THE APOLOGY
OF SOCRATES

Plato

Well then, fellow citizens, I must now make my defence, and must try to clear away in this brief time that calumny which you have entertained so long. I would that this might come to pass, if so it should be better for both you and me, and if it profits me to plead. But I think the task to be a hard one, and what its nature is I am by no means unaware. Still, let the outcome be as it pleases God; the law must be obeyed, and the defence be made.

Let us, then, go back and look at the original accusation from which the slander arose, the slander that gave Meletus his ground for this indictment he has lodged against me. Let us see. Precisely what did the slanderers say when they slandered? We must read their complaint as if it were a legal accusation: 'Socrates is wicked; overdoes inquiry into what occurs below the earth and in the heavens; in arguing makes the worse case win; and teaches others to do the same as he.' Such is in substance the accusation—what you actually saw in the comedy [the *Clouds*] of Aristophanes, where a man called 'Socrates' is swung about, declaring that he treads the air, and sputtering a deal of other nonsense on matters of which I have not one bit of knowledge either great or small. And I do not say so in disparagement of any science such as that, if any one is learned in such matters; I should not wish to be attacked by Meletus upon so grave a charge. But actually, fellow citizens, to me these matters are of absolutely no concern. I call the greater part of you yourselves to witness, and beg all who ever heard me in discussion to tell one another and declare it; many of you are in a position to do this. Declare to one another, therefore, whether any of you ever heard me dealing with such matters either briefly or at length. In that way you will see what all the rest amounts to of what the generality of people say concerning me. . . .

Then perhaps some one of you may be inclined to ask: 'But Socrates, what *is* the matter with you? What is the origin of these charges that are made against you? Unless you acted very differently from everybody else, surely no such story and repute would have arisen—if you did not do something other than most people do. Tell us what it is, in order to keep us from rushing to our own conclusion about you.'

That, I take it, would be fairly spoken; and I shall try to show you what it is that has given me this name and ill repute. Pray listen. Some of you, perhaps, will take me to be joking, but be assured that I shall tell you the simple truth. The fact is, fellow citizens, that I have got this name through my possession of a certain wisdom. What sort of wisdom is it? A wisdom, doubtless, that appertains to man. With respect to this, perhaps, I actually am wise; whereas those others whom I just now mentioned may possibly be wise with a wisdom more than human, or else I do not know what to say of it; as for me, I certainly do not possess it, and whoever says I do is lying, and seeks to injure me.

And, fellow citizens, do not interrupt me even if I say what seems extravagant, for the statement I shall make is not my own; instead, I shall refer you to a witness whose word can be accepted. Your witness to my wisdom, if I have any, and to its nature, is the god at Delphi. You certainly knew Chaerephon. He was a friend of mine from our youth, and a friend of your popular party as well; he shared in your late exile, and accompanied you on your return. Now you know the temper of Chaerephon, how impulsive he was in everything he undertook. Well so it was when once he went to Delphi, and made bold to ask the oracle this question—and, Gentlemen, please do not make an uproar over what I say; he asked if there was any one more wise than I. Then the Pythian oracle made response that there was no one who was wiser. To this response his brother here will bear you witness, since Chaerephon himself is dead.

Now bear in mind the reason why I tell you this. It is because I am going on to show you whence this calumny of me has sprung; for when I heard about the oracle, I communed within myself: 'What can the god be saying, and what does the riddle mean? Well I know in my own heart that I am without wisdom great or small. What is it that he means, then, in declaring me to be most wise? It cannot be that he is lying; it is not in his nature.' For a long time I continued at a loss as to his meaning, then finally decided, much against my will, to seek it in the following way.

I went to one of those who pass for wise men, feeling sure that there if anywhere I could refute the answer, and explain to the oracle: 'Here is a man that is wiser than I, but you said I was the wisest.' The man I went to see was one of our statesmen; his name I need not mention. Him I thoroughly examined, and from him, as I studied him and conversed with him, I gathered, fellow citizens, this impression. This man appeared to me to seem to be wise to others, and above all to himself, but not to be so. And then I tried to show him that he thought that he was wise, but was not. The result was that I gained his enmity and the enmity as well of many of those who were present. So, as I went away, I reasoned with myself: 'At all events I am wiser than this man is. It is quite possible that neither one of us knows anything fine and good. But this man fancies that he knows when he does not, while I, whereas I do not know, just so I do not fancy that I know. In this small item, then, at least, I seem to be wiser than he, in that I do not fancy that I know what I do not.' Thereafter I went to another man, one of those who passed for wiser than the first, and I got the same impression. Whereupon I gained his enmity as well as that of many more.

Thereafter I went from one man to another, perceiving, with grief and apprehension, that I was getting hated, but it seemed imperative to put the service of the god above all else. In my search for the meaning of the oracle I must go to all who were supposed to have some knowledge. And, fellow citizens, by the God, since I have to tell you the truth, here is pretty much what I encountered. The persons with the greatest reputation seemed to me to be the ones who were well-nigh the most deficient, as I made my search in keeping with the god's intent; whereas others of inferior reputation I found to be men superior in regard to their possession of the truth. I needs must tell you all about my wandering course, a veritable round of toils heroic, which I underwent to prove that the oracle was not to be refuted.

After the statesmen, I went to the poets, tragic, dithyrambic, and the rest. There, I thought, my ignorance would be self-evident in comparison with them. So I took those poems of theirs which seemed to me to have been most carefully wrought by them, and asked the authors what they meant, in order that I might at the same time learn from them. Well, Gentlemen, I am ashamed to tell you the truth; and yet it must be done. The fact is, pretty nearly everybody, so to say, who was present could have spoken better than the authors did about the poems they themselves had written. So here again in a short time I learned this about the poets too, that not by wisdom do they make what they compose, but by a gift of nature and an inspiration similar to that of the diviners and the oracles. These also utter many beautiful things, but understand not one of them. And such, I saw, was the experience of the poets. At the same time I perceived that their poetic gift led them to fancy that in all else, too, they were the wisest of mankind, when they were not. So I went away from them as well, believing that I had the same advantage over them as over the statesmen.

To make an end, I went, then, to the artisans. Conscious that I did not, so to say, know anything myself, I was certain I should find that they knew many things and fine. Nor in that was I deceived; they did indeed know things which I did not, and in that they were wiser than I. But, fellow citizens, these excellent workmen seemed to me to have the same defect as the poets. Because they were successful in the practice of their art, each thought himself most wise about all other things of the highest import, and this mistake of theirs beclouded all that wisdom. So I asked myself the question, for the oracle, whether I preferred to be just what I was, neither wise as they were wise nor ignorant as they were ignorant, or to be both wise and ignorant like them. And my response to myself and the oracle was that it paid me to to be as I was.

Such, fellow citizens, was the quest which brought me so much enmity, hatreds so utterly harsh and hard to bear, whence sprang so many calumnies, and this name that is given me of being 'wise'; for every time I caught another person in his ignorance, those present fancied that I knew what he did not. But, Gentlemen, in all likelihood it really is the god who is wise, and by that oracle he meant to say that human wisdom is of little worth, or none. And it appears that when he picked out 'Socrates,' he used my name to take me for an example; it was as if he said: 'O race of men, he is the wisest among you, who, like Socrates, knows that in truth his knowledge is worth nothing.' So even now I still go about in my search, and, in keeping with the god's intent, question anybody, citizen or stranger, whom I fancy to be wise. And when it seems to me that he is not, in defence of the god I show that he is not. And this activity has left me without leisure either to take any real part in civic affairs or to care for my own. Instead, I live in infinite poverty through my service to the god.

In addition, the young men who of their own accord are my companions, of the class who have most leisure, sons of the very rich—they listen with joy to the men who are examined; they often imitate me, and in turn attempt to test out others. And thereupon, I take it, they find a great abundance of men who imagine they have some knowledge, and yet know little or nothing. And then these men whom they examine get angry, not at them, but at me, and say there is one Socrates, a perfect blackguard, who corrupts the young. Yet when anybody asks them how he does it, and by teaching what, they have nothing to tell, nor do they know. But in order not to seem quite at a loss, they make the usual attacks that are leveled at philosophers, namely, about 'things occurring in the heavens and below the earth,' 'not believing in the gods,' and 'making the worse case win.' What they do not care to utter, I imagine, is the truth: that they have been shown up in their pretence to knowledge when they actually knew nothing. Accordingly, since they are proud, passionate, and numerous, and organized and effective in speaking about me, they have long since filled your ears with their violent calumnies.

From among them have come Meletus, Anytus, and Lycon to attack me;

Meletus aggrieved on behalf of the poets, Anytus on behalf of the artists and the politicians, Lycon on behalf of the rhetoricians. Consequently, as I said at the beginning, I shall be surprised if I succeed, within so short a time, in ridding you of all this swollen mass of calumny.

There, fellow citizens, you have the truth. I hide nothing from you, either great or small, nor do I dissimulate. And yet I know that even by this I stir up hatred, which itself proves that I tell the truth, and that it is precisely this that constitutes the charge against me, and is the cause of it. And whether now or later you investigate the matter, you will find it to be so.

Therewith let me close my defence to you on the charges made against me by my first accusers. . . .

No, fellow citizens, that I am guiltless with respect to Meletus' indictment seems to me to call for no long defence; rather, let this argument suffice. But what I have said before, that much antagonism has arisen against me in the minds of many, rest assured that it is true. And this it is that will undo me, if I am undone, not Meletus nor Anytus, but the slander of the many, and their malice. Many another man, and good ones, has it undone, and, me-thinks, it will yet undo. There is no danger that the thing may stop with me.

Perhaps some one will say: 'Well, Socrates, aren't you ashamed that you pursued a course from which you now are in danger of death?' To that it would be right for me to reply: Good sir, it is not well said if you think that a man of any worth at all ought to calculate his chances of living or dying, and not rather look to this alone, when he acts, to see if what he does is right or wrong, and if his are the deeds of a good man or a bad. By your account, the demigods who fell at Troy would be sorry fellows, all of them, and notably the son of Thetis, who so despised all danger in comparison with any disgrace awaiting him, and with what result? When his mother saw him eager to slay Hector, she, the goddess, addressed him, as I recall, approxi-mately thus: "My child, if you avenge the death of your comrade Patroclus by slaying Hector, then you yourself will die. For you the lot of death," she said, "comes straightway after Hector's." But he, on hearing that, made light of death and danger fearing far more to live a coward and not avenge his loved ones. "Straightway let me die," said he, "once I give the villain his reward, and not continue here, a laughing-stock, beside the hollow ships, a burden to the earth." Do you think that he took heed of death or danger?

That, fellow citizens, is the way things really stand. If any one is stationed where he thinks it is best for him to be, or where his commander has put him, there, as it seems to me, it is his duty to remain, no matter what the risk, heedless of death or any other peril in comparison with disgrace.

It would have been dreadful conduct, fellow citizens, had I acted other-wise. When the leaders you had chosen to command me assigned a post to me at Potidaea, at Amphipolis, and at Delium, in the face of death itself I was as steadfast as any one could be in holding the position where they placed me; and when the god, as I believed and understood, assigned to me as my duty that I should live the life of a philosopher, and examine myself and others, it would have been dreadful had I through fear of death, or of anything else whatever, deserted my post. Dreadful indeed would it be, and verily any one would then be justified in bringing me to trial for not believing in gods, when I had disobeyed the oracle, feared death, and thought that I was wise when I was not.

For, Gentlemen, to be afraid of death is nothing else than thinking that one is wise when one is not, since it means fancying that one knows what one does not. Nobody knows, in fact, what death is, nor whether to man it is not perchance the greatest of all blessings; yet people fear it as if they surely knew it to be the worst of evils. And what is this but the shameful ignorance of supposing that we know what we do not? It is there and in that perhaps that I differ, Gentlemen, from the majority of mankind; and if I might call myself more wise than other, it would be in this, that as I do not know enough about what goes on in Hades, so too I do not think that I know. But doing wrong, and disobeying the person who is better than myself, be it god or man, that I know is base and wicked. Therefore never for the sake of evils which I know to be such will I fear or flee from what for all I know may be a good. . . .

All I do is to go about persuading you, both young and old, not to think first of your bodies or your property, nor to be so mightily concerned about them as about your souls, how the spirit shall be at its best; it is my task to tell you that virtue does not spring from wealth, but that wealth and every other good that comes to men in private life or in public proceed from virtue. If it is by saying this that I corrupt the young, then this must be injurious; but any one who holds that I say anything save this says nothing. On that head, fellow citizens, I may assure you that whether you trust Anytus or not, and whether you acquit me or do not acquit me, I shall not alter my course, no matter if I have to die a hundred times.

Now, fellow citizens, do not interrupt, but continue granting my request of you not to cry out at what I may say, but to listen; I do believe that you will profit if you listen. I am, in fact, about to tell you certain other things at which you might possibly protest. Yet please do not. No; for you may rest assured that if you condemn me to death, I being such a person as I say, you will do yourselves more harm than you do me. As for me, Meletus will no more hurt me than will Anytus. It does not lie in his power, for in my belief the eternal order does not permit a better man to be harmed by a worse. Oh yes! quite possibly he might kill or banish me, or rob me of my civil rights; and doubtless this man and the next will think that these are major evils. I do not think them such; no, I think it a far greater evil for a man to do what this man now is doing, namely trying to get a man condemned to death unjustly.

So, fellow citizens, at present I am far from making my defence upon my own account, as one might think; I make it for your sake, in order that you may not, by condemning me, do wrong about the gift of the god to you; for if you have me put to death, you will not easily find another of the sort, fastened upon the City by the god, for all the world (if I may use a rather ludicrous comparison) like a gadfly on a great and noble horse that is somewhat sluggish on account of his size and needs the fly to wake him up. So, it seems to me, the god has fastened me like that upon the City, to rouse, exhort, and rebuke each one of you, everywhere besetting you, and never once ceasing all day long. Another one like that, Gentlemen, you will not come by so easily; but if you listen to me, you will take good care of me. You may, however, quite possibly be annoyed, like people awakened from their slumbers, and, striking out at me, may listen readily to Anytus and condemn me to death. Then you would finish out the rest of your life in sleep, unless the god were in mercy to send you some one else to take my place. That it is the deity by whom I, such as I am, have been given to the City you may see from this: it is not like human nature for me to neglect all my own concerns, to put up with a neglected household all these years, and to attend to your affair, ever going to you individually in private, like a father or an elder brother, urging you to care for your moral welfare. And if I got any profit from it all, if these exhortations brought me any pay, there would seem to be some reason in my conduct. As it is, you see for yourselves that my accusers, who, unashamed, have brought so many other charges against me, have yet not had the effrontery to present a witness to allege that I ever took any sort of fee or sought one. Why not? Because, methinks, the witness I present to show that I speak the truth is quite enough—my poverty. . . .

There you have it, Gentlemen. That is pretty much what I might have to say in my defence, that with possibly some additions, to the like effect. Perhaps, however, one or another of you will be angry when he recalls his own experience, in some trial he was engaged in of less gravity than this; if he besought and with many tears implored the judges, and, in order to arouse the greatest pity, brought in his children along with others of his kin and many friends; while, as for me, I shall do nothing of the sort, although I am in danger, as I might suppose, to the last degree of peril. . . .

These things, fellow citizens, it behoves us not to do if we have any reputation whatsoever; and if we do them, you should not allow it. No; you should make this very thing quite clear, that you will far more readily give your vote against the person who drags in these tearful dramas, and makes the City ridiculous, than against the man who argues quietly.

But apart from the question of propriety, Gentlemen, it does not seem right to me to beg the judge for mercy, or, by doing it, to get away, when one ought rather to enlighten and convince him. He does not take his seat for this, the judge, to render justice as a favor, but to decide on what is just. Indeed he took an oath that he would not favor people according to his notion of them, but that he would give judgment in accordance with the laws. And so we should not get you into the habit of perjuring yourselves, nor should you get into it; neither of us should commit impiety. So do not ask me, fellow citizens, to treat you in a way which I take to be dishonorable, wrong, and impious; above all, by Zeus! when I am under accusation of impiety by this Meletus here present; for obviously, if I swayed you and by begging forced you to act against your oath, I would be teaching you not to believe that there are gods, and by my defence would simply accuse myself of not believing in them. But that be far from me! I do believe in them, my fellow citizens, as none of my accusers does; and to you I commend myself, and to the Deity, to judge concerning me what shall be best at once for me and for you. . . .

AFTER HE IS CONDEMNED TO DEATH

For no great thrift in time, my fellow citizens, you will have from those who wish to vilify the City the name and blame of having put to death the wise man, Socrates; for they will call me wise, even if I am not, they who would defame you. If only you had waited for a little while, the thing would have occurred for you in the course of nature; for you can see my age, that I am far along in life, and near to death. I say this, not to all of you, but only to those who voted for my death. And to them I have also to say this as well. It may be, Gentlemen, that you think I lost my cause for lack of arguments of the sort with which I might have won you over, if I had thought that I ought to say and do all things in order to escape the verdict. Far from it. I lost for a lack, but not of arguments; it was for lack of impudence and daring, and for not being ready to say to you the sort of thing it would have given you most pleasure to hear—me weeping and wailing, and doing and saying any and every sort of thing that I hold to be unworthy of me, but you are accustomed to hear from the rest. No, I did not then believe that, to avoid a danger, I ought to do anything unseemly in a freeman, nor do I now regret my manner of defence. No, far rather would I choose this manner of defence, and die, than follow that, and live. Whether in a court of justice or in war neither I nor any other man should seek by using every means conceivable to escape from death; for in battle you very often see that if you throw away your weapons and beg those who are pursuing you for mercy, you may get out of dying. Indeed, in every sort of danger there are various ways of winning through, if one is ready to do and say anything whatever.

No, Gentlemen, that is not the hard thing, to escape from death; ah no, far harder is it to escape from sin, for sin is swifter than death. And so I, being old and slow, am overtaken by the slower enemy; while my accusers, who are strong and swift, have been caught by the swifter, namely wickedness. And so I now depart, by you condemned to pay the penalty of death; and they by the truth convicted of a base injustice. And as I abide the payment, so do they. Who knows? Perhaps it had to be so, and I think that things are as they ought to be.

Touching the future, I desire to make for you who voted to condemn me, a prediction; for I am at the point where men foresee the future best—when they are soon to die. Let me tell you then, you men who have condemned me, that after I am gone there will straightway come upon you a chastisement far heavier, by Zeus, than the death you have set for me. You have now done this in the belief that you have freed yourselves from giving any reckoning for your life; but I tell you the result will be the very opposite for you. There will be more inquisitors to sift you, men whom I now hold in check without your knowing it. And they will be more critical as they are younger, and will annoy you more; for if you think that by putting men to death you will prevent the slur from being cast at you that you do not live aright, you are in error. This way of getting freedom is neither very sure nor fine; no, the finest and readiest way is this, not to interfere with other people, but to render oneself as good a man as possible. There is the prophecy I make for you who voted to condemn me. And of them I take my leave.

With those of you who voted to acquit me I should be glad to talk about this thing that has occurred, while the magistrates are busy and it is not time for me to go to the place where I must die. So, Gentlemen, please wait with me as long as that. There is nothing to keep us from talking to each other as long as it is allowed. To you as to friends I wish to explain the real meaning of what has just happened to me.

Justices, for when I call you that I am naming you aright, the thing that has come to me is wonderful.

My customary warning, by the spirit, in previous times has always, up to now, come to me very often to oppose me, even when a matter was quite important, if ever I was going to do something amiss. But to-day, as you yourselves have witnessed, that thing has happened to me which anybody might suppose, and which is considered, to be the uttermost of evils. Yet neither did the sign from god oppose me when I left my house this morning, nor at the point when I ascended here to the tribunal, nor in my speech at anything I was about to say; though often when I have been talking elsewhere it has stopped me in the middle of a speech. But to-day, with reference to the whole procedure, not once did it oppose me in a thing I did or said. What, then, do I take to be the cause of this? No doubt this thing that has happened to me is good, and it cannot be that our supposition is correct when any of us think that death is a misfortune. For me, the proof of this is telling: it cannot be but that the customary sign would have opposed me, if I had not been about to do a thing that was good. . . .

But, Justices, you also it behoves to have good hope with reference to death, and this one thing you must bear in mind as true, that, living or dead, to a good man there can come no evil, nor are his affairs a matter of indifference to the gods. Nor has my destiny now come about by chance; rather, it is clear to me that it was better for me now to die and to be released from my troubles. That is why the sign did not at any point deter me, and why I am not very bitter at those who voted to condemn me, or at my accusers. It is true they did not have this notion in condemning and accusing me; no, they thought to injure me, and therein they merit blame.

One thing, however, I do beg of them. When my sons grow up, then, Gentlemen, I ask you to punish them, you hurting them the same as I hurt you, if they seem to you to care for money, or aught else, more than they care for virtue. And if they pretend to be somewhat when they are nothing, do you upbraid them as I upbraided you, for not regarding as important what they ought to think so, and for thinking they have worth when they do not. If you do that, I shall have received just treatment from you, and my sons as well.

And now the time has come for our departure, I to die, and you to live. Which of us goes to meet the better lot is hidden from all unless it be known to God.

AN ESSAY CONCERNING HUMAN UNDERSTANDING

John Locke

1. Every man being conscious to himself that he thinks; and that which his mind is applied about whilst thinking being the *ideas* that are there, it is past doubt that men have in their minds several ideas—such as are those expressed by the words *whiteness, hardness, sweetness, thinking, motion, man, elephant, army, drunkenness,* and others: it is in the first place then to be inquired, *How he comes by them?*

I know it is a received doctrine, that men have native ideas, and original characters, stamped upon their minds in their very first being. This opinion I have at large examined already; and, I suppose what I have said in the foregoing Book will be much more easily admitted, when I had shown whence the understanding may get all the ideas it has; and by what ways and degrees they may come into the mind;—for which I shall appeal to every one's own observation and experience.

2. Let us then suppose the mind to be, as we say, white paper, void of all characters, without any ideas:—How comes it to be furnished? Whence comes it by that vast store which the busy and boundless fancy of man has painted on it with an almost endless variety? Whence has it all the *materials* of reason and knowledge? To this I answer, in one word, from EXPERIENCE. In that all our knowledge is founded; and from that it ultimately derives itself. Our observation employed either about external sensible objects, or about the internal operations of our minds perceived and reflected on by ourselves, is that which supplies our understandings with all the *materials* of thinking. These two are the fountains of knowledge, from whence all the ideas we have, or can naturally have, do spring.

3. First, our Senses, conversant about particular sensible objects, do convey into the mind several distinct perceptions of things, according to those various ways wherein those objects do affect them. And thus we come by those *ideas* we have of *yellow, white, heat, cold, soft, hard, bitter, sweet,* and all those which we call sensible qualities; which when I say the senses convey into the mind, I mean, they from external objects convey into the mind what produces there those perceptions. This great source of most of the ideas we have, depending wholly upon our senses, and derived by them to the understanding, I call SENSATION.

4. Secondly, the other fountain from which experience furnisheth the understanding with ideas is—the perception of the operations of our own mind within us, as it is employed about the ideas it has got;—which operations, when the soul comes to reflect on and consider, do furnish the understanding with another set of ideas, which could not be had from things without. And such are *perception, thinking, doubting, believing, reasoning, knowing, willing,* and all the different actings of our own minds;—which we being conscious of, and observing in ourselves, do from these receive into our understandings as distinct ideas as we do from bodies affecting our senses. This source of ideas every man has wholly in himself; and though it be not sense, as having nothing to do with external objects, yet it is very like it, and might properly enough be called *internal sense.* But as I call the other Sensation, so I call this REFLECTION, the ideas it affords being such only as the mind gets by reflecting on its own operations within itself. By reflection then, in the following part of this discourse, I would be understood to mean, that notice which the mind takes of its own operations, and the manner of them, by reason whereof there come to be ideas of these operations in the understanding. These two, I say, viz. external material things, as the objects of SENSATION, and the operations of our own minds within, as

the objects of REFLECTION, are to me the only originals from whence all our ideas take their beginnings. The term *operations* here I use in a large sense, as comprehending not barely the actions of the mind about its ideas, but some sort of passions arising sometimes from them, such as is the satisfaction or uneasiness arising from any thought.

5. The understanding seems to me not to have the least glimmering of any ideas which it doth not receive from one of these two. *External objects* furnish the mind with the ideas of sensible qualities, which are all those different perceptions they produce in us; and *the mind* furnishes the understanding with ideas of its own operations.

These, when we have taken a full survey of them, and their several modes, [combinations, and relations,] we shall find to contain all our whole stock of ideas; and that we have nothing in our minds which did not come in one of these two ways. Let anyone examine his own thoughts, and thoroughly search into his understanding; and then let him tell me, whether all the original ideas he has there, are any other than of the objects of his senses, or of the operations of his mind, considered as objects of his reflection. And how great a mass of knowledge soever he imagines to be lodged there, he will, upon taking a strict view, see that he has not any idea in his mind but what one of these two have imprinted;—though perhaps, with infinite variety compounded and enlarged by the understanding, as we shall see hereafter.

6. He that attentively considers the state of a child, at his first coming into the world, will have little reason to think him stored with plenty of ideas that are to be the matter of his future knowledge. It is *by degrees* he comes to be furnished with them. And though the ideas of obvious and familiar qualities imprint themselves before the memory begins to keep a register of time and order, yet it is often so late before some unusual qualities come in the way that there are few men that cannot recollect the beginning of their acquaintance with them. And if it were worth while, no doubt a child might be so ordered as to have but a very few, even of the ordinary ideas, till he were grown up to a man. But all that are born into the world, being surrounded with bodies that perpetually and diversely affect them, variety of ideas, whether care be taken of it or not, are imprinted on the minds of children. Light and colours are busy at hand everywhere, when the eye is but open; sounds and some tangible qualities fail not to solicit their proper senses, and force an entrance to the mind;—but yet, I think, it will be granted easily, that if a child were kept in a place where he never saw any other but black and white till he were a man, he would have no more ideas of scarlet or green, than he that from his childhood never tasted an oyster, or a pine-apple, has of those particular relishes.

7. Men then come to be furnished with fewer or more simple ideas from without, according as the objects they converse with afford greater or less variety; and from the operations of their minds within, according as they

more or less reflect on them. For, though he that contemplates the operations of his mind cannot but have plain and clear ideas of them; yet, unless
he turns his thoughts that way, and considers them *attentively*, he will no
more have clear and distinct ideas of all the operations of his mind, and all
that may be observed therein, than he will have all the particular ideas of
any landscape or of the parts and motions of a clock, who will not turn his
eyes to it, and with attention heed all the parts of it. The picture, or clock
may be so placed that they may come in his way every day; but yet he will
have but a confused idea of all the parts they are made up of, till he applies
himself with attention, to consider them each in particular.

8. And hence we see the reason why it is pretty late before most children
get ideas of the operations of their own minds; and some have not any very
clear or perfect ideas of the greatest part of them all their lives. Because,
though they pass there continually, yet, like floating visions, they make not
deep impressions enough to leave in their mind clear, distinct, lasting ideas,
till the understanding turns inward upon itself, reflects on its own operations,
and makes them the objects of its own contemplation. Children, when they
come first into it, are surrounded with a world of new things, which, by a
constant solicitation of their senses, draw the mind constantly to them;
forward to take notice of new, and apt to be delighted with the variety of
changing objects. Thus the first years are usually employed and diverted in
looking abroad. Men's business in them is to acquaint themselves with what
is to be found without; and so growing up in a constant attention to outward
sensations, seldom make any considerable reflection on what passes within
them, till they come to be of riper years; and some scarce ever at all.

THE HOT GATES

William Golding

I had lunch in Lamia, a provincial town of Thessaly which lies on the
route south to Athens. Most people go through Lamia without stopping, but
I was following the route of the Persian invasion, that spectacular combined
operation of almost twenty-five hundred years ago. . . .

It was in these parts, in 480 B.C., that the Persian army had been held up
for a few days on its way to Athens. South of Lamia, the river Spercheios
has cut a valley athwart the invasion route, and the road must crawl round
the corner on the other side of the valley between the cliffs and the sea.
Sitting beneath a tree, and drinking my Demestica, I thought about Athens

and Persia, and the hot springs that bubble out of the cliff where the road is narrowest, so that the Greeks call it the Hot Gates. I thought of myself too—dreaming for twenty years of coming here, poring over ancient maps; and now faced with the duty and the necessity of trying to understand.

I had seen the valley of the Spercheios when I entered Lamia, had glimpsed the vast wall of rock five thousand feet high on the other side of the valley, which lay between me and Athens. Athens was shining Athens, the Athens of history, shining in the mind. Yet when the Persian Xerxes, King of Kings, drove his army at her, she did not shine. At that time she was little but a thorn in his side, a small city which had insisted on running her own affairs—and had an odd knack of encouraging cities which ought to bow to the King of Kings to do the same.

Athens needed thirty years, and then she would shine as no city had shone before or has shone since. For all her faults she would take humanity with her a long, long step—but on that day she was nothing but a pain in the neck of the King of Kings, who had the greatest army in the world poised at her last gate. . . .

At the time of the Persian invasion, when the sea came close to these cliffs, the narrow track had held seven thousand men—Spartans, Thebans, Locrians, Thespians, Phocians—who watched one another as much as they watched the enemy. Greece to the south was in a turmoil as the Persians marched toward it. What to do? Whom to trust? What to believe? The track that summer was thick with dusty messengers bearing appeals for help, or accusations, or denials, or prayers to the gods. In any event, with Xerxes only a few miles away, there was a mixed force to hold the track—groups sent by the cities of Greece, and small groups at that. No city dared strip itself of troops. . . .

I drove on to the Hot Gates proper, where once there had been room for no more than one wagon at a time. Sure enough, there was a memorial, level with the place where that mixed force had once stood in the pass, a nineteenth-century monument, grandiose and expensive. When the battle was fought, the place where the monument stands was out in the sea.

Nature has not done her best here for the story of that battle. The Vale of Tempe would have been a better place, and there are a hundred haunted spots in Greece where the setting would be more striking and the drama more obvious. Quiet, crop-fledged fields lie between the cliffs and the sea, with the scar of the motor road on them. The slopes and cliffs, though sprinkled with shrubs and flowers, aromatic in the hot sun, are arid with outcroppings of rock. There is dust everywhere. Little gullies leading back into the cliffs are marked with low stone walls that look ancient but are recent structures made by farmers and goatherds. If you go to the Hot Gates, take some historical knowledge and your imagination with you.

Just at the mouth of one of these gullies, I came across a mound. It was not very imposing to look at. The Greeks have planted it with laurels; but laurels planted recently in Greece never seem to be doing very well. There are some by the Springs of Daphne, some on the field of Marathon, some at Delphi—and they all look sheepish and a bit scuffy. But it was here, by this very mound, that the mixed force led by Leonidas and his three hundred Spartans came to hold the pass.

Standing by the dusty mound on that April afternoon, in the deserted landscape, where the only sound was an occasional clatter from the laurel leaves in a hot gust of wind, I wondered what Leonidas made of it all. He was, like all the Spartans, a dedicated soldier. But what did he think? As he looked north, where Lamia now lies on the hills across the valley, he must have heard the sound of quarrelling at his back. That is the one certain thing—the mixed force was quarrelling.

You can imagine the sullen afternoon lengthening, the ribaldry, the sudden shouts, perhaps even the clash of arms, the mutter of men who had to do as they were told but knew better than their leaders, the cynical laughter of men who had no faith in anything because Greece behind the wall—Athens, Sparta, Thebes and the rest—was at war not only with Persia but with itself. Then there had come a flash and glitter from the flank of the mountain across the valley.

Mark that Leonidas did not know how Athens needed thirty years to blossom. For him, Sparta, that dull, cruel city, shone brighter than Athens. But as the Persian army seeped down from a dozen pathways into the valley, and the mixed force fell silent at his back, it must have been some inarticulate and bitter passion for freedom as he knew it that kept him there, sullen and fiercely determined as he gazed across the plain.

No man had ever seen anything like this army before. It was patently unstoppable. It came along the neck of the hills on the banks of the Asopus, from the heights of the mountain and along the coastal track from Alope and Phalara. Lengthening rivers of men—Persians in fish-scale armor, turbaned Cissians, bronze-clad Assyrians, trousered Scythians, Indian bowmen, Caspians, Sarangians in bright cloth and high-heeled boots—came down and spread in a flood that filled the plain. Soon there was nothing to see but rising clouds of white dust, pierced and speckled with the flicker of steel. If each of the seven thousand Greeks should kill his ten men, there would be more than enough to press forward—and this was only the vanguard.

At their back, stretching for league after league by Mounts Pelion and Ossa, back through the narrow gorge of the Peneus to the wide plain beneath Olympus, marched the main body of the Persian war machine: Arabs in robes and Negroes in leopard skins; leather-clad Libyans, Thracians with headdresses of foxpelt, Pisidians with their oxhide shields, Cabalians and Milyans, Moschians, Tibareni, Tacrones and Mossynoeci; Marians, Colchians with their wooden helmets, Alarodians, Saspires and Medes; and horses and oxen and mules. There were eighty thousand mounted bowmen and lancers, and chariots in a swarm no one could count.

When that assembly of nations heaved itself off the earth and marched, the ground shuddered like the head of a drum. When that assembly came to a swift Greek river and halted for miles along the bank to drink, the waters shrank to a few pools of mud. This was the army that seeped and flooded into the valley all day, and halted under its own dust before the narrow entrance of the Hot Gates.

Not a man in the pass could be sure that the rest of Greece really meant to fight. And if those panicky cities on the other side of the wall *did* combine, what could they do against such an army? And who could be sure that these lousy Thebans (or Thespians or Locrians, according to your own nationality) really meant to fight? Only the three hundred Spartans were calm, and even cheerful. They were soldiers, and nothing but soldiers, and this was what they were for.

Xerxes pitched his tent and set up his throne. He sent forward a scout. The Spartans saw the horseman coming but ignored him. They were bathing in the sulphur springs and combing their hair. The horseman came thumping along the plain by the shore. He turned toward them and reined back his horse just out of bowshot. He balanced there on his rearing horse and peered sideways at the pass under his lifted hand. Then he wheeled away in dust and spurts of sand. The men in the pass saw him go to a kind of glittering mound, dismount and make his report.

Xerxes waited four days—and nothing happened. The men in the pass would not recognize the obvious. On the fifth day he sent forward a troop; and the result was a pushover for the Greeks. Every time the Persians thrust them back, the Greeks simply plugged the pass more completely. He sent forward his own bodyguard, the Company of Immortals, his best troops. They were defeated. For two days the Persians attacked, and the Greeks held them.

It is said that Xerxes leaped from his throne three times in terror for his whole army. Modern historians have found this incredible, but I cannot see why. Communications between the wings of his army were primitive. At any moment, rumor could have sent those savage levies scrambling away into the mountains. If the soldiers immediately engaging the Greeks had run away, panic would have spread like a heath fire.

I strolled away from the cliff to where the modern but colossal statue of Leonidas stands on its narrow plinth beside the road. He wears a helmet and sword belt, carries a shield, and threatens the mountains with a spear that quivers slightly in the brassy wind. I thought of the messages he sent during those two days. He needed reinforcements—as many as Greece could find. But that summer the roads were thick with messengers.

And then, of course, the inevitable traitor appeared from the wings.

I moved back and peered up at the cliffs. The traitor had led a Persian force over those cliffs at night, so that with day they would appear in the rear of the seven thousand in the pass. For years I had promised myself that I would follow that track. But I should have come twenty years earlier, with knapsack, no money, and plenty of breath. Yet twenty years ago I was fighting, too, and in as bitter a war. If I could climb cliffs less easily now, it was possible that I could understand war better. . . .

Suddenly, the years and the reading fused with the thing. I was clinging to Greece herself. Obscurely, and in part, I understood what it had meant to Leonidas when he looked up at these cliffs in the dawn light and saw that their fledging of pines was not thick enough to hide the glitter of arms.

It was then—and by the double power of imagination and the touch of rock, I was certain of it—that the brooding and desperate thinking of Leonidas crystallized into one clear idea. The last pass was sold. If the rest of Greece beyond the wall did not unite and make its stand, the game was up. Leonidas knew now that he could make one last plea for that stand—a desperate plea, but one which those dull, dedicated Spartans were eminently fitted to give. I clambered and sweated down the cliffside to the place where he made it. He sent away most of his army but moved the Spartans out into the open, where they could die properly and in due form. The Persians came at them like waves of the sea. The Spartans retreated to make their last stand on a little mound.

To most of the Persian army, this must have meant nothing. There had been, after all, nothing but a small column of dust hanging under the cliffs in one corner of the plain. If you were a Persian, you could not know that this example would lead, next year, to the defeat and destruction of your whole army at the battle of Plataea, where the cities of Greece fought side by side. Neither you nor Leonidas nor anyone else could foresee that here thirty years' time was won for shining Athens and all Greece and all humanity.

The column of dust diminished. The King of Kings gave an order. The huge army shrugged itself upright and began the march forward into the Hot Gates, where the last of the Spartans were still fighting with nails and feet and teeth.

I came to myself in a great stillness, to find I was standing by the little mound. This is the mound of Leonidas, with its dust and rank grass, its flowers and lizards, its stones, scruffy laurels and hot gusts of wind. I knew now that something real happened here. It is not just that the human spirit reacts directly and beyond all argument to a story of sacrifice and courage, as a wine glass must vibrate to the sound of the violin. It is also because, way back and at the hundredth remove, that company stood in the right line of history. A little of Leonidas lies in the fact that I can go where I like and write what I like. He contributed to set us free.

Climbing to the top of that mound by the uneven, winding path, I came on the epitaph, newly cut in stone. It is an ancient epitaph though the stone is new. It is famous for its reticence and simplicity—has been translated a hundred times but can only be paraphrased:

'Stranger, tell the Spartans that we behaved as they would wish us to, and are buried here.'

INTRODUCTORY LECTURE
A. E. Housman

The acquisition of knowledge needs no formal justification: its true sanction is a much simpler affair, and inherent in itself. People are too prone to torment themselves with devising far-fetched reasons: they cannot be content with the simple truth asserted by Aristotle: "all men possess by nature a craving for knowledge." πάντες ἄνθρωποι τοῦ εἰδέναι ὀρέγονται φύσει. This is no rare endowment scattered sparingly from heaven that falls on a few heads and passes others by: curiosity, the desire to know things as they are, is a craving no less native to the being of man, no less universal through mankind, than the craving for food and drink. And do you suppose that such a desire means nothing? The very definition of the good, says Aristotle again, is that which all desire. Whatever is pleasant is good, unless it can be shewn that in the long run it is harmful, or, in other words, not pleasant but unpleasant. Mr. Spencer himself on another subject speaks thus: "So profound an ignorance is there of the laws of life, that men do not even know that their sensations are their natural guides, and (when not rendered morbid by long continued disobedience) their trustworthy guides." The desire of knowledge does not need, nor could it possibly possess, any higher or more authentic sanction than the happiness which attends its gratification.

Perhaps it will be objected that we see, every day of our lives, plenty of people who exhibit no pleasure in learning and experience no desire to know; people, as Plato agreeably puts it, who wallow in ignorance with the complacency of a brutal hog. We do; and here is the reason. If the cravings of hunger and thirst are denied satisfaction, if a man is kept from food and drink, the man starves to death, and there is an end of him. This is a result which arrests the attention of even the least observant mind; so it is generally recognised that hunger and thirst cannot be neglected with impunity, that a man ought to eat and drink. But if the craving for knowledge is denied satisfaction, the result which follows is not so striking to the eye. The man, worse luck, does not starve to death. He still preserves the aspect and motions of a living human being; so people think that the hunger and thirst for knowledge can be neglected with impunity. And yet, though the man does not die altogether, part of him dies, part of him starves to death: as Plato says, he never attains completeness and health, but walks lame to the end of his life and returns imperfect and good for nothing to the world below.

But the desire of knowledge, stifle it though you may, is none the less originally born with every man; and nature does not implant desires in us for nothing, nor endow us with faculties in vain. "Sure," says Hamlet,

> Sure, He that made us with such large discourse,
> Looking before and after, gave us not
> That capability and godlike reason
> To fust in us unused.

The faculty of learning is ours that we may find in its exercise that delight which arises from the unimpeded activity of any energy in the groove nature meant it to run in. Let a man acquire knowledge not for this or that external and incidental good which may chance to result from it, but for itself; not because it is useful or ornamental, but because it is knowledge, and therefore good for man to acquire. "Brothers," says Ulysses in Dante, when with his old and tardy companions he had left Seville on the right hand and Ceuta on the other, and was come to that narrow pass where Hercules assigned his landmarks to hinder man from venturing farther: "Brothers, who through a hundred thousand dangers have reached the West, deny not, to this brief vigil of your senses that remains, experience of the unpeopled world behind the sunset. Consider of what seed ye are sprung: ye were not formed to live like brutes, but to follow virtue and knowledge." For knowledge resembles virtue in this, and differs in this from other possessions, that it is not merely a means of procuring good, but is good in itself simply: it is not a coin which we pay down to purchase happiness, but has happiness indissolubly bound up with it. Fortitude and continence and honesty are not commended to us on the ground that they conduce, as on the whole they do conduce, to material success, nor yet on the ground that they will be rewarded hereafter: those whose office it is to exhort mankind to virtue are ashamed to degrade the cause they plead by proffering such lures as these. And let us too disdain to take lower ground in commending knowledge: let us insist that the pursuit of knowledge, like the pursuit of righteousness, is part of man's duty to himself, and remember the Scripture where it is written: "He that refuseth instruction despiseth his own soul."

I will not say, as Prof. Tyndall has somewhere said, that all happiness belongs to him who can say from his heart "I covet truth." Entire happiness is not attainable either by this or by any other method. Nay it may be urged on the contrary that the pursuit of truth in some directions is even injurious to happiness, because it compels us to take leave of delusions which were

pleasant while they lasted. It may be urged that the light shed on the origin
and destiny of man by the pursuit of truth in some directions is not altogether a cheerful light. It may be urged that man stands to-day in the
position of one who has been reared from his cradle as the child of a noble
race and the heir to great possessions, and who finds at his coming of age
that he has been deceived alike as to his origin and his expectations, that he
neither springs of the high lineage he fancied, nor will inherit the vast estate
he looked for, but must put off his towering pride, and contract his boundless hopes, and begin the world anew from a lower level: and this, it may be
urged, comes of pursuing knowledge. But even conceding this, I suppose the
answer to be that knowledge, and especially disagreeable knowledge, cannot
by any art be totally excluded even from those who do not seek it. Wisdom,
said Aeschylus long ago, comes to men whether they will or no. The house
of delusions is cheap to build, but draughty to live in, and ready at any
instant to fall; and it is surely truer prudence to move our furniture betimes
into the open air than to stay indoors until our tenement tumbles about our
ears. It is and it must in the long run be better for a man to see things as they
are than to be ignorant of them; just as there is less fear of stumbling or of
striking against corners in the daylight than in the dark.

Nor again will I pretend that, as Bacon asserts, "the pleasure and delight
of knowledge and learning far surpasseth all other in nature." This is too
much the language of a salesman crying his own wares. The pleasures of the
intellect are notoriously less vivid than either the pleasures of sense or the
pleasures of the affections, and therefore, especially in the season of youth,
the pursuit of knowledge is likely enough to be neglected and lightly
esteemed in comparison with other pursuits offering much stronger immediate attractions. But the pleasure of learning and knowing, though not the
keenest, is yet the least perishable of pleasures; the least subject to external
things, and the play of chance, and the wear of time. And as a prudent man
puts money by to serve as a provision for the material wants of his old age,
so too he needs to lay up against the end of his days provision for the
intellect. As the years go by, comparative values are found to alter: Time,
says Sophocles, takes many things which once were pleasures and brings
them nearer to pain. In the day when the strong men shall bow themselves,
and desire shall fail, it will be a matter of yet more concern than now,
whether one can say "my mind to me a kingdom is"; and whether the
windows of the soul look out upon a broad and delightful landscape, or face
nothing but a brick wall.

Well then, once we have recognised that knowledge in itself is good for
man, we shall need to invent no pretexts for studying this subject or that; we
shall import no extraneous considerations of use or ornament to justify us
in learning one thing rather than another. If a certain department of knowledge specially attracts a man, let him study that, and study it because it

attracts him; and let him not fabricate excuses for that which requires no excuse, but rest assured that the reason why it most attracts him is that it is best for him. The majority of mankind, as is only natural, will be most attracted by those sciences which most nearly concern human life; those sciences which, in Bacon's phrase, are drenched in flesh and blood, or, in the more elegant language of the *Daily Telegraph*, palpitate with actuality. The men who are attracted to the drier and the less palpitating sciences, say logic or pure mathematics or textual criticism, are likely to be fewer in number; but they are not to suppose that the comparative unpopularity of such learning renders it any the less worthy of pursuit. Nay they may if they like console themselves with Bacon's observation that "this same *lumen siccum* doth parch and offend most men's watery and soft natures," and infer, if it pleases them, that their natures are less soft and watery than other men's. But be that as it may, we can all dwell together in unity without crying up our own pursuits or depreciating the pursuits of others on factitious grounds. We are not like the Ottoman sultans of old time, who thought they could never enjoy a moment's security till they had murdered all their brothers. There is no rivalry between the studies of Arts and Laws and Science but the rivalry of fellow-soldiers in striving which can most victoriously achieve the common end of all, to set back the frontier of darkness.

It is the glory of God, says Solomon, to conceal a thing: but the honour of kings is to search out a matter. Kings have long abdicated that province; and we students are come into their inheritance: it is our honour to search out the things which God has concealed. In Germany at Easter time they hide coloured eggs about the house and the garden that the children may amuse themselves in hunting after them and finding them. It is to some such game of hide-and-seek that we are invited by that power which planted in us the desire to find out what is concealed, and stored the universe with hidden things that we might delight ourselves in discovering them. And the pleasure of discovery differs from other pleasures in this, that it is shadowed by no fear of satiety on the one hand or of frustration on the other. Other desires perish in their gratification, but the desire of knowledge never: the eye is not satisfied with seeing nor the ear filled with hearing. Other desires become the occasion of pain through dearth of the material to gratify them, but not the desire of knowledge: the sum of things to be known is inexhaustible, and however long we read we shall never come to the end of our story-book. So long as the mind of man is what it is, it will continue to exult in advancing on the unknown throughout the infinite field of the universe; and the tree of knowledge will remain for ever, as it was in the beginning, a tree to be desired to make one wise.

THE MARKS OF
AN EDUCATED MAN

Alan Simpson

Any education that matters is *liberal*. All the saving truths and healing graces that distinguish a good education from a bad one or a full education from a half-empty one are contained in that word. Whatever ups and downs the term "liberal" suffers in the political vocabulary, it soars above all controversy in the educational world. In the blackest pits of pedagogy the squirming victim has only to ask. "What's liberal about this?" to shame his persecutors. In times past a liberal education set off a free man from a slave or a gentleman from laborers and artisans. It now distinguishes whatever nourishes the mind and spirit from the training which is merely practical or professional or from the trivialities which are no training at all. Such an education involves a combination of knowledge, skills, and standards.

So far as knowledge is concerned, the record is ambiguous. It is sufficiently confused for the fact-filled freak who excels in quiz shows to have passed himself off in some company as an educated man. More respectable is the notion that there are some things which every educated man ought to know; but many highly educated men would cheerfully admit to a vast ignorance, and the framers of curriculums have differed greatly in the knowledge they prescribe. If there have been times when all the students at school or college studied the same things, as if it were obvious that without exposure to a common body of knowledge they would not be educated at all, there have been other times when specialization ran so wild that it might almost seem as if educated men had abandoned the thought of ever talking to each other once their education was completed.

If knowledge is one of our marks, we can hardly be dogmatic about the kind or the amount. A single fertile field tilled with care and imagination can probably develop all the instincts of an educated man. However, if the framer of a curriculum wants to minimize his risks, he can invoke an ancient doctrine which holds that an educated man ought to know a little about everything and a lot about something.

The "little about everything" is best interpreted these days by those who have given most thought to the sort of general education an informed individual ought to have. More is required than a sampling of the introductory courses which specialists offer in their own disciplines. Courses are needed in each of the major divisions of knowledge—the humanities, the natural sciences, and social sciences—which are organized with the breadth of view and the imaginative power of competent staffs who understand the needs of interested amateurs. But, over and above this exciting smattering of knowledge, students should bite deeply into at least one subject and taste its full flavor. It is not enough to be dilettantes in everything without striving also to be craftsmen in something.

If there is some ambiguity about the knowledge an educated man should have, there is none at all about the skills. The first is simply the training of the mind in the capacity to think clearly. This has always been the business of education, but the way it is done varies enormously. Marshalling the notes of a lecture is one experience; the opportunity to argue with a teacher is another. Thinking within an accepted tradition is one thing; to challenge the tradition itself is another. The best results are achieved when the idea of the examined life is held firmly before the mind and when the examination is conducted with the zest, rigor, and freedom which really stretches everyone's capacities.

The vital aid to clear thought is the habit of approaching everything we hear and everything we are taught to believe with a certain skepticism. The method of using doubt as an examiner is a familiar one among scholars and scientists, but it is also the best protection which a citizen has against the cant and humbug that surround us.

To be able to listen to a phony argument and to see its dishonesty is surely one of the marks of an educated man. We may not need to be educated to possess some of this quality. A shrewd peasant was always well enough protected against impostors in the market place, and we have all sorts of businessmen who have made themselves excellent judges of phoniness without the benefit of a high-school diploma; but this kind of shrewdness goes along with a great deal of credulity. Outside the limited field within which experience has taught the peasant or the illiterate businessman his lessons, he is often hopelessly gullible. The educated man, by contrast, has tried to develop a critical faculty for general use, and he likes to think that he is fortified against imposture in all its forms.

It does not matter for our purposes whether the impostor is a deliberate liar or not. Some are, but the commonest enemies of mankind are the unconscious frauds. Most salesmen under the intoxication of their own exuberance seem to believe in what they say. Most experts whose *expertise* is only a pretentious sham behave as if they had been solemnly inducted into some kind of priesthood. Very few demogogues are so cynical as to remain undeceived by their own rhetoric, and some of the worst tyrants in history have been fatally sincere. We can leave the disentanglement of motives to the students of fraud and error, but we cannot afford to be taken in by the shams.

We are, of course, surrounded by shams. Until recently the schools were full of them—the notion that education can be had without tears, that puffed rice is a better intellectual diet than oatmeal, that adjustment to the group is more important than knowing where the group is going, and that democracy has made it a sin to separate the sheep from the goats. Mercifully, these are much less evident now than they were before Sputnik startled us into our wits.

In front of the professor are the shams of the learned fraternity. There is the sham science of the social scientist who first invented a speech for fuddling thought and then proceeded to tell us in his lockjawed way what we already knew. There is the sham humanism of the humanist who wonders why civilization that once feasted at his table is repelled by the shredded and desiccated dishes that often lie on it today. There is the sham message of the physical scientist who feels that his mastery of nature has made him an expert in politics and morals, and there are all the other brands of hokum which have furnished material for satire since the first quacks established themselves in the first cloisters.

If this is true of universities with their solemn vows and limited temptations, how much truer is it of the naughty world outside, where the prizes are far more dazzling and the only protection against humbug is the skepticism of the ordinary voter, customer, reader, listener, and viewer? Of course, the follies of human nature are not going to be exorcised by anything that the educator can do, and I am not sure that he would want to exorcise them if he could. There is something irresistibly funny about the old Adam, and life would be duller without his antics. But they ought to be kept within bounds. We are none the better for not recognizing a clown when we see one.

The other basic skill is simply the art of self-expression in speech and on paper. A man is uneducated who has not mastered the elements of clean forcible prose and picked up some relish for style.

It is a curious fact that we style everything in this country—our cars, our homes, our clothes—except our minds. They still chug along like a Model T—rugged, persevering, but far from graceful.

No doubt this appeal for style, like this appeal for clear thinking, can be carried too far. There was once an American who said that the only important thing in life was "to set a chime of words ringing in a few fastidious minds." As far as can be learned, he left this country in a huff to tinkle his little bell in a foreign land. Most of us would think that he lacked a sense of proportion. After all, the political history of this country is full of good judgment expressed in bad prose, and the business history has smashed through to some of its grandest triumphs across acres of broken syntax. But we can discard some of these frontier manners without becoming absurdly precious.

The road ahead bristles with obstacles. There is the reluctance of many people to use one word where they can get away with a half-dozen or a word of one syllable if they can find a longer one. No one has ever told them about the first rule in English composition: every slaughtered syllable is a good deed. The most persuasive teachers of this maxim are undoubtedly the commercial firms that offer a thousand dollars for the completion of a slogan in twenty-five words. They are the only people who are putting a handsome premium on economy of statement.

There is the decay of the habit of memorizing good prose and good poetry in the years when tastes are being formed. It is very difficult to write a bad sentence if the Bible has been a steady companion and very easy to imagine a well-turned phrase if the ear has been tuned on enough poetry.

There is the monstrous proliferation of gobbledy-gook in government, business, and the professions. Take this horrible example of verbal smog.

> It is inherent to motivational phenomena that there is a drive for more gratification than is realistically possible, on any level or in any type of personality organization. Likewise it is inherent to the world of objects that not all potentially desirable opportunities can be realized within a human life span. Therefore, any personality must involve an organization that allocates opportunities for gratifications, that systematizes precedence relative to the limited possibilities. The possibilities of gratification, simultaneously or sequentially, of all need-dispositions are severely limited by the structure of the object system and by the intra-systemic incompatibility of the consequences of gratifying them all.

What this smothered soul is trying to say is simply, "We must pick and choose, because we cannot have everything we want."

Finally, there is the universal employment of the objective test as part of the price which has to be paid for mass education. Nothing but the difficulty of finding enough readers to mark essays can condone a system which reduces a literate student to the ignoble necessity of "blackening the answer space" when he might be giving his mind and pen free play. Though we have managed to get some benefits from these examinations, the simple fact remains that the shapely prose of the Declaration of Independence or the "Gettysburg Address" was never learned under an educational system which employed objective tests. It was mastered by people who took writing seriously, who had good models in front of them, good critics to judge them, and an endless capacity for taking pains. Without that sort of discipline, the arts of self-expression will remain as mutilated as they are now.

The standards which mark an educated man can be expressed in terms of three tests.

The first is a matter of sophistication. Emerson put it nicely when he talked about getting rid of "the nonsense of our wigwams." The wigwam may be an uncultivated home, a suburban conformity, a crass patriotism, or a cramped dogma. Some of this nonsense withers in the classroom. More of it rubs off by simply mixing with people, provided they are drawn from a wide range of backgrounds and exposed within a good college to a civilized tradition. An educated man can be judged by the quality of his prejudices. There is a refined nonsense which survives the raw nonsense which Emerson was talking about.

The second test is a matter of moral values. Though we all know individuals who have contrived to be both highly educated and highly immoral, and though we have all heard of periods in history when the subtlest resources of wit and sophistication were employed to make a mockery of simple values, we do not really believe that a college is doing its job when it is simply multiplying the number of educated scoundrels, hucksters, and triflers.

The health of society depends on simple virtues like honesty, decency, courage, and public spirit. There are forces in human nature which constantly tend to corrupt them, and every age has its own vices. The worst features of ours is probably the obsession with violence. Up to some such time as 1914, it was possible to believe in a kind of moral progress. The quality which distinguished the Victorian from the Elizabethan was a sensitivity to suffering and a revulsion from cruelty which greatly enlarged the idea of human dignity. Since 1914 we have steadily brutalized ourselves. The horrors of modern war, the bestialities of modern political creeds, the uncontrollable vices of modern cities, the favorite themes of modern novelists—all have conspired to degrade us. Some of the corruption is blatant. The authors of the best sellers, after exhausting all the possibilities of sex in its normal and abnormal forms and all the variations of alcoholism and drug addiction, are about to invade the recesses of the hospitals. A clinical study of a hero undergoing the irrigation of his colon is about all there is left to grafity a morbid appetite.

Some of the corruption is insidious. A national columnist recently wrote an article in praise of cockfighting. He had visited a cockfight in the company of Ernest Hemingway. After pointing out that Hemingway had made bullfighting respectable, he proceeded to describe the terrible beauty of fierce indomitable birds trained to kill each other for the excitement of the spectators. Needless to say, there used to be a terrible beauty about Christians defending themselves against lions or about heretics being burned at the stake, and there are still parts of the world where a public execution is regarded as a richly satisfying feast. But for three or four centuries the West taught itself to resist these excitements in the interest of a moral idea.

Educators are needlessly squeamish about their duty to uphold moral values and needlessly perplexed about how to implant them. The corruptions of our times are a sufficient warning that we cannot afford to abandon the duty to the homes and the churches, and the capacity which many institutions have shown to do their duty in a liberal spirit is a sufficient guaranty against bigotry.

Finally, there is the test imposed by the unique challenge of our own times. We are not unique in suffering from moral confusion—these crises are a familiar story—but we are unique in the tremendous acceleration of the rate of social change and in the tremendous risk of a catastrophic end to all our hopes. We cannot afford educated men who have every grace except the gift for survival. An indispensable mark of the modern educated man is the kind of versatile, flexible mind that can deal with new and explosive conditions.

With this reserve, there is little in this profile which has not been familiar for centuries. Unfortunately, the description which once sufficed to suggest its personality has been debased in journalistic currency. The "well-rounded man" has become the organization man, or the man who is so well rounded that he rolls wherever he is pushed. The humanists who invented the idea and preached it for centuries would recoil in contempt from any such notion. They understood the possibilities of the whole man and wanted an educational system which would give the many sides of his nature some chance to develop in harmony. They thought it a good idea to mix the wisdom of the world with the learning of the cloister, to develop the body as well as the mind, to pay a great deal of attention to character, and to neglect no art which could add to the enjoyment of living. It was a spacious idea which offered every hospitality to creative energy. Anyone who is seriously interested in a liberal education must begin by rediscovering it.

Transition

A FREE MAN'S WORSHIP

Bertrand Russell

To Dr. Faustus in his study Mephistopheles told the history of the Creation, saying:

The endless praises of the choirs of angels had begun to grow wearisome; for, after all, did he not deserve their praise? Had he not given them endless joy? Would it not be more amusing to obtain undeserved praise, to be worshipped by beings whom he tortured? He smiled inwardly, and resolved that the great drama should be performed.

For countless ages the hot nebula whirled aimlessly through space. At length it began to take shape, the central mass threw off planets, the planets cooled, boiling seas and burning mountains heaved and tossed, from black masses of cloud hot sheets of rain deluged the barely solid crust. And now the first germ of life grew in the depths of the ocean, and developed rapidly in the fructifying warmth into vast forest trees, huge ferns springing from the damp mould, sea monsters breeding, fighting, devouring, and passing away. And from the monsters, as the play unfolded itself, Man was born, with the power of thought, the knowledge of good and evil, and the cruel thirst for worship. And Man saw that all is passing in this mad, monstrous world, that all is struggling to snatch, at any cost, a few brief moments of life before Death's inexorable decree. And Man said: "There is a hidden purpose, could we but fathom it, and the purpose is good; for we must reverence something, and in the visible world there is nothing worthy of reverence." And Man stood aside from the struggle, resolving that God intended harmony to come out of chaos by human efforts. And when he followed the instincts which God had transmitted to him from his ancestry of beasts of prey, he called it Sin, and asked God to forgive him. But he doubted whether he could be justly forgiven, until he invented a divine Plan by which God's wrath was to have been appeased. And seeing the present was bad, he made it yet worse, that thereby the future might be better. And he gave God thanks for the strength that enabled him to forgo even the joys that were possible. And God smiled; and when he saw that Man had become perfect in renunciation and worship, he sent another sun through the sky, which crashed into Man's sun; and all returned again to nebula.

"Yes," he murmured, "it was a good play; I will have it performed again."

Such, in outline, but even more purposeless, more void of meaning is the world which Science presents for our belief. Amid such a world, if anywhere, our ideals henceforward must find a home. That Man is the product of causes which had no prevision of the end they were achieving; that his origin, his growth, his hopes and fears, his loves and his beliefs, are but the outcome of accidental collocations of atoms; that no fire, no heroism, no intensity of thought and feeling, can preserve an individual life beyond the grave; that all the labours of the ages, all the devotion, all the inspiration, all the noonday brightness of human genius, are destined to extinction in the vast death of the solar system, and that the whole temple of Man's achievement must inevitably be buried beneath the débris of a universe in ruins—all these things, if not quite beyond dispute, are yet so nearly certain, that no philosophy which rejects them can hope to stand. Only within the scaffolding of these truths, only on the firm foundation of unyielding despair, can the soul's habitation henceforth be safely built.

How, in such an alien and inhuman world, can so powerless a creature as Man preserve his aspirations untarnished? A strange mystery it is that Nature omnipotent but blind, in the revolutions of her secular hurryings through the abysses of space, has brought forth at last a child, subject still to her power, but gifted with sight, with knowledge of good and evil, with the capacity of judging all the works of his unthinking Mother. In spite of Death, the mark and seal of the parental control, Man is yet free, during his brief years, to examine, to criticise, to know, and in imagination to create. To him alone, in the world with which he is acquainted, this freedom belongs; and in this lies his superiority to the resistless forces that control his outward life.

The savage, like ourselves, feels the oppression of his impotence before the powers of Nature; but having in himself nothing that he respects more than Power, he is willing to prostrate himself before his gods, without inquiring whether they are worthy of his worship. Pathetic and very terrible is the long history of cruelty and torture, of degradation and human sacrifices endured in the hope of placating the jealous gods: surely, the trembling believer thinks, when what is most precious has been freely given, their lust for blood must be appeased, and more will not be required. The religion of Moloch—as such creeds may be generically called—is in essence the cringing submission of the slave, who dare not, even in his heart, allow the thought that his master deserves no adulation. Since the independence of ideals is not yet acknowledged, Power may be freely worshipped, and receive an unlimited respect, despite its wanton infliction of pain.

But gradually, as morality grows bolder, the claim of the ideal world begins to be felt; and worship, if it is not to cease, must be given to gods of another kind than those created by the savage. Some, though they feel the demands of the ideal, will still consciously reject them, still urging that naked Power is worthy of worship. Such is the attitude inculcated in God's answer to Job out of the whirlwind: the divine power and knowledge are paraded, but of the divine goodness there is no hint. Such also is the attitude of those who, in our own day, base their morality upon the struggle for survival, maintaining that the survivors are necessarily the fittest. But others, not content with an answer so repugnant to the moral sense, will adopt the position which we have become accustomed to regard as specially religious, maintaining that, in some hidden manner, the world of fact is really harmonious with the world of ideals. Thus Man creates God, all-powerful and all-good, the mystic unity of what is and what should be.

But the world of fact, after all, is not good; and, in submitting our judgment to it, there is an element of slavishness from which our thoughts must be purged. For in all things it is well to exalt the dignity of Man, by freeing him as far as possible from the tyranny of non-human Power. When we have realised that Power is largely bad, that Man, with his knowledge of good and evil, is but a helpless atom in a world which has no such knowledge, the choice is again presented to us: Shall we worship Force, or shall we worship Goodness? Shall our God exist and be evil, or shall he be recognised as the creation of our own conscience?

The answer to this question is very momentous, and affects profoundly our whole morality. The worship of Force, to which Carlyle and Nietzsche and the creed of Militarism have accustomed us, is the result of failure to maintain our own ideals against a hostile universe: it is itself a prostrate submission to evil, a sacrifice of our best to Moloch. If strength indeed is to be respected, let us respect rather the strength of those who refuse that false "recognition of facts" which fails to recognise that facts are often bad. Let us admit that, in the world we know, there are many things that would be better otherwise, and that the ideals to which we do and must adhere are not realised in the realm of matter. Let us preserve our respect for truth, for beauty, for the ideal of perfection which life does not permit us to attain, though none of these things meet with the approval of the unconscious universe. If Power is bad, as it seems to be, let us reject it from our hearts. In this lies Man's true freedom: in determination to worship only the God created by our own love of the good, to respect only the heaven which inspires the insight of our best moments. In action, in desire, we must submit perpetually to the tyranny of outside forces; but in thought, in aspiration, we are free, free from our fellowmen, free from the petty planet on which our bodies impotently crawl, free even, while we live, from the tyranny of death. Let us learn, then, that energy of faith which enables us to live constantly in the vision of the good; and let us descend in action, into the world of fact, with that vision always before us.

When first the opposition of fact and ideal grows fully visible, a spirit of fiery revolt, of fierce hatred of the gods, seems necessary to the assertion of freedom. To defy with Promethean constancy a hostile universe, to keep its evil always in view, always actively hated, to refuse no pain that the malice of Power can invent, appears to be the duty of all who will not bow before the inevit ble. But indignation is still a bondage, for it compels our thoughts to be occupied with an evil world; and in the fierceness of desire from which rebellion springs there is a kind of self-assertion which it is necessary for the wise to overcome. Indignation is a submission of our thoughts, but not of our desires; the Stoic freedom in which wisdom consists is found in the submission of our desires, but not of our thoughts. From the submission of our desires springs the virtue of resignation; from the freedom of our thoughts springs the whole world of art and philosophy, and the vision of beauty by which, at last, we half reconquer the reluctant world. But the vision of beauty is possible only to unfettered contemplation, to thoughts not weighted by the load of eager wishes; and thus Freedom comes only to those who no longer ask of life that it shall yield them any of those personal goods that are subject to the mutations of Time.

Although the necessity of renunciation is evidence of the existence of evil, yet Christianity, in preaching it, has shown a wisdom exceeding that of the Promethean philosophy of rebellion. It must be admitted that, of the things we desire, some, though they prove impossible, are yet real goods; others, however, as ardently longed for, do not form part of a fully purified ideal. The belief that what must be renounced is bad, though sometimes false, is far less often false than untamed passion supposes; and the creed of religion, by providing a reason for proving that it is never false, has been the means of purifying our hopes by the discovery of many austere truths.

But there is in resignation a further good element: even real goods, when they are unattainable, ought not to be fretfully desired. To every man comes, sooner or later, the great renunciation. For the young, there is nothing unattainable; a good thing desired with the whole force of a passionate will, and yet impossible, is to them not credible. Yet, by death, by illness, by poverty, or by the voice of duty, we must learn, each one of us, that the world was not made for us, and that, however beautiful may be the things we crave, Fate may nevertheless forbid them. It is the part of courage, when misfortune comes, to bear without repining the ruin of our hopes, to turn away our thoughts from vain regrets. This degree of submission to Power is not only just and right; it is the very gate of wisdom.

But passive renunciation is not the whole of wisdom; for not by renunciation alone can we build a temple for the worship of our own ideals. Haunting foreshadowings of the temple appear in the realm of imagination, in music, in architecture, in the untroubled kingdom of reason, and in the golden sunset magic of lyrics, where beauty shines and glows, remote from the touch of sorrow, remote from the fear of change, remote from the failures and disenchantments of the world of fact. In the contemplation of these things the vision of heaven will shape itself in our hearts, giving at once a touchstone to judge the world about us, and an inspiration by which to fashion to our needs whatever is not incapable of serving as a stone in the sacred temple.

Except for those rare spirits that are born without sin, there is a cavern of darkness to be traversed before that temple can be entered. The gate of the cavern is despair, and its floor is paved with the gravestones of abandoned hopes. There Self must die; there the eagerness, the greed of untamed desire must be slain, for only so can the soul be freed from the empire of Fate. But out of the cavern the Gate of Renunciation leads again to the daylight of wisdom, by whose radiance a new insight, a new joy, a new tenderness, shine forth to gladden the pilgrim's heart.

When, without the bitterness of impotent rebellion, we have learnt both to resign ourselves to the outward rule of Fate and to recognise that the non-human world is unworthy of our worship, it becomes possible at last so to transform and refashion the unconscious universe, so to transmute it in the crucible of the imagination, that a new image of shining gold replaces the old idol of clay. In all the multiform facts of the world—in the visual shapes of trees and mountains and clouds, in the events of the life of Man, even in the very omnipotence of Death—the insight of creative idealism can find the reflection of a beauty which its own thoughts first made. In this way mind asserts its subtle mastery over the thoughtless forces of Nature. The more evil the material with which it deals, the more thwarting to untrained desire, the greater is its achievement in inducing the reluctant rock to yield up its hidden treasures, the prouder its victory in compelling the opposing forces to swell the pageant of its triumph. Of all the arts, Tragedy is the proudest, the most triumphant; for it builds its shining citadel in the very centre of the enemy's country, on the very summit of his highest mountain; from its impregnable watch-towers, his camps and arsenals, his columns and forts, are all revealed; within its walls the free life continues, while the legions of Death and Pain and Despair, and all the servile captains of tyrant Fate, afford the burghers of that dauntless city new spectacles of beauty. Happy those sacred ramparts, thrice happy the dwellers on that all-seeing eminence. Honour to those brave warriors who, through countless ages of warfare, have preserved for us the priceless heritage of liberty, and have kept undefiled by sacrilegious invaders the home of the unsubdued.

But the beauty of Tragedy does but make visible a quality which, in more or less obvious shapes, is present always and everywhere in life. In the spectacle of Death, in the endurance of intolerable pain, and in the irrevocableness of a vanished past, there is a sacredness, an overpowering awe, a feeling of the vastness, the depth, the inexhaustible mystery of existence, in which, as by some strange marriage of pain, the sufferer is bound to the world by bonds of sorrow. In these moments of insight, we lose all eagerness of temporary desire, all struggling and striving for petty ends, all care for the little trivial things, that, to a superficial view, make up the common life of day by day; we see, surrounding the narrow raft illumined by the flickering light of human comradeship, the dark ocean on whose rolling waves we toss for a brief hour; from the great night without, a chill blast breaks in upon our refuge; all the loneliness of humanity amid hostile forces is concentrated upon the individual soul, which must struggle alone, with what of courage it can command, against the whole weight of a universe that cares nothing for its hopes and fears. Victory, in this struggle with the powers of darkness, is the true baptism into the glorious company of heroes, the true initiation into the overmastering beauty of human existence. From that awful encounter of the soul with the outer world, renunciation, wisdom, and charity are born; and with their birth a new life begins. To take into the inmost shrine of the soul the irresistible forces whose puppets we seem to be—Death and change, the irrevocableness of the past, and the powerlessness of Man before the blind hurry of the universe from vanity to vanity—to feel these things and know them is to conquer them.

This is the reason why the Past has such magical power. The beauty of its motionless and silent pictures is like the enchanted purity of late autumn, when the leaves, though one breath would make them fall, still glow against the sky in golden glory. The Past does not change or strive; like Duncan, after life's fitful fever it sleeps well; what was eager and grasping, what was petty and transitory, has faded away, the things that were beautiful and eternal shine out of it like stars in the night. Its beauty, to a soul not worthy of it, is unendurable; but to a soul which has conquered Fate it is the key of religion.

The life of Man, viewed outwardly, is but a small thing in comparison with the forces of Nature. The slave is doomed to worship Time and Fate and Death, because they are greater than anything he finds in himself, and because all his thoughts are of things which they devour. But, great as they are, to think of them greatly, to feel their passionless splendour, is greater still. And such thought makes us free men; we no longer bow before the inevitable in Oriental subjection, but we absorb it, and make it a part of ourselves. To abandon the struggle for private happiness, to expel all eagerness of temporary desire, to burn with passion for eternal things—this is emancipation, and this is the free man's worship. And this liberation is effected by a contemplation of Fate; for Fate itself is subdued by the mind which leaves nothing to be purged by the purifying fire of Time.

United with his fellow-men by the strongest of all ties, the tie of a common doom, the free man finds that a new vision is with him always, shedding over every daily task the light of love. The life of Man is a long march through the night, surrounded by invisible foes, tortured by weariness and pain, towards a goal that few can hope to reach, and where none may tarry long. One by one, as they march, our comrades vanish from our sight, seized by the silent orders of omnipotent Death. Very brief is the time in which we can help them, in which their happiness or misery is decided. Be it ours to shed sunshine on their path, to lighten their sorrows by the balm of sympathy, to give them the pure joy of a never-tiring affection, to strengthen failing courage, to instil faith in hours of despair. Let us not weigh in grudging scales their merits and demerits, but let us think only of their need—of the sorrows, the difficulties, perhaps the blindnesses, that make the misery of their lives; let us remember that they are fellow-sufferers in the same darkness, actors in the same tragedy with ourselves. And so, when their day is over, when their good and their evil have become eternal by the immortality of the past, be it ours to feel that, where they suffered, where they failed, no deed of ours was the cause; but wherever a spark of the divine fire kindled in their hearts, we were ready with encouragement, with sympathy, with brave words in which high courage glowed.

Brief and powerless is Man's life; on him and all his race the slow, sure doom falls pitiless and dark. Blind to good and evil, reckless of destruction, omnipotent matter rolls on its relentless way; for Man, condemned to-day to lose his dearest, to-morrow himself to pass through the gate of darkness, it remains only to cherish, ere yet the blow falls, the lofty thoughts that ennoble his little day; disdaining the coward terrors of the slave of Fate, to worship at the shrine that his own hands have built; undismayed by the empire of chance, to preserve a mind free from the wanton tyranny that rules his outward life; proudly defiant of the irresistible forces that tolerate, for a moment, his knowledge and his condemnation, to sustain alone, a weary but unyielding Atlas, the world that his own ideals have fashioned despite the trampling march of unconscious Power.

THE REBIRTH OF A FUTURE

Charles A. Reich

Day-to-day events leave us with a feeling of chaos; it seems as if we must be mere powerless spectators at the decline and fall of our country. But these same events are capable of being understood as part of a larger process of social change—a process that is fearsome and yet fundamentally hopeful. And we may be participants—we may regain the power to make our own future—if only we understand what is taking place.

In Spain, the American President rides in an open car with a military dictator who by using lawless force has repressed all meaningful social progress. In Vietnam, halfway around the world, young Americans are compelled to fight in support of another corrupt dictatorship. These are not separate events, they are symptoms of a larger pattern. Women's liberation, Black militancy, the campaign against the S.S.T., Gay Liberation, the long hair of youth are not separate events either; they too are related. The many wars, the many revolutions are one.

The agonies of the great industrial nations, and especially our own, are no mystery. They have been fully predicted and explained by many social thinkers. There is much room for argument among schools of thought, but the main outline is clear. Neither machines nor material progress is inherently bad. But we have achieved our progress by a system which shortsightedly wastes man and nature by failing to protect them in the haste for gain. A rising crime rate, extremes of inequality, neglect of social needs, personal alienation and loss of meaning, disorder and war are all manifestations of the underlying process of corrosive exploitation.

This process has now reached a point where remedial action is desperately urgent. Knowing this, why are we unable to guide our progress along more rational lines? Why is our system so rigid that it ignores even the mild remedies proposed by its own Presidential Commissions? This brings us to a second element of our crisis, an element which also can be explained. American society has been amalgamated into a single monolith of power—the corporate state—which includes both the private and public structures. This monolith is not responsible to democratic or even executive control. The Corporate State is mindless and irrational. It rolls along with a momentum of its own, producing a society that is ever more at war with its own inhabitants. Again, there is plenty of room for different theories of the state, but the major pattern of unthinking and uncontrolled power must by now be accepted.

If our nation's immobility can be explained and understood, we must ask once more: why are we unable to refashion our system? All social systems are merely the creations of men; men make them and men can change them. But the power to act is limited by our consciousness. Today most Americans are not conscious of the realities of their society.

One segment of the American people remains at a level of consciousness that was formed when we were a land of small villages and individual opportunity; Consciousness I is unable to accept the reality of an interdependent society that requires collective responsibility. A second segment of the American people understands the realities of organization life but does not see that organizations and their policies are, by themselves, inhuman. Consciousness II supports the Corporate State and seeks happiness in its artificial rewards, mistakenly believing that such a state is necessary and rational in this industrial age.

These two forms of unreality, Consciousness I and II, render us powerless. We cannot act constructively so long as we are the prisoners of myth. Consciousness I exhausts its energy blaming scapegoats such as Communists, hippies, and liberals. Consciousness II offers solutions that would but strengthen existing structure. But the moment that our eyes are opened to the true causes of our self-destruction, there is hope. . . .

All around us today we see new ways of thinking and living: long hair, student protest, rock music, rejection of old careers. Many people find all of this shocking, frightening, senseless. But against the background of what has gone wrong with America, it all makes sense. There is a logic to it that explains each large and small experiment. Taken as a whole, it represents the only large-scale search for common sense and self-preservation that can be found in America today, the only major effort to come to grips with reality and thereby reassert man's control of his own fate. This is the beginning of a new consciousness, Consciousness III.

If the American Corporate State is, despite the wishes of a majority of its people, mindlessly destroying the land, culture, and people of a country in Southeast Asia, it is rational to refuse to become an instrument of that war, and to refuse obedience to laws that seek to compel a human being, despite his deepest convictions, to kill other human beings. If the State wants its citizens identically boxed and packaged, all the better to serve its rigid organizational structure, it makes sense to wear long hair and beards and clothes that constitute a refusal to be regimented. If the State wants all decisions made by remote central managers or by even more remote computers, it makes sense to insist that real people be allowed to participate in the making of decisions that affect their lives. If official language has been so debased that making war is called "making peace," and human needs are described in terms of manufactured appliances, there is a genuine need for the new language of rock music to aid in the effort to regain truth.

A revolution usually means the seizure of power by one group from another. But the revolution of the new generation is very different. It is not directed against other people, but against an impersonal system. And its objective is to place that system under the guidance of a mind—to reassert values where none are now recognized. The first stage of this revolution must be personal and cultural—the reassertion of values in each individual's life. The revolution will change the political structure of the State only as its final act. This is revolution by consciousness.

Revolution by consciousness is possible—and an orthodox revolution is not—because the Corporate State, while almost impregnable from outside, is astonishingly vulnerable from within. It is operated not by force but by willing workers and willing consumers. They have been persuaded to pursue goals set for them by the State. But if young lawyers will work only in firms that do some public service, if consumers refuse to buy the furs of endangered animal species, the State will be forced to obey, and it will begin to be turned to human ends. Opinion is not enough. People must change their working and consumer lives. And they can do this only by a rediscovery of self. It is only by a renewed self-knowledge that we can learn what work gives our lives meaning, and what material things will not impoverish us but affirm us.

Recovery of self is possible for people of all ages and conditions. The coming revolution has started with youth, but all others can join. They need not adopt the specifics of the youth culture; a sixty-year-old person does not have to wear bellbottoms. All that he needs is to make as honest a search for his own happiness and meaning as youth are making for theirs. There need be no unnatural warfare between generations, incited by promoters of hate. Parents do not want to hate their children. And children—our children of the new generation—desperately want the support and the wisdom of older people, who have too long left it to the young to carry alone the burden of resisting the inhuman Corporate State.

The generation of Consciousness III does not seek anything alien and strange. It is the Corporate State that has turned our country into a foreign and unrecognizable land. The new consciousness dreams the old American dream—of individual fulfillment and brotherly love. It is the old dream restated in terms of the realities and the promise of a technological society, where man must understand and master his machines.

To write about the coming revolution in terms of abstract concepts like "consciousness" is to risk missing its essence. This revolution does not find expression in theories. It is expressed all around us by the bloom of renewed life. Faces are gentler and more beautiful. People are better with each other. There are more smiles, more love. There is new hope, for young people have rediscovered a future, where until recently no future could even be imagined. This is the Revolution: the rebirth of people in a sterile land.

CON III IS NOT THE ANSWER

George F. Kennan

In his recent articles Mr. Charles A. Reich has made himself the spokesman for a condition of the spirit that has characterized the academic New Left generally in these last months.

People already given to this way of looking at things (Mr. Reich calls it a "consciousness") will not, of course, be interested in any attempt to discuss it rationally—it is not, after all, based on reason; and Mr. Reich himself would no doubt dismiss what follows with the same contemptuous disregard which good Russian Communists used to exhibit for the words of anyone who in their opinion was still a captive of the "bourgeois mentality."

But there may be others, particularly among the young, who, however moved by the seductive and contagious quality of the outlook in question, may yet hesitate to take a final departure from the voice of reason; and for them, at least, a critical word may be in order.

No one doubts the reality of the seriousness of the various evils to which Mr. Reich calls attention. He exaggerates them egregiously, of course; and this is no small offense. Such exaggeration of admittedly existing evils has regularly formed the initial ideological basis for fanatical political movements, including the totalitarian ones.

But the evils, I repeat, are real and serious. Inherited institutions are proving quite inadequate to national requirements. The problems of environmental destruction and pollution are dangerous and urgent. The deterioration of certain of our great cities is approaching a state of real crisis. Nobody underestimates the gravity of problems in the areas of crime, drugs and racial conflict. Transportation continues to be chaotic and expensive, geared to expense-account waste rather than to people's needs. The monstrous evil of American advertising and its hold on the mass media shames us as a nation. In foreign affairs we find ourselves still enchained to the folly of Vietnam and the stubborn illusion that there is some sort of security to be obtained by the proliferation of nuclear-weapons systems. There can be no question, finally, but that in the face of all this the two great parties, and political leadership generally, have failed us dreadfully.

This situation calls, of course, for frank recognition, for a clear public refusal to tolerate trends of deterioration, for the frankest and most searching sort of public discussion, and for drastic action. There is no lack of specific tasks. The Constitution needs revision. Some state boundaries no longer make sense. There is probably a need for regional governments, to

467

stand between the Federal government and the states. Environmental problems have to be taken hold of in a wholly new way. Existing arrangements for the settlement of labor disputes need extensive alteration. Unsound external involvements have to be promptly wound up, and the errors of outlook that have led to them—recognized, analyzed and corrected.

Little of the above can be accomplished unless there is a new national political force endowed with a real national program and a real integrity of conviction to give leadership.

There is, in short, plenty to do. But it is clear that if Mr. Reich's philosophy prevails, that will not happen. None of these needs is going to be constructively met by an outlook that takes no account of the problems, or even the concept, of representative government; that denies the need for authority, organization and discipline in the conduct of an immensely complex industrial civilization; that conceives the structure of decision-taking in such a society (or so, at least, we must conclude) as something flowing from a series of spontaneous mass meetings conducted in the spirit of brotherly love; that recognizes no problem of national defense, or of defense of an international order, or even, one must suppose, of defense of the public order at home.

If all that were involved here was Mr. Reich's enthusiasm for the lifestyle of the contemporary undergraduate, there would be no need for this sort of a response. There is a clear repudiation here of the fundamental principles, political and philosophic, on which not only the governmental system of this country but the entire structure of Western democracy has been erected. To be taught to despair of representative government without being given any clear or realistic idea of what might be put in its place; to be led to view with contempt, and to reject entirely, the ideals and strivings of an entire parental generation; to be encouraged to fancy one's self superior to "the rock from which thou wast hewn"; to be asked to believe that if only the profit motive could be removed, man would be in some way liberated from himself: all this is not only to be led down the paths of tragic personal misunderstanding but to be alienated from any constructive participation in the real struggle for a better society.

It is not wholly surprising that students in this country should yield in times of stress to romantic-utopian moods, illusions and hysterias of one sort or another. This has happened in even less disturbed times and places. It is more surprising that teachers, whose function it normally is to give depth and balance to student opinion, should be swayed by similar enthusiasm. Available evidence suggests that the majority of the students, having got various things off their chests last spring, are now settling down to a calmer and more thoughtful view of the world. Could it be that Mr. Reich's teachings, heady as they seem, are six months out-of-date?

GOD IS DEAD

Friedrich Nietzsche

The figs are falling from the trees; they are good and sweet; and, as they fall, their red skin bursts. I am a north wind to ripe figs.

Thus, like figs, these teachings fall to you, my friends; now consume their juice and their sweet meat. It is autumn about us, and pure sky and afternoon. Behold what fullness there is about us! And out of such overflow it is beautiful to look out upon distant seas. Once one said God when one looked upon distant seas; but now I have taught you to say: overman.

God is a conjecture; but I desire that your conjectures should not reach beyond your creative will. Could you *create* a god? Then do not speak to me of any gods. But you could well create the overman. Perhaps not you yourselves, my brothers. But into fathers and forefathers of the overman you could re-create yourselves: and let this be your best creation.

God is a conjecture; but I desire that your conjectures should be limited by what is thinkable. Could you *think* a god? But this is what the will to truth should mean to you: that everything be changed into what is thinkable for man, visible for man, feelable by man. You should think through your own senses to their consequences.

And what you have called world, that shall be created only by you: your reason, your image, your will, your love shall thus be realized. And verily, for your own bliss, you lovers of knowledge.

And now would you bear life without this hope, you lovers of knowledge? You could not have been born either into the incomprehensible or into the irrational.

But let me reveal my heart to you entirely, my friends: *if* there were gods, how could I endure not to be a god! *Hence* there are no gods. Though I drew this conclusion, now it draws me.

God is a conjecture; but who could drain all the agony of this conjecture without dying? Shall his faith be taken away from the creator, and from the eagle, his soaring to eagle heights?

God is a thought that makes crooked all that is straight, and makes turn whatever stands. How? Should time be gone, and all that is impermanent a mere lie? To think this is a dizzy whirl for human bones, and a vomit for the stomach; verily, I call it the turning sickness to conjecture thus. Evil I call it, and misanthropic—all this teaching of the One and the Plenum and the Unmoved and the Sated and the Permanent. All the permanent—this is only a parable. And the poets lie too much.

It is of time and becoming that the best parables should speak: let them be a praise and a justification of all impermanence.

Creation—that is the great redemption from suffering, and life's growing light. But that the creator may be, suffering is needed and much change. Indeed, there must be much bitter dying in your life, you creators. Thus are you advocates and justifiers of all impermanence. To be the child who is newly born, the creator must also want to be the mother who gives birth and the pangs of the birth-giver.

Verily, through a hundred souls I have already passed on my way, and through a hundred cradles and birth pangs. Many a farewell have I taken; I know the heart-rending last hours. But thus my creative will, my destiny, wills it. Or, to say it more honestly: this very destiny—my will wills.

Whatever in me has feeling, suffers and is in prison; but my will always comes to me as my liberator and joy-bringer. Willing liberates: that is the true teaching of will and liberty—thus Zarathustra teaches it. Willing no more and esteeming no more and creating no more—oh, that this great weariness might always remain far from me! In knowledge too I feel only my will's joy in begetting and becoming; and if there is innocence in my knowledge, it is because the will to beget is in it. Away from God and gods this will has lured me; what could one create if gods existed?

But my fervent will to create impels me ever again toward man; thus is the hammer impelled toward the stone. O men, in the stone there sleeps an image, the image of my images. Alas, that it must sleep in the hardest, the ugliest stone! Now my hammer rages cruelly against its prison. Pieces of rock rain from the stone: what is that to me. I want to perfect it; for a shadow came to me—the stillest and lightest of all things once came to me. The beauty of the overman came to me as a shadow. O my brothers, what are the gods to me now?

Thus spoke Zarathustra. . . .

Not long, however, after Zarathustra had got away from the magician, he again saw somebody sitting by the side of his path: a tall man in black, with a gaunt pale face: and *this* man displeased him exceedingly. "Alas!" he said to his heart, "there sits muffled-up melancholy, looking like the tribe of priests: what do *they* want in my realm? How now? I have scarcely escaped that magician; must another black artist cross my way so soon—some wizard with laying-on of hands, some dark miracle worker by the grace of God, some anointed world-slanderer whom the devil should fetch? But the devil is never where he should be: he always comes too late, this damned dwarf and clubfoot!"

Thus cursed Zarathustra, impatient in his heart, and he wondered how he might sneak past the black man, looking the other way. But behold, it happened otherwise. For at the same moment the seated man had already spotted him; and not unlike one on whom unexpected good fortune has been thrust, he jumped up and walked toward Zarathustra.

"Whoever you may be, you wanderer," he said, "help one who has lost his way, a seeker, an old man who might easily come to grief here. This region is remote and strange to me, and I have heard wild animals howling; and he who might have offered me protection no longer exists himself. I sought the last pious man, a saint and hermit who, alone in his forest, had not yet heard what all the world knows today."

"What does all the world know today?" asked Zarathustra. "Perhaps this, that the old god in whom all the world once believed no longer lives?"

"As you say," replied the old man sadly. "And I served that old god until his last hour. But now I am retired, without a master, and yet not free, nor ever cheerful except in my memories. That is why I climbed these mountains, that I might again have a festival at last, as is fitting for an old pope and church father—for behold, I am the last pope—a festival of pious memories and divine services. But now he himself is dead, the most pious man, that saint in the forest who constantly praised his god with singing and humming. I did not find him when I found his cave; but there were two wolves inside, howling over his death, for all animals loved him. So I ran away. Had I then come to these woods and mountains in vain? Then my heart decided that I should seek another man, the most pious of all those who do not believe in God—that I should seek Zarathustra!"

Thus spoke the old man, and he looked with sharp eyes at the man standing before him; but Zarathustra seized the hand of the old pope and long contemplated it with admiration. "Behold, venerable one!" he said then; "what a beautiful long hand! That is the hand of one who has always dispensed blessings. But now it holds him whom you seek, me, Zarathustra. It is I, the godless Zarathustra, who speaks; who is more godless than I, that I may enjoy his instruction?"

Thus spoke Zarathustra, and with his glances he pierced the thoughts and the thoughts behind the thoughts of the old pope. At last the pope began, "He who loved and possessed him most has also lost him most now; behold, now I myself am probably the more godless of the two of us. But who could rejoice in that?"

"You served him to the last?" Zarathustra asked thoughtfully after a long silence. "You know *how* he died? Is it true what they say, that pity strangled him, that he saw how *man* hung on the cross and that he could not bear it, that love of man became his hell, and in the end his death?"

The old pope, however, did not answer but looked aside, shy, with a pained and gloomy expression. "Let him go!" Zarathustra said after prolonged reflection, still looking the old man straight in the eye. "Let him go! He is gone. And although it does you credit that you say only good things about him who is now dead, you know as well as I *who* he was, and that his ways were queer."

"Speaking in the confidence of three eyes," the old pope said cheerfully (for he was blind in one eye), "in what pertains to God, I am—and have the right to be—more enlightened than Zarathustra himself. My love served him many years, my will followed his will in everything. A good servant, however, knows everything, including even things that his master conceals from himself. He was a concealed god, addicted to secrecy. Verily, even a son he got himself in a sneaky way. At the door of his faith stands adultery.

"Whoever praises him as a god of love does not have a high enough opinion of love itself. Did this god not want to be a judge too? But the lover loves beyond reward and retribution.

"When he was young, this god out of the Orient, he was harsh and vengeful and he built himself a hell to amuse his favorites. Eventually, however, he became old and soft and mellow and pitying, more like a grandfather than a father, but most like a shaky old grandmother. Then he sat in his nook by the hearth, wilted, grieving over his weak legs, weary of the world, weary of willing, and one day he choked on his all-too-great pity."

"You old pope," Zarathustra interrupted at this point, "did you see that with your own eyes? Surely it might have happened that way—that way, and also in some other way. When gods die, they always die several kinds of death. But—well then! This way or that, this way and that—he is gone! He offended the taste of my ears and eyes; I do not want to say anything worse about him now that he is dead.

"I love all that looks bright and speaks honestly. But he—you know it, you old priest, there was something of your manner about him, of the priest's manner: he was equivocal. He was also indistinct. How angry he got with us, this wrath-snorter, because we understood him badly! But why did he not speak more clearly? And if it was the fault of our ears, why did he give us ears that heard him badly? If there was mud in our ears—well, who put it there? He bungled too much, this potter who had never finished his apprenticeship. But that he wreaked revenge on his pots and creations for having bungled them himself, that was a sin against *good taste*. There is good taste in piety too; and it was this that said in the end, 'Away with *such* a god! Rather no god, rather make destiny on one's own, rather be a fool, rather be a god oneself!' "

"What is this I hear?" said the old pope at this point, pricking up his ears. "O Zarathustra, with such disbelief you are more pious than you believe. Some god in you must have converted you to your godlessness. Is it not your piety itself that no longer lets you believe in a god? And your overgreat honesty will yet lead you beyond good and evil too. Behold, what remains to you? You have eyes and hands and mouth, predestined for blessing from all eternity. One does not bless with the hand alone. Near you, although you want to be the most godless, I sent a secret, sacred, pleasant scent of long blessings: it gives me gladness and grief. Let me be your guest, O Zarathustra, for one single night! Nowhere on earth shall I now feel better than with you."

"Amen! So be it!" said Zarathustra in great astonishment. "Up there goes the way, there lies Zarathustra's cave. I should indeed like to accompany you there myself, you venerable one, for I love all who are pious. But now a cry of distress urgently calls me away from you. In my realm no one shall come to grief; my cave is a good haven. And I wish that I could put everyone who is sad back on firm land and firm legs.

"But who could take your melancholy off your shoulders? For that I am too weak. Verily, we might wait long before someone awakens your god again. For this old god lives no more: he is thoroughly dead."

Thus spoke Zarathustra.

EXISTENTIALISM AS A SYMPTOM OF MAN'S CONTEMPORARY CRISIS

William C. Barrett

Nowadays we speak quite easily and naturally of the crisis through which our civilization is passing. Without questioning the assumption that we are in the midst of a crisis, I should like to ask whether this feeling of crisis is not something inseparable from human life in any historical period. The more closely we examine the past, the more we find that it, too, is uneasy with its own sense of historical crisis and urgency. Sometimes, in retrospect, these crises look illusory, for mankind has survived some of its worst apprehensions; and then we have to remind ourselves that these men and women of the past felt that bygone crisis in their bones, with the same intimate uneasiness with which we feel ours. We begin to suspect that to live itself is to exist in crisis (more or less actual at any moment), and that only in periods of real historic somnolence and lethargy—real decadence, in short—has mankind been without a sense of crisis. No doubt, there are important differences of degree, and one age may be more plainly a period of breakdown than another; it would be folly to neglect such differences of degree, but the thought that crisis, or the sense of it is a permanent part of human life, does fortify us to see our own contemporary crisis in a much broader light—as a total human condition.

This thought will explain why I prefer to discuss existential philosophy as a symptom, rather than a solution, of our present crisis. For to the degree that we see our crisis as a total and concrete condition, to that degree we shall doubt that any philosophy, no matter how ambitious, can propose itself as the unique path of salvation. Anyone who has had any personal experience of a spiritual crisis will know that recovery does not come through the acquisition of any new abstract ideas. The progress from health to sickness is a change of being, rather than a change in thought. So, if we agree that our civilization is spiritually sick, we should also expect that the recovery will not come through any single set of ideas, or philosophy, but only through a transformation of our whole existence—thus requiring social, economic, and religious change. A new philosophy would be only a necessary *part* of this total change.

Moreover, it is the very characteristic of Existentialism as a philosophy that it must look with irony upon any system of thought that proposes itself as *the* solution for all of life's crises. Let us remember that Kierkegaard, the founder of Existentialism, began to philosophize with the purpose of discovering difficulties, rather than offering easy and readymade solutions. Existentialism as a philosophy attempts to make man aware of certain basic realities of his life. In this sense it seeks to increase, rather than minimize, our human difficulties. The business of finding solutions must come only after a man is aware of the whole depth, import, and, therefore, difficulty, of his human life.

I

This preliminary definition of existential philosophy will be understood better, if we contrast it with the usual kinds of philosophy now taught in our academies. The various schools of philosophy are distinguished from each other by different beliefs. Thus it comes about that a philosophy is understood as a set of beliefs, or propositions, to which a man gives intellectual assent. A man is said to have a philosophy, then, if he has a system of propositions which he holds to be true on purely intellectual or rational grounds. This is the understanding of philosophy that has prevailed particularly in our period of the departmentalization of all human knowledge. But Existentialism seeks to restore a much more primitive sense of the word, "philosophy," than this: namely, the ancient sense of philosophy as a concrete way of life, rather than an abstract set of propositions. Nietzsche, also an Existentialist, pointed out that for ancient man, and even the modern Oriental, the business of achieving a philosophy is one that engaged the whole man, his total being, and was not pursued simply as one specialized department of knowledge among others. Kierkegaard attacked the Hegelian professors of his time as being philosophers without any real philosophic existence: they had a system of propositions to teach, but the system itself was a means of forgetting the concrete realities of human life. For us in America today the philosopher is merely a "professional" savant among many others.

Existentialism, on the contrary, understands philosophy as a thing that is to be lived, and not merely a body of knowledge to be taught to pupils. I have said that Existentialism attempts to bring to human consciousness the basic, even banal, realities of human life: realities such as death, anxiety, choice, love, freedom, guilt, conscience, the willing acceptance of anxiety, etc., etc. In American academic philosophy today these are not the prevailing concepts: philosophers discuss concepts relating to science, knowledge, logic. Existential concepts are thought to belong to literature, perhaps to poetry. This rejection is an evidence of how far one particular tradition among the intellectual elite of our society has tended to set knowledge above life. If the philosopher exists professionally as a member of a department in a university, and if he accepts his role as one that deals with one special department of knowledge among others, then he is inevitably drawn to devote himself to those very special and technical problems that seem to be the peculiar province of the "expert." Our technological civilization has tended more and more to worship the expert and the philosopher, assimilated to his civilization, strives more and more to justify his own professional existence by a high technical competence in the special problems of logic and philosophical analysis. The result is that a great deal of modern philosophy has tended to become divorced from life. Hence it is only natural that Existentialism, which struggles against this tendency, is looked on somewhat askance by a great many American philosophers.

All this has been by way of explaining why it seemed preferable to discuss Existentialism as a symptom, rather than a solution, of our contemporary crisis. But there has also been in the background of my remarks another, and much more drastic point, which will be substantiated by my further discussion, but can be announced now: the point, quite simply, that there is never a solution to any of life's crises. This is one of the cardinal points in existential philosophy itself. The word, "solution," belongs to the vocabulary of science and engineering, suggesting some kind of blueprint that would immediately deliver us from the pain and muddle of suffering, when, in fact, we know that our really deep crises in life are precisely those that we have to live through. Our deepest personal problems do not in the least resemble any problem of engineering, and it is the same, we suggest, with the sickness of civilization, even though the "cure" of a sick civilization might require vast exploits of engineering.

II

That movement in thought should be a symptom of its time, is not in the least a condemnation of this movement as a wild or trivial aberration. I am using the word, "symptom," in its simple and unprejudiced sense of a sign— something that instructs us about the state of the organism from which it arises. Thus Existentialism has a great deal to teach us—which we might otherwise not know—about the condition of the Western civilization that has brought it to birth.

Most Americans connect Existentialism with the current French movement, and particularly with the name of its most brilliant publicist, Jean Paul Sartre. Sartre's is an agile and energetic mind, but his doctrine represents, I believe, a dilution of existential philosophy, and in any case does not take us back to its original sources. These lie in the nineteenth century, and the great innovators are Kierkegaard and Nietzsche—though the latter, unlike Kierkegaard, is not fully aware of his existential point of departure. Existential themes are treated in the fiction of Tolstoi and Dostoievski. In this century the two most important existential philosophers have been the German professors, Martin Heidegger and Karl Jaspers. To these names we might add the considerable figure of the Spanish philosopher, José Ortega y Gasset, who has described his philosophy as one of "vital reason," though it is fundamentally existential in its directions. These names should indicate that Existentialism is not a momentary intellectual fad, derived from the French, but a much wider and deeper movement in Western thought, having roots indeed in the profound upheavals of this civilization during the past two centuries. To see what these roots are, we may find it more convenient to turn, not to an abstruse text in philosophy, but to a work of literature that takes a simpler and more direct grasp of the issues involved: Tolstoi's great story, "The Death of Ivan Ilyich," which by this time has become something of a basic scripture for existential thought.

The plot of Tolstoi's story is slight and almost negligible. Ivan Ilyich is an amiable and undistinguished bourgeois, who has spent his whole life trying to be like everyone else in his social class: a successful and happy man, where happiness means only the absence of suffering. But one day Ivan Ilyich feels a pain in his side, which resists all treatment by doctors, and as his illness progresses, he suddenly realizes that he is going to die. For the first time in his life death becomes a reality for him. In the face of this awful presence, all his disguises fall away: confronting death for the first time in his life, he is also confronting himself for the first time. Hitherto in his life he had hid from himself amid the routine mechanisms of all his social, official, and familial functions. Now, as he is about to die, he asks himself the questions: Who am I? What has been the meaning of my life? In the end Ivan Ilyich dies content, because he has reached the point of knowing that the life he lived was empty, futile, and meaningless.

What Tolstoi is saying here, to put it now as a general thesis, is that modern life has alienated the individual from himself. The materialistic and rationalistic nineteenth century, with its emphasis upon all the bourgeois routines of life, has so externalized the individual that he has lost the feeling and the passion for his own personal existence. Modern man, Tolstoi is saying, has lost the meaning of life, and, as with Ivan Ilyich, it will take nothing less than the presence of death to restore this sense of life.

The sense of decadence haunts the nineteenth century, even at the moments of its most splendid optimism. There is a widespread uneasiness that life has lost its passion, intensity, and meaning; that there has been some secret decline in human vitality. Kierkegaard puts it as eloquently and compactly as one could wish:

> Let others complain that times are bad; I complain that they are petty because they lack passion. Men's thoughts are as flimsy as thin ice and men themselves as insignificant as the thin snow that covers it. Their thoughts are too petty to be sinful. A worm might consider such thoughts to be sinful, but not a man created in the image of God. Their pleasures are circumspect and boring; their passions, sleep; these materialistic souls fulfill their duties, but they collect their usury for it; they believe that although our Lord keeps His accounts in good order, they can hand Him counterfeit. Out with them! This is why my soul always hearkens back to Shakespeare and the Old Testament. There one feels that those who speak are men; there they hate; there they love; there they kill the enemy, curse their descendants for generations to come, there they sin.

This passage might almost have been written by Nietzsche, who launches his plea from the diametrically opposite anti-Christian pole. Modern man, says Nietzsche, lacks a goal, and his existence is, therefore, purposeless and nihilistic. Similar themes appear also in such diverse writers as Stendhal and Burckhardt.

The twentieth century has no reason to forget these fears. Our technological civilization has become even more involved with elaborate apparatus to catch and smother the individual. We have gone beyond the nineteenth century in the development of a fantastic mass culture—in radio, movies, and television—that stamps out all individual differences. Modern society has become more and more a mass society. Cities grow larger, crowds become more and more potent factors, and the individual threatened more than ever by anonymity in the mass. The image of modern man lies in T. S. Eliot's line: "Men and bits of paper, whirled by the cold wind."[1] These fears of the nineteenth century turn out to be prophetic for us: amid this general

---

[1] T. S. Eliot, "Burnt Norton," *Collected Poems of T. S. Eliot, 1909–1935* (New York: Harcourt, Brace & World, Inc., 1936), p. 217.

purposelessness of life, this mass drifting, we set ourselves the task of recapturing the sense and the meaning of life.

III

· When Tolstoi speaks of a loss of the meaning of life, he is not referring to a loss of some rational explanation. Nor is the meaning that is to be restored an intellectual one, some new fact or discovery of the mind. On the contrary, the disorder in modern man that Tolstoi's story speaks of is a disorder in the more primitive and irrational, or non-rational, parts of man's being. Existentialism as a philosophy seeks to deal with these irrational parts of our existence in a way that philosophy has never done before, and by so doing gives reason itself a new place in the human hierarchy.

This is why existential philosophy has been frequently—and, I think, unjustly—criticized as anti-rational. One is not against reason, if one insists that the irrational is an inseparable part of life, and that it is precisely with the irrational parts of our being that modern civilization fails to deal adequately. This so-called "anti-rational" tendency in modern philosophy has now had a long history, from Rousseau to Bergson, Whitehead, and Heidegger in our century, and it embraces too many great names to be dismissed out of hand. Any future rationalism worth its salt will have to assimilate a great deal from these thinkers, and we ourselves would be less than rational, if we did not make an earnest effort to understand in detail how the irrational enters human life.

We gain some idea of the irrational character of life, if we turn back again to Tolstoi's "Ivan Ilyich." As death appears to Ivan Ilyich, it presents itself as something altogether unreasonable and incomprensible. Immersed in the comfortable structure of his life, he sees this strange and dark intruder creep in to destroy everything. Yet, death is a banal fact, and we know that all men have to die; Ivan Ilyich knows all this with his head, but his heart cannot grasp the incomprehensible fact that he, Ivan Ilyich, should have to die. This bewilderment may strike us as childish, but it is Tolstoi's means of showing us how the irrational, like death, may fall upon us in the most incalculable and unpredictable way, upsetting all our plans for life.

Kierkegaard has expounded the presence of the irrational in another area of human life—in the act of choice or decision. We do not doubt that some decisions are more rational than others, and we may even speak of a decision as being the only rational choice under the circumstances. But is a rational choice one from which the irrational is ever completely excluded? Is any choice, however rational it be, free from the uncertain contingencies of risk and adventure? Of course, there are certain trivial choices that we make every day, and that we may reverse the next day, if we are proved wrong. But these are choices that do not commit us deeply, that leave us relatively disengaged from the consequences. As soon, however, as a choice cuts deeply; as soon as it commits our whole life in a certain direction; so soon, then, do the immense difficulties appear, the balance of probabilities becomes harder, and each alternative appears, however we may canvass its possibilities, as a leap into the unknown.

The choice that personally involved Kierkegaard happened to be the question whether or not to marry. Engaged to a young woman in Copenhagen, he desired marriage intensely, but he felt in himself also a certain religious mission that would prevent him from giving himself completely in marriage. The particular psychological facts involved here are important for an understanding of Kierkegaard's biography, but the peculiarly personal difficulties should not obscure for us the fact that the pathos of choice Kierkegaard faced is universal. There are, in short, choices in life that are irreversible. Kierkegaard could not have made an *experimental* choice of marriage, in the expectation that if it "did not work out"—to use the expression that has become common among us these days—he could return to his religious vocation and its tasks, for the vocation might have been lost through his marriage. On the other hand, if he renounced marriage experimentally, he could not hope to return to the young lady, should the other alternative not work out. She might not be there (as in fact she was not) when he returned. Love has to be seized at the moment it is offered; our indecision pollutes and destroys it.

All of this points to the fact that the situation of human choice is not at all a situation of scientific experiment. A situation is experimental in science when certain scientific controls have been established, so that through these controls we can repeat the experiment at any time and place we choose, and indeed repeat it indefinitely. The more precisely scientific the experiment becomes, the more its features of accidental particularity become refined away, and the easier it becomes to repeat it in all its detail. But our fundamental choices in life do not permit us this degree of control, because they do not permit us this degree of detachment. We have to choose here and now, and for the rest of our life, and the alternative we renounce is lost forever. We could be completely experimental about our own lives only if we were immortal, and so could repeat any situation or choice indefinitely.

But as death is real and our lives finite, every choice is also a renunciation, and this is why Kierkegaard speaks of the *pathos* of human choice. It was this sacrificial and pathetic aspect of choice that led Kierkegaard to his great polemic against the excessively rational philosophy of Hegel. The old adage puts the matter quite simply and adequately, "You cannot eat your cake and have it, too"; but Hegel devised a sophisticated dialectic by which it was possible to bring together two conflicting alternatives, thesis and antithesis, into a higher synthesis, so that the speculative philosopher, triumphing over life, could both have his cake and eat it, too. Such a reconciling of opposites is indeed possible in knowledge, where a more inclusive theory may embrace two conflicting alternatives; but it is not possible in life, where the suffering of renunciation cannot be altogether eliminated by reason. This opposition between knowledge and life has been one of the chief themes of Existentialism, as well as of a great deal of modern philosophy and literature.

IV

These two brief illustrations of the irrational—death and human choice—which cannot be altogether expunged from our existence, also illustrate that science, and scientific experiment, cannot take over the whole of life. The fear that science might devour the whole of human life has been a very powerful current of thought in the West, from William Blake onward. Indeed, from the Enlightenment in the eighteenth century to the present day, two deeply opposed attitudes toward science have dominated Western thinking: along with the great hope in science and its possibilities of human liberation, there has developed a great fear that science would somehow mechanize and impoverish human life. This fear of science cannot be dismissed simply as a crude popular superstition, for it embraces too many great names of our culture: Blake, Wordsworth, Kierkegaard, Nietzsche, Dostoievski, Tolstoi, Bergson. Our task, rather, should be to disengage the philosophical traits that characterize this fear of science at its deepest level.

One of the best expressions of the fear of science is found in the first part of Dostoievski's great novel, *Notes from Underground*. The hero is afraid of the scientific society of the future, in which human life can be rationally controlled and ordered, down to the very last detail. When human life is so scientifically precise and predictable, nobody would want to live it. Dostoievski's hero would prefer to smash this machine that would seek to contain him—out of sheer spite, as he puts it—to show that his human will in its liberty transcends the mathematically predictable, even if he has to show this in a destructive way. We come back thus to our principal point: what Dostoevski is saying, through his tormented and oppressed little hero, is that human life must be more than pure reason, and to attempt to reduce it to the latter is to destroy it, even if we make that reduction in the name of universal enlightenment.

It would be a mistake to consider the Underground Man as merely a sick and neurotic individual produced by the stresses of modern society. He is that, of course, but he is also a universal human character. We are all the Underground Man, to some degree or other. He is that dark side of our being, with which we must try to live in peace, and if we take lightly his fulminations against a human regime completely controlled by science and reason, we do so at our own risk.

As he is thus universal, the Underground Man reappears, and perhaps I may drive home my point by turning to the rather extraordinary position advanced in the nineteen hundred and twenties by I. A. Richards, the British critic and psychologist—a position that seems to me to express the extreme of hope that science will master life. (In justice to Richards, however, we must point out that at the time he was much more enamored of the possibilities of psychology than he is today.) Richards contended nothing less than this: that we can anticipate the time when psychological science will have advanced to the point where we can have, if we choose, whatever minds we desire. In the perfectly scientific utopia, in short, you could order your personality at a psychological laboratory the way you might order a prescription at a druggist's. Select your label, follow the prescription carefully, and you will have the personality, or the mind, that you want. Science which has performed so many miracles in the transformation of matter, and has found synthetic substitutes for almost everything, would here have found at last a substitute for life itself. In this psychological utopia it would be possible for a man to have a certain character without living through the risks, anxieties, and uncertain struggles that make it. We need not live to become a certain kind of being, science would provide it readymade.

We notice that this possibility that once inspired Richards with such hopes, is precisely the possibility against which Dostoievski's Underground Man rebels. Sick and resentful though he may be, the Underground Man at least insists upon having his own human life, rather than some mechanized substitute for it. The science of psychology has gone on developing since Richards's remark, but it is now further from maintaining any such utopian claims as once enchanted him. Among some circles in America, psychoanalysis may be regarded as a kind of magic, but not by the analysts themselves. Some people tend to think of psychoanalysis as a process in which the analyst, somewhat like a mechanic, overhauls the patient and gives him a new engine or set of works. But the serious analyst, while hoping to transform the neurotic patient's fundamental orientations toward life, insists that the patient can solve his problems only in actual life and not in the psychoanalytic session. Life has to be lived, there is no substitute for living—not even psychoanalysis.

Existential philosophy, in its insistence that the categories of life cannot be reduced to science, carries this point further. It may seem a rather trivial platitude to say that there can be no substitute for living, but the saying may not strike us as so platitudinous when we reflect upon the vast mechanized passivity that our civilization imposes upon so many of its members. In such circumstances the living rediscovery of certain banalities may represent an immense task and an immense triumph. Some of the greatest chapters in the history of philosophy are its discoveries of what lay obvious, but unnoticed, before every man's eyes. We may recall the great saying of Heraclitus, at the very dawn of philosophy in the sixth century B.C.: "Man is estranged from that with which he is most familiar, and he must continuously seek to rediscover it." This saying might serve as a very good motto for Existentialism. Among other things, it may make clear why the modern Existentialist, Heidegger, finds these early pre-Socratic Greeks his real forebears in the effort to confront human life and the whole life of nature with a primitive directness. The ancestry of existential philosophy thus turns out to be very ancient. I come back thus to a point made at the beginning, which should now be considerably clearer in its import: Existentialism, a modern movement in philosophy, is, in fact, an effort to recapture an old and very primitive sense of philosophy. Philosophy, here, is not the mere putting together of certain abstract propositions into a system; it is rather the concrete effort of the living individual to relate himself to his own life and the life of others around him. Quite literally, philosophy is a task that each individual has to perform for himself.

V

In this search for the primitive, Existentialism is in line with the most considerable movements in art and literature in this century. The word, "primitive," here is bound to arouse misunderstandings, if it is associated with the life of savages, barbarians, or big game hunters. Primitivism suggests to some the beat of tom-toms, Tahiti, maidens in sarongs, Gauguin; in short, an escape from modern civilization into the illusory simplicities of some South Sea island. These forms of primitivism have abounded, but they have always ended in a blind alley, because the desire for escape is itself a very nonprimitive state of being. I am using the word, "primitive," in a much more basic—I almost wrote primitive—sense: the primitive is the primary; and the valid search for the primitive is a search for the sources of our being which a too routinized civilization tends to obscure. In this sense, nearly all the art and literature that matter in the past half century have been primitive.

Modern painting and sculpture, for example, have really succeeded in creating a new kind of vision. In these works we stand in a new and more direct relation to colors, shapes, and forms. It is a vision of things at once simpler and more complex than the Western art of the past. In its distorting simplifications, bold arbitrary forms, it often resembles primitive art, from which indeed it has consciously drawn inspiration in certain cases, though it could not exist without the whole tradition of Western art. Moreover, the artist himself seems to stand in a new and direct relation to the very materials of his art: he seeks naïvely to assert the presence of his paint, stone, or metal, and his art is no longer a device to conceal or transcend this presence.

In literature, in writers such as D. H. Lawrence, James Joyce, and Thomas Mann, we find similar and diverging efforts to deal with the primitive. In his Joseph stories, Mann seeks to restore the primitive mythic consciousness to literature. James Joyce, in his last work, uses the most sophisticated literary technique, drawing upon the whole past of Western literature for its resources, in order to render the most unconscious, inarticulate, and primitive parts of human experience. Of these writers perhaps Lawrence is the most explicitly programmatic in his search for the primitive simplicities that he believes modern life to have lost. The organic unity of being that Lawrence seeks through sexual experience, is something that existential philosophers have sought in other directions. As T. S. Eliot reminds us, Lawrence was a man with an intense spiritual vocation, and his interest in sex was not at all a message of sex-for-sex's sake. Nevertheless, his proposed solution to the sickness of modern civilization seems to us today to be rather onesided. His perception of the sickness was real enough, but his prescription for cure represents a kind of impatient rush toward a solution. We are reminded, again, that when a sickness is total, the recovery can come only through development along many avenues of being at once.

This list could be swelled indefinitely to show that this struggle for rebirth is one of the great themes of modern culture. I have appended these brief indications to my main discussion only to point to the total historical context in which we must try to see the development of modern existential philosophy; and to suggest that this philosophy is not an eccentric movement, but lies in the main stream of modern culture. Existentialism makes clearer the human tasks that our epoch confronts. Unless we realize what the tasks are, we can hardly work significantly toward any solution at all.

RELIGION IN THE AGE OF AQUARIUS

Harvey Cox and T. George Harris

HARRIS: Do you worry, as a theologian, about the general resurgence of superstition and magic? What do you do when students ask about your zodiac sign?

COX: You know, I hate to admit it, but they did bug me at first. When somebody would come up and say, "What's your sign?" I used to say, "I don't know. I'm not interested in that stuff." Then I got to the point where I would say in my skeptical Harvard-professor voice, "If you believe there is really some correlation between signs and character, you ought to tell me what sign I am. What sign am I?" Mine was the typical rationalistic approach: "Look at me. Ask me questions. Guess. Let's test it."

Sometimes they would play my game, but it was wrong. I now know why. Do you know what people are saying when they ask your sign? They are saying *I want to relate to you, to be intimate with you in this kooky, interesting, groovy way—a way that is going to blow the minds of those god-damned rationalists. The logical people who have organized our society have defined us into categories that we can't live in.*

Well, that's true. There's no room to move around in, to grow in, in these little boxes reserved for white people, Protestants, Jews, men, women, students, Americans, Russians, Democrats, suburbanites, New Left, rich people, poor. The whole thing is sick, and we can't do without some kind of empathy.

So along comes this absolutely weird group of categories unrelated to social status or anything else. Nobody's defining you, and you're not putting a tag on him. If you're a Taurus and I'm a Taurus, my god, immediately we've got a secret intimacy. We enter into this little conspiracy . . .

We have spent the last few hundred years with our cultural attention focused dourly on the "outside" factual world—exploring, investigating and mastering it.

Those who had a penchant for fantasy never really felt at home. They were even driven out of religious institutions, the shelter where the fantasies of the mystic would normally be cherished and cultivated. Christianity, especially its Protestant versions, conned itself, and got conned, into providing the spiritual cement and stick-and-carrot values for Western industrialization. Only in the black church and in folk Catholicism such as Mexico has do you find much of Christ's festive spirit still alive.

HARRIS: And the Methodists have cut the gut-busting tunes out of the *Cokesbury Hymnal.* You have to go to a bar to sing an ecstatic hymn.

COX: Sure. A bar certainly is one of the few places remaining where you can really let go without somebody taking you seriously. You can play.

It's my conviction that conventional religion has declined not because of the advance of science or the spread of education or any of the reasons normally advanced for secularization. The reason is simple but hard to see because it is embedded in our total environment: the tight, bureaucratic and instrumental society—the only model we've known since the industrial revolution—renders us incapable of experiencing the nonrational dimensions of existence. The absurd, the inspiring, the uncanny, the awesome, the terrifying, the ecstatic—none of these fits into a production- and efficiency-oriented society. They waste time, aren't dependable. When they appear we try to ban them by force or some brand-name therapy. Having systematically stunted the Dionysian side of the whole human, we assume that man is naturally just a reliable, plane-catching Apollonian.

The blame for this distortion usually gets hung on something called "puritanism" or the "Protestant ethic." But that analysis, I believe, is not entirely adequate. No religion yet tested seems to stand unbent by the pressure of the managerial faith known as "Economic Development." Communism, nationalism and other ideologies have gone the same route elsewhere on the globe.

HARRIS: So how does anybody see out, let alone break out?

COX: We are never completely the captives of our culture or its language. People all over the world are turning, often desperately, to the overlooked corners and freaks that were never completely systematized. Hence our fascination for pop art—and gloriously, for Fellini's films—with the junk and rejects of the industrial process. Also with the slippery stuff that never found a place in it: astrology, madness, witches, drugs, non-Western religions, palmistry and mysticism, shoddy or serious.

Even the current preoccupation with sex and violence can, to some extent, be understood in terms of this reaction. Both blood and sperm are explosive, irregular, feeling-pitched, messy and inexplicably fascinating. You can't store either one safely in the humming memory of an IBM 360, to be smoothly printed out only when needed in the program. To use a theological term, they *transcend* routine experience.

HARRIS: In *The Secular City*, which stirred up many sociologists and city planners, you argued that urban-age man has become the creator of his own world, heaven or hell, including his value system. We can't blame it on fate or God anymore. With that weight on our heads, you now urge us, in *Feast*, to go dancing in the streets.

COX: Maybe I've learned something. Must there be a gap between those who are working and hoping for a better world and those for whom life is affirmative, a celebration? Must the radicals and revolutionaries—the *new militants*—be at cross purposes with the *neo-mystics*—the hippies and Yippies and all those who are experimenting with new styles of being? I think not, and I hope not. They are, I think, tied together.

So *Feast* is not a recantation of *Secular City*; it's an extension, a recognition that the changes we need are much more fundamental than I thought five years ago, and that the method for achieving them must be much more drastic. Man actually took charge of his own history back in the 19th Century. In *City* I was trying to help us face that fact—defatalization—on the conscious level and work out the consequences. In *Feast* the point is that we can't handle the burden of making history if we are ourselves buried in it, unaware of the timeless dimension that we touch only in fantasy and festivity.

Have you noticed, George, how the past has become an intolerable weight? Except for conservatives who want to use the good-old-days as a club to beat everybody else with, people have a desperate impulse to destroy the past, to curse it, blow it up, burn it. That impulse explains the popularity of books like Norman O. Brown's *Life Against Death* and *Love's Body*. Brown calls on us to "be ready to live instead of making history, to enjoy instead of paying back old scores and debts, and to enter that state of Being which has the goal of Becoming." He begins with Freud's view that repression is the price we pay for civilization, and he thinks the price is exorbitant. History to Brown is not just one damned thing after another; it's one big mistake. He wants to get away from it all.

More calmly, Claude Lévi-Strauss and other French structuralists suggest that we are all over-committed to decision-making, temporal aims and historical objectives. Lévi-Strauss argues that Jean-Paul Sartre, the philosopher of free decision and human world-making, must be left behind.

Much of music and theater seeks to immolate the past quite literally. Take John Cage, for instance. He's certainly the most self-conscious avant-gardist in American music. He undermines the whole axiom of continuity by eliminating the idea of melody. He wants us to listen to one sound at a time, not to hear it in terms of the note that came before it.

In his theater of cruelty, Antonin Artaud invited playwrights to deal in the raw, instant aspects of existence. Lights should be selected not to enhance the play but to blister the eyes of the audience. He wanted to destroy our veneration of what had been done so that we would have to create life in our own idiom. Since Artaud, theater has been used to shock, outrage and seduce the audience out of cool spectator seats to participate in violence, magic and, at times, in joy.

HARRIS: Are you putting down such things as guerrilla theater?

COX: Hell, no. Artaud's mix of spoken and written work lights up the visionary quality of some of the student radicals, the ones who are insistently anti-ideological. Cage, on the other hand, symbolizes the mystical, Dionysiac, experience-believing portion of the present generation the *now* mentality that is dedicated to pursuit of direct experience—erotic, visual or auditory.

There's a close connection between sensory overload and sensory deprivation. John Lilly discovered in his experiments that for a man suspended in dark silence, a tiny stimulus becomes agonizingly intense. Now go the other way. With an acid-rock band imploding you with sound and a light show chopping your eyeballs, you are totally isolated and must turn intensely inward. It's not exactly like silent contemplation, but it's one way to cut yourself off from this harried culture.

Why bother? Is there any reason for people's desperate impulse to cut out of the orderly, tense roles assigned to us? Despite the battles between Christianity and Marxism, both have tended to harness us into a sense of doing whatever history bids us do. "History" is the name we give the horizon of consciousness within which we live. It's all we see. We've lost sight of the larger environment—the cosmic phenomena open to us through intuition, awe and ecstasy—because of our enormous self-consciousness about the events of the past, present and future. Michael Polanyi calls this larger reality the "tacit dimension." Teilhard de Chardin called it the "divine milieu." History is defined by time; the cosmic circle suggests eternity. To be fully human we need to be in touch with both—to apprehend, as T. S. Eliot said, the point of intersection of the timeless with time.

Gestalt psychologists and Marshall McLuhan have both pointed out the necessity for an "anti-environment," the background needed to frame anything before we can see it. If something fills our whole environment, we can't see it. . . .

I noticed a while back that my students were reading—really hooked on—six books that ordinarily would not seem to have anything in common. Here they are:

Stranger in a Strange Land, Robert Heinlein's science fiction on the human-from-Mars. Valentine Michael Smith, the hero, could "grok," that beautiful verb for total comprehension, in a way that we earthlings have trained ourselves not to do.

I Ching, the "book of changes" or the sacred books of ancient China.

The Double Helix, the account of how the genetic code was broken—by imagining pretty molecular structures and finding out which one could, by inference, be assumed to exist. Also, there were so many completely nonscientific factors—trying to beat Linus Pauling, and coping with ill-tempered Rosie, the chick in the next lab.

The Teachings of Don Juan, Carlos Castaneda's account of the romantic who refused to see things as practical men did, and do.

The Politics of Experience, psychiatrist R. D. Laing's wild, wonderful application of the theory that schizophrenia is double vision, a survival reaction.

The Mind of the Dolphin, John C. Lilly's research on what the comics of the sea say to each other.

These books all deal with unorthodox, often spooky ways of knowing and feeling, even with seeing things as the dolphin does.

But getting into a nonliteral mode of thought, let alone trying to write about it, is nearly impossible for many people. Remember the weekend we had a few years ago, George, at the American Academy of Arts and Sciences? Henry Murray and Talcott Parsons and Martin Marty and David Riesman—a combination of social scientists and theologians—were all sitting around the table. Remember how miffed Daniel Callahan got over the point you made about the emotional content in religion? He called you a Baptist. Well, my Baptist upbringing helps me to respect the experiential, the validity of the Dionysian. You know, Timothy Leary's wife—second wife—was once a Southern Baptist. I remember spending an evening with them on a hillside, lying under the stars up in New York State. She laughed and said to me, "We Baptists are just natural heads." Beautiful. What she meant was, you know, how could a Unitarian ever see a white flash? What liberal Congregationalist ever had a bad trip in church? . . .

HARRIS: Sister Mary Corita—I guess she'd rather be known as artist Corita Kent—is appropriating secular symbols like bread wrappers for sacramental meaning.

COX: Corita's enormously important. People saw her as just a cute nun, but she's the chick who saw slogans like "the Pepsi generation" and "come alive" and "care enough to send the best" and all that stuff in a way that would let us appropriate it. With her paintings she lets us say that man's creations, even the venial ones, are sacred.

HARRIS: Maybe the whole pop-art movement is a sacramentalizing of the environment. The artist lets us see it in a fresh way so we can laugh at it and celebrate it.

COX: Yeah, yeah. Corita's humanizing the environment and also reminding us that the world is, as she says, unfinished. There's a new universe to create. She brings off these two master strokes at once, and she's got the love to put an ironic twist on slogans that have been used for manipulation. Wouldn't it be great if Corita would paint the cover for this issue of *Psychology Today!*

You know about the thing Corita and some of us did at that discotheque, The Boston Tea Party? We called it "An Evening with God." Everybody came, hundreds, and I started out by saying, a little lamely, "This isn't a church . . ." Somebody in the back yelled, "It *is* a church . . ." The ushers in beads and 20 wonderful girls in miniskirts passed out the wine and the home-baked bread. Dan Berrigan read his poems and Judy Collins sang. Corita had a rock band and strobe lights going, and pretty soon everybody was dancing in the aisles.

It worked well, maybe too well, because people keep coming back to ask when we're going to do it again. What we want is for them to do their own celebrations, not lean on us.

Post-industrial man is rediscovering festivity. In churches all over the country there's been this eruption of multimedia masses, jazz rituals, folk and rock worship services, new art and dance liturgies. You know, there's always a John Wesley around to wonder why the Devil should have all the good things. Judson Memorial in New York and a few other churches have had "revelations," the nude dancers in psychedelic lights at the altar. Some people oppose the guitar and the leotard in church for the same reasons their forebears opposed the use of the pipe organ— it never had been done before, or so they think. Others reject the festive new liturgies as merely the latest example of the Establishment's exploitation of flashy gimmicks to lure the recalcitrant back into the fold. They've got a point. Ecclesiastical imperialism is always a threat.

What matters is that the renaissance of festivity is comprehensive, and at the moment there's far more of it outside the church than inside. That's why Corita and I used a discotheque, not a church.

We're now working on an Easter service—for April 26, the Byzantine Easter, three weeks after the regular one. We'll sing things like *Amazing Grace*; Arlo Guthrie made it an ecumenical hymn. The liturgical dancers in Boston specialize in getting everybody to participate. In the midst of the multimedia rejoicing we'll have small group interactions and meditation. And the Woodstock Eucharist, home-baked bread and jugs. It'll start at 4 a.m. in The Boston Tea Party. At 6 a.m. the trumpets will blow for the resurrection of Christ—whatever that means to you. It's bring-your-own theology. We didn't think too many would come, but so many alienated Protestant and Jewish kids want to participate that we can't find enough things for them to do.

HARRIS: Your emphasis on sensuality blows a lot of clerical minds.

COX: So what do we do, pretend that God created us as disembodied spirits? This is not a new question. Suspicion of the flesh has plagued Christianity off and on for most of its history. I suspect that we've inherited a perverted form of Christianity, deodorized and afraid of smell. That's one reason I used the title *Feast of Fools,* which comes from a Medieval celebration. It was not exactly prim and proper. Ordinarily pious priests and townsfolk put on bawdy masks, sang outrageous ditties and generally kept the world awake with revelry and satire. They made sport of the most sacred royal and religious practices. Of course, the feast was never popular with the higher-ups, who recognized that pure revelry is always radical. As the church became more and more worried about its authority, with running things on time, the bureaucrats managed to stamp out the feast, leaving only a memory of it in Halloween and New Years'.

Our feasting is now sporadic and obsessive, our fantasies predictable and our satire politically impotent. Our celebrations do not relate us, as they once did, to the parade of cosmic history or to the great stories of man's spiritual quest. If discovering that people have bodies is one of the risks we have to take, that seems to be a small—indeed pleasant—price to pay.

HARRIS: How about the risks you've taken in antidraft demonstrations?

COX: I had to be pushed into that. The first time I heard about a guy burning a draft card I was horrified, shocked. Then about three years ago some students who had burned their cards had to go over to South Boston Courthouse for their trial. They were beaten and pummeled by a mob and the police wouldn't intervene. Next day I joined the march—you know, just demanding the right of police protection. That now seems like a long time ago. We were only about 60 people—resistance kids with beards and peace symbols and a couple of black marchers and clergy—but a mob of 300 or 400 came throwing rocks and fruit at us. One guy waved a sword at us with a freshly killed chicken on the point and the blood running down. He had a sense of symbolism.

When we got to the church—it was Good Friday—one of the

resistance kids spoke first. He had a swollen eye from the day before. He said the only thing he was sorry about was that the police had separated us from the mob, kept us from really having an encounter with those people. My first thought was, "this is where I leave you people—you're crazy." And my second thought was, "something's happening here that I don't understand." He really felt warmth and regard for the people who wanted to beat him up. I started out with my speech, but I couldn't say much. It was a turning point for me.

Then came a student who was going to refuse to take the symbolic step forward in the induction center. But he didn't want it to be a dour affair. Since he was doing it to affirm life, refusing to kill, he got his girl friend to make bread and strawberry jam, and all his friends came with him, girls handing out flowers to the military and being festive. Even the people at their desks got caught in the spirit of it.

This kind of thing upsets many adults, not only because they disagree on ideas but because they think the kids are putting them on. They're afraid they're being had. What they don't understand is the whole idea of festivity and celebration. . . .

HARRIS: You're betting on the social sciences to deal with angel feathers, Harvey—things like festivity are too gossamer to inspire serious work.

COX: No, I don't think so. Didn't you publish Jerome L. Singer's research into daydreaming? He and John Antrobus discovered that fantasies are richer among what sociologists call the "marginality" people—richer among immigrant Italians and Jews, richer still among black Americans. Apparently fantasy thrives among the disenfranchised. The symbolism in the black church, which, being marginal, never lost its festivity, should produce very rich possibilities. We may yet see comparative religion turn from its Protestant fixation on the texts of other faiths—surely a distorted and limiting view—to a more promising study of the whole religious ritual of a culture.

HARRIS: Where does that leave the institutional church?

COX: Some form of institutionalized religious expression is going to survive. Man is not only a religious being but a social one as well. He's not going to accept a completely do-it-yourself approach on anything this central to survival. Oh, the denominational type of Christianity headquartered in skyscrapers with branch offices in the suburbs is fated for rapid extinction, and it can't disappear too quickly for me. Yet, some form will rise out of the present resurgence of spiritual concern.

The figure of Christ is ubiquitous. He is now beginning to

appear as Christ the Harlequin: the personification of celebration and fantasy in an age that has lost both. It is a truer sense of Christ than the saccharine, bloodless face we see painted so often. He was part Yippie and part revolutionary, and part something else. On His day of earthly triumph, Palm Sunday, He rode to town on a jackass. One of the earliest representations of Jesus in religious art depicts a crucified figure with the head of an ass. A weak, even ridiculous church somehow peculiarly at odds with the ruling assumption of its day can once again appreciate the harlequinesque Christ.

THE NEW REFORMATION
Paul Goodman

For a long time modern societies have been operating as if religion were a minor and moribund part of the scheme of things. But this is unlikely. Men do not do without a system of "meanings" that everybody believes and puts his hope in even if, or especially if, he doesn't know anything about it; what Freud called a "shared psychosis," meaningful because shared, and with the power that resides in deep fantasy and longing. In advanced countries, indeed, it is science and technology themselves that have gradually, and finally triumphantly, become the system of mass faith, not disputed by various political ideologies and nationalisms that have also had religious uses.

Now this basic faith is threatened. Dissident young people are saying that science is antilife, it is a Calvinist obsession, it has been a weapon of white Europe to subjugate colored races, and scientific technology has manifestly become diabolical. Along with science, the young discredit the professions in general, and the whole notion of "disciplines" and academic learning. If these views take hold, it adds up to a crisis of belief, and the effects are incalculable. Every status and institution would be affected. Present political troubles could become endless religious wars. Here again, as in politics and morals, the worldwide youth disturbance may indicate a turning point in history and we must listen to it carefully.

In 1967 I gave a course on "professionalism" at the New School for Social Research in New York, attended by about 25 graduate students from all departments. My bias was the traditional one: professionals are autonomous individuals beholden to the nature of things and the judgment of their peers, and bound by an explicit or implicit oath to benefit their clients and the community. To teach this, I invited seasoned professionals whom I esteemed—a physician, engineer, journalist, architect, etc. These explained to the students the obstacles that increasingly stood in the way of honest practice, and their own life experience in circumventing them.

To my surprise, the class unanimously rejected them. Heatedly and rudely they called my guests liars, finks, mystifiers, or deluded. They showed that every professional was co-opted and corrupted by the System, all decisions were made top-down by the power structure and bureaucracy, professional peer-groups were conspiracies to make more money. All this was importantly true and had, of course, been said by the visitors. Why had the students not heard? As we explored further, we came to the deeper truth, that they did not believe in the existence of real professions at all; professions were concepts of repressive society and "linear thinking." I asked them to envisage any social order they pleased—Mao's, Castro's, some anarchist utopia—and wouldn't there be engineers who knew about materials and stresses and strains? Wouldn't people get sick and need to be treated? Wouldn't there be problems of communication? No, they insisted; it was important only to be human, and all else would follow.

Suddenly I realized that they did not really believe that there was a nature of things. Somehow all functions could be reduced to interpersonal relations and power. There was no knowledge, but only the sociology of knowledge. They had so well learned that physical and sociological research is subsidized and conducted for the benefit of the ruling class that they did not believe there was such a thing as simple truth. To be required to learn something was a trap by which the young were put down and co-opted. Then I knew that I could not get through to them. I had imagined that the worldwide student protest had to do with changing political and moral institutions, to which I was sympathetic, but I now saw that we had to do with a religious crisis of the magnitude of the Reformation in the fifteen-hundreds, when not only all institutions but all learning had been corrupted by the Whore of Babylon. . . .

Maybe the truth is revealed in the following conversation I had with a young hippie at a college in Massachusetts. He was dressed like an (American) Indian—buckskin fringes and a headband, red paint on his face. All his life, he said, he had tried to escape the encompassing evil of our society that was trying to destroy his soul. "But if you're always escaping," I said, "and never attentively study it, how can you make a wise judgment about society or act effectively to change it?" "You see, you don't dig!" he cried. "It's just ideas like 'wise' and 'acting effectively' that we can't stand." He was right. He was in the religious dilemma of Faith vs. Works. Where I sat, Works had some reality; but in the reign of the Devil, as he felt it, all Works are corrupted, they are part of the System; only Faith can avail. But he didn't have Faith either. . . .

This is an unpleasant picture. Even so, the alienated young have no vital alternative except to confront the Evil, and to try to make a new way of life out of their own innards and suffering. As they are doing. It is irrelevant to point out that the System is not the monolith that they think and that the majority of people are not corrupt, just brow-beaten and confused. What is relevant is that they cannot see this, because they do not have an operable world for themselves. In such a case, the only advice I would dare to give them is that which Krishna gave Arjuna: to confront with nonattachment, to be brave and firm without hatred. (I don't here want to discuss the question of "violence," the hatred and disdain are far more important.) Also, when they are seeking a new way of life, for example when they are making a "journey inward," as Ronald Laing calls it, I find that I urge them occasionally to write a letter home.

As a citizen and father I have a right to try to prevent a shambles and to diminish the number of wrecked lives. But it is improper for us elders to keep saying, as we do, that their activity is "counterproductive." It's our business to do something more productive.

Religiously, the young have been inventive, much more than the God-is-dead theologians. They have hit on new sacraments, physical actions to get them out of their estrangement and (momentarily) break through into meaning. The terribly loud music is used sacramentally. The claim for the hallucinogenic drugs is almost never the paradisal pleasure of opium culture nor the escape from distress of heroin, but tuning in to the cosmos and communing with one another. They seem to have had flashes of success in bringing ritual participation back into theater, which for a hundred years playwrights and directors have tried to do in vain. And whatever the political purposes and results of activism, there is no doubt that shared danger for the sake of righteousness is used sacramentally as baptism of fire. Fearful moments of provocation and the poignant release of the bust bring unconscious contents to the surface, create a bond of solidarity, are "commitment."

But the most powerful magic, working in all these sacraments, is the close presence of other human beings, without competition or oneupping. The original sin is to be on an ego trip that isolates; and angry political factionalism has now also become a bad thing. What a drastic comment on the dehumanization and fragmentation of modern times that salvation can be attained simply by the "warmth of assembled animal bodies," as Kafka called it, describing his mice. At the 1967 Easter Be-In in New York's Central Park, when about 10,000 were crowded on the Sheep Meadow, a young man with a quite radiant face said to me, "Gee, human beings are legal!"—it was sufficient, to be saved, to be exempted from continual harassment by officious rules and Law and Order.

The extraordinary rock festivals at Bethel and on the Isle of Wight are evidently pilgrimages. Joan Baez, one of the hierophants, ecstatically described Bethel to me, and the gist of it was that people were nice to one another. A small group passing a joint of marijuana often behaves like a Quaker meeting waiting for the spirit, and the cigarette may be a placebo. Group thereapy and sensitivity training, with Mecca at Esalen, have the same purpose. And I think this is the sense of the sexuality, which is certainly not hedonistic, nor mystical in the genre of D. H. Lawrence; nor does it have much to do with personal love, that is too threatening for these anxious youths. But it is human touch, without conquest or domination, and it obviates self-consciousness and embarrassed speech.

Around the rather pure faith there has inevitably collected a mess of eclectic liturgy and paraphernalia. Mandalas, beggars in saffron, (American) Indian beads, lectures in Zen. Obviously the exotic is desirable because it is not what they have grown up with. And it is true that fundamental facts of life are more acceptable if they come in fancy dress, e.g. it is good to breathe from the diaphragm and one can learn this by humming "OM," as Allen Ginsberg did for seven hours at Grant Park in Chicago. But college chaplains are also pretty busy, and they are now more likely to see the adventurous and off-beat than, as used to be the case, the staid and square. Flowers and strobe lights are indigenous talismans. . . .

Without doubt the religious young are in touch with something historical, but I don't think they understand what it is. Let me quote from an editorial in New Seminary News, the newsletter of dissident seminarians of the Pacific School of Religion in Berkeley: "What we confront (willingly or not we are thrust into it) is a time of disintegration of a dying civilization and the emergence of a new one." This seems to envisage something like the instant decline of the Roman Empire and they, presumably, are like the Christians about to build, rapidly, another era. But there are no signs that this is the actual situation. It would mean, for instance, that our scientific technology, civil law, professions, universities, etc., are about to vanish from the earth and be replaced by something entirely different. This is a fantasy of alienated minds. Nobody behaves as if civilization would vanish, and nobody acts as if there were a new dispensation. Nobody is waiting patiently in the catacombs and the faithful have not withdrawn into the desert. Neither the Yippies nor the New Seminarians nor any other exalted group have produced anything that is the least bit miraculous. Our civilization may well destroy itself with its atom bombs or something else, but then we do not care what will emerge, if anything.

But the actual situation *is* very like 1510, when Luther went to Rome, the eve of the Reformation. There is everywhere protest, revaluation, attack on the Establishment. The protest is international. There is a generation gap (Luther himself was all of 34 when he posted his 95 theses in 1517, but

Melanchthon was 20, Bucer 26, Münzer 28, Jonas 24; the Movement consisted of undergraduates and junior faculty.) And the thrust of protest is not to give up science, technology, and civil institutions, but to purge them, humanize them, decentralize them, change the priorities, and stop the drain of wealth.

These were, of course, exactly the demands of the March 4 nationwide teach-in on science, initiated by the dissenting professors of the Massachusetts Institute of Technology. This and the waves of other teach-ins, ads and demonstrations have been the voices not of the alienated, of people who have no world, but of protestants, people deep in the world who will soon refuse to continue under the present auspices because they are not viable. It is populism permeated by moral and professional unease. What the young have done is to make it finally religious, to force the grown-ups to recognize that they too are threatened with meaninglessness.

The analogy to the Reformation is even closer if we notice that the bloated universities, and the expanded school systems under them, constitute the biggest collection of monks since the time of Henry VIII. And most of this mandarinism is hocus pocus, a mass superstition. In my opinion, much of the student dissent in the colleges and especially the high schools has little to do with the excellent political and social demands that are made, but is boredom and resentment because of the phoniness of the whole academic enterprise.

Viewed as incidents of a Reformation, as attempts to purge themselves and recover a lost integrity, the various movements of the alienated young are easily recognizable as characteristic protestant sects, intensely self-conscious. The dissenting seminarians of the Pacific School of Religion do not intend to go off to primitive love feasts in a new heaven and new earth, but to form their own Free University; that is, they are Congregationalists. The shaggy hippies are not nature children as they claim, but self-conscious Adamites trying to naturalize Sausalito and the East Village. Heads are Pentecostals or Children of Light. Those who spindle IBM cards and throw the dean down the stairs are Iconoclasts. Those who want Student Power, a say in the rules and curriculum, mean to deny infant baptism; they want to make up their own minds, like Henry Dunster, the first president of Harvard. Radicals who live among the poor and try to organize them are certainly intent on social change, but they are also trying to find themselves again. The support of the black revolt by white middle-class students is desperately like Anabaptism, but God grant that we can do better than the Peasants' War. These analogies are not fanciful; when authority is discredited, there is a pattern in the return of the repressed. A better scholar could make a longer list; but the reason I here spell it out is that, perhaps, some young person will suddenly remember that history was about something.

Naturally, traditional churches are themselves in transition. On college campuses and in bohemian neighborhoods, existentialist Protestants and Jews and updating Catholics have gone along with the political and social activism and, what is probably more important, they have changed their own moral, esthetic and personal tone. On many campuses, the chaplains provide the only official forum for discussions of sex, drugs and burning draft cards. Yet it seems to me that, in their zeal for relevance, they are badly failing in their chief duty to the religious young: to be professors of theology. They cannot really perform pastoral services, like giving consolation or advice, since the young believe they have the sacraments to do this for themselves. Chaplains say that the young are uninterested in dogma and untractable on this level, but I think this is simply a projection of their own distaste for the conventional theology that has gone dead for them. The young are hotly metaphysical—but alas, boringly so, because they don't know much, have no language to express their intuitions, and repeat every old fallacy. If the chaplains would stop looking in the conventional places where God is dead, and would explore the actualities where perhaps He is alive, they might learn something and have something to teach.

ON DUALISTIC THINKING— FROM MANI TO THE NEW LEFT

Walter Kaufmann

It is time to move beyond black and white and to start thinking in color. Dualism is as colorblind in ethics as it is in aesthetics. Those who approach the riches of the moral life with the traditional dichotomies of good and evil or just and unjust are like aestheticians who know only two terms, "beautiful" and "ugly," and possibly pride themselves on their progressiveness because they actually recognize degrees of beauty and ugliness.

The radicals of the New Left, who see the world in black and white, lend this issue intense urgency. Were it not for them, the problem might seem merely philosophical.

Radicalism traditionally facilitates progress by pushing old errors to the extremes of absurdity, making plain what is wrong with ideas that had seemed quite tolerable as long as they were taken none too seriously. Traditional morality had become reasonably comfortable by means of endless compromises, and it had come to be taken less and less seriously. Our new radicals remind us that millions have long found security in world views that reduce an inexhaustible variety to black and white, and many will not even suffer shades of grey.

On the whole, the ancient Greeks and Indians were remarkably free from this dualistic tendency. But in Persia, Zarathustra (also called Zoroaster) proclaimed two great cosmic forces, that of light and good and that of darkness and evil, and he called on man to help the former vanquish the latter. His teaching left its mark upon the Hellenistic world and on Christianity. But the church never followed Zarathustra all the way.

In the third century A.D. another Persian prophet, Mani, preached a more Zoroastrian version of Christianity. He was martyred at the instigation of Magian priests but was survived by the doctrine that still bears his name: Manichaeism. For a while its impact in the Roman empire rivalled that of Christianity, and Augustine came under its spell. Eventually the church condemned the Manichean heresy, and as a religion it died. Yet Manichaeism is far from dead if we use the name inclusively to label that view in which history is a contest between the forces of light and darkness, and men are divided into two camps, with all right on one side. In the following pages the term is used in this broad sense, and "Mani" is not an ancient martyr but a symbol of this outlook.

The virus of Mani has taken a fearful toll in Christianity, but in our time the churches are going far towards ridding themselves of this disease—or the plague is leaving the sinking ship of Christianity to smite our ideologues. When Manichaeism struck the Right in the 19th Century, it was apparent that the infection had come from the church. In the Dreyfus affair the clerical background of anti-Semitism met the eye, and even in the Nazis' leading anti-Semitic journal, *Der Stürmer*, no text was quoted more often than Jesus' dictum in the fourth Gospel that the Devil was the father of the Jews. Joe McCarthy and the Birch Society left anti-Semitism behind and cast the Communists in the role of the forces of darkness, while still trying to explain all social evils in terms of conspiracies; but the Nazis had destroyed the intellectual respectability of the far Right, and few have taken McCarthy or the Birchers seriously on an intellectual level. Their attempts to explain events in Manichaean terms have not been dignified with the name of philosophy.

When the New Left appeared, the dreadful silence, apathy, and despair of the McCarthy period gave way to a new ferment in the intellectual community. But almost at birth the New Left succumbed to the virus of Mani.

Why? However unfortunate it is that the New Left swallowed the basic scheme of the Old Right, merely reversing the value signs, the case is anything but exceptional. When the tables are turned, the tables themselves are not subjected to critical scrutiny.

It may seem as if the Old Right could not have had that much influence.

But precisely its Manichaeism triumphed internationally; and the young radicals of the New Left grew up during the period of the Cold War. For their elders, whose memories extend back to Hitler and World War II, McCarthyism was a shameful interlude that is recalled only as a brief and wretched excess. But for those who entered colleges and universities in the 1960s, it was neither brief nor an excess. Nazism and Pearl Harbor happened before their time. These student radicals were born under the aegis of Hiroshima and Nagasaki, their childhood was dominated by the Cold War and, if they are Americans, by McCarthyism, and their adolescence by the civil rights struggle. It is all too understandable that democracy seems much sicker to them than to their parents who lived through World War II.

To understand the New Manichaeans, one must further consider the color problem. Like the Cold War, it is international; but one must begin somewhere, and we shall focus on the United States first.

American Negroes are visually a heterogeneous group and look no more alike than do whites, but whether the actual color of their skin is black, dark brown, light brown, or white, they have been classified and treated as Negroes and made to see the world in black and white, whether they liked it or not; and until the 1960s few of them did.

At the same time, black and white were by no means neutral terms. In Horace's *Satires* "he that backbites an absent friend" is called black, *niger*, and Horace also speaks of "the whitest souls earth ever bore." In his *Genealogy of Morals* Nietzsche surmised that the Latin *malus* (bad) was probably related to Greek *melas* (black), and that such words reflect the ancient contempt of blond conquerors for the black-haired native population. Perhaps there is some truth in this hypothesis; but the notion that darkness is uncanny, dangerous, and the enemy, while the light dispels threats and is friendly, a saviour, and the force of good, is probably far older.

Clearly, "black" hearts, "black" days, "blackmail," "blacken," and the connotations of "dark" were not invented by American whites to make the Negro feel inferior. Nevertheless, the value judgments embedded in such language did undermine the self-esteem of American Negroes. To regain that, it would not do to suggest a more pluralistic perspective and insist that men do not fall into one of two categories, that there are an indefinite number of shadings, and that it is arbitrary to lump the almost white with the truly black. There was nothing for it but to insist that "black is beautiful."

Why should millions of people model themselves on an alien ideal of beauty, admire light skin and straight hair, despise their own looks, and either try to change them by straightening their hair or feel ugly and hopeless? Taken out of its historical context, "black is beautiful" seems as silly as the insistence that white is beautiful. In its context, it was a long overdue cry of humanity. Nor is it any wonder that it was often accompanied by the charge that white is wicked and that white men are devils. This turning of the tables by some of the radicals is one source of the Manichaeism of the New Left, but it is not the major source, not even in the United States.

One might discount these facts altogether because the virus of Mani has struck the New Left in Europe, too, where no comparable color problem exists; but this would be a mistake. The white man's oppression of the non-whites furnishes the prime example of the kind of conflict that lends itself to a black and white diagram. White radicals could agree with Negro rebels that the way white America had treated the Negroes for centuries was indeed wicked and inexcusable. And then the question arose whether the A-bombs dropped on Hiroshima and Nagasaki were not of a piece with this wickedness: were not the Japanese also colored people? The Algerian war could be seen in the same perspective: non-white people fighting successfully against their white oppressors. And the Vietnam war fell into place.

Intellectuals, of course, did not suppose that all whites were devils or that all non-whites were beautiful or virtuous. But many did come to see the world divided into two camps: white oppressors who did not shrink from using atom bombs, napalm, and torture—against the oppressed, mostly non-white, who were fighting for their freedom. Given this model, one could readily cut through the complexities of Latin-American politics and the Palestinian situation. One need hardly wonder at the popularity of a world view that makes so many crucial and exasperating problems so simple; that makes it so easy to choose sides; and that provides the assurance that, having done that, one is wholly in the right and in the company of the vast majority of struggling humanity. . . .

Nobody could have persuaded millions of adults that we are witnessing a vast, possibly world-wide, clash of two parties if so many people were not preconditioned to think in terms of two parties. Being used to a two-party system, to the cold war, to believers and unbelievers, good and evil, right and wrong, healthy and sick, just and unjust, "us" and "them," people are quite willing to believe that our social problems are due to, or marked by, the collision between whites and blacks or those over and those under thirty. But these two suggestions are incompatible unless we interpret them to mean, for example, that one party consists of all non-whites as well as all whites under thirty, while the other one is composed of all whites over thirty. That would be logically possible, but it is obviously false.

There are tremendous tensions among non-whites in Asia, in Africa, and in Latin-America. China and Taiwan come to mind, Korea, Vietnam, India and Pakistan, Nigeria and Biafra; and there are immense upheavals in China, enormous conflicts in Pakistan, and anything but serene harmony in India. The American Negro community is so profoundly split that the very word "community" may be quite inappropriate, and most Negroes certainly do not feel any great sense of solidarity with Puerto Ricans, Mexican Americans, and Indians. Nor are the whites under thirty one party: they are scattered over the whole spectrum from George Wallace to Eugene McCarthy, as their fathers at one time ranged all the way from Joe McCarthy to Henry Wallace.

Even the radical students are far from forming a single party: the SDS tends to be shunned by most radical Negro groups, which in turn are often on bad terms with each other—Malcolm X was shot by the Black Muslims, Eldridge Cleaver and the Panthers are against the Muslims, all these groups are against the movement started by Martin Luther King Jr.; and Roy Wilkins and Whitney Young have still different ideas. Meanwhile the SDS is deeply divided, too, and the hippies' revolt against the establishment is something else again: more radical in some ways than most of the other groups, the hippies call into question the Manichaean intolerance that most other rebellious groups share with so many reactionaries. But even the hippies do not go all the way toward tolerance and pluralism: in practice they represent another extreme conformism in hairstyle, dress, and way of life; and most of them seem to consider themselves the children of light and the non-hippies children of darkness.

It is crucial for any informed and sensitive analysis of the contemporary situation to have some sense of this infinite variety and to think of a multitude of intersecting spectra instead of reducing such colorful multiplicity to black and white. But the courage to face chaos is only a beginning and no substitute for an analysis. . . .

There are no opposites of this rose or that Austrian Pine? Of this rock? Of the sun, the sky, this shadow? This human being has no opposite, neither does the hue of his skin, the light on his hair, or the way he speaks.

Only human thought introduces opposites. Neither individual objects nor classes of objects—such as roses, pines, rocks, and human beings—have opposites; nor do colors, sounds, textures, and feelings.

But are not hard and soft opposites? As abstract concepts, they are; but the feel of a rock and the feel of moss are not opposites. It is only by disregarding most of the qualities of both experiences and classifying one as hard and the other as soft that we *think* of them as opposites. Playing with fire and rolling in the snow are not opposites—far from it—but hot and cold are. No specific degree of heat or coldness has any opposite, only the concepts of hot and cold do. The starry heavens and a sunny sky are not opposites, but day and night are. And Mani's minions look everywhere for day-concepts and night-concepts.

Hot and cold are not like day and night. Temperatures are arranged on a linear scale, like hard and soft, fast and slow. Day and night, like summer and winter, form a cycle and have to be represented by a circle, like colors. And colors that are across from each other on a color wheel are not called opposite but conplementary colors. Black and white may be opposite, but no two colors are; nor are any two times of day, indeed nothing temporal, nothing living, nothing that is in process.

Hegel grasped this; also that only the understanding introduces opposites. But in the history of ideas, what has influence is usually a misunderstanding: either a man's errors and prejudices prevail, or *he* is misunderstood. Hegel was soon taken to have taught that nature and history abound in opposites, and this was believed to be the essence of his dialectic. Marx and Engels liked this dialectic better than anything else in Hegel's thought and gave the world dialectical materialism.

Now that Marx's memory is sacred not only to billions of Marxists but also to millions of others, even as Jesus' name is sacred not only to Christians, one is bound to arouse wide resentment if one points to the Manichaean elements in both. Jesus is held to have been love incarnate, and Marx a major social scientist, though both denied the bare integrity and decency of their opponents, substituting gross invective and vituperation for attempts at dialogue. They saw the world in black and white. "Whoever is not for me is against me."

The work of the understanding is of the utmost importance: to understand complex situations that initially strike us as chaotic, we need concepts and abstractions; we disregard what for the moment is irrelevant and focus our attention on a few factors that we idealize, ignoring, as it were, the imperfections of their actual existence. Hegel always associated this power of the understanding, which he hailed repeatedly, with the negative and even with destruction. Let us call it analysis.

Scientists and engineers and analytical philosophers do not need to be told how important it is, but growing numbers of young people see it as the enemy, along with the computer, and they extol concrete existence and direct experience, intuition, feeling, confrontation. These neo-romantics fall prey to the virus of Mani much more often than do the devotees of analysis. Why?

As Hegel recognized, philosophy requires the understanding as well as intuition, and reason does not do its job as long as either analysis or direct experience are held to be sovereign. Although no other philosopher had made so much of this theme, the partiality of both approaches is felt widely, and the partisans of each feel a need for the other. Thus the analytically minded tend to leave the realms of faith and morals, if not politics, to feeling and intuition, while the prophets of direct experience indulge in a bare minimum of analysis and have a fondness for polarities.

Unimpeded, neither analysis nor experience stops with the recognition of opposites; both lead to pluralism, and so does any thinking that subjects even faith and morals to analysis, without ignoring the concrete experiences of the moral and religious life. Those who see things in black and white limp on both legs: they curtail both the understanding and direct experience, settling for a little of each.

I am prepared to push my anti-Manichaeism to the point of saying that we should not hate or detest any human being. You should always remain mindful of the other man's humanity and of the ways in which he is "as yourself." Why? I cannot invoke as an authority Moses' "You shall love your neighbor as yourself" (Lev. 19.18) or the extension of the same commandment to the stranger (19.34). If authority is out of the picture, what reasons remain?

Even if a man's views, actions, and behavior are detestable, it might be held that there is more to the man than his views, actions, and behavior and that we therefore ought not to detest or hate *him*. This argument admits of variations, but the refutation is the same in all cases:this reasoning proves too much. By the same token it would be unreasonable to admire a person whose views, actions, and behavior deserved admiration.

This refutation does not depend merely on our desire to go on admiring some people. Rather it shows that the first argument in its desire to protect the other person against negative feelings removes him altogether out of our world to the point where no contact between human beings remains possible at all. The refutation is thus intended as a reduction to the absurd. But those who find such extreme alienation from their fellow men true to their own experience are bound to reject the refutation and insist that we can respond only to behavior, never to another person. They will neither love nor hate, admire or detest other human beings.

Another argument would allow us to admire but not to detest others, to love but not to hate. But it is a pragmatic argument, no strict proof; or in Kantian language, it is merely a hypothetical imperative and not a categorical one. Within these limits it is a sound argument: There are two good reasons for not hating any man but loving some.

First, it is difficult to discover some of our own faults; they are much plainer in others. If we always make excuses and end up by not accounting them faults at all, we are almost bound to become lax with ourselves. But if we hate and detest as inhuman those in whom we find grievous faults we are more than apt to overlook the same faults or tendencies in ourselves because we do not see the continuity between "us" and "them." Hence it is essential for our own moral health to see those who offend us in their full humanity while judging their faults clearly. Judge your neighbor and remember that he is "as yourself."

Secondly, our ideas and "truths"—especially in faith, morals, and politics —have an inveterate tendency to be one-sided. What helps more than anything else is to go out of one's way to consider with an effort at sympathy the views of those whom we are tempted to detest. Without suspending our critical faculties, we should ask ourselves how human beings not essentially different from ourselves have come to see things that way. For the sake of truth, insight, and psychological understanding, it is important to cultivate the habit of not hating other men.

There is no parallel argument against love and admiration. On the contrary, the effort to become a better person and the quest for knowledge can be greatly helped by both. What obviously cannot be squared with my position is *blind* admiration or love. Even as we do not always admire or love those with whom we agree, we need not agree with those we love or admire. Nor need we deny their faults. . . .

We must liberate the imagination even of the young. They now seek freedom by asking all schools to abolish the same requirements and to introduce the same options. They all want the same. We should encourage them to think and imagine for themselves instead of copying their peers.

For we need far more imagination than the middle-aged possess, and *we* are no longer likely to come up with bold plans for new institutions and new ways of life. Time is running out on us, and if our children and students show as little imagination as their elders have done, Western civilization could well come to an end around the year 2000. If those now young are even more inept than their elders, that is scarcely grounds for gloating.

Time is running out on us. Many of the students have very little patience. Their experience of time differs from ours. Even if we fly far more often than our students, we can also remember taking two weeks to cross the Atlantic in a boat, and longer than that to hitchhike across the United States. Our sense of time was molded by experiences like that and we are prone to feel that the condition of the Negro in America has changed a great deal in the last two decades. But our students know that we have landed men on the moon less than ten years after Kennedy proclaimed this as a goal, and the speeds reached by the rockets rushing toward the moon have a place in the experience of youth, while we still think in pre-rocket terms.

Time is running out on us. In a few more decades all who worry about student radicals will be dead, and those now young will run or ruin the world. We might use what little time is left us to say what most needs saying: It is time to move beyond black and white and to start thinking in color.

Aspiration

ON REDISCOVERING JESUS

Malcolm Muggeridge

Sex is the mysticism of a materialist society—in the beginning was the Flesh, and the Flesh became Word—with its own mysteries—this is my birth pill; swallow it in remembrance of me!—and its own sacred texts and scriptures—the erotica which fall like black atomic rain on the just and unjust alike, drenching us, blinding us, stupefying us. To be carnally minded is life! So we have ventured on, Little Flowers of D. H. Lawrence; our Aphrodites rising, bikini'd and oiled, from Côte d'Azur beaches; drive-in Lotharios, Romeos of the motorways, glowing and burning like electric log fires, until—cut!—the switch is turned off, leaving the desolate, impenetrable night. Did I sometimes, staring sleepless into it, even then catch a glimpse, far, far away, of a remote shading of the black into grey? A minuscule intimation of a dawn that would break? You!

It was padding about the streets of Moscow that the other dream—the kingdom of heaven on earth—dissolved for me, never to be revived. Those grey anonymous figures, likewise padding about the streets, seemed infinitely remote, withdrawn, forever strangers, yet somehow near and dear. The grey streets were paradise, the eyeless buildings, the many mansions of which heaven is composed. I caught another glimpse of paradise in Berlin after it had been liberated—there the mansions made of rubble, and the heavenly hosts, the glow of liberation still upon them, bartering cigarettes for tins of

Spam, and love for both. (Later, this paradise was transformed by means of mirrors into a shining, glowing one, running with *schlag* and fat cigars, with bartered love still plentifully available, but for paper money, not Spam). So many paradises springing up all over the place, all with many mansions, mansions of light and love; the most majestic of all, the master-paradise on which all the others were based—on Manhattan Island! Oh, what marvelous mansions there, reaching into the sky! What heavenly Muzak overflowing the streets and buildings, what brilliant lights spelling out what delectable hopes and desires, what heavenly hosts pursuing what happiness on magic screens in living color!

And You? I never caught even a glimpse of You in any paradise—unless You were an old, colored, shoeshine man on a windy corner in Chicago one February morning, smiling from ear to ear; or a little man with a lame leg in the Immigration Department in New York, whose smiling patience as he listened to one Puerto Rican after another seemed to reach from there to eternity. Oh, and whoever painted the front of the little church in the woods at Kliazma near Moscow—painted it in blues as bright as the sky and whites that outshone the snow? That might have been You. Or again at Kiev, at an Easter service when the collectivization famine was in full swing, and Bernard Shaw and newspaper correspondents were telling the world of the bursting granaries and apple-cheeked dairymaids in the Ukraine. What a congregation that was, packed in tight, squeezed together like sardines! I myself was pressed against a stone pillar, and scarcely able to breathe. Not that I wanted to particularly. So many grey, hungry faces, all luminous, like an El Greco painting; and all singing. How they sang—about how there was no help except in You, nowhere to turn except to You; nothing, nothing, that could possibly bring any comfort except You. I could have touched You then, You were so near—not up at the altar, of course, where the bearded priests, crowned and bowing and chanting, swung their censers—one of the grey faces, the greyest and most luminous of all.

It was strange in a way that I should thus have found myself nearest to You in the land where for half a century the practice of the Christian religion had been most ruthlessly suppressed; where the very printing of the Gospels is forbidden, and You are derided by all the organs of an all-powerful State as once you were by the Roman soldiers when they decked you out as a ribald King of Jews. Yet on reflection not so strange. How infinitely preferable it is to be abhorred, rather than embraced, by those in authority. Where the distinction between God and Caesar is so abundantly clear, no one in his senses—or out of them, for that matter—is likely to suggest that any good purpose would be served by arranging a dialogue between the two of them. In the Communist countries an unmistakable and unbridgeable abyss divides the kingdoms of the earth into the Devil's gift and Your kingdom, with no crazed clerics gibbering and grimacing in the intervening no-man's-land. It provides the perfect circumstances for the Christian faith to bloom anew, so uncannily like the circumstances in which it first bloomed at the beginning of the Christian era. I look eastward, not westward, for a new Star of Bethlehem.

It would be comforting to be able to say: Now I see! To recite with total satisfaction one of the Church's venerable creeds—"I believe in God, the Father Almighty. . . ." To point to such a moment of illumination when all became miraculously clear. To join with full identification in one of the varieties of Christian worship. Above all, to feel able to say to You: "Lord!" and confidently await Your command. Comforting—but alas it would not be true. The one thing above all others that You require of us is, surely, the truth. I have to confess, then, that I see only fitfully, believe no creed wholly, have had no all-sufficing moment of illumination.

And You? What do I know of You? A living presence in the world; the one who, of all the billions and billions and billions of our human family came most immediately from God and went most immediately to God, while remaining most humanly and intimately here among us, today, as yesterday and tomorrow; for all time. Did you live and die and rise from the dead as they say? Who knows, or for that matter, cares? History is for the dead, and You are alive. Similarly, all those churches raised and maintained in Your name, from the tiniest, weirdest conventicle to the great cathedrals rising so sublimely into the sky—they are for the dead, and must themselves die; are, indeed, dying fast. They belong to time, You to eternity. At the intersection of time and eternity—nailed there—You confront us; a perpetual reminder that, living, we die, and, dying, we live. An incarnation wonderful to contemplate; the light of the world, indeed.

Fiat lux! Let there be light! So everything began at God's majestic command; so it might have continued till the end of time—history unending—except that You intervened, shining another light into the innermost recesses of the human will, where the ego reigns and reaches out in tentacles of dark desire. Having seen this other light, I turn to it, striving and growing toward it as plants do toward the sun. The light of love, abolishing the darkness of hate; the light of peace, abolishing the darkness of strife and confusion; the light of life, abolishing the darkness of death; the light of creativity, abolishing the darkness of destruction. Though, in terms of history, the darkness falls, blacking out us and our world, You have overcome history. You came as light into the world, that whoever believed in You should not remain in darkness. The promise stands forever. Your light shines in the darkness, and the darkness has not overcome it. Nor ever will.

THE SERMON AT BENARES

Gautama Buddha

Kisa Gotami had an only son, and he died. In her grief she carried the dead child to all her neighbors, asking them for medicine, and the people said: "She has lost her senses. The boy is dead."

At length, Kisa Gotami met a man who replied to her request: "I cannot give thee medicine for thy child, but I know a physician who can."

And the girl said: "Pray tell me, sir; who is it?" And the man replied "Go to Sakyamuni, the Buddha."

Kisa Gotami repaired to the Buddha and cried: "Lord and Master, give me the medicine that will cure my boy."

The Buddha answered: "I want a handful of mustard-seed." And when the girl in her joy promised to procure it, the Buddha added: "The mustard-seed must be taken from a house where no one has lost a child, husband, parent or friend."

Poor Kisa Gotami now went from house to house, and the people pitied her and said: "Here is mustard-seed; take it!" But when she asked, "Did a son or daughter, a father or mother, die in your family?" they answered her: "Alas! the living are few, but the dead are many. Do not remind us of our deepest grief." And there was no house but some beloved one had died in it.

Kisa Gotami became weary and hopeless, and sat down at the wayside, watching the lights of the city, as they flickered up and were extinguished again. At last the darkness of the night reigned everywhere. And she considered the fate of men, that their lives flicker up and are extinguished again. And she thought to herself: "How selfish am I in my grief! Death is common to all; yet in this valley of desolation there is a path that leads him to immortality who has surrendered all selfishness."

The Buddha said: "The life of mortals in this world is troubled and brief and combined with pain. For there is not any means by which those that have been born can avoid dying; after reaching old age there is death; of such a nature are living beings. As ripe fruits are early in danger of falling, so mortals when born are always in danger of death. As all earthen vessels made by the potter end in being broken, so is the life of mortals. Both young and adult, both those who are fools and those who are wise, all fall into the power of death; all are subject to death.

"Of those who, overcome by death, depart from life, a father cannot save his son, nor kinsmen their relations. Mark! while relatives are looking on and lamenting deeply, one by one mortals are carried off, like an ox that is led to the slaughter. So the world is afflicted with death and decay, therefore the wise do not grieve, knowing the terms of the world.

"Not from weeping nor from grieving will any one obtain peace of mind; on the contrary, his pain will be the greater and his body will suffer. He will make himself sick and pale, yet the dead are not saved by his lamentation. He who seeks peace should draw out the arrow of lamentation, and complaint, and grief. He who has drawn out the arrow and has become composed will obtain peace of mind; he who has overcome all sorrow will become free from sorrow, and be blessed."

THE STOIC CODE

Marcus Aurelius

Begin the morning by saying to thyself, I shall meet with the busybody, the ungrateful, arrogant, deceitful, envious, unsocial. All these things happen to them by reason of their ignorance of what is good and evil. But I who have seen the nature of the good that it is beautiful, and of the bad that it is ugly, and the nature of him who does wrong, that it is akin to me, not [only] of the same blood or seed, but that it participates in [the same] intelligence and [the same] portion of the divinity, I can neither be injured by any of them, for no one can fix on me what is ugly, nor can I be angry with my kinsman, nor hate him. For we are made for co-operation, like feet, like hands, like eyelids, like the rows of the upper and lower teeth. To act against one another, then, is contrary to nature; and it is action against one another to be vexed and to turn away.

Whatever this is that I am, it is a little flesh and breath, and the ruling part. Throw away thy books; no longer distract thyself: it is not allowed; but as if thou wast now dying, despise the flesh; it is blood and bones and a network, a contexture of nerves, veins, and arteries. See the breath also, what kind of a thing it is; air, and not always the same, but every moment sent out and again sucked in. The third, then, is the ruling part; consider thus: Thou art an old man; no longer let this be a slave, no longer be pulled by the strings like a puppet to unsocial movements, no longer be either dissatisfied with thy present lot, or shrink from the future.

All that is from the gods is full of providence. That which is from fortune is not separated from nature or without an interweaving and involution with the things which are ordered by providence. From thence all things flow; and there is besides necessity, and that which is for the advantage of the whole universe, of which thou art a part. But that is good for every part of nature which the nature of the whole brings, and what serves to maintain this nature. Now the universe is preserved, as by the changes of the elements so by the changes of things compounded of the elements. Let these principles be enough for thee; let them always be fixed opinions. But cast away the thirst after books, that thou mayest not die murmuring, but cheerfully, truly, and from thy heart thankful to the gods.

Remember how long thou hast been putting off these things, and how often thou hast received opportunity from the gods, and yet dost not use it. Thou must now at last perceive of what universe thou art a part, and of what administrator of the universe thy existence is an efflux, and that a limit of time is fixed for thee, which if thou dost not use for clearing away the clouds from thy mind, it will go and thou wilt go, and it will never return.

Every moment think steadily as a Roman and a man to do what thou hast in hand with perfect and simple dignity, and feeling of affection, and freedom, and justice, and go give thyself relief from all other thoughts. And thou wilt give thyself relief if thou doest every act of thy life as if it were the last, laying aside all carelessness and passionate aversion from the commands of reason, and all hypocrisy, and self-love, and discontent with the portion which has been given to thee. Thou seest how few the things are, the which if a man lays hold of, he is able to live a life which flows in quiet, and is like the existence of the gods; for the gods on their part will require nothing more from him who observes these things.

Do wrong to thyself, do wrong to thyself, my soul; but thou wilt no longer have the opportunity of honoring thyself. Every man's life is sufficient. But thine is nearly finished, though thy soul reverences not itself, but places thy felicity in the souls of others.

Do the things external which fall upon thee distract thee? Give thyself time to learn something new and good, and cease to be whirled around. But then thou must also avoid being carried about the other way; for those too are triflers who have wearied themselves in life by their activity, and yet have no object to which to direct every movement, and, in a word, all their thoughts.

Through not observing what is in the mind of another a man has seldom been seen to be unhappy; but those who do not observe the movements of their own minds must of necessity be unhappy.

This thou must always bear in mind, what is the nature of the whole, and what is my nature, and how this is related to that, and what kind of a part it is of what kind of a whole, and that there is no one who hinders thee from always doing and saying the things which are according to the nature of which thou art a part.

Theophrastus, in his comparison of bad acts—such a comparison as one would make in accordance with the common notions of mankind—says, like a true philosopher, that the offences which are committed through desire are more blamable than those which are committed through anger. For he who is excited by anger seems to turn away from reason with a certain pain and unconscious contraction; but he who offends through desire, being overpowered by pleasure, seems to be in a manner more intemperate and more womanish in his offences. Rightly, then, and in a way worthy of philosophy, he said that the offence which is committed with pleasure is more blamable than that which is committed with pain; and on the whole the one is more like a person who has been first wronged and through pain is compelled to be angry; but the other is moved by his own impulse to do wrong, being carried towards doing something by desire.

Since it is possible that thou mayest depart from life this very moment, regulate every act and thought accordingly. But to go away from among men, if there are gods, is not a thing to be afraid of, for the gods will not involve thee in evil; but if indeed they do not exist, or if they have no concern about human affairs, what is it to me to live in a universe devoid of gods or devoid of providence? But in truth they do exist, and they do care for human things, and they have put all the means in man's power to enable him not to fall into real evils. And as to the rest, if there was anything evil, they would have provided for this also, that it should be altogether in a man's power not to fall into it. Now that which does not make a man worse, how can it make a man's life worse? But neither through ignorance, nor having the knowledge but not the power to guard against or correct these things, is it possible that the nature of the universe has overlooked them; nor is it possible that it has made so great a mistake, either through want of power or want of skill, that good and evil should happen indiscriminately to the good and the bad. But death certainly, and life, honor and dishonor, pain and pleasure,—all these things equally happen to good men and bad, being things which make us neither better nor worse. Therefore they are neither good nor evil.

How quickly all things disappear,—in the universe the bodies themselves, but in time the remembrance of them. What is the nature of all sensible things, and particularly those which attract with the bait of pleasure or terrify by pain, or are noised abroad by vapory fame; how worthless, and contemptible, and sordid, and perishable, and dead they are,—all this it is the part of the intellectual faculty to observe. To observe too who these are whose opinions and voices give reputation; what death is, and the fact that, if a man looks at it in itself, and by the abstractive power of reflection resolves into their parts all the things which present themselves to the imagination in it, he will then consider it to be nothing else than an operation of nature; and if any one is afraid of an operation of nature, he is a child. This, however, is not only an operation of nature, but it is also a thing which conduces to the purposes of nature. To observe too how man comes near to the Deity, and by what part of him, and when this part of man is so disposed.

Nothing is more wretched than a man who traverses everything in a round, and pries into the things beneath the earth, as the poet says, and seeks by conjecture what is in the minds of his neighbors, without perceiving that it is sufficient to attend to the daemon within him, and to reverence it sincerely. And reverence of the daemon consists in keeping it pure from passion and thoughtlessness, and dissatisfaction with what comes from gods and men. For the things from the gods merit veneration for their excellence; and the things from men should be dear to us by reason of kinship; and sometimes even, in a manner, they move our pity by reason of men's ignorance of good and bad; this defect being not less than that which deprives us of the power of distinguishing things that are white and black.

Though thou shouldest be going to live three thousand years, and as many times ten thousand years, still remember that no man loses any other life than this which he now lives, nor lives any other than this which he now loses. The longest and shortest are thus brought to the same. For the present is the same to all, though that which perishes is not the same; and so that which is lost appears to be a mere moment. For a man cannot lose either the past or the future: for what a man has not, how can any one take this from him? These two things then thou must bear in mind; the one, that all things from eternity are of like forms and come round in a circle, and that it makes no difference whether a man shall see the same things during a hundred years, or two hundred, or an infinite time; and the second, that the longest liver and he who will die soonest lose just the same. For the present is the only thing of which a man can be deprived, if it is true that this is the only thing which he has, and that a man cannot lose a thing if he has it not.

Remember that all is opinion. For what was said by the Cynic Monimus is manifest: and manifest too is the use of what was said, if a man receives what may be got out of it as far as it is true.

The soul of man does violence to itself, first of all, when it becomes an abscess, and, as it were, a tumor on the universe, so far as it can. For to be vexed at anything which happens is a separation of ourselves from nature, in some part of which the natures of all other things are contained. In the next place, the soul does violence to itself when it turns away from any man, or even moves towards him with the intention of injuring, such as are the souls of those who are angry. In the third place, the soul does violence to itself when it is overpowered by pleasure or by pain. Fourthly, when it plays a part, and does or says anything insincerely and untruly. Fifthly, when it allows any act of its own and any movement to be without an aim, and does anything thoughtlessly and without considering what it is, it being right that even the smallest things be done with reference to an end; and the end of rational animals is to follow the reason and the law of the most ancient city and polity.

Of human life the time is a point, and the substance is in a flux, and the perception dull, and the composition of the whole body subject to putrefaction, and the soul a whirl, and fortune hard to divine, and fame a thing devoid of judgment. And, to say all in a word, everything which belongs to the body is a stream, and what belongs to the soul is a dream and vapor, and life is a warfare and a stranger's sojourn, and after-fame is oblivion. What then is that which is able to conduct a man? One thing, and only one, philosophy. But this consists in keeping the daemon within a man free from violence and unharmed, superior to pains and pleasures, doing nothing without a purpose, nor yet falsely and with hypocrisy, not feeling the need of another man's doing or not doing anything; and besides, accepting all that happens, and all that is allotted, as coming from thence, wherever it is, from whence he himself came; and, finally, waiting for death with a cheerful mind, as being nothing else than a dissolution of the elements of which every living being is compounded. But if there is no harm to the elements themselves in each continually changing into another, why should a man have any apprehension about the change and dissolution of all the elements? For it is according to nature, and nothing is evil which is according to nature.

THE SERMON ON THE MOUNT

Matthew

And seeing the multitudes, he went up into a mountain; and when he was set, his disciples came unto him: and he opened his mouth, and taught them, saying, Blessed are the poor in spirit: for theirs is the kingdom of heaven. Blessed are they that mourn: for they shall be comforted. Blessed are the meek: for they shall inherit the earth. Blessed are they which do hunger and thirst after righteousness: for they shall be filled. Blessed are the merciful: for they shall obtain mercy. Blessed are the pure in heart: for they shall see God. Blessed are the peacemakers: for they shall be called the children of God. Blessed are they which are persecuted for righteousness' sake: for theirs is the kingdom of heaven. Blessed are ye, when men shall revile you, and persecute you, and shall say all manner of evil against you falsely, for my sake. Rejoice, and be exceeding glad: for great is your reward in heaven: for so persecuted they the prophets which were before you.

Ye are the salt of the earth: but if the salt have lost his savour, wherewith shall it be salted? it is thenceforth good for nothing, but to be cast out, and to be trodden under foot of men. Ye are the light of the world. A city that is set on a hill cannot be hid. Neither do men light a candle, and put it under a bushel, but on a candlestick; and it giveth light unto all that are in the house. Let your light so shine before men, that they may see your good works, and glorify your Father which is in heaven. Think not that I am come to destroy the law, or the prophets; I am not come to destroy, but to fulfil. For verily I say unto you, Till heaven and earth pass, one jot or one tittle shall in no wise pass from the law, till all be fulfilled. Whosoever therefore shall break one of these least commandments, and shall teach men so, he shall be called the least in the kingdom of heaven: but whosoever shall do and teach them, the same shall be called great in the kingdom of heaven For I say unto you, That except your righteousness shall exceed the righteousness of the scribes and Pharisees, ye shall in no case enter into the kingdom of heaven.

Ye have heard that it was said by them of old time, Thou shalt not kill; and whosoever shall kill shall be in danger of the judgment: but I say unto you, That whosoever is angry with his brother without a cause shall be in danger of the judgment: and whosoever shall say to his brother, Raca, shall be in danger of the council: but whosoever shall say, Thou fool, shall be in danger of hell fire. Therefore if thou bring thy gift to the altar, and there rememberest that thy brother hath ought against thee; leave there thy gift before the altar, and go thy way; first be reconciled to thy brother, and then come and offer thy gift. Agree with thine adversary quickly, while thou art in the way with him; lest at any time the adversary deliver thee to the judge, and the judge deliver thee to the officer, and thou be cast into prison. Verily I say unto thee, Thou shalt by no means come out thence, till thou hast paid the uttermost farthing.

Ye have heard that it was said by them of old time, Thou shalt not commit adultery; but I say unto you, That whosoever looketh on a woman to lust after her hath committed adultery with her already in his heart. And if thy right eye offend thee, pluck it out, and cast it from thee: for it is profitable for thee that one of thy members should perish, and not that thy whole body should be cast into hell. And if thy right hand offend thee, cut it off, and cast it from thee: for it is profitable for thee that one of thy members should perish, and not that thy whole body should be cast into hell. It hath been said, Whosoever shall put away his wife, let him give her a writing of divorcement: but I say unto you, That whosoever shall put away his wife, saving for the cause of fornication, causeth her to commit adultery: and whosoever shall marry her that is divorced committeth adultery.

Again, ye have heard that it hath been said by them of old time, Thou shalt not forswear thyself, but shalt perform to the Lord thine oaths: but I say unto you, Swear not at all; neither by heaven; for it is God's throne: nor by the earth; for it is his footstool: neither by Jerusalem; for it is the city of the great King. Neither shalt thou swear by thy head, because thou canst not make one hair white or black. But let your communication be, Yea, yea; Nay, nay: for whatsoever is more than these cometh of evil.

Ye have heard that it hath been said, An eye for an eye, and a tooth for a tooth: but I say unto you, That ye resist not evil: but whosoever shall smite thee on thy right cheek, turn to him the other also. And if any man will sue thee at the law, and take away thy coat, let him have thy cloak also. And whosoever shall compel thee to go a mile, go with him twain. Give to him that asketh thee, and from him that would borrow of thee turn not thou away.

Ye have heard that it hath been said, Thou shalt love thy neighbor, and hate thine enemy. But I say unto you, Love your enemies, bless them that curse you, do good to them that hate you, and pray for them which despitefully use you, and persecute you; that ye may be the children of your Father which is in heaven; for he maketh his sun to rise on the evil and on the good, and sendeth rain on the just and on the unjust. For if ye love them which love you, what reward have ye? do not even the publicans the same? And if ye salute your brethren only, what do ye more than others? do not even the publicans so? Be ye therefore perfect, even as your Father which is in heaven is perfect.

Take heed that ye do not your alms before men, to be seen of them: otherwise ye have no reward of your Father which is in heaven. Therefore when thou doest thine alms, do not sound a trumpet before thee, as the hypocrites do in the synagogues and in the streets, that they may have glory of men. Verily I say unto you, They have their reward. But when thou doest alms, let not thy left hand know what thy right hand doeth: that thine alms may be in secret: and thy Father which seeth in secret himself shall reward thee openly. And when thou prayest, thou shalt not be as the hypocrites are: for they love to pray standing in the synagogues and in the corners of the streets, that they may be seen of men. Verily I say unto you, They have their reward. But thou, when thou prayest, enter into thy closet, and when thou hast shut thy door, pray to thy Father, which is in secret; and thy Father which seeth in secret shall reward thee openly. But when ye pray, use not vain repetitions, as the heathen do: for they think that they shall be heard for their much speaking. Be not ye therefore like unto them: for your Father knoweth what things ye have need of, before ye ask him. After this manner therefore pray ye: Our Father which art in heaven, Hallowed be thy name. Thy kingdom come. Thy will be done in earth, as it is in heaven. Give us this day our daily bread. And forgive us our debts, as we forgive our debtors. And lead us not into temptation, but deliver us from evil: for thine is the kingdom, and the power, and the glory, for ever. Amen. For if ye forgive men their trespasses, your heavenly Father will also forgive you: but if ye forgive not men their trespasses, neither will your Father forgive your trespasses.

Moreover when ye fast, be not, as the hypocrites, of a sad countenance: for they disfigure their faces, that they may appear unto men to fast. Verily I say unto you, They have their reward. But thou, when thou fastest, anoint thine head, and wash thy face; that thou appear not unto men to fast, but unto thy Father which is in secret; and thy Father, which seeth in secret, shall reward thee openly.

Lay up not for yourselves treasures upon earth, where moth and rust doth corrupt, and where thieves break through and steal: but lay up for yourselves treasures in heaven, where neither moth nor rust doth corrupt, and where thieves do not break through nor steal: for where your treasure is, there will your heart be also. The light of the body is the eye: if therefore thine eye be single, thy whole body shall be full of light. But if thine eye be evil, thy whole body shall be full of darkness. If therefore the light that is in thee be darkness, how great is that darkness! No man can serve two masters: for either he will hate the one, and love the other; or else he will hold to the one, and despise the other. Ye cannot serve God and mammon. Therefore I say unto you, Take no thought for your life, what ye shall eat, or what ye shall drink; nor yet for your body, what ye shall put on. Is not the life more than meat, and the body than raiment? Behold the fowls of the air: for they sow not, neither do they reap, nor gather into barns; yet your heavenly Father feedeth them. Are ye not much better than they? Which of you by taking thought can add one cubit unto his stature? And why take ye thought for raiment? Consider the lilies of the field, how they grow; they toil not, neither do they spin: and yet I say unto you, That even Solomon in all his glory was not arrayed like one of these. Wherefore, if God so clothe the grass of the field, which to day is, and to morrow is cast into the oven, shall he not much more clothe you, O ye of little faith? Therefore take no thought, saying, What shall we eat? or, What shall we drink? or, Wherewithal shall we be clothed? (For after all these things do the Gentiles seek:) for your heavenly Father knoweth that ye have need of all these things. But seek ye first the kingdom of God, and his righteousness; and all these things shall be added unto you. Take therefore no thought for the morrow: for the morrow shall take thought for the things of itself. Sufficient unto the day is the evil thereof.

Judge not, that ye be not judged. For with what judgment ye judge, ye shall be judged: and with what measure ye mete, it shall be measured to you again. And why beholdest thou the mote that is in thy brother's eye, but considerest not the beam that is in thine own eye? Or how wilt thou say to thy brother, Let me pull out the mote out of thine eye; and behold, a beam is in thine own eye? Thou hypocrite, first cast out the beam out of thine own eye; and then shalt thou see clearly to cast out the mote out of thy brother's eye.

Give not that which is holy unto the dogs, neither cast ye your pearls before swine, lest they trample them under their feet, and turn again and rend you. Ask, and it shall be given you; seek and ye shall find; knock, and it shall be opened unto you: for every one that asketh receiveth; and he that seeketh findeth; and to him that knocketh it shall be opened. Or what man is there of you, whom if his son ask bread, will he give him a stone? Or if he ask a fish, will he give him a serpent? If ye then, being evil, know how to give good gifts unto your children, how much more shall your Father which is in heaven give good things to them that ask him? Therefore all things whatsoever ye would that men should do to you, do ye even so to them: for this is the law and the prophets.

Enter ye in at the strait gate: for wide is the gate, and broad is the way, that leadeth to destruction, and many there be which go in thereat: because strait is the gate, and narrow is the way, which leadeth unto life, and few there be that find it. Beware of false prophets, which come to you in sheep's clothing, but inwardly they are ravening wolves. Ye shall know them by their fruits. Do men gather grapes of thorns, or figs of thistles? Even so every good tree bringeth forth good fruit; but a corrupt tree bringeth forth evil fruit. A good tree cannot bring forth evil fruit, neither can a corrupt tree bring forth good fruit. Every tree that bringeth not forth good fruit is hewn down, and cast into the fire. Wherefore by their fruits ye shall know them. Not every one that saith unto me, Lord, Lord, shall enter into the kingdom of heaven; but he that doeth the will of my Father which is in heaven. Many will say to me in that day, Lord, Lord, have we not prophesied in thy name? And in thy name have cast out devils? and in thy name done many wonderful works? And then will I profess unto them, I never knew you: depart from me, ye that work iniquity. Therefore whosoever heareth these sayings of mine, and doeth them, I will liken him unto a wise man, which built his house upon a rock: and the rain descended, and the floods came, and the winds blew, and beat upon that house; and it fell not: for it was founded upon a rock. And every one that heareth these sayings of mine, and doeth them not, shall be likened unto a foolish man, which built his house upon the sand: and the rain descended, and the floods came, and the winds blew, and beat upon that house; and it fell: and great was the fall of it. And it came to pass, when Jesus had ended these sayings, the people were astonished at his doctrine: For he taught them as one having authority, and not as the scribes.

THE UPANISHADS: SVETASVATARA

OM . . .
With our ears may we hear what is good.
With our eyes may we behold thy righteousness.
Tranquil in body, may we who worship thee find rest.
OM . . . Peace—peace—peace.
OM . . . Hail to the supreme Self!

Disciples inquire within themselves:

What is the cause of this universe?—is it Brahman? Whence do we come? Why do we live? Where shall we at last find rest? Under whose command are we bound by the law of happiness and its opposite?

Time, space, law, chance, matter, primal energy, intelligence—none of these, nor a combination of these, can be the final cause of the universe, for they are effects and exist to serve the soul. Nor can the individual self be the cause, for, being subject to the law of happiness and misery, it is not free.

The seers, absorbed in contemplation, saw within themselves the ultimate reality, the self-luminous being, the one God, who dwells as the self-conscious power in all creatures. He is One without a second. Deep within all beings he dwells, hidden from sight by the coverings of the gunas— *sattwa, rajas,* and *tamas.* He presides over time, space, and all apparent causes.

This vast universe is a wheel. Upon it are all creatures that are subject to birth, death, and rebirth. Round and round it turns, and never stops. It is the wheel of Brahman. As long as the individual self thinks it is separate from Brahman, it revolves upon the wheel in bondage to the laws of birth, death, and rebirth. But when through the grace of Brahman it realizes its identity with him, it revolves upon the wheel no longer. It achieves immortality.

He who is realized by transcending the world of cause and effect, in deep contemplation, is expressly declared by the scriptures to be the Supreme Brahman. He is the substance, all else the shadow. He is the imperishable. The knowers of Brahman know him as the one reality behind all that seems. For this reason they are devoted to him. Absorbed in him, they attain freedom from the wheel of birth, death, and rebirth.

The Lord supports this universe, which is made up of the perishable and the imperishable, the manifest and the unmanifest. The individual soul, forgetful of the Lord, attaches itself to pleasure and thus is bound. When it comes to the Lord, it is freed from all its fetters.

Mind and matter, master and servant—both have existed from beginningless time. The Maya which unites them has also existed from beginningless time. When all three—mind, matter, and Maya—are known as one with Brahman, then is it realized that the Self is infinite and has no part in action. Then is it revealed that the Self is all.

Matter is perishable. The Lord, the destroyer of ignorance, is imperishable, immortal. He is the one God, the Lord of the perishable and of all souls. By meditating on him, by uniting oneself with him, by identifying oneself with him, one ceases to be ignorant.

Know God, and all fetters will be loosed. Ignorance will vanish. Birth, death, and rebirth will be no more. Meditate upon him and transcend physical consciousness. Thus will you reach union with the lord of the universe. Thus will you become identified with him who is One without a second. In him all your desires will find fulfillment.

The truth is that you are always united with the Lord. But you must *know* this. Nothing further is there to know. Meditate, and you will realize that mind, matter, and Maya (the power which unites mind and matter) are but three aspects of Brahman, the one reality.

Fire, though present in the firesticks, is not perceived until one stick is rubbed against another. The Self is like that fire: it is realized in the body by meditation on the sacred syllable OM.

Let your body be the stick that is rubbed, the sacred syllable OM the stick that is rubbed against it. Thus shall you realize God, who is hidden within the body as fire is hidden within the wood.

Like oil in sesame seeds, butter in cream, water in the river bed, fire in tinder, the Self dwells within the soul. Realize him through truthfulness and meditation.

Like butter in cream is the Self in everything. Knowledge of the Self is gained through meditation. The Self is Brahman. By Brahman is all ignorance destroyed. . . .

The one absolute, impersonal Existence, together with his inscrutable Maya, appears as the divine Lord, the personal God, endowed with manifold glories. By his divine power he holds dominion over all the worlds. At the periods of creation and dissolution of the universe, he alone exists. Those who realize him become immortal.

The Lord is One without a second. Within man he dwells, and within all other beings. He projects the universe, maintains it, and withdraws it into himself.

His eyes are everywhere; his face, his arms, his feet are in every place. Out of himself he has produced the heavens and the earth, and with his arms and his wings he holds them together.

He is the origin and support of the gods. He is the lord of all. He confers bliss and wisdom upon those who are devoted to him. He destroys their sins and their sorrows.

He punishes those who break his laws. He sees all and knows all. May he endow us with good thoughts!

O Lord, clothed in thy most holy form, which is calm and blissful, and which destroys all evil and ignorance, look upon us and make us glad.

O Lord, thou hast revealed thy sacred syllable OM, which is one with thee. In thy hands it is a weapon with which to destroy ignorance. O protector of thy devotees, do not conceal thy benign person.

Thou art the supreme Brahman. Thou art infinite. Thou hast assumed the forms of all creatures, remaining hidden in them. Thou pervadest all things. Thou art the one God of the universe. Those who realize thee become immortal.

Said the great seer Svetasvatara:

I have known, beyond all darkness, that great Person of golden effulgence. Only by knowing him does one conquer death. There is no other way of escaping the wheel of birth, death, and rebirth.

There is nothing superior to him, nothing different from him, nothing subtler or greater than he. Alone he stands, changeless, self-luminous; he, the Great One, fills this universe.

Though he fills the universe, he transcends it. He is untouched by its sorrow. He has no form. Those who know him become immortal. Others remain in the depths of misery.

The Lord God, all-pervading and omnipresent, dwells in the heart of all beings. Full of grace, he ultimately gives liberation to all creatures by turning their faces toward himself.

He is the innermost Self. He is the great Lord. He it is that reveals the purity within the heart by means of which he, who is pure being, may be reached. He is the ruler. He is the great Light, shining forever.

This great Being, assuming a form of the size of a thumb, forever dwells in the heart of all creatures as their innermost Self. He can be known directly by the purified mind through spiritual discrimination. Knowing him, men become immortal.

This great Being has a thousand heads, a thousand eyes, and a thousand feet. He envelops the universe. Though transcendent, he is to be meditated upon as residing in the lotus of the heart, at the center of the body, ten fingers above the navel.

He alone is *all this*—what has been done and what shall be. He has become the universe. Yet he remains forever changeless, and is the lord of immortality.

His hands and feet are everywhere; his eyes and mouths are everywhere. His ears are everywhere. He pervades everything in the universe.

Without organs of sense, yet reflecting the activities of the senses he is the lord and ruler of all.

He is the friend and refuge of all.

He resides in the body, the city of nine gates. He sports in the world without in innumerable forms. He is the master, the ruler, of the whole world, animate and inanimate.

He moves fast, though without feet. He grasps everything, though without hands. He sees everything, though without eyes. He hears everything, though without ears. He knows all that is, but no one knows him. He is called the Supreme, the Great One.

Subtler than the subtlest, greater than the greatest, the Self is hidden in the heart of all creatures. Through his grace a man loses his cravings, transcends grief, and realizes him as Brahman Supreme.

MEDITATION XVII

John Donne

Nunc lento sonitu dicunt,
morieris[1]

Perchance he for whom this bell tolls may be so ill as that he knows not it tolls for him; and perchance I may think myself so much better than I am as that they who are about me and see my state may have caused it to toll for me, and I know not that. The church is catholic, universal, so are all her actions; all that she does belongs to all. When she baptizes a child, that action concerns me; for that child is thereby connected to that body which is my head too and ingrafted into that body whereof I am a member. And when she buries a man, that action concerns me. All mankind is of one author, and is one volume; when one man dies, one chapter is not torn out of the book, but translated into a better language; and every chapter must be so translated. God employs several translators; some pieces are translated by age, some by sickness, some by war, some by justice; but God's hand is in every translation, and his hand shall bind up all our scattered leaves again for that library where every book shall lie open to one another. As therefore the bell that rings to a sermon calls not upon the preacher only but upon the congregation to come, so this bell calls us all; but how much more me who am brought so near the door by this sickness! There was a contention as far as a suit—in which piety and dignity, religion and estimation, were mingled —which of the religious orders should ring to prayers first in the morning; and it was determined that they should ring first that rose earliest. If we understood aright the dignity of this bell that tolls for our evening prayer, we would be glad to make it ours by rising early, in that application, that it

[1] Now this bell tolling softly says, you must die.

might be ours as well as his, whose indeed it is. The bell doth toll for him that thinks it doth; and though it intermit again, yet from that minute that that occasion wrought upon him he is united to God. Who casts not up his eye to the sun when it rises? but who takes off his eye for a comet when that breaks out? Who bends not his ear to any bell which upon any occasion rings? but who can remove it from that bell which is passing a piece of himself out of this world? No man is an island entire of itself; every man is a piece of the continent, a part of the main. If a clod be washed away by the sea, Europe is the less, as well as if a promontory were, as well as if a manor of thy friend's or of thine own were. Any man's death diminishes me, because I am involved in mankind, and therefore never send to know for whom the bell tolls; it tolls for thee. Neither can we call this a begging of misery or a borrowing of misery, as though we were not miserable enough of ourselves but must fetch in more from the next house, in taking upon us the misery of our neighbors. Truly it were an excusable covetousness if we did, for affliction is a treasure, and scarce any man hath enough of it. No man hath affliction enough that is not matured and ripened by it and made fit for God by that affliction. If a man carry treasure in bullion or in a wedge of gold and have none coined into current money, his treasure will not defray him as he travels. Tribulation is treasure in the nature of it, but it is not current money in the use of it, except we get nearer and nearer our home, heaven, by it. Another man may be sick, too, and sick to death, and this affliction may lie in his bowels as gold in a mine and be of no use to him; but this bell that tells me of his affliction digs out and applies that gold to me, if by this consideration of another's danger I take mine own into contemplation and so secure myself by making my recourse to my God, who is our only security.

MAN WILL PREVAIL

William Faulkner

*Speech of Acceptance upon the award of
the Nobel Prize for Literature, delivered
in Stockholm on the tenth of December,
nineteen hundred fifty.*

I feel that this award was not made to me as a man, but to my work—a life's work in the agony and sweat of the human spirit, not for glory and least of all for profit, but to create out of the materials of the human spirit something which did not exist before. So this award is only mine in trust. It will not be difficult to find a dedication for the money part of it commensurate with the purpose and significance of its origin. But I would like to do the same with the acclaim too, by using this moment as a pinnacle from which I might be listened to by the young men and women already dedicated to the same anguish and travail, among whom is already that one who will some day stand here where I am standing.

Our tragedy today is a general and universal physical fear so long sustained by now that we can even bear it. There are no longer problems of the spirit. There is only the question: When will I be blown up? Because of this, the young man or woman writing today has forgotten the problems of the human heart in conflict with itself which alone can make good writing because only that is worth writing about, worth the agony and the sweat.

He must learn them again. He must teach himself that the basest of all things is to be afraid; and, teaching himself that, forget it forever, leaving no room in his workshop for anything but the old verities and truths of the heart, the old universal truths lacking which any story is ephemeral and doomed—love and honor and pity and pride and compassion and sacrifice. Until he does so, he labors under a curse. He writes not of love but of lust, of defeats in which nobody loses anything of value, of victories without hope and, worst of all, without pity or compassion. His griefs grieve on no universal bones, leaving no scars. He writes not of the heart but of the glands.

Until he relearns these things, he will write as though he stood alone and watched the end of man. I decline to accept the end of man. It is easy enough to say that man is immortal simply because he will endure: that when the last ding-dong of doom has clanged and faded from the last worthless rock hanging tideless in the last red and dying evening, that even then there will still be one more sound: that of his puny inexhaustible voice, still talking. I refuse to accept this. I believe that man will not merely endure: he will prevail. He is immortal, not because he alone among creatures has an inexhaustible voice, but because he has a soul, a spirit capable of compassion and sacrifice and endurance. The poet's, the writer's, duty is to write about these things. It is his privilege to help man endure by lifting his heart, by reminding him of the courage and honor and hope and pride and compassion and pity and sacrifice which have been the glory of his past. The poet's voice need not merely be the record of man, it can be one of the props, the pillars to help him endure and prevail.

INDEX